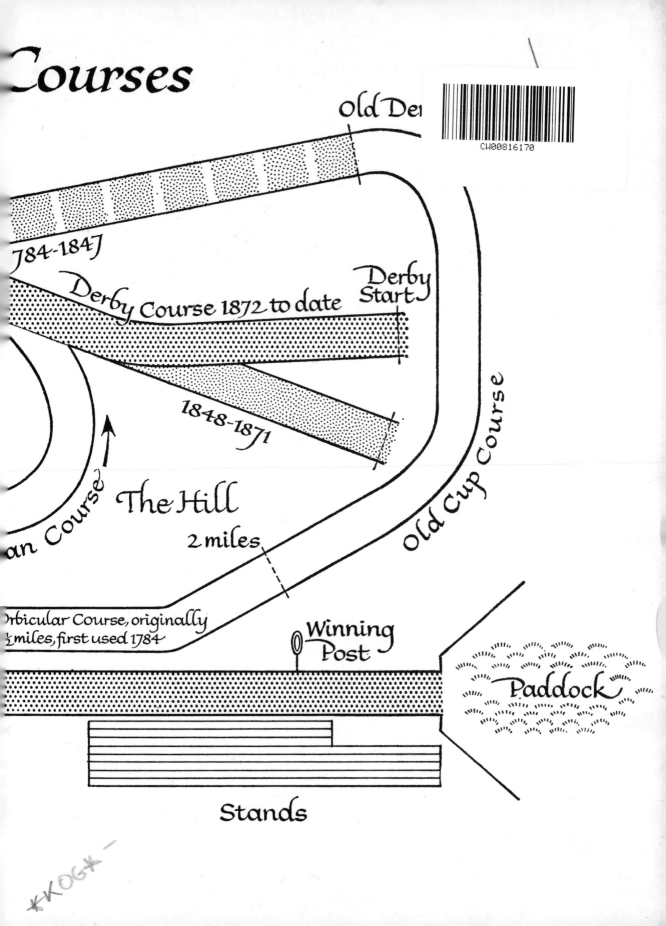

Courses

Old Der...

784-1847

Derby Course 1872 to date

Derby Start

1848-1871

...an Course

The Hill

2 miles

Old Cup Course

...rbicular Course, originally
...miles, first used 1784

Winning
Post

Paddock

Stands

THE HISTORY OF
THE DERBY STAKES

The start of the Memorable Derby of 1844; by J. F. Herring Senior

THE HISTORY

OF THE

DERBY STAKES

New Edition

ROGER MORTIMER

MICHAEL JOSEPH · LONDON

First published in Great Britain in 1961 by Cassell & Co. Limited
This edition first published in 1973 by Michael Joseph Limited
52 Bedford Square, London WC1B 3EF
1973

© 1961, 1973 by Roger Mortimer

ISBN 0 7181 1183 4

Printed in Great Britain by
Fletcher & Son Ltd, Norwich

Colour Plates

Black and White Illustrations

ILLUSTRATIONS

ILLUSTRATIONS

Acknowledgements

I should like to acknowledge with gratitude the invaluable assistance derived from the late Mr E. Moorhouse's *Romance of the Derby*, which recorded the race from its inception until 1907; and from Mr V. Orchard's *The Derby Stakes* (1900–53). Equally helpful, particularly over pedigrees, have been various editions of the *Bloodstock Breeders' Review*.

Other sources of information include:

Memories of Racing and Hunting. The Duke of Portland.
British Racecourses. B. W. R. Curling.
The Classic Races of the Turf. Guy B. H. Logan.
Famous Gentlemen Riders at Home and Abroad. Charles Adolph Voigt.
Famous Racing Men and Tales of the Turf. 'Thormanby'.
Memories of Men and Horses. William Allison.
Turf Memories of Sixty Years. Alexander Scott.
Admiral Rous and the English Turf. T. H. Bird.
Sixty Years on the Turf. George Hodgman.
John Porter of Kingsclere, an autobiography written in conjunction with E. Moorhouse.
Trainer to Two Kings. Richard Marsh.
Racing Life of Lord George Cavendish Bentinck, M.P. John Kent and Hon. Francis Lawley.
The Romance of the Derby Stakes. Alan Macey.
From Gladiateur to Persimmon. Sydenham Dixon.
My Sixty Years of the Turf. Charles Morton.
History of the British Turf. James Rice.
Finishing Post. Charlie Smirke.
The Derby (1919–47). George Melton.
The Aga Khan's Horses. R. C. Lyle.
Bloodstock Breeding. Sir Charles Leicester.
Reminiscences of the Turf. William Day.
Just My Story. Stephen Donoghue.
Men and Horses I have Known. The Hon. George Lambton.
Racing Reminiscences and Experiences of the Turf. Sir George Chetwynd.
The History of the Racing Calendar and the Stud-Book. C. M. Prior.
The Jockey Club and its Founders. Robert Black.
Memoirs of a Racing Journalist. Sidney Galtrey.

ACKNOWLEDGEMENTS

The Autobiography of Robert Standish Sievier.
My Story. Sir Gordon Richards.
Kings of the Turf. 'Thormanby'.
Come Racing with Me. Eric Rickman.
A Great Year. Alfred E. T. Watson.
John Gully. Bernard Darwin.
The Rae Johnstone Story. Rae Johnstone.
Silk and Scarlet. 'The Druid'.
Post and Paddock. 'The Druid'.
Race Horses and Racing. F. Gray Griswold.

The colour plates are reproduced by permission of the Jockey Club, with the exception of the frontispiece (Messrs Fores) and the portrait of Lord Derby (Crown Copyright reserved). Monochrome illustrations are reproduced by permission of the following (numbers indicate the page facing the plate, *a* and *b* upper and lower illustrations): The Jockey Club: 119, 215*a*, 311*b*, 407*b*, 534*b*; Lord Rosebery: 247*a*; the *British Racehorse*: 23*b*, 151*b*, 215*b*, 246*b*, 310*a* & *c*, 406*b*, 407*a*, 503, 534*a*, 598*b*, 599, 630*a*; Radio Times Hulton Picture Library: 22*a*, 151*a*, 214, 342*b*, 502*a*; the Mansell Collection: 226, 118, 150, 246*a*, 247*b*, 311*a*; Sport and General: 439*a* & *b*, 598*a*, 630*b*, 631; Press Association: 342*a*, 535*a*; Associated Press: 438, 535*b*; W. W. Rouch: 310*b*, 406*a*; Messrs Fores: 55; Victoria and Albert Museum: 33*a*; J. Bernard: 343; Messrs John R. Freeman: 54; Fox Photos: 439*c*.

The Foundation

It is arguable that but for Henry Whicker there would never have been a Derby.

The summer of 1618 was one of exceptional drought and there was great difficulty in many parts of the country in finding sufficient water for the cattle. Whicker, a herdsman in the little Surrey village of Epsom, some fourteen miles from the centre of London, was surprised and delighted to find water in a small hole on the common between Ashtead and Epsom. He returned home for a spade and proceeded to widen the area of the spring until he had made a sizeable drinking place for the cattle.

To Whicker's astonishment the cattle refused to drink. He took a sip of the water himself and found it remarkably nasty. In due course the spring was visited by local physicians and apothecaries who entirely failed to appreciate its true properties, so that for the next fourteen years the waters were used externally for the cure of simple wounds.

The real nature of the waters was only made apparent in 1632 when some labourers elected to drink deeply from the spring and half an hour later were uncomfortably aware of its effect. At first only local fame attended this second discovery, but gradually the reputation of the spring was extended and it became fashionable for rich Londoners, whose livers and stomachs had been ravaged by over-indulgence, to visit Epsom and take the waters, while for the benefit of those who were unable to make the journey, the salts were extracted and sold at five shillings an ounce. The village itself was enlarged into a town with tree-lined avenues and comfortable inns, and for a time at least it supplanted Tunbridge Wells as the most popular and frequented of spas. A local historian, Mr Pownall, wrote fondly of Epsom in the heyday of its popularity towards the end of the seventeenth century:

> Soon after the improvements made by Mr Parkhurst at the Wells, the village was enlarged to a considerable extent. It became the centre of fashion; several houses were erected for lodgings, and yet the place would not contain all the visitors, many of whom were obliged to seek accommodation in the neighbouring villages. Taverns, at that time reputed to be the largest in England, were opened; sedan chairs and numerous coaches attended. There was a public breakfast, with dancing and music every morning at the Wells. There was also a Ring as in Hyde Park; and on the Downs races were held daily at noon, with cudgelling and wrestling matches, foot races, etc., in the afternoon. The evenings were usually spent in private parties, assemblies, or cars, and we may add that neither Bath nor Tunbridge ever boasted of more noble visitors than Epsom, or exceeded it in splendour at the time we are describing.

After the Restoration, Charles II spent much of his time at Epsom, racing, hawking, and hunting, and built himself a hunting-box, The Warren, on the Downs immediately above the town. Pepys mentioned the racing there in his diary and on 25 May 1663 he wrote: 'Having intended this day to go to Banstead Downs to see a famous race, I sent Will to get himself ready to go with me; but I hear it is put off because the Lords do sit in Parliament to-day.' Two days later he wrote: 'This day there is a great throng to Banstead Downs upon a great horse-race and foot-race. I am sorry I could not go thither.' In those days the term Banstead Downs embraced an area that ran from Croydon to Farnham and included Epsom. According to a seventeenth-century writer, Richard Blome, the Downs 'affordeth great delight for Hawking, Hunting, and Horse-races'.

When races were first held at Epsom it is impossible to say, but in 1648, during the Civil War, the Earl of Clarendon recorded that a party of Royalists met on the Downs 'under pretence of a horse-race, intending to cause a diversion on the King's behalf'. This certainly suggests that race-meetings were not an unusual feature then. After the fall of the Commonwealth, the first recorded race-meeting on the Downs took place on 7 March 1661 and the King himself was present.

The popularity of Epsom as a spa began to decline early in the eighteenth century owing, according to Mr Pownall, to 'the knavery of an apothecary'. In 1704 a certain Dr Levingston bought some land, sank a well, and erected ball-rooms, gambling-rooms, and a pump. Every type of diversion was provided for visitors, and the centre of these attractions was named the New Wells. Unfortunately Dr Levingston's well possessed no medicinal qualities whatsoever, the rapid discovery of which did considerable damage to Epsom's reputation. A further blow was inflicted by another member of the medical profession, who bought the Old Wells, which he kept locked up till he died in 1727.

In the seventeen thirties Epsom had a brief revival of popularity owing to the presence of a woman usually known as 'Crazy Sally', who had remarkable skill as a bonesetter. Unfortunately 'Crazy Sally' fell passionately in love with a certain Mr Mapp of London and determined to marry him. The townsfolk of Epsom, fearing that romance might interrupt her work, did everything they could to prevent the marriage. Their efforts were all in vain, however, for eventually a child with a dislocated neck was brought to her and she refused to handle the case until opposition to her marriage was withdrawn. The citizens of Epsom acknowledged themselves defeated; 'Crazy Sally' duly became Mrs Mapp, went off with her husband to London, and never returned.

Between 1760 and 1770 a London surgeon, Mr Dale Ingram, made a final effort to restore Epsom as a spa, but his advertisements offering a series of public breakfasts, the food washed down with a mixture of magnesia and Epsom salts in allegedly palatable form, met with only a limited response. In 1804 the buildings at the Old Wells were pulled down and a private house was erected on the site.

Although Epsom town had its reversals of fortune, these had little effect on the racing there which continued to prosper, largely due to the course being so handily placed for visitors from London. Regular spring and summer meetings were established as far back as 1730, but the real turning point in Epsom's history as a sporting centre came in 1773 when the twelfth Lord Derby, then aged twenty-one, took over the lease of The Oaks, a country house at Woodmansterne on the outskirts of Epsom, from his uncle by marriage, General Burgoyne.

The Oaks was part of a property that the Lambert family had owned for over five hundred years. When the General first took a fancy to it, The Oaks was nothing more than a primitive ale-house, but he spent a lot of money on improvements and eventually converted it into a comfortable home. Burgoyne is perhaps more widely remembered in the United States than in England as it was he who surrendered Saratoga to the rebels in the War of Independence. An illegitimate son of Lord Bingley, he was stationed as a young officer at Preston Barracks in Lancashire, and while there, he met and fell in love with Lady Charlotte Stanley, daughter of the eleventh Earl of Derby. Lady Charlotte's family were greatly displeased when she married Burgoyne, who, however, was a man of considerable wit and charm, and in due course was accepted, and even regarded with affection, by his wife's relations.

The twelfth Earl of Derby succeeded his grandfather. His father, who insisted on calling himself 'Lord Strange' though he had no claim to that title, had been a member of the Jockey Club and had done well both for himself and for his descendants by marrying the daughter of an extremely rich man, Mr Hugo Smith. The twelfth Earl, popular, hospitable, easy-going, and self-indulgent, devoted to racing but even more so to cock-fighting, married Lady Elizabeth Hamilton, sister and heiress to the seventh and eighth Dukes of Hamilton, when he was little more than a boy. To celebrate his engagement he organized a magnificent fête at The Oaks, the programme including amateur theatricals and the masque *The Maid of the Oaks* written by General Burgoyne. Unfortunately the marriage proved an unhappy one, and after a son and three daughters had been born, the Earl and his wife parted. It was generally expected that the Earl would sue for divorce, but he declined to do so, being determined that his wife should not be free to marry her lover, the Duke of Dorset. The marriage, therefore, remained undissolved until Lady Derby died in 1792. Six months later the Earl married Miss Farren, an accomplished actress and a very amiable woman as well, although she did draw the line at cock-fights staged in her drawing-room.

The Earl entertained in great style both at Knowsley, 'where more good ale was drunk than in any servants' hall in England', and also at The Oaks. He almost killed his chef by demanding late suppers, and when that unfortunate man was inconsiderate enough to remonstrate, he was airily told to put down a fixed sum to 'wear and tear of life'. At Epsom races the Earl invariably acted as steward and used to invite a party of friends for the week. The May meeting of 1778 was of the traditional type, being composed entirely of races run in heats over two or four miles. Possibly inspired by the example of the St Leger, which had been instituted two years previously, Lord Derby and his friends decided to enliven proceedings by founding a race for three-year-old fillies, to be called the Oaks, and to be run the following year over a mile and a half.

At this period the great majority of races were for mature horses over at least two miles, but there was a growing tendency, particularly in the north, to race horses younger and to encourage the development of speed by matching them over a shorter distance.

There were seventeen subscribers at fifty guineas each for the first Oaks. Twelve fillies took the field and appropriately enough the race was won by Lord Derby's Bridget, who started favourite. The experiment was considered a success, and another three-year-old race, this time both for colts and fillies and to be run over a mile,* was proposed for the following year. The archives at Knowsley throw no light at all on the details of the founding of this race, but the story goes that a toss of the coin decided whether it should be named the Derby Stakes, or alternatively the Bunbury Stakes after Sir Charles Bunbury, the foremost racing man of the day, who was staying at The Oaks. It seems at least equally probable though, that the guests at The Oaks insisted that the race should be named in honour of their host. As the late Lord Rosebery said a century later: 'A roystering party at a country house founded two races, and named them gratefully after their host and his house, the Derby and the Oaks. Seldom has a carouse had a more permanent effect.'

* The distance was increased to a mile and a half in 1784 and has remained so ever since.

1780

4 May 1780 was the date of the first Derby. It was the first race on the card and the programme was enlivened by a main of cocks between birds belonging to the Gentlemen of Middlesex and Surrey and the representatives of the Gentlemen of Wiltshire. Nine of the thirty-six horses entered for the Derby went to the post, and the conditions being '50 guineas, half forfeit', the prize was 1,075 guineas. The winner was Diomed, owned by Sir Charles Bunbury and ridden by Sam Arnull. Because the race was then deemed of no particular importance, few details concerning it have been handed down, and it is not even known how far Diomed finished in front of the runner-up, Major O'Kelly's Budrow.

Diomed, by Florizel, a son of Herod, was out of a mare by Spectator and was a well-made, powerfully built chestnut standing fifteen hands three inches. In his only previous outing he had won a Sweepstakes of 500 guineas each at Newmarket, and he passed through the whole of his three-year-old career without defeat. Soon afterwards, though, he went wrong and he did not race at all the two following years. He reappeared as a six-year-old, but was not particularly successful, his sole victory being in a King's Purse at Guildford. Finally, having pulled up very lame after a race at Lewes, he was retired by his owner to the stud.

Five guineas was deemed sufficient for Diomed's services, firstly at Up Park, not far from Petersfield, and later at his owner's place, Great Barton in Suffolk. At one point his fee did go up to ten guineas, but he was not a great success as a sire and eventually it sank as low as two.

When the old horse was twenty years of age and his sphere of usefulness apparently at an end, Sir Charles sold him for fifty guineas to be exported to the United States. The most notable of Diomed's stock in England were Grey Diomed and Young Giantess. Grey Diomed, winner of many races, went to Russia, where he exerted a considerable influence on bloodstock breeding; Young Giantess became the dam of Eleanor, who won the Derby and The Oaks for Sir Charles in 1801.

Doubtless Sir Charles never thought to hear of Diomed again, once he had sold him, but the first Derby winner was a tough old customer and survived what was then the long and exacting journey across the Atlantic. Soon after landing he was sold to Colonel John Hoomes of Virginia for a thousand guineas. This looked a stiff price to pay for an elderly and somewhat discredited stallion, but the Colonel's judgement was vindicated in no uncertain fashion. Not only did Diomed live for another ten years, but he founded a dynasty, and from him are descended many of the greatest horses, such as Lexington, in American racing history. When at last he died, there was as much grief among the horse-loving Virginians as there had been at the passing of George Washington, and his death was regarded in the light of a national catastrophe.

Sir Charles Bunbury (1740–1821), whose name is still remembered at Newmarket through the 'Bunbury Mile', represented Mildenhall in Parliament for many years and was at one time Chief Secretary for Ireland. He played an important part not only in the development of English racing, but even more so in the gradual extension of the authority of the Jockey Club, of which he was regarded as the 'Perpetual President'. His word became law on the Turf, and it was his action after the in-and-out running of the Prince of Wales's horse Escape that led to the Prince (afterwards George IV) shaking the dust of Newmarket off his heels for good. He won the Derby three times, with Diomed, Eleanor, and Smolensko, but the best horse he ever bred was Highflyer, whom he sold to Lord Bolingbroke.

Diomed's rider Sam Arnull, who died in 1800, was a member of a famous racing family. He himself won the Derby four times, his brother John five times, and his nephew William three times. Quiet and temperate, he loved a good hunter and was usually attended by a groom as well turned out as himself.

1780: Thursday, 4 May . . . 36 Entries. £1,065 15s.

SIR C. BUNBURY'S ch.c. DIOMED by Florizel		
out of Pastorella's dam	S. ARNULL	1
MAJOR O'KELLY'S b.c. BUDROW brother to Vertumnus		2
MR WALKER'S c. SPITFIRE by Eclipse		3

Also ran:

Mr Panton junior's colt by Herod; Sir F. Evelyn's colt by Vauxhall Snap; H.R.H. Duke of Cumberland's colt by Eclipse; Mr Sulsh's colt by Cardinal Puff; Mr Delmé's colt by Gimcrack; Duke of Bolton's colt by Matchem.

9 ran.

Betting:

6–4 Diomed; 4–1 Budrow; 7–1 Spitfire; 10–1 Duke of Bolton's colt by Matchem.

1781

Major O'Kelly's Young Eclipse, winner in 1781, was one of the three Derby winners sired by Eclipse, the other two being Sergeant and Saltram. Like Diomed, he was out of a mare by Spectator. He remained in training for a further three seasons but the rest of his career was undistinguished.

Major (later Colonel) O'Kelly derived his rank from his allegiance to a Middlesex militia regiment of a highly irregular nature. Born in 1720, he was a typical Irish adventurer with quick wit, considerable charm, and the thickest of skins. He was twenty-four when he came to England to seek his fortune, and at one time things were going so ill for him that he was glad to pick up a few shillings by acting as a sedan chairman or a billiards marker. He had a short spell in Fleet Prison as a debtor, but was released on the death of George II. From that point the tide turned in his favour and he began to prosper.

O'Kelly had a house at Clay Hill on Epsom Downs and there, no doubt, he must have seen Eclipse, who was trained nearby. Bred by William, Duke of Cumberland, Eclipse was sold as a yearling after his breeder's death to Mr Wildman, a meat salesman of Leadenhall Market, for seventy-five guineas. The horse had his first race when he was five years old; the following year, 1770, Major O'Kelly first bought a half share in him for 650 guineas, and then paid 1,750 guineas to buy him outright.

Eclipse was without question one of the greatest horses ever seen on the English Turf. Not only was he never beaten, he was never even extended, and in the famous words of O'Kelly, it was always 'Eclipse first, the rest nowhere'. He won £25,000 in stakes himself, and at the stud he sired three hundred and thirty-five winners of nearly £160,000. When he died at Cannons in Middlesex at the age of twenty-five, he was still advertised to cover fifty mares a season. Admirers, on hearing of his death, came in hundreds to pay their last respects and were regaled with cakes and wine. Chance can play a great part in the breeding of famous horses; Squirt, grandsire of Eclipse, was being led off to a dog-kennel for execution when a groom persuaded the horse's owner, Sir Harry Harpur, to spare his life, and he was reprieved at the very last moment.

O'Kelly died at his house in Piccadilly in 1787. He was a rich man by then, and his one grievance was the failure of the Jockey Club to elect him a member. He was not noticeably devout, and it was said that the nearest he ever got to religion was to own a parrot that could whistle one of the psalms.

Second to Young Eclipse in the 1781 Derby was Crop, owned by Sir John Lade, whose wife Letty had been the mistress of a notorious highwayman. Lade, a brilliant whip, was a close friend of the Prince of Wales, whose coachman he subsequently became when he had squandered his fortune. Possibly his greatest claim to fame today rests on his reputation of having been the first man to appear in public wearing long trousers.

1781: Thursday, 24 May . . . 35 Entries. £1,312 10s.

MAJOR O'KELLY'S b.c. YOUNG ECLIPSE by Eclipse out of Juno	HINDLEY	1
SIR J. LADE'S gr.c. CROP by Turf		2
LORD CLERMONT'S c. PRINCE OF ORANGE by Herod		3

Also ran:

H.R.H. Duke of Cumberland's colt by Eclipse; Duke of Queensberry's colt by Sweet William; Lord Derby's King William; Lord Clermont's Arbutus; General Smith's colt by Florizel; Mr Walker's Seducer; Mr Kingsman's filly by Herod; Mr Douglas's colt by Metaphysician; Lord Milsintown's Scarf; Sir C. Danver's colt by Herod; Lord Craven's colt by Marske; Mr Sulsh's colt by Herod.

15 ran.

Betting:

5–4 Crop; 10–1 Young Eclipse; long odds against all the rest.

1782

Sam Arnull rode his second Derby winner in 1782 when the winner was Lord Egremont's Assassin, by Sweetbriar. Assassin was never rated a particularly good horse and when he retired to his owner's stud at Petworth, his fee was fixed at three guineas. His name soon vanished from the list of advertised stallions and he was evidently a hopeless failure as a sire.

The third Earl of Egremont was a man of immense wealth and remarkable benevolence. He gave away about £20,000 every year and it was said that he delighted in giving as other rich men delighted in accumulating. He was a generous patron of the arts, and an agriculturalist far in advance of his times. He never married, and when he died in 1837 his estates passed to his illegitimate son, Colonel Wyndham, who later in life was created Baron Leconfield.

For many years Lord Egremont ran a great race meeting in his park at Petworth, and it was the discontinuance of this fixture that led the third Duke of Richmond to establish the Goodwood meeting in 1801. Lord Egremont's other Derby winners were Hannibal (1804), Cardinal Beaufort (1805), Election (1807), and Lapdog (1826). There had always been rumours that if the teeth of some of Lord Egremont's Derby winners had been examined, they would have been found unnaturally long for three-year-olds, and Bird, who trained for Lord Egremont, admitted on his deathbed that he had twice won the Derby with four-year-olds through the simple expedient of slipping two-year-olds into the yearling paddocks. There were usually over three hundred horses at Petworth, and as management there was notoriously lax, discovery was extremely unlikely. Bird unfortunately did not divulge which of his Derby winners were the fraudulent ones. Needless to say, Lord Egremont himself was entirely ignorant of the deception practised by his trusted servant.

1782: Thursday, 9 May . . . 35 Entries. £1,155.

LORD EGREMONT's b.c. ASSASSIN by Sweetbriar
   out of Angelica   S. ARNULL   1
LORD GROSVENOR's b.c. SWEET ROBIN by Sweetbriar   2
SIR C. BUNBURY's b.c. FORTUNIO by Florizel   3

Also ran:

Duke of Bolton's Achilles; Major O'Kelly's Confederate; Mr Napier's Glancer; Mr Turner's colt by Ranthos; Mr Vernon's Berwick; Lord Clermont's Flirtator; H.R.H. Duke of Cumberland's Epaminondas; Mr Parker's Ascot; Mr Fox's Brutus; Sir W. Moore's Plutus.

13 ran.

Betting:

3–1 Sweet Robin; 5–1 Assassin; 10–1 Fortunio.

1783

There were only six runners in 1783 when the winner was Eclipse's son Saltram, owned by Mr Parker and ridden by Hindley. When his owner died the following year, Saltram passed into the possession of the Prince of Wales, who retired him to the stud at the end of the season. For the Prince he sired a top-class horse in Whiskey and at one period his stud fee soared to twenty guineas. His reputation did not last, though, and in 1798 he was quartered at a livery stable in Great Portland Street. Eventually he was exported to the United States but, unlike Diomed, he failed to meet with any success there.

Mr Parker, owner of Saltram, was a close friend of the Prince of Wales and lived at Saltram in the county of Devonshire. From 1762 he represented Devonshire in Parliament, and in 1784 he was created Baron Boringdon. His son and successor, created Earl of Morley in 1815, was a leader in the movement for compulsory vaccination.

Phenomenon, who finished last in the Derby, won the St Leger and was the first horse to compete in both events. In those days, before the development of transport, horses had to walk to the meetings where they ran. In consequence, horses from the south rarely ran at the big northern meetings, while those from the north seldom ventured on the long and tiring journey south. Like Saltram, Phenomenon was exported to the United States, but he died very soon after landing.

1783: Wednesday, 29 May . . . 34 Entries. £945.

MR PARKER'S b.c. SALTRAM by Eclipse   HINDLEY   I

COLONEL O'KELLY'S b.c. DUNGANNON by Eclipse   2

MR WALKER'S PARLINGTON by Morwick Ball   3

Also ran:

Duke of Queensberry's Gonzales; Colonel O'Kelly's Cornet; Mr Davis's Phenomenon.

6 ran.

Betting:

5–2 Saltram and Cornet; 5–1 Dungannon; 8–1 Gonzales; 10–1 Parlington; 20–1 Phenomenon.

1784

Colonel O'Kelly won the Derby again in 1784, this time with Sergeant, ridden by John Arnull. Sergeant, by Eclipse out of Aspasia, a daughter of Herod, was just a moderate racehorse and there is nothing in the records to show that he was ever retired to the stud.

In this year there were signs that the Derby was already regarded as a race of some consequence, for in the Sion Sweepstakes at Newmarket in October, winners of the Cumberland or Derby Stakes were required to carry six pounds extra.

The first four races for the Derby had been run over a mile. This year the distance was increased to a mile and a half.

1784: Wednesday, 20 May . . . 30 Entries. £1,076 5s.

COLONEL O'KELLY's b.c. SERGEANT by Eclipse out of Aspasia	J. ARNULL	1
LORD GROSVENOR's gr.c. CARLO KHAN by Mambrino		2
LORD DERBY's ch.c. DANCER by Herod		3

Also ran:

H.R.H. Duke of Cumberland's Fencer; Duc de Chartres's Cantator; Lord Derby's Collector; Sir C. Danver's Pitch; Sir C. Bunbury's Pharamond; Mr Stapleton's colt by Herod; Mr Douglas's Ishmael; Lord G. H. Cavendish's Steady.

11 ran.

Betting:

3–1 Sergeant; 5–1 Pitch and Steady; 7–1 Pharamond; 8–1 Dancer and Mr Stapleton's colt; 20–1 Carlo Khan.

1785

Hindley, of whom strangely little seems to be known, rode his third Derby winner in 1785 when Aimwell won for Lord Clermont. Neither Aimwell nor any of the horses that he beat established anything of a reputation afterwards and in all probability it was an extremely moderate field. In fact Lord Clermont owned a considerably better colt in Trumpator, from whom Barcaldine is directly descended. Barcaldine, unbeaten on the racecourse, sired several classic winners and is largely responsible for the maintenance of the Matchem line in this country.

Lord Clermont, a leading figure on the Irish Turf, was in later years a close friend of the Prince of Wales. He had, however, in his private life a somewhat unsavoury reputation, and it was probably an understatement when a contemporary described him as a 'hoary reprobate'. It is proof, though, of his status in the racing world that one of the Newmarket courses, which has long ago passed into oblivion, was named after him.

1785: Thursday, 5 May . . . 29 Entries. £1,023 15s.

LORD CLERMONT's b.c. AIMWELL by Marc Antony	HINDLEY	1
LORD GROSVENOR's gr.c. GRANTHAM by Mambrino		2
MR WASTELL's c. VERJUICE by Highflyer		3

Also ran:
Colonel O'Kelly's Chaunter (4th); Colonel O'Kelly's colt by Eclipse; Mr Bullock's Balloon; Lord Grosvenor's Vulcan; Sir F. Standish's Lepicq; Lord Foley's Backbite; Lord Sherborne's Rollo.

10 ran.

Betting:
2–1 Lord Grosvenor's representatives and Balloon; 7–1 Aimwell.

1786

Noble, owned by Mr Panton and ridden by White, won in 1786. He was a 30–1 outsider in a field of fifteen and no horse won the Derby at longer odds until Sam scored at 50–1 in 1818. Noble's record outside his Derby success was an indifferent one. As a five-year-old he was retired to the stud at Farnham, his fee being two guineas with half a crown extra for the groom. A little later he stood at Yately in Hampshire, but did no good there and was undoubtedly a failure as a sire. His owner, Mr Panton, was a prominent member of the Jockey Club and was a Steward at the time of the Escape scandal.

Noble was the first of three Derby winners sired by Highflyer. Bred by Sir Charles Bunbury, Highflyer was sold to Lord Bolingbroke, who gave him his name through being foaled in a field where some highflyer walnut trees were growing. In 1779 Lord Bolingbroke re-sold him for £800 to Mr Richard Tattersall of the well-known firm of auctioneers.

Highflyer, by Herod out of a mare by Blank, was never beaten, won £8,920 in stakes and was without question the outstanding horse of his day. His pedigree combined the blood of the Byerly Turk, the Godolphin Arabian, and the Darley Arabian in almost equal proportions. Mr Tattersall always had implicit faith in Highflyer's excellence and was never shy in expressing his confidence. Moreover he had the wit to realize that Eclipse mares were the ideal mates for Highflyer, and as long as the price was not too stiff, he always bought an Eclipse mare if one happened to come on the market. He was probably the first thoroughbred breeder to sell his young stock rather than race them, and in so doing he made for himself a very handsome fortune.

In view of the money he made out of the horse, it is hardly surprising that Mr Tattersall worshipped Highflyer. He built a great house near Ely, naming it Highflyer Hall, and it was a very happy moment for the old gentleman when he proposed the toast 'The Hammer and Highflyer' at the dinner he gave every year to the Newmarket jockeys at the end of the season. When Highflyer died in his twentieth year in 1793, Mr Tattersall had the following words engraved on the memorial stone: 'Here lieth the perfect and beautiful symmetry of the much lamented Highflyer, by whom and his wonderful offspring the celebrated Tattersall acquired a noble fortune, but was not ashamed to acknowledge it.'

1786

It is always difficult to compare the merits of horses of different epochs, but the great Admiral Rous was a firm believer in the constant improvement of the thorough-bred, and some sixty years after Highflyer's death he gave it as his opinion that 'the form of Flying Childers might not now win a £30 plate, winner to be sold for £40; and Highflyer and Eclipse might pull through in a £50 plate, winner to be sold for £200'. How those words must have made poor Mr Tattersall shudder in his grave!

1786: Wednesday, 31 May . . . 29 Entries. £1,155.

MR PANTON's c. NOBLE by Highflyer out of Brim	J. WHITE	1
LORD GROSVENOR's ch.c. METEOR by Eclipse		2
SIR H. FETHERSTON's b.c. CLARET by Bourdeaux		3

Also ran:

H.R.H. Prince of Wales's Braganza (4th); Lord Egremont's colt by Highflyer; H.R.H. Prince of Wales's Little Henry; Duke of Orleans's colt by Highflyer; Lord Grosvenor's Balsam; Mr Wyndham's Prodigal; Duke of Queensberry's Young Giant; Lord Clermont's Mark Ho!; Colonel O'Kelly's colt by Vertumnus; Colonel O'Kelly's Scota; Mr Douglas's Macbeth; Duke of Rutland's Brother to Imperator.

15 ran.

Betting:

2–1 Scota; 3–1 Meteor; 9–1 Prodigal; 19–1 Claret; 30–1 Noble.

1787

This year saw another victory for one of Highflyer's sons, the winner being the twelfth Earl of Derby's Sir Peter Teazle, ridden by Sam Arnull. It is curious that despite long and liberal support of the Turf, the Stanley family was unable to repeat this success until the seventeenth Earl of Derby won with Sansovino in 1924.

Sir Peter Teazle was bred by his owner at Knowsley, his dam being Papillon, a mare by Snap, that Lord Derby had bought from one of the two Shafto brothers, both famous in racing circles in the north. Papillon was an outstanding success at the stud. Apart from Sir Peter Teazle, who won seventeen races, she bred Sincerity, winner of five races; Lady Teazle, winner of eleven; and The Wren, winner of fifteen. From The Wren are descended many famous French horses, as well as the Fisherman family, prominent in the Australian Stud Book. Sir Peter Teazle and Lady Teazle were both named in compliment to Lord Derby's second wife, who had won a great reputation on the stage in the part of Lady Teazle in *The School for Scandal*.

The Derby was Sir Peter Teazle's first race, but he had been well galloped and started second favourite in a field of seven. Unbeaten as a three-year-old, he was clearly a high-class colt and had a good record the next two seasons as well. In October 1789 he broke down and was sent to the stud. There he maintained his high reputation, siring four Derby winners, four St Leger winners, and two winners of the Oaks. It was sometimes said that his stud record would have been even better if Lord Derby had not persisted in carrying out his theories on in-breeding to excess. Lord Derby was also accused of weakening his own strain of fighting-cocks in the same way.

At this period there was a great demand for our best bloodstock in the United States. The Americans offered 7,000 guineas for Sir Peter Teazle, but Lord Derby declined to do business.

1787: Wednesday, 24 May . . . 33 Entries. £1,050.

LORD DERBY's br.c. SIR PETER TEAZLE by Highflyer
   out of Papillon   S. ARNULL 1
COLONEL O'KELLY's ch.c. GUNPOWDER by Eclipse   2
MR VERNON's ch.c. BUSTLER by Florizel   3

Also ran:

Lord Grosvenor's Mentor; Lord Grosvenor's colt by Justice; Mr Charlton's colt by Pontifex; Lord Clermont's Ospray.

7 ran.

Betting:

7–4 Bustler; 2–1 Sir Peter Teazle; 3–1 Lord Grosvenor's representatives; 8–1 Gunpowder.

1788

The ninth Derby marked the first success in that race of the royal colours, the winner being the Prince of Wales's Sir Thomas, ridden by William South, who was then in his fifty-fourth year. Bred by a Mr Dawson, Sir Thomas was by Pontac, a son of Eclipse's sire Marske, out of Sportsmistress, dam of that famous horse Pot-8-os. Sir Thomas won his only race as a two-year-old and was then sold to the Prince. He was still unbeaten when he went to the post for the Derby, and such was the confidence behind him, that he started at 6–5 on in a field of eleven, the first odds-on favourite in the history of the race. Sir Thomas ran for two more seasons, but then vanished into obscurity. There is no record of him at the stud, and his ultimate fate is unknown.

The Prince of Wales began his racing career in 1784 at the age of twenty-one. As was only to be expected, his ownership was conducted in an absurdly extravagant manner and two years later he was heavily in debt. Parliament, however, rescued him from that predicament and rendered him solvent again. He thereupon came back to racing in the same old lavish style and in 1790 he ran no fewer than thirty-nine horses. The following season, though, came the Escape scandal, which separated him a second time temporarily from the Turf, although it must be emphasized that his own integrity was never called in question.

1788: Wednesday, 8 May . . . 30 Entries. £971 15s.

H.R.H. PRINCE OF WALES'S ch.c. SIR THOMAS by Pontac
out of Sportsmistress W. SOUTH 1
LORD GROSVENOR'S ch.c. AURELIUS by Eclipse 2
LORD BARRYMORE'S br.c. FEENOW by Tandem 3

Also ran:

Lord Foley's Altamont (4th); Mr Fox's Grey Diomed; Duke of St Albans's Brother to Cowslip; Mr Taylor's Star; Lord Clermont's Ponto; Duke of Queensberry's Goliath; Mr Lade's Constans; Mr Hull's colt by Jupiter.

11 ran.

Betting:

6–5 on Sir Thomas; 5–2 Aurelius; high odds against all the rest.

1789

Men did not live as long a hundred and sixty years ago as they are apt to do now, and heirs came into their fortunes quicker. There were no death duties either, and in consequence there were far more young owners in racing than in modern times. Feenow, who ran third to Sir Thomas in 1788, was owned by the disreputable Lord Barrymore, then only nineteen years of age. Skyscraper, winner of the Derby in 1789, was owned by the fifth Duke of Bedford, who was then in his twenty-fifth year.

A competent race-rider himself, the Duke of Bedford, unlike his descendants, was a great supporter of racing and won the Derby on two other occasions, with Eager in 1791, and with the unnamed colt by Fidget out of Sister to Pharamond in 1797. He was also successful three times in the Oaks. In his ventures on the Turf he had the advantage of an extremely shrewd confederate in Mr Ralph Dutton. He died when he was only thirty-seven as the result of an old injury he had received when playing cricket as a boy at Westminster.

There is some doubt as to who bred Skyscraper; it may have been the Duke or it may have been Lord Egremont. By Highflyer out of a mare by Eclipse, he did not race at all as a two-year-old, but won three races the following season before the Derby, for which he started a 7–4 on favourite in a field of eleven and justified the confidence placed in him by winning from his owner's second string, Sir George. Unbeaten as a three-year-old, he raced for five more seasons before retiring to the stud at Woburn, where he was apparently a failure, all trace of him soon being lost.

Skyscraper was ridden by Sam Chifney senior, the most skilful rider of his day. A native of Norfolk and a man whose personality was a curious compound of genius, cunning, and conceit, he claimed that he was entirely self-taught in respect of race-riding, a subject on which he was inclined to theorize at considerable length. There is, however, little doubt that his unself-conscious claim—'I could ride horses in a better manner in a race than any other person known in my time'—was in fact justified. Moreover he was responsible for the training of his son, Sam Chifney junior, who in due course became an even better rider than his father.

It was the Escape affair that set Chifney on the road to ruin. On 20 October 1791, he rode the Prince of Wales's Escape in a race at Newmarket and finished last in a field of four. Escape had started a hot favourite and there was a widely held suspicion that Chifney had not done his best to win. Chifney's own explanation was that Escape was short of a gallop, and when the Prince decided to run Escape again the following day, Chifney told him that he thought the horse would win.

Escape duly won his second race and then the trouble started. It began by an inquiry by the Stewards, and ended with Sir Charles Bunbury telling the Prince that no gentleman would run his horse against him if he continued to employ Chifney. To his eternal credit, the Prince stood up for Chifney, and so greatly did he resent the action of the Stewards, that he never raced at Newmarket again. He even made a solemn promise to continue to pay Chifney his retaining fee of 200 guineas every season, but that promise, like others that he made, may not have been fulfilled as Chifney eventually died in Fleet Prison, to which he had been committed for debt.

It is probable that in more modern times Chifney's explanation would have been accepted. Not only was his statement that Escape was in need of a race a reasonable one, but Escape's form had never been consistent, while the two races were over entirely different distances. A possible reason for the action of the Stewards is that Chifney, like certain other leading jockeys since, had for some considerable time been under strong suspicion with regard to his integrity, and the authorities were determined to drop on him. In their anxiety to do so, though, they selected an unsuitable occasion.

That great sporting writer Henry Hall Dixon, more usually known as 'The Druid', has left an interesting description of jockeys' attire at this period: 'Those were the days when jockeys might as fitly have appeared Esquimaux-fashion as in "peg-tops"; and brown breeches with bunches of ties which might have made them pass muster for "The Driving Club", white stockings and short gaiters encased the nether man. This was Chifney's and Singleton's wonted attire, but there are those still alive who remember how the former wore ruffles and a frill whenever he "took silk" of an afternoon, while love-locks hung on each side from beneath his jockey cap.'

1789: Thursday, 28 May . . . 30 Entries. £1,076 5s.

DUKE OF BEDFORD's b.c. SKYSCRAPER by Highflyer
   out of Everlasting   S. CHIFNEY, SEN. 1
DUKE OF BEDFORD's SIR GEORGE brother of Lovemore   2
LORD GROSVENOR's b.c. BROTHER TO SKYLARK   3

Also ran:

H.R.H. Prince of Wales's Soujah ul Doulah (4th); H.R.H. Prince of Wales's Serpent; Lord G. H. Cavendish's Competitor; Lord Grosvenor's colt by Pot-8-os;

Duke of St Albans's Bashful; Mr Lade's Pantaloon; Lord Barrymore's Sir Christopher; Lord Egremont's Sublimate.

11 ran.

Betting:

7–4 on Skyscraper; 7–2 Soujah ul Doulah; 100–8 Pot-8-os' colt; 100–7 Sublimate.

1790

The winner in 1790 was Rhadamanthus, ridden by John Arnull and owned by the first Earl Grosvenor (1731–1802), who raced on a gigantic scale; his hobby, it was said, costing him a quarter of a million pounds during his lifetime.

Horses in Earl Grosvenor's colours had been second in the Derby in 1784, 1785, 1786, and 1788, a record only approached by the late Lord Astor, who was second four times between 1919 and 1924. This year, however, the luck changed and not only did Rhadamanthus, who started favourite, win, but Earl Grosvenor's second string, Asparagus, was runner-up.

The winner was by Justice out of a mare called Flyer, who also bred the 1794 Derby winner Daedalus, a full brother to Rhadamanthus. Only seven other mares have bred two Derby winners; their names are given in the appendix.

Like most Derby winners of that period, Rhadamanthus did not run as a two-year-old. He remained in training until he was six, but his form deteriorated and it was apparently not reckoned worth while to send him to the stud.

1790: Thursday, 20 May . . . 32 Entries. £1,102 10s.

LORD GROSVENOR's b.c. RHADAMANTHUS by Justice
out of Flyer   J. ARNULL   I
LORD GROSVENOR's ch.c. ASPARAGUS by Pot-8-os   2
LORD DERBY's b.c. LEE BOO   3

Also ran:

H.R.H. Prince of Wales's Cambooe (4th); Mr Panton's Griffin; H.R.H. Prince of Wales's Fitzwilliam; Lord Foley's Rattler; Lord Clermont's Bag-ho!; Duke of Queensberry's Burgundy; Mr Panton's Ostrich.

10 ran.

Betting:

5–4 Rhadamanthus; 4–1 Asparagus; 5–1 Griffin; 7–1 Lee Boo.

Sir Charles Bunbury

The Third Earl of Egremont;
after T. Philips

The Road to Epsom; after Rowlandson

Sam Chifney

1791

The young Duke of Bedford won again in 1791, this time with a colt that was merely known at the time as Brother to Fidget, but having won the Derby, was honoured with the name of Eager. Eager, who did not race as a two-year-old, had run once before the Derby, in which he started at 5–2 and defeated the favourite Vermin, owned in partnership by Lord Foley and Mr Charles James Fox, both notoriously heavy gamblers. The result, a very expensive one for the two partners, may have been one of those flukes that sometimes happen in racing as subsequent form showed that Vermin was undoubtedly the better colt of the two. Eager continued to race until he was six, but his career was far from distinguished and towards its close he had the indignity, unique in the case of a Derby winner, of running in a selling race. There is no record of his ever retiring to the stud.

1791 : Thursday, 9 June . . . 32 Entries. £1,076 5s.

DUKE OF BEDFORD's EAGER by Florizel out of Fidget's dam	STEPHENSON 1
LORD FOLEY's br.c. VERMIN by Highflyer	2
LORD EGREMONT's PROTEUS by Mercury	3

Also ran :

H.R.H. Prince of Wales's St David (4th); H.R.H. Prince of Wales's colt by Highflyer; Mr Vernon's colt by Garrick; Sir C. Bunbury's Playfellow; Mr Graham's colt by Eclipse; Lord Grosvenor's Gumcistus.

9 ran.

Betting :

5–4 Vermin; 5–2 Eager; 8–1 St David; 10–1 Proteus.

1792

Lord Grosvenor had his second Derby winner in 1792, John Bull, by Fortitude, a 6–4 on favourite, winning from the 100–1 outsider Speculator owned by Lord Clermont. John Bull had very little racing; he did not run as a two-year-old, had only one other race, which he won, besides the Derby as a three-year-old, and was beaten in his one and only outing the following season. He was then retired to the stud where he enjoyed a modest measure of success.

Probably the best horse in this Derby was Saltram's son Whiskey, owned by the Prince of Wales. He failed to run up to form on this occasion, but subsequently won some good races and was an outstanding success as a sire, one of his daughters being Eleanor, winner of both the Derby and the Oaks. Eleanor's son Muley sired Marpessa, dam of the famous mare Pocahontas. Moreover Clove, Marpessa's dam, was by Whiskey's son Marmion, so that Pocahontas, dam of Stockwell, Rataplan, and King Tom, was closely in-bred to the Prince of Wales's horse.

Frank Buckle (1766–1832), who rode John Bull, was a great rider, enjoying in his heyday a popularity equal to that in later times of Fred Archer, Steve Donoghue, and Sir Gordon Richards. He won the Derby five times, the Oaks nine times, and the St Leger twice.

Son of a Newmarket saddler, Buckle had a very long career as a jockey, his final ride being in 1831, fifty years to a day after he had joined Mr Vernon's stable as a very small boy. Unlike most of his fellow riders, he was invariably neat in his dress and always wore beautifully made boots and breeches; unlike many of them, too, he was scrupulously honest. For much of his life he lived at Peterborough, where he farmed successfully, being famous for his butter, and he also bred greyhounds, bulldogs, and fighting-cocks. At one time, too, he was a Master of Hounds.

He must have been a tough little man—he could go to scale at 7 st. 10 lb. without wasting—as he thought nothing of hacking over to Newmarket to ride work and then riding home to Peterborough in time for tea, a total distance of ninety miles. His whip, covered in silver and bearing the record of his classic successes, was for many years a coveted racing trophy in Germany. He was comfortably off and widely respected when he died rather suddenly in 1832.

1792

No better rider ever crossed a horse;
Honour his guide, he died without remorse.
Jockeys, attend—from his example learn
The meed that honest worth is sure to earn.

1792: Thursday, 24 May . . . 32 Entries. £834 15s.

LORD GROSVENOR's ch.c. JOHN BULL by Fortitude out of Xantippe	F. BUCKLE	1
LORD CLERMONT's b.c. SPECULATOR by Trumpator		2
LORD DERBY's b.c. BUSTARD by Woodpecker		3

Also ran:

Mr Graham's Lycias (4th); Mr Wyndham's St George; H.R.H. Prince of Wales's Whiskey; Duke of Queensberry's colt by Pharamond.

7 ran.

Betting:

6–4 on John Bull; 5–2 Bustard; 8–1 Whiskey; 100–1 Speculator.

1793

The Derby of 1793 was perhaps the most important one since its foundation, both Waxy, who won, and Gohanna, who was second, being horses of outstanding merit. Both, moreover, and in particular Waxy, have left their mark in the Stud Book.

Waxy carried the colours of his breeder, Sir Ferdinand Poole, head of a well-known Cheshire family, and was ridden by William Clift. He was trained by Robson, the greatest trainer of his day, and far less severe and drastic in his methods than the majority of his contemporaries. Besides Waxy, Robson trained six other Derby winners including Whalebone, Whisker, and Emilius, and ten winners of the Oaks. On his retirement in 1828 he was presented with a handsome piece of plate by leading members of the Turf in recognition of his professional skill and his character. He died at Newmarket in 1838.

Waxy's sire was Eclipse's son Pot-8-os, a good horse and a very tough one, too, as he won thirty-five races altogether, seventeen of them being over the Beacon Course, more than four miles long, at Newmarket. He was extremely successful at the stud, siring 165 winners, including two other Derby winners in Champion and Tyrant. In Waxy's Derby he sired six of the thirteen runners.

In the Derby Waxy started at 12–1 and beat the odds-on favourite Gohanna, owned by Lord Egremont, by half a length. The rest of his racing career was distinguished by a series of tremendous battles with Gohanna. In the spring of 1794 he beat his rival in the Jockey Club Plate after a long and stirring duel. Not long afterwards Gohanna, receiving three pounds, beat him by a short head in a Match, but at Lewes later in the same year, Waxy again won when they met on level terms. In 1796 they met at Guildford in the King's Plate, which was run in four mile heats. In the first heat Waxy won by a short head, in the second they dead-heated, and in the third Waxy won again by half a length. Gohanna, named after a hill near Petworth, where he was foaled, was only a small horse, but had the courage of a lion. He was a success as a sire, one of the best of his winners being Election, winner of the Derby in 1807.

Waxy equalled Gohanna in tenacity and courage and was just the better race-horse of the two. He eventually became the property of the third Duke of Grafton and most of his stud career was passed at Euston Hall in Norfolk. He sired 190 winners of over £70,000, including the Derby winners Pope, Whalebone, Blücher, and Whisker. Whalebone, the greatest of the four, became a most powerful influence in thoroughbred breeding, being the tail male ancestor of such horses as Blandford, Tracery, Bend Or, Hermit, Hampton, and Carbine. Waxy lived until he was twenty-seven and was buried close to All Saints Church at Newmarket.

William Clift, Waxy's rider in the Derby, was a rough, hardy Yorkshireman, who began life as a shepherd's boy. Success never smoothed down his rough edges and a contemporary described him as 'a rough, uncultivated Indian'. His manners towards his employers were notoriously brusque, and when the Duke of Dorset asked him whether he liked a certain horse he had ridden, he replied curtly, 'Hang me, you see I won; that's enough for you'! He was perfectly honest, but unpolished in his methods and was frequently very hard on the horses he rode; in fact it was remarkable that he was so widely patronized. He was a man of considerable physical endurance himself, and when he was close on eighty years of age, he used to walk from Newmarket to Bury St Edmunds and back, a distance of twenty-eight miles, 'just to give my legs a stretch'.

1793: Thursday, 16 May . . . 50 Entries. £1,653 15s.

SIR F. POOLE's b.c. WAXY by Pot-8-os out of Maria	W. CLIFT 1
LORD EGREMONT's b.c. GOHANNA by Mercury	2
LORD GROSVENOR's b.c. TRIPTOLEMUS	3

Also ran:

Lord Grosvenor's Druid (4th); Mr Hull's Xanthus; Sir F. Standish's Darsham; Lord Derby's colt by Pot-8-os; Lord Strathmore's colt by Mercury; Lord Grosvenor's Lilliput; Lord Grosvenor's colt by Pot-8-os; Mr Kaye's colt by Phenomenon; Sir F. Poole's Mealy; Mr Philips's Brother to King David.

13 ran.

Betting:

11–10 on Gohanna; 8–1 Xanthus; 10–1 Druid; 12–1 Waxy.

Won by half a length.
Winner trained by Robson.

1794

The Derby of 1794 was a sad come-down from the previous year. There were only four runners, the smallest field in the history of the race, and they certainly did not atone by their quality for the deficiency in numbers.

The winner, ridden by Buckle, was Lord Grosvenor's Daedalus, a full brother to the 1790 winner Rhadamanthus. He had never run before, and neither he nor his stable companion Drone was reckoned to have the slightest chance against the odds-on favourite Leon, who, however, could only finish third. Daedalus was twice defeated at Newmarket in the autumn and from then on all trace of him is lost.

1794: Thursday, 5 June . . . 49 Entries. £1,391 5s.

LORD GROSVENOR's br.c. DAEDALUS by Justice out of Flyer	F. BUCKLE	I
LORD EGREMONT's br.c. by Highflyer out of Camilla		2
DUKE OF BEDFORD's ch.c. LEON		3

Also ran:
Lord Grosvenor's Drone.

4 ran.

Betting:
5 and 6–4 on Leon; 2–1 the Highflyer colt; 6–1 Daedalus.

1795

Lord Egremont's Arun started favourite for the Derby in 1795, but he finished near the tail-end of the field, the winner being the well-backed Spread Eagle, ridden by Wheatley.

By Eclipse's son Volunteer out of a mare by Highflyer, Spread Eagle had been nominated for the Derby by the Duke of Dorset, but carried the colours of Sir Frank Standish of Duxbury, Lancashire, a member of the Jockey Club and a man much respected on the Turf. Spread Eagle was the first of his three Derby winners and he also won the Oaks on two occasions. It was for poisoning Sir Frank's Eagle colt by placing arsenic in a drinking trough at Newmarket that Daniel Dawson was hanged at Cambridge in 1812. There is little doubt that Dawson was the agent of two villainous bookmakers called Bland.

Spread Eagle did not run as a two-year-old, but won two races at Newmarket before the Derby. He only ran once more that season after Epsom, being soundly beaten when a 5–1 on favourite at Newmarket. He continued to race until he was six, but his later career was undistinguished. It is believed that he was eventually exported to America.

1795: Thursday, 21 May . . . 45 Entries. £1,470.

SIR F. STANDISH's b.c. SPREAD EAGLE by Volunteer
out of a mare by Highflyer   A. WHEATLEY   1
LORD EGREMONT's b.c. CAUSTIC, brother of Precipitate   2
SIR F. POOLE's br.c. PELTER by Fortunio   3

Also ran:
Mr Dawson's Diamond (4th); Lord Grosvenor's colt by Pot-8-os; Lord Egremont's Arun; Duke of Bedford's Brass; Mr Durand's colt by Saltram; Mr Hallett's colt by Volunteer; Mr O'Kelly's colt by Volunteer; Mr Turner's Miller.

11 ran.

Betting:
5–2 Arun; 3–1 and 5–2 Spread Eagle; 3–1 the colt by Pot-8-os; 9–1 Pelter.

1796

The following year Sir Frank Standish won the Derby again and the Oaks as well, thereby achieving a double success that had been previously accomplished by Lord Clermont in 1785 with Aimwell and Trifle, and by the Duke of Bedford in 1791 with Eager and Portia. The last time this feat was accomplished was in 1950 when M. Boussac won with Galcador and Asmena.

Didelot, a half-brother by Trumpator to Spread Eagle, was only Sir Frank's second string, the stable selected being Mr Teazle, who started favourite at 11–8, while history has not even recorded the odds that were offered against the winner, who was ridden by John Arnull. Mr Teazle had some good form as a two-year-old and had won impressively at Newmarket the following spring. It seems probable that he broke down at Epsom, as the Derby was his final appearance on the race-course.

Didelot's form both before and after the Derby was moderate, and there is no further mention of him in the *Calendar* after 1799. Evidently very little was thought of him as in the advertisements for his sire Trumpator, a grandson of Matchem, his name was not included in the list of Trumpator's most notable winners.

1796: Thursday, 12 May . . . 45 Entries. £1,470.

SIR F. STANDISH's b.c. DIDELOT by Trumpator out of Spread Eagle's dam	J. ARNULL	I
MR HALLETT's STICKLER by Highflyer		2
DUKE OF BEDFORD's LEVIATHAN by Highflyer		3

Also ran:

Mr Smith's Little Devil; Duke of Queensberry's colt by King Fergus; Mr Bullock's Hanger; Lord Egremont's colt by Mercury; Sir H. V. Tempest's colt by Volunteer; Sir F. Standish's Mr Teazle; Mr Hammond's Arthur; Mr Lade's colt by Dungannon.

11 ran.

Betting:

11–8 Mr Teazle; 9–2 Leviathan; 7–1 Stickler.

1797

In 1797 Sir Frank Standish was expected to win his third Derby in succession, but his colt Stamford, who started favourite, was unplaced in a field of seven. The winner was the Duke of Bedford's unnamed colt by Fidget out of a Sister to Pharamond. The Fidget colt had never run before and only ran once afterwards, finishing well down the course in a race at Newmarket as a four-year-old.

Stamford started a 7–4 on favourite for the St Leger, but was beaten by Lounger. However, he won the Doncaster Cup the following day, a victory he repeated in 1798.

John Singleton, who rode the Fidget colt, was a Yorkshireman and a member of a famous family of jockeys. His parents planned to make him a doctor and he was placed in the care of his uncle, a Sheffield surgeon, but he ran away to Newmarket and attached himself to the stable of Stephenson, who had won the Derby on Eager and who was then training for the Duke of Bedford. He soon established himself as a first-rate rider, but his career was a short one as he died in 1802 aged twenty-six.

1797: Thursday, 1 June . . . 37 Entries. £1,155.

DUKE OF BEDFORD's br.c. by Fidget out of a sister of Pharamond	J. SINGLETON	1
LORD GROSVENOR's ch.c. ESCULUS		2
LORD DARLINGTON's b.c. PLAISTOW		3

Also ran:

Sir F. Standish's Stamford (4th); Sir C. Bunbury's Wrangler; Lord Egremont's Chameleon; Lord Egremont's colt by Woodpecker or Precipitate.

7 ran.

Betting:

11–8 Stamford; 2–1 Plaistow; 10–1 the colt by Fidget; 20–1 Esculus.

1798

Perhaps the chief claim to fame of Sir Harry, who won in 1798, is that he was the first Derby winner to be sired by a previous winner of that race, his sire being the 1787 winner, Sir Peter Teazle. He was bred at Preston, Lancashire, not far from where Sir Peter Teazle stood, by Sir Harry Houghton, and his dam, Matron, is said to have been hunted in Leicestershire at one stage of her career.

Sir Harry was owned by Mr Joseph Cookson of Newcastle, who had served as a young man in the Guards, but who later adopted the more profitable profession of banker. He enjoyed a considerable reputation for astuteness and it was widely believed that he won a great deal of money on the Turf. Sir Harry had never seen a racecourse before the Derby, but he had been highly tried and, partnered by Sam Arnull, he started a 7–4 favourite in a field of ten. The remainder of his career was lacking in distinction, although as a five-year-old, receiving half a pound, he did beat the 1798 St Leger winner Symmetry in a Match. He eventually retired to the stud at Epsom at a fee of five guineas, but made little mark although his name appears in the pedigree of the 1855 Derby winner, Wild Dayrell.

1798: Thursday, 24 May . . . 37 Entries. £1,233 15s.

MR JOSEPH COOKSON's br.c. SIR HARRY by Sir Peter Teazle out of Matron	S. ARNULL	1
MR BALDOCK's br.c. TELEGRAPH		2
MR DELMÉ's b.c. YOUNG SPEAR		3

Also ran:

Lord Egremont's colt by Precipitate; Lord Grosvenor's Admiral Nelson; Lord Grosvenor's Brother to Waxy; Lord Clarendon's Brother to Recruit; Mr Durand's Sheet Anchor; Mr Concannon's Sparrowhawk; Mr Perren's Young Javelin.

10 ran.

Betting:

6 and 7–4 against Sir Harry; 3–1 the colt by Precipitate; 6–1 Admiral Nelson; 8–1 Young Spear; 100–3 Telegraph.

1799

In 1799 Sir Frank Standish repeated his performance of 1796 and won the race with 'the stable neglected'. His colt Eagle, a full brother to Spread Eagle, started favourite but could only finish third, the winner being Sir Frank's other runner Archduke, ridden by John Arnull, whose chance had been reckoned as negligible. Archduke, by Sir Peter Teazle and a full brother to the 1797 Derby favourite Stamford, never did much good subsequently and disappeared completely from the scene the following year. There is no record of his ever going to the stud.

1799: Thursday, 9 May . . . 33 Entries. £1,155.

SIR F. STANDISH'S br.c. ARCHDUKE by Sir Peter Teazle out of Horatia	J. ARNULL	1
LORD EGREMONT'S b.c. GISLEBERT		2
SIR F. STANDISH'S b.c. EAGLE by Volunteer		3

Also ran:

Mr R. Heathcote's Vivaldi (4th); Mr Cookson's Expectation; Mr Wilson's Kite; Duke of Grafton's Vandal; Lord Grosvenor's Canterbury; Mr Waller's colt by Satellite; Lord Oxford's Dart; Mr Lake's colt by Sir Peter Teazle.

11 ran.

Betting:

Evens Eagle; 7–2 Canterbury; 8–1 Vivaldi; 10–1 Kite; 12–1 Archduke; 17–1 Gislebert.

*   *   *

At the close of the eighteenth century, the English Turf was only just emerging from the dark ages. Meetings were generally conducted on extremely primitive lines and horses competed on rough, unprepared ground for very small stakes. Most races were still run in heats, trials of stamina for mature animals being the order of the day rather than mere tests of speed for two- and three-year-olds, although the picture was gradually changing in that respect. Hardly a thought was spared for the comfort, convenience, or control of spectators, who wandered at large all over the crudely marked tracks, while stray horsemen not infrequently impeded the progress of a race. The authority of the Jockey Club, though growing, was far from fully developed. The sport was completely ignored in the newspapers, details for those who desired them being available only in the *Racing Calendar*.

Before the establishment of railways, visitors who attended the Epsom Summer Meeting usually took lodgings in the town or at Cheam, Ewell, or Leatherhead. Epsom itself, still rural and unspoiled, was converted during race-week into a seething city, doubtless to the great satisfaction and profit of the local shopkeepers who charged famine prices for food. Until the local constabulary was instituted, race-week invariably heralded a crime wave, and a contemporary writer observed: 'The vicious and unprincipled form a tolerable proportion of the crowd, and it generally follows that many atrocities are committed.'

In the early days of the Derby, the Stewards watched the racing from a little stand on the south side of the course, opposite the present grandstand. On the north side was Prince's Stand, built for the Prince Regent; this still exists and is known today as the Warwick Stand. There was no permanent stand for visitors at all, but in 1828 a Doncaster speculator called Bluck, a thorough rogue, got permission to erect a permanent building. Bluck soon got into difficulties and for £750 was bought out by some prominent citizens of Epsom, who formed the Epsom Grand Stand Association and raised £20,000 for building and maintaining the stand, which was opened for public use in 1830.

As has been pointed out, up till 1784 the Derby was run over a mile. It then started at Burgh Heath, three furlongs east of Tattenham Corner, that is to say beyond the present five furlong starting-gate. When the distance was increased, the start used to take place on the south side of the Downs, beyond Down House. Until 1847, when the course was altered, the start and the first three furlongs were invisible from the stand.

The growth of the Derby into the great race that it eventually became was a gradual process; not until some fifty years or so after its foundation did it attain true eminence and then it was very largely due to the boosting it received in *Bells Life in London*, the popular sporting paper founded in 1822. In its early years the Derby was witnessed by a mere five thousand or so spectators; by the eighteen fifties the number had risen to sixty thousand, and by the twentieth century to a quarter of a million, although it is, of course, impossible to assess with any degree of accuracy the total of spectators on the Downs, which are open and free to all.

Other factors contributing towards the Derby's development were improved roads and transport facilities, which made it easier for the public to get to the course and enabled horses to be sent to Epsom from any part of England without undue risk of fatigue. By 1847 the race had attained such a position that it became the custom, now discontinued, for Parliament to adjourn from Tuesday till Thursday in Epsom week. Needless to say, this parliamentary holiday met with unrelenting disapproval from the Radicals. In 1848 Lord George Bentinck described Derby Day as a recognized holiday in the metropolis, Earl Russell declared it was a national fête, while Lord Palmerston, an enthusiastic racing man himself, styled Epsom week 'our Olympian Games'.

1800

Mr Christopher Wilson's Champion, winner of the first Derby of the nineteenth century, was the first horse to complete the double by winning the St Leger as well. Moreover, he remained the only horse to accomplish it until Surplice won both races forty-eight years later. Possibly the chief reason why the feat remained unique for so long was the lack of transport facilities. Until the development of railways, the best horses from the south rarely made the long and arduous journey up to Doncaster.

Champion, who was ridden by Clift at Epsom, was a son of Pot-8-os. He had never seen a racecourse before the Derby, but he had been highly tried and, starting favourite at 7–4, he duly won from another well-backed runner, Lord Egremonts' colt by Precipitate out of Tag. In the St Leger Champion started at 2–1 and was ridden by Buckle. At the end of that year Mr Wilson sold Champion to the Earl of Darlington, for whom the colt won three races in 1801. In May 1802 he broke down in a race at York, was sold to a Colonel Lumm, and disappeared from the records.

Mr Christopher Wilson, of Tadcaster, Yorkshire, was a staunch supporter of racing for over sixty years. An upright and hospitable man, who delighted in keeping up old customs, he was held in much affection and respect. He was nearly eighty years of age when he dropped dead in London on the morning of Derby Day, 1842.

1800: Thursday, 9 May . . . 33 Entries. £1,207 10s.

MR WILSON'S b.c. CHAMPION by Pot-8-os out of Huncamunca	CLIFT	1
LORD EGREMONT'S ch.c. by Precipitate out of Tag		2
LORD EGREMONT'S ch.c. MYSTERY by Woodpecker		3

Also ran:

Lord Grosvenor's Quick (4th); Lord Donegall's Fortitude; Sir H. T. Vane's Glenarm; Duke of Grafton's Chuckle; Mr Watson's Triumvir; Mr White's Statesman; Mr Panuwell's colt by Rockingham; Mr Heming's Sir Sidney; Mr Ladbroke's Lazarus; Mr Wilson's Surprise.

13 ran.

Betting:

7–4 Champion; 4–1 the colt by Precipitate; 5 and 6–1 Lazarus; 10–1 Glenarm; high odds the rest.

1801

In 1801 a filly, Sir Charles Bunbury's Eleanor, won the Derby for the first time in the history of the race. The only other fillies to win the greatest race on the English Turf are Blink Bonny (1857), Shotover (1882), Signorinetta (1908), Tagalie (1912), and Fifinella (1916)*. Eleanor, Blink Bonny, Signorinetta, and Fifinella all won the Oaks as well. Shotover won the Two Thousand Guineas and Tagalie the One Thousand Guineas.

Bred by her owner, Eleanor was by Whiskey, a grandson of Eclipse, out of Young Giantess, a daughter of Diomed. Young Giantess was a great mare; she bred Sorcerer, by Trumpator, winner of sixteen races and later a successful sire. Comus, a son of Sorcerer, sired Humphrey Clinker, from whom is descended Melbourne, sire of the 1853 Derby winner West Australian and also of Blink Bonny. After producing Sorcerer, Young Giantess had eight foals, all by Whiskey. The three colts were useless, but of the fillies Eleanor won twenty-eight races; Julia was the dam of the 1811 Derby winner, Phantom; while Cressida was the dam of Priam, winner of the Derby in 1830.

Just before the Derby Eleanor's trainer, Cox, was suddenly stricken with a mortal illness. A parson was summoned and the dying man indicated that he wished to impart one final message. The parson duly bent his head to receive it: 'Depend on it, that Eleanor is the hell of a mare,' croaked Cox and fell back dead. Cox's opinion of Eleanor was fully justified by her racing record. She won her only race before the Derby, for which, with Saunders riding, she started favourite at 5–4. Conditions for fillies this year had been made a bit easier, and carrying 7 st. 12 lb., she received a sex allowance of five pounds from the colts. The following day she started a 2–1 on favourite for the Oaks and had no difficulty in accounting for her five opponents. Like many another Epsom hero and heroine, she then came to grief at Ascot, being beaten in a race over the New Mile by the Asparagus colt. Later in the season, however, she won two more races at Newmarket.

She continued to race until she was seven, frequently competing at small meetings for insignificant prizes, and she is probably the only winner of the Derby to have won a race at Huntingdon as well. At the stud her most notable achievement was to breed Muley, the sire of Marpessan, who became the dam of Pocahontas.

* Owing to the war, the Derby and Oaks were run at Newmarket this year.

1801

1801: Thursday, 21 May . . . 31 Entries. £1,102 10s.

SIR C. BUNBURY's b.f. ELEANOR by Whiskey
out of Young Giantess   SAUNDERS   1
MR WYNDHAM's br.c. by Fidget   2
DUKE OF GRAFTON's ch.f. REMNANT by Trumpator   3

Also ran:

Mr Watson's Gaoler (4th); Lord Grosvenor's Mathew; Sir W. Gerard's Belleisle;
Lord Derby's colt by Sir Peter Teazle; Lord Clermont's Brother to Young Spear;
Lord Donegall's Curb; Mr Heming's Pugilist; Mr Hoomes's Horns.

11 ran.

Betting:

5–4 Eleanor; 7–2 Gaoler; 7–1 Remnant; 10–1 Brother to Spear; 12–1 Belleisle.

1802

The third Duke of Grafton, who won with Tyrant in 1802, the first of his three successes in the race, was a great-grandson of Charles II; the first Duke, whom his royal father married at the age of nine to a little girl of five, being a son of Charles's mistress, Barbara Villiers. Born in 1735, the third Duke succeeded to the title in 1757 and at the age of thirty-one he took office as Prime Minister of England. Unfortunately his morals were hardly in keeping with his proud office, and his political career came to an end largely owing to the indiscreet, even shameless manner of his conduct with the notorious Nancy Parsons, with whom he was sufficiently ill-judged to walk arm-in-arm at Ascot and Newmarket. He could hardly have offered a less missable target to his enemies, and he was savagely and not undeservedly attacked in the 'Letters of Junius'.

Whatever may be thought of his morals and his politics, and few people apparently thought highly of either, he was a notable agriculturalist, and the development of the thoroughbred owed not a little to his judgement and foresight. The foundation mare of his eminently successful stud was Julia, by Blank. Bought from Mr Panton, Julia produced a filly by Snap called Promise. Promise in her turn foaled Prunella, by Highflyer, and Prunella bred eleven first-rate horses, whose names all began with the letter 'P'.

The Duke's first marriage was dissolved by Act of Parliament. His former wife immediately wed the Earl of Upper Ossory, while he himself selected as his second bride the daughter of the Dean of Windsor. He had twelve children by his second marriage, the eldest son of this union being the Rev. Lord Henry Fitzroy, who did very nicely in a financial sense from his calling, his numerous livings affording him little labour but an income of £6,000 a year. In fact he elected to devote his mind and his energy to racing and breeding, on both of which subjects he became an expert and from his knowledge of which he augmented his income still further.

> Behold the reverend Lord, good Fitzroy, stand
> With Holy Bible in his precious hand;
> Or so it seems. I doubt it as I look;
> Is it his Bible or his betting book?

Like many another graceless old sinner before and since, the Duke, who died in

1811, switched hopefully to religion when declining health rendered self-indulgence no longer enjoyable or even practical. While his reverend son looked after the horses, he himself published religious tracts and regularly attended the Unitarian Chapel in Essex Street, just off the Strand.

To return to Tyrant: a son of Pot-8-os, he was an indifferent racehorse, and although he won the Derby easily enough, it was his solitary success. In fact all trace of him is lost after 1803. He was certainly nothing like as good a horse as Orville, who won the St Leger in 1802.

Tyrant was ridden at Epsom by Buckle, who stood to win a big bet if he could ride the winner of the Oaks as well. Scotia was his mount in that race, and after she had looked well beaten on at least three occasions, he coaxed one final effort out of her and forced her head in front right on the post.

1802: Thursday, 3 June . . . 30 Entries. £1,024 16s.

DUKE OF GRAFTON's b.c. TYRANT by Pot-8-os		
out of Tuneful's dam	F. BUCKLE	1
MR C. WILSON's b.c. by Young Eclipse, dam by Highflyer		2
SIR C. BUNBURY's br.c. ORLANDO by Whiskey		3

Also ran:

Mr Whaley's Gulliver (4th); Sir F. Standish's Duxbury; Lord Clermont's Piscator; Sir F. Standish's Master Eagle; Lord Grosvenor's Margery; Lord Camelford's Omnium.

9 ran.

Betting:

11–8 the colt by Young Eclipse; 4–1 Piscator; 7–1 Tyrant; 10–1 Orlando; very high odds against any other.

Won easily.
Winner trained by Robson.

1803

In 1803 the weights were changed, colts carrying 8 st. 5 lb. and fillies eight stone, as opposed to 8 st. 3 lb. and 7 st. 12 lb. in the previous year.

The winner was Ditto, the property of a leading north-country owner, Sir Hedworth Williamson, who had the singular distinction of making only two attempts to win the Derby and of succeeding on each occasion. Ditto was by Sir Peter Teazle, who sired three of the six runners, these three occupying the first three places. Sir Peter's achievement was subsequently equalled by Stockwell, who sired the first three to finish in 1866.

Ditto's only race as a three-year-old was the Derby and, ridden by Clift, he won very easily. Again as a four-year-old he only ran once, winning the Claret Stakes at Newmarket. The following year he won the Craven Stakes at Newmarket, was beaten in a Match over the Beacon Course, won a King's Purse at Guildford, and then vanished into obscurity.

1803: Thursday, 26 May . . . 35 Entries. £929 5s.

SIR H. WILLIAMSON'S b.c. DITTO by Sir Peter Teazle out of a mare by Dungannon	W. CLIFT	1
LORD GREY'S b.c. SIR OLIVER by Sir Peter Teazle		2
SIR F. STANDISH'S b.c. BROTHER TO STAMFORD by Sir Peter Teazle		3

Also ran:

Mr G. Watson's Dreadnought (4th); Sir H. T. Vane's Discussor; Colonel Kingscote's Wheat-ear.

6 ran.

Betting:

7–4 Brother to Stamford; 7–2 Ditto; 5 and 6–1 Discussor; 9–1 Sir Oliver.

Won very easily.

1804

The Times honoured Epsom with a few lines in 1804, when the following brief notice appeared in its columns:

Notwithstanding the unpromising appearance of the morning, Epsom Races were very fully attended yesterday. Much expectation was formed from the characters of the horses that were entered to run for the Derby Stakes. The bets at starting were:

> 20 to 10 against Mr Wilson's Waxy colt.
> 22 to 10 against Hannibal.
> 35 to 10 against Zodiac.
> 40 to 10 against Hippocampus.

The Waxy colt made all the play, and there was severe running between him and Hippocampus till Hannibal came up at Tattenham Corner and won easy. The race was run in less time than was ever remembered; and so good a one has not happened for many years.

Hannibal, owned by Lord Egremont, was by Driver, a descendant of the Godolphin Arabian. He was, in fact, a very indifferent racehorse, and apart from receiving a walk-over in a Match, the Derby was his solitary success.

William Arnull, who on this occasion rode the first of his three Derby winners, was nineteen years old at the time. He had the reputation of being a poorish judge of pace, but possessed the not too common asset in his profession of being absolutely honest. He was described by a contemporary writer, who was probably endeavouring to be complimentary, as 'a merry little fellow up to all sorts of queer games'. As a matter of fact he was rather a buffoon and some queer little games were played on him; for example, on one occasion, with the curious humour of the time, a friend inserted a dwarf in a hamper of wine that Arnull was expecting. In later years he became very gouty and his disposition correspondingly less merry.

1804: Thursday, 17 May . . . 33 Entries. £1,076 5s.

LORD EGREMONT's b.c. HANNIBAL by Driver		
out of Fractious	W. ARNULL	1
MR WILSON's b.c. PAVILION by Waxy		2
MR DAWSON's b.c. HIPPOCAMPUS by Coriander		3

1804

Also ran:

Lord Darlington's Zodiac (4th); Mr Lake's Lynceus; Sir F. Poole's Sir Walter Raleigh; Mr Warrington's Woodcot; Mr Warrington's colt by Guildford.

8 ran.

Betting:

2–1 Pavilion; 5–2 and 3–1 Hannibal; 7–2 and 3–1 Zodiac; 9–2 Hippocampus; 12–1 Sir Walter Raleigh.

Won very easily.

1805

Lord Egremont won again in 1805, this time with Cardinal Beaufort, a son of his old favourite Gohanna. Lord Egremont was very keen on the theory of in-breeding, and one of his fillies was by Little John, by Octavius, out of Rectory, also by Octavius. She received the appropriate if unattractive name of Incest.

Cardinal Beaufort had never run before the Derby, and as he was thought to have no chance of beating the favourite, his stable companion Imposter, odds of 20–1 against him were freely available. Imposter, however, lived up to his name and was in full retreat some distance from home, whereas Cardinal Beaufort battled on with great courage to beat the second favourite, Plantagenet, by a neck. There was a nasty accident in the race when the Dungannon colt was brought down by an imprudently straying spectator. Fortunately the jockey concerned received only superficial injuries.

At Brighton later in the season Cardinal Beaufort won two races, but was then beaten twice at Lewes. Lord Egremont promptly sold him to a Mr Ladbroke, who quickly re-sold him to a Mr Arthur; for both of these gentlemen he won races at Newmarket. In 1807 he had three different owners, Mr Shakspear, Mr Mellish, and Mr Lloyd, and won races for all three. The following year he belonged to General Gower, for whom he won prizes at Brighton and Newmarket. After that, all trace of him is lost.

Dennis Fitzpatrick, who rode Cardinal Beaufort at Epsom, was an Irishman, who had made his reputation at the Curragh. He died the following year aged forty-one.

1805: Thursday, 30 May . . . 39 Entries. £1,338 15s.

LORD EGREMONT's b.c. CARDINAL BEAUFORT by Gohanna
out of Colibri   D. FITZPATRICK 1
LORD GROSVENOR's b.c. PLANTAGENET by John Bull 2
LORD GROSVENOR's b.c. GOTH by Sir Peter Teazle 3

Also ran:

Mr Biggs's Bassanio (4th); Lord Foley's Little Peter; Lord Egremont's Imposter; General Gower's Swinley; H.R.H. Prince of Wales's Barbarossa; Mr Wilson's Newmarket; Mr Howorth's Honesty; Mr Glover's Sigismunda; Mr Robert Jones's

Freedom; Mr Robert Jones's Junius; Mr Best's colt by Dungannon; Mr Harris's Farmer.

15 ran.

Betting:

7–4 Imposter; 5–2 and 2–1 Plantagenet; 9–1 Little Peter, Newmarket, and Bassanio; 20–1 Cardinal Beaufort.

Won by a neck.

1806

In 1806 Lord Egremont's Trafalgar was beaten after a desperate battle by a short head by Lord Foley's Paris. Lord Egremont won again in 1807 with Election, so those few inches by which Trafalgar was defeated deprived him of the wonderful achievement of winning the race four years in succession.

Paris was by Sir Peter Teazle out of Horatia, and was thus a full brother to Stamford, the unsuccessful Derby favourite of 1797, and also to Brother to Stamford, unsuccessful favourite in 1803. Both the Stamfords belonged to Sir Frank Standish, who must have tired of the mare and her offspring and sold both her and her foal to Lord Foley. To make matters even more vexatious for him this year, Sir Frank owned the filly by Mr Teazle out of the Yellow mare that started favourite.

Paris had only run once before the Derby. Later in Epsom week he was beaten by a brother to Cardinal Beaufort, to whom he conceded five pounds. In the autumn he met Cardinal Beaufort himself in a 200-guinea Match over the Abingdon Mile. Cardinal Beaufort conceded eight pounds and won. Horses had to be tough in those days, and the very same afternoon Paris competed for a Sweepstakes Across The Flat and was defeated.

Next year Paris won three Matches at Newmarket in the spring, but then ran unsuccessfully in Sweepstakes, twice at York and once at Newmarket. His final appearance was in 1808 when he met his old Derby rival Trafalgar in a Match for 500 guineas over the Beacon Course and was beaten. After that there is no trace of him at all in the records.

Lord Foley was a supporter of racing for many years. His father was said to have dissipated the best part of a million pounds at cards and on the Turf, while he himself reduced the family fortune even further by reckless gambling.

John Shepherd, who rode Paris in the Derby, was a Yorkshireman, forty-one years of age at the time. He came down to Newmarket to act as trainer and jockey to Lord Foley at an annual salary of £200, and by his skill did something to weaken the Newmarket prejudice against north-country riders. He did not retire from the saddle until he was nearly sixty, but he died a poor man, his large and hungry family having accounted for most of his savings.

1806

1806: Thursday, 22 May . . . 39 Entries. £1,348 15s.

LORD FOLEY's b.c. PARIS by Sir Peter Teazle out of Horatia	J. SHEPHERD	1
LORD EGREMONT's b.c. TRAFALGAR by Gohanna		2
THE MARGRAVINE OF ANSPACH's gr.c. HECTOR by Highover		3

Also ran:

Mr Wilson's Smuggler; Duke of Grafton's Podargus; Lord Egremont's Hedley; Mr S. Arthur's Achilles; Sir J. Shelley's Clasher; Mr Mellish's Luck's All; Sir F. Standish's filly by Mr Teazle; Mr S. Batson's Rapture; Mr Croft's Ploughboy.

12 ran.

Betting:

7–2 the filly by Mr Teazle; 5–1 Paris and Achilles; 6–1 Trafalgar.

Won by a short head.

1807

The weights were altered to 8 st. 7 lb. and 8 st. 5 lb. in 1807 when Election gave Lord Egremont his fourth success. Election was a son of Gohanna, whose stud fee at that time was fifty guineas, a considerable sum in those days, and double the fee, for example, of Sir Peter Teazle.

Election, ridden by John Arnull, had never run before the Derby, which was his only race as a three-year-old. He had evidently been well galloped though, as he started favourite at 3–1, the only other runners seriously backed being the Duke of Grafton's Musician, Lord C. Somerset's Job Thornberry, and Mr Christopher Wilson's Giles Scroggins. It proved to be a good and exciting race. Giles Scroggins led to the distance where he was headed by the outsider Coriolanus. Election then put in a very determined challenge and, running on strongly, he won all out by a length from Giles Scroggins, who had re-passed Coriolanus close home. The Prince of Wales had two runners, Mungo and Lewis, but they ran in the name of his manager, Mr Delmé Radcliffe. The Prince had taken up racing again five years previously and his horses were then trained at Albury Grange, near Winchester, by a man called Smallman who was a brother-in-law of Sam Chifney senior.

Election remained in training till 1811 and won a good many races, mostly of minor importance. He finally retired to the Hampton Court Stud at a fee of ten guineas, but met with little success. He died at Euston in 1821. Giles Scroggins was bought by Lord Darlington, who changed his somewhat bucolic name to Master Goodall, but the change of name failed to bring about a change of luck.

1807: Thursday, 14 May . . . 38 Entries. £1,333 10s.

LORD EGREMONT'S ch.c. ELECTION by Gohanna
  out of Chestnut Skim   J. ARNULL 1
MR WILSON'S GILES SCROGGINS by Sir Solomon   W. CLIFT   2
MR LAKE'S b.c. CORIOLANUS by Gohanna   WHEATLEY   3

Also ran:
  Mr Ladbroke's Corsican; Mr Biggs's Rosario; Duke of Grafton's Pioneer; Duke of Grafton's Musician; Mr Delmé Radcliffe's Mungo; Mr Delmé Radcliffe's Lewis;

Lord C. Somerset's Job Thornberry; Lord Foley's Chaise-and-one; Sir F. Standish's colt by Sir Peter Teazle; Lord Darlington's Brother to Expectation.

13 ran.

Betting:

   3–1 Election; 7–2 Musician; 4–1 Job Thornberry and Giles Scroggins; very high odds against Coriolanus.

Won by a length.

1808

Sir Hedworth Williamson's Pan, winner in 1808, was a half-brother by Highflyer's son St George to Ditto, winner in 1803. Pan had never seen a racecourse before Epsom, and so little was thought of him that he started at 25–1 in a field of ten.

This year's favourite was the Duke of Grafton's Vandyke, by Sir Peter Teazle, while other well-backed runners were the Prince of Wales's Rubens, and another colt by Sir Peter Teazle, Clinker, owned by Mr Sitwell. Clinker became the sire of Clinkerina, dam of Humphrey Clinker, the sire of Melbourne.

It was a magnificent race to watch. Lord Egremont's Brighton Lass made the running till just past Tattenham Corner where she was headed by Vandyke and Clinker. Just as these two were battling it out, they were headed at the distance by Rubens and at that point it looked any odds on a royal victory. All of a sudden, however, Pan appeared on the scene with a devastating late run and mastered the tiring Rubens close home to win by half a length from Vandyke, who re-passed Rubens near the post.

The following spring Pan again beat Vandyke, this time in a Sweepstakes at Newmarket, but in the autumn Vandyke obtained his revenge on the Derby winner by beating him in a King's Plate over the Beacon Course. Soon afterwards Pan was sold to Lord Sackville, for whom he won eleven races in the course of the next three seasons. He eventually retired to the stud near Luton at a fee of five guineas, but proved only moderately successful.

Frank Collinson, a Yorkshire farmer's son, rode a brilliant race on Pan at Epsom, but in his triumph were the seeds of disaster as well. On his journey south he slept in a damp bed at an inn and contracted an illness that was the cause of his death three years later.

1808: Thursday, 2 June . . . 38 Entries. £1,260.

SIR H. WILLIAMSON's ch.c. PAN by St George out of Arethusa	F. COLLINSON	1
DUKE OF GRAFTON's br.c. VANDYKE by Sir Peter Teazle	W. CLIFT	2
LORD GROSVENOR's b.c. CHESTER by Sir Peter Teazle	F. BUCKLE	3

Also ran:

H.R.H. Prince of Wales's Rubens (4th); Mr Sitwell's Clinker; Lord Egremont's Scorpion; Lord Egremont's Brighton Lass; Lord Stawell's No Conjuror; Mr Ladbroke's Tristram; Mr Mellish's Bradbury.

10 ran.

Betting:

9–4 Vandyke; 10–3 Rubens; 4 and 5–1 Clinker; 6–1 Scorpion; 9–1 No Conjuror; 20–1 Chester; 25–1 Pan.

Won by half a length.

1809

The Duke of Grafton triumphed again in 1809, the victor being his colt Pope (frequently known as Waxy Pope), by Waxy, winner of the 1793 Derby, out of Prunella.

Waxy, closely in-bred on both the male and female side to the Darley Arabian, transmitted to many of his descendants the astonishing vitality that was a feature both of himself and of his sire Pot-8-os. The Duke of Grafton had observed and carefully noted the successful combination of Eclipse with Herod mares, and accordingly he mated Prunella, a daughter of Herod's best son, Highflyer, with Waxy.

Previously Prunella had produced Penelope, by Trumpator; Parasol, by Pot-8-os; Pelisse and Pioneer, both by Whiskey; and Podargus, by Worthy. Penelope, dam of the Derby winners Whalebone and Whisker, won eighteen races, Parasol thirty-one, Pelisse seventeen (including the Oaks), and Podargus two.

Besides Pope, Prunella bred two full sisters to him, Pledge and Pope Joan. Pledge won twice and was dam of the 1819 Derby winner, Tiresias, while Pope Joan produced in successive years Tontine, winner of the One Thousand Guineas; Turcoman, winner of the Two Thousand Guineas; and Turquoise, winner of the Oaks. No wonder Prunella is generally recognized as one of the greatest mares in the Stud Book, and it only remains to add that two recent Derby winners, Ocean Swell (1944) and Never Say Die (1954), are both descendants of Chelandry, who traces in tail female to the Duke of Grafton's famous mare.

The Derby was Pope's first race and his victory came as a complete surprise. The red-hot favourite was Mr Christopher Wilson's Wizard, who had won the first contest for the newly founded Two Thousand Guineas. Wizard started at 11–8 on and came very close to winning, but after taking the lead on the turn for home he was caught less than half a dozen strides from the post by Pope, the unconsidered 20–1 outsider.

Unbeaten as a three-year-old, Pope met Wizard in a 200-Guinea Match at Newmarket the following spring. Such was Mr Wilson's confidence that he agreed for his colt to concede the Derby winner three pounds. Moreover, the result fully justified his opinion, as Wizard defeated the odds-on Pope. Towards the close of 1810, Pope was sold to Lord Sligo, for whom he won three races before being retired to the stud in Ireland, where he died in 1831.

Pope was ridden at Epsom by Tom Goodisson, a son of Dick Goodisson, the blunt, rough-tongued, slovenly dressed Yorkshireman who for many years acted as trainer and jockey to the Duke of Queensberry, generally known as 'Old Q'. Tom, a very sound rider and an admirable judge of pace, was retained for many years by the Duke of York, and he also rode frequently for the Duke of Grafton and Sir Charles Bunbury. He rode four winners of the Derby, and in 1813 and again in 1815 he rode the winners of both the Epsom classics. He died at Newmarket in 1840 aged fifty-eight.

1809: Thursday, 18 May . . . 45 Entries. £1,443 15s.

DUKE OF GRAFTON's b.c. POPE by Waxy out of Prunella	T. GOODISSON	1
MR C. WILSON's ch.c. WIZARD by Sorcerer	W. CLIFT	2
DUKE OF RUTLAND's br.c. SALVATOR by Trumpator	No jockey recorded	3

Also ran:

Sir C. Bunbury's Fair Star; Mr Wyndham's Trusty; Lord Foley's Ospray; Mr Lake's Break; Sir J. Shelley's Robin; Sir J. Mawbey's Botleys; Lord Lowther's Blue Ruin.

10 ran.

Betting:

11–8 on Wizard; 9–2 Fair Star; 10–1 Salvator; 20–1 Pope.

Won by a neck.
Winner trained by Robson.

1810

Whalebone, who won for the Duke of Grafton in 1810, was described by old Dry-
man, Lord Egremont's stud-groom, as 'the lowest and longest and most double-
jointed horse, with the best legs and the worst feet I ever saw'. 'The Druid' was even
less flattering; 'Whalebone,' he wrote, 'was as shabby to the eye as old Prunella
herself. He had rather a Turkish pony look, and was broad and strong, with a
shortish neck. His own feet grew very pumiced, and his mares lost their speed early.'

However, the fact remains that this mottled brown horse with a white off-hind
fetlock, standing just over fifteen hands, not only won the Derby, but exercised a
profound influence on bloodstock breeding. In the last century his descendants,
through his son Camel, included Touchstone, Newminster, Lord Clifden, and
Hampton; while through Sir Hercules came Birdcatcher, The Baron, Stockwell,
Doncaster, Bend Or, Ormonde, Oxford, Sterling, and Isonomy. In modern times
among the great horses descended from him in tail male are Blandford, Tracery,
Phalaris, Teddy, Orby, Son-in-Law, Gainsborough, Spearmint, Hyperion, Sardanapale, and Whisk Broom. A very high proportion, therefore, of the great horses in
racing history include his name in their pedigree.

Whalebone was by Waxy out of Prunella's daughter Penelope. The Duke of
Grafton was a firm adherent of in-breeding and he mated Penelope with Waxy
because she herself was in-bred to the Godolphin Arabian and was therefore, in his
opinion, ideally suited to Waxy, in whom there were three strains of the Godolphin
Arabian, two of which he obtained from his sire Pot-8-os.

Penelope has been described as 'the most epoch-making mare in the Stud Book',
and undoubtedly her owner's decision to mate her with Waxy produced astonishingly
successful results. Altogether she produced nine offspring by Waxy:

1806	Bay filly	unnamed	Won 1 race	
1807	Brown colt	Whalebone	Won 20 races	Including the Derby. Sired 252 winners (two Derby winners) of £81,683.
1808	Bay filly	Web	Won 2 races	Dam of Middleton (winner of the Derby), and grand-dam of Cobweb, winner of the One Thousand Guineas and the Oaks.

54

Sir Peter Teazle; after S. Gilpin

Above: Bay Middleton. *Below:* Saddling in the Warren, 1836; after J. Pollard

1809	Bay colt	Woful	Won 12 races	Sire of 58 winners of £33,589. Exported to Germany.
1810	Chesnut filly	Wilful	Won 12 races	Went to Ireland.
1811	Brown filly	Wire	Won 9 races	Went to Ireland.
1812	Bay colt	Whisker	Won 13 races	Including the Derby. Sire to 167 winners of £55,140.
1816	Bay colt	Wildfire	Won 0 races	Went to Germany.
1817	Chesnut colt	Windfall	Won 0 races	Only ran once.

Apart from her offspring by Waxy, Penelope produced two colts and two fillies. These included Waterloo, by Walton, winner of the St Leger; and Whizgig, by Rubens, winner of seven races and dam of the One Thousand Guineas winner Oxygen.

As regards Whalebone's racing career, he made his first appearance at the Newmarket First Spring Meeting in 1810 when he won the Newmarket Stakes after first dead-heating with Treasurer, a grey colt by Stamford. His next outing was the Derby and, ridden by Clift, he started favourite at 2–1. He triumphed with the utmost ease and is one of the few horses to have won the race after making every yard of the running. At the Newmarket Houghton Meeting he attempted to concede Treasurer seven pounds over the Ditch In Course and was beaten. However, that week he won two Matches and received forfeit in two more.

Whalebone won more races in 1811 and 1812, and towards the end of the latter year he was sold to Mr R. Ladbroke, a banker, for whom he won the Northampton Gold Cup and a number of other events. His racing record was a good one, but in the course of it he was defeated on six occasions and it can hardly be said to have foretold his striking success at the stud. Mr Ladbroke was evidently of the opinion that Whalebone would never make much of a sire and sold him as a seven-year-old to Lord Egremont for the modest sum of 510 guineas. In 1815, therefore, Whalebone retired to the Petworth Stud, his fee at the outset being a mere ten guineas.

It only remains to add that Whalebone will always have his place in French racing history as well, as his son Defence was the great-grandsire of the immortal Gladiateur, the first French horse to win the Derby and the so-called 'Avenger of Waterloo'.

1810: Thursday, 3 June . . . 45 Entries. £1,365.

DUKE OF GRAFTON's b.c. WHALEBONE by Waxy
   out of Penelope   W. CLIFT   1
LORD KINNAIRD's ch.c. THE DANDY by Gohanna   W. PEIRSE   2
LORD G. H. CAVENDISH's b.c. ECCLESTON by Cesario   S. CHIFNEY   3

Also ran:

Lord Grosvenor's Hephestion; Mr Thompson's O.P.; Duke of Grafton's Pledge; Lord Egremont's Interloper; Major Wilson's Erebus; Mr Lake's Breslaw; Mr Howorth's Revoke; General Gower's Abdiel.

11 ran.

Betting:

2–1 Whalebone; 3–1 Pledge and Hephestion; 7–1 Eccleston; 8–1 The Dandy.

Won easily.
Winner trained by Robson.

1811

Sir John Shelley won his first Derby in 1811 with Phantom; he was to win again in 1824 with Phantom's son Cedric. Sir John, the sixth baronet, was head of a family for many years resident at Michel Grove in Sussex. His father had been a well-known racing man and a member of the Jockey Club; he himself was closely identified with the Turf for many years and for a considerable period was the racing confederate of Lord Jersey. Forty years of age when Phantom won, he was not elected to the Jockey Club till 1835, which suggests that he was not by any means universally popular.

Phantom was by Walton, own brother to Ditto and half-brother to Pan, the two Derby winners owned by Sir Hedworth Williamson. In all probability Walton was Sir Peter Teazle's best son; he won nineteen of his twenty-six races, and besides Phantom he sired Nectar, winner of the Two Thousand Guineas, and St Patrick, winner of the St Leger. Bred by his owner, Phantom was out of Julia, a full sister to that great mare Eleanor, winner of the Derby and the Oaks in 1801. Julia's only other produce was Vexation, winner of fourteen races.

Phantom's first race was a Produce Stakes at the Newmarket Craven Meeting as a three-year-old and he must have been very well galloped as he started favourite at 3–1 on. However, he was beaten by Lord Grosvenor's filly Barossa, a daughter of the 1797 Oaks winner Niké. Possibly his defeat was due to inexperience, as Barossa was far from outstanding and failed to get a place in the Oaks.

The Derby was Phantom's next race. Favourite was Trophonius, a black colt by Sorcerer that had won the Two Thousand Guineas. Phantom and Lord Darlington's Hit or Miss were joint second favourites at 5–1, while Magic was quite well backed as well. Wellington and Merrygoround, both sons of Trumpator, were the leaders up to the distance where Magic headed them, hotly pursued by Phantom. Buckle rode a superb finish on Phantom and succeeded in forcing his mount's head in front in the very last stride.

Phantom won several other prizes before he retired. His last race was at Newmarket in 1813 when he met Mr Gascoigne's Soothsayer, who had beaten Magic in the 1811 St Leger, in a Match Across The Flat. It was a great race in which Soothsayer prevailed by a narrow margin. Phantom did well at the stud; he sired two Derby winners, Cedric and Middleton; two Two Thousand Guineas winners,

Pindaric and Enamel; and Cobweb, winner of the One Thousand Guineas and the Oaks. While at the stud he became completely blind.

1811: Thursday, 30 May . . . 48 Entries. £1,680.

SIR J. SHELLEY's b.c. PHANTOM by Walton out of Julia	F. BUCKLE	1
MR ASTLEY's ch.c. MAGIC by Sorcerer	T. CARR	2

No horse was officially placed third.

Also ran:

Sir C. Bunbury's Rival; Mr Payne's Mountebank; Sir F. Standish's Wellington; Lord G. H. Cavendish's Merrygoround; Mr Lake's colt by Sorcerer; Mr Wilson's colt by Sir Solomon; Lord Darlington's Hit or Miss; Lord Darlington's Timour; Sir F. Standish's colt by Mr Teazle; Mr Blake's Rapid; Duke of Rutland's Momus; Mr Shakespear's Jolter; Mr Norton's colt by Cockfighter; Mr Andrew's Trophonius.

16 ran.

Betting:

3–1 Trophonius; 5–1 Hit or Miss and Phantom; 7–1 Magic; 10–1 Mountebank; 12–1 Merrygoround and Wellington.

Won by a head in the last stride.

1812

The Derby of 1812 was regrettably marred by foul play. Manuella, owned by a Mr Hewett, had never run in public, but had been so highly tried at home that her owner was persuaded to run her against the colts, although she was engaged in the Oaks as well.

Ridden by Sam Chifney junior, Manuella started second favourite at 7–2. Chifney, however, was not the first or the last great jockey to be thoroughly dishonest when the financial incentive was deemed sufficient, and he deliberately stopped the filly. The next day he booked a bet of 2,000 to 100 about her for the Oaks, in which she was ridden by Pierce. She duly won that race, beating the odds-on favourite Elizabeth, owned by the Duke of Rutland. Unfortunately, the Oaks victory failed to save Mr Hewett, who had lost more than he could pay on the Derby and who fled to France with his family. Later in the year Manuella started favourite for the St Leger, but was sexually amiss and finished down the course.

With Manuella 'a dead 'un', the Derby was won by Octavius, a son of Orville, belonging to Mr Ladbroke, the London banker who at one time had owned Whalebone. Orville, owned by Lord Fitzwilliam, won the St Leger in 1802. He was inclined to be lazy and needed a great deal of driving, but there was no doubt about his merit as he won twenty races besides his classic success. He was also sire of Emilius, winner of the Derby in 1823.

Octavius did not run as a two-year-old, and his first outing was at the Newmarket Craven Meeting when he won a Sweepstakes although apparently little fancied. On the strength of that victory he was made second favourite for the Two Thousand Guineas, but could do no better than finish third to Cwrw, whose name must have tested the bookmakers, and Cato. In the Derby Sir John Shelley's Comus was favourite, and both Manuella and Whitburn were more strongly supported than Octavius.

Mr Christopher Wilson's Wisdom led until Tattenham Corner where he was headed by Octavius, Comus, and Lord Egremont's Sweep. The three raced abreast till just over a furlong out, at which point Comus began to falter a little. Octavius and Sweep continued to battle it out, Octavius, ridden by W. Arnull, obtaining a slight advantage close home to win by the margin of 'half a neck'.

Octavius only raced once more that season, finishing a dismal last in a field of four for the Magna Charta Stakes at Egham. The following year he won the Epsom Gold Cup, beating the Oaks winner Sorcery, and then an insignificant prize at Stockbridge. After three defeats in 1814 he was sold to Lord Egremont. He did not prove a second Whalebone, though, for his new owner, his most notable achievement at the stud being to sire Little John, whose son Frederick won the 1829 Derby.

1812: Thursday, 14 May . . . 47 Entries. £1,601 5s.

MR R. LADBROKE's br.c. OCTAVIUS by Orville out of Marianne	W. ARNULL	1
LORD EGREMONT's b.c. SWEEP by Gohanna	W. WHEATLEY	2
SIR J. SHELLEY's COMUS by Sorcerer	F. BUCKLE	3

Also ran:

Mr Wilson's Wisdom; Mr Stafford's Whitburn; Duke of Rutland's Ptolemy; Lord Lowther's Brother to Briseis; Sir F. Standish's colt by Young Eagle; Mr Hewett's Manuella; General Gower's Anastasia; Mr Mellish's Flash; Mr Mellish's Bodkin; Mr Lake's Pointers; Mr Booth Grey's colt by Sir Oliver.

14 ran.

Betting:

3–1 Comus; 7–2 Manuella; 6–1 Whitburn; 7–1 Octavius; 9–1 Brother to Briseis.

Won by half a neck.

1813

At the age of seventy-three Sir Charles Bunbury won his third and final Derby, the winner in 1813 being his black colt Smolensko, the only horse of that colour to win the most coveted race of the year until Grand Parade's victory in 1919. Smolensko was by Sorcerer, a son of Trumpator, whose grandsire was Matchem. Wouski, Smolensko's dam, had run second in the Oaks in 1800 when owned by Mr Hallett, and was subsequently bought by Sir Charles.

Smolensko had the distinction of being the first horse to win both the Two Thousand Guineas and the Derby. He started a 7–4 favourite for the Newmarket classic and the very next day he turned out for the Newmarket Stakes, which he won as well. He was made an even money favourite for the Derby, the only horse seriously fancied to beat him being the Duke of Rutland's Solyman. Far from winning with the ease expected, Smolensko had to fight very hard indeed for his victory and it was only in the last few strides that he mastered Lord Jersey's Caterpillar, who, ridden by Buckle, had led from the very start.

There was an interesting little sequel to the race that showed that 'The First Dictator of the Turf', like so many rich men, had a curious streak of meanness in his character. After the Derby a bookmaker called Brograve, unable to meet his creditors of whom Sir Charles was one, saw fit to shoot himself. Sir Charles, therefore, handed Goodisson three ten-pound notes for his three victories on Smolensko, explaining that owing to Brograve's default, he was unfortunately unable to afford any more. It is a matter of regret that Goodisson's comments on this transaction have not been handed down to posterity.

Smolensko won the Magna Charta Stakes at Egham that year, but at Newmarket in October he was beaten as a 4–1 on favourite for a Subscription Purse. He won a Match later that autumn and two prizes the following spring, at which point, for some reason, his racing career came to an end. When his owner died in 1821 he was sold to Mr R. Wilson for 1,300 guineas, being subsequently re-sold to Mr Theobald of Stockwell. He did fairly well at the stud, siring 116 winners of £35,262, and his name appears in the pedigree of that good horse Robert the Devil, who so nearly beat Bend Or in the 1880 Derby.

1813: Thursday, 3 June . . . 51 Entries. £1,653 15s.

SIR C. BUNBURY'S bl.c. SMOLENSKO by Sorcerer out of Wouski	T. GOODISSON	1
LORD JERSEY'S br.c. CATERPILLAR by Haphazard	F. BUCKLE	2
MR GLOVER'S b.c. ILLUSION by Haphazard	W. WHEATLEY	3

Also ran:

Duke of Rutland's Solyman; Duke of Rutland's Rastopchin; Lord Suffield's Hocuspocus; Mr Lake's Eurus; Mr Lake's Aladdin; Lord Darlington's Brother to Pan; Lord Derby's Viceroy; Lord Grosvenor's Onyx; Mr Kellerman's Alcohol.

12 ran.

Betting:

Evens Smolensko; 4–1 Solyman; 7–1 Caterpillar; 9–1 Viceroy; 17–1 Aladdin.

Won by half a length.

1814

Blücher, winner in 1814, belonged to Lord Stawell, who was for many years a prominent racing man and who had inherited his title from his mother. He left no successor when he died in 1820.

Blücher, not one of the outstanding Derby winners, was by Waxy out of Pantina, by Buzzard, so once again the Eclipse–Herod cross proved successful. Unlike the vast majority of early Derby winners, Blücher was seen in public as a two-year-old, running three times at that age, and winning a Sweepstakes at the Newmarket Houghton Meeting.

The following season Blücher won a Sweepstakes at the Newmarket Craven Meeting and a fortnight later the Newmarket Stakes. As a result he was made favourite for the Derby at 5–2. He duly won, but it was only in the last few strides that William Arnull forced his head in front of Perchance, who had led from the start.

Blücher had only three races subsequently, winning the Magna Charta Stakes at Egham and being beaten in the other two. He retired to the stud at Farnham and sired a number of winners, though none as useful as himself.

1814: Thursday, 26th May . . . 51 Entries. £2,706 5s.

LORD STAWELL'S b.c. BLÜCHER by Waxy
  out of Pantina   W. ARNULL   1
MR PRINCE'S ch.c. PERCHANCE by Haphazard   W. CLIFT   2
No horse was officially placed third.

Also ran:

Lord Lowther's Bourbon; Duke of Rutland's Kutusoff; Lord Egremont's Wanderer; Sir G. Webster's Grand Duchess; Duke of Rutland's Osman; Lord F. Bentinck's Monkey; Mr Warwick Lake's colt by Zodiac; Mr Lake's Brother to Sagana; Duke of Grafton's Jeweller; Mr Andrews's Robin Adair; Mr Newnham's Wilmington; Mr S. Pearce's colt by Eagle.

14 ran.

Betting:

5–2 Blücher; 3–1 and 7–2 Bourbon; 4–1 Perchance; 7–1 Grand Duchess; 10–1 Wanderer and the colt by Zodiac.

Won by a head.

1815

The third Duke of Grafton, owner of three Derby winners, died in 1811. His son, who succeeded him, only won the Derby once, with Whisker in 1815, but thanks to the profound knowledge of racing and breeding on the part of his brother, the Rev. Lord Henry Fitzroy, and to the scientific methods of his trainer Robson, his successes on the Turf in fact exceeded those enjoyed by his father. He won the Two Thousand Guineas five times; the Oaks seven times; and the One Thousand Guineas eight times within a period of nine years. No doubt because of the difficulties of travel, he never ran a horse in the St Leger. He died in 1844, having for several seasons before his death made a practice of selling the majority of his yearlings.

Whisker, a full brother to Whalebone, is said to have been one of the most perfectly formed horses ever foaled. His career, however, began somewhat disappointingly, for after walking over for a Match, he was unplaced in the Two Thousand Guineas, in which he had started second favourite. Furthermore, in the Newmarket Stakes, he was soundly beaten by Busto, a son of Clinker.

Busto was owned by General Gower, who, however, owned another colt, Raphael by name, that had been tried at home to be greatly superior to Busto. On form, therefore, Raphael had little to fear in the Derby from Whisker.

Raphael started favourite for the Derby at 7–2; Whisker was quite well backed at 8–1, but Busto was without a quotation in the market. Busto's task, in fact, was to make the running for Raphael, and so well did he carry it out that he was still in front with just under a furlong to go. At that point Raphael came with a perfectly judged run and headed him, but just when the race looked to be at the favourite's mercy, Goodisson brought Whisker with a storming late challenge to seize the advantage just as the winning post was reached. The judge's verdict was a short head; the gallant Busto was only a neck behind the second, and the other runners were never in the picture at all. Some of the crowd took Raphael's defeat very ill indeed, and the unfortunate Jackson, who had ridden an admirable race on the favourite, was dragged from his horse and mauled, fortunately without serious injury being inflicted.

In the autumn Whisker was unplaced in the Newmarket St Leger, and before the season was over he had won a couple of matches and lost one. As a four-year-old he won four times and was then sold to Lord Darlington. The rest of his racing career was without distinction and he eventually retired to the stud at a fee of fifteen guineas, which was later on raised to twenty. He sired The Colonel, winner of the 1828 St Leger, and his daughter Emma was dam of Mowerina, dam of the 1853 Derby winner West Australian. In fact his mares did remarkably well, as the Derby winners Cotherstone and Mündig, the St Leger winner Mango, and Euclid, who dead-heated for the 1839 St Leger with Charles XII, only to be beaten in the run-off, were all out of Whisker mares.

1815: Thursday, 25 May . . . 51 Entries. £1,680.

DUKE OF GRAFTON'S b.c. WHISKER by Waxy out of Penelope	T. GOODISSON	1
GENERAL GOWER'S b.c. RAPHAEL by Rubens	J. JACKSON	2
GENERAL GOWER'S br.c. BUSTO by Clinker	W. PEIRSE	3

Also ran:

Lord Foley's colt by Selim; Mr Lake's Castanet; Mr Lake's Scrapall; Lord Rous's Equator; Mr Wyndham's Frolic; Mr Andrews's Garus; Mr Payne's Quinola; Mr Stonehewer's Delville; Mr Duncombe's colt by Sir David; Sir B. Graham's Sir Christopher.

13 ran.

Betting:

3–1 and 7–2 Raphael; 7–2 Frolic; 7–1 Castanet; 8–1 Whisker and the colt by Selim.

Won by a short head.
Winner trained by Robson.

1816

Frederick, Duke of York, one of the unattractive and unsatisfactory sons of George III, won the Derby twice, with Prince Leopold, who actually ran in the name of Mr Warwick Lake, the Duke's master of horse, in 1816, and with Moses in 1822. This is not the place to comment on the Duke of York's activities as Commander-in Chief of the Army, it will suffice to say here that he was an inveterate gambler, and although not unsuccessful on the Turf, he left a mountain of debts behind him when he died. To discharge these, the Government is said to have ceded Cape Breton to his creditors.

Prince Leopold, by Hedley, out of a mare by Sorcerer, can be fairly summed up as the best of a moderate lot. He had never run before Epsom, and although his owner supported him to win some thousands, the general public ignored him completely and he started at 20–1. Nectar, winner of the Two Thousand Guineas, was favourite and led from the start, but was tackled a furlong and a half out by Prince Leopold and Pandour, Prince Leopold finishing just the stronger to win by half a length.

Prince Leopold did not win again that season. The following year he won the Port Stakes, again beating Nectar, but gradually became so bad-tempered that it was decided to cut him. Unfortunately the operation proved fatal.

1816: Thursday, 30 May . . . 51 Entries. £1,635 15s.

MR LAKE's b.c. PRINCE LEOPOLD by Hedley out of Gramarie	W. WHEATLEY	1
LORD CAVENDISH's b.c. NECTAR by Walton	F. BUCKLE	2
LORD STAWELL's ch.c. PANDOUR by Walton	W. ARNULL	3

Also ran:

Lord Foley's colt by Selim; Duke of Grafton's Alien; Mr Blake's John of Paris; Mr Blake's Expectation; Mr Terrel's Sovereign; Mr Duncombe's colt by Stavely; Mr Scaith's Bacchus; Mr Wyndham's Skim.

11 ran.

Betting:

10–6 Nectar; 7–4 Skim; 7–1 Alien; 16–1 Pandour and John of Paris; 20–1 Prince Leopold.

Won by half a length.

1817

The three-year-old form in 1817 was very erratic and there can be little doubt that it was far from a vintage year. The best-backed horse in the Derby was Mr Udney's The Student, who had won Sweepstakes on three successive days at Newmarket; next in demand was Mr Stephenson's Manfred, winner of the Two Thousand Guineas, but subsequently unplaced in the Newmarket Stakes. Neither made much of a show in the race, and to the consternation of the crowd, the finish was fought out by two 50–1 outsiders, Azor and Young Wizard, Azor gaining the advantage well inside the final furlong to win by half a length. Azor, owned by Mr John Payne, uncle of the famous figure in mid-Victorian racing circles, Mr George Payne, had a mediocre record outside his Derby success, and all trace of him is lost after he was on offer for sale the following year.

The most interesting point of Azor's Derby was in affording that great rider Jem Robinson the first of his six successes in the race. That number has yet to be exceeded, but it was equalled a century later by Steve Donoghue, two of whose victories were however wartime substitute races at Newmarket, and later by Lester Piggott.

Born at Newmarket in 1794, Robinson showed high promise from an early age, and before long it was a frequent source of argument whether he or young Sam Chifney was the greater artist. Both were marvellous judges of pace, and both extremely strong finishers. There is no doubt, though, that Robinson was by far the more honest and dependable of the two. When he was getting on in years, Robinson had a very bad fall on a two-year-old and broke his thigh. This accident left him with one leg four inches shorter than the other for the rest of his life. He had a great deal of trouble with his weight, and on one occasion was found insensible by the side of the road, having collapsed and fainted from sheer weakness after wasting.

1817: Thursday, 22 May . . . 56 Entries. £1,811 5s.

MR PAYNE'S ch.c. AZOR by Selim
   out of Zoraida   J. ROBINSON 1
MR WILSON'S ch.c. YOUNG WIZARD by Wizard   No jockey recorded 2
No horse was officially placed third.

1817

Also ran:

Duke of Rutland's Sylvanus; Mr Stephenson's Manfred; Mr Vansittart's Pendulum; Mr Udney's The Student; Lord Darlington's Brother to Crispin; Mr Hallett's Boroughmonger; Lord Stawell's Merrymaker; Mr Lake's Gazelle; Mr Lake's Roller; Mr Lake's Doctor Busby; Mr Forth's Waterloo.

13 ran.

Betting:

7–4 The Student; 4–1 Manfred; 8–1 Merrymaker; 10–1 Sylvanus; 12–1 Brother to Crispin and Gazelle; 15–1 Roller; 50–1 Azor and Young Wizard.

Won by half a length.
Winner trained by Robson.

1818

Sam Chifney junior, Jem Robinson's great rival, won the first of his two Derbys in 1818 on Sam, who had been named after himself, and who belonged to his patron and friend, Mr Thomas Thornhill, the Squire of Riddlesworth in Norfolk.

A member of the Jockey Club and a fine judge of a horse, Squire Thornhill was a good-humoured, friendly man of immense size, weighing well over twenty stone. Towards the end of his life he had to give up riding the fine weight-carrying hacks, Tiger and Tobacco Stopper, that were bred by Mr Dobito, a Suffolk farmer of comparable girth, and take to a yellow phaeton instead. 'Not,' he said, 'because I can't get a horse to carry me, but because I can't get one to stand still under me.' He won the Derby again in 1820 with Sailor. When he died in 1844, he left his house and stables in Newmarket to young Sam Chifney for life.

Young Sam Chifney was thirty-two when he won on Sam. He won the Derby again on Sailor two years later and was fifty-seven when he won his last classic race, the One Thousand Guineas on Extempore in 1843.

Old Sam Chifney had taken endless pains in the training of his sons. William, the more intelligent, was taught training and stable management. Young Sam, phlegmatic but resolute, was coached in riding. From the time that he could first sit on a pony young Sam was instructed in every aspect of the art of race-riding, and during his boyhood he was rarely out of the saddle. Like his father, he specialized in waiting races, and it was he rather than old Sam who perfected the famous 'Chifney rush'.

Young Sam stood 5 ft. 7 in. and was strongly built. As he grew older his weight began to bother him, but unfortunately his phlegmatic nature degenerated into sloth and inertia; he could rarely be persuaded to take any exercise, and in consequence missed hundreds of winning rides, a deprivation that failed to disturb him in the least. Occasionally he would go for a short stroll across some fields with a gun and his favourite white pointer, Banker, but what he really enjoyed most was just sitting quietly for hours at a time and watching his pet foxes play in their enclosure. Towards the end of his life he moved to Hove and there he died in his seventieth year. His last visit to a racecourse had been to see his nephew Frank Butler win the Derby on West Australian.

To revert to the horse Sam: he was by Scud, and according to 'The Druid', he was a low, lengthy, and plain sort of horse with a sour countenance and a delicate constitution. He ran once before the Derby, being beaten in The Riddlesworth Stakes at Newmarket by Sir John Shelley's Prince Paul, who started favourite at 11–5 at Epsom. Sam was on offer at 7–2, a remarkably short price considering that he had been amiss ten days previously, and his owner had seriously considered hedging his bets.

The going was as hard as a moneylender's heart; there were ten false starts, which caused Prince Paul to become extremely unsettled; and the race was run from start to finish in a choking cloud of dust. In fact it was only when the majority of the field dropped back beaten that Chifney could pick out Prince Paul, the one rival that he feared. As soon as he spotted him, he made his challenge and beat him.

The remainder of Sam's career was undistinguished, and the following year he was sold to a Mr Charlton, who retired him to the stud at Ludlow at a ten-guinea fee. He was not a success as a sire.

1818: Thursday, 28 May . . . 56 Entries. £1,890.

MR T. THORNHILL's ch.c. SAM by Scud out of Hyale	S. CHIFNEY, JUN.	1
LORD DARLINGTON's gr.c. RABY by Sorcerer	W. PEIRSE	2
SIR J. SHELLEY's b.c. PRINCE PAUL by Walton	EDWARDS	3

Also ran:

Mr Crockford's Rob Roy; Mr Scaith's Aethon; Duke of Rutland's colt by Walton; Mr Watson's Warsaw; Mr Vansittart's Slim; Mr Lake's colt by Seymour; Duke of Grafton's Moeonides; Mr Calley's Guy Mannering; Mr Goddard's Strephon; Lord Stawell's colt by Waxy; Mr Payne's Fitzcloddy; Mr Blake's Dictator; Mr Morgan's Caractacus.

16 ran.

Betting:

11–5 Prince Paul; 7–2 Sam; 7–1 Fitzcloddy; 10–1 Slim; 17–1 Dictator; 18–1 Moeonides; 20–1 the Waxy colt and Guy Mannering.

Won by three parts of a length.
Winner trained by W. Chifney.

1819

The fourth Duke of Portland, who won with Tiresias in 1819, was the father of Lord George Bentinck, who succeeded Sir Charles Bunbury as the most influential racing man of the day. The Duke, however, was a man of some consequence in the racing world himself. When he died in 1854, he had been a member of the Jockey Club for over fifty years and an active member for most of that period as well. In 1831 he advanced money to the Jockey Club for the purchase of the freehold of the Coffee Room, New Rooms, and adjuncts. He owned part of Newmarket Heath and did much work at his own expense in improving the Heath as a centre for racing. In addition he bought land surrounding the Heath in case it should ever fall into the hands of persons hostile to racing.

In 1827 he was instrumental in establishing the Jockey Club's right to warn allegedly undesirable individuals off Newmarket Heath. There was a disputed bet, and the Jockey Club's decision on that matter greatly displeased a Mr Hawkins, who gave an uncouth demonstration of his sentiments by swearing horribly at Lord Wharncliffe. The Jockey Club thereupon warned him off the Heath. Mr Hawkins fought back gamely and brought an action against the Jockey Club. The case was defended by the Duke of Portland on behalf of the Club, and the Club's right to the action taken against Mr Hawkins was upheld by the judge.

Tiresias, by Soothsayer out of Pledge, by Waxy, began his three-year-old career by winning a Sweepstakes, two Matches, the Newmarket Stakes, and the Palace Stakes. Not surprisingly he was made favourite for the Derby, but Sultan, owned by the notorious gaming-house keeper, Mr Crockford, met with almost equal support. These two, in fact, had the race very much to themselves. Tiresias, ridden with tremendous drive and vigour by Clift, made all the running, but a strong late challenge by Sultan was only held at bay by 'half a neck'.

Tiresias, a well-made horse standing sixteen hands, broke down the following season after winning a King's Plate at Ipswich. He retired to the stud at Ollerton, Nottinghamshire, at a ten-guinea fee and got a number of useful winners. His own sire Soothsayer was exported to Russia. Sultan became sire of Glencoe, who got the famous mare Pocahontas and subsequently did extremely well at the stud in America.

1819

1819: Thursday, 27 May . . . 54 Entries. £1,837 10s.

DUKE OF PORTLAND's br.c. TIRESIAS by Soothsayer
  out of Pledge   W. CLIFT   1
MR CROCKFORD's SULTAN by Selim   No jockey recorded 2
No horse was officially placed third.

Also ran:

  Lord Rous's Euphrates; Lord Foley's The Dominie; Mr Watson's Philip; Mr Lake's Banker; Lord G. H. Cavendish's colt by Rubens; Mr Forth's Lovemore; Mr Payne's Shreckhorn; Mr Gardiner's colt by Haphazard; Mr Charlton's Conjuror; Mr Crockford's Emperor; Mr Butler's Cetes; Mr Andrews's colt by Orville; Mr Goddard's Topaz; Mr Farrall's Dahlia.

16 ran.

Betting:

  2–1 and 5–2 Tiresias; 5–2 and 3–1 Sultan; 7–1 Euphrates; 8–1 the colt by Rubens; 12–1 The Dominie; 14–1 Topaz; 20–1 Conjuror.

Won by a head.

1820

In 1819 Squire Thornhill won the Oaks with Shoveller, a filly by Scud out of Gooseander, by Hambletonian. The following year he won his second Derby with Shoveller's full brother Sailor, a plain, rather leggy colt that was at his best when the going was really heavy.

Sailor had one race before Epsom, winning a Sweepstakes at Newmarket over the Abingdon Mile. He was well backed in consequence for the Derby, but that race was generally regarded as a 'good thing' for the Duke of Grafton's Pindarrie, winner of the Two Thousand Guineas.

The night before the Derby there was a terrible storm. For hours the rain teemed down, while a tearing wind blew the tents and booths on the Downs around as if they were bits of old newspaper. When William Chifney, who trained Sailor, got up at four in the morning to go down to Mr Ladbroke's place, where Sailor was stabled, he had to pick his way through a morass of mud and was soaked to the skin after a few minutes. His own discomforts, though, were submerged by his delight in the knowledge that conditions were now exactly right for Sailor. Mr Thornhill's confidence, too, was vastly increased, and he at once took eight thousand to two thousand about Sailor, so that in all he stood to win some £23,000.

Sailor fully justified the trust of his owner and trainer and, ridden by Sam Chifney, he won by two lengths from Mr Udney's Abjer, with Tiger third and the favourite well down the course. Two of the runners, Arbutus and the oddly named Anti-Gallican, both ran out.

The Derby was Sailor's last race. A few months later he broke a blood-vessel in his chest while at exercise and died almost immediately. He is probably the only Derby winner to have won the race on **his birthday**, which happened to be 18 May.

1820: Thursday, 18 May . . . 52 Entries. £1,758 15s.

MR T. THORNHILL's ch.c. SAILOR by Scud
  out of Gooseander   S. CHIFNEY, JUN.   1
MR UDNEY's br.c. ABJER by Truffle   F. BUCKLE   2
LORD G. H. CAVENDISH's TIGER by Middlethorpe   No jockey recorded 3

73

Also ran:

Lord Warwick's Selma; Duke of Grafton's Pindarrie; Mr Peirse's Arbutus; Lord Stawell's Anti-Gallican; Mr Wilson's Locksley; Mr Milnes's The Duke; Mr Payne's Jobson; Mr Fox's Gambler; Lord Jersey's colt by Waxy; Duke of Rutland's colt by Haphazard; Mr Lake's Prodigious; Lord Rous's Hoopoe.

15 ran.

Betting:

5–2 and 3–1 Pindarrie; 4–1 and 7–2 Sailor; 9–2 Selma; 13–1 Anti-Gallican; 15–1 Abjer and The Duke; 18–1 Locksley; 25–1 Arbutus.

Won by two lengths.
Winner trained by W. Chifney.

1821

Until the late Mr E. Kennedy imported Roi Hérode to his stud in Co. Kildare in the early years of this century with the primary object of restoring the Herod male line, grey horses were comparatively rare on the English Turf. In fact when the grey filly Tagalie won the Derby in 1912, there had been only one previous grey winner of that race and that was Gustavus in 1821. Two more greys have won since Tagalie, Mahmoud in 1936 and Airborne in 1946.

Gustavus belonged to Mr J. Hunter, a member of the Jockey Club and a big betting man. Bred at the Six Mile Bottom Stud, which belonged to George IV when Prince Regent and was subsequently bought by Colonel Leigh, Gustavus was purchased by Mr Hunter at a sale at Hampton Court for twenty-five guineas. His sire Election had won the Derby for Lord Egremont; his dam, from whom he inherited his colour, was Lady Grey, by Stamford. Unless 'The Druid' was unjust to him, he was by no means handsome, that writer summing him up as 'a shabby little grey'.

As a two-year-old Gustavus surprised his owner by winning the July Stakes at Newmarket at 100–6. The following season he won the Newmarket Stakes and was made favourite for the Derby at 2–1, 4–1 being available about the Duke of Grafton's Reginald, who had won the Two Thousand Guineas in a field of four. As it turned out, these two had the Derby more or less to themselves, Reginald leading till just short of the final furlong when he was challenged by Gustavus, who finished just the stronger to win by half a length.

In those days the Derby was run at half past one, after which there was a prolonged interval while any royal personages present went off to lunch with Mr Ladbroke at his place at Headley. The public in the meantime had lunch as well, either in the town or at booths on the course. Much liquid refreshment was consumed and proceedings afterwards were apt to get somewhat out of hand, being conducted 'in a very vinous mist'.

This year trouble began while the Derby was actually in progress and the ground-keepers, hired at the rate of eighteenpence a day, proved totally unable to keep control. The crowd surged wildly on to the course, and according to Sam Day, who rode Gustavus, 'Buckle and I wound in and out all the way from Tattenham Corner like a dog at a fair.' This can have been little to the liking of Buckle, as that great rider was losing some of his dash and confidence by then.

Gustavus started favourite for the St Leger, but failed to stay, the race being won by Mr Orde Powlett's Jack Spigot. The following year Gustavus won the Claret Stakes at the Craven Meeting, but was beaten by Sultan in a Match over the Rowley Mile. He was beaten four more times that season and was then retired to the stud at York at a ten-guinea fee; by 1827, when he was standing at the Rose and Crown at Beverley, he had done sufficiently well for his fee to be doubled. He was exported to Prussia in 1836.

Sam Day was a member of a famous nineteenth-century racing family, the Days of Danebury. Sam, nicknamed 'Uncle Sam', and his elder brother John were both first-rate riders. John never had any luck in the Derby, but won the Oaks on five occasions. Sam had three Derby victories, but only one in the Oaks. Cheerful, hardy, and a great deal more honest than some of the prominent members of the Day family, two of whom, William and John junior, were both 'warned off', Sam Day retired from the Turf after winning the 1830 Derby on Priam. However, his farming venture near Reading proved unprofitable, and reducing his weight from 11 st. 6 lb. to 7 st. 12 lb., he returned to the saddle to win the Derby and the Oaks for Mr Gully on Pyrrhus the First and Mendicant. When he finally retired, he trained a few horses at Ascot. He died in 1866 aged sixty-four.

1821: Thursday, 7 June . . . 54 Entries. £1,758 15s.

MR J. HUNTER's gr.c. GUSTAVUS by Election
   out of Lady Grey   S. DAY   I
DUKE OF GRAFTON's br.c. REGINALD by Haphazard   F. BUCKLE 2
MR RAMSBOTTOM's br.c. SIR HULDIBRAND by Octavius
                                            No jockey recorded 3

Also ran:

   Mr Bouverie's Tressilian; Lord Jersey's Richard; Mr R. Milnes's Jock the Laird's brother; Mr Fox's North Wester; Duke of Rutland's filly by Waxy; Mr S. Duncombe's colt by Smolensko; H.R.H. Duke of York's colt by Walton; Mr Calley's The Hetman; Mr Batson's Rioter; Lord Exeter's Mokanna.

13 ran.

Betting:

   2–1 Gustavus; 4–1 Reginald; 5–1 Jock the Laird's brother; 7–1 Tressilian; 10–1 Rioter; 50–1 Sir Huldibrand.

Won by half a length.

1822

The Duke of York had his second Derby winner in 1822 when Moses, ridden by Goodisson, was the victor. Moses was by Whalebone or Seymour, probably the latter, out of a mare by Gohanna, and was well in-bred to Herod. He can certainly not be numbered among the great Derby winners. He began his career when a three-year-old by winning a Sweepstake at Newmarket. This success apparently made little impression, and he was not a strong public fancy for the Derby, in which the two best-backed horses were the Duke of Grafton's Hampden, well galloped with his owner's fillies Pastille and Whizgig, winners of the Two Thousand and One Thousand Guineas respectively; and Lord Darlington's Brother to Antonio.

From Tattenham Corner it was a great race between Moses, Mr Roger's Figaro, and Hampden. Moses, however, always held a slight advantage and retained it in a desperate battle to the winning post which he passed a head in front of Figaro.

Three weeks after Epsom, Moses won the Albany Stakes at Ascot. The following year he won the Claret Stakes at Newmarket but was then beaten in a Match by a horse to whom he was conceding ten pounds. At the end of the season he retired to the Hampton Court Stud, but was subsequently sold to the Duke of Richmond and stood at Goodwood. He sired a number of winners, but not one of any distinction.

When Moses won, the Duke of York's finances were in such a deplorable state that he was unable to have as big a bet as he desired. His stable was then managed by Mr Charles Greville, who was related on his mother's side to the Duke of Portland. Greville was closely connected with racing in many capacities all his life, although there were times when the seamy side of the sport and its less attractive adherents filled his aristocratic soul with deep disgust. When the Duke of York had to sell his horses in 1827, Greville managed the fourth Duke of Portland's stable for a short time. He then became a racing confederate, firstly of Lord Chesterfield, and secondly of his imperious cousin, Lord George Bentinck. He eventually quarrelled with Bentinck, whose arrogance and hypocrisy were the subjects of some scathing paragraphs in his famous diary.

1822: Thursday, 23 May . . . 53 Entries. £1,706 5s.

H.R.H. DUKE OF YORK's b.c. MOSES by Whalebone or Seymour
out of Sister to Castanea   T. GOODISSON 1
MR ROGER's b.c. FIGARO by Haphazard   No jockey recorded 2
DUKE OF GRAFTON's ch.c. HAMPDEN by Rubens   No jockey recorded 3

Also ran:

General Grosvenor's Marcellus; Lord Exeter's Stamford; Lord Egremont's
Wanton; Mr Pearce's colt by Juniper; Mr Walker's Magnus Troil; Mr Rush's colt
by Selim; Mr Bouverie's Moresco; Mr Batson's Mystic; Lord Darlington's Brother
to Antonio.

12 ran.

Betting:

3–1 Hampden; 9–2 Brother to Antonio; 6–1 Moses, Mystic, and Moresco:
10–1 Stamford; 14–1 Wanton; 20–1 Marcellus.

Won by a head.

1823

A far more distinguished horse than Moses was Emilius, owned by Mr John Udney of Aberdeen, a member of the Jockey Club who had won the One Thousand Guineas and the Oaks in 1818 with Corinne.

Emilius was by Orville, sire of the 1812 Derby winner Octavius, out of Emily, by Stamford. He did not run as a two-year-old, and as a three-year-old he was undefeated. At the Craven Meeting he won the Riddlesworth Stakes and was given a walk-over in the Dinner Stakes. At the Newmarket First Spring Meeting he deadheated for a Sweepstake with Lord Exeter's Fanatic, who, by mutual arrangement, was not opposed in the run-off. Then came the Derby; Emilius and Mr Roger's Tancred, the first and second favourites, had the race very much to themselves. Emilius made the running to Tattenham Corner, where Buckle gave him a breather and he was headed by Tancred. Inside the final furlong, however, Buckle balanced Emilius for a final effort, and mastered Tancred to win by a length.

Emilius won a Sweepstakes at Ascot and then rested till the autumn. He then won the Grand Duke Michael Stakes Across The Flat, beating Zinc, winner of both the fillies' classics that year, and concluded the season by winning a 400-guinea Sweepstakes at the Newmarket Second October Meeting.

Tancred's only other appearance that season was in the St Leger, a race that turned out to be a farce. The Clerk of the Course acted as starter and proved singularly ill-fitted for the task. There were four false starts and after the fourth, twenty-three of the twenty-seven runners completed the course, the Rosanne colt winning from Barefoot. The Clerk of the Course at once complained that there had not been a proper start and, by order of the Stewards, the race was re-run. Only twelve horses then went to the post, Barefoot winning from Sherwood.

In 1824 Emilius was sold to Mr Thornhill, for whom he won one Match, but he was defeated in two other Matches and also in the Audley End Stakes at Newmarket. He was then retired to the stud at Riddlesworth, where he sired two Derby winners in Priam and Plenipotentiary. When Mr Thornhill died in 1844, Lord George Bentinck bought Emilius privately. The old horse was then twenty-four years of age and very weak, but his new owner nursed him back to vigour and he was reputed as fresh as a four-year-old when leased in 1846 to Mr Jaques of Easby Abbey, Yorkshire. He died in 1847, the cause of his death being a meal of whole oats, which he was quite unable to masticate. According to 'The Druid', he was 'a muscular, compact horse, with great chest and arms, short legs and peculiarly straight hind ones. Add to this a great middle piece and good back ribs, with a muscular neck not too long and rather inclined to arch. He looked, in fact, quite as much a hunter as a blood horse.'

In those days the status of jockeys was appreciably lower than it is today, and the authorities liked to regard them as no more than grooms. However, thanks to men like Robinson, Buckle, and Chifney, their standing and prestige was improving. This year the *Racing Calendar* made for the first time the concession, no doubt begrudged, of giving the name of the successful rider when recording the result of the Derby.

1823: Thursday, 29 May . . . 60 Entries. £1,863 15s.

MR J. R. UDNEY's b.c. EMILIUS by Orville out of Emily	F. BUCKLE	I
MR J. ROGER's b.c. TANCRED by Selim	W. WHEATLEY	2

No horse was officially placed third.

Also ran:

Duke of Grafton's Talisman; Mr Biggs's Bertram; Mr Roger's Nicolo; Duke of Grafton's Cinder; Mr Ramsbottom's Cephalus; Mr Naylor's Triumph; Mr Duncombe's Young Quiz; Mr Turner's colt by Phantom; Mr Tomes's Felix.

11 ran.

Betting:

5–4 and 11–8 Emilius; 6–4 and 13–8 Tancred; 10–1 Nicolo; 14–1 Bertram; high odds against any other.

Won by a length.
Winner trained by Robson.

1824

In 1824 Jem Robinson brought off a remarkable wager, having betted that in one week he would ride the winner of the Derby, the winner of the Oaks, and get married. He won the Derby on Sir John Shelley's Cedric; the Oaks on Lord Jersey's Cobweb, and on the Saturday he completed the treble by leading a certain Miss Powell to the altar.

Cedric was by Phantom, a son of Walton, out of a Walton mare. The theory of close in-breeding may have been successful in so far as racecourse merit went, but when Cedric retired to the stud, he failed to get a single foal.

Cedric ran four times as a three-year-old before the Derby. He beat a solitary opponent for a Sweepstakes at the Craven Meeting, but was beaten the very same day in the Dinner Stakes by the Duke of Grafton's Rebecca. At the First Spring Meeting he won a Sweepstakes and a Match, both over a mile. This record did not suffice to make him favourite for the Derby, that distinction being held by Mr Thornhill's Reformer. There were three false starts in each of which Sir W. Milner's Osmond was first away and covered a considerable amount of ground. In the true start Osmond was very much slower off the mark, but nevertheless finished second to Cedric, who ran out a comfortable winner.

Cedric won twice at Ascot after the Derby and twice at Newmarket. The following season he only ran twice before retiring to the stud, winning a Match at Newmarket and being beaten by Lottery in the Doncaster Cup.

1824: Thursday, 3 June . . . 58 Entries. £1,968 15s.

SIR J. SHELLEY's ch.c. CEDRIC by Phantom
out of a mare by Walton   J. ROBINSON   1
SIR W. MILNER's br.c. OSMOND by Filho da Puta   T. NICHOLSON   2
No horse was officially placed third.

Also ran:
   Mr Tomes's Sir Gray; Mr Rush's M'Adam; Lord G. H. Cavendish's Dragoman; Mr Greville's Don Carlos; Duke of Grafton's Skiff; General Grosvenor's Lyrnessa; Mr Udney's Grenadier; Lord Egremont's colt by Phantom; Lord Stradbroke's

Cyndus; Mr Forth's Swallow; Mr Thornhill's Reformer; Mr Houldsworth's Elephant; Mr Dundas's colt by Anticipation; Mr Batson's Serab.

16 ran.

Betting:

   5–2 Reformer; 9–2 Cedric; 5–1 Elephant; 9–1 Serab; 16–1 Osmond; 17–1 Swallow; 20–1 the Phantom colt; 33–1 Sir Gray.

Won easily.

1825

Cedric's owner, Sir John Shelley, was for many years the racing confederate, as the saying went in those days, of the fifth Lord Jersey, who himself won the Derby in 1825 with Middleton, a success he was to repeat in 1827 with Mameluke and in 1836 with Bay Middleton. Tall, handsome, fearless, and a great favourite with the ladies, Lord Jersey was Lord Chamberlain to William IV and Master of the Horse to Queen Victoria. He was a great patron of the Turf, but despite his ten successes in classic races, his devotion to the sport is said to have cost him over £400,000. Throughout his life hunting was an even stronger passion than racing, for which he lost much of his zest in the closing years of his life. He was a great man to hounds, and took part in the famous Billesden Coplow run in 1800, which has been immortalized in song as one of the unforgettable events in the history of hunting in Leicestershire. He died in 1859 and his successor, the sixth Earl, died three weeks later. The seventh Earl took to the Turf, backed more by money than good sense, but even the former commodity ran short, and in 1867 he had to flee the country owing the Ring the best part of £50,000. Eventually his creditors accepted £25,000 in settlement and he returned to England, but not to the racecourse. The rest of his life was spent in public service and he became an Alderman of the Middlesex County Council and Governor of New South Wales.

Middleton, by Phantom, was a big, clumsy sort of horse and for a long time Lord Jersey and his trainer Edwards reckoned he was useless. However, his action improved as he grew older and he showed that he possessed a considerable turn of speed. He never ran before the Derby, but no doubt he had been very highly tried as he started favourite at 7–4, the Duke of Grafton's Rufus being the only horse seriously backed to beat him. It was a great race between the pair of them till well inside the final furlong when Middleton, beautifully ridden by Robinson, produced a sudden burst of speed to win by a couple of lengths.

Middleton's backers were unaware how lucky they were to draw their money. Middleton's lad had been 'got at' and, entrusted with a bucket of water to help in plaiting the colt's mane, he allowed him to swallow the lot so that when the head-lad came into the box there was nothing in the bucket but the sponge. Utter consternation was the first reaction, but Edwards's spirits rose as he walked Middleton from Mickleham to The Warren, a distance of some four miles. Nevertheless, the colt looked so barrel-like at the post that Lord Jersey declared he must have swallowed more than they knew. Edwards, however, remained optimistic and remarked that 'even with five gallons inside, nothing would touch him'. Edwards had considerable experience with the descendants of Web, sister to Whalebone and Whisker and dam of Middleton. 'They're as fat as pigs,' he said; 'if I work them two days together, they're lame, and if their bellies touch the ground, they are good enough to get through.' It only remains to add that the coachmen of Lord Jersey and the Duke of Wellington both won well over a thousand pounds on the race.

Probably because of navicular disease, Middleton never ran again. He went to the stud at a ten-guinea fee at the beginning of 1827 at the Horse Bazaar, King Street, Portman Square. His stud advertisement stated that 'mares may be turned out in the Park, within half a mile of the Bazaar, fenced in the most safe and secure manner, from whence it is impossible they can be stolen'. He was exported to Russia in 1833.

1825: Thursday, 19 May . . . 58 Entries. £1,995.

LORD JERSEY's ch.c. MIDDLETON by Phantom
out of Web ... J. ROBINSON ... 1
DUKE OF GRAFTON's ch.c. RUFUS by Election ... W. ARNULL ... 2
MR BATSON's ch.c. HOGARTH by Rubens ... S. CHIFNEY, JUN. ... 3

Also ran:

Mr Udney's colt by Muley; Mr Roger's Muleteer; Mr Smith's Tamar; Mr Benson's Dauntless; Mr Scaith's Whipcord; Mr Shard's Hougoumont; Mr Wyndham's colt by Granicus; Mr Heathcote's Oberon; Mr Roger's Flounder; H.R.H. Duke of York's Frogmore; Mr Milnes's Actaeon; Mr Benson's Comrade; Mr Yates's Cain; Lord Orford's Fleance; Captain Bevan's Bitton.

18 ran.

Betting:

7–4 Middleton; 11–5 Rufus; 10–1 Hogarth, Hougoumont, and Muleteer; 18–1 Dauntless; and very high odds against any other.

Won by two lengths.
Winner trained by Edwards.

1826

Lord Egremont won his last Derby in 1826 with Lapdog, by Whalebone out of a mare by Canopus. Lapdog was a moderate racehorse and, judging from the rest of his form, his victory may have been one of those strange flukes that sometimes happen in racing. On the other hand he may have been suited by the appalling conditions, as it was a terrible Derby Day, heavy rain falling without a break from dawn till dusk. Whatever the reason, the fact remains that Lapdog, starting at 50–1 and ridden by an unfashionable jockey called Dockeray, won by a length and a half from Mr West's Shakespeare. After an unsuccessful autumn Lord Egremont decided that Lapdog should run no more, and he is last heard of as a stallion standing at Houghton Down, Stockbridge, at a fee of seven guineas.

Dockeray was not at all a well-known jockey. He had continual trouble with his weight, and after drastic reducing, was compelled by ill-health to give up riding.

1826: Thursday, 25 May . . . 57 Entries. £1,800.

LORD EGREMONT's b.c. LAPDOG by Whalebone
out of a mare by Canopus   G. DOCKERAY   I

MR WEST's br.c. SHAKESPEARE by Smolensko   2

No horse was officially placed third.

Also ran:

Duke of Grafton's Dervise; Lord Egremont's Black Swan; Lord Exeter's Tirailleur; Lord Exeter's Hobgoblin; Mr Mockford's Scamper; Mr Goddard's Composer; Mr Wilson's The Justice; Mr Rush's Carthago; Mr Roger's Monarch; Duke of Grafton's Bolivar; Lord Verulam's The Moslem; Mr Marriott's Clothier; Mr Croft's Truth; Mr Heathcote's Syntax; Mr Pettit's Baron Münchhausen; Mr Wyndham's Colleger; Mr Forth's Premier.

19 ran.

Betting:

5–2 Premier; 5–1 Tirailleur; 7–1 Dervise and Monarch; 10–1 Carthago; 13–1 Shakespeare; 25–1 Black Swan; 50–1 Lapdog.

Won by a length.

Winner trained by Bird.

1827

There were twenty-three runners in 1827, the largest field so far in the history of the race, and Lord Jersey owned both the winner, Mameluke, by Partisan out of Miss Sophia, by Buzzard; and the runner-up, Glenartney, a full brother to Middleton, by Phantom out of Web.

Both colts had run in the Riddlesworth Stakes, for which Mameluke started favourite. Glenartney in fact won, but only after a filly of Lord Clarendon's had been disqualified for carrying the wrong weight. In the Derby Lord Jersey made no declaration to win with either, but Glenartney, ridden by Harry Edwards, was the better backed of the two. Glenartney was in front with a couple of furlongs to go and his rider appeared to be sitting there comfortably with any amount in hand, when along came Robinson on Mameluke and beat him by quite a decisive margin.

There were some unpleasant rumours after the race, and it was commonly believed that Lord Jersey and his friends were better suited by Mameluke's victory than they would have been by Glenartney's. That view was strengthened soon afterwards when Mameluke was sold for 4,000 guineas, while a bid of 5,000 guineas for Glenartney was refused.

Whether in fact Lord Jersey was himself implicated in a piece of sharp practice it is impossible to say. What is certain is that Edwards some time previously had had a substantial bet on Mameluke, and his riding certainly did not give the impression that he was anxious for Glenartney to win. Edwards had one eye, superb professional ability, and a disposition as crooked as a corkscrew. He would far rather have won twenty pounds crooked than a hundred pounds straight, and in his own words he 'enjoyed doing a bit on the quiet on his own account and putting the double dodge on the swells'.

Mameluke was bought by Mr John Gully, a former prize-fighter, a power in the Betting Ring, and a future M.P. He had risen in life the hard way, and a quiet contempt for the aristocracy was linked with an ability to take on some of the 'warmest' men on the Turf at their own game. He could be hard, vindictive, and unscrupulous, but when he lost he settled without complaint, even when the dice had been loaded against him.

If Mameluke was fortunate in the Derby, he was desperately unlucky not to win the St Leger. Gully had gone for a big win and stood to land some £40,000, but it

The twelfth Earl of Derby, in his robes as Chancellor of the Duchy of
Lancaster; by J. F. Hoppner

was noticeable that however much money was stacked on Mameluke, the price never shortened. Before long there was a whisper that Mameluke was not going to be permitted to win, and there was talk of a conspiracy in which the former fish-peddler, Crockford, who had laid heavily against Mameluke, and Ridsdale, a smooth-tongued little crook, who had strongly supported Mr Petre's filly Matilda for the race, were said to be implicated. There was also a Guards officer all set to flee to the Continent if Mameluke won.

A plot there certainly was, and the Starter, later dismissed, was successfully bribed. Mameluke did not possess the smoothest of temperaments and a series of false starts was organized to bring his restiveness to the boil. Finally the word 'Go!' was given when Matilda was well clear in front and Mameluke flat-footed far behind. That Mameluke started at all was largely due to Gully standing by with a cart-whip, but he had the best part of a hundred yards to make up. He made a superb effort to regain the lost ground and in fact drew almost level with the filly close home, but she still had a little bit in reserve and retained her advantage to win by 'a short half length'.

Gully was able to settle the following week although he was badly hit. 'Is it convenient for you?' asked one of his creditors. 'It is always convenient,' Gully replied, 'but it is not always pleasant.' With the money he won over Mameluke, Crockford was able to open his gaming-house in St James's Street.

The following year Mameluke won the Oatlands Stakes and the Portland Stakes, but was beaten in the Doncaster Cup. In 1829 he won three more races and Gully then sold him to Mr Theobald, a retired linen draper usually known as 'Old Leather-breeches' from the garments he habitually wore and in which he was believed to retire to bed. Gully evidently regretted the sale afterwards and offered Mr Theobald a profit, saying that Mrs Gully was very distressed indeed at the horse's sale. Mr Theobald replied that Gully must make it up with his wife as best he could, as he himself had no intention of parting with the horse. Eventually Mameluke was exported to America, but he was not a stud success.

Mameluke was bred by Mr R. C. Elwes, who also bred the 1847 Derby winner Cossack. Miss Sophia, Mameluke's dam, was very small and her owner wished to have her put down. However she was spared, thanks to the entreaty of Mrs Christopher Wilson, wife of Elwes's racing confederate, and she bred Mameluke when she was eighteen years of age.

1827

1827: Thursday, 31 May . . . 89 Entries. £2,800.

LORD JERSEY'S b.c. MAMELUKE by Partisan
out of Miss Sophia   J. ROBINSON   1

LORD JERSEY'S b.c. GLENARTNEY by Phantom   H. EDWARDS   2

MR YATES'S b.c. EDMUND by Orville   W. SCOTT   3

Also ran:

Lord G. H. Cavendish's Rapid Rhone; Mr Yates's Tamworth; Lord Egremont's Gaberlunzie; Mr Haffenden's Pontiff; Mr Payne's Bachelor; Mr Gauntlett's Gamelius; Lord Egremont's Grampus; Duke of Grafton's Roderick; Mr Forth's Intruder; Mr Sadler's Defence; Mr Haffenden's Trumpeter; Mr Forth's Spondee; Mr Charlton's Raymond; Mr Payne's colt by Rainbow; Captain Locke's Fairlawn; Captain Standen's Conrad; Lord Exeter's colt by Captain Candid; Duke of Grafton's Turcoman; Mr Radclyffe's Windermere; Mr Berkeley Bond's Sparkler.

23 ran.

Betting:

5–1 Glenartney; 6–1 Windermere; 6 and 7–1 Roderick; 7–1 Defence; 9–1 Mameluke.

Won by two lengths.
Winner trained by Edwards.

1828

There have been two dead-heats in the Derby, the first in 1828 between Cadland and The Colonel, the second in 1884 between St Gatien and Harvester.

Cadland belonged to the fifth Duke of Rutland, who succeeded to the title at the age of nine in 1787 and died in 1857. He never raced on a large scale, but was remarkably successful and won three classic races besides the Derby. The Colonel was owned by the Hon. Edward Petre, a fat, jovial character, who had won the St Leger the year before with Matilda.

Cadland was by Andrew, a son of Orville, out of Sorcery, by Sorcerer out of a mare by Andrew, so his victory delighted the adherents of close in-breeding. The Colonel, a small neat horse, was by the 1815 Derby winner Whisker. The Colonel started favourite for the Derby at 7–2, Cadland being second favourite at 4–1.

As a two-year-old The Colonel had won three races, including the Champagne Stakes at Doncaster, the winner of that event being then required to give to the Club six dozen bottles of champagne. As a three-year-old, he never ran before the Derby. Cadland did not run as a two-year-old; the following season he won a Sweepstakes at the First Spring Meeting, and the following day he triumphed in the Two Thousand Guineas.

There were fifteen runners in the Derby, and as the field swung into the straight, Cadland was in the lead. Almost at once The Colonel closed with him and the pair ran on together with Alcaston and Zinganee close behind. With less than a furlong to go Alcaston dropped back beaten and Zinganee, after looking all over a winner, faded in the final twenty yards. The other two passed the post as if locked together, neither flinching under pressure although The Colonel, somewhat unjustly, had been described as 'ready to creep into a mousehole if tackled'. Amidst tremendous excitement the judge pronounced a dead-heat, and the tension rose still further when it was announced that the run-off would take place later that afternoon.

For this second contest The Colonel started favourite at 6–5 on. Jem Robinson on Cadland made the running to the distance where he 'gammoned' Bill Scott that he was beaten. Scott at once made his effort and forged ahead with the race apparently at his mercy; but Cadland still had a bit in reserve, and coming with a great run in the final fifty yards, he got up to win by a neck. It was a perfectly judged, intelligent piece of riding on the part of Robinson.

Later that year Cadland won the Grand Duke Michael Stakes and the New-market St Leger; in 1828 he won a King's plate, the Oatland Stakes, and the Audley End Stakes, while in 1830 he won four races including The Whip. He won again the following year and then retired to the stud in Staffordshire. A handsome, hardy, genuine bay standing fifteen hands two, his legs were as unmarked when he finished with racing as on the day that he went into training. Unfortunately he proved a disappointing sire. He went to France in 1833 and died there in 1837.

The Colonel started favourite for the St Leger, which he won. The following year he was bought by the King in the hope that he would win the Ascot Cup, but in that event he was defeated by Zinganee. He was exported to Germany a few years later.

In all probability the best horse in the 1828 Derby was Zinganee, owned by the Chifney brothers. Unfortunately he picked up a throat infection at Epsom and was far below his best. The next season he beat Mameluke, Cadland, and The Colonel in a memorable race for the Ascot Cup. Just before that event he was sold to Lord Chesterfield with the proviso that Lord Chesterfield should keep the Cup and the Chifney brothers the stake.

1828: Thursday, 22 May . . . 89 Entries. £2,600.

DUKE OF RUTLAND's br.c. CADLAND by Andrew
out of Sorcery   J. ROBINSON   1*
MR PETRE's ch.c. THE COLONEL by Whisker   W. SCOTT   2*
No horse was officially placed third.

Also ran:

Mr W. Chifney's Zinganee; Mr Benson's Alcaston; Mr Payne's colt by Walton; Lord Ailesbury's Rioter; Duke of Grafton's Omen; Duke of Grafton's Lancastrian; Lord Grosvenor's Navarino; Mr Sadler's Challenger; Mr Houldsworth's Lambtonian; Mr Thornhill's Merchant; Mr Sowerby's Palemon; General Grosvenor's John de Bart; Mr Heathcote's Scipio.

15 ran.

Betting:

7–2 The Colonel; 4–1 Cadland; 5, 6, 7 and 10–1 Zinganee; 8–1 the colt by Walton; 14–1 Lambtonian; 18–1 Omen; 20–1 Challenger and Lancastrian; after a dead-heat, even money and 5–4 on The Colonel.

Cadland won the run-off by half a length.

* After a dead-heat.

1829

The 1829 Derby was a classic example of beginner's luck. The winner was Frederick, bred and owned by Mr G. W. Gratwicke, whose family had for many years lived in the little Sussex village of Ham, not far from Goodwood. Mr Gratwicke came of age and into a considerable fortune in 1815. Desiring to start racing in a modest manner, he bought for £30 a mare by Phantom. She was duly sent to be covered by Little John, by Octavius, who belonged to her owner's friend and neighbour, Lord Egremont. The result was a colt called Sir John, who eventually made a considerable name for himself as a sire in Australia.

In 1826 the mare produced another colt by Little John; he was named Frederick, and Forth, who then acted both as trainer and jockey for Mr Gratwicke, advised that he should be entered for the Derby. This was done and in due course Frederick won that race, ridden by Forth, who was then over sixty years of age. At that time the Phantom mare was the only brood mare that Mr Gratwicke owned, while Frederick was his only horse in training. Nor did the luck end there; in 1830 the mare produced a filly by Little John called The Margravine; she became the dam of The Merry Monarch, who won the Derby for Mr Gratwicke in 1845.

Frederick had never run before the Derby for which Lord Exeter's Patron, winner of the Riddlesworth Stakes, the Two Thousand Guineas, the Newmarket Stakes, and the Dinner Stakes, was reckoned a certainty. Patron looked sure to win half-way up the straight, but like many another Guineas winner he failed to stay, and was headed by Frederick with just under a furlong to go. The Exquisite, a grey colt also trained by Forth, put in a very strong challenge, but Frederick held on grimly to his advantage to win by a head. Both winner and runner-up were returned at 40–1.

In 1828 old Forth had had a good bet with Crockford that he would ride and win on The Exquisite, but later on he came to like Frederick the better and accordingly asked permission to transfer his bet. Crockford agreed to that, adding contemptuously that for all he cared Forth could ride them both, as neither of them stood the remotest chance.

In the St Leger Frederick was well beaten by Rowton, who gave Mr Petre his third consecutive St Leger victory and who was in all probability the outstanding colt of that year. Frederick did not run at all in 1830 and failed in all his three races in 1831. He then retired to the stud at Ham at a fee of three and a half guineas.

Mr Gratwicke was a rather weak character, who was apt to pay too much attention to the views of the person he had been talking to last. Like so many men of his type, he was plagued by a very suspicious nature. At one stage his horses were trained at Goodwood by permission of the Duke of Richmond, but he was always complaining that they were run in the interests of other members of the stable. Eventually the Duke could tolerate this no longer. 'If Mr Gratwicke,' he pronounced, 'is dissatisfied with the management of the Goodwood stable, and thinks his horses can be better trained and better managed elsewhere, by all means let him make the experiment at once and take them away.' So away the horses went to Newmarket, where they were leased to the Duke of Bedford on terms suggested by Admiral Rous, who managed the Duke of Bedford's stable and who was commonly believed to be able to twist Mr Gratwicke round his finger.

1829: Thursday, 4 June . . . 89 Entries. £2,650.

MR GRATWICKE's b.c. FREDERICK by Little John
   out of a mare by Phantom   J. FORTH   I
MR FORTH's gr.c. THE EXQUISITE by Whalebone F. BUCKLE, JUN. 2
No horse was officially placed third.

Also ran:

Mr Rush's Oatlands; Lord Sligo's Prince Eugene; Lord G. H. Cavendish's Spaniard; Lord Sefton's Morris-dancer; Lord Exeter's Patron; Lord Egremont's Lapwing; Mr Hunter's Alington; Mr Payne's colt by Orville; Mr Allwood's Leonardo; Mr Greville's Mohican; Lord Grosvenor's Ebury; Mr Stonehewer's Chiron; Mr Young's Lazarus; Mr Begbie's Aaron; Sir G. Heathcote's Centaur.

17 ran.

Betting:

6–5 Patron; 7–1 The Rhoda colt; 8–1 Ebury; 12–1 Morris-dancer and The Espagnolle colt; 22–1 the colt by Orville; 30–1 Prince Eugene; 40–1 Frederick and The Exquisite.

Won easily by a head.
Winner trained by J. Forth.

1830

By 1830, it is fair to say that the Derby was firmly established as the great event of the racing year.

The structure and conduct of the Turf had altered considerably since the century began, and further changes were to come in the next two decades. Racing was no longer the recreation of the privileged few, but the business and pleasure of many. The railways were not only to do away with the long and tedious journeys on foot for horses but were also to enable followers of the sport to travel with comparative ease, speed, and comfort from meeting to meeting. Newspapers were beginning to realize and to exploit the growing public interest, *Bells Life* in particular devoting more and more space to racing topics.

Stakes were still small, and owners competed almost entirely for their own money. Matches were dwindling in popularity, and heats were disappearing altogether, whereas two-year-old racing was greatly on the increase. Amenities for the public were still inclined to be primitive, but Lord George Bentinck was to introduce number-boards, punctuality, and the organized parade in the paddock. The status of jockeys was improving, while trainers were being recognized as something rather better than grooms, and tended to come from a slightly superior class.

As against the improvements made, it can be stated without contradiction that Turf morals have never stood at a lower ebb than they did between 1820 and 1860. There were romance and excitement in plenty, but there was also an unwholesome air of suspicion and chicanery, and time and again the great races were marred by some calculated act of villainy. It is a miracle that the sport not only survived some of the murkier episodes, but continued to attract as patrons men of the utmost distinction and unquestioned integrity. If Lord George Bentinck had not declared war on crooks and defaulters, racing, like the prize-ring, might well have fallen into utter disrepute.

There are various reasons for the deplorable standard that prevailed. To start with, sporting ethics were very different from those that prevailed at the close of the nineteenth century. Hard blows were given and accepted, and even if the blow was of dubious fairness, the loser was expected to pay up and not waste time with complaint. After all, Lord George Bentinck undoubtedly did things that would have got him 'warned off' today. The Rev. Lord Henry Beauclerk, the undisputed monarch

93

of Lord's, made £700 a year out of cricket by methods that were far from being attractive, while the great professional cricketer Lambert unhesitatingly sold his side for a bribe. 'Play or pay' was the rule, with no foolish nonsense about chivalry.

The age itself was a rough and harsh one. Life may have been fine and elegant for the few, but for many the appalling conditions in mines and factories were only equalled in misery by the squalor of existence in the new industrial slums. For thousands life was endless drudgery punctuated by intervals of sodden insobriety. It was a time when the penal code possessed hardly a glimmer of humanity, and executions were still a popular public spectacle. No wonder racecourse crowds were sometimes brutal and dangerous, while Derby Day in particular was notorious for riot and drunkenness. The standards and morals of the Queen and her Consort had yet to influence the life of the country, and *Eric, or Little by Little* was still several decades away.

A new type of owner, too, had arrived and the ranks of the patricians were leavened by a growing number of men of humble birth and varied background. Many of these new owners were genuine sportsmen and an asset to the Turf, but among their number were men like Gully, the former prize-fighter, whose finger was to poke into many unsavoury pies; the smooth Yorkshireman Ridsdale, 'that most dangerous and dexterous manipulator of jockeys'; the villainous gaming-house keeper Crockford, with a semi-idiot expression on his pallid face and with hands 'as soft as raw veal and white as paper'; and worst of them all, the scheming money-lender Padwick, whose delight it was to encompass the ruin of rich young men, whose wits were not in equal proportion to their bank-rolls.

There had been a change also in the manner of betting. Formerly, owners for the most part had wagered with each other; now the day of the professional bookmaker had begun. It is impossible to pretend that these early representatives of the profession were a reputable collection. For the most part they were foul-mouthed, illiterate, and dishonest. They knew no law but the law of the jungle. In the great ante-post betting races such as the Derby, the St Leger, and the Chester Cup, they went to endless pains to have lame or even dead horses boosted in order to attract the money of the less well informed. The majority would have skinned their own sister without a moment's hesitation had that operation offered the prospect of financial advantage. Their speciality was the corruption of trainers, jockeys, and stable employees. The cripple, 'Cruch' Robinson, was one of the better representatives, but he was domineering, ill-mannered, ill-spoken, and uncouth. The two Blands, Joe and 'Facetious Jemmy', were both the lowest type of scoundrel and had been behind the poisoning of horses on Newmarket Heath, a deed for which Daniel Dawson was eventually hanged. In betting their motto was 'Win, lie, or wrangle'.

Of Jemmy it was said that 'if you had met him eating birds' nests with chopsticks in Pekin, you would have known at once he was a leg'. Then there were Crockford, sinister, repulsive, and capable of anything; 'Ludlow' Bond, a vain, greasy, over-dressed crook who appeared at Newmarket on a grey hack and was subsequently known as 'Death on the Pale Horse'; and Frank Richardson, up to every dirty trick in the game and renowned as a 'nobbler' of favourites.

Finally, the control of the Jockey Club was nothing like as firm or as far-reaching as it ultimately became, while many local stewards and officials were either corrupt or inept or both. At one meeting in the Midlands, the Clerk of the Course owed the Ring a great deal of money and showed no disposition to settle. A plot was hatched, therefore, to hustle him out of his office into Tattersalls; once there, he could be declared a defaulter and ejected from his own premises. However, the official got to hear of all this and at once had erected outside his office door a stout wooden palisade; over the top of this rampart his grinning face would appear at intervals while racing was in progress in order to pass a few mocking comments at the expense of his thwarted opponents.

It is easy enough to understand what Mr Charles Greville's feelings were when he made the following entry in his diary:

> I grow more and more disgusted with the atmosphere of villainy I am forced to breathe . . . it is not easy to keep oneself undefiled. It is monstrous to see high-bred and high-born gentlemen of honoured names and families, themselves marching through the world with their heads in the air, all honourable men, living in the best, the greatest and most refined society, mixed up in schemes, which are neither more nor less than a system of plunder.

Later he added:

> The sport of horse-racing has a peculiar and irresistible charm for persons of un-blemished probity. What a pity it is that it makes just as strong an appeal to the riff-raff of every town and city.

*   *   *

Priam, winner in 1830, was by the 1823 Derby winner Emilius out of Cressida, sister to the Derby and Oaks heroine Eleanor. He was bred by Sir John Shelley and sold to Will Chifney as a yearling for a thousand guineas. Unbroken when bought, he was never tried as a two-year-old, but so convinced were the Chifney brothers of his merit that he was entered for all the important races. The opinion of him held by the Chifneys was reinforced by that of Lord Chesterfield, who said that he could gaze at

1830

the colt all day and that he considered him the only faultless blood horse he had ever seen. Lord Darlington, on the other hand, disliked him and was convinced he would never stay a mile and a half. 'The Druid' described him as follows: 'In height he was a trifle above 15·3, rather light-limbed and with lightish back ribs, from which the critics drew their "short-course" inferences. His greatest merit lay in his forehand; he had deep, oblique shoulders, and one of the most expressive and blood-like of heads.'

As a three-year-old Priam contracted a chill in March as the result of a prolonged inspection in a cold wind by Lord Darlington. However, he recovered sufficiently to win two races at the Craven Meeting; in the Riddlesworth Stakes he beat Mahmoud, subsequently third in the Derby, and in the Column Stakes he beat Lord Exeter's Augustus, who won the Two Thousand Guineas a fortnight later.

Nowadays the journey from Newmarket to Epsom can be accomplished smoothly and comfortably in a horse box in something around three hours. Priam left for Epsom at four o'clock in the morning almost a fortnight before the Derby was run, and for much of the way Will Chifney walked beside him, while sporting inn-keepers came to their doors to give the travellers a cheer as they went their way. They had started off on a Friday and that night they stopped at Newport. On Saturday they rested at the Cock Inn at Epping, and before midday on Sunday they were at Smith's stables in Sloane Street, where various members of the Jockey Club came to inspect the colt. By Monday they were at Epsom, and thus had just over a week for rest and quiet preparation.

Priam was favourite for the Derby at 4–1, but Little Red Rover, owned by a very 'warm' combination in Messrs Gully and Ridsdale, was almost equally well supported and Gully alone had backed him to win over £50,000. Little Red Rover, not to be confused with Red Rover who also ran in the Derby, was hardly more than a pony. As a two-year-old he looked very weedy and dried-up, possibly because he was kept cooped up too long in a stuffy stable. However, acting on expert advice Gully had him turned out into a paddock and given as much corn as he could eat, while he himself came down to the paddock every morning with a whip and made the little horse gallop for half an hour or so. This new treatment proved eminently successful, and Little Red Rover would have been good enough to win the Derby in eight years out of ten.

In those days it was nothing unusual for a great deal of trouble to occur at the start of a big race. Sometimes the starter was inefficient, sometimes the reason was the bitter rivalry between jockeys from the north and those from the south, but the most common cause of delay and disturbance was that horses with no chance whatsoever were sent to the post with the sole object of upsetting the better-backed runners for the benefit of persons financially interested.

On this occasion there were fourteen false starts with the rain pouring down in torrents. Fortunately Priam possessed an equable temperament and did not become unduly excited, but even so he was badly away and lost several lengths. However, his class soon enabled him to make good the lost ground and at Tattenham Corner he was so handily placed and going so well that Sam Day, who rode him because Sam Chifney and Robinson both had to conform to prior claims, was able to take a pull. Little Red Rover led down the straight with Augustus and Mahmoud hard on his heels, but passing the grandstand Day gave Priam his head. The favourite responded as only a good horse can and in half a dozen strides he settled the issue and went on to win by a comfortable two lengths. The Chifney brothers were reputed to have won a fortune but in fact their joint gains were not more than £12,000, including the stake, which was £2,800.

Priam won a Sweepstakes over a mile at Ascot and was then put by for the St Leger. Unfortunately for him and for his owners, conditions at Doncaster that year were appalling. Rain had fallen almost unceasingly for several days and there were pools of water all over the course. Priam struggled gamely enough in the mud, but was worn down and beaten half a length by Birmingham, a great, slashing seventeen-hand colt that had been sold for forty-five guineas as a foal. While still a foal Birmingham was seriously ill and his owner, Mr Beardsworth, decided to have him put down. Mrs Beardsworth, however, interceded and nursed him back to health and strength herself. Birmingham adored his benefactress ever afterwards and until he grew too big for it to be convenient, he used to follow her around the house like a dog.

Two days after the St Leger, Priam beat Lord Glasgow's Retriever in a Match for £500 over a mile and a half. That was his final appearance that year; in the spring of 1831 he turned out again, apparently as good as ever, winning the Craven Stakes and the Port Stakes at the Craven Meeting. At that point in his career he was sold to Lord Chesterfield for 3,000 guineas.

The sixth Lord Chesterfield was born in 1805. Good-tempered, easy-going, extravagant, and idle, he got increasingly slothful as he grew older. He seldom got up before midday; when in London he sat in his club till the early hours of the morning, and if he was at home at Bretton Park, he spent hours on the terrace gazing into space through a telescope manipulated by his butler. That his estates went to rack and ruin and that his immense fortune rapidly dwindled failed to disturb him at all. He just became more and more inert and died at the age of sixty-one.

Priam's new owner at once matched him against Sir Mark Wood's five-year-old mare Lucetta, who had won the Ascot Cup the previous year, beating The Colonel, Zinganee, and the Oaks winner Green Mantle. The Match, which was for £200 over the Middle Two Miles at Newmarket at level weights, aroused the greatest interest and there was immense confidence behind Lucetta, declared by Robinson to be one of the finest stayers he had ever ridden. Priam, however, won easily by four lengths, much to the surprise of Robinson who had set such a pace that he expected Priam to 'fold up' a long way from home.

Will Chifney had entered Priam for the Ascot Cup, but although the nomination was transferred to Lord Chesterfield it was declared void, as entries that year had been limited to horses owned by members of the Jockey Club, White's, or Brooks's. This rule, which was soon repealed, was said to have been initiated, somewhat pettily, to prevent men like Gully from winning the race; an alternative theory was that it formed a reprisal, some insubordinate, non-titled owner having gone to the Royal Stand at Ascot and demanded in most peremptory fashion to see Lord Maryborough in order to complain about some defect in the arrangements.

Priam next won the Goodwood Cup for which he was prepared, to spare him the long journey from Newmarket, in Goodwood Park by John Kent, senior. In 1832 he was beaten in somewhat mysterious circumstances in the Craven Stakes, but beat Lucetta for a King's Plate over four miles, won the Eclipse Foot at Ascot, and finally the Goodwood Cup for the second time. He then retired to the stud at Bretby Park, Burton-on-Trent, at a fee of thirty guineas. Three years later he was sold for 3,500 guineas and went to America. After he had gone, his daughters, Miss Letty and Industry, both won the Oaks, while Crucifix, another filly, won the Two Thousand Guineas, the One Thousand Guineas, and the Oaks. An effort was then made to buy him back again for the benefit of British breeders, but all offers were firmly refused. In America, as in England, his fillies proved very much better than his colts.

Defeated only twice in a strenuous career and possessed of great speed as well as abundant stamina, Priam takes rank as one of the greatest of Derby winners. John Kent, junior, who rode him when he was a boy, who later trained for Lord George Bentinck, and whose experience of racing lasted till late in the nineteenth century, wrote as follows:

I have seen all the best horses that have flourished and had their day for more than sixty years past, and I now repeat my well-considered opinion that Priam was the most perfect racehorse I ever saw. His constitution was magnificently sound; his temperament and nervous system beautifully attuned; his shape, make, and action were faultless. No weight known to the *Racing Calendar* could crush his spirit. All courses came alike to him. I well remember how frequently I rode him at exercise when, in 1831, he came to our stables to run for the Goodwood Cup of that year, which as a four-year-old he won in a canter, carrying 9 st. 5 lb. two miles and a half. That was sixty-one years ago, and I question whether there is any other man still living who ever crossed the back of that 'bright particular star' among horses, the beautiful and incomparable Priam . . . the peer of Flying Childers and Eclipse . . . *the* horse of the nineteenth century.

1830: Thursday, 27 May . . . 89 Entries. £2,800.

MR W. CHIFNEY's b.c. PRIAM by Emilius out of Cressida	S. DAY	1
MR RIDSDALE's ch.c. LITTLE RED ROVER by Tramp	S. TEMPLEMAN	2
LORD EXETER's b.c. MAHMOUD by Sultan	J. DAY	3

Also ran:

Lord Exeter's Augustus (G. Dockeray); H.M. The King's Young Orion (G. Nelson); Lord Exeter's Red Rover (A. Pavis); Sir Mark Wood's Cestus (T. Robinson); Sir Mark Wood's The Mummer (G. Edwards); Mr Petre's Brunswicker (W. Scott); Lord Cleveland's colt by Emilius (S. Chifney); Lord Sefton's Captain Arthur (H. Edwards); Mr Roger's Firman (W. Wheatley); Mr Ramsbottom's Zucharelli (T. Goodisson); Lord G. H. Cavendish's Burlington (W. Arnull); Mr Tomes's Port (S. Darling); Lord Sligo's Brine (P. Conolly); Mr Griffith's Throngrove (G. Calloway); Mr Rush's Ivanhoe (J. Robinson); Sir D. Baird's Snooks (Boyce); Lord Grosvenor's Thermometer (Chapple); Colonel Wilson's Ringleader (F. Buckle); Mr Gully's Disraeli (J. Spurr).

22 ran.

Betting:

4–1 Priam; 5–1 Little Red Rover; 6–1 Young Orion; 13–2 Brunswicker; 12–1 Augustus; 15–1 Captain Arthur; 16–1 Mahmoud; 17–1 The Mummer; 40–1 Brine.

Won by two lengths.
Winner trained by W. Chifney.

1831

If Priam was one of the best of Derby winners, Spaniel, who won the following year, was one of the worst. Bred by Lord Egremont, Spaniel was sold across the dinner-table for 150 guineas to Lord Lowther, who had asked his host how much he wanted for 'that Whalebone weed'. Lord Lowther, afterwards the second Earl of Lonsdale, became Lord President of the Council in 1852 and died in 1872.

Spaniel's two-year-old form did nothing to suggest that he would become the winner of a classic race, and he ran several times without success. The following season he won firstly a Handicap at the Craven Meeting, and then the Shirley Stakes at Epsom two days before the Derby was run. These victories, however, can hardly have been of an impressive nature since his starting price in the Derby was 50–1. Lord Jersey's Riddlesworth, winner of the Riddlesworth Stakes, the Two Thousand Guineas, and the Newmarket Stakes, was a very warm favourite, as indeed his form entitled him to be. A furlong out he was in front and his backers were beginning to count up their winnings when he was strongly challenged by Spaniel, who had been third at the entrance to the straight. Either Riddlesworth failed to stay or else he had little heart for a struggle; the fact remains that he put up only a feeble resistance, and Spaniel, ridden by Wheatley, won fairly comfortably by three parts of a length.

The result left the onlookers dumbfounded, and Spaniel's subsequent form made his success look all the more astonishing. In the autumn he was beaten by a filly belonging to Sir Mark Wood, and after three defeats in 1832 he was sold to Mr Meyrick, who was content to let the Derby winner pick up trifles at Haverfordwest, Carmarthen, and Brecon. In 1833 Spaniel broke down when running in a minor handicap at Canterbury and was immediately destroyed. Riddlesworth was bought by Sir Mark Wood, who sold him to go abroad soon after.

King William IV had a runner in this Derby. He was not, however, greatly interested in racing although he carried out improvements at the Royal Stud and increased the number of King's Plates. He also presented to the Jockey Club one of Eclipse's hoofs, set in gold, to be competed for annually at Ascot by horses owned by members of the Club. The race apparently failed to catch on, and so the hoof was converted into a snuff-box and rests today in the Jockey Club Rooms at Newmarket.

Conditions for the Derby were altered this year. Instead of receiving £100 out of the stakes, the owner of the second was to save his stake of fifty pounds only. In addition, the owner of the winner was called upon to provide £100 towards the expenses of the police, who were now being employed in increasing numbers to keep the course clear and maintain some sort of order on the Downs.

1831: Thursday, 19 May ... 105 Entries. £3,000.

LORD LOWTHER's b.c. SPANIEL by Whalebone out of a mare by Canopus	W. WHEATLEY	1
LORD JERSEY's ch.c. RIDDLESWORTH by Emilius	H. EDWARDS	2
MR COOKE's b.c. INCUBUS by Phantom	WAKEFIELD	3

Also ran:

Sir G. Heathcote's Ferdousi (F. Buckle); Mr Thornhill's Africanus (C. Day); H.M. The King's colt by Mustachio (G. Nelson); Lord Exeter's Hoemus (J. Chapple); Mr S. Day's Caleb (S. Day); Duke of Richmond's Ciudad Rodrigo (T. Lye); Mr Vansittart's Rubini (F. Boyce); Lord Sligo's Bras de Fer (Spring); Mr Beardworth's Colwick (S. Darling); Mr W. Chifney's Exile (W. Macdonald); Mr W. Chifney's filly by Emilius (S. Chifney, jun.); Lord Egremont's Conscript (W. Arnull); General Grosvenor's Sarpedon (Farlow); Lord Verulam's Vestris (P. Conolly); Lord Chesterfield's colt by Middleton (W. Scott); Mr Rush's Roadster (J. Robinson); Mr Petre's Rattler (G. Boast); Sir R. W. Bulkeley's Pickpocket (G. Calloway); Duke of Grafton's Aeneas (J. Day); Lord Jersey's Blunderer (G. Edwards).

23 ran.

Betting:

6–4 on Riddlesworth; 12–1 Vestris; 16–1 Blunderer; 20–1 Bras de Fer; 25–1 the colts by Middleton and Roadster; 30–1 the colt by Mustachio; 50–1 Caleb, Spaniel, Colwick, and the filly by Emilius; 100–1 Incubus.

Won easily by three-quarters of a length.

1832

St Giles, winner in 1832, was owned in partnership by Messrs Robert Ridsdale and John Gully. Ridsdale, a Yorkshireman, was originally groom to Mr Lambton, afterwards first Lord Durham. Smooth, intelligent, with considerable charm and the ability to play the gentleman, Ridsdale soon got tired of stable drudgery and decided to take to the Turf and live by his wits. This he did with remarkable success and before long he had won a considerable fortune. His methods were based on the systematic corruption of trainers, jockeys, and stable employees, and while he flourished he exercised a thoroughly evil influence on the sport. Just occasionally his plans misfired. For instance he laid against Jerry heavily for the 1824 St Leger, first taking the precaution of bribing Harry Edwards to pull the horse. By sheer chance Jerry's trainer discovered the plot on the eve of the race, and when Edwards the following afternoon appeared in Jerry's colours all ready to mount, he was told that his services were not required. Another rider, Ben Smith, 'the most quiet, simple-minded creature that ever trod Yorkshire ground', was substituted and Jerry duly won. Ridsdale and his friends had no time to hedge and were badly hit.

For some time Ridsdale and Gully were in ignoble, if profitable confederacy, but they quarrelled after St Giles's Derby. Further disputes followed and Gully struck Ridsdale with his crop one afternoon out hunting. Ridsdale brought an action for assault, which was heard before Mr Justice Taunton and a special jury at York. As Gully had been a prize-fighter and Ridsdale was only a small man, sympathy was very much on the side of the latter, and an award of £500 damages was greeted in court by his supporters with a tremendous view-holloa, in which even the Bench and Bar are said to have joined.

From that moment, though, Ridsdale's luck deserted him. Two years later he was 'broke', and when he died in a hayloft at Newmarket, three halfpence was all that was left of his possessions.

John Gully was the son of an impecunious butcher at Bath. Six foot tall and powerfully built, he was a champion of the prize ring as a young man, but in fact he only fought two men during the whole of his boxing career: Pearce, the 'Game Chicken', who had rescued him from the Fleet Prison to which he was confined for debt; and the gigantic, lumbering Lancastrian, John Gregson, a fifteen-stone former steam-boat captain, 'poet laureat of the ring, and even in the company of laureats, where the standard of badness is high, probably the worst poet that ever lived'. Gully was beaten in a fierce and punishing fight by the 'Game Chicken', but when the latter decided to retire, he was offered the championship and accepted. He beat Gregson firstly in a fight at Six Mile Bottom, and secondly in Sir Giles Sebright's park in Hertfordshire.

After his second win over Gregson, Gully himself retired and took a public-house in Carey Street, where he began to operate as a bookmaker. Aided by a good head for figures, toughness, and a complete lack of scruples that made him eminently suited to his new profession, he was extremely successful and before long was the owner of a racing stud. After falling out with Ridsdale, he teamed up with Harry Hill, whose speciality was the laying of 'dead 'uns'. Harry Hill was dirty in person and lewd in speech, 'cracking his sides with laughter at his own personal and ill-timed gibes, not being ashamed to utter what others would blush to hear'. Originally a boot-black, he wormed his way into familiarity with every tout and card-sharper on the racecourse, and his knowledge of the seamy side of the sport was quite unrivalled. He knew how to make himself useful when wanted and he was the only professional betting man ever admitted to the bedroom of Lord George Bentinck, whose commissions he frequently carried out. It was his extraordinary knowledge of the racing underworld that supplied vital evidence for Bentinck's exposure of Running Rein after the 1844 Derby. For years he was commonly credited with complete control over a number of jockeys, and over a good many horses, too, that did not run in his name. He must have made a fortune at one period but, despite miserly habits, there was not much left when he died, blind and friendless.

Gully became Member of Parliament for Pontefract in 1832 and held the seat till 1837. It was said that it was not so much his powerful oratory that swayed the voters towards the liberal interest as his foresight in placing barrels of beer in the streets on polling day. Later in life he became a great colliery owner in Durham. He lived till 1863, but he had a narrow escape from death many years earlier when he fell foul of the redoubtable Squire Osbaldeston, who 'called him out'. The Squire sent a bullet slap through Gully's hat: 'better through my hat than through my head' is Gully's only recorded comment on the incident.

St Giles, bred by Ridsdale, was by Tramp out of Arcot Lass, by Ardrossan. As a two-year-old he ran twice without success. The following spring he won a Match over the Rowley Mile, and on the following day, a handicap over the Ditch Mile. There was nothing, therefore, in his record to justify St Giles being favourite for the Derby, a position which he nevertheless justified in no uncertain manner by winning with considerable ease and thereby netting the best part of £100,000 for his joint owners.

1832

Not surprisingly, in view of the circumstances and the characters of the joint owners, there was a strong suspicion of fraud, and it was commonly alleged that not only was St Giles a four-year-old, but that all but four jockeys participating in the race had been successfully squared. It seems highly probable that both allegations were true. There was in fact an objection to the winner on the grounds of an incorrect entry, but after due consideration it was overruled.

St Giles's only other race that year was the Goodwood Cup, in which he finished unplaced behind Priam. He was then sold to Mr Kirby of York. The following year he again failed in the Goodwood Cup and fell lame when competing for some minor event at Plymouth. He was patched up in 1835 to win at York and Catterick, after which he was exported to America, where he made no mark as a sire.

Bill Scott, who rode St Giles in the Derby, was born at Chippenham, near Newmarket and was one of the foremost riders of his time. He rode no fewer than nine winners of the St Leger, four of them in succession, while in addition he had four successes in the Derby and three in the Oaks. His brother John won equal fame as a trainer, and for many years they proved an extremely formidable combination. Drink, unfortunately, was Bill Scott's weakness, and towards the end of his career he was frequently in no condition to ride. If he had not been drunk, he would almost certainly have won the Derby on his own horse Sir Tatton Sykes in 1846. He died in 1848.

1832: Thursday, 7 June ... 101 Entries. £3,075.

MR R. RIDSDALE's ch.c. ST GILES by Tramp out of Arcot Lass	W. SCOTT	I
MR VANSITTART's ch.c. PERION by Whisker	F. BOYCE	2
MR RIDSDALE's ch.c. TRUSTEE by Catton	G. EDWARDS	3

Also ran:

Mr Gully's Margrave (S. Day); Mr Forth's Gratis (J. Forth); Sir G. Heathcote's Damascus (Wright); Mr Mills's Kate (A. Pavis); Lord Exeter's Beiram (W. Arnull); Mr. W. Chifney's Emiliana (S. Chifney, jun.); Lord Mountcharles's Minster (H. Edwards); Lord Chesterfield's Non Compos (P. Conolly); Lord Lowther's Lazarone (J. Chapple); Mr West's Creeper (G. Calloway); Lord Exeter's Spencer (S. Darling); Lord Portarlington's Bedouin (F. Buckle); Mr Wheeler's Revealer (J. Jacques); Lord Orford's The General (N. Flatman); Mr Hunter's Rouncival (T. Robinson); Mr Batson's Mixbury (T. Lye); Lord Lowther's Messenger (W. Wheatley); Lord Worcester's Haymaker (J. Robinson); Mr Garritt's Wallace (carried 9 st. 6 lb., no rider given).

22 ran.

Betting:

3–1 St Giles; 6–1 Perion; 7–1 Margrave; 15–2 Mixbury; 12–1 Kate; 20–1 Minster and Beiram; 25–1 Trustee and Gratis; 30–1 Non Compos; 50–1 Damascus.

Won easily by a length and a half.

1833

Dangerous, by Tramp out of Defiance, the winner in 1833, was very strongly suspected of being a four-year-old. Owned and bred by a Mr Sadler and trained at Stockbridge, he ran three times as a two-year-old, or rather as a reputed two-year-old, being placed at Ascot and also at Stockbridge, where he was second to General Grosvenor's Glaucus, who was subsequently sold to the notorious Mr Ridsdale.

Neither Dangerous nor Glaucus ran the following season before the Derby, for which Glaucus, heavily backed by Ridsdale, was favourite at 3–1, whereas 30–1 was available at the off about Dangerous. Early in the race Dangerous was a long way behind the leaders, but he was handily placed at Tattenham Corner and, taking the lead at the distance, he was not unduly troubled to hold off the challenge of John Scott's 100–1 outsider Connoisseur, whom he beat by a comfortable length. Chapple, the quiet, unassuming Devonshire man who partnered Dangerous, stated afterwards that his mount was lame at the start and that he would not have given a pint of porter for his chance. However, the stiffness wore off during the race, although the horse was lame again as soon as he was pulled up.

Dangerous never ran again. For a short time he was at the stud near Cheltenham, but in 1835 he was exported to France where he was used as a Government sire. Glaucus subsequently won some good races including The Whip, the Claret Stakes, the Eclipse Foot, and the Ascot Cup. At the conclusion of his racing career he was sold for export to America.

The day that Dangerous won the Derby was one of glorious sunshine from an unbroken blue sky. There was an enormous crowd on the Downs, and it was reported that 'as much order was maintained as was possible, having regard to the eccentricities and buoyant spirits of the multitude'.

1833: Thursday, 23 May ... 124 Entries. £3,725.

MR SADLER's ch.c. DANGEROUS by Tramp out of Defiance	J. CHAPPLE	1
MR J. SCOTT's br.c. CONNOISSEUR by Chateau Margaux	S. TEMPLEMAN	2
MR RAWLINSON's REVENGE by Fungus	T. COWLEY	3

Also ran:

Mr Sowerby's Catalonian (S. Mann); Lord Exeter's Sir Robert (W. Arnull); Mr Hunter's Forester (Wright); Mr Greville's Whale (W. Scott); Mr Forth's Imbar (Norman); Mr Houldsworth's Despot (T. Lye); Mr Wood's Titian (C. Edwards); Sir G. Heathcote's Astracan (F. Buckle, jun.); Mr Cooper's colt by Catton (N. Flatman); Mr Cosby's The Bravo (S. Day); Mr Chifney's Moorhen (S. Chifney, jun.); Mr Goodwin's Pagan (W. Macdonald); Duke of Grafton's Aegyptus (J. Day); Lord Exeter's Cactus (S. Darling); Duke of Rutland's Shylock (J. Robinson); Lord Jersey's Glenmore (G. Edwards); Mr Ridsdale's Glaucus (W. Wheatley); Mr Payne's colt by Wrangler (Spring); Mr W. Chifney's Prince Llewellyn (H. Edwards); Lord Verulam's Little Cassino (P. Conolly); Mr Champion's Robin Roughhead (W. Coleman); Mr Bristow's Uncle Toby (Wakefield).

25 ran.

Betting:

3–1 Glaucus; 7–1 Forester and Whale; 9–1 Little Cassino; 10–1 Sir Robert; 12–1 Moorhen; 15–1 Revenge; 20–1 the colt by Catton; 30–1 Dangerous; 100–1 Connoisseur.

Won by a length.

1834

It was a vintage year in 1834. The winner, Plenipotentiary, was undoubtedly a great horse at his best: Glencoe, winner of the Two Thousand Guineas, not only sired Pocahontas, dam of Stockwell, Rataplan, and King Tom, but proved an outstanding stud success when sent to America; while Touchstone, winner of the St Leger, was not only a top-class racehorse, but extraordinarily successful as a stallion as well.

Plenipotentiary—invariably known on the racecourse as 'Plenipo'—was owned and bred by Mr Stanlake Batson, a most respected member of the Jockey Club. Like Priam, he was by Emilius, while his dam Harriet was by Pericles out of a mare by Selim. He never ran as a two-year-old, but made a successful first appearance the following season at the Craven Meeting when he won a small Sweepstakes. Two days later he took on Lord Jersey's Glencoe in the Craven Stakes. Glencoe, who had just won the Riddlesworth Stakes, started at 6–4 on as, apart from his own merit, 'Plenipo', who always carried a lot of flesh, was still physically backward. However it was 'Plenipo' that won, much to the disgust of Glencoe's rider Robinson, who thought he had the race at his mercy when he happened to look round and saw 'that great bullock cantering at my side'.

A fortnight later Glencoe enhanced the value of that form by winning the Two Thousand Guineas, and not unnaturally Plenipotentiary, who did not run again before Epsom, became a short-priced favourite for the Derby, despite reports that he had been coughing and was short of work.

Second favourite was Shilelagh, bought from the Chifney brothers by the Duke of Cleveland, formerly Lord Darlington. Two days before the Derby, the Chifneys wanted to increase their bet on Shilelagh, but did not fancy the current price. Accordingly they sent out with blistered legs and bandages a horse they had that looked very like Shilelagh. The touts were completely taken in, the rumour spread that Shilelagh was wrong, and the Chifneys' commission was carried through promptly at extremely favourable odds. Such ingenuity really deserved to succeed!

The weather for Epsom week was superb and the crowd on Derby Day enormous. When the twenty-two runners went to the post there were five false starts before they were really away. Glencoe and Plenipotentiary were the first two to show in front, but Conolly soon gave the favourite a pull and was content to lie about sixth. Coming down the hill 'Plenipo' moved up on the rails and was fourth on the final bend behind Glencoe, Intriguer, and Darius. At the distance he challenged Glencoe, and accelerating with wonderful smoothness, drew clear to win by two lengths to the immense delight of the crowd, who gave him a tumultuous reception. It was a fast run race, and close home Glencoe weakened a little and lost second place by half a length to Shilelagh, a big, leggy, brown colt that had never been seen on a racecourse before. Mr Batson won some £5,000 on the race, which was generally accounted to have been a wonderfully profitable one for the 'swells'.

'Plenipo' walked over for the St James's Palace Stakes at Ascot, and his next appearance was in the St Leger, which was regarded as more or less a match between himself and Shilelagh. He could hardly have run worse; six furlongs from home he was stone cold, and he finished a furlong behind Touchstone at the tail-end of the field, even being beaten by Bubastes who had finished plumb last in the Derby. There were some who said he was grossly unfit, and one writer, who may not have seen him before and probably did not know his physical characteristics, said that 'he was carrying as much blubber as would have swamped a South Sea whaler'. Another story was that he had had an accident and injured himself on the road from Newmarket to Doncaster, but the lad in charge of him had been too scared to tell anyone. In all probability, though, he had been drugged, and not long afterwards it was rumoured that the head-lad, who died very suddenly, had laid bare the whole sordid story on his death-bed. Usually 'Plenipo' was a difficult horse to saddle, plunging and kicking in alarming fashion, but on this occasion he had to be kicked before he got up, and he tripped and was almost down three times on the way to the starting-post. Conolly had to spur him to get him to canter, and turning to John Scott he exclaimed, 'My horse is as dead as a stone'!

A lot of scurrilous talk was directed against Mr Batson, but it is highly unlikely that he was in any way implicated. A writer in a paper called *The Age* produced an article called 'The Safety or Plenipo Pills'. He gave the following receipt for the pills: '6 lb. Jacobi Blandini; 7 oz. Ridsdalian powder; 8 oz. Gullianae Boxianae; ½ lb. Hunteri sex mili Bottomi Batsoni Bottleholderi; ¼ lb. Out of the Way Traineri Payni, Matino Currente etc'. The writer concluded: 'The legs won all the money and the gentlemen had nothing for it but to fork out the dibs. Who would have been the losers had Plenipo won? The wriggling Jamie—the well-known hand at a cross, the horse-whipped groom Ridsdale, who not only stood in himself, but told his friends to follow suit; the out-and-outer Wagstaffe,* the chum of Richardson, the Pontefract Boxing M.P.'

* A singularly audacious and repulsive crook, whose teeth fitted into each other, like two cross-cut saws set together.

Plenipotentiary won the Craven Stakes the following spring; and during the same week a Plate. Having proved that his horse was all right again, Mr Batson retired him to the stud at Linton, near Newmarket, at a fee of twenty-five guineas. He was not a stud success, and before he died in 1854 at Denham he had been serving half-bred mares for a fiver.

In 1835 Colonel Jackson of Alabama sent a commission to buy the best horse on the market, expressing a preference for Plenipotentiary, Priam, or Glencoe. Glencoe was the one he obtained, and that horse's name figures in the pedigree of many famous American winners. He died aged twenty-seven at Georgetown, Kentucky.

1834: Thursday, 29 May . . . 123 Entries. £3,625.

MR S. BATSON's ch.c. PLENIPOTENTIARY
by Emilius out of Harriet . P. CONOLLY 1
DUKE OF CLEVELAND's b.c. SHILELAGH
by St Patrick S. CHIFNEY, JUN. 2
LORD JERSEY's ch.c. GLENCOE by Sultan J. ROBINSON 3

Also ran:

Mr Yates's Bentley (A. Pavis); Mr W. Edwards's Intriguer (Wright); Mr Houldsworth's Darius (S. Darling); Mr Walls's Bubastes (W. Scott); Mr Hunter's Morotto (W. Arnull); Duke of Grafton's Olympic (J. Day); Mr Gully's Viator (J. Forth); Mr Sadler's Defensive (J. Chapple); Mr Gardnor's Cornet (G. Edwards); Duke of Rutland's Dacre (F. Boyce); Sir G. Heathcote's Nisus (F. Buckle); Lord Orford's Paris (Wakefield); Mr Greatrex's colt by Lottery (C. Edwards); Mr Cosby's Stradbally (S. Mann); Mr Mills's Patapan (N. Flatman); Sir Mark Wood's Flatterer (W. Wheatley); Lord Lowther's Rioter (Rogers); Mr E. Peele's Noodle (Spring); Duke of Cleveland's Guardian (T. Lye).

22 ran.

Betting:

9–4 Plenipotentiary; 11–4 Shilelagh; 8–1 Bubastes; 11–1 Glencoe; 20–1 Bentley and Cornet; 22–1 Intriguer.

Won in a canter by two lengths.

1835

Mr John Bowes of Streatlam Castle, Durham, won the Derby four times, with Mündig in 1835, with Cotherstone in 1843, with Daniel O'Rourke in 1852, and with West Australian in 1853. A member of the Jockey Club, he owned horses for more than fifty years, and until John Scott's death in 1871, he was a patron of the famous Whitehall stable at Malton.

Bowes was a son of Lord Strathmore and would have succeeded to that title but for the fact that he was born nine years before his parents married. Possibly the circumstances of his birth left their mark on his character, as he was always a shy and rather solitary figure, living for the most part quietly in Paris and tending in later years to become a complete recluse. In fact for thirty years before his death, which took place in 1885, he never set foot on a racecourse. Unlike so many rich young men who take to racing at an early age, he always had a very good idea of the value of money, and he had increased his fortune substantially when he died, despite the fact that at great expense he had been in the habit of hiring the Variétés Theatre in Paris for the benefit of his wife, who was a somewhat indifferent French actress.

Bowes was only twenty-one and still at Cambridge when Mündig (the German word meaning 'of age') won the Derby. The horse had been entered for the Derby by his trustees, one of whom was the Duke of Cleveland. When it became clear that Mündig was a colt of considerable promise, the trustees backed him at a long price without informing the owner or offering him a share in the commission. With considerable coolness, Bowes summoned a meeting of his trustees to discover the circumstances in which his colt had been so heavily backed. The trustees attempted to bluff him, but were eventually compelled to transfer the most favourable bets to him when he threatened to have his horse scratched. 'What an owdacious young 'un!' exclaimed John Scott in admiration when he heard of this episode.

Mündig was a rather plain chesnut by Catton, who was twenty-three years old when Mündig was foaled. He had never seen a racecourse before the Derby, but he had done enough at home to suggest that he might easily win in a moderate year. At all events he started a well-backed third favourite. The actual favourite was Lord Jersey's Ibrahim, winner of the Two Thousand Guineas, and second favourite was Lord Offord's Ascot, winner of a Sweepstakes at the Craven Meeting. Lord Jersey also ran Silenus, who had at one period been favourite, but who started without a quotation, his mission being to make the pace for Ibrahim. Oddly enough, there was another horse called Ibrahim in the field as well.

After four false starts Silenus went off in front and was still in the lead at Tattenham Corner with Mündig, Ascot, Ibrahim, and Pelops hard on his heels. Silenus was stone cold at the distance, and a hundred yards later both Ibrahim and Pelops began to falter. That left Mündig and Ascot out in front, and the pair had a tremendous battle home, Mündig being adjudged the winner by a head, while Pelops, Ibrahim, and Valentissimo finished almost abreast only a length behind Ascot. Bill Scott, it was said, never rode a severer race than he did on the winner, and apart from punishing his own horse, he was roaring at Nat Flatman, Ascot's jockey, throughout the final furlong, urging him to stop his horse from hanging on to Mündig. Scott's anxiety to win is understandable as he and his brother collected £20,000 between them and Mr Bowes a further £20,000. That night the successful young owner celebrated his victory by dining quietly by himself at Crockford's.

Mündig was by no means an outstanding Derby winner and was well down the course in the St Leger. He did, however, win a £100 Foal Stakes at Doncaster the following day. In 1836 he was beaten twice at Liverpool, won three King's Plates, and then suffered three more defeats. At the end of the season he retired to the stud at Market Harborough at a ten-guinea fee. His sole claim to fame as a stallion was his exceptional savagery, and on one occasion he ran amok and killed a man.

1835: Thursday, 4 June . . . 128 Entries. £3,550.

MR J. BOWES's ch.c. MÜNDIG by Catton
   out of Emma   W. SCOTT   I
LORD ORFORD's ASCOT by Reveller   NAT FLATMAN   2
No horse was officially placed third.

Also ran:

   Lord Warwick's Pelops (G. Calloway); Lord Jersey's Ibrahim (J. Robinson); Lord Jersey's Silenus (E. Edwards); Duke of Richmond's Elizondo (F. Boyce); Duke of Cleveland's colt by Memnon (S. Chifney, jun.); Mr Ridsdale's Coriolanus (P. Conolly); Mr Pettit's Ibrahim (E. Wright); Sir G. Heathcote's Valentissimo (F. Buckle); Mr J. Robinson's Stockport (S. Darling); Mr J. Peel's Trim (J. Chapple); Mr Ridsdale's Luck's All (G. Edwards); Duke of Rutland's Florestan (W. Wheatley).

14 ran.

Betting:

2–1 Lord Jersey's Ibrahim; 3–1 Ascot; 6–1 Mündig; 10–1 Elizondo; 12–1 Coriolanus; 20–1 the colt by Memnon; 50–1 Trim and Valentissimo; 100–1 Pelops.

Won by a head.
Winner trained by John Scott at Malton.

1836

Lord Jersey had his third and final victory in 1836 with Bay Middleton, a beautifully bred colt by Sultan, who ran Tiresias to a head in the Derby, out of the Oaks winner Cobweb, a Phantom mare whose great grand-dam was the famous Penelope.

A handsome bay standing 16·1½, Bay Middleton was bred by his owner. He never ran as a two-year-old, but such was his promise from his earliest days that he was backed to win the Derby at 8–1 before he had even done a serious gallop. As a three-year-old he won the Riddlesworth Stakes, beating Destiny, who later won the One Thousand Guineas, and he then went on to win the Two Thousand Guineas himself. Among the horses he beat in the Guineas was Elis, who won the St Leger in the autumn. Elis carried Lord Lichfield's colours, but in fact belonged to Lord George Bentinck, who had reckoned him unbeatable in the first of the season's classics.

Bay Middleton was a strong favourite for the Derby despite a number of detrimental rumours which may have been based on the fact that he always had one doubtful leg as well as a temper that at times was quite ungovernable. John Day's Venison was heavily backed to beat him, but Lord Jersey was supremely confident and made no secret of his feelings.

There were several false starts, and the real start was ragged and unsatisfactory, the Chifneys' colt Athenian being hopelessly left, while Gladiator, ridden by Bill Scott, was very badly away. Bay Middleton, however, was always commanding his field, and although Gladiator recovered from his early ill-fortune so well that he was almost level at the distance, the favourite had no difficulty in shaking him off and went on to win by a very easy two lengths. Bay Middleton's rider, Robinson, was given a present by Lord Jersey of £200, a very large sum for a jockey in those days.

Lord Jersey and his friends took a lot of money out of the Ring, and in general the bookmakers were heavy losers. Another loser was the Hon. Berkeley Craven, who had staked £800 on the race and shot himself at his home in Connaught Terrace that evening. He was an experienced gambler and was sixty years of age at the time.

At Ascot Bay Middleton won the Buckhurst Stakes, and at Newmarket in October he again defeated Elis, this time in the Grand Duke Michael Stakes. He finished the season by winning a Match against Muezzin, to whom he gave thirteen pounds, and shortly afterwards was sold for 4,000 guineas, a very stiff price at this period, to Lord George Bentinck, who had held an extremely high opinion of him since the Guineas. Bentinck, who won a lot of money over Bay Middleton in the Derby, was hoping to win the Ascot Cup with him the following season, but that doubtful leg went for good and all soon after the purchase, so instead he retired him to the stud at the Turf Inn, Doncaster, at a fee of thirty guineas.

At the stud Bay Middleton was for a long time a disappointment, and a costly one, too, to his owner, who had sent him a great many mares and had heavily engaged the produce, many of whom were unsound and impossible to train. Alas, Bentinck was dead when at last Bay Middleton justified his owner's faith and sired a really good horse, The Flying Dutchman. He also sired the 1854 Derby winner Andover, and Kalipyge, a filly that broke down at Epsom, but was thought by Sir Joseph Hawley, whose standards were high, to be the best of her sex that he had ever owned. Bay Middleton died at Danebury in 1857.

1836: Thursday, 19 May . . . 128 Entries. £3,725.

LORD JERSEY's b.c. BAY MIDDLETON by Sultan out of Cobweb	J. ROBINSON	1
LORD WILTON's ch.c. GLADIATOR by Partisan	W. SCOTT	2

No horse was officially placed third.

Also ran:

Mr J. Day's Venison (J. Day); Colonel Peel's Slane (A. Pavis); Lord Chesterfield's Alfred (S. Rogers); Lord Egremont's Hock (G. Edwards); Mr Batson's Taishteer (Wakefield); Lord Exeter's Muezzin (P. Conolly); Sir G. Heathcote's Willesden (F. Buckle); Mr W. Chifney's The Athenian (F. Butler); Duke of Richmond's Sepoy (F. Boyce); Colonel Peel's Mr Waggs (Nat Flatman); Mr Osbaldeston's Ebberston (W. Wheatley); Sir L. Glyn's Recruit (S. Day, jun.); Mr J. Robertson's Whaley (S. Darling); Lord Lichfield's Toss-up (J. Cartwright); Mr Allen's Master of the Rolls (T. Lye); Mr E. Peel's Morison (W. Macdonald); Mr Gardnor's Idiot (J. Chapple); Duke of Beaufort's Hatfield (E. Wright); Lord Chesterfield's Weighton (F. Edwards).

21 ran.

Betting:

7–4 Bay Middleton; 7–2 Venison; 8–1 Colonel Peel's two; 11–1 Gladiator; 14–1 Sepoy; 25–1 Alfred; 30–1 Hock and Muezzin; 50–1 Recruit.

Won by two lengths.

1837

The first Derby winner of Queen Victoria's reign was Phosphorus, owned by Lord Berners, better known on the Turf, perhaps, as Colonel Ralph Wilson. Lord Berners was a mildly eccentric old bachelor, who loved the country and every form of sport and visited London as rarely as possible. Wherever he was, his costume invariably consisted of an enormous hat that might have been white when it left the shop many years previously, a frock-coat made of some material that looked suspiciously like green baize, and a pair of immensely thick breeches, the colour of a well-used hunting saddle. He invariably smoked a cigar, was very careful with his money in his later years, and appeared perfectly satisfied both with the world in general and himself. His favourite sport was hawking, a taste perhaps inherited from his ancestress Dame Julia Berners, Prioress of the Nunnery of Sopwell, who in 1481 published 'A Treatise on Hawking, with something of Hunting, and a little of Heraldry'.

Phosphorus, by Lamplighter, was a ewe-necked colt, lacking in power and anything but handsome. He began his racing career by being second to the Duke of Rutland's Rat-trap in the Newmarket Stakes, and at the Second Spring Meeting he won a £50 Plate from a very big field. This latter performance was evidently quite impressive, as two days before the Derby he was quoted at 11–1 for that race. In fact he was seriously fancied, and 'Vates', who turned out some deplorable doggerel for *Bells Life* every Sunday, concluded his Derby epic as follows:

> 'Tis over, the trick for the thousands is done,
> George Edwards on Phosphorus the Derby has won.

Forty-eight hours before the Derby 'Vates' was no doubt kicking himself for having tipped Phosphorus, as the news had leaked out that the colt was lame and his price had drifted to 40–1, with no takers. The story current at the time was that Lord Berner's trainer went to him to advise him to scratch the horse, but the old gentleman kept on reiterating 'Run, I always run', so it was decided that Phosphorus must take his chance. A more probable version, though, is the following, given thirty years later by Lord Berners's nephew, and his successor to the title:

Phosphorus reached Epsom about a week before the race, thoroughly fit. In one of his first gallops on the Downs, he sprained a foreleg and pulled up lame. In-

116

flammation and swelling ensued. He was put into a loose-box, out of which he was not removed for four days until the evening before the Derby, when, after reaching Epsom with his owner, I found, on examination, and on moving him round the box, that he walked sound, and that the inflammation had subsided; but that a thickening of the sheath of the tendon remained. Knowing how perfectly he had been prepared, I ordered him to be taken out at four the next morning and walked, until I came to him. At eight he was brought in perfectly sound, and being still so at ten o'clock, he was ordered to be prepared for the race. He was ridden by George Edwards with judgment and patience, but no extra exertion was used or required.

The race proved to be an exceptionally exciting one. The favourite, Rat-trap, like many another Derby favourite, was done with at Tattenham Corner, and from then on it was a gruelling battle between Lord Suffield's Caravan, the second favourite, and Phosphorus, with Phosphorus, his lameness forgotten, forcing his head in front almost on the post to win by a head. Possibly the best horse in the race was Mango, owned by Mr Greville. He was still physically backward at Epsom, but improved steadily throughout the summer and won the St Leger. He was eventually exported to America. Phosphorus never ran again, and when Lord Berners died ten months later, he was sold for a thousand guineas to the Duke of Brunswick for export.

It only remains to add a few minor points. This was the first Derby to be started by flag and the last one to be run on a Thursday, Wednesday being the appointed day from then on. Finally, it is perhaps worth noting that the 1837 Derby has its permanent place in literature, Disraeli having described at the opening of his novel, *Sybil*, not only the race itself, but the scene in Crockford's the night before when the ineffable Mr Mountchesney remarked: 'I rather like bad wine. One gets so bored with good wine.'

1837: Thursday, 25 May . . . 131 Entries. £3,700.

LORD BERNERS's b.c. PHOSPHORUS by Lamplighter out of a mare by Rubens	G. EDWARDS	1
LORD SUFFIELD's br.c. CARAVAN by Camel	A. PAVIS	2

No horse was officially placed third.

Also ran:

Mr Osbaldeston's Mahometan (H. Edwards); Lord Exeter's Hibiscus (P. Conolly); Lord Exeter's Dardanelles (S. Darling); Mr C. Greville's Mango (Nat Flatman); Mr Gardnor's Benedict (J. Chapple); Duke of Rutland's Rat-trap

(J. Robinson); Mr Wreford's Wisdom (J. Day); Lord Exeter's Troilis (S. Nelson); Mr Bowes's Mickle Fell (W. Scott); Mr Osbaldeston's The Pocket Hercules (S. Rogers); Lord Chesterfield's Critic (S. Chifney, jun.); Mr Theobald's Sir Frederick (W. Macdonald); Mr Barclay's Pegasus (Mr Bartley); Mr Cooke's Norgrove (C. Edwards); Mr Phillimore's colt by Catton (F. Buckle).

17 ran.

Betting:

7–4 Rat-trap; 7–2 Caravan; 11–2 Mango; 6–1 Hibiscus; 16–1 Wisdom; 25–1 Benedict; 30–1 Dardanelles; 40–1 Mahometan and Phosphorus.

Won by a head.

Tattenham Corner, 1847

F. Buckle jun.

J. Robinson

Will Scott

John Scott

by Abraham Cooper

John Day

1838

This year for the first time the railways ran special trains from Nine Elms Station, Battersea, to Epsom. The innovation was hardly an unqualified success as the trains provided could only accommodate a fraction of the vast number of would-be travellers, many of whom were stranded on the platform at Nine Elms after a curt explanation from the railway staff that they 'were short of engines'. In fact it must have been a scene quite reminiscent of present-day travelling on suburban lines.

It was an Epsom triumph this year. The winner Amato was trained on the Downs by Ralph Sherwood, and had been bred by his owner Sir Gilbert Heathcote at The Durdans, which belonged to the Heathcote family before being bought by Lord Rosebery. The Durdans adjoins Epsom racecourse, and the paddock and parade ring for a long time formed part of the estate. Sir Gilbert Heathcote, a member of the Jockey Club, was extremely well liked locally, and with Baron de Tessier of Woodcote Manor, invariably acted as Steward at the Epsom meetings. There has only been one Epsom-trained winner of the Epsom Derby since Amato, and that was April The Fifth in 1932.*

The favourite in 1838 was Grey Momus, winner of the Two Thousand Guineas. Bred by Sir Tatton Sykes, Grey Momus had twice carried Mr John Bowes's colours successfully at Goodwood as a two-year-old, but had then been sold to Lord George Bentinck, who ran horses in his own name for the first time this season. Second favourite was Mr Combe's Cobham, while Colonel Peel's Ion was strongly supported as well. Amato, a little fifteen-hand horse by Velocipede, had never run before, but had shown up well in his gallops and there had been quite a lot of money for him until he started to cough a few days before the race. After that, 'the coughing pony', as he was then called in the sporting press, drifted right out in the market.

Once again it was a deplorable start. After three false starts several jockeys were caught unprepared when the flag fell, and both Young Rowton and St Francis were hopelessly left. Bretby made the early running at a fast gallop, but he was beaten at half-way and Amato then went to the front. Grey Momus was under pressure without response at Tattenham Corner, and the only serious challenge to Amato came from Ion. He, however, was comfortably held at bay by 'the coughing pony', who passed the post a length to the good with Grey Momus three lengths away third.

* Straight Deal won a substitute Derby at Newmarket in 1943.

Although he started at 30–1 Amato's victory, no doubt due to his local associations, was well received, and Chapple, 'the honest and civil little Jock who rode the baronet's colt, received many and hearty shakes of the hand'.

Amato broke down soon afterwards and never ran again. He died in 1843 and was buried at The Durdans. Grey Momus redeemed his reputation later that year by winning the Ascot Cup, two races at Goodwood, the Grand Duke Michael Stakes, and the Newmarket St Leger. The following season he won the Port Stakes and three other races, so there can be little doubt that he was a high-class colt and must have failed for some reason to show his very best form in the Derby. Ion only ran once again and was then second to Don John in the St Leger. He retired to the Royal Stud at Hampton Court and sired the 1855 Derby winner, Wild Dayrell. No doubt the best three-year-old in 1838 was Don John, unbeaten that year and the previous year as well. He had been bought as a foal by Mr Robert Ridsdale, and when that gentleman crashed financially, Lord Chesterfield bought him for 145 guineas. Lord Chesterfield did not win much in bets over Don John's St Leger, his failure to do so incurring the contempt of Lord George Bentinck, whose avowed objective was to break the Ring. 'If I had such a horse as Don John,' Bentinck remarked, 'I would not have left the last card-seller in Doncaster with a rag to his back.'

Velocipede, sire of Amato, had a pair of indifferent forelegs but did well at the stud, siring the winners of over £100,000 in stakes. Other good winners by him were Queen of Trumps, who won the Oaks and the St Leger in 1835, and Carolina, winner of the Oaks in 1839.

Amato has an inn at Epsom named in his honour. Close to the inn there is a well, known as 'The Amato Well', on the side of which a tip for the Derby is traditionally chalked up every year on the eve of the race.

1838: Wednesday, 30 May . . . 134 Entries. £4,005.

SIR G. HEATHCOTE's br.c. AMATO by Velocipede out of Jane Shore	J. CHAPPLE	1
COLONEL PEEL's br.c. ION by Cain	A. PAVIS	2
LORD GEORGE BENTINCK's gr.c. GREY MOMUS by Comus	J. DAY	3

Also ran:

Lord Westminster's Albemarle (J. Holmes); Mr Buckley's Tom (S. Darling); Mr Worrall's Dormouse (S. Rogers); Mr Forth's Conservator (Owner); Lord Jersey's Phoenix (J. Robinson); Lord George Bentinck's D'Egville (J. Day, jun.);

1838

Mr Payne's Young Rowton (S. Chifney, jun.); Captain Berkeley's Bullion (P. Conolly); Mr E. Peel's The Early Bird (S. Templeman); Mr Edwards's Drum Major (G. Edwards); Duke of Grafton's Chemist (W. Wheatley); Sir J. Boswell's Constantine (T. Lye); General Grosvenor's Daedalus (Nat Flatman); Mr Stirling's Orange Boy (G. Boast); Sir J. Mills's Volunteer (E. Edwards); Mr Bond's colt by Reveller (Wakefield); Mr Pettit's St Francis (Pettit, jun.); Mr Tarleton's Blaise (Perren, jun.); Mr Combe's Cobham (W. Scott); Lord Chesterfield's Bretby (H. Edwards).

23 ran.

Betting:

5–2 Grey Momus; 7–2 Cobham; 7–1 Phoenix; 8–1 D'Egville; 13–1 Ion; 15–1 Young Rowton; 25–1 The Early Bird; 30–1 Amato and Albemarle; 40–1 Conservator and Chemist; 50–1 Bullion; 1,000–15 Drum Major and Bretby.

Won by a length.
Winner trained by R. Sherwood at Epsom.

1839

The Derby of 1839 was unpleasant and unsatisfactory. The weather was vile; there were disputes and insinuations with regard to the winner, about whom 'public opinion favoured the belief that he had a year in hand'; and there was a strong suspicion that the runner-up was prevented from winning by her rider.

When Mr Robert Ridsdale came to grief and was forced to sell his horses, there was one ugly little foal for whom there was no bid and who accordingly was taken over by Robert Ridsdale's brother, William. The foal was named Bloomsbury and apparently improved immensely in appearance as he grew older.

At this period William Ridsdale had for some time been acting as trainer to Lord Chesterfield, who entered Bloomsbury for the Derby. Ridsdale and his patron, however, parted company somewhat abruptly and there was a wrangle about Bloomsbury's ownership, Ridsdale claiming the colt as his own. Nevertheless, in April 1839 Lord Chesterfield was still threatening to scratch the colt from every engagement. A little later, though, it was announced that the horse's engagements would be allowed to stand if someone would come forward and pay all the forfeits due on him. This was done by a certain bookmaker, possibly Harry Hill, who is known to have won a great deal of money over Bloomsbury at Epsom.

Bloomsbury had never run before the Derby, for which he started at 25–1, nor had the favourite Sleight-of-Hand from John Scott's stable. Mr Thornhill's Euclid and Lord Jersey's Caesar were both well backed, and there was a certain amount of support for Mr Fulwar Craven's filly Deception. Lord Lichfield's Corsair, however, winner of the Two Thousand Guineas, was more or less neglected in the market.

There was frost in the morning, sleet at midday, snow while the race was in progress, and a cutting east wind throughout the entire proceedings. The new starter, Mr Perren of Newmarket, got the twenty-one runners off quickly and evenly. Deception made the running at a moderate gallop from Lord Exeter's Bosphorus and Bloomsbury. Once the straight was reached, Trenn on Deception began to ride the filly like one possessed and drove her into a five lengths' lead from Bloomsbury and Euclid. Not surprisingly, she failed to last it out and was unable to resist the challenge of Bloomsbury, which the north-country jockey Sim Templeman had delayed till he was well inside the final furlong. Bloomsbury passed the post a length ahead of Deception, with Euclid two lengths away third and the rest of the field nowhere in the picture. It was generally agreed that Trenn had ridden a singularly ill-judged race, and it was strongly rumoured that it had never been his purpose to win. Two days later, with John Day up, Deception won the Oaks in a canter.

Two days after the Derby Mr Craven, owner of Deception, objected to Bloomsbury on the grounds that the colt was entered for the race as 'by Mulatto', whereas the Stud Book described him as being 'by Tramp or Mulatto'. However, when the Stewards met to hear the case, no one appeared in support of the objection. Apparently Mr Craven had an ominous difficulty in finding anyone prepared to give evidence on his behalf, and a letter he sent to the Stewards requesting an adjournment arrived too late. The objection, therefore, was overruled.

At Ascot Bloomsbury won two races, one the Ascot Derby, but started for both under protest. Lord Lichfield, who owned the runner-up in the Ascot Derby, agreed with Mr Craven that the whole question of Bloomsbury's description and identity should be referred to the Jockey Club. Lord Lichfield, however, subsequently withdrew his consent to the case being settled in that manner as the witnesses he needed refused to give evidence unless compelled to.

The matter then went to law, and the case of Lichfield *v.* Ridsdale was heard before a special jury at Liverpool. The jury found for Ridsdale, a decision that was popular enough in some circles where the view was taken that it was a case of might against right, or a wealthy and influential member of the aristocracy vindictively persecuting a comparatively poor and possibly honest man. There is little doubt that Lord Lichfield himself had recourse to law against his better judgement, but allowed himself to be persuaded by Lord George Bentinck, who was convinced that there had been trickery of some sort. In all probability there had been, and perhaps it would have been exposed if a little more patience had been exercised and action delayed until decisive evidence was available. There is no doubt that Bentinck was too impulsive on this occasion and in consequence came off second best.

In the autumn Bloomsbury was defeated in the St Leger and also in another race at Doncaster. The following year he ran third in the Ascot Cup, and second, carrying nine stone, in the Cesarewitch. It was a wonderful finish for the Cesarewitch with Robinson on Clarion, the winner, and Chifney on Bloomsbury both at their best; in the words of a contemporary writer, 'A more beautiful race in every meaning of the phrase it would be impossible to conceive.' In 1841 Bloomsbury was last but one in the Ascot Cup and at the end of the season was exported to Germany.

Mr Fulwar Craven, the owner of Deception, was a well-known eccentric, famous as a story-teller in the manner of Baron Münchausen and with a pronounced taste for extremely low company. His manner of dress was unique.

'He wore light-coloured kerseymere breeches and gaiters, the tongues of the latter nearly covering his boots, which, in their turn, were more dandified than substantial. The hinder part of the calves of his legs was uncovered for some two inches in width, the better to display his flesh-coloured silk stockings. He wore a claret-coloured coat, buff waistcoat, and a large-frilled shirt. From the outside breast-pocket of his coat hung a large yellow silk handkerchief, covering half his side. His shirt collar was Gladstonian, of an immense size, and round it was loosely wound a gaudy necktie, secured with a pin nearly the size of a small saucer. He had long, flowing, and very bushy red or auburn whiskers, and wore a white hat, characteristically high. He took an immense quantity of snuff from a huge gold box, which he carried in his waistcoat pocket.'

1839: Wednesday, 15 May . . . 143 Entries. £4,100.

MR W. RIDSDALE's b.c. BLOOMSBURY by Mulatto out of Arcot Lass	S. TEMPLEMAN	1
MR FULWAR CRAVEN's b.f. DECEPTION by Defence	TRENN	2

No horse was officially placed third.

Also ran:

Mr Thornhill's Euclid (P. Conolly); Colonel Peel's Bey of Algiers (A. Parvis); Mr Sadler's Dart (W. Sadler); Captain Williamson's Melbourne (Nat Flatman); Lord Albemarle's Domino (C. Cotton); Lord Jersey's Caesar (J. Robinson); Mr S. Herbert's Clarion (W. Day); Lord Lichfield's The Corsair (Wakefield); Mr G. Clark's The Dragsman (H. Edwards); Sir G. Heathcote's Valaincourt (J. Chapple); Duke of Grafton's Aethur (J. Day); Lord Jersey's Ilderim (E. Edwards); Lord Exeter's Bosphorus (S. Darling); Mr Bowes's King of Kelton (C. Edwards); Duke of Grafton's Montreal (W. Wheatley); Mr Worrall's Peon (S. Rogers); Lord Westminster's Sleight-of-Hand (W. Scott); Mr. Dixon's Hyllus (S. Day); Mr Eddison's Rory O'More (J. Holmes).

21 ran.

Betting:

5–1 Sleight-of-Hand; 6–1 Euclid; 7–1 Caesar; 8–1 Clarion; 12–1 Deception; 16–1 Corsair; 20–1 Dragsman; 24–1 Dart; 25–1 Montreal and Bloomsbury; 30–1 Valaincourt and Melbourne; 50–1 Aethur and Ilderim.

Won by two lengths.
Winner trained by W. Ridsdale.

1840

In 1840 the Derby received recognition as a national occasion through a semi-state visit of the Queen and the Prince Consort. It was a perfect summer afternoon and the Queen looked charming, 'all smiles and dimples', but the masses had little affection for royalty in the 'hungry forties' and the Queen's reception was lacking not only in enthusiasm, but in respect. No doubt because of that, the visit was not repeated.

A minor misfortune that year was the conduct of the owner of The Warren. He developed religious scruples, which impelled him to forbid the saddling of horses in his paddock. They were saddled, therefore, at Langley Bottom instead, and the Prince rode down on his cob to watch them.

It was a poor-class field for the big race. The favourite at 9–4 was Lord Westminster's Launcelot, a full brother to Touchstone, and winner the year before of the Champagne Stakes at Doncaster. Equal second favourites at 7–2 were Lord Albemarle's Assassin and Mr Etwall's Melody colt. Among the 50–1 outsiders completely ignored by the public was Little Wonder, a colt by Muley that stood less than fifteen hands. Little Wonder was entered by Mr Robertson of Ladybank, Berwick-on-Tweed, and had cost a mere sixty-five guineas at the sale of the Underley yearlings. Mr Robertson did not risk a shilling on his colt, but his trainer William Forth, who had a well-deserved reputation for guile, was said to have won some £18,000, and to have concealed from Mr Robertson the very important fact that Little Wonder had a year in hand!

There was a long delay at the start, but they were all well enough away in the end. At the distance Launcelot was in front and looked very much like winning, but Little Wonder, ideally suited to the very hard ground, challenged strongly in the final furlong and eventually mastered the favourite to win by a length. The winner was admirably handled by little Macdonald, who was only a lad and one of the youngest riders in the race. When Little Wonder was making his run Bill Scott on Launcelot shouted at Macdonald, 'A thousand pounds for a pull!' to which Macdonald coolly replied, 'Too late, Mr Scott, too late!'

Little Wonder only ran once again as a three-year-old, finishing second in the Ascot Stakes. The following season, after several failures, he broke down in a race at Kelso and was never heard of again. Launcelot won the St Leger, for which he started favourite, but was distinctly lucky to do so as his stable companion Maroon could have beaten him, and it was said that 'Scott had as much difficulty to win on Launcelot as Holmes had to lose on Maroon'.

There is no doubt that the best three-year-old in 1840 was Lord George Bentinck's Crucifix, who had been bought, together with her dam, at Lord Chesterfield's sale for fifty-four guineas the pair. Crucifix, 'all wire and whipcord', was a mass of nervous energy and vitality with an action 'like a dancing master's whose ribs you could count'. She won over £18,000 in stakes, a very large sum for those days, and her three-year-old victories included the Two Thousand and One Thousand Guineas and the Oaks. The hard ground at Epsom finished her racing career, but at the stud she bred Surplice, winner of the Derby in 1848.

There was a strange sequel to this Derby five years later when John Day, senior, suddenly charged Mr Thomas Crommelin, a bookmaker and a leading member of Tattersalls, with having offered John Day, junior, a bribe to secure the defeat of the Danebury Derby candidate, the Melody colt, owned by Mr Etwall, Member of Parliament for Andover.

The case was heard by the Stewards of the Jockey Club, and evidence was given that Mr Crommelin, somewhat inadequately disguised in a pair of green spectacles and a false moustache, had met John Day, junior, in an hotel at Winchester. Mr Crommelin stated that far from offering a bribe, he had merely gone to Winchester to get information, as regularly supplied to him by members of the Day family, about the horses at Danebury; he made no attempt to explain, though, why a disguise had been considered necessary. Mr Crommelin was no doubt a considerable villain, but the affair having taken place five years previously, the Stewards considered it unnecessary to take further action in his case beyond expressing their opinion that the intimacy between him and the Days was discreditable. On the other hand, as John Day, junior, was judged to have given false evidence before them, he was warned off Newmarket Heath.

Some years later Mr Crommelin emigrated to Australia, where he emulated Mr Micawber by becoming a magistrate.

Before leaving Little Wonder's Derby, it only remains to add that old Forth's riding orders to Macdonald were, 'Now you mind and catch tight hold of his head and come truly through with him, for he is an early foal.' 'Short and to the point,' Sir John Astley wrote, 'for there is little doubt he was foaled a year earlier than his competitors were.'

1840

1840: Wednesday, 3 June . . . 144 Entries. £3,775.

MR D. ROBERTSON's b.c. LITTLE WONDER by Muley out of Lucerta	W. MACDONALD	1
LORD WESTMINSTER's br.c. LAUNCELOT by Camel	W. SCOTT	2
MR ETWALL's c. by Mulatto out of Melody	J. DAY, JUN.	3

Also ran:

Mr Houldsworth's Confederate (S. Rogers); Lord Albemarle's Assassin (E. Edwards); Lord Exeter's Amurath (N. Flatman); Lord Kelburne's Pathfinder (G. Nelson); Sir G. Heathcote's Bokhara (J. Chapple); Lord Exeter's Scutari (S. Darling); Captain Gardnor's Monops (W. Wakefield); Lord Jersey's Muley Ishmael (J. Robinson); Duke of Cleveland's colt by Emilius (J. Day); Mr Forth's colt by Muley (Owner); Lord Orford's Angelo (P. Conolly); Duke of Cleveland's Theon (T. Lye); Colonel Wyndham's Nongifted (S. Templeman); Sir G. Heathcote's Sophocles (F. Buckle).

17 ran.

Betting:

9–4 Launcelot; 7–2 Assassin and the Melody colt; 6–1 Theon; 20–1 Scutari and Bokhara; 25–1 Pathfinder; 28–1 Confederate; 30–1 the colt by Muley; 40–1 Nongifted and Angelo; 50–1 Little Wonder; 1,000–15 Muley Ishmael.

Won by half a length.
Winner trained by W. Forth.

1841

The run of victories by outsiders ended in 1841, when the winner was the favourite, Mr A. T. Rawlinson's Coronation, a son of Sir Hercules.

It was strange that Coronation should be favourite. To start with, he was trained privately in Heythrop Park by Mr Rawlinson's stud-groom, and secondly his successes had been gained at minor meetings like Oxford and Warwick. However Isaac Day, who had something to do with the management of the horse, had great confidence in him, and not only backed him heavily himself, but advised his friends to do so, too.

The race took place on a perfect summer afternoon in front of an immense crowd. There were twenty-nine runners—a record for the race at that time—and some idea of the ordeal that horses had to undergo in big races at that period can be gathered when it is stated that the field came under orders at half past two and the 'off' was at four o'clock.

Lord Albemarle's Ralph, winner of the Two Thousand Guineas, made the running from Potentia, winner of the One Thousand, and Lord Orford's Arundel. The pace was a really hot one and two-thirds of the field were in a hopeless position before half a mile had been covered. Approaching Tattenham Corner Ralph was still in front, but Coronation had moved up second and Potentia was still in a handy position on the rails. At the distance Coronation took the lead and Lord Westminster's second string, Van Amburgh, improved into second place, but Van Amburgh could make no impression on Coronation, who, in Conolly's hands, ran on strongly to win by a decisive three lengths. Mustapha Muley was third, and then came Galaor, Ralph, and Belgrade. Marshal Soult, with whom Lord Westminster had declared to win, was well beaten before Tattenham Corner was reached.

The race was a bad one for the Ring. Some bookmakers had refused to take Coronation's credentials seriously and had laid against him with abandon. One of them, a man called Gurney, was unable to settle. With the consent of most of his creditors and also of the Stewards of the Jockey Club, who then took cognizance of betting, Gurney placed his affairs in the hands of 'three persons of high respectability', who invited all who owed money to Gurney to pay it over to them. Lord George Bentinck, who evidently smelled a rat, declined to comply with this request until he was given an undertaking in writing that Gurney's account would be settled in full.

1841

After the Derby, Coronation had a walk-over for the Ascot Derby and won a cup at his local meeting at Oxford. He started a 2–1 on favourite for the St Leger, but to the general astonishment he was beaten by Lord Westminster's Satirist, no one being more surprised than Lord Westminster himself. Coronation's defeat was generally attributed to an inadequate preparation. For a week before the race he had been quartered at Thirberg, Mr T. Fullerton's estate, and there he had had 'plenty to eat and drink and nothing to do'. His rider, John Day, complained that ever since the Derby the horse had been treated like a spoiled child. Coronation never ran again and retired to the stud at Chadlington, Oxfordshire, at a fee of twenty guineas.

As a result of Satirist's St Leger victory, Lord Westminster removed all his horses from John Scott to Osborne, who trained near Delamere Forest. Scott had won four classic races for Lord Westminster, who, however, objected to the 'jugglery' that had taken place in regard to his horses, complaining that he had been kept in the dark and had been made to look as if he was 'putting his friends away'. There was a considerable outcry in the north, where John Scott had a host of admiring adherents, but responsible opinion on the Turf for the most part endorsed Lord Westminster's action.

John Scott's wonderful record of sixteen St Leger victories and five in the Derby is proof of his outstanding professional ability, and in many respects he was a most likeable and entertaining man. Sometimes, though, he was inclined to be just a little bit too crafty, and when he gave evidence on the question of gambling before a Select Committee of the House of Commons, he showed that he was capable of a barefaced lie. As one who knew him intimately wrote: 'His greatest fault was, as his face indicated, a lack of moral courage.'

1841: Wednesday, 26 May . . . 154 Entries. £4,275.

MR A. T. RAWLINSON's b.c. CORONATION by Sir Hercules
out of Ruby   P. CONOLLY   1
LORD WESTMINSTER's b.c. VAN AMBURGH
by Pantaloon   J. HOLMES   2
No horse was officially placed third.

Also ran:

Mr Copeland's Mustapha Muley (Marlow); Mr Thornhill's E.O. (Pettit); Lord Orford's Arundel (S. Mann); Lord Albemarle's Ralph (S. Day); Mr Vansittart's Galaor (R. Hesseltine); Mr Goodman's Belgrade (Wakefield); Lord Jersey's Joachim (E. Edwards); Mr Dixon's Knightsbridge (F. Buckle); Duke of Rutland's Sir Hans (Boyce); Colonel Peel's Cameleon (Stagg); Mr Greville's Paloemon (Nat

1841

Flatman); Mr Thornhill's Eringo (Hornsby); Mr Combe's The Nob (Bartley); Mr Sadler's Protection (S. Rogers); Lord Exeter's Cesarewitch (S. Darling); Mr Wimbush's Finchley (W. Cotton): Captain Ridge's colt by Coelebs (G. Calloway); Mr Griffith's Hereford (Whitehouse); Mr Batson's Potentia (Sly); Mr Buckley's Gilbert (M. Jones); Mr Negus's Portsoken (A. Perren); Colonel Crawford's Ermengardis (S. Templeman); Lord Westminster's Marshal Soult (W. Scott); Colonel Wyndham's Monsieur le Sage (W. Day); Sir G. Heathcote's Mongolian (J. Chapple); Captain Williamson's St Cross (W. Macdonald); Mr Rush's colt by Plenipotentiary (J. Robinson).

29 ran.

Betting:

5–2 Coronation; 5–1 Ralph; 7–1 Marshal Soult; 11–1 Belgrade and Galaor; 12–1 Van Amburgh; 18–1 Knightsbridge; 25–1 Joachim; 30–1 Ermengardis and Sir Hans; 33–1 Potentia; 50–1 E.O.

Won by three lengths.

1842

John Scott won the Derby in 1842 with Attila, ridden by his brother Bill and owned by Colonel Anson, who had bought the colt for £120. Colonel Anson had fought at Waterloo as an ensign in the Foot Guards. A well-known and well-liked figure at White's and in fashionable London, his opinion was much sought after in disputes and affairs of honour. It was his skilful handling of the duel between Lord George Bentinck and Squire Osbaldeston that in all probability saved Bentinck's life. Much to the surprise of his friends, for he liked to soldier within striking distance of Newmarket, he accepted quite late in life a high appointment in India. In due course he became Commander-in-Chief there, and while holding that position, the Sepoy Mutiny occurred. Telegrams notifying him of the outbreak arrived during a dinner party, but the old gentleman's manners were too punctilious to permit him to open them in front of his guests. There was in consequence a lamentable and far from unavoidable delay before orders were issued. A few days later General Anson had to take the field himself, but years of easy living had left him unprepared both mentally and physically for hard campaigning, and within a very few days he was dead.

Attila, by Colwick, won the Champagne Stakes at the Potteries Meeting, the Champagne Stakes at Doncaster, and the Clearwell Stakes at Newmarket as a two-year-old. The following season he was a very easy winner in the spring of a mile Sweepstakes at Newmarket. However, he did not start favourite for the Derby, the best-backed horse being Mr Trelawny's Coldrenick, who had never run before and who apparently never ran afterwards.

There was a tedious delay at the start caused by certain riders persistently attempting to snatch an unfair advantage. When at last the field was despatched, Combemere made the running from Attila, Lasso, and Belcoeur. At Tattenham Corner Coldrenick was already in trouble, and Belcoeur led with Attila still second and obviously going very well. At the distance Attila put in a storming challenge and swept past Belcoeur to win by two lengths from Robert de Gorham, who had headed Belcoeur close home. Robert de Gorham had won a couple of races at Gorhambury, near St Albans, a meeting that for a brief period threatened to rival Goodwood in popularity.

The rest of Attila's racing career was totally undistinguished. In the St Leger he was unplaced to Blue Bonnet, who was savagely punished by her jockey, Tommy Lye, who had backed her to win £2,000. ' Mr "Bloody" Lye will never ride for me again,' remarked the filly's trainer, George Dawson, afterwards, and in fact Blue Bonnet never really got over that gruelling race. In 1844 Attila was second in the Royal Hunt Cup, trying to concede a stone and a half to The Bishop of Romford's Cob, and a day later he broke down in the Ascot Cup. He was sold for export to Germany, but died in the boat on the way out.

1842: Wednesday, 25 May . . . 180 Entries. £4,900.

COLONEL ANSON's br.c. ATTILA by Colwick
out of Progress   W. SCOTT   1
LORD VERULAM's br.c. ROBERT DE GORHAM   COTTON   2
by Sir Hercules
MR ALLEN's BELCOEUR by Belshazar   J. MARSON   3

Also ran:

Lord Westminster's Auckland (T. Lye); Mr Meiklam's colt by Agreeable (S. Chifney, jun.); Mr Forth's Policy (F. Butler); General Yates's Seahorse (Nat Flatman); Mr Etwall's Palladium (W. Day); Mr Connop's The Oneida Chief (Sly); Mr Charlton's Lasso (Hesseltine); Sir G. Heathcote's Hydaspes (J. Chapple); Mr Herbert's Nessus (Whitehouse); Lord Chesterfield's Jack (J. Holmes); Mr Goodman's Rover (W. Macdonald); Mr Forth's The Golden Rule (Ball); Mr Osbaldeston's Devil among the Tailors (S. Darling); Lord George Bentinck's Chatham (S. Rogers); Mr Pryse Pryse's Cheops (W. Wakefield); Mr G. Clark's The Baronet (S. Templeman); Colonel Wyndham's Singleton (Francis); Lord Westminster's William de Fortibus (Cartwright); Mr Copeland's Combemere (Marlow); Mr Trelawny's Coldrenick (J. Day); Mr Gregory's Defier (J. Robinson).

24 ran.

Betting:

11–8 Coldrenick; 5–1 Attila; 12–1 Jack and Mr Forth's lot; 14–1 Seahorse; 20–1 the colt by Agreeable; 30–1 Chatham; 40–1 Combemere, William de Fortibus, Lasso, and Hydaspes; 50–1 Auckland; 100–1 any other.

Won by two lengths.
Winner trained by John Scott at Malton.

1843

Mr John Bowes had his second Derby success in 1843, Cotherstone, whom he bred himself, being a half-brother to Mündig by Touchstone. The outstanding sire of his era, Touchstone got 343 winners of 738 races worth £223,150. He was by Camel out of Banter, whose dam Boadicea was a hunter so little esteemed that her owner, Sir Charles Knightley, willingly swapped her for a cow. Touchstone was Banter's first foal and a somewhat weakly one as well. Lord Westminster had an implacable prejudice against first foals and invariably gave them away, the only reason that he kept Touchstone being his despair at finding anyone ready to accept him. Touchstone developed into an immensely powerful horse, and according to 'The Druid', 'if you looked at him from behind and missed his fine blood-like head, he seemed as strong and as coarse as a cart-horse'.

Cotherstone, who had been named after a Durham village, was rather a sickly specimen as a yearling, and even as a two-year-old he was very frequently amiss. However, in the autumn he did succeed in dead-heating at Newmarket with a filly of Mr Payne's for the Ditch Mile Nursery, having been unplaced previously that week to Lord George Bentinck's Bay Middleton colt Gaper in the Criterion Stakes. Mr Bowes was very disappointed with his colt at the end of the season and all but sold him to his trainer John Scott, but ultimately the deal fell through.

Cotherstone improved tremendously during the winter, and in a trial at Malton early in the spring he went so well that Bill Scott deliberately eased him in order to avoid showing him up too clearly. Colonel Anson, who watched the trial, was reluctant to believe that Cotherstone was as good as Bill Scott said, but Mr Bowes at once departed for London, where he backed his colt for the Derby to win £23,000. Long odds were readily available as certain bookmakers were convinced they possessed the means of rendering Cotherstone 'safe', but once the money was on, acting on Colonel Anson's advice, the colt was guarded with the utmost vigilance.

A week or two later Cotherstone was despatched to Newmarket, where he won the Riddlesworth Stakes, the Column Produce Stakes, and the Two Thousand Guineas. In consequence he started a short-priced favourite for the Derby, in which Gaper was judged to be his most formidable opponent. Gaper had great ability but extremely dubious joints, and he was noticeably upright on his pasterns as well. On firm ground he could hardly gallop at all, and John Day, senior, confident that he could never be trained for the Derby, laid heavily against him. Gaper however, kept sound and in his two trials before the Derby he did everything that his trainer John Kent had asked. Lord George Bentinck backed him as if defeat was out of the question and eventually stood to win £135,000. He had the sense, though, to cover himself on Cotherstone, and in fact after paying his losses on Gaper, was £30,000 up on the race.

All the jockeys riding in the Derby had been warned of penalties for misbehaviour at the start and for once there was no delay. Gaper made the running at a very strong gallop followed by Khorassan, Cotherstone, and Gorhambury. Gaper dropped back beaten early in the straight and Cotherstone at once took the lead, running on strongly to win by a comfortable two lengths from Gorhambury, with Sirikol three lengths away third. Cotherstone had rather a high, round action, but the smooth manner in which he came down the hill dumbfounded those who said he could never win a Derby 'unless it was run upstairs'.

Gorhambury was owned by Colonel Charrettie, who had charged with the Life Guards at Waterloo and was the acknowledged authority on duelling procedure. The Colonel had bought the colt for £400 from Lord Verulam after it had been injured in a two-year-old race at Gorhambury Park.

John Kent was far from satisfied with the way that Sam Rogers had handled Gaper. From the stands it certainly looked as if Gaper, whom Rogers insisted on riding in a severe curb bridle, had been ridden into the ground, considering the going was heavy and conditions were testing. It may be significant that a year later Rogers was 'warned off' for his riding of Ratan in the Derby.

Cotherstone won the Gratwicke Stakes at Goodwood, again beating Gaper, but in the St Leger he was beaten a head by Nutwith, with Prizefighter a head away third. One version of the race is that Frank Butler, who rode Cotherstone on this occasion, was over-confident and was caught napping; an alternative theory is that Butler did not do his best on the favourite, but was hoping to let up Prizefighter, whom John Gully had backed to win £50,000.

Cotherstone won two more races as a three-year-old, and the following season was defeated at Goodwood in his only outing. He was then sold to Lord Spencer and retired to the stud at Althorp. As a sire he was a failure, most of his stock being soft, but it must be added in extenuation that he himself was kept as fat as a Christmas goose, he was never exercised, and he never left his box for years at a time.

1843

1843: Wednesday, 31 May ... 155 Entries. £4,225.

MR J. BOWES'S b.c. COTHERSTONE by Touchstone
out of Emma   W. SCOTT I

COLONEL CHARRETTIE'S b.c. GORHAMBURY
by Buzzard   F. BUCKLE 2

SIR G. HEATHCOTE'S br.c. SIRIKOL by Sheet Anchor G. EDWARDS 3

Also ran:

Lord George Bentinck's Gaper (S. Rogers); Sir G. Heathcote's Khorassan
(J. Chapple); Mr Bateman's Cotornian (S. Mann); Mr Combe's Fakeaway
(Bartholomew); Mr J. Brown's A British Yeoman (S. Templeman); Mr. T. Taylor's
Gamecock (Nat Flatman); Mr Griffith's Newcourt (Whitehouse); Mr Mostyn's
General Pollock (Marlow); Mr Yarborough's Dumpling (J. Holmes); Lord Chester-
field's Parthian (F. Butler); Mr Bell's Winesour (Hesseltine); Lord Westminster's
Ameer (S. Darling); Mr Theobald's Humbug (W. Macdonald); Mr Theobald's
Highlander (J. Day, jun.); Mr Baxter's Magna Charta (W. Boyce); Colonel
Wyndham's Murton Lordship (Crouch); Lord Eglinton's Aristides (J. Robinson);
Mr Gratwicke's Hopeful (Bell); Lord Orford's colt by St Patrick (W. Wakefield);
Mr Thornhill's Elixir (S. Chifney, jun.).

23 ran.

Betting:

13–8 Cotherstone; 5–1 Gaper; 14–1 Newcourt; 15–1 Gamecock; 18–1 General
Pollock; 20–1 Winesour; 28–1 Dumpling; 30–1 Elixir, Aristides, Parthian, and
A British Yeoman; 50–1 Sirikol and Ameer; 66–1 Magna Charta, Gorhambury,
Humbug, and the colt by St Patrick.

Won by two lengths.
Winner trained by John Scott at Malton.

1844

The 1844 Derby was a sordid story of fraud and intrigue, which, thanks to the energy and determination of Lord George Bentinck, was eventually fully exposed. Inevitably, though, the revelations did a great deal of harm to racing, the disgraceful incidents that occurred giving many an honest man the impression that the Turf was little more than a playground for crooks and swindlers.

The first horse past the post in the Derby was described as Mr A. Wood's Running Rein. He was, in fact, a four-year-old called Maccabaeus.

The real Running Rein, bred by Mr Cobb, a Malton chemist, was a bay colt by The Saddler out of Mab, by Duncan Grey, and as such he was entered for the Derby. As a foal he was sold to a disreputable gambler who went by the name of Goodman, though his real name was Goodman Levy. The foal was at once sent to Goodman's stables in London. The horse that won the Derby was Maccabaeus, a four-year-old bred by Sir C. Ibbotson and purchased by Goodman as a yearling. The change-over took place in 1842, and in 1843 the new Running Rein was transferred to Mr A. Wood, an Epsom corn merchant, to whom Goodman owed a considerable sum for forage. There is no reason to believe that Wood was ever more than Goodman's ignorant dupe.

In 1843 Running Rein (as Maccabaeus must be called in future) was sent to run in a two-year-old race at Newmarket. He looked precisely what he was, a well-developed three-year-old, and one writer stated in forthright terms: 'There were grounds for supposing that Mr Goodman's Running Rein was a year older than he ought to be to qualify him for a two-year-old race; and to speak plainly, the colt is as well furnished as many of our bona fide three-year-olds.'

Running Rein, backed down from 10–1 to 3–1, duly won his race and Goodman brought off a substantial gamble. However, the Duke of Rutland, owner of the runner-up, immediately lodged an objection, a procedure in which he had the backing of Lord George Bentinck.

The inquiry was held a fortnight later, bets having been paid under protest in the meantime. A stable employee of Mr Cobb's, who had been present when Running Rein was foaled, was expected to prove the decisive witness. Brought down from Malton to Newmarket, he was kept under constant watch until taken before the Stewards and confronted with the horse. To the consternation of the Duke of Rutland and of Lord George Bentinck, he identified it without hesitation as the genuine Running Rein. The objection, of course, immediately collapsed.

Encouraged by this victory, Goodman laid plans for even greater successes the following year. Bentinck's temporary disappointment, however, only drove him on to pursue his inquiries with ever-increasing energy. By the spring he had amassed a considerable amount of evidence and was prepared to act if Running Rein ran in the Two Thousand Guineas, but Goodman decided to bide his time till Epsom.

Five days before the Derby, a petition signed by Bentinck, Mr Bowes, and John Scott was presented to the Epsom Stewards, requesting them to investigate Running Rein's identity and, above all, to have his mouth examined by veterinary surgeons of eminence before he was permitted to start.

An examination would no doubt have been the sensible solution. The Stewards, however, acting on the advice of Captain Rous, came to the extraordinary decision that the horse should be permitted to run, but that, if he won, the stakes would be withheld pending further inquiry.

Running Rein duly won by three parts of a length from Colonel Peel's Orlando. The Colonel, spurred on by Bentinck, immediately claimed the stakes. The Stewards sent for Mr Wood, ostensibly Running Rein's owner, but he was nowhere to be found. Complete chaos reigned with regard to the settling of bets and the paying out on many valuable lotteries and sweepstakes.

A number of legal actions were entered, and the Jockey Club wisely stood back and awaited a settlement by law. The real test case was that of Wood v. Peel before Baron Alderson and a special jury. Obviously the whole matter could have been settled by the production of Running Rein, and it was no wonder that the Judge reiterated, 'Produce the horse! Produce the horse!' That, however, was a step that the plaintiff could not afford to take. Eventually Cockburn, subsequently Lord Chief Justice, the plaintiff's counsel, more or less threw in his hand; Mr Wood withdrew from the case, and Peel and Bentinck were left victorious on the field of battle. All that remained were a few scathing comments from the Judge, who acidly remarked that 'if gentlemen condescended to race with blackguards, they must condescend to expect to be cheated'.

Goodman and his confederates, who had stood to win £50,000, fled the country. Running Rein never saw a racecourse again and ended his life peacefully on a Northamptonshire farm, while Lord George's sterling efforts were rewarded with a testimonial, from which was founded the 'Bentinck Benevolent Fund' for the dependants of trainers and jockeys who are left in necessitous circumstances.

The Running Rein business was not the only bit of dirty work in the Derby by any means. Two days before the race Lord Maidstone made an appeal to the Stewards about a horse called Leander, similar to the one that had been presented in respect of Running Rein. Leander, however, was allowed to start with the same proviso that had been made with regard to Goodman's horse.

During the race, Leander, who was leading, was struck into by Running Rein and his leg was broken. He was destroyed that evening, but the Stewards ordered his jaws to be cut off and examined by veterinary surgeons. The examination disclosed them to be those of a four-year-old, and accordingly the owners, a pair of German brothers called Lichtwald, were barred from entering horses again on the English Turf for life. One of the Lichtwalds was extremely angry and denounced the English as a race of appalling liars, adding as an afterthought that Leander had not been four at all, but six!

Nor was that all. The favourite for the race, Ugly Buck, was the victim of deliberate foul riding and his chance was effectively ruined. The second favourite Ratan, owned by the sinister Crockford, was not only 'got at' the night before, but was pulled by Sam Rogers in the race to make doubly sure. The shock was too much for old Crockford, who died two days later, 'dead of a Derby favourite', it was commonly said. For his riding of Ratan, Sam Rogers was in due course 'warned off'.

Orlando, proclaimed the winner on Running Rein's disqualification, was a bay colt with flat knees and somewhat heavy shoulders by Touchstone out of a very fast mare called Vulture, who was killed by a kick not long after Orlando had been weaned. As a two-year-old Orlando ran second at Ascot and then won four races in succession, including the July Stakes at Newmarket and the Ham Stakes at Goodwood. The following year he won the Riddlesworth Stakes before the Derby and received a walk-over at Ascot after it. He never ran as a four-year-old and broke down badly at Ascot in 1846. He was then retired to the stud at Newmarket at a fee of ten guineas. Subsequently he was moved, firstly to Bonehill, and finally to Hampton Court. At the sale of Colonel Peel's horses he was sold to Mr Charles Greville and his fee was raised to fifty guineas. Most of his stock were rather light-framed, came to hand early, and possessed plenty of speed. Teddington, winner of the 1851 Derby, was among his first crop of runners, and his other good winners included Fazzoletto, Fitzroland, and Diaphantus, who all won the Two Thousand Guineas, and Imperieuse, winner of the One Thousand Guineas and the St Leger. He died at Hampton Court in 1868.

Colonel (later Major-General) Peel, who also owned Ionian, runner-up to Orlando in the Derby, was a brother of the Tory Prime Minister, Sir Robert Peel. He was commissioned into the army at the age of fifteen, three days before Waterloo, and he never saw active service throughout his career in the 71st Highlanders, the

Rifle Brigade, and the Foot Guards, his applications to proceed to the Crimea being turned down on account of his age. He sat in the House of Commons for forty-two years and acted as Secretary of State for War in Lord Derby's Ministry. A prominent member of the Jockey Club, he was the most upright and likeable of men and there was never a breath of suspicion against him during his long career on the Turf. He trained firstly with Coope, who prepared Orlando, and during his later years with Joseph Dawson. He died in 1879.

Nat Flatman, who rode Orlando, was Colonel Peel's favourite jockey, and the pair of them used to go off ratting together on fine evenings at the July or First October Meetings. A thoroughly honest and straightforward man, Flatman was the son of a Suffolk yeoman farmer and had joined Coope's stable as a very small boy when he weighed rather less than four stone. His first ride was in 1829, and his last one thirty years later. He never had much trouble with his weight, and for most of his career he could go to scale without any difficulty at 7 st. 5 lb. He was always in great demand to ride in trials, as he was one of the very few jockeys that could be trusted to keep his mouth shut afterwards. He died aged fifty in 1860 and is buried under the tower of All Saints Church, Newmarket.

1844: Wednesday, 22 May . . . 153 Entries. £4,450.

COLONEL PEEL's b.c. ORLANDO by Touchstone
out of Vulture   NAT FLATMAN   1
COLONEL PEEL's b.c. IONIAN by Ion   G. EDWARDS   2
COLONEL ANSON's BAY MOMUS by Bay Middleton   F. BUTLER   3

Also ran:

Mr J. Day's The Ugly Buck (J. Day, jun.) ; Sir G. Heathcote's Akbar (J. Chapple) ; Mr Crockford's Ratan (S. Rogers) ; Mr J. Day's Voltri (W. Day) ; Mr Bowes's T'Auld Squire (J. Holmes) ; Sir G. Heathcote's Campunero (Perren) ; Mr Ford's Qui Tam (J. Robinson) ; Mr J. Osborne's Mount Charles (Bumby) ; Mr Ford's Phalaris (Whitehouse) ; Lord George Bentinck's Croton Oil (W. Howlett) ; Mr A. W. Hill's Beaumont (G. Calloway) ; Mr Lichtwald's Leander (Bell) ; Mr Gratwicke's Needful (W. Cotton) ; Mr Herbert's colt by Elis (Sly) ; Mr Forth's The Ashstead Pet (Boyce) ; Mr Gregory's Loadstone (S. Darling) ; Lord Glasgow's colt by Velocipede (Hesseltine) ; Lord Westminster's Lancet (S. Templeman) ; Mr St Paul's Telemachus (J. Marson) ; Mr Ongley's King of the Gipsies (Marlow) ; Mr M. Jones's British Tar (M. Jones) ; Mr Cuthbert's Beaufront (J. Howlett) ; Lord Maidstone's Cockmaroo (Simpson) ; Mr Dixon's Dick Thornton (Darling, jun.) ;

Mr Thornhill's Elemi (S. Chifney, jun.); Mr A. Wood's Running Rein (S. Mann) finished first but was disqualified.

29 ran.

Betting:

5–2 The Ugly Buck; 3–1 Ratan; 10–1 Running Rein; 14–1 Leander; 15–1 Ionian; 20–1 Orlando, Akbar, Qui Tam, and Bay Momus.

Running Rein won by three-quarters of a length; two lengths between Orlando and Ionian.
Winner trained by Cooper at Newmarket.

1845

Mr Gratwicke won his second Derby in 1845, the winner on this occasion being The Merry Monarch, a colt by Colonel Peel's stallion Slane out of The Margravine, a sister of Frederick, who won the Derby for Mr Gratwicke in 1829.

The Merry Monarch, trained by Forth, was a bay standing sixteen hands, high in the withers and long in the pasterns. In all probability he was an indifferent horse. In his only outing before the Derby he had been unplaced in the Ham Stakes at Goodwood as a two-year-old. He was certainly considerably less fancied at Epsom than Mr Gratwicke's other runner Doleful and in consequence he was partnered by a little-known rider named Bell. Under the circumstances it is not surprising that he was without a quotation in the market, although 'Forth's lot' was on offer at 15–1.

The favourite was Lord Stradbroke's Idas, winner of the Two Thousand Guineas, and others well-backed were Mr Greville's Alarm, and Mr Gully's pair Weatherbit, subsequently the sire of the Derby winner Beadsman, and Old England.

Alarm, bought by Mr Greville from the breeder Captain Delmé, had been particularly well galloped and Mr Greville had backed him to win a considerable sum. Unfortunately Alarm grew restive at the start and suddenly lashed out at The Libel. The Libel responded by rearing up at Alarm and striking Alarm's jockey, Flatman. Flatman came off, and Alarm thereupon charged the chains at the side of the course and bolted towards the Stewards' Stand, a proceeding that Lord George Bentinck, who had recently quarrelled with Greville, was able to observe with an equanimity undoubtedly born of rancour. Alarm was eventually caught, remounted, and took a prominent part in the race despite a number of injuries that were later declared to be severe. Considering how well he ran after his escapade, he may well have been a somewhat unlucky loser. Later in the year he won the Cambridgeshire, and the following season the Ascot Cup.

There was another mishap in the race as well, as Pam fell and interfered considerably with both Weatherbit and Old England.

Owing to the Alarm affair, the race was an hour late in starting. The favourite was beaten at Tattenham Corner, and Kedger and Doleful went on up the straight with The Merry Monarch in hot pursuit. At the distance The Merry Monarch took the lead and ran on strongly to hold off the late challenge of Annandale by a length with Old England close up third.

1845

The Merry Monarch was beaten as a 4–1 on favourite for the Gratwicke Stakes at Goodwood, and then went wrong during his St Leger preparation. After running once unplaced as a four-year-old, he retired to the stud where he made no mark.

The race was not without its seamy side. Gully discovered that certain bookmakers were laying his horse Old England at well above the market price. A visit to Danebury, where, in a formidable rage, he confronted the entire Day family, confirmed his opinion that all was very far from well. He next hurried off to London, where his destination was Tattersalls. There he mounted a chair, addressed the members, and accused a certain Mr Hargreaves of Manchester, 'a lucky, screaming gentleman with a large face and pink eyes', of attempting to corrupt William Day and John Day, junior. Hargreaves was a notorious scoundrel and had made a fortune in conjunction with Sam Rogers through the nobbling of Ratan.

The Jockey Club felt compelled to take action. Unfortunately sufficient evidence to convict Hargreaves was not available, but William Day, together with two men called Bloodworth and Stebbings, were warned off for their part in the conspiracy. Stebbings had proposed to wrap a silk handkerchief round one of Old England's legs and to beat that leg with a stick until a sinew was sprung. An alternative suggestion was that a powder should be administered to cause internal bleeding, but Bloodworth drew the line at that, not on the grounds of conscience or of tender-heartedness, but because such a crime 'was a lagging affair'. Stebbings admitted that for years he had received stable information from William Day and had betted heavily on his behalf. William Day was a great student of Shakespeare, whom he was very fond of quoting; a man of considerable ability, he eventually wrote his reminiscences, and while he had some very nasty things to say about Gully, he delicately avoided the subject of Old England altogether. He was undoubtedly a person who would betray anyone or anything for money, and his condemnations of others are best treated with a considerable reserve.

1845: Wednesday, 28 May ... 137 Entries. £4,225.

MR GRATWICKE's b.c. THE MERRY MONARCH by Slane
out of The Margravine   F. BELL   1
MR A. JOHNSTONE's br.c. ANNANDALE by Touchstone   J. MARSON   2
MR GULLY's b.c. OLD ENGLAND by Mulatto   S. DAY   3

Also ran:

Lord Mostyn's Pantasa (4th) (Marlow); Lord Exeter's Wood Pigeon (Boyce); Mr Gratwicke's Doleful (H. Bell); Colonel Anson's Kedger (Simpson); Lord Stradbroke's Idas (G. Edwards); Mr Parry's Adonis (Hornsby); Mr Gully's Weather-

bit (J. Day, jun.) ; Lord Chesterfield's Pam (F. Butler) ; Mr Ford's Fuzbos (Sly) ;
Colonel Cradock's Jinglepot (Templeman) ; Duke of Richmond's The Laird
o' Cockpen (Whitehouse) ; Mr Wreford's Worthless (J. Howlett) ; Mr St Paul's
Mentor (Lye) ; Colonel Peel's King Cob (E. Edwards) ; Mr Waller's Columbus
(Wakefield) ; Mr Worley's John Davis (Crouch) ; Mr A. W. Hill's Salopian (Den-
man) ; Lord Glasgow's colt by Bay Middleton (Holmes) ; Sir G. Heathcote's Gwalior
(J. Chapple) ; Mr T. Theobald's Desperation (Bartholomew) ; Lord Verulam's
Hawkesbury (Cotton) ; Mr Lingott's Cabin Boy (F. Buckle) ; Mr Greville's Alarm
(Nat Flatman) ; Mr Ferguson's Clear-the-way (J. Robinson) ; Mr Coleman's Young
Eclipse (W. Coleman) ; Mr Mytton's The Black Prince (Copeland) ; Mr Mack's
Little Jack (Balchin) ; Mr A. W. Hill's The Libel (Calloway).

31 ran.

Betting :

3–1 Idas ; 7–2 Weatherbit ; 6–1 The Libel ; 10–1 Alarm ; 15–1 Doleful ; 20–1 Pam ;
22–1 Fuzbos and Old England ; 25–1 Pantasa and Jinglepot ; 40–1 Mentor and The
Laird o' Cockpen ; 50–1 Columbus and Annandale ; 66–1 the colt by Bay Middleton
and Wood Pigeon ; 200–1 Clear-the-way and 15–1 Forth's lot.

Won by a length ; a length between second and third.
Winner trained by J. Forth.

1846

This was John Gully's year without a doubt, the former prize-fighter seeing his colours carried to victory by Pyrrhus the First in the Derby and by Mendicant in the Oaks. Luck was certainly on Gully's side as far as the Derby was concerned, as there is very little doubt that the race should have been won by Sir Tatton Sykes, owned and ridden by Bill Scott, then drawing to the close of a long and frequently brilliant career.

Sir Tatton Sykes, originally called Tibthorpe, was bred by Mr Hudson, an East Riding farmer, and Bill Scott having heard the colt well spoken of, drove over one day to have a look at him. He approved of him, bought him for £100, a sum that was not paid in full until the Two Thousand Guineas was won, and renamed him in honour of his old master.

Sir Tatton went to be trained by William Oates and his son. To start with he was extremely sluggish, but gradually he disclosed his merit in no uncertain form, and after one particularly impressive gallop Bill Scott, not a noticeably religious man as a rule, went down on his knees and thanked God 'for at last having given me the hell of a horse'.

Sir Tatton, who was a long, low bay by Melbourne, won the Two Thousand Guineas ridden by his owner and survived a subsequent examination of his mouth which took place at the instigation of Lord Maidstone. He was naturally well fancied for the Derby, but shortly before the race, the Ring began to field against him in an ominous manner, greatly to Bill Scott's annoyance. On the Derby afternoon, Scott, who had been drinking hard all day, was having a glass of brandy with a friend when he heard what he considered to be extravagant odds being offered against his horse. He rushed out of the bar shouting, 'I'll take eight thousand to a thousand Sir Tatton wins in a trot!' As the recorder of that incident justly remarked: 'Had he not shaken hands with his brother Bacchus, we verily believe his words would have come true.'

Scott was undoubtedly very drunk when he rode Sir Tatton down to the start. There he abused the starter in the crudest terms after being reproved for a breach of discipline, and he was still arguing the toss when the flag fell and he forfeited several lengths. Sir Tatton, however, soon made up the lost ground and was in front with two furlongs to go. At that point he looked almost certain to win, but Scott was very far gone by then, and Sir Tatton, deprived of a guiding hand, veered away from the rails and across the course to the stands. Seizing his opportunity, Sam Day rode Pyrrhus the First for all he was worth and, coming up on the inside, secured the lead in the last few strides to win by a neck.

Had Bill Scott been sober, Sir Tatton would have been the first horse to win the Triple Crown, as he duly won the St Leger in September although Scott was exhausted and a complete passenger in the final quarter of a mile. That was Scott's ninth and last St Leger victory. His iron constitution had been worn out and he died in 1848.

Pyrrhus the First, a handsome chesnut standing fifteen hands three, was a halfbrother to Old England by Epirus. He was bred by Colonel Bouverie in Northamptonshire and he and his dam Fortress were bought by old John Day for 300 guineas the pair. John Gully went halves in the purchase and subsequently bought Day's share in the colt for a hundred guineas, although that is denied by William Day in his reminiscences. Pyrrhus's first race was the Newmarket Stakes, which he duly won, beating Iago, who subsequently ran second in the St Leger to Sir Tatton Sykes. After the Derby he won a number of minor events and changed hands twice before his final owner, a Mr Harrison, retired him to the stud at Easby Abbey in Yorkshire at a fee of ten guineas. Undoubtedly the best animal he sired was that fine filly Virago, who not only won the One Thousand Guineas but also achieved the almost incredible feat of winning both the City and Suburban and the Great Metropolitan on the same afternoon as a three-year-old.

Before the Derby Lord Maidstone, who seems to have developed something approaching a mania on this point, demanded that The Conjuror's mouth should be examined on the grounds that he was over age. Mr Clark, owner of the Conjuror, retaliated by requesting an examination of Lord Maidstone's colt Tom Tulloch.

Finally it must be said that this was the first occasion that the time was officially recorded. It took Pyrrhus two minutes fifty-five seconds to cover the course, nearly twenty-two seconds longer than Mahmoud's time in 1936.

1846: Wednesday, 27 May . . . 193 Entries. £5,500.

MR J. GULLY's ch.c. PYRRHUS THE FIRST by Epirus out of Fortress	S. DAY	I
MR W. SCOTT's b.c. SIR TATTON SYKES by Melbourne	OWNER	2
GENERAL SHUBRICK's br.c. BROCARDO by Touchstone	HOLMES	3

Also ran:

Sir R. W. Bulkeley's Joinville (Bumby); Lord Maidstone's Tom Tulloch (Nat

Flatman); Lord E. Russell's Sting (H. Bell); Colonel Anson's Iago (F. Butler);
Mr Meiklan's Fancy Boy (Templeman); Sir G. Heathcote's colt by Hetman Platoff
(J. Chapple); Mr A. Johnstone's Grimston (T. Lye); Mr J. Drake's Bold Archer
(G. Edwards); Lord Chesterfield's Ginger (Dufflo); Sir J. Hawley's Humdrum
(R. Sly); Mr O'Brien's The Traverser (Cartwright); Mr Drinkald's Widred (Mann);
Mr E. Peel's Spithead (Francis); Mr Merry's colt by Don John (J. Robinson);
Mr Mostyn's colt by Phoenix (Marlow); Mr E. R. Clark's The Conjuror (E. Edwards); Mr Walls's The Crown Prince (Wakefield); Mr Gurney's Cantley (Pettit);
Mr Ramsay's Malcolm (Robertson); Lord Orford's Blackie (Whitehouse); Count
Batthyany's Tragical (Crouch); Mr Balchin's Sir Edmund (W. Balchin); Mr T.
Powell's Holloway (Bartholomew); Lord Eglinton's Sotades (J. Marson).

27 ran.

Betting:

5–1 Fancy Boy; 8–1 Pyrrhus the First; 10–1 Tom Tulloch, Sting, and The Conjuror; 11–1 Humdrum; 15–1 the colt by Don John; 16–1 Crown Prince and Sir
Tatton Sykes; 25–1 Brocardo; 40–1 the colt by Hetman Platoff; 50–1 the colt by
Phoenix; 100–1 Spithead.

Won by a neck; a length between second and third.   2 m. 55 s.
Winner trained by John Day at Danebury.

1847

The Danebury stable won the Derby again in 1847, the winner being Cossack, owned by a Mr Pedley, who was John Gully's son-in-law. Pedley was a Huddersfield bookmaker with a loud voice and of ungainly appearance. He fancied himself considerably as a singer, and at convivial gatherings would oblige with a rendering of 'The cats on the housetops are mewing, love'. At one time he had amassed a considerable fortune, but most of it had gone before he died.

Cossack was by Hetman Platoff, by Brutandorf, a son of Blacklock; his dam Joannina was by Priam, and went back on her dam's side to Filligree, the dam of Riddlesworth and of Bay Middleton's dam Cobweb. Old John Day bought Cossack in Northamptonshire as a yearling for 200 guineas and a Derby contingency of 1,000 guineas, at which price he passed the colt on to Mr Pedley.

Cossack only ran once as a two-year-old, finishing third in the July Stakes, for which he started an odds-on favourite. The following season he won the Newmarket Stakes and was backed down to 5–1 for the Derby, in which Sir R. Pigot's Conyngham, winner of the Two Thousand Guineas, was favourite, while another much fancied candidate was Lord Eglinton's Van Tromp, a half-brother by Lanercost to the 1849 Derby winner, The Flying Dutchman.

There were thirty-two runners—a new record—but Mr Hubburd, the starter, had them all well away on time. Gabbler led to begin with, but after a mile Cossack, ridden with great confidence by Sim Templeman, went to the front, and there he stayed till the winning-post was reached except for half a dozen strides when War Eagle had his head in front on the approach to Tattenham Corner. The favourite, like so many winners of the Guineas, failed to stay, and Cossack resisted War Eagle's rally in the final furlong to win by a length. Van Tromp was four lengths away third. At this point of the season Van Tromp, who had been ridden by Job Marson, was still physically backward and nothing like the horse he was in the autumn. Lord Eglinton, who, together with various friends, including Lord George Bentinck, had backed him heavily, was convinced he had been pulled and accordingly gave Marson the sack, in all probability an act of gross injustice.

Cossack, who stood fifteen hands three, was a delightful horse to ride and a thoroughly genuine one as well. He was no doubt fortunate, though, in finding Van Tromp below his best as Van Tromp defeated him comfortably in the St Leger and

1847

asserted his superiority twice at Goodwood the following year and also in the Ascot Cup in 1849. Cossack continued to race until 1852 when he retired to the stud at a fee of ten guineas. Not long afterwards he was sold for export to France.

1847: Wednesday, 19 May . . . 188 Entries. £5,500.

MR PEDLEY's ch.c. COSSACK by Hetman Platoff out of Joannina	S. TEMPLEMAN	1
MR BOUVERIE's br.c. WAR EAGLE by Lanercost	W. BOYCE	2
LORD EGLINTON's br.c. VAN TROMP by Lanercost	J. MARSON	3

Also ran:

Sir R. Pigot's Conyngham (A. Day); Duke of Richmond's Red Heart (Cotton); Mr Merry's Limestone (S. Darling, jun.); Mr Mostyn's Mr Martin (Calloway); Duke of Richmond's Halo (H. Bell); Lord E. Russell's Nottingham (E. Edwards); Lord Caledon's Wanota (Marlow); Mr Irwin's Oxonian (Sly); Mr Mostyn's Planet (W. Abdale); Mr Mostyn's Gabbler (Kitchener); Mr Mostyn's Crozier (Ford); Lord Strathmore's Signet (Crouch); Captain Delmé's Resolution (Pettit); Mr Meiklam's Deloraine (Hornsby); Sir R. Bulkeley's Montpensier (Bumby); Lord Warwick's Aliwal (Wakefield); Mr O'Brien's The Liberator (Cartwright); Lord Glasgow's Chainbearer (Whitehouse); Mr Bateman's The Questionable (J. Sharpe); Colonel Anson's Bingham (F. Butler); Mr Bowes's Epirote (Holmes); Sir G. Heathcote's Bellerophon (J. Chapple); Mr Robertson's Good Coin (W. Howlett); Mr Lowther's The Admiral (Bartholomew); Mr Greville's Mirmillo (Nat Flatman); Mr Osbaldeston's Pantomime (S. Mann); Mr S. Conway's Christopher (W. Scott); Mr Worley's Old Port (J. Robinson); Mr Ford's Clarendon (G. Edwards).

32 ran.

Betting:

5–2 Conyngham; 5–1 Cossack; 7–1 Van Tromp; 16–1 Mirmillo, Red Heart, and Oxonian; 20–1 War Eagle, Planet, and Wanota; 40–1 Bingham and Old Port; 50–1 Halo; 1,000–15 Deloraine; 100–1 Crozier.

Won by a length; four lengths between second and third.　　　2 m. 52 s.
Winner trained by John Day at Danebury.

1848

In 1846 Lord George Bentinck decided, in the impulsive way that he had, to throw up his racing interests in order to concentrate on politics. Accordingly he sold his entire racing stud during the Goodwood Meeting to Mr Mostyn (later Lord Mostyn) for £10,000. Included in the stud was Surplice, destined to win the Derby two years later. Before that occurred, however, Mostyn had sold Surplice to Lord Clifden, who from all accounts was a singularly unattractive individual. One writer summed him up as 'reserved, selfish, and indolent. Many thought him proud, but in reality he was not so, for that would have cost him an exertion he did not care to make.'

Surplice, by Touchstone out of Priam's daughter Crucifix, winner of the Two Thousand Guineas, the One Thousand Guineas, and the Oaks, was a bay standing just over sixteen hands; he was noticeably 'in' at the elbows, a defect that he inherited from his dam. Bentinck had specially requested that the colt should remain after the sale with his trainer, John Kent, and his wishes in that respect were carried out, at any rate until after the Derby.

As a two-year-old Surplice won the Ham Stakes and the Produce Stakes at Goodwood, the Municipal Stakes at Doncaster, and was given a walk-over for the Buckenham Stakes at Newmarket. His form had been sufficiently impressive for him to be heavily supported for next year's Derby, but all through the winter he was the subject of adverse rumour. The cause of these rumours was the conduct of Mr Francis Villiers, who managed Lord Clifden's racing affairs. Villiers, a foolish, vain, and rather objectionable young man, had the weakness not uncommon to youth of assuming he knew everything that there was to know about racing. He took the line, quite contrary to John Kent's advice, that a horse in the stable called Loadstone was greatly superior to Surplice. Accordingly he backed Loadstone for the Derby and laid Surplice whenever the opportunity occurred. He did not grow more sensible as he became older; seven years later, when a Steward of the Jockey Club, he fled the country owing £100,000.

As a three-year-old Surplice did not run before the Derby for which he started favourite, the best backed of the others being Mr George Payne's Glendower and Mr J. D. Day's Nil Desperandum. Surplice, ridden by Templeman, held a good position throughout and, taking the lead at the distance, just held off a terrific late challenge by Mr Bowes's Springy Jack, ridden by Frank Butler. Shylock was third and Glendower fourth. Surplice was a very genuine horse, but inclined to be lazy and to consider he had done enough as soon as he found himself in front. On this occasion Sim Templeman had to ride him for all he was worth to retain his advantage until the winning-post was reached. Although he started favourite, Surplice's victory was not a particularly popular one, some people taking the view that the adverse rumours the previous winter had been deliberately circulated to obtain a more favourable price. Lord Clifden and his friend Mr Lloyd, who had a half-share in the horse, both had a substantial win and so had Lord George Bentinck.

Despite his financial gain, the race must have been a bitter blow to Bentinck. To win the Derby had always been one of his foremost ambitions, and it can be readily understood that he was unable to bring himself to go and watch the race. Every schoolboy knows the story of how Disraeli found him a day or two later in the Library of the House of Commons, of how Disraeli's consolation evoked from Lord George 'a sort of superb groan', and how Disraeli himself coined that now famous phrase for the Derby, 'The Blue Riband of the Turf'.

Surplice disliked heavy ground and was twice beaten at Goodwood in the mud. He then left Kent's stable, and for his St Leger victory he was prepared by Robert Stephenson at Newmarket. He won a race at Newmarket in the autumn, but was unplaced in the Cesarewitch in which he carried 8 st. 5 lb. and started favourite. He ran three times in the two following seasons, his one success being a walk-over. He then retired to the stud at Doncaster at a fee of twenty-five guineas, but he did not prove a success. He died in Suffolk in 1871.

The Derby Course was altered this year. Previously it had been the last twelve furlongs of the Cup Course, and the start and the opening phase of the race had been invisible from the grandstand. The boredom of the spectators, therefore, during some of those long delays at the start must have been almost intolerable. The New Course, which remained in use till 1871, started in Langley Bottom. It provided a far better view for spectators and a much stiffer climb for the first half-mile for the competitors.

Travellers to the Derby by rail could now go direct on the Brighton line to Epsom itself; previously they had had to alight at Kingston or Croydon. The first year of the innovation had been a chaotic experience for many racegoers. Tickets could not be issued quickly enough and London Bridge Station was jammed. Thousands of would-be passengers never got near a train at all, while some were left stranded on the way, as the engines were not powerful enough for their task and could not pull their loads up the hills.

Voltigeur

Derby Day,
1871

Galopin

1848

1848: Wednesday, 24 May . . . 215 Entries. £5,800.

LORD CLIFDEN's b.c. SURPLICE by Touchstone out of Crucifix	S. TEMPLEMAN	1
MR J. BOWES's b.c. SPRINGY JACK by Hetman Platoff	F. BUTLER	2
MR B. GREEN's bl.c. SHYLOCK by Simoom	S. MANN	3

Also ran:

Mr Payne's Glendower (4th) (Nat Flatman); Mr J. B. Day's Nil Desperandum (A. Day); Mr Nunn's The Fowler (J. Holmes); Mr Lillie's The Great Western (J. Howlett); Lord Clifden's Loadstone (J. Marson); Mr Baker's Oscar (Bumby); Duke of Rutland's The Fiddler (J. Robinson); Mr E. R. Clark's Weathercock (Tant); Mr T. Parr's Sponge (Owner); Sir J. B. Mills's Deerstalker (Donaldson); Mr Rolt's Comet (R. Pettit); Lord Eglinton's Eagles Plume (Marlow); Major Pitt's Fern (E. Edwards); Mr Osbaldeston's Fugleman (S. Rogers).

17 ran.

Betting:

Evens Surplice; 4–1 Glendower and Nil Desperandum; 14–1 Shylock; 15–1 Springy Jack; 20–1 Loadstone; 40–1 The Great Western, The Fiddler, and Fugleman; 50–1 The Fowler; 1,000–15 Fern and Eagles Plume; 100–1 Deerstalker.

Won by a neck; a length between second and third. 2 m. 48 s.
Winner trained by J. Kent at Goodwood.

1849

Van Tromp, winner of the 1846 St Leger, had been bought by Lord Eglinton from Colonel Vansittart for £300 and a Derby contingency. Towards the end of Van Tromp's three-year-old career, Lord Eglinton came to an agreement with Vansittart to buy for 1,000 guineas every perfectly formed foal produced by Van Tromp's dam Barbelle. In that way he came to possess one of the most famous of Derby winners, The Flying Dutchman, by Bay Middleton out of Barbelle, by Sandbeck.

Born in 1812, Lord Eglinton succeeded to the title when at Eton. Not over-burdened with brains and rather too susceptible to flattery, he was nevertheless a man of remarkable charm, a chivalrous sportsman, and outstandingly generous. In 1839 he organized at a personal cost of £50,000 the famous Eglinton Tournament that was ruined by rain. In Ireland he achieved at least a superficial popularity with the local inhabitants when Lord-Lieutenant by his princely and open-handed methods. He died of apoplexy when still a comparatively young man in 1861.

The Flying Dutchman was prepared at Middleham by Fobert, who had recently succeeded Tom Dawson as Lord Eglinton's trainer. As a two-year-old he ran five times and won on each occasion, his victories including the July Stakes at Newmarket and the Champagne Stakes at Doncaster. His great rival was Colonel Peel's Tadmor, who had won six races including the Ham Stakes at Goodwood. The following spring Tadmor won the Column Produce Stakes, but The Flying Dutchman did not run before the Derby, for which the pair of them started joint-favourites at 2–1. Other fancied competitors were Nunnykirk, winner of the Two Thousand Guineas, and Vatican, winner of the Newmarket Stakes. Nunnykirk was one of the six horses saddled for the race by John Scott.

The weather was perfect, the going somewhat heavy after rain, and the two co-favourites looked fit to run for their lives. The appearance of The Flying Dutchman, a dark bay standing fifteen hands three, roman nosed, distinctly 'over' at the knees, and immensely powerful behind the saddle, at once dispelled rumours circulating that he was considerably short of work.

Vatican led from the start, and he was still in front at Tattenham Corner though hard pressed by The Flying Dutchman, Tadmor, and the 50–1 outsider Hotspur. With two furlongs to go Vatican was beaten and The Flying Dutchman held a narrow lead from Hotspur, with Tadmor a couple of lengths away third. In the final two hundred yards it looked as if Hotspur might win, but 'The Dutchman' rallied in the last ten yards to win a great race by half a length, with Tadmor only another half-length away third. The race was worth £6,575 to the winner and was the richest Derby run up till then.

Lord Eglinton and his friends had a very big win, and members of the Army and Navy Club—then usually called 'The Ragged Famine Club', a nickname subsequently abbreviated to 'The Rag'—cleared over £30,000. Fobert had an ox killed and fed over a hundred poor families at Middleham. Marlow, who rode the winner, was given a generous present, but he was never a man to worry about the future. He died some thirty years later, forgotten and friendless, a pauper in Devizes workhouse. Davis, 'the Leviathan', one of the most notable bookmakers of the time, had a disastrous race and paid out £40,000 the following Monday.

Hotspur, who ran so gallantly, was a half-bred by Sir Hercules; he was never able to produce anything like such good form again. Vatican's end was a truly terrible one. At the stud he became savage, and after biting off one lad's thumb and another one's ear, he was roped to the stable wall. As an experiment he was given a donkey as a companion. The next morning the donkey was found decapitated and disembowelled. Beatings, starvation treatment, cajoling, all had no effect, but no one had the sense to shoot the unfortunate animal, who existed in the utmost squalor as no lad dared enter his box. One day, with unimaginable folly and a savagery not untypical of the age, he was chloroformed and his eyes burnt out with hot irons. When he came round from the chloroform he was a heart-rending sight and naturally in appalling pain. His screams were terrible to hear and at long last the poor, mad, suffering creature was put down.

The Flying Dutchman, an odds-on favourite, won the St Leger easily enough in pouring rain, and later in the autumn he gave Vatican seven pounds and an eight lengths' beating over a mile at Newmarket. He went into winter quarters unbeaten and emerged the following season as brilliant as ever, winning the Ascot Cup in a canter by eight lengths, and then defeating Vatican by ten lengths at Goodwood. At that point he appeared to be invincible, but then came his unforeseen and sensational defeat in the Doncaster Cup. The Flying Dutchman's only opponent in the Cup was Lord Zetland's three-year-old Voltigeur, also unbeaten and winner of both the Derby and the St Leger. His St Leger victory, though, was only achieved after first dead-heating with Russborough, whom he then defeated in the run-off, and it was asking a lot of him to take on a champion of The Flying Dutchman's calibre a mere forty-eight hours later.

'The Dutchman', ridden by Marlow, carried 8 st. 12 lb., and had to give nineteen pounds to Voltigeur, partnered by Flatman, who was always at his best in a match. Odds of 4–1 were freely laid on the older horse although for the first time in his life he had been off his feed two days previously, despite which Fobert had seen fit to subject him to a really searching gallop on the Cup course only twenty-four hours before the race.

Both riders had received instructions to wait, but unfortunately Marlow had been drinking. No sooner had the flag fallen than he emitted a cry of 'I'll show you what I've got under me today' and off he went at a tremendous gallop. Voltigeur kept two or three lengths behind him for most of the way, but with three furlongs to go he gradually drew closer and at the distance he made his challenge. Marlow began to ride the favourite for all he was worth, but there was no response. 'The Dutch-man' had given all he had and Voltigeur forged ahead to win all out by half a length.

The great crowd assembled to witness this duel between unbeaten champions was almost too dumbfounded by the result to cheer the victor, whose success would have been received almost in silence but for the vociferous jubilation of some two or three hundred supporters of his from Swaledale, who had backed him in doubles to win both the St Leger and the Cup. Lord Eglinton, white and shaken, had every reason to be furious with Marlow, but he stood beside him, trying vainly to console him, while tears of alcoholic remorse streamed down the jockey's cheeks.

Matters could hardly be allowed to rest there, and the respective owners agreed to a £1,000 Match to be run over two miles at York the following spring. Admiral Rous was asked to adjust the weights and allotted 8 st. 8½ lb. to The Flying Dutch-man, eight stone to Voltigeur.

The interest in the match was tremendous and many big bets were struck, The Flying Dutchman nearly always being fractionally the favourite. Both horses under-went a searching preparation, and Voltigeur's may have been a shade too strenuous as he looked noticeably light when he cantered down to the post in front of the biggest crowd seen on the Knavesmire since Eugene Aram was hanged there nearly a hundred years before. Most of the professional racing men supported The Flying Dutchman, but the sympathies of Yorkshire were with Voltigeur, who was owned by a Yorkshire peer, whereas 'The Dutchman' was owned by a Scottish one.

The same two jockeys were employed as at Doncaster, but this time the tactics were reversed and it was Voltigeur who made the running. Five furlongs out he was still three lengths clear, but then 'The Dutchman' gradually began to close the gap and just below the distance he drew level. It was then a question of which of the two was going to crack. With less than a hundred yards to go Voltigeur faltered a little and his rival drew ahead to win by just under a length. The victory was by no means easily gained, and the winner's flanks showed clearly enough the marks of his rider's spurs when he returned to the unsaddling enclosure.

The Flying Dutchman never ran again and retired to the stud at a fee of thirty guineas. He was a great horse and great things were expected of him, but at first he was hardly the success anticipated, many of his stock being light and narrow. Possibly unintelligent management was partially to blame, as he was asked to cover fifty mares his very first season. He did sire a moderate Derby winner in Ellington and an Oaks winner in Brown Duchess, but in 1858 he was sold for £4,000 for export to France. He did well there, the most important horse he sired being Dollar, who came over to England and won the Goodwood Cup, and who is largely responsible for the strength of the Herod male line in France. From him was descended in tail-male that highly successful stallion Tourbillon.

It only remains to add that The Flying Dutchman's dam, Barbelle, 'looking like a worn-out hack', was sold in her old age for forty pounds and is said to have ended her days pulling a cart and performing other menial tasks.

1849: Wednesday, 23 May . . . 237 Entries. £6,575.

LORD EGLINTON'S br.c. THE FLYING DUTCHMAN
   by Bay Middleton out of Barbelle   MARLOW   1
MR GODWIN'S br.c. HOTSPUR by Sir Hercules   WHITEHOUSE   2
COLONEL PEEL'S TADMOR by Ion   NAT FLATMAN 3

Also ran:

   Lord Clifden's Honeycomb (4th) (J. Robinson); Sir C. Monck's Vanguard (Bumby); Mr J. Bowes's The Knout (F. Butler); Lord Bateman's Goodwood (Sly); Mr Farrance's The Old Fox (Hornsby jun.); Sir C. Cockerell's Thibault (H. Darling); Lord Eglinton's Elthiron (J. Prince); Mr A. Nichol's Nunnykirk (Marson); Lord Exeter's Glenalvon (Bartholomew); Mr Campbell's Robert de Brus (H. Bell); Lord Stanley's Uriel (J. Holmes); Mr H. Hill's Henry of Exeter (W. Boyce); Mr Walls's Chatterer (A. Day); Mr B. Green's Westow (Wintringham); Sir J. Hawley's Vatican (S. Rogers); Sir G. Heathcote's Companion (R. Sherwood); Mr Burgess's The Crowner (J. Sharp); Mr Pedley's Old Dan Tucker (S. Templeman); Mr Disney's Montague (W. Abdale); Mr Gratwicke's Landgrave (Kitchener); Mr Jaques's Chantrey (G. Simpson); Mr F. Nicholl's Woolwich (W. Oates); Duke of Rutland's Fire-eater (Pearl).

26 ran.

Betting:

   2–1 The Flying Dutchman and Tadmor; 6–1 Nunnykirk; 10–1 Chatterer; 20–1

Vatican; 25–1 Elthiron and Honeycomb; 30–1 The Knout and Uriel; 40–1 Old Dan Tucker and Robert de Brus; 50–1 Hotspur and Montague.

Won by half a length; the same between second and third.　　　　3 m.
Winner trained by Fobert at Middleham.

1850

Voltigeur, a brown colt by Voltaire out of Martha Lynn, by Mulatto, was bred near Hartlepool by Mr Robert Stephenson. He came up for sale as a yearling with a reserve of £350 on him, but Mr Tattersall failed to attract a bid of even £100. Hill, Lord Zetland's private trainer, tried to induce his patron to buy the colt, but without success. However the following spring, Lord Zetland, largely on the advice of his brother-in-law, Mr Williamson, changed his mind and purchased the Martha Lynn colt, whom he then named Voltigeur. The price was 1,000 guineas with a Derby contingency of 500 guineas.

In the autumn Voltigeur was given a trial and disclosed his merit in no uncertain fashion by conceding twelve pounds to a three-year-old filly called Castanette and beating her with ease. Soon afterwards he had his only race as a two-year-old, winning the Wright Stakes at Richmond. He was not given another race, nor subjected to a further trial, before the Derby.

All through the winter Yorkshire money poured on to Voltigeur for the Derby, but the sporting pundits in London steadfastly opposed him, and on the day of the race Clincher, Mildew, Bolingbroke, The Nigger, and the Two Thousand Guineas winner Pitsford were all preferred in the market to Lord Zetland's colt. The hundreds of racing enthusiasts from the Richmond area of Yorkshire who had travelled down to Epsom were delighted to find Voltigeur on offer at 16–1, but their exuberance was slightly dimmed when they heard that he had gone distinctly 'short' in his gallop on the Downs. That, however, was no doubt due to stiffness after a long and tiring journey in the train.

Voltigeur's unimpressive gallop, however, was not the only cause for worry. Far more serious was Lord Zetland's discovery that forfeits of £400 were due from Voltigeur's nominator, and unless these were paid, Voltigeur would not be permitted to run. Lord Zetland was furious, and with aristocratic disregard for the feelings or the pockets of the thousands who had backed his horse, gave orders for Voltigeur to be scratched. Servants and tenants on the Zetland estates who, to a man, had had their limit on the horse, were in despair, and a deputation from among them was despatched to Mr Williamson. He agreed to see what he could do, and when the hardship and disappointment involved in his proposed action was made clear to him, Lord Zetland changed his mind and paid all the forfeits due.

Luckily for their nerves, which by then must have been in a shattered condition, Voltigeur's backers suffered little anxiety in the race. From Tattenham Corner he never looked in danger of defeat, and he duly won by a comfortable length from Pitsford, who beat Clincher for second place in the last few strides. The cheers of the Yorkshiremen mingled with those from thousands of Freemasons, who had staked a shilling or two on the winner because Lord Zetland at that time was the head of English Freemasonry. Lord Zetland, who rarely betted and then only in moderate sums, won £600, his coachman £200. Davis, 'The Leviathan', had a shocking race, but an Irish gentleman, who had taken a considerable fancy to the winner, won £27,000, with which he prudently bought himself an estate.

In the St Leger Voltigeur, an odds-on favourite, was again ridden by Marson who had partnered him at Epsom. In his two memorable races against The Flying Dutchman, Voltigeur was ridden by Flatman, but that was because Marson was unable to do the weight. No doubt Voltigeur would have won the St Leger comfortably enough, but he was so consistently interfered with by Chatterbox that Marson was compelled to take him to the front a good deal sooner than he intended. As a result, Voltigeur faltered a little close home, and in the last few strides Russborough, a stable companion of Chatterbox, got up to force a dead-heat. In the run-off Voltigeur had a very hard struggle before Russborough was finally mastered, and he must have been a horse of remarkable toughness to have turned out again two days later and to have defeated The Flying Dutchman.

Voltigeur's two battles against 'The Dutchman' have already been described. After the Match at York, Voltigeur was asked to run the very next day in the York and Ainsty Cup, worth £100, and was beaten by a filly called Nancy after a farcical contest in which the runners scarcely raised a gallop throughout. The following week Lord Zetland and his trainer Hill parted company. The cause of the trouble was that Lord Zetland's colt Lightfoot, which the public and Hill had backed for the Derby, ran very badly indeed at Chester and was immediately scratched by his owner.

In 1852 Voltigeur, appropriately enough, won The Flying Dutchman Handicap at York, but was beaten in both the Ascot Cup and the Ebor. Lord Zetland then retired him to the stud, and in 1853 he was leased to stand at Hampton Court, but soon afterwards he was transferred to Mr Smallwood's stud at Middlethorpe, where his fee was twenty-five guineas. His best sons were Vedette and Skirmisher. Vedette won the Two Thousand Guineas for Lord Zetland and when mated with The Flying Duchess, a mare by The Flying Dutchman, he sired Galopin, who in his turn sired St Simon, one of the greatest horses in the history of the English Turf.

Voltigeur was badly kicked by a mare in 1874 and died soon after. Harry Hall, who painted most of the classic winners of that period, described him as follows: 'A brown horse standing only 15 hands 3 inches in height, with a rather coarse head, small ears, and muscular neck with very good oblique shoulder, deep-girthed, high in the leg, and rather light, but with a good back and powerful quarters rather dropping towards his light thin tail.' Voltigeur's favourite companion was a cat who, once the horse was rugged up, would sit on his back for hours at a time.

Lord Zetland, an honourable and upright man of somewhat impulsive temperament, was born in 1795. He succeeded to the title in 1839 and died in 1873. The most important public office he held was that of Lord-Lieutenant of Ireland.

1850: Wednesday, 29 May . . . 205 Entries. £4,975.

LORD ZETLAND'S br.c. VOLTIGEUR by Voltaire out of Martha Lynn	J. MARSON	1
MR H. HILL'S ch.c. PITSFORD by Epirus	A. DAY	2
LORD AIRLIE'S br.c. CLINCHER by Turcoman	F. BUTLER	3

Also ran:

Mr Gratwicke's The Nigger (4th) (Nat Flatman); Mr Ford's Penang (Sly); Mr W. Edward's Bolingbroke (J. Robinson); Mr Jaques's Mildew (Bartholomew); Mr Hussey's Royal Hart (Simpson); Mr Gannon's Deicoon (J. Sharp); Mr Gurney's St Fabian (Pettit); Mr Greville's Cariboo (S. Rogers); Mr Davidson's Charley (Abrahams); Mr Meiklam's The Italian (Templeman); Lord Exeter's Nutshell (Norman); Mr T. Stevens's The Knight of Gwynne (Dockeray); Count Batthyany's Valentine (Crouch); Duke of Richmond's Ghillie Callum (S. Mann); Mr Merry's Brennus (J. Prince); Lord Eglinton's Mavors (Marlow); Major Martyn's The Swede (W. Abdale); Mr Disney's Captain Grant (Wynne); Mr Moseley's Alonzo (Whitehouse); Sir G. Heathcote's colt by Sir Hercules (R. Sherwood); Mr Lawson's Augean (H. Edwards).

24 ran.

Betting:

4–1 Clincher; 9–2 Mildew; 5–1 Bolingbroke; 6–1 The Nigger; 12–1 Pitsford; 16–1 Voltigeur; 20–1 Deicoon; 33–1 Nutshell; 40–1 The Italian and Ghillie Callum; 50–1 Cariboo and The Swede; 1,000–15 Captain Grant, Brennus, The Knight of Gwynne, and Royal Hart.

Won by a length; half a length between second and third.   2 m. 50 s.
Winner trained by R. Hill.

1851

The 1851 Derby was won by Sir Joseph Hawley's Teddington ridden by Job Marson.

The circumstances in which Hawley bought Teddington are not entirely clear. Teddington was bred by Mr Tomlinson, who kept the toll bar at Godmanchester, and he was foaled in a barn at Great Stukeley, two miles from Huntingdon. His dam Miss Twickenham, in foal to Orlando, had been given to Tomlinson by Colonel Peel, who was Member of Parliament for Huntingdon.

According to 'The Druid', Hawley gave Tomlinson £250 for Teddington and Miss Twickenham when Teddington was three months old, a contingency of £1,000 being added should the foal by any chance win the Derby. An alternative version was that Teddington was seen with his dam by Hawley at Newmarket, where Miss Twickenham had gone to be mated with Orlando, and that taking a liking to Teddington he bought him for £500 down, £300 more if he won the Chesterfield Stakes, and £1,000 more if he won the Derby.

The weakness in this second version is that Orlando did not stand at Newmarket at all, but at his owner's stud at Bonehill in Staffordshire. Whatever the truth happened to be, there was undoubtedly a misunderstanding, to say the least of it, with regard to the Derby contingency, and after Teddington's victory at Epsom, Hawley refused to pay Tomlinson a penny more than £300.

Teddington was well galloped as a two-year-old, but he disappointed considerably in his first two races, being beaten at the Second Spring Meeting at Newmarket and subsequently in the Woodcote Stakes at Epsom. However, in July he won the Chesterfield Stakes at Newmarket and the Molecomb Stakes at Goodwood, although his success at Goodwood was only achieved after an earlier defeat at the same meeting.

The following year Teddington beat a single opponent in a race at the Craven Meeting, but in a trial not long afterwards he showed that he was something out of the ordinary by giving six pounds and an easy beating to a good-class five-year-old in Vatican. That gallop clearly gave him a favourite's chance at Epsom, but there were some anxious moments to be gone through first. A week before the big race he developed sore shins, and on the morning of Derby Day itself he was off his feed. Nevertheless, he started favourite at 3–1, Marlborough Buck being almost as heavily backed at 7–2, while there was strong support as well for Hernandez and The Prime Minister.

160

It was the year of the Great Exhibition and the crowd was enormous, distinction, so some people alleged, being added by the presence of a number of German royalties. The weather was perfect and the field of thirty-three constituted a fresh record for the race. It proved to be a case of 'the bigger the field, the bigger the certainty', as Teddington won with ridiculous ease. He was pulling over his rivals at Tattenham Corner, and when Marson gave him a touch of the spur, he responded so violently that he almost knocked over Ariosto, ridden by Flatman. 'Where do you think you're going to?' shouted Flatman. 'I'm sorry, I can't hold my horse,' Marson replied. 'I wish I couldn't hold mine,' said Flatman, but by then Marson had passed out of hearing. Teddington won literally in a canter by two lengths from Marlborough Buck with Neasham a length away third. Sir Joseph, who in later years declaimed about the iniquities of heavy betting, won something like £80,000. Among the unplaced horses was Newminster, winner of the St Leger and sire of two Derby winners. His weakness was very thin feet, a defect that frequently interfered with his racing career. On this occasion he was quite unfancied and started at 100–1.

Teddington did not run in the St Leger, but in the autumn he won a £1,000 Match against Mr Osbaldeston's Mountain Deer. He won three of his six races as a four-year-old, beating Newminster in the Doncaster Cup. As a five-year-old he was better than ever; he won the Ascot Cup, giving nine pounds and a beating to Stockwell, and he ran a valiant race in the Cesarewitch carrying 9 st. 7 lb. Horses had to be tough in those days, and on the same afternoon as the Cesarewitch he was beaten by Kingston over The Beacon Course, both of them carrying ten stone. After that effort he retired to the stud at Deans Hill, Stafford. He was not a success, though, many of his stock being 'soft'. He ended his days abroad.

Sir Joseph Hawley, heir to the Laybourne estates in Kent, was born in 1814 and won the Derby on four occasions. He served for a time in the 9th Lancers, but being intelligent, well-read, and artistic, life in the light cavalry was not very much to his taste. On leaving the army he settled down for a time in Florence, and it was there, strangely enough, that his passion for racing developed, largely through the influences of his friend Mr J. M. Stanley, later Sir J. Massey Stanley Errington. Stanley became his racing confederate for a time, and there were strong rumours that he was really the owner of Teddington.

Hawley's association with the English Turf began in 1844 when he had horses in partnership with Stanley that were trained by Beresford at Newmarket. Once he had learnt the rudiments of the sport though, his instincts were strongly in favour of a private stable run under his personal control. Accordingly he installed Alec Taylor at Fyfield in Wiltshire, and it was Taylor who prepared Teddington for the Derby. Subsequently, after a brief period with the Days at Danebury, Hawley's horses were trained by George Manning at Cannons Heath, and after Manning's death by John Porter, firstly at Cannons Heath and then at Kingsclere. The trainer's job was to keep the horses fit and well; the owner did the entering and placing. Even when the horses were tried, Hawley often weighed-out the lads himself, refusing to tell either them or the trainer the actual weight that they carried. At one time he betted very heavily indeed, and that practice, combined with his habit of giving extravagant presents to his jockeys, incurred the implacable hostility of Admiral Rous.

In later life, as a member of the Jockey Club, he interested himself in Turf reform, and there was much to be said in favour of his plans to restrict two-year-old racing and to extend the privilege of membership of the Jockey Club to a rather wider circle. He was not a popular man though, and his speeches on the iniquities of heavy gambling, in view of his own record in that respect, laid him open to the charge of hypocrisy. In fact he never really enjoyed the confidence or trust of his contemporaries, and largely for that reason, combined with the bitter opposition of Admiral Rous, his proposals for reform were defeated. He died after much suffering in 1875.

1851: Wednesday, 21 May . . . 192 Entries. £5,325.

SIR J. HAWLEY'S ch.c. TEDDINGTON by Orlando out of Miss Twickenham	J. MARSON	1
MR J. CLARKE'S br.c. MARLBOROUGH BUCK by Venison	G. WHITEHOUSE	2
MR WILKINSON'S br.c. NEASHAM by Hetman Platoff	J. HOLMES	3

Also ran:

Lord Enfield's Hernandez (4th) (S. Mann); Mr J. Powney's Lamartine (A. Day); Mr Halford's The Prime Minister (W. Sharpe); Sir J. Hawley's The Ban (Pearl); Lord Chesterfield's Heart Breaker (F. Butler); Mr Waller's Ephesus (Wakefield); Mr Greville's Ariosto (Nat Flatman); Mr Higgins's Theseus (S. Rogers); Mr Osbaldeston's Mountain Deer (Maton); Mr E. R. Clark's Glenhawk (Dockeray); Lord Exeter's Midas (Norman); Mr Moore's Alompra (Simpson); Mr A. Nichols's Newminster (Pettit); Mr Wentworth's Azeth (Bumby); Mr Morris's Hungerford (Fenn); Mr Delamere's Guy Mannering (Bartholomew); Sir T. Burke's Cock-crow (H. Robertson); Baron Rothschild's colt by Tearaway (J. Robinson); Mr Nevill's Telescope (H. Bell); Lord Eglinton's Bonny Dundee (Cartwright); Lord Eglinton's Hippolytus (C. Marlow); Mr Meiklam's Constellation (Templeman); Mr Saxon's The Black Doctor (W. Abdale); Mr H. J. Thomson's Gholah Singh (Wintringham); Mr F. Garner's Serus (H. Edwards); Mr Worthington's Goliath (Osborne, jun.);

Mr Merry's Louis Napoleon (J. Howlett); Duke of Richmond's Buckhound (Kitchener); Sir R. Pigot's Aeolus (W. Boyce); Sir R. Pigot's Runnymede (Sly).

33 ran.

Betting:

3–1 Teddington; 7–2 Marlborough Buck; 7–1 Hernandez and The Prime Minister; 15–1 Constellation, Theseus, and Neasham; 22–1 The Black Doctor; 30–1 Lamartine and Hippolytus; 40–1 Bonnie Dundee; 50–1 Ariosto; 1,000–15 Guy Mannering, Glenhawk, Telescope, and the colt by Tearaway; 100–1 Newminster; 200–1 Cock-crow.

Won by two lengths; a length between second and third.   2 m. 51 s.
Winner trained by A. Taylor at Fyfield.

1852

Undoubtedly the best three-year-old in 1852 was Lord Exeter's Stockwell. Bred by Mr Theobald, Stockwell was by The Baron out of Pocahontas, by Glencoe. Pocahontas was an indifferent racehorse and a 'roarer', but besides Stockwell she produced Rataplan, winner of forty-two prizes, and King Tom, second in the Derby and twice Champion Sire. She lived to the age of thirty-three, and when she was twenty-five she foaled Auricula, dam of colts that won the Two Thousand Guineas and the Derby.

Lord Exeter bought Stockwell as a yearling, somewhat reluctantly, it was said, for £180 and a Derby contingency of £500. As a two-year-old the colt was too big to be properly trained, but the following season he won the Two Thousand Guineas and the St Leger. No doubt he would have won the Derby as well, but he had to have a septic gumboil lanced not long before the race and ran far below his usual form in consequence. In addition he got into every sort of trouble in running, being forced on to the rails and getting badly cut when his rider, Norman, was trying to go for an opening.

Stockwell did not have the best of shoulders and in consequence was not a good mover in his slower paces, but he had tremendous depth and power as well as wonderful bone, and taking him all in all he could rightly be described as a magnificent stamp of weight-carrying thoroughbred. At the stud he was an outstanding success and fully earned his title of 'Emperor of Stallions'. He transmitted to his stock the stoutness for which he was famous and it would be difficult to exaggerate the value of his services as a sire. On seven occasions he headed the list of winning sires, and four other times he was second. He sired three Derby winners in Blair Athol, Lord Lyon, and Doncaster, and in 1866 the first three horses in the Derby were all sired by him. Stockwell is the ancestor of the Phalaris male line, the most powerful one in England today. To him also traces the line of The Boss, a dominant sprinting influence in modern breeding, and that of Teddy, to whom French and American bloodstock owe so much. Stockwell died at Mr R. C. Naylor's stud in Cheshire in 1870.

Profiting from Stockwell's ill-fortune, Mr John Bowes won the Derby with Daniel O'Rourke. It was the third of his four successes in the race. Trained by John Scott and ridden by Frank Butler, Daniel O'Rourke was a chesnut by the Irish horse Birdcatcher our of Forget-me-not, by Hetman Platoff. Though well enough made, he was in fact little more than a pony and stood only fourteen hands three inches. Both before the Derby and after it his form was of small account, and he must be rated one of the less distinguished winners of the Blue Riband.

As a two-year-old he ran second in the Champagne Stakes at Doncaster and unplaced in the Criterion Stakes at Newmarket. He did not appear again before Epsom, where he started at 25–1, but he had evidently shown John Scott some form at home as Mr Bowes had backed him at very long odds and so had Mr Greville, among others. In fact it was the worst of the many bad Derbys experienced by Davis, 'the Leviathan', who lost the best part of £80,000. 'You have had a bad race, I hear,' remarked Greville after Daniel O'Rourke's number was hoisted into the frame. 'So everybody says,' replied Davis, 'but you can have a cheque now for your money,' and he paid his debts, it was recorded, 'with as little concern as he paid his laundry bill'.

The going was soft after hours of heavy rain when the field of twenty-seven runners went to the post. The favourite was Little Harry, the Danebury candidate, who owed his position almost entirely to what he was said to have accomplished in a trial at home. Hobbie Noble was second favourite at 4–1; as a two-year-old he won the New Stakes and the July Stakes, being subsequently sold to Mr Merry for £6,500.

Little Harry made the running to Tattenham Corner with Harbinger and Hobbie Noble close behind. In the straight, however, Barbarian, who carried a stack of Irish money, went on from Hobbie Noble, Chief Baron Nicholson, and Daniel O'Rourke. Below the distance the four leaders split into two groups, Chief Baron Nicholson and Hobbie Noble fighting it out on the rails, Barbarian and Daniel O'Rourke on the stand side. The two on the stand side, though, were always dominating their opponents, and in a tremendous finish Daniel O'Rourke won by a short half-length from Barbarian, with Chief Baron Nicholson another half-length away third. The time was the slow one of three minutes two seconds. The general opinion was that Barbarian, owned by Mr Bradshaw, would have won had he been more than three parts fit, and had his rider Hiett been the equal in skill of Frank Butler.

There was an unpleasant background to the race. It was strongly rumoured that Hobbie Noble had been 'got at' the night before the race. If he had been, he certainly ran a wonderfully good race under the circumstances. He was trained at Hednesford by Saunders, who numbered among his patrons Dr William Palmer, a heavy betting man and a notorious poisoner, subsequently hanged for murder.

Furthermore Chief Baron Nicholson, backed by his trainer George Ducker to win £100,000, was not ridden to win by his jockey Kitchener, who subsequently admitted that fact. Kitchener was a late substitute for another rider who had been successfully rendered *hors de combat* by interested parties. Ducker himself died some time afterwards in mysterious circumstances. It was said that he went up to London with a lot of ready money to bet on a prize fight, and was given an overdose of some drug by a gang of thieves intent on robbing him.

After winning the Derby Daniel O'Rourke beat a solitary opponent in the St James's Palace Stakes at Ascot, but was beaten in the Ebor Handicap and then in the St Leger, which Stockwell won by ten lengths. As a four-year-old he was defeated twice at Goodwood and was subsequently sent overseas.

Frank Butler was a nephew of young Sam Chifney and inherited a touch of his genius. His early life was passed in comparatively easy circumstances as his father was quite a successful trainer and was able to give him a good education. As a rider the turning-point in his career came when he went up north to join John Scott's powerful stable. A tremendously strong finisher, his favourite method was to come from behind with a late run, but sometimes he ran things a little bit too fine and it was generally thought that he would have beaten Surplice in the Derby on Springy Jack if he had made his effort a little bit sooner. He rode two Derby winners, both for Mr Bowes, and six winners of the Oaks, four of them in succession. He died in 1856 after a long illness at the age of thirty-eight.

1852: Wednesday, 26 May ... 181 Entries. £5,200.

MR J. BOWES'S ch.c. DANIEL O'ROURKE
    by Birdcatcher out of Forget-me-not   F. BUTLER   1
MR BRADSHAW'S b.c. BARBARIAN by Simoom   HIETT   2
MR DORRIEN'S bl.c. CHIEF BARON NICHOLSON
    by The Baron   KITCHENER   3

Also ran:

Mr Merry's Hobbie Noble (4th) (W. Sharple); Lord Zetland's Augur (S. Rogers); Mr Farrance's Joe Miller (Dockeray); Duke of Richmond's Homebrewed (Sly); General Anson's King Pepin (Charlton); Mr Arnold's Little Harry (A. Day); Lord Ribblesdale's Kingston (G. Brown); Lord Ribblesdale's Nabob (Pettit); Mr P. Booth's Missive (Wakefield); Duke of Richmond's Harbinger (Nat Flatman); Lord Orford's Alcoran (Bartholomew); Major Martyn's Convulsion (Doyle); Mr Duncombe's Alfred the Great (Bumby); Mr J. M. Stanley's Orelio (Pearl); Mr Meiklam's Wormesley (Templeman); Mr G. Barton's The Surveyor (J. Marson); Lord Exeter's Stockwell (Norman); Lord Exeter's Ambrose (W. Boyce); Mr J. Clark's

Elcot (Whitehouse); Duke of Bedford's Maidstone (J. Howlett); Mr R. S. Walker's Treasurer (Simpson); Lord Eglinton's Claverhouse (Marlow); Mr Davidson's Vortex (Maton); Mr Harrison's King of Trumps (Cartwright).

27 ran.

Betting:

7–2 Little Harry; 4–1 Hobbie Noble; 11–1 Harbinger and Alcoran; 12–1 Claverhouse; 14–1 Kingston; 16–1 Stockwell; 20–1 Alfred the Great and Wormesley; 25–1 Daniel O'Rourke, King of Trumps, and Joe Miller; 30–1 Augur and Orelio; 40–1 Chief Baron Nicholson; 50–1 Missive; 100–1 Barbarian.

Won by half a length; the same distance between second and third.　　3 m. 2 s. Winner trained by John Scott at Malton.

1853

This year was another triumph for John Scott's stable, the winner being West Australian, the last and the best of Mr John Bowes's four Derby horses.

West Australian, in fact, was one of the greatest of English racehorses. Not only did he win the Two Thousand Guineas, the Derby, and the St Leger, being the first horse to gain the Triple Crown, but in addition he won the Ascot Cup as a four-year-old.

Bred by his owner, 'The West', as he was generally called, was by Melbourne, who had run unplaced in the 1838 Derby, out of Mowerina, by Touchstone out of Emma, the dam of the Derby winners Mündig and Cotherstone. Melbourne, held in great esteem by breeders, was almost the only male line descendant of Trumpator, and the names of Waxy, Whalebone, and Whisker were not to be found in his pedigree. But for him the Matchem family in all probability would have ceased to exist.

'The West', whom John Scott reckoned the best horse he ever trained, stood fifteen hands three inches and was described as 'a yellowish bay, rather long in the body, with a low stealing action that gave nothing away'. He was given plenty of time to develop his strength and as a two-year-old he did not run until the Houghton Meeting at Newmarket. In the Criterion Stakes he was beaten by Speed the Plough, with Filbert third, but later that week he reversed the form and won the Glasgow Stakes with Filbert second and Speed the Plough third. He had in fact been very well tried in August, as the result of which Mr Bowes took the train to London, and seeking out 'The Leviathan', backed 'The West' to win him £30,000 in the Derby.

West Australian's first race as a three-year-old was the Two Thousand Guineas, in which he started favourite at 6–4 on and won by half a length from the Duke of Bedford's Sittingbourne. In the Derby, ridden by Frank Butler wearing the jacket and cap which Bill Scott had worn on Cotherstone ten years previously, he was a 6 4 favourite in a field of twenty-eight. He won, but not with the ease anticipated, for it was only after a desperate struggle in the final furlong that he mastered Sittingbourne to win by a neck, with the Danebury representative Cineas only a head away third. Rataplan, full brother to Stockwell, was fourth and Rattle fifth. Mr Bowes, who tended to become more and more a recluse, did not come to Epsom to see the race. It was yet another bad Derby for Davis, who only just succeeded in settling and had barely

£200 left when he went to Ascot a fortnight later. Luckily for him, he won £12,000 on the very first day of that meeting.

Davis's career as a bookmaker was drawing to a close. Not long afterwards he fell through the grandstand roof at Rochester; it may have been the fall, or it may have been his insistence on running twice round the course 'to ward off the effects of shock', but he was never quite the same man afterwards. He finally retired from racing in 1857. He had started life as a joiner, augmenting his wages by accepting shilling bets from his mates. The main source of his fortune in later years was his lists on future events which he kept posted in the Durham Arms, Lincolns Inn Fields. Business there was so brisk that the lady who managed the Durham Arms was able to retire in comfort within three years of Davis making the place his headquarters.

'The West' won the St Leger in a canter and Frank Butler remarked afterwards: 'I only touched him once with the whip and I was glad to get him stopped.' As a four-year-old he won a Triennial Stakes at Ascot, the Ascot Cup, beating Kingston by a head, and a Sweepstakes at Goodwood by twenty lengths. He was then bought for 5,000 guineas by Lord Londesborough, who retired him to the stud at Tadcaster at a fee of thirty guineas. Lord Londesborough re-sold him some years later for 1,000 guineas less to the Duc de Morny, on whose death the horse passed into the hands of the French Emperor. West Australian was not a success at the stud either in England or France, but through Solon, Barcaldine, and Marco, Hurry On is descended from him in tail-male. Hurry On sired three Derby winners, Captain Cuttle, Coronach, and Call Boy, as well as the Gold Cup winner Precipitation, sire of Airborne, winner of the Derby in 1946.

1853: Wednesday, 25 May . . . 194 Entries. £4,450.

MR J. BOWES's b.c. WEST AUSTRALIAN by Melbourne
out of Mowerina   F. BUTLER   1
DUKE OF BEDFORD's ch.c. SITTINGBOURNE by Chatham S. ROGERS   2
MR POWNEY's b.c. CINEAS by Touchstone or Epirus   BUMBY   3

Also ran:

Mr Howard's Rataplan (4th) (Wells); Baron Rothschild's Orestes (Charlton); Lord Londesborough's The Mayor of Hull (J. Holmes); Count Batthyany's Stone Plover (W. Abdale); Mr E. R. Clark's Mr Sykes (Bartholomew); Mr Mare's Pharold (Pettit); Lord Exeter's Filbert (Norman); Mr Perren's Ionic (Hornsby); Lord Derby's Umbriel (Templeman); Duke of Richmond's Pharos (Nat Flatman); Captain D. Lane's Ninnyhammer (Sly); Lord Clifden's Cheddar (A. Day); Lord Caledon's Prince Leopold (W. Sharpe); Mr B. Way's Brocket (Thick); Mr Knowles's

Talfourd (Basham); Mr J. M. Stanley's Orinoco (J. Marson); Mr Howard's Lascelles (W. Day); Mr Oliver's Ethelbert (Crickmere); Mr Surtee's Honeywood (J. Osborne); Mr Rowan's Fioun-ma-Coul (Wynne); Mr J. Alying's Rattle (E. Sharp); Mr Thompson's Coomburland Stathesmon (Aldcroft); Lord Glasgow's Barbatus (Whitehouse); Lord Eglinton's Vanderdecken (Marlow); Mr Wilkins's Peggy (H. Neale).

28 ran.

Betting:

6–4 West Australian; 6–1 Honeywood; 7–1 Orestes; 8–1 Sittingbourne; 20–1 Umbriel, Pharos, and Cineas; 25–1 Ninnyhammer; 30–1 Peggy and Rataplan; 50–1 Cheddar, Barbatus, Orinoco, and Brocket; 100–1 Filbert, Vanderdecken, Rattle, and Coomburland Stathesmon.

Won by a neck, a head between second and third. 2 m. 55 s.
Winner trained by John Scott at Malton.

1854

Mr John Gully won the Derby in 1854 with Andover, trained by old John Day at Danebury and ridden by one of John's sons, Alfred.

Bred at Longstock by Mr W. Etwall, at one time M.P. for Andover, Andover was a bay colt standing fifteen hands two inches by Bay Middleton. He was bought by Gully as a yearling and made his first racecourse appearance at Goodwood, running third in the Ham Stakes and winning the Molecombe Stakes. A fortnight later he won a £100 Plate at Brighton and that was the last that was seen of him before the Derby.

The fact that Andover started second favourite at Epsom at 7–2 can be attributed to the fact that in a trial at Danebury he showed himself considerably superior to Hermit, another Bay Middleton colt owned by Gully and winner of the Two Thousand Guineas. Hermit also took part in the Derby, but he started at 14–1 and his mission was to make the running for Andover. The actual favourite was Lord Derby's Dervish, who had some good form to his credit as a two-year-old, while another fancied runner was Stockwell's half-brother by Harkaway, King Tom.

Hermit led into the straight followed by Dervish, still fighting for his head, Andover, King Tom, and Early Bird. Approaching the distance Hermit's stride began to shorten and Day at once sent Andover to the front. Sim Templeman then asked Dervish for his effort, but there was no response at all, and without putting up the semblance of a struggle the favourite allowed himself to be passed by both Early Bird and King Tom. Inside the final furlong King Tom made a valiant effort to get on terms with Andover, who, however, was always going just a bit too well for him and stayed on to win by a comfortable length. Hermit was third, half a length behind King Tom, and Early Bird close up fourth. Gully and the Days had a very big win indeed, but luck was undoubtedly on their side, as ten days before the race King Tom sprained a tendon and could not leave his box for a week.

Andover won further races that season at Stockbridge, Goodwood, Brighton, and Doncaster. At the end of the year he was sold to Sir Tatton Sykes who sent him to the stud at Sledmere. He was not a success as a sire, though, and was eventually exported to Russia.

Alfred Day was twenty-four years old at the time of Andover's Derby victory. This was his only success in that race, but he was second on Pitsford in 1850, and also on Kingstown in 1855. As was the case with certain other members of his family, his conduct was sometimes open to suspicion. He was a well-educated, quiet sort of man, whose one distinction outside racing was to be president of a local Rabbit Club.

1854: Wednesday, 31 May . . . 217 Entries. £6,100.

MR J. GULLY's b.c. ANDOVER by Bay Middleton out of a mare by Defence	A. DAY	1
BARON ROTHSCHILD's b.c. KING TOM by Harkaway	CHARLTON	2
MR J. GULLY's b.c. HERMIT by Bay Middleton	WELLS	3

Also ran:

Mr Copperthwaite's The Early Bird (4th) (Aldcroft); Lord Derby's Dervish (Templeman); Mr R. E. Cooper's Autocrat (G. Manning); Mr R. E. Cooper's Woodcote (Whitehouse); Lord Zetland's Hospodar (G. Oates); Lord Lonsdale's Welham (S. Rogers); Mr Cookson's The First Lord (Sly); Mr Powney's Marc Anthony (Maton); Baron Rothschild's Middlesex (Simpson); Mr C. Spence's Canute (Pearl); Mr S. Walker's Winkfield (W. Abdale); Mr E. R. Clark's Punchbox (F. Marson); Sir T. Burke's Grey Plover (Osborne); Mr Clarkson's Neville (Bartholomew); Mr Newland's Bracken (Holmes); Mr Shepherdson's New Warrior (Nat Flatman); Mr Gregory's Papageno (Yates); Mr Morris's Knight of St George (Basham); Lord Clifden's Alembic (J. Marson); Lord Clifden's Rodo-Meli (G. Mann); Sir R. Pigot's Coup d'Etat (Pettit); Mr Merry's Wild Huntsman (C. Marlow); Mr Osbaldeston's Champagne (Dockeray); Mr Knowles's Marsyas (Bumby).

27 ran.

Betting:

5–2 Dervish; 7–2 Andover; 8–1 King Tom; 10–1 Wild Huntsman; 12–1 Neville; 14–1 Hermit and Hospodar; 20–1 Marsyas and The Early Bird; 25–1 New Warrior; 40–1 Knight of St George; 50–1 Alembic and Canute; 1,000–15 Bracken; 100–1 Champagne, Woodcote, Welham, Middlesex, Grey Plover, and Papageno.

Won by a length; half a length between second and third. 2 m. 52 s. Winner trained by John Day at Danebury.

1855

Wild Dayrell may not have been among the greatest of Derby winners, but few can have had a stranger or more romantic story.

Mr Francis Popham, born in 1809, was a country squire, whose estate was at Littlecote, near Hungerford, in the County of Berkshire. He loved every form of sport, and eventually began to breed thoroughbreds in a small and somewhat amateurish way. The second mare he ever owned was Ellen Middleton, by Bay Middleton. She had been advertised for sale, and his stud-groom Rickaby, a member of a family that still plays a prominent part on the English Turf, persuaded him to buy her from Lord Zetland for fifty pounds.

The following year Rickaby took Ellen Middleton to Newmarket to look for a suitable mate, and finally decided on the Herod horse Ion, who had finished second to Amato in the Derby.

In due course Ellen Middleton produced a colt foal, the first ever bred at Little-cote, where the event caused considerable excitement. The birth took place soon after midnight and on being informed of it, Mr Popham's butler appeared on the scene wearing a nightcap and bearing a bottle of wine. It was decided to move the foal into a warmer box, and the butler insisted on transferring it there in a wheel-barrow, being determined, as he explained, 'to wheel the winner of the Derby once in my life'. From the very first day Rickaby insisted that there was something fateful about the foal, as on the way back to his cottage at five o'clock that April morning, he saw a wild duck and a wild drake sitting on a quickset hedge close to the highroad. Whether that was a portent for good or for evil he was unable at the time to decide.

The colt was duly named Wild Dayrell after a sixteenth-century owner of Little-cote, who, among other crimes, was said to have killed a new-born baby by throwing it on the fire. He escaped the gallows, but died after a bad fall from his horse and was reputed to haunt Littlecote ever after.

As a yearling Wild Dayrell was sold to Lord Henry Lennox, a son of the Duke of Richmond, for 100 guineas. Trained by John Kent at Goodwood, he was big, backward, and unpromising at the start of his two-year-old career. Accordingly, when the Duke of Richmond's stud was dispersed, he was sent up with the other horses to Tattersalls. There Mr Popham bought him back for 250 guineas, disposing of a share to his friend, Lord Craven.

At first Wild Dayrell was trained by Rickaby, together with a five-year-old gelding and a three-year-old filly, on the banks of the Kennet, but in May 1854 all three were transferred to Lord Craven's place, Ashdown Park, where Rickaby and his two sons, Sam and John, continued to look after them.

Wild Dayrell thrived under the Rickabys, and in the autumn he won a Sweepstakes at Newmarket from two opponents. That was his only appearance as a two-year-old and he never ran again before the Derby. He continued to be trained in Ashdown Park, but Robert Sherwood, a son of Amato's trainer Ralph Sherwood, was engaged to partner him in the Derby and used to come and ride him in his gallops. Various lead horses were purchased, but Wild Dayrell broke them down one after the other, so eventually Mr Popham paid £1,600 for Jack Sheppard, a four-year-old that had recently won quite a good-class race at Chester. Ten days before the Derby Wild Dayrell was given his final trial; he gave eight pounds to Jack Sheppard and twenty-eight pounds to another four-year-old and beat them both with ease. Charlton, who rode Jack Sheppard, exclaimed, 'I thought King Tom's trial a good one last year, but I never rode against such a horse as this before.'

Wild Dayrell's merits had become known far beyond Hungerford, and he was heavily backed by the public for the Derby. Mr Popham, though, was alarmed to find that however much money was poured on to Wild Dayrell, his price never shortened and the bookmakers displayed an ominous desire to lay him at generous odds. Suspicion that villainy was afoot was confirmed when Mr George Hodgman, a professional betting man, was approached by a well-known racing character of singularly doubtful reputation, who strongly advised him to lay Wild Dayrell for all his worth as the horse was due 'to be settled' before the race. Hodgman at once passed the information on to a Mr Roberts, who had been entrusted with the backing of Wild Dayrell for the stable. Immediate precautions were taken and the only person in Rickaby's yard who could possibly be regarded as a suspect was sacked on the spot without a word of explanation.

That, however, was not the end of the business by any means. First of all the indignant Mr Popham, who had been under the illusion that racing was purely a sport, was approached by an individual who offered him £5,000 not to run Wild Dayrell at Epsom. Finally, there was an attempt to interfere with the van in which Wild Dayrell was to travel. Rumours of this plot luckily reached the stable, and as an experiment a bullock was put in the van, which was then paraded past Mr Popham. As soon as the van moved, the wheels collapsed and the van toppled over on to its side, breaking one of the bullock's legs in the process.

The gang which had planned to stop Wild Dayrell from running had also backed Kingstown, trained by young John Day, for all they were worth, and with the failure of their plans they were left in a hazardous position. They were compelled to back Wild Dayrell at the last minute at whatever odds were available, with the result that Wild Dayrell started at even money. Kingstown belonged to Harry Hill, a bookmaker and one of the most villainous characters that the Turf has ever known. If ever there was a sordid racing plot it was inevitable that Hill's dirty fingers would have some part in shaping it, except on the few occasions that he did a bit of informing for a change. He had lost a lot of money on West Australian's Derby, believing, no doubt with very good reason, that he had Frank Butler 'in his pocket'. Unfortunately for him, Colonel Anson, who had backed West Australian and who had heard that something crooked was afoot, sent for Frank Butler shortly before the race and warned him in no uncertain terms what his fate would be if there was the slightest suspicion that he had not played straight.

The difficulties of those who wished to back Wild Dayrell at the last moment were increased when Lord Derby's De Clare, who was reckoned to have an outstanding chance, broke down shortly before the race, while there was also a mishap to Rifleman, who had been substantially backed as well. Rifleman was said to have been found lame on the journey to Epsom, but unkind people said that his retreat home was caused by the fact that certain inquiries had been set on foot with regard to his eligibility for the race. The chief danger to Wild Dayrell, therefore, was Mr Merry's Lord of the Isle, winner of the Two Thousand Guineas and trained by William Day.

The weather was cold and dull, the field the smallest since 1823, and the attendance, no doubt because of the Crimean War, extremely meagre. Lord of the Isles pulled his way to the front and retained his lead until Kingstown headed him at the top of the hill. Approaching Tattenham Corner Wild Dayrell began to make up ground and in the straight he joined Kingstown and Lord of the Isles. Approaching the distance Kingstown and Lord of the Isles were both in trouble, and Wild Dayrell forged ahead to win by a comfortable two lengths from Kingstown, with Lord of the Isles, who had hung badly in the closing stages, only a head away third.

Mr Popham, who understandably declared that he never wanted to own a Derby horse again, won £10,000, the bulk of which he shared with his friends. There was a row over the running of Lord of the Isles. One view was that he had not fully recovered from a very hard race in the Guineas; an alternative theory held that his rider Aldcroft had not done his best to win and had been more concerned with ensuring Kingstown's victory. The upshot was that soon afterwards Mr Merry removed Lord of the Isles and his other horses from William Day's stables. William Day had been 'warned off' some years previously, but the ban had since been lifted.

Robert Sherwood was twenty years old when he won on Wild Dayrell. He soon began to have trouble over his weight, and in the early sixties he went out to Hong

Kong to manage the racing interests of Messrs Gardiner, Mattheson and Company. Later he returned to England, set up as a trainer at Newmarket, and prepared St Gatien, who dead-heated with Harvester for the Derby in 1884. Among his patrons was Sir Winston Churchill's father, Lord Randolph Churchill. A popular man and extremely able professionally, Sherwood's weaknesses were an explosive temper, which, however, rapidly subsided, and a tendency to blame his jockey unjustly if a fancied horse of his failed to run up to expectations.

Wild Dayrell won the Ebor St Leger at York, beating a good horse in Toulston, who started favourite, but at Doncaster he broke down badly in the Cup, which was won by Rataplan, and was never able to race again. Rataplan, besides being a very good horse, was an extremely indolent one. He used to lie down in his box to have his mane plaited, and invariably had a prolonged siesta after every meal. If disinclined for exercise, he used to kick his lad off and walk quietly back to his box.

Wild Dayrell retired to the stud at Chilton Folliat, near Hungerford, at a fee of thirty guineas. He was not a success as a sire though, the most notable horses he got being The Rake, grandsire of Grey Leg, and Buccaneer, sire of the 1876 Derby winner, Kisber.

1855: Wednesday, 23 May . . . 191 Entries. £5,075.

MR F. L. POPHAM's br.c. WILD DAYRELL by Ion out of Ellen Middleton	R. SHERWOOD	1
MR H. HILL's br.c. KINGSTOWN by Tearaway	A. DAY	2
MR MERRY's b.c. LORD OF THE ISLES by Touchstone	ALDCROFT	3

Also ran:

Mr Atkins's Flatterer (4th) (Bartholomew); Mr J. J. Henderson's Rylstone (G. Oates); Mr Norton's Courtenay (J. Prince); Lord Anglesey's Stroud (H. Goater); Mr W. Garret's Little Brownie (J. Marson); Mr W. Smith's The Cave Adullam (Collins); Lord Eglinton's Dirk Hatteraick (Marlow); Lord Eglinton's Coroebus (Waddington); Mr J. Osborne's Lord Alfred (J. Osborne).

12 ran.

Betting:

Evens Wild Dayrell; 7–4 Lord of the Isles; 12–1 Dirk Hatteraick and Kingstown; 20–1 Flatterer; 30–1 Rylstone; 50–1 The Cave Adullam; 1,000–15 Lord Alfred; 100–1 Stroud and Little Brownie.

Won by two lengths; a head between second and third.   2 m. 54 s.
Winner trained by Rickaby at Ashdown Park.

1856

Ellington, winner in 1856, was owned by Admiral Harcourt and trained at Middleham by Thomas Dawson, eldest of a famous Scottish training family from Gullane. Ellington's sire was The Flying Dutchman, his dam Ellerdale, by Lanercost. A brown horse standing $15 \cdot 2\frac{1}{2}$, he was of the 'long and low' variety, with powerful quarters, a rather coarse head, and big feet that assisted him to plough through the heavy going on Derby Day. He was not an outstanding horse by any means, and it was his particular good fortune to be foaled in a moderate year.

As a two-year-old he won two of his three races, including the Champagne Stakes at Doncaster. During the winter he was used as a hack by the Admiral's coachman round the estate, but his owner must have had a shrewd idea of his potentialities as he turned down an offer for him of £4,000.

In the early spring Ellington was sent back to Dawson and at the York Spring Meeting he failed by a neck to concede six pounds to Fisherman, who was destined to become an outstanding success at the stud in Australia. In his only other race before the Derby, Ellington was second in the Dee Stakes at Chester.

The favourite for the Derby was Lord Derby's Fazzoletto, who had beaten Yellow Jack by half a length in the Two Thousand Guineas and had then survived an objection for crossing. Other well-backed horses were Wentworth, winner of the Newmarket Stakes, Cannobie, and Artillery. Ellington's starting price was 20–1. The Prince Consort, unaccompanied by the Queen, saw the twenty-four runners canter to the post on going made heavy by recent rain. Vandermulin led at Tattenham Corner with Yellow Jack and Ellington hard on his heels, and Fazzoletto, Cannobie, and Wentworth all well placed. With two furlongs to go the favourite and Wentworth were both in trouble and Vandermulin was beaten not long after. The race was then between Yellow Jack and Ellington, and as soon as Ellington's rider, Aldcroft, went for his whip, Admiral Harcourt's colt responded in great style to win by a length, with Cannobie only half a length away third. Aldcroft summed the race up afterwards by saying: 'Well, I don't know. I just gave him one crack of the whip and he did jump tremendous.'

Yellow Jack was a good horse with the unfortunate propensity of always finding one just better than him in almost every race in which he ran. To this day a horse that is habitually second is often referred to as 'a regular Yellow Jack'. He was owned by a Mr Padwick, who raced under the name of Mr Howard. Padwick was a moneylender, clever, unscrupulous, and utterly ruthless. He was perhaps the most evil man on the Turf in his day.

Tom Dawson won £25,000 on the race, largely because he was unable to hedge his money as he had hoped. He drew his winnings in bank notes at Tattersalls the following Monday, stuffed them into an old hat-box, and took the train for home. Unfortunately he was very sleepy when he changed trains at Northallerton and left the precious hat-box on the rack. It was missing for a week and went as far north as Aberdeen, but eventually Dawson got it back with all the money intact.

Ellington never won another race. He started an odds-on favourite for the St Leger, but finished down the course behind Warlock. After being beaten in a handicap at Kelso, his owner retired him to the stud at Kilburn, Middlesex, at a fee of ten guineas, but he was not a success as a sire.

Aldcroft, who rode Ellington, came from Manchester where his father was an omnibus proprietor. He succeeded Tommy Lye as Dawson's stable jockey, and after leaving Dawson he rode for John Scott. A heavy smoker, he was noted as a fashionable, if somewhat flashy dresser, and claimed to have introduced peg-top trousers into Middleham.

1856: Wednesday, 28 May . . . 211 Entries. £5,875.

ADMIRAL HARCOURT's br.c. ELLINGTON			
by The Flying Dutchman out of Ellerdale	ALDCROFT	1
MR HOWARD's ch.c. YELLOW JACK by Birdcatcher	WELLS	2
LORD J. SCOTT's b.c. CANNOBIE by Melbourne	R. SHERWOOD	3

Also ran:

Lord Derby's Fazzoletto (Nat Flatman); Mr Howard's Coroner (J. Goater); Mr Moseley's Bay Hilton (Ashmall); Mr Bowes's Fly-by-Night (Bartholomew); Lord J. Scott's Wandering Willie (Templeman); Mr Halford's Leamington (Kendall); Mr Hart's Aleppo (J. Marson); Mr Fitzwilliam's Wentworth (A. Day); Mr W. Cookson's Bird in Hand (J. Osborne); Mr Murland's Forbidden Fruit (E. Harrison); Mr E. R. Clark's Vandermulin (Charlton); Mr F. S. Swindell's Puck (J. Quinton); Mr Hobson's Mr Verdant Green (J. Mann); Mr Morris's Artillery (Basham); Lord Anglesey's Astrologus (G. Mann); Mr H. Hill's Rogerthorpe (S. Rogers); Mr Barber's Pretty Boy (J. Forster); Lord Wilton's Dramatist (Whitehouse); Mr Night's Cotswold (Sly); Mr Gratwicke's The Prince (T. Sherwood).

23 ran.

Betting:

5–2 Fazzoletto; 7–2 Wentworth; 6–1 Cannobie; 7–1 Artillery; 12–1 Fly-by-Night and Vandermulin; 15–1 Yellow Jack; 20–1 Bird in Hand and Ellington; 25–1 Puck; 40–1 Bay Hilton, Leamington, Rogerthorpe, and Coroner; 50–1 Astrologus; 100–1 any other.

Won by a length; half a length between the second and third.   3 m. 4 s.
Winner trained by T. Dawson at Middleham.

1857

In 1857 Blink Bonny emulated the great achievement of Sir Charles Bunbury's filly Eleanor and won both the Derby and the Oaks.

Blessed with a perfect racing temperament, Blink Bonny was a bay standing 15·2½ with a neat, lean head, a longish neck, and the best of shoulders. She had immense ribs and unusually powerful quarters. Her sire was Melbourne and her dam Queen Mary, by Gladiator. Owing to the successes of a horse called Braxey, Mr William I'Anson, a Scotsman who trained at Malton, determined to acquire Queen Mary. Her whereabouts were entirely unknown to him but he ran her to ground in Scotland and bought her for thirty pounds. Apart from producing Blink Bonny, she was the grand-dam of Blair Athol, winner of the Derby, and of Caller Ou, winner of the St Leger.

Mr I'Anson certainly did not spare Blink Bonny as a two-year-old as she ran eleven times, winning eight races, including the Gimcrack Stakes at York. During the season Lord Londesborough offered 3,000 guineas for her, and I'Anson would have accepted if he had been permitted to retain her in his stable, but that Lord Londesborough declined to do. Later offers of £5,000 and £6,000 from other sources were firmly refused.

In the late autumn Blink Bonny had a lot of dental trouble, a common weakness with Melbourne's stock. She suffered a great deal of pain and faded away to nothing. She could not touch corn, and green stuff was all that she could eat. Despite that, she remained winter favourite for the Derby. In the new year she began to pick up, but she was still far from her best when she ran fifth of eight in the One Thousand Guineas, a race that I'Anson had mistakenly reckoned her good enough to win half-trained.

This failure resulted in Blink Bonny's Derby price receding to 1,000–30, and it was freely rumoured that she would not run. In fact, some bookmakers traded on the assumption that she would not go to the post, so that when her number went up on the board there was a rush to cover certain bets that had been laid and she actually started at 20–1. The favourite was Tournament, George Fordham's first mount in the Derby, and other fancied runners were Lord Zetland's Skirmisher, M.D., Saunterer, Arsenal, Anton, and Adamas.

The favourite sweated profusely while being saddled and no doubt his chance was further affected by a tedious delay of nearly an hour at the start, this being caused by the indiscipline of a number of jockeys, four of whom were subsequently fined for continual disobedience to the starter. The pace, when at last they were off, was a fast one, and Tournament, Skirmisher, and Saunterer were all in trouble before Tattenham Corner was reached. The Danebury candidate Anton led into the straight, and he was still in front at the distance where he was joined by Arsenal, Blink Bonny, and M.D., the last of whom had been rather slowly away. With just under a furlong to go M.D. looked very much like winning, but just as his supporters were starting to shout him home, he broke down badly on his off foreleg and his chance had gone.

In the meantime Anton was passed by Blink Bonny, Black Tommy, Strathnaver, and Adamas. The four passed the post almost in line but well apart, and nobody knew which had won until the judge ordered Blink Bonny's number to be hoisted into the frame. She had won by a neck from Black Tommy, with Adamas a short head away third and Strathnaver only a neck behind Adamas. It had been a wonderfully close and exciting race, and a length and a half covered the first seven horses to finish. The time, 2 m. 45 s., set up a new record for the race.

Black Tommy, who came within inches of winning, was a 200–1 outsider, owned by Mr Drinkald, and saddled on Derby Day, it is said, by Mr Drinkald's valet. Despite the contemptuous odds at which he started, Black Tommy was very much fancied by his owner, who had backed him to win a fortune for a very small outlay, one of his bets being £20,000 to a coat, waistcoat, and hat. As the horses flashed past the post Mr Drinkald was convinced that Black Tommy's head was in front. 'Thank God I've won the Derby,' he shouted, and then added a trifle ungenerously, 'and not a soul is on but myself!' When Blink Bonny was declared the winner, Mr Drinkald could not believe it, and a friend who was with him has described how the unfortunate man turned green and gasped as if he had been struck a heavy blow just below the heart. It is impossible not to sympathize with his feelings at that moment of dire disappointment.

Tournament, who was such a disappointing favourite, later showed that sprinting was his game, and the money lost on him at Epsom was largely retrieved two months later when, with seven stone on his back, he succeeded in winning the six-furlong Stewards Cup at Goodwood.

Blink Bonny, none the worse for her gruelling battle in the Derby, came out again on the Friday and won the Oaks with ease. Not surprisingly she was a short-priced favourite for the St Leger, but Charlton, who had ridden her in both her victories at Epsom, deliberately pulled her. The Doncaster crowd gave the filly a very hostile reception on her return, and but for the intervention of Tom Sayers, the prize-fighter, the unfortunate Mr I'Anson, who had taken no part in the plot, might well have been lynched.

The man behind the pulling of Blink Bonny was John Jackson, a Yorkshire farmer's son and one of the leading bookmakers of his day. Quick-witted and thoroughly unscrupulous, his death at a comparatively early age was certainly no loss to the Turf. As some bookmakers had done before him and others have done since, he specialized in the corruption of jockeys. He himself had backed Imperieuse heavily and had laid Blink Bonny, acting on the well-founded assumption that Charlton would not hesitate to betray his employer if offered sufficient incentive. I'Anson had been warned of what was afoot, but he stood by his jockey and declined to replace him with a rider of greater integrity. His loyalty was very ill-rewarded.

Blink Bonny won a Sweepstakes at Ascot, the Lancashire Oaks, and the Bentinck Memorial Stakes at Goodwood before the St Leger tragedy, and the Park Hill Stakes at Doncaster immediately after it. She only had one outing as a four-year-old and that was at Goodwood, where she ran so badly that she had to be pulled up. She died in 1862 and her fame as a brood mare rests on her son, the 1864 Derby winner Blair Athol. Her skeleton was set up in the museum at York.

1857: Wednesday, 27 May ... 202 Entries. £5,700.

MR W. I'ANSON's b.f. BLINK BONNY by Melbourne
out of Queen Mary   CHARLTON   1
MR DRINKALD's bl.c. BLACK TOMMY by Wormesley   COVEY   2
MR MELISH's b.c. ADAMAS by Touchstone   WELLS   3

Also ran:

Mr C. Harrison's Strathnaver (4th) (Bumby); Lord Zetland's Skirmisher (W. Abdale); Lord John Scott's Lady Hawthorn (Ashmall); Mr Wilkins's Oakball (T. Cliff); Admiral Harcourt's Wardermarske (Aldcroft); Mr W. S. S. Crawford's Zuyder Zee (S. Oates); Mr F. Robinson's Anton (A. Day); Mr T. Parr's M.D. (Templeman); Mr Jackson's Saunterer (J. Osborne); Mr J. S. Douglas's Tournament (Fordham); Baron Rothschild's Sydney (D. Hughes); Lord Exeter's Turbit (Norman); Mr Ford's Laertes (J. Holmes); Lord Clifden's colt by Surplice (Bray); Lord Clifden's Loyola (Sly); Mr Taylor's Newton-le-Willows (J. Quinton); Mr Barber's Commotion (Kendall); Mr E. Parr's Lambourn (Sopp); Mr J. Merry's Special Licence (Chillman); Lord Anglesey's Ackworth (C. Hornsby); Mr Copperthwaite's Sprig of Shillelagh (Bates); Lord Ribblesdale's Glee Singer (W. Day); Mr Howard's Arsenal (J. Goater); Mr Howard's Chevalier d'Industrie (H. Goater);

Diomed with his jockey, Sam Arnull; by F. Sartorius

Mr Bowes's The Bird in the Hand (Nat Flatman); Sir J. Hawley's Gaberlunzie (G. Mann); Mr S. Williams's Dusty Miller (G. Quinton).

30 ran.

Betting:

4–1 Tournament; 100–15 Skirmisher; 7–1 M.D.; 8–1 Saunterer; 9–1 Arsenal and Anton; 12–1 Adamas; 20–1 Blink Bonny; 25–1 Wardermarske, Strathnaver, Lady Hawthorn, Zuyder Zee, and Sydney; 40–1 The Bird in the Hand, Commotion, and the colt by Surplice; 50–1 Oakball; 1,000–15 Sprig of Shillelagh and Glee Singer; 100–1 Lambourn and Chevalier d'Industrie; 200–1 Black Tommy and 30–1 Lord Clifden's two.

Won by a neck; a short head between second and third.   2 m. 45 s.
Winner trained by the owner at Malton.

1858

Sir Joseph Hawley removed his horses from Danebury in 1857 and set up George Manning, a former head-lad, as his private trainer at Cannons Heath. While the Cannons Heath stables, unused since the Duke of Bolton and Sir John Lade had their horses trained there fifty years previously, were being renovated, Hawley had a fit of depression and decided to sell his entire stud. His reputation for shrewdness, however, was such that no one imagined he would contemplate selling his horses if they possessed any prospects for the future, and a buyer at Sir Joseph's price was not to be found. Events soon proved that fortune was on his side, as the very next year he won the Two Thousand Guineas with Fitz-Roland, bought from the Royal Stud as a yearling for 430 guineas, and the Derby with Beadsman, whom he bred himself. Beadsman was a dark brown, almost black horse standing 15·2½. He was described as rather heavy in the shoulder and deficient in bone, but with a good back and powerful thighs. His sire was Weatherbit, a sturdy stayer that had been trained at Danebury and whose dam Miss Letty had won the Oaks; his own dam was Mendicant, who won the Oaks in 1847 for Mr Gully, and who was later on sold to Sir Joseph for £2,500.

As a two-year-old Beadsman had a couple of outings at Goodwood, being placed third on each occasion. The following season he won Sweepstakes at both the Newmarket Craven and First Spring Meetings, and then dead-heated with Eclipse, owned by the villainous Padwick, for the Newmarket Stakes. In the meantime his stable companion Fitz-Roland won the Two Thousand Guineas, and about a fortnight before the Derby, Sir Joseph had the pair of them tried against each other. Manning thought Fitz-Roland had gone just the better, Sir Joseph's preference was for Beadsman, while the stable jockey, 'Tiny' Wells, was far from being certain but finally gave his vote in favour of Beadsman. Soon afterwards the two horses were galloped together again, and this time Beadsman's superiority was unquestioned. Inevitably news of the gallop leaked out and Fitz-Roland's Derby price receded, but there was no wild rush by the betting public to support Beadsman, whose starting price on Derby Day was 10–1, the favourite being Toxophilite, trained by John Scott and owned by Lord Derby, who at that time held office as Prime Minister.

In the race both Beadsman and Fitz-Roland were well to the fore from the start, and Fitz-Roland went to the front soon after Tattenham Corner with Beadsman,

Eclipse, and Toxophilite in hot pursuit. With just over a furlong to go Toxophilite was travelling so well that he looked almost certain to win, but in the last two hundred yards he was challenged by Beadsman, who ran on with the greater determination to win rather cleverly by a length. The Hadji, owned by Mr Harrison, was third and Eclipse fourth. Sir Joseph won the best part of £70,000 on the race, but he had to undergo one or two anxious moments first. It was a day of intense heat and several jockeys returned lighter than when they weighed out. Wells was one of them, and not until the bridle was obtained was he able to draw out his proper weight.

Beadsman's only other race was a Triennial Stakes at Stockbridge, which he won. He then retired to the stud at Hurstbourne Park, Whitchurch. His most notable offspring were Blue Gown, winner of the Derby in 1868, Green Sleeve, Rosicrucian, and Pero Gomez. After Blue Gown's victory his fee was raised to 100 guineas, a noticeably high one in those days. He died in 1872.

Toxophilite won several more races before he was sent to the stud, where eventually he became completely blind. He was the sire of Musket, who in turn sired Carbine, a great horse both in New Zealand, where he was bred, and in Australia. Imported to England in 1895 by the Duke of Portland, Carbine sired the 1906 Derby winner Spearmint, and became grandsire of Spion Kop, winner of the Derby in 1920, and great-grandsire of Felstead, winner in 1928.

John Wells, associated with so many of Sir Joseph Hawley's greatest successes, was born at Sutton Coldfield in 1833. He was so small when apprenticed to a trainer called Flintoff in Hednesford that he received the somewhat obvious nickname of 'Tiny'. This he retained for much of his life even when he was exceptionally tall for a jockey and somewhat portly as well, but towards the end of his career he was usually, for some reason history has not disclosed, referred to as 'Brusher'. For some time he was attached to the Danebury stable and thus came to ride that famous mare Virago. As a jockey he was no great stylist, but he suited Sir Joseph because he was capable, obedient, and absolutely honest. His retaining fee from Sir Joseph was only £100 a year, but he was very generously treated in respect of presents whenever he won a good race. He was careful with his money, some of which he invested in a flourishing pen factory at Birmingham, and was comfortably off when he died. He was both vain and eccentric over matters of dress. In his book of reminiscences, Custance described him as follows:

You would see him one day in a tall hat very much turned up at the sides, and the next day he would be wearing a cream coloured one, with a deep black band. On one occasion when he was riding Pero Gomez at exercise on the course at Doncaster on the Tuesday morning before Sir Joseph Hawley's horse won the

St Leger, Wells appeared in an Alpine hat with several feathers, a suit of clothes made from a Gordon plaid, and a pair of red morocco slippers.

'I don't care how he dresses,' the practical Sir Joseph once remarked. 'He's a good enough jockey for me.'

1858: Wednesday, 19 May . . . 200 Entries. £5,575.

SIR J. HAWLEY's br.c. BEADSMAN by Weatherbit out of Mendicant	J. WELLS	1
LORD DERBY's TOXOPHILITE by Longbow	NAT FLATMAN	2
MR HARRISON's THE HADJI by Faugh-a-Ballagh	ALDCROFT	3

Also ran:

Mr Howard's Eclipse (4th) (G. Fordham); Mr Howard's Sudbury (J. Goater); Mr Howard's Carmel (Porter); Sir J. Hawley's Fitz-Roland (Templeman); Mr Crawfurd's East Langton (Hughes); Mr Robinson's Pelissier (Owner); Mr La Mert's Dumfries (French); Captain White's Jordan (Plumb); Mr Sargent's Physician (Kendall); Mr S. Murland's Longrange (S. Rogers); Mr R. Jones's Ditto (Bumby); Mr Higgins's Harry Stanley (Cresswell); Captain Lamotte's King of Sardinia (Pettit); Sir J. B. Mills's colt by Bay Middleton (A. Day); Mr Gratwicke's Deceiver (R. Cotton); Mr Gratwicke's Ethiopian (Ashmall); Mr Saxon's The Ancient Briton (Charlton); Lord Glasgow's Brother to Bird on the Wing (J. Osborne); Mr T. Parr's Kelpie (Bates); Lord Ribblesdale's The Happy Land (Bray).

23 ran.

Betting:

100–30 Toxophilite; 6–1 Eclipse; 8–1 Ethiopian; 10–1 Beadsman; 12–1 Fitz-Roland, The Ancient Briton, and Ditto; 20–1 The Happy Land, Physician, and The Hadji; 25–1 Sudbury, East Langton, and Longrange; 40–1 Jordan and Deceiver; 50–1 Kelpie; 1,000–15 Bird on the Wing's Brother and King of Sardinia; 100–1 the colt by Bay Middleton; 1,000–6 Pelissier.

Won easily by a length; two lengths between second and third.　　　2 m. 54 s.
Winner trained by G. Manning at Cannons Heath.

1859

Sir Joseph Hawley was again successful in 1859, this time with Musjid, a son of New-minister. A brown horse standing fifteen hands three, Musjid had a blood-like head, great length of body, tremendous depth, and a perfect racing temperament. As a yearling he showed singularly little promise, and at the Doncaster Sales failed to reach his modest reserve of 300 guineas. Subsequently, however, Sir Joseph bought him from his breeder Lord Scarborough for £200 with a Derby contingency of £500.

Musjid's two-year-old form was not of a very inspiring character, his solitary success being in the Mottisfont Stakes at Stockbridge. The following spring in a Match at Newmarket over the Ditch Mile he gave a filly of Lord Glasgow's fourteen pounds and beat her by ten lengths. On that form it seems extraordinary that Musjid started a 9–4 favourite for the Derby in a field of thirty, but he had been very highly tried at home, and his owner had backed him to win £75,000.

Musjid's most formidable opponents were reckoned to be The Promised Land, winner of the Two Thousand Guineas and owned in partnership by William Day, who rode him, and a Mr Robinson of High Wycombe; and Trumpeter, owned by the odious Harry Hill and ridden by Alfred Day. The Promised Land came into the straight with a long lead and his rider looking over his shoulder for danger, while Trumpeter seemed to be going the best of the remainder. Musjid at that point was well behind, having received some very rough treatment from a couple of horses, whose riders were later alleged to have been handsomely paid by some bookmakers to do everything that they could to prevent the favourite from winning. In fact it was only by means of some friendly assistance from Fordham and French that Wells was able to extricate Musjid in the straight.

In the last two furlongs Musjid began to make up ground very rapidly indeed, while The Promised Land showed every sign of flagging. From the distance Wells rode Musjid for all he was worth and Musjid, responding in the most gallant manner possible, got up to win close home by half a length from Marionette, with Trumpeter a neck away third and The Promised Land fourth. The first three horses to finish had all been bought as yearlings, the total sum paid for them being well under £1,000.

There were some ugly rumours after the race in which, as usual, members of the

Day family were implicated. It was generally agreed that William Day rode an ill-judged race on The Promised Land, made far too much use of him, and made no attempt to utilize the Two Thousand Guineas winner's speed. It was even hinted that he had deliberately ridden to lose. It was also alleged that William's brother Alfred, who rode Trumpeter, stood to win £30,000 on Mr C. E. Johnstone's Marionette, ridden by Sam Rogers, and it was suggested that while he was holding Trumpeter and yelling to Rogers to go on and win, Musjid swooped down on them and beat them both. It is possible that Alfred Day's explanation that Trumpeter broke down near the finish was correct, but the fact remains that he owned a share in Marionette, and soon after the race he was informed that if he did not at once dispose of all his interests in the horse, he would not be permitted to continue riding.

The Promised Land won the Goodwood Cup and started an odds-on favourite for the St Leger, in which he was ridden by Alfred Day. He ran very badly, and the crowd, disliking his rider's tactics, gave Day a very rough reception when he returned to unsaddle.

Musjid was matched for £2,000 to run against The Promised Land over two miles at Newmarket in October, but Sir Joseph elected to pay forfeit of £500. In fact Musjid never ran again and retired to the stud, firstly at Rufford Abbey, secondly at Benham Park, Newbury, at a fee of twelve guineas, subsequently raised to fifteen. He died in 1865 before he had made his mark.

1859: Wednesday, 1 June . . . 246 Entries. £5,400.

SIR J. HAWLEY's br.c. MUSJID by Newminster
out of Peggy   J. WELLS   1
MR C. E. JOHNSTONE's br.c. MARIONETTE by Touchstone   S. ROGERS   2
MR H. HILL's TRUMPETER by Orlando   A. DAY   3

Also ran:

Mr W. Day's The Promised Land (4th) (W. Day); Lord Chesterfield's Volcano (Ashmall); Sir J. Hawley's Gallus (Cresswell); Captain Gray's Glenbuck (Hammond); Mr Towneley's Ticket of Leave (G. Oates); Mr G. Payne's Harlestone (Charlton); Mr T. Walker's Bankrupt (Aldcroft); Mr Wentworth's Schuloff (Pearl); Baron Rothschild's Magnum (Musgrove); Mr Nichols's Phantom (Templeman); Mr Barratt's Electric (J. Goater); Mr Ford's Polonius (T. Sherwood); Mr Hawkins's Enfield (E. Marlow); Mr C. Capel's Highwayman (J. Mann); Mr Parr's Gaspard (W. Boyce); Sir C. Monck's Gamester (Withington); Mr Towneley's Gladiolus (J. Snowden); Mr Parker's Nimrod (Roe); Lord Dorchester's Reynard (French); Mr A. Worsley's Newcastle (G. Fordham); Mr W. I'Anson's Balnamoon (Kendall);

1859

Mr Saxon's Defender (L. Snowden); Mr J. Osborne's Red Eagle (J. Osborne); Mr C. Peck's Napoleon (Bumby); Mr Merry's Lord of the Manor (Plumb); Mr J. Hawkins's Sir Hercules (E. Sharp); Mr Ferguson's Lovett (Bullock).

30 ran.

Betting:

9–4 Musjid; 7–2 The Promised Land; 4–1 Trumpeter; 15–1 Balnamoon and Newcastle; 20–1 Ticket of Leave; 22–1 Marionette; 25–1 Glenbuck; 33–1 Gamester; 40–1 Phantom and Electric; 50–1 Defender and Volcano; 1,000–15 Harlestone; 1,000–10 Red Eagle, Lovett, Gaspard, Schuloff, Reynard, and Bankrupt; 1,000–8 Napoleon; 1,000–5 Magnum and Lord of the Manor.

Won by half a length; a neck between second and third.   2 m. 59 s.
Winner trained by G. Manning at Cannons Heath.

1860

Mr James Merry, owner of Thormanby, the winner in 1860, was an uncouth, ill-educated, suspicious-minded Scot, whose character was admirably set off by his hard, unfriendly countenance. He inherited a fortune from his father, who was originally an itinerant pedlar, but who had had the wit and good fortune to discover and develop the high iron content that lay in the Ayrshire hills.

Merry's three great loves in order of precedence were money, cock-fighting, and racing. At one time he kept well over a thousand cocks and betted on them shrewdly enough to make his hobby pay. As regards racing, like most men of his type, he had a great many trainers during his lifetime. George Dawson, senior, William I'Anson, Saunders, William Day, Prince, Matthew Dawson, James Waugh, and Robert Peck all had his horses at one time or another, but his greatest period of success was between 1859 and 1870 when Matthew Dawson, a son of George Dawson, senior, was his private trainer at Russley in Wiltshire. That era came to an end when Dawson elected to set up as a public trainer at Newmarket.

Merry's closest associates were Norman Buchanan, a wine merchant, and Tass Parker, a retired prize-fighter. Parker, whose speciality was beating up anyone suspected of touting Merry's horses, was certainly the less odious of the two. Buchanan was a rich man's hanger-on of the most contemptible type, dishonest himself, and constantly implying dishonesty in others. He lived on Merry for years, being an adept in mixing up his own betting accounts with those of his benefactor, but the friendship ended in a sordid dispute over money. This led to Buchanan bringing an action against Merry for the recovery of a sum of money said to be due to him. The case was adjusted out of court, and it was widely believed that although Buchanan's claims were completely false, Merry elected to settle them in part since Buchanan knew far too much about him to make a suitable subject as a witness.

Merry died at his house in Eaton Square in 1877. Needless to say, he was never elected to the Jockey Club. The best that can be said of him is that his horses appeared to be run in a straightforward manner, and for that reason alone his colours were popular enough with the racing public.

Bred by Mr Plummer, Thormanby was by Melbourne or Windhound, almost certainly the latter, out of the famous mare Alice Hawthorn, who won no fewer than fifty-two races and ten gold cups. She was said to have 'an action like a hare and could steal along over the ground with her ears pricked'. By Muley Moloch, she was half-sister to a good horse called The Provost, and also to Annadale, who ran second in the St Leger. She herself was dam of Oulston, probably the best colt of his year and eventually sold for 6,000 guineas. In view of his breeding, it is strange to record that Mr Plummer had considerable difficulty in disposing of Thormanby as a yearling, and several prospective clients had turned the colt down before Matthew Dawson bought him on Mr Merry's behalf for £350. Mr Merry's first opinion of Thormanby was distinctly unfavourable, and with typical meanness he made his trainer keep the colt for several weeks at his own expense before the purchase was ratified.

Thormanby, to use a favourite expression of his trainer's, was made 'to sweat for the brass' as a two-year-old. Low, lengthy, light-fleshed, and with legs like bars of steel, he ran no fewer than fourteen times, winning on nine occasions. He ran twice at Ascot, winning a Biennial Stakes and being beaten in the New Stakes, while he appeared on no fewer than three occasions at the York August Meeting, being third in the Convivial Produce Stakes, and winning the Eglinton and Gimcrack Stakes.

Thormanby's soundness and tough constitution enabled him to stand up to all this hard work without difficulty and the following year he was better than ever. A week before Epsom he was very highly tried by Dawson, who from that moment was convinced that the colt was virtually certain to win. In fact when old John Scott wrote to him from Whitehall to say that he had just tried The Wizard, winner of the Two Thousand Guineas, to be 'a tremendous horse', Dawson laconically replied 'Who's afraid?' The Wizard in fact started favourite at 3–1, Thormanby was at 4–1, while there was a lot of money, too, for the American-bred Umpire, owned by a much-liked American sportsman, Mr Ten Broeck. Mr John Wyatt, owner of a fancied outsider called Nutbourne, objected to Umpire on the grounds that he was not the stipulated age, but the objection was later withdrawn with a very humble apology indeed.

It was generally expected that young Custance was to ride Thormanby, but on the very morning of the race Dawson learned that Merry, without a word to him, had engaged a jockey from Russia called Sharpe to ride his horse. There was a very heated argument in the paddock, but eventually Merry reluctantly agreed that Custance should ride Thormanby, and Sharpe the stable second string, Northern Light.

None of the runners made a better impression than Thormanby as they cantered down to the start. In the words of a contemporary writer: 'His coat was like a mirror, his muscle as developed as that of Heenan at the battle of Farnborough, and when he galloped past the stand, he hardly seemed to touch the ground.'

The pace was only moderate to start with, but Nutbourne and Umpire accelerated after Tattenham Corner and led the field with just under three furlongs to go. A furlong later Nutbourne broke down badly on both forelegs, while Umpire was obviously tiring. At that point The Wizard went to the front, but almost immediately he was challenged by Thormanby, who, after one tap with the whip from Custance, ran on in the most determined fashion to win by a length and a half. Captain Christie's Horror was a moderate third, four lengths behind The Wizard, and Count Lagrange's Dangu, who had run unplaced in the French Derby three days previously, fourth.

Mr Merry won something like £85,000 and an eye-witness declared he had never seen such a sight as Merry and his wife at home the following Monday evening counting up the money and sorting out the cheques. Dawson received a present of £1,000, not an unduly generous reward considering the magnitude of the win and also that at one period he had been obliged to keep the winner at his own expense. The loathsome Buchanan was sent to give Custance £100, a gift that was coupled with an expression of hope that the young man's head would not be turned. According to Custance, that was the only present he ever received from his employer during the three years that he rode for him, although he won many valuable races in Merry's colours and had to waste hard continually to keep his weight down.

Thormanby did not run again until the St Leger, for which he started favourite, but was unplaced behind a very good stayer in St Albans. Probably he was not at his best that autumn, as he met with three further defeats before the season ended. The following summer he did much to restore his reputation by beating St Albans in the Ascot Cup, but after finishing unplaced in the Goodwood Cup, his owner retired him to the stud at Croft, near Darlington, at a fee of thirty guineas. He was the sire of Rouge Rose, dam of the 1880 Derby winner Bend Or, and he also sired Feronia, whose daughter Atalanta was the dam of Ayrshire, winner of the Derby in 1888. His old Derby rival, The Wizard, was only beaten a head in the Goodwood Cup as a four-year-old and ran a very good race in the Cambridgeshire carrying 9 st. 11 lb. He was eventually sold for 4,000 guineas to go to Prussia.

Born at Peterborough in 1841, Harry Custance was having his very first ride in the Derby when he was given the mount on Thormanby. He won the race subsequently on Lord Lyon in 1866, and on George Frederick in 1874. Better educated than most of his fellow jockeys, he was also better conducted and more reliable, having little taste for the company of the less reputable type of bookmaker. He kept the money he made, and on retirement he acted for some time as starter. He is the only man to have ridden in the Derby and to have started it as well, for he despatched the field in 1885, the year that Melton won, in faultless fashion. For a period he owned the

1860

George Inn at Oakham and was very well known and well liked in hunting circles in the Midlands.

1860: Wednesday, 23 May . . . 224 Entries. £6,350.

MR J. MERRY's ch.c. THORMANBY by Melbourne or
   Windhound out of Alice Hawthorn   H. CUSTANCE   1
MR NICHOLS's b.c. THE WIZARD by West Australian
   out of a mare by The Cure   A. FRENCH   2
CAPTAIN CHRISTIE's br.c. HORROR by Wild Dayrell
   out of Sally   CHALONER   3

Also ran:

Count F. de Lagrange's Dangu (4th) (J. Quinton); Lord Palmerston's Mainstone (S. Rogers); Mr I'Anson's Cramond (Robertson); Mr Tate's The Drone (G. Fordham); Mr Wyatt's Nutbourne (D. Hughes); Mr H. Harland's Sutton (J. Osborne); Lord Stamford's Bentinck (A. Edwards); Lord Strathmore's Leprochaun (Covey); Mr T. Dawson's Sir William (Bullock); Baron Rothschild's Restes (Charlton); Lord Derby's Cape Flyaway (Clement); Mr Howard's The Rap (W. Boyce); Mr Gibbs's Wallace (E. Sharp); Mr Heslop's The Tiger (J. Snowden); Captain Little's Man at Arms (Perry); Lord Portsmouth's Buccaneer (J. Goater); Lord Glasgow's Tom Bowline (Aldcroft); Lord Zetland's Lanchester (Marchant); Sir C. Monck's Vesta (Hibberd); Mr Ten Broeck's Umpire (L. Snowden); Mr Merry's Northern Light (J. Sharp); Sir J. Hawley's Loiterer (Wells); Sir J. Hawley's Largesse (Payter); Mr Crawfurd's Winton (Norman); Mr Copperthwaite's The Rising Sun (J. Mann); Mr Gratwicke's Ebony (D. Plum); Mr Jaques's High Treason (Withington).

30 ran.

Betting:

3–1 The Wizard; 4–1 Thormanby; 6–1 Umpire; 7–1 Nutbourne; 100–6 Buccaneer; 25–1 Horror and High Treason; 30–1 Restes; 40–1 The Drone, Mainstone, and Cramond; 50–1 Wallace and Tom Bowline; 1,000–15 Lanchester and Sutton; 1,000–10 Loiterer; 1,000–5 Dangu.

Won by a length and a half; four lengths between second and third.   2 m. 55 s. Winner trained by M. Dawson at Russley.

1861

Mr Merry very nearly won the Derby again in 1861, this time with Dundee, a son of his Two Thousand Guineas winner Lord of the Isles. Bought for 170 guineas as a yearling, Dundee won six of his seven races as a two-year-old, his only defeat being first time out at Liverpool. His great weakness, though, was the fact that he was extremely straight in front. A week before the Derby his legs were causing considerable anxiety, but as he had been heavily backed by his owner and the public, it was decided to run him and hope for the best. One of his legs 'went' early in the straight, but he ran on with superb courage and looked all over a winner till about a hundred yards from the winning post when he broke down on the other foreleg and Kettledrum beat him by a length. The suspensory ligament of his near foreleg had gone so badly that the fetlock touched the ground and it was with the greatest difficulty that he returned to his box at Sherwood's. Needless to say he never ran again.

Kettledrum was owned by Colonel Towneley, a member of an old north-country Catholic family that still flourishes in Lancashire today. Born in 1803, Colonel Towneley married a daughter of Lord Sefton and when a young man he had a few horses in training with John Scott. For a time he gave up racing and concentrated on breeding short-horns, but later, with his estate agent Mr Eastwood as his partner, he took to the Turf once again. He was not long in meeting with success for in 1860 Butterfly, running in Mr Eastwood's name, won the Oaks.

Oates, Colonel Towneley's trainer, had narrowly missed buying some very good horses. He had very much wanted to acquire Thormanby, had bid for Musjid, and would certainly have bought Caller Ou, who won the St Leger, from Mr I'Anson, if Mrs I'Anson and her daughters had not put their combined feet down firmly when they heard of the impending transaction. Furthermore, having bought Kettledrum as a yearling for 400 guineas, Oates did his level best to persuade his patrons to buy the very next yearling offered, which happened in fact to be Dundee.

Bred by Mr Cookson at Croft, near Darlington, Kettledrum was a big slashing colt, rather too heavily topped for some people's taste, by Rataplan, full brother to Stockwell, out of Hybla, by The Provost. Mr Cookson's aim in breeding was that the sire should return to the dam the best strain in her pedigree. Hybla, therefore, required the Whalebone cross that Rataplan was able to provide.

Kettledrum was a delicate feeder and took plenty of time to develop his strength.

He was still only half trained when he made a winning first appearance at York in August, but he was beaten in another race that week and ran indifferently in September in the Champagne Stakes at Doncaster. The following spring he had trouble with his teeth, and he was still by no means at his best when second in the Two Thousand Guineas to Diophantus, with the favourite, John Scott's Klarikoff, third. After that race he was sent to Prince's stable at Lambourn, but remained under the supervision and control of Oates.

Dundee started a slightly better favourite for the Derby than Diophantus, who had won the Two Thousand Guineas with considerable ease, while there was plenty of money for Klarikoff, whose Guineas running was thought to be all wrong and for a half share of whom Lord St Vincent had just paid 5,000 guineas. Dictator, a strong but rather coarse-looking north-country colt, was also well fancied, and there was plenty of money for Kettledrum at 12–1.

The start of the race was regrettable to say the least. Mr McGeorge, harassed and hemmed in by part of the enormous crowd, lost his head and dropped his flag while Klarikoff, Rouge Dragon, and Lopcatcher were a good thirty yards behind the others and as Lupus was actually walking back. After a furlong, these four were the best part of a hundred yards behind the others, but by the time the top of the hill had been reached, Klarikoff had raced up second. There can be little doubt that his rider George Fordham was sadly at fault in making his ground up quite so quickly.

Approaching Tattenham Corner Diophantus was in front 'with his head in the air and his mouth wide open', while Klarikoff, soon fated to be burnt to death in his box, Aurelian, and Kettledrum were all close up. In the straight they were joined by Dundee, who faltered a little as the first leg went, but responded gallantly when Custance gave him a couple of taps with the whip. At the distance Dundee was two lengths in front of Kettledrum, but inside the final furlong the other leg gave out and he was unable to withstand the powerful challenge of Kettledrum, who won by a length. Diophantus was third, only a head behind Dundee, and Aurelian, some lengths behind the first three horses, fourth. Colonel Towneley, who won £2,000 on the race, a large sum for him, was the first to admit that Kettledrum would never have won if Dundee had been able to keep going till the finish.

Kettledrum had been a little bit off colour before the St Leger for which he started favourite at 6–4. In a desperate finish he lost by a head to Mr I'Anson's filly Caller Ou, whom he had so nearly purchased as a yearling. Caller Ou, a 66–1 chance, had been offered to Lord Stamford for £1,500 the evening before the race. Two days later Kettledrum was pulled out again for the Doncaster Cup, in which he dead-heated with the Oaks winner Brown Duchess, to whom he conceded sixteen pounds.

These two hard races so close together, when not entirely at his best, finished him and he never ran again. He retired to his owner's stud at Clitheroe, Lancashire, at a fee of thirty guineas and was sire of Hampton's dam, Lady Langden. Hampton was Champion Sire himself and founded the sire line which includes Gainsborough, Son-in-Law, and Hyperion. Kettledrum's stud career was not a distinguished one, and he was sold to Sir T. B. Lennard in 1870 for 550 guineas.

Bullock, who rode Kettledrum at Epsom, was still in his early twenties when he died from a growth in his throat in 1863. Born at Morpeth, he was a decent and honest young man who rode chiefly for stables in the north. A contemporary writer described him as 'not only a very first rate jockey, in the saddle, but his conduct out of it was beyond all reproach, for he had none of the impertinent familiarity about him that characterizes so many jockeys of the present day'. His nephew, W. Bullock, won the Derby on Signorinetta in 1908.

Before leaving Kettledrum's Derby for good, it must be said that there was considerable trouble after it. Firstly, as was only to be expected, there was a good deal of resentment at the indifferent start, and a spirited debate took place in the Press on McGeorge's fitness for his office. Secondly, it was generally agreed that the course was in a deplorable condition, ill-tended and with broken glass and other debris scattered over it in abundance.

1861: Wednesday, 29 May . . . 236 Entries. £6,350.

COLONEL TOWNELEY's ch.c. KETTLEDRUM by Rataplan
out of Hybla   BULLOCK   1
MR J. MERRY's b.c. DUNDEE by Lord of the Isles
out of Marmalade   CUSTANCE   2
LORD STAMFORD's ch.c. DIOPHANTUS by Orlando
out of Equation   A. EDWARDS   3

Also ran:

Mr Hamilton's Aurelian (4th) (J. Goater); Lord Stamford's Imaus (A. French); Count F. de Lagrange's Royallieu (H. Grimshaw); Mr Merry's Russley (Withington); Mr Mann's Seven Dials (Sopp); Mr Thomas's Dictator (J. Osborne); Lord Glasgow's The Drake (Aldcroft); Colonel Towneley's Yorkminster (J. Snowden); Sir C. Monck's Gardener (D. Hughes); Sir J. Hawley's Rouge Dragon (Wells); Mr T. Parr's Kildonan (Clement); Mr Henry's Klarikoff (G. Fordham); Lord Lincoln's Lupus (A. Day); Mr Penton's Atherstone (S. Rogers); Mr J. Osborne's Lopcatcher (Chaloner).

18 ran.

Betting:

3–1 Dundee; 4–1 Diophantus; 6–1 Dictator; 7–1 Klarikoff; 12–1 Kildonan; 14–1 Rouge Dragon; 16–1 Kettledrum; 20–1 Royallieu; 25–1 The Drake; 40–1 Yorkminster; 1,000–15 Atherstone and Aurelian.

Won by a length; a head between second and third. 2 m. 45 s.
Winner trained by Oates at Lambourn.

1862

Bell's Life used to publish a set of verses every year a day or two before the Derby was run. In 1862 one of the verses ran as follows:

> And if, of the outsiders there,
> Just one should pass the winning chair,
> Enrolled in the successful three,
> Be sure Caractacus is he.

The author was a better tipster than he was poet, for Caractacus duly won at 40–1.

Caractacus was by Kingston out of Defenceless, by Defence. Bred at Mr Blenkiron's Middle Park Stud, he was bought as a yearling by William Day for 250 guineas on behalf of Mr Snewing, a prosperous publican from the Tottenham Court Road. The colt remained with Day until the spring of 1861, but was then removed to be trained at Harpenden, Hertfordshire, by a man called Zachary. In fact the person largely responsible for Caractacus's preparation was a certain Mr Bob Smith, who managed Snewing's racing affairs.

As a two-year-old Caractacus ran three times in moderate company without success. His Derby preparation the following year was unorthodox to say the least. First of all he was beaten a head in the Great Metropolitan at Epsom, receiving thirty-three pounds from the winner. He evidently made a good impression as Mr Snewing was at once offered £3,000 for his colt. He refused without hesitation, adding that his price was £10,000 and an annuity of £100 for his trainers! Caractacus was then unplaced in the Chester Cup, third in the two-mile Great Northern Handicap at York, and finally won the two-mile Somersetshire Stakes at Bath. This last victory was watched by Sir John Astley, who at once backed Caractacus for the Derby at long odds, thereby gaining for himself a brief and unaccustomed period of financial stability.

Caractacus thus had four races over two miles or more before Epsom, as well as some searching gallops on Harpenden racecourse. He thrived on the treatment, however, and an observer who described him as 'a short-legged, powerful, trussy horse', stated that he came out 'big and above himself for the Derby'.

Public interest in Caractacus as a possible winner was lessened by the fact that

Mr Snewing had an interest in another Derby candidate, Spite, to whom Goater, who had been retained by Mr Snewing and given the choice of mounts, decided to pin his faith, a decision he must have later regretted since he had been promised an annuity of £100 if he won the race. Caractacus, rejected by Goater, was partnered by a sixteen-year-old stable lad called Parsons, who knew the colt well but had little experience of race-riding. Parsons was not informed of his good fortune immediately, but was merely told that he was wanted to ride in a trial and was to increase his weight by eating as much as he could.

The field numbered thirty-four, a new record for the race. The favourite was the Two Thousand Guineas winner The Marquis, a 5–2 chance trained by John Scott, while almost equally backed was Buckstone, a Voltigeur colt, owned by Mr Merry. Unfortunately Mr McGeorge again made a nonsense of the start. There had been three false starts and he himself, together with the bulk of the field, was standing well in advance of the starting-point with only three or four horses in the correct position. To the general amazement he proceeded to drop his flag and away they went. One of the horses left belonged to Lord Stamford, who complained to the Stewards. McGeorge received a severe reprimand and was informed that any repetition of his conduct would lead to instant dismissal.

At Tattenham Corner Brighton, Nottingham, and The Marquis were the leaders with Caractacus and Buckstone not far behind. Caractacus, still on a tight rein, struck the front with just over two furlongs to go, and ridden with wonderful coolness and assurance by Parsons, withstood a very strong challenge from the distance by The Marquis and won by a neck. Buckstone was third, a length and a half away, and Neptunus fourth. Spite broke down and had to be pulled up. Mr Snewing won £20,000 and entertained the poor of Watford to a gigantic fête, at which many clergymen of the district were present to lend a hand. Mr Bob Smith was a big winner, too, but before long his gains were returned to the bookmakers with interest. Parsons retired into obscurity. Years later he was seen, middle-aged and shabby, leading a yearling round the sale ring at Newmarket.

Caractacus broke down in his final St Leger gallop and never ran again. He was retired to the stud at Highfield Paddocks, St Albans, at a fee of twenty guineas. The Marquis beat Buckstone by a head in the St Leger, and the following year Buckstone won the Ascot Cup after first dead-heating with Tim Whiffler.

This year the conditions for the Derby, unchanged since 1807, were altered. The weight for colts was raised from 8 st. 7 lb. to 8 st. 10 lb., and the weight for fillies from 8 st. 2 lb. to 8 st. 5 lb.

1862

1862: Wednesday, 4 June . . . 233 Entries. £6,675.

MR SNEWING's b.c. CARACTACUS by Kingston
  out of Defenceless   J. PARSONS   1
MR S. HAWKE's b.c. THE MARQUIS by Stockwell
  out of Cinizelli   ASHMALL   2
MR J. MERRY's br.c. BUCKSTONE by Voltigeur
  out of Burlesque   H. GRIMSHAW   3

Also ran:

Mr Jackson's Neptunus (4th) (Bullock); Lord Glasgow's colt by Stockwell (Aldcroft); Lord Glasgow's colt by Barbatus out of Clarissa (Basham); Lord Glasgow's colt by Barbatus out of Brown Bess (Withington); Mr Merry's The Knave (Lynch); Mr Savile's Harlequin (W. Cotton); Sir J. Hawley's Argonaut (Wells); Sir J. Hawley's St Alexis (S. Rogers); Mr Angell's Lord Burleigh (Chaloner); Lord Chesterfield's colt by Voltigeur (J. Mann); Mr Coleman's Surrey (J. Reeves); Mr Elphinstone's Maharajah (Brewty); Lord Stamford's Ensign (A. Edwards); Baron Rothschild's Norroy (E. Sharp); Mr Bevill's Alvediston (Mr W. Bevill); Duke of Beaufort's Gemse (Salter); Mr Parr's Star of the West (C. Marlow); Mr Parr's Tolurno (Clement); Lord Annesley's Ace of Clubs (W. Boyce); Mr Goater's Spite (J. Goater); Mr Henry's Malek (G. Fordham); Mr Sutton's Nottingham (A. Day); Mr Ward's Ellangowan (Keeler); Mr Bowes's Welcome (Custance); Lord St Vincent's Schehallion (Hibberd); Lord Coventry's Exchequer (J. Adams); Mr South's Michel Grove (T. Clay); Lord Fitzwilliam's Vanguard (Norman); Mr Osborne's Zetland (J. Osborne); Mr Gratwicke's Ashford (H. Bell); Mr Thomas's Brighton (Hughes).

34 ran.

Betting:

5–2 The Marquis; 100–30 Buckstone; 7–1 Neptunus; 12–1 Argonaut and Zetland; 100–6 the Stockwell colt; 20–1 St Alexis; 25–1 Ensign; 100–3 Ace of Clubs; 40–1 Caractacus; 50–1 Harlequin, Spite, Nottingham, and Lord Burleigh; 200–3 the Clarissa colt; 100–1 Star of the West, Tolurno, Malek, Alvediston, the Brown Bess colt, Gemse, Surrey, and the Voltigeur colt; 1,000–5 Norroy, The Knave, Welcome, Ellangowan, Schehallion, Exchequer, and Ashford.

Won by a neck; a length and a half between second and third.   2 m. 45½ s.
Winner trained by Zachary at Harpenden.

1863

Macaroni, winner of the Derby in 1863, was bred by the Marquis of Westminster at Eaton and was by Sweetmeat out of Jocose, by Pantaloon. Sweetmeat, bought as a foal for twenty guineas, was unbeaten as a three-year-old and might well have won the Derby had he been entered. He was the sire not only of Macaroni, but of Mincemeat and Mincepie, both winners of the Oaks, and of Parmesan, sire of the Derby winners Favonius and Cremorne. He was exported to Germany in 1861, but died in Hamburg from injuries received on the voyage.

In 1861 there was an epidemic of strangles at Eaton. Six yearlings were badly affected and took so long to recover that it was decided to sell them as soon as it was possible to do so. A few miles from Eaton Mr R. C. Naylor, a former Liverpool banker who had inherited a fortune from a maternal uncle, had recently founded a stud at Hooton Park. His stud-groom Griffiths was a friend of the stud-groom at Eaton, who suggested that Mr Naylor might care to buy the yearlings. Mr Naylor agreed to the proposal and bought the six for approximately £700, a wonderful bargain for the buyer, as five of the six, which included Macaroni, won races, the sixth having died before it had a chance to prove its merits.

Carnival was at first thought to be the pick of the batch. As a two-year-old he was tried seven pounds better than Macaroni in the spring and then won the Mostyn Stakes at Chester. Macaroni's first appearance was at Newmarket in the autumn. He had been slightly amiss and was defeated by his solitary opponent in a race over the Abingdon Mile. During the winter there was considerable public support for Carnival for the Derby, but Mr Naylor was convinced that Macaroni was the better prospect and backed him at very long odds to win the best part of £100,000.

As a three-year-old Macaroni soon showed that his owner's high opinion of him was justified. He won a Sweepstakes over a mile at the Craven Meeting and then won the Two Thousand Guineas, starting at 10–1, by half a length from Lord Strathmore's Saccharometer. Despite this victory, he started at 10–1 for the Derby, the favourite for which was Lord St Vincent's Lord Clifden, winner of the Woodcote Stakes at Epsom and the Champagne Stakes at Doncaster the previous year.

Bred by Mr Hind, Lord Clifden, who was by Newminster, had been sold as a two-year-old to Captain Christie for £4,000 and a Derby contingency of £1,000. Soon afterwards Captain Christie re-sold him to Lord St Vincent, whose connexion with

1863

the Turf cost him a great deal of money, for £5,000 and a contingency of £2,000. After wintering at Lord St Vincent's place at Canterbury, Lord Clifden was sent for his Derby preparation to Telscombe, just outside Lewes. There an attempt was made to 'get at' him, some villain digging holes in the gallops and filling them up with flints. Luckily the trap was discovered before any harm could be done.

From the weather point of view it was an appalling Derby. The rain fell in torrents and the attendance was very much smaller than usual. The Prince of Wales paid his first visit to the race and was given a tumultuous reception. Possibly his subsequent love of racing and of the atmosphere of the racecourse was stimulated by the spontaneous warmth of his greeting, just as Queen Victoria's coldness towards the sport may well have been influenced by the unflattering way in which the Epsom crowd had received her in 1840.

Mr McGeorge, after the previous year's fiasco, was determined that everything should be carried out in accordance with regulations. No doubt, as the rain teemed down, the spectators wished he was rather less meticulous, as there were no fewer than thirty-four false starts, largely caused by the intractable behaviour of Tambour Major, who was eventually left.

From the final bend it was a thrilling duel between Lord Clifden and Macaroni. For most of the way Lord Clifden was a neck in front, but in the final furlong Chaloner asked Macaroni for one supreme effort, and Macaroni responded in the most gallant fashion possible. With less than fifty yards to go Fordham on the favourite had to transfer his whip from his right hand to his left and Lord Clifden faltered for a couple of strides. This was Macaroni's opportunity and as the pair swept past the post, it was Macaroni's head that was an inch or two in front. Only half a length behind Lord Clifden was Lord Glasgow's Rapid Rhone, who might well have won had he not been twice baulked of an opening. Among the unplaced horses was Mr Savile's Ranger, who a few days later went to Paris and won the newly instituted Grand Prix. There was a nasty accident coming down the hill to Tattenham Corner when Saccharometer fell, brought down King of the Vale, and seriously interfered with Fantastic.

The victory of Macaroni was received with a peal of bells at All Saints Church, Newmarket. This celebration had been arranged with the vicar by Macaroni's trainer, Godding. If there was one thing that Godding, who lived just by All Saints, really disliked it was church bells, and to spare his feelings the vicar had them rung as seldom as possible. Godding, therefore, felt it was only fair to give the vicar the opportunity of a peal, especially as he himself would be at Epsom and far out of hearing. A subsequent vicar of All Saints was less accommodating with the bells and nearly drove the unfortunate Godding out of his mind.

Lord St Vincent was very hard hit and later became involved with the unscrupulous moneylender, Padwick. Fordham took the favourite's defeat very much to heart, and when Mr Oldaker, Clerk of the Course at Harpenden, remarked in the hearing of Fordham, whom he had not recognized, that Lord Clifden had been deliberately pulled, Fordham threw him into a furze bush and proceeded to beat him severely. The scene has been vividly described by Mr Hodgman in his book *Sixty Years on the Turf*, but it is difficult to believe that Oldaker, while being thrashed in a bed of prickles, really shouted to Fordham: 'Cheese it! Here, sir, you cheese it!'

After the Derby Macaroni won the Drawing Room Stakes at Goodwood, the York Cup, and the Doncaster Cup. He did not run in the St Leger and at the end of the season he retired to the Hooton Park Stud at a fee of thirty guineas. He proved outstanding as a sire of brood mares, and his mares 'nicked' in remarkably successful manner with Bend Or. Mated to Macaroni mares, Bend Or sired the Triple Crown winner Ormonde and his sister Ornament, dam of Sceptre, winner of every classic bar the Derby; Martagon, winner of the Goodwood Cup; Kendal, sire of the Triple Crown winner Galtee More and of Tredennis; Bonavista, winner of the Two Thousand Guineas and sire of Cyllene; Medora, dam of the Ascot colt Gold Cup winner Zinfandel; and Doremi, grand-dam of Teddy.

Lord Clifden failed in the Grand Prix but won the St Leger. As a four-year-old he lost his form completely and failed to win a race. He retired to the stud at Moorlands Farm near York, his most distinguished son being Hampton, who became Champion Sire, sired three Derby winners, Merry Hampton, Ayrshire, and Ladas, and founded the Hampton male line of which Hyperion is perhaps the most notable member in modern times. Lord Clifden died in 1875, twelve years before Macaroni.

Tom Chaloner, who rode Macaroni in both his classic successes, had learnt much of his skill from John Osborne, senior at Middleham. He only rode one Derby winner, but was successful five times in the St Leger and three times in the Two Thousand Guineas. He had the reputation of being not only a first-class jockey, but a quiet, honest, reliable, and unassuming man.

1863: Wednesday, 20 May . . . 255 Entries. £7,100.

MR R. C. NAYLOR'S b.c. MACARONI by Sweetmeat
  out of Jocose   T. CHALONER   I
LORD ST VINCENT'S b.c. LORD CLIFDEN by Newminster
  out of The Slave   G. FORDHAM   2
LORD GLASGOW'S ro.c. RAPID RHONE
  by Young Melbourne out of a mare by Lanercost   DOYLE   3

Also ran:

Captain D. Lane's Blue Mantle (4th) (Lynch); Lord Glasgow's colt by Young Melbourne (Withington); Lord Glasgow's Clarior (Aldcroft); Mr J. Bowes's Early Purl (Ashmall); Mr H. J. Smith's Avondale (J. Mann); Mr Sale's Safeguard (H. Covey); Mr Naylor's Aggressor (Perry); Mr H. Savile's The Ranger (J. Goater); Mr G. Bryan's Fantastic (Custance); Lord Palmerston's Baldwin (G. Gray); Count Batthyany's Tambour Major (Wells); Sir F. Johnstone's The Ghillie (J. Adams); Lord Durham's Michael Scott (W. Boyce); Lord Strathmore's Saccharometer (D. Hughes); Lord Stamford's Onesander (A. Edwards); Mr Whitaker's King of Utopia (H. Grimshaw); Count F. Lagrange's Hospodar (A. Watkins); Count F. Lagrange's Jarnicoton (Hunter); Count Henekel's Giles the First (E. Sharp); Baron Rothschild's King of the Vale (Daley); Mr E. Brayley's Tom Fool (A. Cowley); Mr J. Gilby's Donnybrook (S. Rogers); Mr Beaumont's Golden Pledge (J. Osborne); Mr Cartwright's Scamander (Drew); Mr Wall's National Guard (E. Harrison); Mr Elphinstone's Trojanus (Midgeley); Mr Capel's Bright Cloud (Reeves).

31 ran.

Betting:

4–1 Lord Clifden; 9–1 Hospodar and The Ghillie; 10–1 Macaroni and Saccharometer; 13–1 King of the Vale; 100–7 Fantastic; 20–1 Scamander and National Guard; 25–1 Tom Fool; 40–1 Early Purl; 50–1 Baldwin, Blue Mantle, King of Utopia, Avondale, Golden Pledge, and Lord Glasgow's lot; 1,000–10 Onesander and Trojanus.

Won by a head; half a length between second and third.   2 m. 50½ s.
Winner trained by Godding at Newmarket.

1864

Blair Athol, winner in 1864, was certainly bred to be a champion, being by that mighty sire Stockwell out of the immortal Blink Bonny, winner of the Derby and the Oaks in 1857. A handsome, rangy chesnut with a white face and a flaxen tail—he was commonly known as 'the bald-faced chesnut'—Blair Athol was bred at Malton by Mr William I'Anson, who subsequently sold a share in him to Captain Cornish. The colt was slow to come to hand and never ran as a two-year-old. He did sufficient in his work at home, though, to show that he was something out of the ordinary and I'Anson had no compunction in refusing a bid of 4,000 guineas from an overseas buyer, as well as one of 7,000 guineas from John Jackson, the bookmaker. Jackson reckoned that for his offer to be refused, Blair Athol must be of quite exceptional merit and backed him forthwith for the Derby to win a very large stake indeed, an action that proved of the utmost significance the subsequent year.

In his early three-year-old days Blair Athol, like his dam, suffered from tooth trouble and was unable to feed properly. No sooner had this trouble been cleared up than he developed an intermittent lameness, the source of which completely baffled the vets. Luckily Mr Colpitts, a close friend of I'Anson, overheard a conversation in the barber's shop at Malton and thereby ascertained that Blair Athol's lad had been suborned to prevent the colt from running in the Derby and was in the habit of kicking him savagely from time to time in the genitals. Mr Colpitts at once informed I'Anson, who extracted a confession from the culprit, gave him a tremendous thrashing, and kicked him out of the yard.

Nor was that the final worry. A number of leading bookmakers had backed Lord Glasgow's General Peel, winner of the Two Thousand Guineas, very heavily indeed for the Derby and wished to exert their influence to prevent Blair Athol from running at Epsom and to back him for the St Leger instead. A conference of those involved was held, and despite the opposition of Steel and Hargreaves, Jackson's determination that Blair Athol should run just carried the day.

Blair Athol, therefore, had never seen a racecourse before the Derby. Nevertheless he was well supported at 14–1, and the officers of two cavalry regiments had combined to back him to win some £23,000. The bulk of the public money, though, was for General Peel and Mr Merry's candidate Scottish Chief. One tipster selected Blair Athol, whose claims he advocated in the following verse:

In short, if you'd summer in clover
And send to the devil the Jews
Believe me, the Derby is over,
Blair Athol can't possibly lose!

The day was fine and the crowd enormous. There were eight false starts and Blair Athol, who had been saddled at Tattenham Corner and led down to the start by Caller Ou, was one of those badly away. His Yorkshire jockey Jim Snowden, however, was in no particular hurry to make up the lost ground and delayed his effort till well on up the straight, at which point General Peel was being shouted home as the winner. When Snowden really got down to business—and he used his spurs on Blair Athol with little restraint—the big chestnut began to make up ground rapidly and overtook General Peel inside the distance to win by a clear two lengths with Scottish Chief a further three lengths away third. All Yorkshire supported the winner: Jackson won the best part of £40,000 and I'Anson £15,000.

Jim Snowden was a fine rider at his best and excelled at waiting tactics. Although a genial weakness for wine and women sometimes hampered his career, his ready wit and thoroughly likeable personality made him a great favourite with the racing public in the north. 'Take those blinkers off, boy,' he once remarked to the lad leading round an old plater he was just going to ride. 'It's bad enough to have a blind jockey without having a blind horse as well.'

At the end of Epsom week Blair Athol was sent to run in the Grand Prix at Longchamps, but a rough and tiring journey coupled with his strenuous exertions at Epsom resulted in his defeat by Vermont and the Oaks winner Fille de l'Air. In addition, Tom Chaloner, who rode him, Snowden for some reason being unavailable, was not a little intimidated by the open hostility shown to Blair Athol and his rider by the French crowd, which was violently anglophobe at this period.

Blair Athol won a Triennial at Ascot and the Gratwicke Stakes at Goodwood, but at York he was beaten by a three-year-old called The Miner, to whom he conceded seven pounds. The Miner, owned by the Rev. J. W. King, the rector of Basingham, was no match for Blair Athol in the St Leger, 'the bald-faced chestnut' winning very comfortably from General Peel with Cambuscan third. The race was run almost in darkness owing to an impending storm, and in the gloom Blair Athol was struck into by another competitor just as he was pulling up. He suffered an injury to a tendon, and although he seemed to recover, he completely lost his action and it was found impossible to race him again. I'Anson thereupon sold a two-thirds share in the horse to Jackson, retaining the remainder for himself. When Blair Athol left Malton, the route to Jackson's stud at York was lined by cheering spectators, who gave the gallant chestnut a reception a king might have envied.

1864

In 1868 Jackson, his health undermined by over-indulgence of every description, was a dying man and he decided to sell off his stud. Blair Athol was bought for 5,000 guineas by Mr Blenkiron of the Middle Park Stud, but in 1871 Mr Blenkiron himself died and Blair Athol came under the hammer once again. This time he was bought on behalf of the Cobham Stud Company for 12,500 guineas. It was assumed at first that he had been purchased by one of the many overseas buyers who were present, and when it was announced that he was to remain in England, there was a tumultuous outburst of cheering.

While at Cobham Blair Athol on four occasions headed the list of winning sires. After his son Silvio had won the Derby and the St Leger for Lord Falmouth, his fee was raised from 100 to 200 guineas. Lord Falmouth and nearly every other leading breeder considered that the fee demanded was exorbitant and unreasonable. Blair Athol, in consequence, was more or less boycotted and not unnaturally his record soon began to suffer most noticeably. In an attempt to redeem the situation, his fee was lowered to seventy-five guineas, but he never recovered his position. In 1879 the Cobham Stud was in financial difficulties and had to be dispersed; Blair Athol was sold for 4,500 guineas and was sent to the nearby Pound Stud where he died in 1882.

The year 1864 was the last in which the owner whose horse had won the Derby was compelled to contribute towards the cost of the police at Epsom, as well as towards the fee that was paid to the Judge.

1864: Wednesday, 25 May . . . 234 Entries. £6,450.

MR W. I'ANSON'S ch.c. BLAIR ATHOL by Stockwell
out of Blink Bonny   J. SNOWDEN   1
LORD GLASGOW'S b.c. GENERAL PEEL
by Young Melbourne out of a mare by Orlando   ALDCROFT   2
MR MERRY'S b.c. SCOTTISH CHIEF by Lord of the Isles
out of Miss Ann   J. ADAMS   3

Also ran:

Captain A. Cooper's Knight of Snowdon (4th) (F. Adams); Mr Bowes's Baragha (Ashmall); Lord Falmouth's Hollyfox (T. French); Lord Glasgow's Strafford (Doyle); Mr John Day's Master Richard (Deacon); Captain Christie's Warrior (J. Grimshaw); Mr W. Hudson's Cathedral (Whiteley); Mr Eastwood's Surat (Buck); Mr W. G. Craven's Planet (Morgan); Mr Ten Broeck's Paris (Fordham); Mr H. Hill's Copenhagen (S. Rogers); Mr H. Hill's Ackworth (Rogers); Mr E. Brayley's Outlaw (A. Cowley); Mr Cartwright's Ely (Custance); Lord Westmorland's Signalman (S. Adams); Lord Westmorland's Birch Broom (J. Goater);

Mr W. Steward's The Major (H. Grimshaw); Captain J. White's Cambuscan (J. Mann); Sir J. Hawley's Washington (Wells); Mr Naylor's Appenine (A. French); Mr Naylor's Coast-Guard (Chaloner); Mr Savile's Privateer (E. Sharp); Sir F. Johnstone's Historian (Daley); Mr Cathcart's Prince Arthur (J. Osborne); Mr A. H. Baily's Dormouse (W. Boyce); Mr Hodgman's Valiant (Perry); Mr J. Starky's Izaak Walton (H. Sopp).

30 ran.

Betting :

9–2 Scottish Chief and General Peel; 11–2 Birch Broom; 6–1 Cambuscan; 13–1 Paris; 14–1 Blair Athol; 16–1 Ely; 20–1 Coast-Guard; 25–1 Ackworth; 28–1 Valiant; 100–3 Baragah; 40–1 Strafford and Historian; 50–1 Hollyfox; 100–1 Copenhagen; 200–1 Washington.

Won by two lengths; three lengths between second and third.　　　2 m. 43 s.
Winner trained by Mr I'Anson at Malton.

1865

In modern times we have become inured to defeat, even humiliation, in every branch of international sport, and there is something almost pathetic in our elation that our chosen representatives are successful. Even on the Turf we have been hard put to it to hold our own, and since 1946 a distressingly high percentage of our most coveted races has been won by horses bred in France, the United States, or Italy.

A hundred years ago the situation was very different. Not only did Britannia rule the waves, but English supremacy in the sphere of sport was unchallenged, the easy-going contempt with which the average Englishman regarded every foreigner being extended to the foreigner's horses as well. The victory of the French colt Gladiateur, therefore, in the 1865 Derby came as a painful shock to national pride and prestige, and as such it gave immense pleasure to thousands of Frenchmen, who rejoiced in the discomfiture of the haughty, self-satisfied inhabitants of 'Perfide Albion'. Not for nothing was Gladiateur nicknamed 'The Avenger of Waterloo'.

Count F. de Lagrange, owner and breeder of Gladiateur, was born in 1816, and inherited a considerable fortune from his father, one of Napoleon's generals. His interest in the Turf was encouraged by Lord Pembroke, who was then living in Paris, and in 1855 he bought M. Aumont's stud of twenty-eight horses for £11,200. A racing partnership with Baron Nivière ended in 1863, but there is no foundation for the supposition that Baron Nivière's place was taken by Napoleon III.

When the Franco-Prussian war broke out, the Count sent the whole of his stud to England on a three-year lease to M. Lefevre. His estate in Normandy was occupied by the invading Prussians, who emptied his cellars and subjected him to personal humiliation. He resumed his racing career in 1874 and had a particularly good season in 1879. Soon after that, however, he began to suffer severely from attacks of gout and his racing interests had been greatly reduced when he died in 1883, leaving behind him, in the words of a contemporary writer, 'the reputation of a model French gentleman, an intellectual companion, a genuine sportsman, and a perfect host'.

The Count's horses in England were trained by Tom Jennings, those in France by Charles Pratt. His first English classic success was with Fille de l'Air in the Oaks in 1864. In 1876 his filly Camelia won the One Thousand Guineas and dead-heated for the Oaks, while he won the Two Thousand Guineas with Chamant in 1876 and the St Leger with Rayon d'Or in 1879. Fille de l'Air had run deplorably when favourite for the Two Thousand Guineas and her victory at Epsom caused an ugly demonstration which nearly deteriorated into a serious riot. It was at a banquet after Epsom in 1864 that Admiral Rous warned English owners and breeders of the challenge that in future they would have to face from France: 'Our French neighbours are difficult to beat at any game. By clever investments they have secured our best blood. Look to your laurels, gentlemen! They have gone "bang up your heads".'

Among the horses bought from M. Aumont was Monarque, a four-year-old that in due course became an outstanding success at the stud. Monarque was described as by The Baron or Sting or The Emperor. The credit is usually given to The Emperor, a son of Defence and a grandson of Whalebone that was imported into France in 1850 and died the following year. Gladiateur was by Monarque out of Miss Gladiator, by Gladiator. He started life badly by being trodden on as a foal in the paddock. This mishap left him with an unsightly enlargement on a point of his off foreleg. When he went into training, the vet advised the Count to have him fired, but Tom Jennings expressed strong disagreement and in the end nothing was done. Gladiateur in fact was intermittently lame throughout his racing career, but that was due to navicular. His dam, Miss Gladiator, was notably unsound and it had proved quite impossible to train her.

Gladiateur, a tall angular bay, was given plenty of time to come to hand by Jennings, an outstanding trainer of stayers, and his first appearance as a two-year-old was in the Clearwell Stakes at Newmarket in October. He duly won, and 'The Druid' observed that with his flowing mane and hairy heels, the big colt already looked a three-year-old. Owing to the indifferent judgement of his rider, Gladiateur was narrowly beaten in the Prendergast Stakes three days later. At the Houghton Meeting he was unplaced in the Criterion Stakes, but he was coughing at the time so there was a valid excuse for his defeat.

During the winter Gladiateur was continually lame. His forelegs were blistered and he hardly left his box in January and February. When the Two Thousand Guineas came along he was still physically backward, but starting at 7–1 he won an exciting race from Archimedes and Liddington.

Between Newmarket and Epsom Gladiateur for once remained perfectly sound. His final trial was run over a mile and a half on the Limekilns against three four-year-olds, of whom Fille de l'Air, winner of the Oaks the previous year and of several races during the current season, received eight pounds, the other two both thirty-five. Gladiateur beat them all without the slightest difficulty and showed beyond a shadow of doubt that he was virtually a certainty for the greatest race of the year.

Gladiateur, a 5–2 favourite at Epsom, had his task rendered easier by the fact that his opponents were a second-rate collection. Mr Chaplin had just paid William

I'Anson £11,000 for Breadalbane and Broomielaw. A lot was thought of Breadalbane, a full brother to Blair Athol, but both he and his stable companion ran deplorably, so badly in fact that Mr Chaplin removed them forthwith from I'Anson's
care. Liddington, close up third in the Guineas, and the Marquis of Hastings's fancied
colt, The Duke, both went wrong shortly before the race and were unable to run.

Gladiateur, ridden by Harry Grimshaw, a competent but very short-sighted rider
who was killed in a driving accident not long after, was only tenth at Tattenham
Corner. However, he then began to make up ground in the smoothest fashion
imaginable and ran on strongly to the finish to win by a decisive two lengths from
Christmas Carol, with the rank outsider Eltham a bare half-length away third. The
crowd, who love a good horse, particularly when they have backed it, gave the winner
a great reception and the ill-feeling over Fille de l'Air was evidently forgiven and
forgotten. As a precaution, though, certain arrangements had been made for the
security of Gladiateur and his connexions. A French newspaper made the most of
that fact and published a highly imaginative account of a protective shield of six
hundred pugilists, to say nothing of an alleged plot to seize and bleed Grimshaw in
order to render him too weak to be able to ride!

Immediately after Epsom Gladiateur departed for Paris where he won the Grand
Prix with the utmost ease amid scenes of remarkable enthusiasm. On returning to
England he won twice at Goodwood—one race was a walk-over—and at Doncaster
he completed the rare distinction of the Triple Crown by defeating the Oaks winner
Regalia in the St Leger. He had been desperately lame a few days previously, but
seemed to forget about his weakness on the racecourse.

After the St Leger Regalia's owner, Mr Graham, a former wrestler who had made
a fortune from the production of gin, objected to Gladiateur on the grounds of his
being a four-year-old. The objection, for which there was no justification at all,
was speedily overruled.

Gladiateur won the Newmarket Derby by forty lengths and on his final appearance that season he was unplaced in the Cambridgeshire carrying 9 st. 12 lb., a
stupendous task for a three-year-old. Even so he would probably have been placed
had not the semi-blind Grimshaw lain so far out of his ground in the early stages of
the race.

The following year Gladiateur was more unsound than ever, but on iron-hard
ground he beat Regalia by forty lengths in the Ascot Gold Cup despite having been
the best part of 300 yards behind the pacemaker Breadalbane at one stage. He
finished his career by winning the Grand Prix de l'Empereur in Paris and then retired to the Middle Park Stud at a fee of 100 guineas. Unfortunately he proved a
sad disappointment as a sire.

1865

Such was Gladiateur, the only horse that has so far won the English Triple Crown and the Grand Prix as well. Without question he was one of the greatest horses of the nineteenth century and his achievements were all the more remarkable in view of his chronic infirmities. He certainly earned the memorial statue of himself that stands in the paddock at Longchamps and to this day he remains the outstanding performer in French racing history.

1865: Wednesday, 31 May . . . 249 Entries. £6,875.

COUNT F. DE LAGRANGE's b.c. GLADIATEUR	
by Monarque out of Miss Gladiator	H. GRIMSHAW 1
MR R. WALKER's br.c. CHRISTMAS CAROL	
by Rataplan out of Mistletoe	T. FRENCH 2
MR W. ROBINSON's ch.c. ELTHAM by Marsyas	
out of Butterfly	S. ADAMS 3

Also ran:

Mr Spencer's Longdown (4th) (J. Osborne); Mr Palmer's Kate Hampton (Norman); Duke of Beaufort's Todleben (G. Fordham); Count F. de Lagrange's Le Mandarin (Hunter); Lord Stamford's Archimedes (T. Chaloner); Mr Haig's Roderick Random (G. Noble); Baron Rothschild's Zephyr (J. Daley); Mr Chaplin's Breadalbane (Aldcroft); Mr Chaplin's Broomielaw (J. Mann); Mr Merry's Wild Charley (A. Edwards); Mr Mackenzie's The Oppressor (J. Doyle); Marquis of Hastings's Kangaroo (J. Grimshaw); Captain Gray's Audax (F. Adams); Sir J. Hawley's Bedminster (Wells); Mr C. P. Hudson's Tilt (Perry); Lord Poulett's Nutfinder (J. Reeves); Lord Durham's Ariel (J. Adams); Lord Glasgow's Rifle (H. Covey); Mr J. B. Morris's Puebla (A. Cowley); Lord Westmorland's Brahma (J. Goater); Count Batthyany's King Charming (Custance); Mr Watt's Olmar (J. Snowden); Mr Bowes's Farewell (Ashmall); Mr C. E. Johnstone's First-born (Maidment); Mr T. Parr's Friday (Clement); Mr G. Reynold's Richmond (Morris); Captain White's Joker (E. Sharp).

30 ran.

Betting:

5–2 Gladiateur; 7–2 Breadalbane; 10–1 Archimedes and Longdown; 12–1 Oppressor; 100–7 Wild Charley; 100–6 Christmas Carol; 25–1 Zephyr; 50–1 Broomielaw, Bedminster, Ariel, and Brahma; 100–1 King Charming, Kangaroo, Olmar, Friday, Farewell, Roderick Random, and Eltham; 1,000–8 Richmond.

Won by two lengths; half a length between second and third.   2 m. 56 s.
Winner trained by T. Jennings at Newmarket.

1866

Lord Lyon, by Stockwell out of Paradigm, winner of the Triple Crown in 1866, was bred at Oakley Hall, Kettering, by Colonel (later General) Mark Pearson, a member of the Jockey Club who raced for love of the sport and had very little interest in betting. Some years previously Colonel Pearson had wanted a hack for his wife and for eighteen guineas bought Ellen Horne, a thoroughbred filly by Redshank out of Delhi, by Plenipotentiary. Evidently Ellen Horne was not a success as a hack as she was sent to the stud, and mated with Touchstone's son Paragone, produced Paradigm, who in successive seasons was the dam of Lord Lyon and of that magnificent filly Achievement, winner of the One Thousand Guineas and the St Leger.

Colonel Pearson raced Achievement himself, but Lord Lyon was leased to Mr Richard Sutton, second son of Sir Richard Sutton, a celebrated Master of the Quorn and the Cottesmore, whose hunting was said to have cost him £300,000. Mr Richard Sutton, who eventually succeeded to the baronetcy, was born in 1821 at Sudbrooke Hall, Lincolnshire. He entered the Navy as a boy and served under Captain (later Admiral) Rous in the *Pique* when she made her famous rudderless voyage across the Atlantic. Perhaps that hazardous and uncomfortable experience gave Mr Sutton a certain distaste for the sea, as he subsequently transferred his services to the Life Guards. However, even duty in the Household Cavalry conflicted at times with his sporting inclinations and his stay in the Army was a brief one. A member of the Jockey Club, he very much liked a gamble, and no doubt 'a gentleman who owns all Piccadilly' could afford to bet heavily. He began his racing career in 1856, and in 1865 he won a lot of money when his filly Gardevisure, leased from Colonel Pearson, won the Cambridgeshire.

Lord Lyon, trained by James Dover at Ilsley, showed exceptional promise from his earliest days. Before he had run as a two-year-old, he was tried over six furlongs in August against the three-year-old filly Gardevisure, who won the Cambridgeshire that autumn with 6 st. 2 lb. He received eighteen pounds from the filly and beat her by seven lengths. A fortnight later, receiving only ten pounds, he was tried against her again and this time won easily by three lengths. He made his first racecourse appearance in the Champagne Stakes at Doncaster, dead-heating with Redan, who was then allowed to walk over. At Newmarket in the autumn he won both the Troy and the Criterion Stakes.

Lord Lyon wintered well and started a 7–4 on favourite for the Two Thousand Guineas. Ridden by a little-known jockey called Thomas, as Custance had broken a collar-bone at the Epsom Spring Meeting, he won by a length from Monarch of the Glen. He continued to thrive afterwards, and with Custance available to partner him there was unshakable confidence in his ability to win the Derby. Despite having twenty-five opponents, he started at 6–5 on, the first odds-on favourite for thirty-five years.

Lord Lyon, however, was not the certainty that his supporters imagined and in fact he only pulled an apparently lost race out of the fire in the last few strides. Soon after Tattenham Corner he went to the front, but was immediately headed by Lord Ailesbury's Bribery colt, later named Savernake. Rustic, a Stockwell colt that Colonel Pearson had sold to the Duke of Beaufort for 5,000 guineas, was close up as well and it looked like being a tremendous race between the three.

With two furlongs to go Rustic was going the best but, coming under pressure below the distance, he could find no more. Inside the final 200 yards the Bribery colt was a neck in front of the favourite, who looked a beaten horse but, just as the crowd was shouting the Bribery colt home, Custance called on his mount for one final, supreme effort, Lord Lyon responded in the bravest way imaginable and, lengthening his stride, pushed his head in front literally on the post. It was a wonderful race, and Lord Lyon's supporters were almost too overwrought to cheer. Mr Sutton won over £50,000 and it is worthy of note that the first three horses were all by Stockwell.

At Ascot Lord Lyon, conceding six pounds, was beaten by Rustic in the Prince of Wales's Stakes. Not surprisingly, his exertions at Epsom had told on him for the time being and he was described as looking as 'dry as a chip'. In October he met Rustic in a £1,000 Match over the Ditch In Course and beat him by twenty lengths. Rustic was shortly afterwards exported to Prussia.

In the St Leger Lord Lyon had a second tremendous battle with Savernake and again he won by a matter of inches. According to Custance Savernake was decidedly unlucky, as he was hopelessly shut in at the distance, and when at last he got clear, the winning post came a couple of strides too soon. Custance never had a great opinion of Lord Lyon, regarding him as a lucky horse rather than a champion, and certainly not a true stayer. In his reminiscences he wrote: 'It is not generally known that Lord Lyon was a very slight whistler, and was fired with a flat-iron. Whether it did him any good or not I cannot say.'

Lord Lyon was pulled out again two days after the St Leger for the Doncaster Cup, but he could not stay the distance and was beaten by Rama. He won two subsequent races that season and the following year he won six times in succession until Rama beat him again, this time in a Queen's Plate at Lincoln. In all he won seven-

Tattenham Corner, 1875;
after Doré

Derby Day, 1875

Sir Joseph Hawley; by J. F. Herring

Matthew Dawson

teen of his twenty-one races and over £26,000 in stakes. He retired to the Hurst-bourne Park Stud in Hampshire at a fee of thirty guineas, the best horse he sired being Minting, whose misfortune it was to have been foaled the same year as Ormonde. Lord Lyon was destroyed in 1887.

1866: Wednesday, 16 May . . . 274 Entries. £7,350.

MR R. SUTTON's b.c. LORD LYON by Stockwell out of Paradigm	H. CUSTANCE	1
LORD AILESBURY's ch.c. SAVERNAKE by Stockwell out of Bribery	T. FRENCH	2
DUKE OF BEAUFORT's ch.c. RUSTIC by Stockwell out of Village Lass	CANNON	3

Also ran:

Lord Exeter's Knight of the Crescent (J. Adams); Mr Bowes's Westwick (Ash-mall); Mr W. C. Brown's Harefield (Nightingall); Mr Rickards's Knapsack (Deacon); Lord St Vincent's Redan (H. Grimshaw); Marquis of Hastings's Blue Riband (A. Cowley); Count F. de Lagrange's Plutus (Parry); Lord Stamford's Freedom (A. Edwards); Mr T. Dawson's The Stabber (Morris); Baron Rothschild's Janitor (Wells); Baron Rothschild's Robin Hood (J. Daley); Captain Barron's Hidalgo (Carroll); Prince Soltykoff's Duke of York (J. Mann); Mr H. Chaplin's Vespasian (J. Grimshaw); Mr Wall's Strathconan (J. Snowden); Mr Rigby's Aber-geldie (J. Goater); Mr R. C. Naylor's Monarch of the Glen (Chaloner); Mr Savile's The Corsair (Loates); Mr G. Bryan's Laneret (Lynch); Mr Savile's Sealskin (Doyle); Lord Glasgow's colt by Toxopholite (J. Osborne); Mr Lincoln's Tacitus (Maid-ment); Mr J. Johnstone's The Czar (Cameron).

26 ran.

Betting:

6–5 on Lord Lyon; 5–1 Rustic; 12–1 Redan; 100–7 The Toxophilite colt; 20–1 Savernake, Monarch of the Glen, and Blue Riband; 30–1 Vespasian; 33–1 Knight of the Crescent; 40–1 Abergeldie; 50–1 Strathconan; 1,000–15 Westwick and Janitor, and 1,000–5 Plutus.

Won by a head; three lengths between second and third.　　　　　　2 m. 50 s.
Winner trained by J. Dover at Ilsley.

1867

Hermit, winner in 1867, was owned by Mr Henry Chaplin, later Lord Chaplin, who was twenty-five years of age at the time. The son of a Lincolnshire parson, Chaplin inherited the Blankney estate and a splendid fortune from an uncle when he was still a minor. Blankney looked a magnificent possession at the time, but the day was to come, years later, when Chaplin found himself compelled to dispose of it after a succession of bad harvests and during a period of agricultural depression.

In 1864 Chaplin was engaged to marry the beautiful Lady Florence Paget, but just before the wedding she jilted him and went off with the foolish, irresponsible, but far from unattractive Marquis of Hastings, a reckless gambler whose ruin was hastened by the gigantic losses he incurred over Hermit's astonishing victory at Epsom.

Chaplin had taken to racing on a modest scale almost as soon as he came of age, but after his desertion by Lady Florence he at once increased the scope of his activities on the Turf. In fact at this early stage of his career it was said of him that 'he bought horses as though he were drunk and backed them as if he were mad'. He paid William I'Anson, towards the end of 1864, £11,000 for Breadalbane, a brother of Blair Athol, and Broomielaw, who was out of Blink Bonny's dam, Queen Mary. Possibly this transaction was effected in the hope of defeating Hastings's The Duke in the Derby.

Breadalbane and Broomielaw remained with I'Anson, who had bred them, but neither turned out much good and there was a row between Chaplin and I'Anson after Breadalbane's failure at Epsom. Chaplin was vexed at the colt's poor showing, while I'Anson complained that he alone understood the peculiarities of the Queen Mary breed, but his training plans were constantly disrupted by the interference of Chaplin and his friend Sir Frederick Johnstone. The upshot was that Chaplin took his horses away from I'Anson and sent them to Newmarket to be trained by Bloss under the management of Captain Machell.

Machell, born at Beverley in 1838, was originally an impecunious member of an unfashionable line regiment and was noted chiefly for his prowess at running and jumping. During a period of service at the Curragh, however, he developed, with profit to himself, his undoubted flair for horses and for racing, and in 1862 he decided to send in his papers in order to devote himself entirely to the Turf.

216

Machell was a good judge of a horse, particularly of a steeplechaser, and a fearless bettor. He had his ups and downs and was sometimes desperately short of ready money, but by and large he did well, not only for himself—he was able to buy back the family estate in Westmorland—but also for the young men whose horses he managed. He won the Grand National twice with horses owned by himself, while on the flat the most famous winners he was concerned with were Hermit, Harvester, and Isinglass. He was very much a man of moods. He could be a charming and generous host, but not infrequently he displayed a cold, calculating, ruthless, and suspicious side to his character. In later years he suffered atrociously from gout and underwent long periods of intense depression. He died in 1902.

In 1865 Machell bought on Chaplin's behalf a colt by Newminster out of the Tadmor mare Seclusion for 1,000 guineas at the sale of the Middle Park Stud yearlings. The colt was subsequently named Hermit. The very next yearling to enter the ring was Marksman, whom Mr Merry bought for 1,000 guineas, and who was destined to finish second to Hermit in the Derby.

Hermit, a dark chesnut standing $15 \cdot 2\frac{1}{2}$, soon began to show signs of exceptional promise and in December it was decided to make some sort of test of his merit. Accordingly he was tried over four furlongs against a filly called Problem, to whom he conceded thirty-five pounds. He beat her by two lengths, and the value of his performance was proved two and a half months later when Problem won the Brocklesby Stakes at Lincoln from a very big field. Machell at once began to back Hermit for the Derby at 20–1. Some of these wagers were being ratified one evening at Long's Hotel when in walked the Duke of Hamilton, a very young man with a great deal of money and not much sense. In a distinctly truculent manner he offered to lay 30,000 to 1,000 against Hermit six times; Machell, never the man to let an opportunity slip, booked a bet of £180,000 to £6,000. Subsequently Machell was offered a considerable sum of money to cancel the bet, but he refused to compromise and eventually declared the wager off.

Hermit's first outing as a two-year-old was at the Newmarket First Spring Meeting in a race in which Marksman was also a competitor. He beat Marksman, but largely through inexperience was himself defeated by a filly called Cellina. Shortly afterwards at Bath, however, he met Cellina again, and conceding her three pounds won by a neck. In the Woodcote Stakes at Epsom he finished second to a very good filly in Achievement, who also defeated him on the other two occasions that they met. He won a Biennial Stakes at Ascot and then won twice at Stockbridge, beating in one of his races there the Duke of Beaufort's Vauban.

Vauban, by Muscovite, did not have the best of joints, but he was hardier than he looked and won seven of his fifteen races as a two-year-old. The following season he won the Two Thousand Guineas quite comfortably and was made a short-priced favourite for the Derby. In the Guineas, however, Knight of the Garter, a stable companion of Hermit's, had beaten Marksman and finished within a couple of lengths of Vauban although not one hundred per cent at his best. When, therefore, Hermit was tried to give Knight of the Garter ten pounds over a mile and beat him, Machell had every justification for thinking that he had little to fear from any of the horses that had run in the first of the classics.

Custance was engaged to partner Hermit in the Derby and exactly a week before the race he came down to Newmarket to ride him in a gallop over a mile and a half. For a mile Hermit could hardly have gone better, but then suddenly he gave a tremendous cough and all but fell. He had broken a blood-vessel in his nostril and his chance in the Derby looked hopeless. Mr Chaplin, on hearing the news, was in favour of scratching him forthwith, but Machell refused to give up hope and persuaded Hermit's owner to delay drastic action and to await any further developments.

When the news of Hermit's mishap leaked out, it was naturally assumed that he was most unlikely to run and Custance was invited to take the mount instead on Mr Pryor's much-fancied candidate, The Rake. Chaplin eventually agreed to this on the grounds that he did not wish to deprive Custance of the chance of winning the race. By an almost incredible coincidence, The Rake broke a blood-vessel in his final gallop, too. As Hermit was responding to treatment Machell urged Chaplin to re-claim Custance, but Pryor was determined that The Rake should run and refused to release him. The matter was referred to the Stewards who decided that Chaplin's letter to Pryor constituted a release and gave the latter the right, but as both horses had broken blood-vessels, they considered that in all fairness Pryor should relinquish his claim. This, however, Pryor declined to do. Custance, therefore, had to ride The Rake, who ran abominably, while Johnny Daley, a tall young man, twenty years of age, a sound jockey but hardly a fashionable one, was engaged for Hermit, the terms being £100 for the ride, £100 if he was placed, and £3,000 if he won. This wonderful piece of good fortune for Daley, who was Newmarket-born and the son of a trainer, was followed by victory in the Oaks on Hippia. He never rode another winner of a classic race.

Hermit in the meantime had been allowed very little hay and was covered with the lightest of rugs in order to keep his blood as cool as possible. He did a fair amount of work, but all downhill, and on the Saturday he was given no fewer than six canters over a mile.

The weather on Derby Day was atrocious. It was bitterly cold and snow fell heavily both before and after the race. Most of the horses in the paddock appeared tucked up and Hermit himself was a picture of misery. In fact if looks went for any-thing, the bookmakers were being far from generous in laying 1,000–15 against him. However Machell, who, unlike Chaplin, had hedged most of his earlier bets, backed him to win £3,000 as the horses were on their way to the post.

To add to the misery of the soaked and shivering crowd, there were ten false starts and an interminable delay in consequence. When at last they were off, the Danebury colt Vauban was soon to the fore and led down the hill to Tattenham Corner with Wild Moor, Marksman, and Julius hard on his heels, and Hermit some distance behind in the middle division. On reaching the straight Julius and The Rake dropped back beaten, while Van Amburgh, The Corporal, The Palmer, and Hermit began to improve. With two furlongs to go the leaders were Marksman, Van Amburgh, and Vauban; Van Amburgh was done with at the distance, and with Fordham uneasy on Vauban, it looked any odds on a victory for Marksman, who established a clear advantage with just under a furlong to go.

All of a sudden Hermit appeared on the scene apparently going twice as fast as any other horse in the race. Daley had obeyed to the letter his instructions to come with one long run, and sweeping past Vauban as if the favourite was standing still, he rapidly closed with Marksman and headed him a few strides from the post to win a sensational race by a neck.

James Waugh, trainer of Marksman, blamed Grimshaw for his horse's defeat. Grimshaw was notoriously short-sighted, and according to Waugh he was peering for Vauban, whom he reckoned the only danger, and entirely failed to notice Hermit until it was too late. Mr Merry, however, was slightly consoled by the fact that Marksman had beaten the Duke of Beaufort's colt, for if there were two men whom Merry particularly disliked, they were the Duke of Beaufort and Lord Stamford. There was dissatisfaction, too, with Fordham's riding of Vauban, it being considered that he had made far too much use of the favourite.

Chaplin himself won the best part of £120,000 on the race, while Hastings, who was the first man to pat Hermit on the neck on the return to the unsaddling en-closure, was said to have lost a similar amount. Some £20,000 of Hastings's losses were due to Chaplin, who generously sent him a note telling him he need not worry about settling until it was convenient. The following Monday Hastings paid out £102,000 at Tattersalls.

Hermit's victory was a blow from which Hastings never recovered, but even if Hermit had lost, the ultimate result would have been the same as far as Hastings was concerned. Although a reckless gambler, he was not a complete fool about racing and he enjoyed some very big wins in his day. It was not so much the Turf that ruined him as the futility and extravagance of his day-to-day existence.

Hermit won a Biennial Stakes and the St James's Palace Stakes at Ascot, but was beaten a length in the St Leger by Colonel Pearson's great filly Achievement. Two days later Achievement beat him again in the Doncaster Cup, and that very same afternoon he was called upon to run in a mile and three-quarter Sweepstakes, which he won. Probably those three Doncaster races got to the bottom of him, as he was beaten three times in the autumn, and never won a race at all the two following seasons.

Hermit was retired to the stud at Blankney at a fee of twenty guineas, but such was his success that it was eventually raised to 300 guineas and there were cases of 500 guineas being paid for a nomination. He was Champion Sire six seasons in succession, and between 1873 and 1897 his offspring won 846 races worth over £356,000. His stock also did well in France, and although the Hermit sire line has long since faded out in England, it may conceivably be revived through the importation of the French stallion Guersant to Ireland. Hermit sired two Derby winners in Shotover and St Blaise, and two Oaks winners in Thebais and Lonely. He died in 1890.

1867: Wednesday, 22 May . . . 256 Entries. £7,000.

MR H. CHAPLIN'S ch.c. HERMIT by Newminster out of Seclusion	J. DALEY	1
MR J. MERRY'S ch.c. MARKSMAN by Dundee out of Shot	GRIMSHAW	2
DUKE OF BEAUFORT'S br.c. VAUBAN by Muscovite out of Palm	G. FORDHAM	3

Also ran:

Mr Eastwood's Master Butterfly (Hardcastle); Mr Eastwood's Lord Hastings (Doyle); Mr F. Elliot's Leases (Jeffries); Mr Bignell's Man of Ross (Loates); Mr Godding's colt by Rataplan (French); Mr G. Angell's Ben Nevis (Parry); Mr J. Bowes's Taraban (Carroll); Mr Savile's Roquefort (H. Covey); Mr Savile's D'Estournel (Edwards); Mr Fleming's Van Amburgh (Chaloner); Count F. Lagrange's Dragon (Hibberd); Lord Exeter's Grand Cross (Norman); Mr J. Johnstone's The Corporal (Cameron); Mr F. Pryor's The Rake (Custance); Duke of Newcastle's Julius (J. Mann); Mr H. Temple's Fitz-Ivan (Payne); Sir J. Hawley's The Palmer (Wells); Marquis of Hastings's Uncas (Salter); Mr. A. Heathcote's Gipsy King (Snowden); Mr Gilby's Skysail (Huxtable); Duke of Hamilton's Wild Moor (Clement); Sir R. Bulkeley's Owain Glyndwr (Goater); Lord Coventry's The Rescue (J. Adams); Mr Crawley's Redbourne (Morris); Mr Wynn's Bedlamite (R. Viney); Lord Uxbridge's Distin (Cannon).

30 ran.

1867

Betting:

    6–4 Vauban; 7–1 The Palmer; 8–1 Van Amburgh; 9–1 The Rake; 10–1 Marksman; 16–1 Julius and D'Estournel; 30–1 Dragon and Grand Cross; 50–1 Tynedale; 1,000–15 Master Butterfly, Hermit, and Fitz-Ivan; 100–1 Taraban, Gipsy King, and Owain Glyndwr; 1,000–8 Leases, The Corporal, Wild Moor, and The Rescue; 1,000–6 Redbourne.

Won by a neck; a bad third.   2 m. 52 s.

Winner trained by Bloss at Newmarket.

1868

In 1867 the Marquis of Hastings owned a two-year-old filly of quite exceptional brilliance called Lady Elizabeth. There is no better medium for a gamble than a high-class two-year-old, and no doubt largely because of that Lady Elizabeth was raced unsparingly throughout the season. She went to the post on thirteen occasions, her one defeat being in the Middle Park Stakes, a failure that was alleged to be largely due to over-confidence on the part of Fordham.

Two days after the Middle Park, Hastings, with scant regard for the filly's future, matched her for £1,000 over the Bretby Course against Julius, who had finished third in the St Leger and who had just won the Cesarewitch with eight stone on his back. Julius only conceded the filly nine pounds and was favourite at 11–10 on, but in one of the most punishing struggles ever seen, Lady Elizabeth battled on with wonderful gameness to win by a matter of inches.

Unfortunately the glorious achievements of Lady Elizabeth were unable to rescue Hastings from his financial predicament. He had gone for a vast win in the Middle Park Stakes and he lost £49,000 on the meeting. He settled, but with difficulty. At the Houghton Meeting a fortnight later he lost another £40,000 and could not pay.

By then his Scottish estates had already gone, sold to Lord Bute for £300,000. He had sacrificed securities and had given a reversion on his Donington estate. He sold his hunters, and at the end of the season he sold nearly all his racehorses bar Lady Elizabeth and another top-class two-year-old called The Earl. Even so he had to apply to the dreadful Padwick for a loan, and Padwick demanded in addition to other securities, a bill of sales on various other assets, including The Earl.

Now that they had Hastings on the run, the bookmakers pursued him without mercy. Some of them applied to the Jockey Club to have his name struck off the list of members, but he resigned without being asked to. A close friend almost brought about a reasonable settlement—the outstanding liabilities were not more than £50,000—but the attempt was thwarted by one bookmaker who declined to be kept waiting for his pound of flesh.

The one good card that Hastings seemed to hold was Lady Elizabeth for the Derby, but alas, the battle with Julius had broken her heart. She grew bad-tempered and was frequently off her feed. Her trainer, John Day, who, whatever his faults, was not a fool, must have suspected the worst, and it is significant that the filly was not given a race or subjected to any sort of trial before the Derby. Her deterioration, however, was carefully concealed from Hastings, while no news leaked out to disturb the confidence of the public.

The real tragedy of the situation from Hastings's point of view lay in the fact that in all probability he could have won the Derby with The Earl had the colt been permitted to run. Unfortunately, though, persons connected with the stable—including, no doubt, Padwick, Hill, and possibly Day himself—had laid so much money against The Earl the previous year when it was considered certain that Lady Elizabeth would triumph at Epsom, that there were very good reasons for not running him, and accordingly, the day before the race, Hill was sent round to Weatherbys with an order in his pocket to scratch the colt.

Sir Joseph Hawley had been having a comparatively lean spell with his horses, but with John Porter as his trainer, his luck changed for the better in 1867 when he had three top-class two-year-olds—the colts Blue Gown and Rosicrucian, and the filly Green Sleeve—all bred by himself, and all by his Derby winner Beadsman.

Blue Gown and Rosicrucian both won at the Ascot Spring Meeting, but Blue Gown was shortly afterwards beaten by Lady Elizabeth at Bath. However he won the Fern Hill Stakes at the Royal Ascot Meeting, and in September the Champagne Stakes at Doncaster. Unfortunately Wells, who was getting somewhat portly and increasingly reluctant to take exercise, carried about five pounds more than he ought to have done in the Champagne Stakes. After some unsuccessful trickery on his part when returning to the scales, he failed to draw the weight, and to the justifiable fury of Sir Joseph, Blue Gown was disqualified. The same week Blue Gown ran very badly in another race and finished last of five.

Before the Newmarket Second October Meeting, Sir Joseph decided to try Green Sleeve, who had yet to run, Rosicrucian, and Blue Gown against a useful and very reliable four-year-old called Xi. The result of the trial was as follows: 1st, Rosicrucian (8 st. 4 lb.); 2nd, Green Sleeve (7 st. 12 lb.); 3rd, Blue Gown (7 st. 12 lb.): 4th, Xi (9 st. 8 lb.). Won by a length; five lengths between second and third.

The subsequent Newmarket Meeting was a triumph for Hawley's three two-year-olds. Green Sleeve won the Middle Park Stakes by a head from Rosicrucian, who was conceding her six pounds. She may have been a bit lucky to beat her stable companion, as they were racing on opposite sides of the course and Huxtable, who rode Rosicrucian, was under the impression that he was lengths ahead and took matters somewhat easily in consequence. Green Sleeve also won the Prendergast Stakes at the same meeting, while Rosicrucian won the Criterion and the Troy Stakes and Blue Gown the Clearwell Stakes.

During the winter Hawley's horses moved into the new yard at Kingsclere, but unfortunately the boxes were still damp; both Green Sleeve and Rosicrucian caught chills which lingered on to the spring and retarded their preparation. They both ran in the Two Thousand Guineas but with little hope of success, and both finished unplaced behind the dead-heaters, Mr Stirling Crawfurd's Moslem and Mr Graham's filly Formosa, who subsequently won the One Thousand Guineas, the Oaks, and the St Leger. Blue Gown, who had wintered well, did not run in the Two Thousand Guineas, but was started instead in the Tenth Biennial, in which The Earl, running in the name and colours of Padwick, beat him by a head. Blue Gown, however, did win two minor events at the First Spring Meeting.

Before the Derby there was a trial at Kingsclere which took place in secret, the assembled touts having been caught napping and carefully locked up in an old toll-house. The result of the trial was as follows: 1st, Rosicrucian (8 st. 7 lb.); 2nd, Blue Gown (8 st. 7 lb.); 3rd, The Palmer, four-year-old (9 st. 10 lb.). Won by a neck; two lengths between second and third.

Later that morning Hawley informed Porter that he had decided to start all his three candidates—Green Sleeve, Rosicrucian, and Blue Gown—in the Derby. Blue Gown would run on his merits, but a declaration would be made to win with either of the other two. Hawley himself never had a high opinion of Blue Gown. The public on the other hand had always placed considerable confidence in the colt since his abortive victory in the Champagne Stakes. What is more, they refused to be swayed either by rumours of trials or by the opinion of Sir Joseph himself. They continued to pour money steadily on to Blue Gown for the Derby and it was that fact above all that influenced Hawley in permitting the colt to take part. Despite Hawley's declaration to win with either of the other two, Blue Gown was a firm second favourite at 7–2, whereas Green Sleeve was on offer at 25–1 and Rosicrucian at 30–1.

Lady Elizabeth, a 7–4 favourite, was always a bit fractious before a race and on Derby Day permission was given to saddle her on her own away from the paddock. When Hastings walked down to see her, followed by John Day and Padwick, he was sympathetically received by the crowd who gave him a cheer. He was cheered again when he took his place with his wife to watch the race from Lord Anglesey's stand.

As usual, Lady Elizabeth played up at the start and tried to buck Fordham off, but she was facing the right way when the flag fell. Unfortunately it was soon all too clear that her old brilliance had vanished. She had completely lost her action and was never in the race with a chance. Nor did she run any better in the Oaks two days later.

Coming down the hill to Tattenham Corner the leaders were Orion, See Saw, and

Speculum. See Saw was beaten soon afterwards and King Alfred then went on from Blue Gown, Speculum, St Ronan, and Rosicrucian. Speculum began to falter with two furlongs to go, and from the distance it was a match between King Alfred and Blue Gown. At first King Alfred, a 50–1 chance, appeared to be drawing away, but Wells, who had selected Blue Gown as his mount, then sat down to ride for all he was worth. Inch by inch the gap was reduced, and with fifteen yards to. go Blue Gown forced his head in front and won a most exciting race by half a length. Sir Joseph did not win nearly as much in bets as he had done over his previous Derbys, but that did not stop him from presenting Wells with the stake.

Incidentally the staff 'poet' on *Bells Life* tipped the winner in the following verse:

> For Lady Elizabeth in spite of her wins,
> Will have to cave in when the fighting begins,
> And all you gay gallants of old London Town
> Must put your spare cash on the Bonny Blue Gown.

Blue Gown next won the Ascot Gold Cup, for which he was a 'post entry', beating Speculum and King Alfred, the only other runners. He won the Fitzwilliam Stakes at Doncaster, but was unplaced with 8 st. 11 lb. in the Cesarewitch. He then ran a good second in the Cambridgeshire, carrying nine stone and conceding the winner, See Saw, twelve pounds. He finished the season by carrying top weight to victory in the Free Handicap. He did not improve as he grew older and at the end of his four-year-old season, during which Brigantine beat him in the Gold Cup, he was sold for 5,000 guineas to Prince Pless. He was a complete failure at the stud and died on the journey to America in 1880.

John Porter, born at Rugeley in Staffordshire in 1838, was one of the greatest trainers of the Victorian era. Besides Blue Gown, he trained Shotover, St Blaise, Ormonde, Sainfoin, Common, and Flying Fox to win the Derby, and had sixteen other classic successes as well. At one time he trained for the Prince of Wales, later Edward VII. When he retired from training, he was largely instrumental in planning the construction of Newbury racecourse, where the John Porter Stakes commemorates his memory today. Not long after Blue Gown's Derby, Lord Hastings asked him to take his horses, having apparently had enough of John Day, but on Hawley's instructions Porter declined the invitation.

The Earl went to Paris and won the Grand Prix, returning in time for Royal Ascot, where he won three races. The public then began to ask why The Earl, who had defeated Blue Gown earlier in the season, had not been permitted to run in the Derby. What most people thought was summarized in a typically bold and indiscreet letter to *The Times* from Admiral Rous.

Sir,—Observing in your paper today the following paragraph quoted from the *Pall Mall Gazette*: 'The *Sporting Life*, with more audacity, mentions what Admiral Rous said on the course, that if he had taken as much laudunum as had been given to the mare he would have been a dead man'—permit me to state that it is perfectly untrue.

My belief is that Lady Elizabeth had a rough spin with Athena in March when the Days discovered she had lost her form, a very common occurrence with fillies that have been severely trained at two years old: that when the discovery was made they reversed a commission to back her for the One Thousand Guineas Stakes at Newmarket, and they declared that Lord Hastings would not bring her out before the Derby on which he stood to win a great stake.

I am informed that when Lord Hastings went to Danebury to see her gallop they made excuses for her not to appear. If he had seen her move, the bubble would have been burst.

But the touters reported she was 'going like a bird'. £10 will make a horse fly if the trainer wishes it to rise in the market.

She has never been able to gallop the whole year. Lord Hastings has been shamefully deceived, and with respect to scratching The Earl, Lord Westmoreland came up to town early on Tuesday to beseech Lord Hastings not to commit such an act.

On his arrival in Grosvenor Square he met Mr Hill going to Weatherbys with the order in his pocket to scratch The Earl, and Padwick closeted with Lord Hastings.

In justice to the Marquess of Hastings, I state that he stood to win £35,000 by The Earl, and did not hedge his stake money. Then you will ask: 'Why did he scratch him?' 'What can the poor fly demand from the spider in whose web he is enveloped?'

> I am, Sir,
> Your obedient servant,
> H. J. Rous.

13, Berkeley Square, June 15, 1868.

The letter, of course, created a considerable sensation. Lord Hastings and Padwick both denied its accuracy and its implications, but their statements in explanation were met with an incredulity that was not even polite. Padwick tried every dodge he knew to try and get Rous to apologize, but without success, and he was wily enough to realize that he would be ill-advised to take the matter to law. John Day, who quite correctly judged that his professional reputation had been gravely damaged, instructed his solicitors to take legal proceedings against the Admiral, who was subjected to considerable pressure from various sources to withdraw his allegations. That, however, he declined to do, but the death of Lord Hastings in the autumn removed the chief witness in the case, which was thereupon settled out of court, the Admiral withdrawing his original letter. No doubt this conclusion was a welcome relief to Day, who might have had some embarrassing questions to answer in the witness-box.

The Earl was heavily backed for the St Leger but broke down shortly before the race. Hastings, ruined in health as well as in pocket, died on 10 November. He was twenty-six years of age. Just before he died he said to a friend: 'Hermit's Derby broke my heart. But I didn't show it, did I?'

1868: Wednesday, 27 May . . . 260 Entries. £6,800.

SIR J. HAWLEY's b.c. BLUE GOWN by Beadsman
out of Bas Bleu — J. WELLS 1
BARON ROTHSCHILD's b.c. KING ALFRED by King Tom
out of Schelass Dam — NORMAN 2
DUKE OF NEWCASTLE's b.c. SPECULUM by Vedette
out of Doralice — KENYON 3

Also ran:

Mr Chaplin's St Ronan (4th) (Jeffery); Mr Hodgman's Paul Jones (Parry); Mr Beadman's Orion (Clement); Sir J. Hawley's Green Sleeve (J. Adams); Sir J. Hawley's Rosicrucian (Custance); Marquis of Hastings's Lady Elizabeth (G. Fordham); Lord Ailesbury's Franchise (Chaloner); Sir L. Newman's The Forest King (J. Snowden); Mr John Day's Cock o' the Walk (H. Day); Lord Glasgow's Brother to Bird on the Wing (Cameron); Mr Padwick's Samson (T. French); Mr J. Scott's Viscount (J. Osborne); Colonel Pearson's Cap-a-Pie (Grimshaw); Lord Wilton's See Saw (Maidment); Baron Rothschild's Suffolk (J. Daley).

18 ran.

Betting:

7–4 Lady Elizabeth; 7–2 Blue Gown; 8–1 Paul Jones; 10–1 Suffolk; 100–7 Speculum; 100–6 Orion; 25–1 Green Sleeve; 30–1 Rosicrucian; 40–1 Cap-a-Pie and St Ronan; 50–1 King Alfred and The Forest King; 100–1 Franchise, See Saw, and Viscount.

Won by half a length; a bad third. — 2 m. 43½ s.

Franchise broke a leg, and was destroyed. Baron Rothschild declared to win with Suffolk, Sir J. Hawley with Green Sleeve or Rosicrucian in preference to Blue Gown. Winner trained by J. Porter at Kingsclere.

1869

The winner in 1869 was Pretender, trained at Tupgill by Thomas Dawson. Since then not one Yorkshire-trained horse has won the Epsom Derby, although Dante won a substitute race at Newmarket in 1945.

Pretender was bred by Mr Sadler, a Yorkshire plasterer, and was a brown colt standing sixteen hands by Adventurer out of Ferina, by Venison. His dam was twenty-two years of age when he was foaled. He was bought as a yearling by Mr John Johnstone, a member of a well-known sporting family and the master of the Dumfriesshire Hounds. Mr Johnstone was at that time owner of the Sheffield Lane Stud, founded by his brother Andrew, who had died some time previously. Mr John Johnstone had bought Adventurer, who stood at Sheffield Lane from the start of his stud career. Pretender was one of the first of Adventurer's stock to run.

Pretender ran four times as a two-year-old, winning the North of England Biennial at York and finishing third to Sir Joseph Hawley's Pero Gomez and the Duke of Beaufort's Scottish Queen in the Middle Park Stakes. During the winter he was fourth favourite for the Derby, those preferred being Pero Gomez, the Duke of Hamilton's Wild Oats, and Mr Merry's Belladrum, a Stockwell colt that had won ten of his twelve races.

Unfortunately, Belladrum had gone in his wind and treatment for the defect during the winter proved unavailing. When news of his infirmity leaked out, certain bookmakers laid against him recklessly for the Two Thousand Guineas and the Derby. He gave them a nasty shock in the Guineas as he looked very much like winning at one stage, and in the end Pretender only beat him by half a length. James Waugh, Belladrum's trainer, blamed Kenyon for not waiting with the colt and Daley was engaged to partner him at Epsom. Pretender was made a short-priced favourite for the Derby and eventually started at 11–8. Pero Gomez, who had gone most disappointingly in his final trial, was at 11–2, and then came Belladrum at 6–1. Nothing else appeared to be seriously fancied.

Pretender was accompanied to the post by Lord Hawthorn and Thorwaldsen, whose task it was to make the running, while King Cophetua was started to perform a similar office for Pero Gomez. Coming down the hill to Tattenham Corner, Lord Hawthorn held the lead. At the corner itself there was nearly a nasty accident as

Duke of Beaufort swerved, nearly bringing down Thorwaldsen and causing Pero Gomez to be checked and pulled to the outside.

With two and a half furlongs to go Pretender, Ryshworth, The Aegean, and Thorwaldsen were almost in line. At the distance The Aegean dropped back beaten, The Drummer took a slight lead to Pretender, while Pero Gomez began to make steady progress. Inside the final furlong Pretender, admirably ridden by John Osborne, headed The Drummer and looked to have the race at his mercy, but Pero Gomez came with a tremendous late run and only failed by a head to get up. The Drummer was third and Duke of Beaufort fourth. Belladrum, who was beaten after a mile, was at the tail end of the field, and the last of all to finish was Ladas, owned by a future Prime Minister of England in Lord Rosebery. Twenty-five years later another Ladas was to win for Lord Rosebery the first of his Derby successes.

John Porter was inclined to blame Wells for the defeat of Pero Gomez, alleging that Wells had not fancied the colt after his disappointing trial, had been badly away, and had ridden a thoroughly careless race. He did not deny, though, that Pero Gomez had been badly hampered at Tattenham Corner.

Pretender deteriorated as he grew older and eventually went wrong in his wind. He started an odds-on favourite for the St Leger but was soundly beaten by Pero Gomez, who again defeated him in the Doncaster Stakes two days later. In the autumn he was beaten by Count de Lagrange's Boulogne in the Newmarket Derby.

Pretender's record the next two seasons was an inglorious one and eventually he was retired to the stud at the modest fee of fifteen guineas. He proved a complete failure as a sire. Pero Gomez, a game, honest horse but straight in front and difficult to train, sired a good number of winners at the stud, the best of them being Peregrine, winner of the Two Thousand Guineas in 1881.

John Osborne, a member of a Suffolk family that migrated to Yorkshire, had his first ride in 1846 and his last one in 1892. He then trained quite successfully for a number of years and lived to a very great age. Not a stylish jockey, he was a very effective one and could be relied on to use his head. Above all, he was absolutely incorruptible.

During the winter of 1868-9, there was a quarrel between the Epsom Executive and Mr Studd, who had bought some land that was crossed by part of the Derby course. At one time the dispute had become so bitter that it seemed quite possible that the Derby would not be run, but eventually a satisfactory solution was found.

1869

1869: Wednesday, 26 May . . . 247 Entries. £6,225.

MR J. JOHNSTONE's br.c. PRETENDER by Adventurer out of Ferina	J. OSBORNE	1
SIR J. HAWLEY's br.c. PERO GOMEZ by Beadsman out of Salamanca	WELLS	2
MR G. JONES's b.c. THE DRUMMER by Rataplan out of My Niece	MORRIS	3

Also ran:

Mr Brayley's Duke of Beaufort (4th) (Cannon); Sir J. Hawley's King Cophetua (J. Adams); Mr J. Johnstone's Lord Hawthorn (Hudson); Mr J. Johnstone's Thorwaldsen (Chaloner); Mr H. E. Surtees's The Aegean (Parry); Sir C. Legard's Border Knight (Snowden); Lord Calthorpe's Martyrdom (Fordham); Mr J. Merry's Belladrum (J. Daley); Mr Savile's Ryshworth (Maidment); Mr Savile's Neuchatel (Hammond); Lord Rosebery's Ladas (Custance); Lord Royston's Alpenstock (Mr W. Bevill); Lord Strafford's Rupert (French); Mr T. Jenning's Perry Down (Butler); Mr J. Dawson's De Vere (Grimshaw); Duke of Newcastle's Tenedos (Metcalfe); Sir R. Bulkeley's Tasman (Kenyon); Mr Padwick's Ethus (J. Goater); Mr J. Denman's Defender (Roper).

22 ran.

Betting:

11–8 Pretender; 11–2 Pero Gomez; 6–1 Belladrum; 100–8 Perry Down; 20–1 The Drummer and Martyrdom; 33–1 Border Knight and Thorwaldsen; 50–1 Ryshworth, Duke of Beaufort, Rupert, and De Vere; 66–1 Ethus and Ladas; 1,000–8 King Cophetua; 1,000–5 The Aegean, Tenedos, and Defender.

Won by a head; a length between second and third.   2 m. 52½ s.
Mr Johnstone declared to win with Pretender.
Winner trained by T. Dawson at Tupgill.

1870

The winner in 1870 was Lord Falmouth's Kingcraft, a bay horse standing sixteen hands, bred by his owner, by King Tom out of Woodcraft, by Voltigeur.

Kingcraft made his first appearance in a Triennial at Ascot, where he was beaten a head by the King Tom filly, Mahonia. He then won six races in succession, including the Chesterfield Stakes and the Ham Stakes, but in the Middle Park Stakes he was beaten a head and a short head by the fillies Frivolity and Sunshine, to whom he conceded six pounds and three pounds respectively. It was a gruelling race and Kingcraft had not fully recovered from its effects when he was beaten in the Criterion Stakes a fortnight later.

Kingcraft wintered well and started favourite for the Two Thousand Guineas, but could only finish third to Mr Merry's Macgregor, who made mincemeat of his opponents and was perhaps the easiest and most impressive winner of that event until Tudor Minstrel's runaway victory in 1947.

Macgregor, by Macaroni, first showed his quality in a yearling trial in which he had no difficulty in accounting for Sunshine and a four-year-old filly, who was conceding twelve pounds. Soon afterwards, though, James Waugh discovered a weakness in the suspensory ligament of the colt's off foreleg, and from that day onwards Macgregor had to be trained with considerable caution.

That may have been partly the reason why Macgregor never ran as a two-year-old, but the main cause was Mr Merry desiring as much honour and glory as possible for Sunshine, who was by his own stallion Thormanby. Sunshine, in fact, ran ten times and her one defeat was in the Middle Park Stakes. There was yet another top-class two-year-old in the stable, Sunlight, by Stockwell. He was a pound or two in front of Sunshine, but when tried with Macgregor in the autumn, Macgregor proved clearly the superior. Merry thereupon decided not to run Macgregor as had been planned at the Houghton Meeting, but to keep secret from the public the merits of a colt he now believed to be a champion of champions.

Before the Derby Macgregor was sent to compete in a mile and a half race at Bath. Daley, who had had to put up a pound over weight in the Guineas, had not got a hope of doing 8 st. 7 lb. and Grimshaw was given the ride. Grimshaw elected to lie a long way out of his ground so that Macgregor had a hundred yards to make up in the last half-mile. He accomplished it easily enough, but had a harder race on very firm going than was suitable for a colt with a doubtful leg. Kingcraft in the meanwhile was being given an easy time, Matt Dawson having come to the conclusion that the colt had not been suited by his severe preparation for the Guineas.

The public had been completely carried away by Macgregor's runaway victory in the Guineas, and as far as betting went, it was a one-horse race. Macgregor, partnered on this occasion by Fordham, started at 9–4 on. Camel was on offer at 100–9, Prince of Wales at 100–7, while Kingcraft was almost neglected at 20–1. The Derby was never Fordham's lucky race, and on this occasion he was pale and agitated beforehand and the very reverse of confident.

Approaching the straight Bonny Swell and Palmerston were the leaders, with King o' Scots and Macgregor close behind. With three furlongs to go the crowd saw with a certain apprehension that while Kingcraft was steadily making up ground, Fordham was niggling uneasily at the favourite. A quarter of a mile from home a tremendous shout, in which dismay and incredulity were mingled, went up from the stands and the Downs when it was clearly seen that the hottest favourite in the history of the race was hopelessly beaten. Kingcraft on the other hand kept going in splendid style to win by a decisive four lengths from Palmerston, who later in life was sold for seventy-five pounds and ran over fences. Muster was third and the exhausted favourite fourth.

Kingcraft's victory was well received because of the respect that was felt for his owner, but the question that was uppermost in every mind was what had caused the overthrow of the favourite? Fordham said that one of the colt's legs had gone at Tattenham Corner, but this was denied by Waugh. Merry, suspicious and cantankerous at the best of times, was even more odious in defeat. He declared that Macgregor had been got at—certainly the race was a triumph for the bookmakers—but Waugh denied all possibility of that as well. Merry furthermore alleged that if Sunshine had been trained for the classics, she would undoubtedly have won them all, conveniently forgetting that she had gone in the wind and had also met with a serious accident in the spring. This last insinuation was the final straw as far as Waugh was concerned; not without reason he disliked his employer very much indeed and handed in his resignation soon after.

A few weeks later Macgregor broke down and was retired to the stud. He was not a success as a sire, although he did get the Two Thousand Guineas winner Scot Free. Possibly his Derby failure was due to lack of stamina—Tudor Minstrel, the so-called 'Horse of the Century', also failed to stay—or perhaps he felt his doubtful leg on the very hard going on which the race was run.

Kingcraft started favourite for the St Leger but was beaten half a length by Hawthornden. The rest of his career was very disappointing and at one period he had amassed a sequence of eighteen defeats. In 1874 he retired to the stud at a fee of twenty-five guineas. He was eventually sold for export to America, but died in the course of the sea journey.

Tom French, the very capable jockey who rode Kingcraft at Epsom, was a native of Liverpool. He died in 1873 at the age of twenty-five, and his death opened the door of opportunity to young Fred Archer, who had been apprenticed to Matt Dawson.

The sixth Viscount Falmouth was born in 1819, the son of a parson, and succeeded a cousin in the Viscounty in 1852. He began to own horses in 1857 and won the One Thousand Guineas with Hurricane in 1862 and the Oaks with Queen Bertha in 1863. Both these fillies were trained for him by John Scott. After Scott's death, his horses were sent to Matthew Dawson at Newmarket, and between 1870 and his retirement from racing in 1883 he enjoyed an era of unparalleled success with animals bred by himself at Mereworth in Kent. In that period he won the Two Thousand Guineas three times, the One Thousand Guineas three times, the Derby twice, the Oaks three times, and the St Leger three times. He never had a bet and enjoyed the respect of everyone connected with racing. He died in 1889.

Matthew Dawson, one of the greatest of trainers, was a Scotsman who cared little for petty economies and liked to run his stable on lavish lines. A strong and fearless character who was never reluctant to speak his mind, he was invariably courteous both to his employers and to those whom he employed. He was widely respected on the Turf and much loved by those who knew him best. He had no patience with weak men or bad horses, and heavy betting he abhorred. In fact he had a certain contempt for money, unlike Fred Archer with whom he was so closely associated and whom he summarized as 'that damned, long-legged, tin-scraping young devil'. He was as good a gardener as he was a trainer and used to appear on the gallops in a tall hat, varnished boots, and with a wonderful flower in his buttonhole. He spoke with a pronounced Scottish accent, which made even his strongest language sound like a benediction. In later years he won the Derby for the Duke of Portland with Ayrshire and Donovan, and for Lord Rosebery with Ladas and Sir Visto. He also trained the mighty St Simon, whom the Duke of Portland bought on his advice on the death of Prince Batthyany.

Dawson died in 1897 during a summer heatwave. As he lay dying he was told that his secretary, of whom he was very fond, had just departed on his honeymoon. 'Poor fellow, how damned hot he will be,' he murmured, and those were the last words he spoke.

1870

1870: Wednesday, 1 June . . . 252 Entries. £6,175.

LORD FALMOUTH's b.c. KINGCRAFT by King Tom
   out of Woodcraft   T. FRENCH   I

MR W. S. CRAWFURD's br.c. PALMERSTON by Brocket
   out of Rita   T. CHALONER   2

LORD WILTON's br.c. MUSTER by Tim Whiffler
   out of Charade   MAIDMENT   3

Also ran:

   Mr Merry's Macgregor (4th) (G. Fordham); Mr J. Dawson's King o' Scots (J. Covey); Mr J. Dawson's Camel (Custance); Captain Machell's Bonny Swell (Jeffery); Sir R. Pigot's Bay Roland (E. Martin); Mr J. B. Morris's Prince of Wales (Cannon); Lord Stamford's Normanby (Grimshaw); Mr. J. J. Ellis's Cymbal (Lynch); Mr Bowes's Nobleman (Morris); Mr F. Murphy's Sarsfield (Murphy); Mr W. Roger's The Cockney Boy (Robertson); Mr Cartwright's Ely Appleton (J. Adams).

15 ran.

Betting:

   9–4 on Macgregor; 100–9 Camel; 100–7 Prince of Wales; 100–6 Palmerston; 20–1 Kingcraft; 30–1 King o' Scots; 33–1 Cymbal and Normanby; 50–1 Bonny Swell; 100–1 Ely Appleton and Nobleman.

Won by four lengths; a neck between second and third.   2 m. 45 s.
The Cockney Boy, hopelessly tailed off after two hundred yards, collided with a spectator and fell. Trained by an East London veterinary surgeon on Hackney Marshes, he had been well galloped against a local pedestrian!
Winner trained by M. Dawson at Newmarket.

1871

The year 1871 was known as 'The Baron's Year' as Baron Meyer de Rothschild, the first Jew to become a member of the Jockey Club, won four of the five classic races. His King Tom filly Hannah, named after his daughter who married Lord Rosebery, won the One Thousand Guineas, the Oaks, and the St Leger, while Favonius, by Parmesan out of Zephyr, a full sister to Hannah, won the Derby.

Baron Rothschild, who died three years later, was a lavish patron of the Turf and his colours enjoyed considerable popularity with the racing public. Loyal and generous to those who worked for him, he bred most of his horses himself and his particular enthusiasm was for the stock of King Tom, whose statue stands at Mentmore to this day.

Favonius, who was not named until a day or two before the Derby, never ran as a two-year-old. It had been intended to run him at Ascot but he fell lame, and after that it was decided to give him every chance to develop his strength, as he was a big colt and not the type to come to hand early. He had his first race as a three-year-old in the Newmarket Biennial and was beaten a head by Albert Victor. Nevertheless there was considerable confidence in his ability to win the Derby as before that race he was tried to be sixteen pounds better than Hannah. His starting price at Epsom was 9–1, the better-backed horses than himself being the Yorkshire-trained Bothwell, an easy winner of the Two Thousand Guineas; Albert Victor, who had won the Middle Park Stakes the year before; and Mr Chaplin's Newminster filly, The Pearl.

Favonius, who was trained by Joe Hayhoe, won comfortably by a length and a half. He tackled the leader Digby Grand half-way up the straight, and once in the lead he had no difficulty in Tom French's capable hands in withstanding the efforts of Albert Victor and King of the Forest, who dead-heated for second place. It was an exceedingly popular victory, and both Favonius and his owner were given a wonderful reception.

Favonius was not engaged in the St Leger, but he won the Midsummer Stakes at Newmarket, was second to the 50–1 chance Shannon in the Goodwood Cup, and then won the Brighton Cup. He was unplaced in the Cambridgeshire with 8 st. 11 lb., but finished the season with a win in a minor event at the Houghton Meeting. The following season he won two races at Newmarket in the spring, was second to Henry in the Gold Cup at Ascot, and then won the Goodwood Cup in a canter. He ran only once as a five-year-old, finishing second in the Goodwood Cup, before he was retired to the stud at Mentmore. He unfortunately died in 1877, but in his brief stud career he sired Sir Bevys, winner of the Derby in 1879.

1871: Wednesday, 24 May . . . 208 Entries. £5,125.

BARON ROTHSCHILD's ch.c. FAVONIUS
   by Parmesan out of Zephyr   T. FRENCH   I
MR CARTWRIGHT's ch.c. ALBERT VICTOR
   by Marsyas out of Princess of Wales   H. CUSTANCE
MR J. MERRY's KING OF THE FOREST   } dead-heat
   by Scottish Chief out of Lioness   J. SNOWDEN

Also ran:

Mr G. G. Keswick's Digby Grand (4th) (Fordham); Mr Merrik's The Count (Cannon); Mr T. Lombard's Ravenshoe (Chaloner); Mr Johnstone's Bothwell (J. Osborne); Mr Johnstone's Columbus (Hudson); Mr Savile's Ripponden (Maidment); Mr R. C. Naylor's Noblesse (Morris); Mr H. Chaplin's The Pearl (Jeffery); Mr H. Jenning's Eneide (Watkins); Mr Lancelot's Grand Coup (Parry); Mr Lancelot's Hyperion (Wyatt); Mr H. Delamarre's Mr Feeder (Carver); Mr Beverley's Blenheim (J. Goater); Mr Bowes's Field Marshal (H. Grimshaw).

17 ran.

Betting:

5–2 Bothwell; 4–1 Albert Victor; 8–1 The Pearl; 9–1 Favonius; 14–1 King of the Forest; 100–7 Grand Coup; 20–1 Ravenshoe; 25–1 The Count; 30–1 Noblesse and Digby Grand; 50–1 Ripponden; 100–1 Field Marshal and Mr Feeder; 200–1 Eneide.

Won by a length and a half; dead-heat for second place.   2 m. 50 s.
Mr Johnstone declared to win with Bothwell.
Winner trained by J. Hayhoe at Newmarket.

1872

The present Derby course was used for the first time in 1872. The alteration resulted in the first part of the course being farther away from the Grand Stand but on a somewhat higher level; consequently the opening stages of the race were less steeply uphill than had formerly been the case. The reason for the change was not dissatisfaction with the old course, but a determination to be rid of the slightest liability to that difficult and unco-operative gentleman, Mr Studd, who had in 1868 bought the manor of Walton-on-the-Hill through which part of the old course ran.

The Derby course as it exists today rises about one hundred and fifty feet at varying gradients for the first six furlongs, and then falls until the final fifty yards, which are uphill. The first six furlongs are not straight, but the width of the course minimizes the effect of the bend. The next two furlongs run on a gradual turn, but sharply downhill, to Tattenham Corner. The straight run-in is half a mile long.

It can be said that the Derby course and distance provide an admirable test of the thoroughbred. A true-run mile and a half—there is seldom any loitering in the Derby —demands speed and stamina combined, and eliminates both the fast short-runner and the plodder devoid of acceleration. The gradients require from a horse the ability to race both uphill and down, and as a rule only a horse of good conformation can negotiate the steep descent to Tattenham Corner without becoming to some extent unbalanced. Competitors that are too straight in front or heavy in the shoulder are at a considerable disadvantage. Furthermore, the atmosphere of tension and excitement on Derby Day, the crowds that throng round a fancied runner in the paddock, and above all the lengthy parade in front of the stands, combine to make the race a considerable test of temperament as well.

Cremorne, winner in 1872, was owned and bred by Mr Henry Savile, of Rufford Abbey, a member of the Jockey Club, a notable patron of the Turf and an extremely popular man. He was famous for his loyalty and generosity to those whom he employed, and when he died in 1880, he left to his trainer William Gilbert the pick of any five horses in his stable. The five that Gilbert selected fetched £12,000 at the subsequent sale.

Cremorne was by Favonius's sire Parmesan out of Rigolboche, a mare with such bad legs that she could not be trained. Besides remarkable racing ability, Cremorne had two outstanding characteristics, gluttony and sloth. He was a tremendous eater and used to eat his bed till sawdust was substituted for straw. When not actively engaged in feeding, he was usually in a condition of torpor and sometimes used to fall asleep when walking out to the gallops. He roused himself, though, when his clothing was removed and he was invited to canter or gallop.

He first showed his ability in a yearling trial and he confirmed that promise in no uncertain fashion as a two-year-old, winning nine of his eleven races, including the Woodcote, Chesterfield, and Champagne Stakes. His defeats were in the Prince of Wales's Stakes at York and in the Criterion Stakes at Newmarket. At York he had had a hard race earlier in the afternoon; at Newmarket he was only just pulling round from a severe attack of colic caused by stuffing himself with straw.

The Two Thousand Guineas in 1872 was regarded as virtually a match between Cremorne and Prince Charlie. A seventeen-hand son of Blair Athol, Prince Charlie always ran in the name and colours of his trainer, Joseph Dawson, but in fact he was owned by his breeder, Mr Jones, a Littleport farmer, and he had been brought to Dawson's stables as a yearling by a labourer wearing a smock. He showed brilliant promise as a two-year-old, winning the Middle Park Stakes on his first appearance and then the Criterion Stakes, beating Nuneham and Cremorne. Unfortunately he went wrong in his wind shortly afterwards and his stamina was seriously affected, even though he maintained his brilliant speed. In due course he became a magnificent sprinter, and his performances over the Newmarket five furlongs earned him the title of 'The Prince of the T.Y.C.'. He won twenty-five of his twenty-nine races and was then exported to America, where he sired a really good horse in Salvator. He was certainly one of the most popular horses ever known in this country, and a set of verses in his honour began as follows:

> Let hoary veterans, past their prime,
> Dilate on the steeds of a bygone time,
> And their genealogical tree;
> On Charlie's form can they name a patch?
> What flyer of old would they bring to scratch,
> What 'modern Eclipse' could they dare to match
> With the Prince of the T.Y.C.?

In the Guineas public opinion proved correct and in the last two furlongs Prince Charlie and Cremorne came right away from the others. Cremorne, ridden by Maidment, made tremendous efforts to get on terms as he met the rising ground, but Prince Charlie, ridden by John Osborne, just held on to win by a neck. As regards jockeyship, the advantage was with Prince Charlie as Maidment was hardly in the top flight and certainly lacked the strength to get to the bottom of a big, lazy horse like Cremorne.

Ten days before the Derby Cremorne was tried over the full distance with the four-year-old Ripponden, to whom he gave fourteen pounds and a six lengths' beating. This was considered highly satisfactory, but the full significance only became apparent at Ascot when Ripponden won the Hunt Cup very easily carrying 7 st. 2 lb. Gilbert was confident that Cremorne could beat Prince Charlie over a mile and a half, but just before the race old Alec Taylor warned him that his colt Pell.Mell was the best horse he had ever tried and he fully expected him to win. Pell Mell's potentialities had become apparent in his final trial, after which he was backed to win a fortune at extended odds.

Approaching Tattenham Corner Westland, Wenlock, and Cremorne were the leaders. Prince Charlie improved his position on the final bend but was beaten soon afterwards, and with three furlongs to go Cremorne began to draw away with Pell Mell in hot pursuit, this pair being well clear of the remainder. Cremorne would probably have won by a decisive margin if Maidment had seen Pell Mell, who was racing wide of him, but Maidment remained in happy ignorance of Pell Mell's challenge and took matters so easily in consequence that Cremorne only passed the post a head to the good.

Cremorne next went to Paris for the Grand Prix, which he won quite comfortably, a victory which irritated the French considerably as they thought that England had been unhelpful during their catastrophic war against the Prussians. Cremorne's reception in consequence was extremely hostile and Mr Savile was urged to get his horse out of the country at the earliest possible opportunity. Cremorne was hurried away to Boulogne and had to endure a terribly stormy crossing to Folkestone, the boat arriving two and a half hours late. However, by Monday evening he was at Ascot, where he won a Biennial and enjoyed a walk-over in another event. He won two races at York and the Newmarket Derby, but failed to concede fourteen pounds to Laburnum in the Newmarket St Leger.

As a four-year-old Cremorne was better than ever before. He was not really fit when he just failed to concede the five-year-old Mornington seventeen pounds in the City and Suburban, but he accomplished a highly satisfactory trial before Ascot and was at the top of his form for the Gold Cup, in which he beat an unusually strong field by eight lengths. The following day he won the Alexander Plate by fifteen lengths.

Ascot was really the end of his racing career as in July he sprang a curb. He did in fact canter round at the rear of the field in the Goodwood Cup, but that was only to get the better of a bookmaker who was in illegal receipt of stable information and who had rashly laid long odds against him going to the post. Attempts to get him sound again next season were fruitless and he retired to his owner's stud at a fee of a hundred guineas. When Mr Savile died, he was bought for 5,400 guineas by Mr A. S. Lumley, but dropped dead fourteen months later. Gilbert had given ample warning that Cremorne would need plenty of exercise at the stud or he would become unhealthily gross. Unfortunately this advice was neglected and he died of fatty degeneration of the heart. The most notable winner he sired was Lord Rosebery's good filly Kermesse.

1872: Wednesday, 29 May . . . 191 Entries. £4,850.

MR H. SAVILE's b.c. CREMORNE by Parmesan out of Rigolboche	MAIDMENT	1
MR J. N. ASTLEY's br.c. PELL MELL by Young Melbourne out of Makeshift	T. CHALONER	2
LORD FALMOUTH's b.c. QUEENS MESSENGER by Trumpeter out of Queen Bertha	T. FRENCH	3

Also ran:

Lord Wilton's Wenlock (4th) (W. Pratt); Mr I. Woolcot's The Druid (J. Goater); Lord Royston's Ruffle (Salter); Mr J. Dawson's Prince Charlie (J. Osborne); Lord Falmouth's Patriarch (Huxtable); Mr W. Nicholl's Raby Castle (J. Snowden); Mr Hatfield's Quainton (Gregory); Mr A. E. Hope's Young Sydmonton (Jeffery); Lord Aylesford's Vanderdecken (Marsh); Mr John Parry's Marshal Bazaine (E. Martin); Mr Bruton's Landmark (Custance); Baron Rothschild's Laburnum (Parry); Mr Holdaway's Westland (Wyatt); Duke of Beaufort's Almoner (Cannon); Mr Lefevre's Drummond (Morris); Mr G. G. Keswick's Helmet (F. Webb); Mr A. C. Barclay's Bertram (Jewitt); Mr T. E. Walker's Statesman (Jones); Mr Somerville's Misserrimus (S. Mordan); Mr Delamarre's Condor (Carver).

23 ran.

Betting:

5–2 Prince Charlie; 3–1 Cremorne; 6–1 Queens Messenger; 7–1 Wenlock; 25–1 Marshal Bazaine and Drummond; 30–1 Almoner; 33–1 The Druid; 40–1 Laburnum; 50–1 Pell Mell and Bertram; 66–1 Helmet; 100 1 Young Sydmonton, Statesman, Vanderdecken, Condor, Landmark, and Misserrimus; 1,000–6 Raby Castle and Westland.

Won by a head; three lengths between second and third. 2 m. 45½ s. Winner trained by W. Gilbert at Newmarket.

1873

Mr Merry had parted with his trainer James Waugh in 1870 and engaged Robert Peck in his place, with Martin Gurry as head-lad. Peck, quick-witted, a wonderful judge of horses and racing, and full of vitality, probably had a somewhat easier time than his predecessors, since he was failing in health and lacked the energy to be as actively unpleasant as in the past. In fact his interest in racing was rapidly dwindling and he no longer found pleasure or excitement in heavy betting.

In 1871 Peck very much wanted Merry to buy one of the Sledmere yearlings, a golden chesnut colt by Stockwell out of Marigold, a mare that had run second to Queen Bertha in the Oaks in 1863. Merry showed little enthusiasm for the project, but eventually consented to bid up to 1,000 guineas for the colt, who then bore the cumbersome name of All Heart and No Peel. Nine hundred and fifty guineas proved sufficient, and the colt's name was immediately changed to Doncaster.

It was the absurd custom in those days to send yearlings pig-fat into the sale-ring. So gross was Doncaster, in fact, that it was impossible to get him anything like fit as a two-year-old; he never ran that season, and he went so badly in a gallop in the autumn that his lack of promise had to be concealed from his owner, who would otherwise have weeded him out.

Early the following year Doncaster still showed no sign whatever of future greatness. One morning on the downs, however, Peck, who weighed over eleven stone, stuck his umbrella into the ground and climbed on the colt's back himself. Doncaster went as he had never gone before. When Peck dismounted he exclaimed, 'There's the winner of the Derby!' and promptly went off and backed him at 66–1.

Starting at 33–1, Doncaster made his début in the Two Thousand Guineas, but failed to get a place. Peck blamed Tom Cannon for waiting too long, but Merry was convinced that his colt did not stay. In fact he wanted to scratch him and keep him for a race at Ascot; luckily he was persuaded to change his mind after Doncaster had accomplished an excellent trial a week or two later. The winner of the Two Thousand Guineas was Mr Crawfurd's Gang Forward, by Stockwell, who beat Mr Savile's Skirmisher colt Kaiser by a short head. Gang Forward and Kaiser ran amazingly true to form in their next two races, as they dead-heated for second place in the Derby, while at Ascot, Kaiser beat his rival by a head.

Gang Forward was favourite for the Derby at 9–4; Kaiser was 4–1, while a

German horse called Hochstapler was strongly supported as well. Doncaster was virtually friendless at 45–1. Jimmy Snowden had been given the mount on Doncaster, but he was a very heavy drinker at times and omitted to turn up to ride Doncaster in an exercise gallop on the morning of the Derby. Young Fred Webb, who had picked up a horse-shoe a minute or two previously, was therefore engaged instead.

Hochstapler was in front with a mile to go, but was headed before Tattenham Corner by Kaiser, Gang Forward, and Suleiman. The German horse, who had been severely bumped coming down the hill, gave up the struggle soon afterwards, whereas Doncaster began to improve his position at a great rate on the rails. With two furlongs to go Doncaster had clearly taken the measure of his opponents and he ran on strongly to win by a length and a half from Gang Forward and Kaiser, who dead-heated for second place. The victory of this little-considered outsider was received in almost complete silence, and even Merry did not look particularly pleased. In fact the only signs of jubilation came from Robert Peck, who had won a small fortune in bets.

Merry owned a really good filly this year in Marie Stuart, who won the Oaks. She was a little bit better than Doncaster over a mile and a half, but the colt was her superior over two miles; it was a problem, therefore, which would prove the better over the St Leger distance. Both were strongly supported by the public and Merry decided that both should take their chance. In a great race the filly beat the colt by a head, with Kaiser, who started favourite, close up third. That struggle undoubtedly took the edge off Doncaster for the rest of the season, and in the autumn he failed in both the Grand Duke Michael Stakes and the Newmarket Derby.

As a four-year-old Doncaster dead-heated for second place with Flageolet in the Gold Cup behind that very good French stayer Boiard; Gang Forward, Kaiser, and Marie Stuart all being unplaced. In his only other race that season he won the Goodwood Cup, giving seven pounds to Kaiser and beating him by a neck. The following year he won the Gold Cup very easily indeed and was immediately bought by Robert Peck for £10,000. Within a fortnight he had been re-sold for £14,000 to the Duke of Westminster and went off to start his stud career at Eaton. Among his first crop of runners was Bend Or, winner of the Derby and sire of that great horse Ormonde, who was the grandsire of Flying Fox. Today Doncaster is renowned as the tail-male ancestor not only of the Phalaris sire line, so wonderfully successful in recent years, but also of the Teddy sire line, which has proved such a strong influence in French and American racing, and of those famous sprinting sires Gold Bridge and Panorama. Doncaster was eventually sold for export to Austria for £5,000 and died there in 1892. Mr Crawfurd bought Marie Stuart as a brood mare, but she proved very unsuccessful at the stud.

1873

1873: Wednesday, 28 May . . . 201 Entries. £4,825.

MR J. MERRY's ch.c. DONCASTER
  by Stockwell out of Marigold   F. WEBB   1

MR W. S. CRAWFURD's ch.c. GANG FORWARD
  by Stockwell out of Lucky Mary   T. CHALONER ⎫
                                                          ⎬ dead-heat
MR SAVILE's b.c. KAISER   ⎪
  by Skirmisher out of Regina   MAIDMENT   ⎭

Also ran:

Lord Aylesford's Chandos (4th) (T. Cannon); Count de Juigné's Montargis (Carrat); Mr W. S. Crawfurd's Beadroll (Low); Lord Falmouth's Andred (T. French); Mr Dane's Snail (Baverstock); Count Renard's Hochstapler (J. Osborne); Mr F. Gretton's Suleiman (Fordham); Lord Lonsdale's Somerset (Custance); Mr H. Levy's Meter (Parry).

12 ran.

Betting:

9–4 Gang Forward; 4–1 Kaiser; 9–2 Hochstapler; 9–1 Montargis; 10–1 Chandos; 20–1 Somerset and Suleiman; 45–1 Doncaster; 50–1 Andred; 1,000–15 Meter.

Won by a length and a half; dead-heat for second place.   2 m. 50 s.
Winner trained by R. Peck at Russley.

1874

They were not a good lot of three-year-olds in 1874, and in all probability George Frederick, who won the Derby, was well below the average standard of winners of that race.

George Frederick was bred near Swansea by Mr W. S. Cartwright, who had originally been a solicitor, but who had extensive mining interests in Wales. As far as racing went, Mr Cartwright's fortunes were largely founded on a mare by Melbourne called The Bloomer. As a six-year-old The Bloomer was given by Mr John Stanley to Alec Taylor, senior, who sold her to Tom Olliver for twenty-five pounds, a sum, incidentally, that was never paid. Olliver, who was training at Wroughton for Mr Cartwright, re-sold her to his patron, for whom she produced Princess of Wales and Ely, the latter the winner of the Ascot and Goodwood Cups. Princess of Wales, by Stockwell, was repeatedly mated with Marsyas, the offspring, all named after a member of the Royal family, being Albert Victor, one of the best colts of his year, Louise Victoria, Victoria Alexandra, George Frederick, Maud Victoria, Albert Edward, and George Albert. History has not related whether Queen Victoria accepted Mr Cartwright's nomenclature as a compliment.

By 1873 Tom Olliver, that once great rider and winner of three Grand Nationals, was poor in pocket and poorer still in health. Accordingly Tom Leader, a young man of twenty-six who had been born at Wroughton and who managed Mr Cartwright's stud, was sent to give him a hand with the training. In fact from the moment of his arrival Leader really took over the stable, poor Olliver being too sick and too listless to take much interest.

George Frederick was a big, gross, heavy-shouldered colt that had not been getting nearly enough work before Leader began to take him in hand. He was hog-fat when he ran unplaced at York in August, and he was still hardly a quarter fit when he went to Doncaster to run in the Municipal Stakes on St Leger day. Early that morning, a very wet and unpleasant one, Tom Chaloner rode the colt in what was meant to be a brisk six furlongs, beginning at the St Leger start. At the end of the six furlongs the rain was teeming down and, not wishing to return under such conditions at a walk, Chaloner proceeded to complete the entire St Leger course. What with the rain and the sweat which were cascading down him, George Frederick was a sorry picture when he returned. However, Leader took him behind the stands, removed his clothing, scraped him down, and made him a little bit more presentable before he walked him home. As it happened the exercise had done George Frederick good and he beat his solitary opponent, Apology, a filly owned by the Rev. Mr King, who raced under the name of 'Mr Launde', by a length and a half. It would have been difficult to foretell at the time that George Frederick would win the Derby the following year, and Apology the Oaks and the St Leger.

George Frederick was beaten in a second race at Doncaster, but he was gradually improving and won the Boscawen Stakes and another event at the First October Meeting. At the Second October Meeting, the last fixture that Tom Olliver attended before his death a few months later, George Frederick ran in the Middle Park Stakes, but was unplaced in a big but moderate field behind Newry, who never won another race before or after. He remained up at Newmarket with Leader and did some very strong work before the Houghton Meeting, but his trainer tried to cram just a bit too much into a fortnight, and although George Frederick looked lighter and fitter, he was utterly stale and failed completely when he ran in the Criterion Stakes.

George Frederick wintered well, but got extremely gross again and his preparation was hindered by the interference of his owner, who kept on telling Leader that he was pushing the colt along too fast. Fortunately George Frederick had two races before Epsom, a Biennial in which he was third and the Newmarket Stakes, which he won, and they did him the world of good. He acquitted himself splendidly, too, in his final gallop, after which both Leader and Mr Cartwright were supremely confident. In fact on the morning of the Derby, Mr Cartwright, who was usually anything but sanguine, wrote out thirty telegrams to friends telling them that his horse had won.

The favourite was Mr Merry's Glenalmond but he owed his position less to actual accomplishment than to the prestige enjoyed by his stable. Atlantic, winner of the Two Thousand Guineas, had had his preparation interrupted by a slight mishap and was rather less fancied than his stable companion Aquilo. Lord Rosebery's Couronne de Fer was well supported, and George Frederick would undoubtedly have started at shorter odds than 9–1 if so many alleged experts had not declared that a colt with shoulders like his could never come down the hill. As a matter of fact he came down the hill like the handiest of polo ponies and gave Custance a wonderfully smooth ride to win in a canter by two lengths from Couronne de Fer with Atlantic a neck away third. His victory was received with tremendous rejoicings in Wales, where every sporting Welshman had had his little bit on, and also at Swindon, the nearest town to the Wroughton Stables. There the church bells were pealed and brass bands paraded the streets till late on into the night. Backers of Atlantic naturally declared that their selection would have won but for his mishap, but the fact remains that George Frederick triumphed with the proverbial ton in hand.

George Frederick met with a mishap soon after the Derby and was unable to run at Ascot. He was trained for the St Leger, however, but became lame again the day before the race and had to be scratched. The following year he ran in the Claret Stakes when nothing like fit and was easily beaten. That ended his racing career and he was retired to the stud at Mr Hume Webster's place, Morden Deer Park.

George Frederick was a failure as a sire. Furthermore, he became increasingly savage. After three of his attendants had been mauled and suffered broken arms, no one could be found who was willing to enter his box until Mr Webster appeared on the scene in person. After a few preliminary sarcasms at the expense of those who were holding back, he approached the box with jaunty confidence: 'I have never yet come across a horse I could not master,' he remarked, and having removed his coat and armed himself with a cudgel, he stepped inside. A roar of rage greeted him, and only the speed and agility of his retreat saved him from serious injury. Eventually George Frederick was exported to America where he died in 1896.

1874: Wednesday, 3 June . . . 212 Entries. £5,350.

MR W. S. CARTWRIGHT's ch.c. GEORGE FREDERICK by Marsyas
   out of Princess of Wales   H. CUSTANCE   1
LORD ROSEBERY's br.c. COURONNE DE FER by Macaroni
   out of Miss Agnes   T. CHALONER   2
LORD FALMOUTH's ch.c. ATLANTIC by Thormanby
   out of Hurricane   T. OSBORNE   3

Also ran:

   Lord Falmouth's Aquilo (Parry); Mr W. S. Cartwright's Volturno (Constable); Colonel Carleton's Reverberation (H. Jeffery); Mr J. Johnstone's Tipster (J. Osborne); Mr Lefevre's Ecossais (Fordham); Mr Merry's Glenalmond (F. Webb); Sir R. Bulkeley's Leolinus (J. Goater); Mr Evington's First Lord (Butler); Mr W. R. Marshall's Trent (T. Cannon); Mr Johnstone's King of Tyne (F. Archer); Mr F. Gretton's Algebra (Huxtable); Mr J. Bowes's Whitehall (Morris); Mr W. Hall's Selsea Bill (G. Lowe); Mr Peddie's Sir Arthur (J. Snowden); Mr F. Fisher's Rostrevor (Jewitt); Mr Laurie's Belford (Griffiths); Mr Savile's filly by Skirmisher out of Vertumna (Maidment).

20 ran.

Betting:

   9–2 Glenalmond; 100–15 Aquilo; 7–1 Couronne de Fer; 9–1 George Frederick;

Ormonde and The Bard

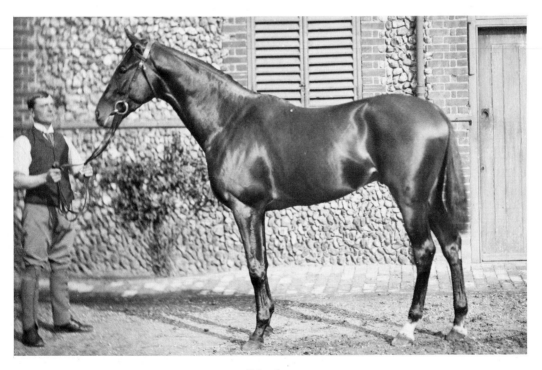

Isinglass

The Fifth Earl of Rosebery with Ladas (J. Watts up)

Persimmon winning the 1896 Derby

11–1 Leolinus; 100–8 Atlantic; 16–1 Ecossais; 20–1 Tipster and the filly by Skirmisher; 22–1 King of Tyne; 33–1 Rostrevor and Reverberation; 40–1 Trent and First Lord; 100–1 Algebra, Whitehall, Selsea Bill, and Sir Arthur.

Won by two lengths; a neck between second and third.   2 m. 46 s.
Winner trained by T. Leader at Wroughton.

1875

Prince Batthyany, who won the Derby in 1875 with Galopin, was by birth a Hungarian, but he came to England in his early twenties, and like other central Europeans of his class and type, he was greatly attracted to the life that was then open to a good-looking young man with plenty of money and sporting proclivities. He became to all intents and purposes a naturalized Englishman and for many years he was a familiar and much-liked figure on English racecourses. He started his stud in 1843 and was elected to the Jockey Club sixteen years later. For a considerable period he met with only limited success on the Turf, but from the middle sixties, with Matt Dawson's brother John as his trainer, his luck took a change for the better. His training establishment was maintained in appropriately princely style, the horses' clothing being of scarlet, while the lads were decked out in dark blue livery and tall hats. He died of a heart attack at Newmarket in 1884 on the threshold of the Jockey Club luncheon-room, having become fatally over-excited at the prospect of the Two Thousand Guineas being won by Galliard, a son of his beloved Galopin. One of his horses that was sold after his death was St Simon, who was bought by the young Duke of Portland. Unbeaten, and in fact never extended on the racecourse, St Simon was perhaps the most successful sire this country has ever known.

Galopin, bred by Mr Taylor Sharpe of Baumber Park, Lincolnshire, was by Voltigeur's son Vedette out of Flying Duchess, by The Flying Dutchman. His grand-dam Merope was by Voltaire, the sire of Voltigeur. Mr Sharpe had bought Flying Duchess for eighty guineas at the break-up of the Norfolk Stud, and in 1871 he sent her to the Diss Stud to be covered by Vedette. In due course she returned home and the following spring foaled Galopin. It was sometimes alleged in later years that Galopin was really by Delight, another horse standing at Diss. The Diss stud-groom stated that Vedette was paralysed at the time of the mare's visit, and it was common knowledge in addition that affairs at Diss were conducted in a thoroughly haphazard manner. However, Galopin exhibited so many of the characteristics of the Blacklock family that it is safe to assume that Vedette was indeed his sire.

Galopin, a bay standing fifteen hands three, showed great promise in both his yearling trials and started favourite for his first race, the Hyde Park Stakes at the Epsom Spring Meeting. In a bumping finish he was beaten a head by a filly called

Cachmere, but was awarded the race on an objection. At Ascot he won the Fern Hill Stakes and the New Stakes, both with the utmost ease, and was then given a rest until the Middle Park Stakes in October. In that event he was most unluckily beaten a couple of heads by Plebian and Per Se after being almost knocked over by another competitor in the Dip. So fast was Galopin as a two-year-old that John Dawson wanted to match him over five furlongs against that redoubtable sprinter Prince Charlie, 'The Prince of the T.Y.C.', but Prince Batthyany was too fond of his colt to subject him to so arduous a test.

Galopin wintered well and his only outing before the Derby was a match over the Rowley Mile for £500 against Mr Chaplin's filly Stray Shot. Galopin gave her ten pounds and won by ten lengths in a canter. Possibly the achievement did not add up to much, but it was sufficiently impressive to have him made favourite for the Derby, although not a few experienced judges considered that a colt with his exceptional speed was unlikely to stay the distance.

Dawson's trust in Galopin was such that he never subjected him to a formal trial before the Derby, and Galopin repaid that confidence by winning at Epsom by a comfortable length from Claremont with the Repentance colt a further six lengths away third. Undoubtedly Galopin's task had been made easier by the fact that Camballo, winner of the Two Thousand Guineas, was unsound, while Holy Friar was unable to run owing to the death of his nominator, the Rev. J. W. King. Backers of Holy Friar were naturally vexed and there was an agitation, often repeated in later years, to abolish the rule whereby an entry became void on the death of the nominator. It was maintained for many years that legal difficulties barred the way to reform, and the rule continued to exist until a friendly legal action by Mr Edgar Wallace against the Jockey Club, which Mr Wallace won on appeal, paved the way for its abolition in 1929.

Galopin was ridden at Epsom by Morris, a sound jockey who obeyed orders, but who was handicapped by his deafness. Morris's belief in the superiority of Galopin was such that he had no qualms in taking him on the very wide outside at Tattenham Corner, reckoning it was well worth while to lose ground in the certainty of avoiding trouble. Undoubtedly Morris took matters a bit easily at the finish and it was just as well that Fordham yelled at him 'Go on, Deafie!' to warn him that Claremont was getting dangerously close. Poor Morris, he died years later, penniless and forgotten, in a cellar.

Galopin showed his versatility by returning to sprinting at Ascot and making hacks of some good-class two-year-olds in the Fern Hill Stakes. Unfortunately he was not engaged in the St Leger, but in the autumn, receiving twelve pounds, he defeated the five-year-old Lowlander in a £1,000 Match over the Rowley Mile.

1875

Two days later he won the Newmarket Derby, beating Craig Millar, who had won the St Leger, quite comfortably. That was the end of Galopin's racing career. His owner's heart was weak and it was feared that the excitement of seeing his favourite run might prove to be the death of him.

Galopin made rather a slow start as a sire, but in 1883 he was second to Hermit, while he was Champion Sire in 1888, 1889, and, finally, when twenty-six years of age, in 1898. A great horse himself, he sired an even greater one in St Simon, who was denied success in the classics through Prince Batthyany's death. He was also sire of Galliard and Disraeli, winners of the Two Thousand Guineas; of Galeottia, winner of the One Thousand Guineas; and of Donovan, winner of both the Derby and the St Leger. On Prince Batthyany's death, Galopin was bought for 8,000 guineas by Mr Henry Chaplin and stood at the Blankney Stud till he died in 1899.

1875: Wednesday, 26 May . . . 198 Entries. £4,950.

PRINCE BATTHYANY's b.c. GALOPIN by Vedette		
out of Flying Duchess	MORRIS	1
LORD AYLESFORD's b.c. CLAREMONT, by Blair Athol		
out of Coimbra	MAIDMENT	2
LORD FALMOUTH's b.c. by Macaroni		
out of Repentance	F. ARCHER	3

Also ran:

Lord Falmouth's Garterly Bell (H. Jeffery); Mr C. Vyner's Camballo (J. Osborne); Lord Aylesford's Telescope (Glover); Prince Soltykoff's Balfe (T. Cannon); Mr W. S. Cartwright's The Bay of Naples (Custance); Lord Fitzwilliam's Breechloader (F. Webb); Mr H. Savile's Earl of Dartrey (W. Plate); Mr John Watson's Earlston (Constable); Mr F. E. Brace's Fareham (T. Osborne); Count F. de Lagrange's Gilbert (Fordham); Count F. de Lagrange's Punch (Carver); Mr C. Bush's Lord Berners (Parry); Mr J. Dawson's Seymour (C. Wood); Lord Ailesbury's Temple Bar (T. Chaloner); Mr F. Swindell's Woodlands (J. Goater).

18 ran.

Betting:

2–1 Galopin; 100–12 Balfe; 9–1 Camballo; 100–8 Repentance colt; 100–7 Claremont and The Bay of Naples; 20–1 Woodlands; 22–1 Temple Bar; 25–1 Seymour, Breechloader, and Earl of Dartrey; 30–1 Telescope; 100–3 Fareham; 1,000–15 Lord Berners and Gilbert; 100–1 Garterley Bell and Punch.

Won by a length; six lengths between second and third.   2 m. 48 s.
Winner trained by J. Dawson at Newmarket.

1876

Kisber, who won in 1876, was bred at the Hungarian Imperial Stud at Kisber, but his pedigree was exclusively English, his sire being Buccaneer, by Wild Dayrell, and his dam Mineral, by Rataplan out of Manganese, by Birdcatcher. He was bought as a yearling for the equivalent of £500 by the Baltazzi brothers and ran in the name and colours of Mr Alexander Baltazzi, who was well under thirty years of age at the time. The Baltazzis were the sons of a Levantine merchant in Turkey, but had been educated at Rugby, where they developed a love of sport. After leaving school, they spent a short period in Constantinople and Vienna before returning to England, where they had a few horses in training with Joseph Hayhoe, whose chief patrons were, of course, the Rothschilds.

As a two-year-old Kisber shaped like a stayer of exceptional promise when he won the Dewhurst Plate at Newmarket in the autumn, and from that moment onwards he was looked upon as a likely candidate for the Derby. His chief rival was Mr Spencer's Petrarch, by Lord Clifden. Petrarch was a convincing winner of the Middle Park, beating no fewer than twenty-eight opponents, and shortly afterwards he was bought by Lord Dupplin for £10,000. In the spring Petrarch, when far from fit, was galloped against his stable companion Kaleidoscope. The gallop, which took place against John Dawson's advice and on the direct order of Lord Dupplin, resulted in an easy win for Kaleidoscope, whom Lord Dupplin then backed heavily for the Two Thousand Guineas. In the Guineas, however, Petrarch, who ran as second string and started at 20–1, was a very easy winner indeed and became in consequence a short-priced favourite for the Derby.

Kisber meantime was completing a highly satisfactory preparation. Nevertheless certain bookmakers were ominously keen to lay him and there was a nasty rumour that he might not go to the post. The fact was that the Baltazzi brothers were in the hands of a moneylender, who threatened to seize the horse and prevent it from running. Luckily the situation was saved by Mr Sam Lewis, a moneylender himself, who stepped into the breach, settled the debt, and advanced the brothers a further £500 as well. Once that little matter was dealt with, Hayhoe's confidence knew no bounds. On the eve of the race he said to Gilbert, who had won in 1872 with Cremorne: 'Bill, I shall win the Derby tomorrow; there's not the slightest doubt about it.'

Coming down the hill to Tattenham Corner Petrarch was in front and going so easily that he looked sure to win. He continued to lead up the straight with the crowd all cheering him home, but when Kisber moved up to tackle him at the distance he did not put up the semblance of a struggle and Kisber ran on to win with the greatest ease by five lengths from Forerunner and Julius Caesar, who both were owned by Robert Peck. The Baltazzis won the best part of £100,000 on the race and Maidment received a very generous present, which he invested for the benefit of his wife and children.

Kisber was sent to Paris for the Grand Prix, which he won, while Petrarch went on to Ascot. He won his race on the first day most convincingly, but was soundly beaten in two other events at the meeting. The circumstances of those two defeats gave rise to considerable gossip, and Lord Dudley, who had lost £9,000 on one of them, refused to settle for a long time on the grounds that the colt had not been beaten on his merits. As in the Derby, certain bookmakers showed an alarming willingness to oppose Kisber in the St Leger. This time they won their money as Kisber was undoubtedly 'got at' and finished unplaced. In the words of John Osborne who rode him: 'He was beaten before he even started.' The winner was the erratic Petrarch, who beat the outsider Wild Honey by a neck. It is possible that Petrarch's in-and-out form was due to an intermittent kidney disease from which he suffered.

Kisber never ran again. He stood for many years at the Morden Deer Park Stud, but although he sired a fair number of winners, he was not an outstanding success by any means.

1876: Wednesday, 31 May . . . 226 Entries. £5,575.

MR A. BALTAZZI's b.c. KISBER by Buccaneer
    out of Mineral   MAIDMENT   I
MR R. PECK's b.c. FORERUNNER by The Earl or The Palmer
    out of Preface   F. WEBB   2
MR R. PECK's JULIUS CAESAR by St Albans
    out of Julie   T. CANNON   3

Also ran:

Lord Dupplin's Petrarch (4th) (Morris); Lord Rosebery's All Heart (Constable); Lord Rosebery's Bay Wyndham (J. Goater); Lord Rosebery's Father Claret (Morbey); Lord Falmouth's Skylark (F. Archer); Lord Falmouth's Great Tom (J. Osborne); Mr J. Houldsworth's Coltness (T. Osborne); Lord Zetland's Hardrada (J. Snowden); Count F. de Lagrange's Braconnier (Glover); Duke of Hamilton's

Wild Tommy (Custance); Mr Gomm's Advance (Chaloner); Lord Wilton's Wisdom (Parry).

15 ran.

Betting:

2–1 Petrarch; 4–1 Kisber; 100–15 Skylark and Forerunner; 100–12 All Heart; 33–1 Great Tom and Wild Tommy; 40–1 Julius Caesar; 50–1 Hardrada, Braconnier, and Bay Wyndham; 100–1 Wisdom and Coltness; 1,000–5 Advance and Father Claret.

Won by five lengths; three lengths between second and third.   2 m. 44 s.
Winner trained by J. Hayhoe at Newmarket.

1877

The most interesting feature of Silvio's Derby was the fact that Lord Falmouth's colt was partnered by Fred Archer, perhaps the greatest rider ever seen on the English Turf.

Fred Archer was born in 1857 at Cheltenham, his father being William Archer, a well-known steeplechase jockey who won the 1858 Grand National on Little Charlie. In 1868 Fred was apprenticed to Matt Dawson, with whose stable he was to remain in close association for the remainder of his life. He rode his first winner in 1870 and won the Cesarewitch in 1872, but the turning-point of his career came in 1874 when Lord Falmouth chose him to succeed Tom French, who had died in 1873. The very first season he rode for Lord Falmouth he won the Two Thousand Guineas, the One Thousand Guineas, and the Oaks, while he was third in the Derby on the Repentance colt. From then till his death in 1886 his career was one of unbroken and unprecedented success. He won the Derby five times, the St Leger six times, the Oaks four times, the Two Thousand Guineas four times, and the One Thousand Guineas twice. He rode in 8,084 races and won no fewer than 2,471 of them. Only Sir Gordon Richards has ridden a greater total of winners and Sir Gordon's career was of considerably longer duration.

Archer was tall for a jockey, five foot ten inches, good-looking but with a hint of melancholy in his expression, quiet in dress and in manner, and possessed of considerable charm. He weighed between ten and eleven stone in the winter and during the flat-racing season he was only able to keep his weight down by the constant application of the most drastic methods. A water biscuit and half a glass of champagne often composed his dinner, and the medicine he took acted like dynamite upon an ordinary man. It was a miracle, really, that his health endured for as long as it did.

His success was due to a variety of factors. He had a wonderful nerve and it was typical of him that he was invariably at his best at Epsom. His determination to win was coupled with an almost uncanny appreciation of the characteristics of any horse he rode and a consequent ability to induce its very best form. He used his brain and was exceptionally observant during a race. He rode a very strong finish although his method of sitting rather forward with a loose rein was reckoned to be more effective than elegant. There was no draw in those days and he usually left the paddock first to make sure of obtaining the best position. He had two weaknesses; he was some-times desperately severe on a horse he had backed—jockeys were permitted to bet in those days—and sometimes he was anything but scrupulous in his tactics against a fancied opponent.

Not surprisingly Archer had a tremendous public following and up in the north crowds used to assemble outside his hotel to cheer him as he left for the races. He had every excuse for becoming swollen-headed—he could have married a duchess had he desired to—but success and adulation never turned his head. Throughout his career there is no doubt that he owed much to the steadying influence of Matt Dawson, as shrewd and exacting a judge of men as he was of horses. He kept well clear of the riff-raff in racing and was intensely loyal to his few intimate friends.

In 1883 Archer married a daughter of John Dawson, but she died after giving birth to a daughter a year later. It was a blow from which he never really recovered. In the autumn of 1886 his health was deteriorating under the fearful demands that he made upon it, and a chill after the Cambridgeshire was followed by typhoid fever. In the course of that illness, and in a moment of terrible depression, he took a revolver and shot himself. Sporting England went into mourning and Lord Marcus Beresford spoke his epitaph when he said, 'Backers have lost the best friend they have ever had.'

Silvio was bred by his owner Lord Falmouth and was by Blair Athol out of Silverhair. He won the Ham Stakes at Goodwood on his first appearance and had three successes at Newmarket in the autumn, but in the Buckenham Stakes he was well beaten by Count Lagrange's Verneuil. His record was a thoroughly satisfactory one, but he had never beaten any two-year-old of importance and there was little disposition to regard him as a serious contender for the Derby.

He started the following season none too well by being unplaced at the Craven Meeting in the Newmarket Biennial. Possibly, however, the form was unreliable as the race took place under appalling weather conditions. In the Two Thousand Guineas he did very much better, finishing a good third to the French-bred Chamant and the American-bred Brown Prince. That performance, however, did not seem to impress the public much and he started at 100–9 in the Derby. Perhaps if his owner had given a lead the public would have followed it, but as usual Lord Falmouth did not bet.

The favourite for the Derby was Rob Roy, a rather flashy chestnut that had not seen a racecourse since his two-year-old days, but who had been galloped unbeatable at home. The Guineas winner Chamant was strongly supported despite having pulled up noticeably sore after his final gallop, while Brown Prince, Altyre, and Plunger were all preferred to Silvio in the market. At Tattenham Corner, where Glen Arthur led, Silvio was well behind the leaders, but together with Touchet he soon began to make up ground in the straight. Touchet faltered at the distance, but Silvio continued to make headway and mastering Glen Arthur, whose French jockey Dodge sported a beard, just under a hundred yards from the post, he won a thrilling race all out by half a length, with Rob Roy, who was flying at the finish, three parts of a length away third. Rhidorroch was close up fourth, only a head behind Rob Roy. Chamant, who hated the hard ground, was beaten a long way out. He pulled up lame and was taken out of training soon afterwards. It was generally agreed that young Archer had ridden with the coolness and judgement of a veteran.

Silvio beat Glen Arthur much more easily in the Ascot Derby and was then put by until the St Leger, which he won from his stable companion Lady Golightly, who had been fourth in the Oaks, and Manœuvre, a one-eyed mare that was subsequently the dam of the 1892 Derby winner Sir Hugo. In the autumn, however, Silvio's limitations were clearly exposed, as the four-year-old Springfield, a really good horse, conceded him twelve pounds in the Champion Stakes and beat him very comfortably indeed.

The following year Silvio won twice at Newmarket in the spring, but in the Gold Cup at Ascot he was well trounced by the French horse Verneuil. He was beaten by his stable companion Jannette in the Champion Stakes, but he was far from disgraced on that occasion as he was giving her fifteen pounds and had Verneuil, Petrarch, and Glen Arthur a long way behind him. He finished the season by a fine performance in the Jockey Club Cup in which he gave nineteen pounds successfully to Insulaire, who had won the French Derby and had been second in both the Epsom Derby and the Grand Prix.

As a five-year-old Silvio failed to win, but he ran creditably twice at Ascot, finishing second to Isonomy, who received seven pounds, in the Gold Vase and second to Chippendale, who received eighteen pounds, in the Hardwicke Stakes. He retired to the stud at a fee of twenty-five guineas, but failed to make his mark, and after three seasons he was exported to France, where he did very much better, once heading the list of winning sires.

1877: Wednesday, 30 May . . . 245 Entries. £6,050.

LORD FALMOUTH's b.c. SILVIO by Blair Athol out of Silverhair	F. ARCHER	1
MR W. S. MITCHELL-INNES's b.c. GLEN ARTHUR by Adventurer out of Maid of the Glen	DODGE	2
MR J. T. MACKENZIE's ch.c. ROB ROY by Blair Athol out of Columba	CUSTANCE	3

Also ran:

Mr W. Bevill's Rhidorroch (4th) (H. Jeffery); Mr H. E. Beddington's Altyre (T. Cannon); Mr M. Sandford's Brown Prince (J. Osborne); Count F. de Lagrange's Chamant (J. Goater); Mr C. J. Langland's Don Carlos (R. Wyatt); Lord Anglesey's The Grey Friar (Hunt); Mr Bowes's Jagellon (Griffiths); Mr W. Roger's Lady Miller (Weston); Mr Gerard's Orleans (F. Webb); Mr H. Baltazzi's Plunger (T. Chaloner); Mr C. Alexander's Thunderstone (Morley); Mr J. H. Houldsworth's Tantalus (T. Osborne); Lord Rosebery's Touchet (Constable); Mr H. Bird's Covenanter (Morris).

17 ran.

Betting:

3–1 Rob Roy; 4–1 Chamant; 100–15 Altyre and Brown Prince; 9–1 Plunger; 100–9 Silvio; 100–7 Touchet; 40–1 The Grey Friar; 50–1 Glen Arthur, Jagellon, Thunderstone, Orleans, and Tantalus.

Won by half a length; three parts of a length between second and third. 2 m. 50 s. Winner trained by M. Dawson at Newmarket.

1878

Mr W. Stirling Crawfurd, who won with Sefton in 1878, was born in 1819. He came from an old Scottish family and assumed the additional name of Crawfurd shortly before he was twenty-one. A member of the Jockey Club, he had a long and successful career as an owner. Apart from Sefton's victory, he won the One Thousand Guineas with Mayonnaise, Thebais, and St Marguerite, the Oaks with Thebais, and the St Leger with Craig Millar. In addition his colt Moslem dead-heated with Formosa for the Two Thousand.

In 1876 Mr Stirling Crawfurd married Caroline, widow of the fourth Duke of Montrose, a lady more familiarly known as 'Carrie Red'. She raced under the nom de course of 'Mr Manton' and at one time owned a useful mare called Corrie Roy that won the Cesarewitch. There was a little rhyme at that period that went as follows:

> Corrie Roy and Carrie Red,
> One for the stable, t'other for bed.
> Carrie Red and Corrie Roy,
> Isn't Craw a lucky boy?

'Carrie Red' was one of the outstanding personalities of her day. She knew as much about form and the stud book as any man, and conducted her racing affairs with considerable efficiency. Tall and upright, her features in later years were unsparingly adorned with paint, and her hair was dyed that particular shade of gold that makes not the slightest attempt at deception. Her clothes were of an essentially masculine and 'horsy' cut and she usually wore a stock and a homberg hat. When things were going well she could be very amusing company, but she was fickle and vindictive if thwarted in any respect, and when she was in one of her moods, she was apt to make cruel, cutting, and frequently untrue comments in a singularly soft and charming voice. When thoroughly roused, her language and power of expression was more than a match for the roughest bookmaker in Tattersalls. At one time it was widely believed that she intended to marry Fred Archer, and she was parodied in a musical comedy called *The Sporting Duchess*. At times she was utterly ruthless on the Turf, and insisted on her husband scratching Thebais at the eleventh hour when the filly was favourite for the Cambridgeshire. When Thebais won a small race the following day, there was nearly a riot at Newmarket. 'Carrie Red' tried to brazen it out, but eventually she broke down and was driven from the course amid a storm of jeers and invective.

Once, when a spell of bad weather threatened the harvest, the vicar of St Agnes, Newmarket, offered up prayers for fine weather. The Duchess stumped out of church forthwith, sent for the vicar afterwards and abused him thoroughly on the grounds that he ought to have known that her St Leger candidate only went well in the mud. On another occasion she approached Major Egerton, a somewhat portly handi-capper, and addressed him as follows: 'Major Egerton, I see from the way you handicap my horses that you are desirous of riding them yourself. I only intend to say that on no account will your wish be gratified.' After Mr Stirling Crawfurd's death she carried on his stud and the stable, and when seventy years of age she brought off a final surprise by marrying Mr Henry Milner, who was then aged twenty-four.

Sefton was by the Goodwood Cup winner Speculum out of the dam of Liverpool, by West Australian. Speculum, a son of Vedette, founded an important sire line which was carried on to Santoi and Achtoi in one stirp and to Sunstar, Mon Talis-man, Admiral Drake, and Phil Drake in another. Sefton himself was bred at the Glasgow Stud, Enfield, and was a bright bay, long in the back and low on the leg, with plenty of good points. Bought by Mr Stirling Crawfurd as a yearling for 1,000 guineas, he hardly looked like proving a bargain as a two-year-old as he ran on four occasions without winning a race.

He began his three-year-old career by running second in the Craven Stakes to Thurio, who gave him five pounds. A few days later, carrying 5 st. 8 lb., he won the City and Suburban by a head from Lord Lonsdale's Advance. There were some good horses in the field for the handicap including Petrarch, who carried 9 st. 4 lb., and Verneuil, with fourteen pounds less on his back. Sefton continued to improve and he was a creditable third in the Two Thousand Guineas behind Lord Lonsdale's good filly Pilgrimage, whom her breeder Mr Cookson had sold as a yearling for 200 guineas, and the little black French-bred colt Insulaire. Two days later Pil-grimage won the One Thousand Guineas as well.

Pilgrimage was not entered for the Derby and the favourite accordingly was Insulaire, who had won the Prix du Jockey Club the previous Sunday. A tough, hardy colt, Insulaire was none the worse for his exertions and the journey, and made a bold bid for victory at Epsom, but found one just too good for him in Sefton, who started at 100–12. Ridden by Constable, Sefton took up the running at least a mile from home. He ran on strongly in the straight, and when he beat off Childeric's challenge at the distance, he looked like winning quite comfortably. Constable, in fact, showed signs of over-confidence, and Fred Archer always declared that Constable would have been caught napping but for his warning shout 'Look out! Old Jim Goater's coming!' as Insulaire made his effort. Constable then rode Sefton home for all he was worth and he passed the post a length and a half in front of Insulaire, who had not really liked the sticky going, with Childeric a similar distance away third. As soon as Epsom was over, the hard-worked Insulaire departed for Paris again, where he was beaten a head in the Grand Prix by Thurio.

At Ascot Sefton only dead-heated for third place in the Prince of Wales's Stakes with Bonnie Scotland behind Glengarry and Childeric, but he was conceding four pounds to Childeric and sixteen pounds each to the other two. In the Newmarket St Leger he put up perhaps the best performance of his career, giving two pounds and a six lengths' beating to Insulaire, with Thurio and Childeric both a very long way behind. In his next race, the Cesarewitch, he broke down badly and could never be trained again. He retired to the stud at a fifty-guinea fee, but was a failure and was put down in 1891.

Sefton was trained by old Alec Taylor, father of Alec Taylor, 'the wizard of Manton', who turned out so many famous winners during the first quarter of this century. 'Old Alec' was a fearlessly outspoken man, who stood no nonsense from anyone, and even the formidable 'Carrie Red' was said to stand in some awe of him. Contrary to the general opinion that Sefton was a mediocre Derby winner, Taylor had quite a high opinion of the colt. 'I never had him quite to my liking, but he stayed very well and would have made a Cup horse if only I could have kept him sound.'

Harry Constable was a good and stylish rider, a sound judge of a horse and of the form-book, and a man of intelligence and integrity. He often bemoaned the fact that he had never ridden a really good horse in the whole of his career and he certainly never put Sefton into that category. He rode many winners for Lord Rosebery, whom he greatly admired and respected and for whom he was extremely proud to ride. When he died of tuberculosis in the prime of life, Lady Rosebery helped to nurse him during the final stages of his illness.

1878: Wednesday, 5 June . . . 231 Entries. £5,825.

MR W. STIRLING CRAWFURD's b.c. SEFTON by Speculum
out of Liverpool's dam   H. CONSTABLE   I
COUNT F. DE LAGRANGE's bl.c. INSULAIRE
by Dutch Skater out of Green Sleeve   J. GOATER   2
LORD FALMOUTH's b.c. CHILDERIC by Scottish Chief
out of Gertrude   F. ARCHER   3

Also ran :

'Mr Acton's' Topaz (4th) (Dodge); Mr R. N. Ball's Castlereagh (J. Osborne); Prince Soltykoff's The Callant (Hopkins); Prince Soltykoff's Thurio (Rossiter); Mr J. R. Peyton's Zanoni (Chaloner); Mr Houldsworth's Attalus (Custance); Lord Rosebery's Bonnie Scotland (F. Webb); Lord Wilton's Censer (C. Wood); Mr T. Gee's Cyprus (Fordham); Mr T. Melville's John Frederick (Huxtable); Mr J. N. Barlow's Knighthood (Snowden); Mr F. Gretton's Knight of the Cross (T. Cannon); Mr T. J. Monk's Noble (S. Mordan); Count Festetic's Oasis (Morgan); Count F. de Lagrange's Pontoise (Morris); Mr Mitchell-Innes's Potentate (Morbey); Mr Pulteney's Priscillian (H. Jeffery); Lord Rosebery's Ridotto (Wyatt); Mr W. J. Legh's Sir Joseph (Glover).

22 ran.

Betting :

100–30 Insulaire; 4–1 Bonnie Scotland; 6–1 Sir Joseph and Thurio; 100–12 Sefton and Cyprus; 100–8 Childeric; 100–7 Attalus; 50–1 Knight of the Cross; 66–1 Zanoni; 100–1 Oasis.

Won by half a length; the same distance between second and third.   2 m. 56 s. Winner trained by A. Taylor, senior, at Manton.

1879

Sefton may only have been moderate, but he was in all probability a considerably better racehorse than Sir Bevys, winner of the centenary Derby for Baron Lionel Rothschild, who raced under the name of 'Mr Acton'. The Baron owned considerable property, including a stud, in Acton, which is now an unattractive and densely populated suburb of London. Sir Bevys's opponents at Epsom were indisputably mediocre, and Peter, the best colt of the year, was unable to run on account of the death of his nominator, General Peel.

Bred by Lord Norreys at Wytham, near Oxford, Sir Bevys was a smallish brown colt by Favonius out of Lady Langden, by Kettledrum, and was thus a half-brother to Hampton, who proved to be a great sire after a strenuous racing career. As a two-year-old Sir Bevys succeeded in winning a race at Newmarket, but in general his form was uninspiring. He did not run again before the Derby in which, with George Fordham riding, he started at 20–1.

Although Derby Day itself was fine, there had been a lot of heavy rain just previously and the going was heavy. In the early stages of the race Sir Bevys was nearly a hundred yards behind the leaders, but Fordham refused to be hustled. In the straight Fordham wisely made for the sounder going on the extreme outside of the course and Sir Bevys at once began to make headway. Staying on stoutly, he mastered the 100–1 outsider Palmbearer a hundred yards from home to win by three parts of a length, with Visconti, another outsider, a further length away third.

Everyone was pleased to see Fordham win the race that had so long eluded him, and largely on that account Sir Bevys's victory was very well received. Few people in fact backed the winner, but among the visitors to the course who did so was Alfred Tennyson, then Poet Laureate, who had £100 to £5 about Sir Bevys 'because Sir Bevys was the hero of one of my early poems'. Shortly afterwards Sir Bevys went wrong in his wind, and after a poor display in the St Leger, he retired to the stud at a fee of ten guineas, approved mares and the dams of winners free. He had gained few honours as a sire when he died in 1896 at Morden Deer Park, having passed into the possession of Mr Hume Webster.

Born at Cambridge in 1837, George Fordham won his first race at Brighton in 1851 and a year later he won the Cambridgeshire riding at the remarkable weight of 3 st. 12 lb. As he grew older and stronger, so did his skill increase, and in his hey-day he was second, and a very close second at that, only to Archer. Year after year, though, despite many fancied mounts in the race, he failed in the Derby and he had in fact retired from the Turf without a solitary success in the 'Blue Riband' when, owing to some highly unsuccessful business ventures, he returned to the saddle and won the race on Sir Bevys.

In *Turf Memories of Sixty Years* Mr Alexander Scott described Fordham's style as follows:

I saw him ride at nearly every meeting in England under Jockey Club Rules between 1868 and 1883, a period of fifteen years, and shall never forget his peculiar seat, unlike that of any other jockey of his time. He rode with fairly short leathers, got well down on his mount's back, and slewed his head and body almost side-ways during a race with his shoulders hunched up high. This last mannerism was very effective in keeping his intentions up his sleeve, because he kept to that posture throughout a race, very seldom taking up his whip, but riding his mount home with his hands. In fact he got more out of a horse with his hands than any other jockey I remember.

His judgement of the winning post was of the first order, and to see him get up and win, body and head cocked on one side, with only his hands asking the horse a question, was an education in the art of timing a finish. It was by no means uncommon to hear the cry go up of 'Fordham's beat' in races which he eventually won, and no jockey could wish for a greater compliment than that.

He was a man of complete integrity, a great lover of children and animals. He hated to give a two-year-old a hard race first time out. 'When I get down to the post on these two-year-olds,' he once said to Mr Leo Rothschild, 'and I feel their little hearts beating under my legs, I think why not let them have an easy race, win if they can, but don't frighten them first time out.' His closing years were spent quietly at Slough, where he died in 1887. He never talked much about racing when he was at home and, detesting every sort of gambling, he did everything he could to prevent his son from coming into contact with the racing world.

Of those horses that finished unplaced behind Sir Bevys at Epsom, Rayon d'Or won the St Leger, while Muley Edris earned notoriety by savaging Fred Archer the following year.

1879

1879: Wednesday, 28 May . . . 278 Entries. £7,025.

'MR ACTON'S' br.c. SIR BEVYS by Favonius out of Lady Langden by Kettledrum	G. FORDHAM	1
MR J. TROTTER'S ch.c. PALMBEARER by The Palmer out of Schehallion	J. OSBORNE	2
LORD ROSEBERY'S br.c. VISCONTI by Parmesan out of Lady Audley	H. CONSTABLE	3

Also ran:

Duke of Westminster's Victor Chief (T. Chaloner); Sir G. Chetwynd's Abbot of St Mary's (H. Jeffery); Lord Ellesmere's Alpha (Huxtable); Captain Machell's Blue Blood (F. Webb); Lord Douglas Gordon's Cadogan (Custance); Lord Anglesey's Caxtonian (Morbey); Lord Falmouth's Charibert (F. Archer); Mr C. Blanton's Exeter (Rossiter); Mr F. Gretton's Falmouth (T. Cannon); Mr W. S. Cartwright's George Albert (C. Wood); Lord Dupplin's Marshall Scott (Luke); Lord Falmouth's Muley Edris (Morgan); Mr R. Shier's Nutbush (W. Platt); Count F. de Lagrange's Prologue (Dodge); Lord Bateman's Protectionist (R. Wyatt); Count F. de Lagrange's Rayon d'Or (J. Morris); Mr J. H. Houldsworth's Ruperra (J. Snowden); 'Mr Acton's' Squirrel (J. McDonald); Mr F. Davis's Whackum (Glover); Count F. de Lagrange's Zut (J. Goater).

23 ran.

Betting:

9–2 Cadogan; 5–1 Victor Chief; 6–1 Charibert; 8–1 Ruperra; 10–1 Zut; 100–7 Falmouth; 100–6 Caxtonian and Rayon d'Or; 20–1 Sir Bevys; 33–1 Abbot of St Mary's; 40–1 George Albert; 50–1 Muley Edris; 66–1 Visconti and Marshall Scott; 100–1 Blue Blood, Exeter, Palmbearer, Protectionist, Squirrel, and Whackum; 200–1 Alpha; 500–1 Nutbush and Prologue.

Won by three-quarters of a length; a length between second and third. 3 m. 2 s. Winner trained by J. Hayhoe at Newmarket.

1880

The Derby of 1880 provided one of the best and most exciting races in its history, only marred by a sensational sequel which left a lingering doubt in some minds as to the true identity of the winner.

In 1874 Hugh Lupus Grosvenor, first Duke of Westminster and reputedly the richest man in England, had paid the then almost unprecedented sum of 14,000 guineas to Robert Peck for Doncaster, winner of the Derby the previous year. From among Doncaster's first crop of foals the Duke bred at his stud at Eaton a colt, in due course named Bend Or, out of Rouge Rose, by Thormanby out of Ellen Horne. Rouge Rose had been bought as a ten-year-old from General Pearson, and was a half-sister to Paradigm, dam of Lord Lyon and Achievement. Ellen Horne was in her twenty-second year when she foaled Rouge Rose.

Bend Or was a chesnut with a white blaze on his face and a round black mark like a small cannon-ball in the middle of his near quarter. He stood sixteen hands one and combined power and quality in a quite unusual degree. In the autumn of 1878 he was sent with other yearlings from Eaton to be trained by Robert Peck at Russley. The following year he made his first racecourse appearance at Newmarket in the Chesterfield Stakes, which he duly won, beating among others Illuminata, who was destined to be the dam of Lord Rosebery's Derby winner Ladas. Bend Or then won the Richmond Stakes at Goodwood, the Prince of Wales's Stakes at York, and a Triennial and the Rous Memorial Stakes at Goodwood. He finished the season unbeaten, and so did his future rival Robert the Devil, but the latter had only two races. Another good two-year-old was Beaudesert, winner of the Middle Park Plate, but he broke down at an early stage of his three-year-old career, a bitter blow to Lord Alington, who had bought him the previous autumn for 5,000 guineas from Lord Anglesey.

The following year Bend Or did not run before the Derby for which he was made a clear favourite. Robert the Devil, however, turned out in a Newmarket Biennial and was narrowly beaten by Lord Falmouth's Apollo, to whom he conceded five pounds. The Bend Or camp, however, had plenty of worries to contend with. Not only did the favourite develop sore shins shortly before Epsom so that his trainer was up treating him all night, but Fred Archer was badly savaged by the four-year-old Muley Edris and one of his arms was painfully injured. While Archer was under treatment for his wounds, his weight went up to 9 st. 10 lb., and he had to undergo a drastic and weakening course of wasting to rid himself of a stone within four days.

There were nineteen runners and the start was one of McGeorge's best. Robert the Devil, heavily backed at 7–1, took the lead at the top of the hill, followed by Teviotdale, Mask, Mariner, and Bend Or. At Tattenham Corner Archer spotted the slenderest of openings on the rails and through it he drove the favourite though he had to lift his left leg to the level of Bend Or's head to prevent it from being crushed. This daring manœuvre placed Bend Or in a handy position and despite twisting a plate, he was second with two furlongs still to go. Robert the Devil, however, was two lengths clear and showed not the slightest sign of weakening. In fact, if his rider Rossiter had then ridden him home for all he was worth, he must surely have won, but nerves and indecision overcame the unfortunate Rossiter just when the goal was in sight. Of all fatal follies to commit, he steadied his mount and looked over his shoulder. To his amazement and horror he saw Bend Or very nearly alongside and Archer riding for all he was worth. The sight unmanned him and he lost his head completely. Archer immediately grasped the situation, and with a final, almost superhuman, effort landed the favourite in front on the post. Mask was a bad third, and Apollo fourth.

The winner, his owner, his trainer, and in particular his rider, were all given a wonderful reception, and there were cheers, too, for the gallant runner-up, owned in partnership by Mr Charles Brewer and his trainer Blanton. 'Robert's' dam Cast Off, by the Promised Land, had been barren for years when she was mated with Bertram. She was then turned out on some Fen land in Cambridgeshire and was left to get her living as best she could. There she remained in fact until Robert was foaled.

A fortnight after the Derby came the sequel. Mr Brewer approached Sir George Chetwynd, then Senior Steward of the Jockey Club, and informed him that he intended to object to Bend Or on the grounds that the colt was really Tadcaster, and that the identities had been mixed up on the hand-over from Eaton to Robert Peck's stable. Sir George suggested that Mr Brewer might speak to the Duke of Westminster on the subject first, but Mr Brewer was a man of humble origin and class distinctions were more clearly defined in those days. 'What,' he replied, quite shocked at the idea, 'me go up to the Duke of Westminster's front door, ring the bell and ask to see him?' It seemed to Mr Brewer an unthinkable liberty, and no doubt the Duke would have agreed.

Sir George, having won money on Bend Or, did not sit on the inquiry, and after a protracted hearing, the Stewards of Epsom published the following announcement:

We, as Stewards of Epsom, unanimously decide that the chesnut colt Bend Or, which came in first for the Derby of 1880, is by Doncaster out of Rouge Rose, and therefore the objection lodged by Messrs Brewer and Blanton is overruled.

(Signed) W. G. Craven.

James Lowther.

Calthorpe (for Sir G. Chetwynd).

Most of the evidence produced by Mr Brewer emanated from the Eaton stud-groom, who was under notice to quit, and from people closely connected with him. Under the circumstances, it is perhaps not surprising that the objection was over-ruled. The fact remains that as he lay dying some years later, the chief witness re-affirmed the truth of his statements, while Mr Lowther declared that additional facts which came to his knowledge later made him doubt whether he and his fellow-Stewards had given the right decision. One thing was quite clear; the Eaton stud book had been maintained in lamentably haphazard fashion.

At Ascot Bend Or won the St James's Palace Stakes, but he failed signally to stay the distance in heavy going when an odds-on favourite for the St Leger, and Robert the Devil, ridden by Tom Cannon, won in the drenching rain by an easy three lengths from Lord Rosebery's filly Cipolata. In the Great Foal Stakes Across The Flat at Newmarket early in October 'Robert' again beat the Derby winner, but this time only by a head. At the Second October Meeting 'Robert' proved beyond all doubt what an outstanding racehorse he was, winning the Cesarewitch carrying 8 st. 6 lb. and giving Cipolata a stone, while two days later he slammed Bend Or by a clear ten lengths in the Champion Stakes.

The following year Bend Or won the City and Suburban with nine stone on his back, giving thirty-five pounds to the three-year-old Foxhall, who won both the Cesarewitch and Cambridgeshire in the autumn. The fifth and final meeting between himself and Robert the Devil took place in the Epsom Gold Cup—now called the Coronation Cup—over the Derby course at the Derby meeting. When the two horses came on to the course there was a sudden silence; betting stopped and everyone gazed at the two champions. It was a splendid battle and from the distance the rivals raced home neck and neck, Bend Or, ridden with superb confidence by Archer, gaining the mastery close home to win rather cleverly by a neck. Bend Or won the Champion Stakes in the autumn, but was unplaced in the Cambridgeshire with 9 st. 8 lb. He then retired to the stud at Eaton at a fee of fifty guineas, which later was raised to a hundred.

Robert the Devil, a great slashing bay horse slightly on the leg, had won the Grand Prix de Paris as a three-year-old and as a four-year-old he won the Gold Cup at Ascot and also the Alexandra Plate. He went wrong shortly afterwards and was sent to the stud, having won twelve of his sixteen races and over £23,000 in stakes. When Mr Brewer died he was sold to Mr Bowes for approximately £8,000, and was later re-sold to Mr Henry Waring, dying at the Benham Park Stud near Newbury in 1889. He was not a stud success, the best of his progeny being that good but rather unsound performer Chittabob.

It is arguable that 'Robert' was a better horse than Bend Or as he defeated him three times out of five, twice by decisive margins, and was desperately unlucky not to have won the Derby. He was unquestionably the better stayer of the two. Bend Or, however, did a great deal better at the stud and was twice second and twice third in the winning sires' list before his death at the age of twenty-six. He himself was Doncaster's best son and came from Doncaster's first crop of foals, while the best horse he himself ever got was the mighty Ormonde, who came from his own first crop of runners. Ormonde, in his turn, got Orme in his very first season at the stud.

The Duke of Westminster was one of the leading owners and breeders on the English Turf in the last twenty years of the century. He was born in 1825, and before his death in 1899 he had won the Two Thousand Guineas with Shotover, Ormonde, and Flying Fox, the One Thousand Guineas with Farewell, the Derby with Bend Or, Shotover, Ormonde, and Flying Fox, and the St Leger with Ormonde and Flying Fox. He was a tall, upright man of patrician appearance, with a rather ascetic cast of countenance, dignified, reserved, and self-contained, but endowed with considerable charm which he chose to use sparingly. He was an exceptional horseman, and knew as much as any man about the breeding, training, and riding of thoroughbreds.

1880: Wednesday, 26 May . . . 256 Entries. £6,375.

DUKE OF WESTMINSTER's ch.c. BEND OR by Doncaster
   out of Rouge Rose   F. ARCHER   1
MR C. BREWER's b.c. ROBERT THE DEVIL by Bertram
   out of Cast Off   ROSSITER   2
PRINCE SOLTYKOFF's ch.c. MASK by Carnival
   out of Meteor   GLOVER   3

Also ran:

Lord Falmouth's Apollo (4th) (C. Wood); Lord Rosebery's Ercildoune (H. Constable); Lord Rosebery's Pelleas (Luke); Mr F. Gretton's Mariner (T. Cannon); Mr R. Jardine's Teviotdale (J. Osborne); Duke of Westminster's Muncaster (J. Snowden); Lord Wilton's Cylinder (Hopkins); Mr L. de Rothschild's Valentino (J. Morris); Mr P. Lorrilard's Boreas (H. Jeffery); Lord Hastings's Fire King

(Morgan); Lord Calthorpe's Von der Tann (Fordham); Mr J. Gretton's Draycott (F. Webb); Mr H. Savile's Proctor (J. Goater); Lord Bradford's Zealot (W. McDonald); Mr B. C. Lane's Death or Glory (Maidment); Mr W. Bourke's colt by Uncas out of Hetty (Lynch).

19 ran.

Betting:

2–1 Bend Or; 100–15 Von der Tann; 7–1 Robert the Devil; 8–1 Muncaster; 100–8 Apollo; 100–7 Ercildoune; 20–1 Mask and Valentino; 25–1 Teviotdale; 33–1 Fire King; 40–1 Cylinder; 50–1 Mariner and Draycott; 66–1 Zealot.

Won by a head; a bad third.   2 m. 46 s.
Winner trained by R. Peck at Russley.

1881

The first American Derby victory—the second was that of Never Say Die in 1954—came in 1881, the winner being Iroquois, owned by Mr Pierre Lorillard, a tobacco millionaire who raced on the very best lines. In 1879 Mr Lorillard sent some yearlings over to Newmarket, Iroquois among them, accompanied by his trainer Jacob Pincus, who relied largely on the clock when he worked his horses, and whose methods were viewed in this country, at any rate to start with, with considerable scepticism. Pincus remained in England after Mr Lorillard had temporarily given up racing here and became a much-liked member of the Newmarket community.

Iroquois was bred by Mr Aristides Welch at the Erdenheim Stud near Philadelphia and was by Leamington out of Maggie B.B., by Australian. Leamington had been imported from England and was by Faugh-a-Ballagh, a full brother to Birdcatcher. A handsome horse with a beautiful action, Iroquois ran on twelve occasions as a two-year-old, his four successes including the Chesterfield Stakes at Newmarket and the Lavant Stakes at Goodwood. He began his three-year-old campaign by running second to the Duke of Westminster's Peregrine in the Two Thousand Guineas, a performance that was extremely gratifying to Pincus as the American colt had been amiss and was a long way from being at his best. Peregrine, who ran in the name of Mr Grosvenor owing to the recent death of the Duchess of Westminster, won the Guineas with considerable ease and there was a tendency to regard him as a colt of exceptional merit. Fred Archer, however, thought otherwise, and he went to Pincus and asked for the ride on Iroquois. Needless to say, his request was speedily granted.

Iroquois beat a solitary opponent in the Newmarket Stakes and then had a walkover in the Burwell Stakes. Pincus in the meantime was working him hard at home and most critics thought that the American colt had run up light when they saw him in the paddock at Epsom. In fact he was trained to the minute, and with Archer supremely confident, he started a heavily supported second favourite at 11–2.

Seldom has the Derby been run on a hotter afternoon and the thousands of spectators on the shadeless Downs were grilled. Mr Lorillard himself had not made the journey to Epsom, but his wife was there with a big American contingent. The early stages of the race were uneventful and at Tattenham Corner the leader was Lord Rosebery's Voluptuary, who, in the hands of Mr E. P. Wilson, won the Grand

National Steeplechase three years later. With just over two furlongs to go, however, Voluptuary was in trouble and was headed by Scobell, Town Moor, and Cumberland. Almost immediately these three were joined by Peregrine, ridden by Webb who had finished fifth in the Grand National that year on The Scot. Unfortunately, as soon as Webb went for his whip, Peregrine, who was close to the rails, swerved sharply away to the right. Archer had been tracking the favourite, and as soon as this happened, he seized his opportunity and steered his mount straight through the gap. Iroquois rapidly closed with the favourite, who, despite his swerve, had shaken off the remainder, and mastered him well inside the final furlong to win rather cleverly by a neck. Town Moor was third, two lengths behind Peregrine, and Scobell fourth.

Although the winner was a 'foreigner', his victory was heartily applauded, no doubt largely because Archer rode him and a great many people had backed him. There were scenes of wild enthusiasm when the news was received in New York. Business on Wall Street was temporarily suspended and the Stock Exchange reverberated to prolonged outbursts of cheering. There was particular jubilation among the thousands of Irish-Americans who regarded England as their deadly enemy and the success of Iroquois as a long-overdue blow at English arrogance and self-esteem. In kindlier vein were the following lines:

> Flushed red are American faces!
> Hurrah! for old Leamington's son.
> You'll show the pale Briton how races
> Across the Atlantic are run.
> Dash on as if life was at Venture
> And news shall unloosen the cork
> From seas of champagne at Newmarket
> And oceans of 'fizz' in New York!

Iroquois won the Prince of Wales's Stakes and the St James's Palace Stakes at Ascot, and then the St Leger, for which he started a 2–1 favourite despite rumours, due no doubt to Pincus's unconventional training methods, that he was a 'dead 'un'. He ran well below his best in the Champion Stakes and was only third to Bend Or and Scobell, but two days later he won the Newmarket Derby very easily. He never ran at all the following season and finished his career in 1883 by beating Scobell in the Stockbridge Cup. Unquestionably a really good horse at his best, he retired to the stud at the Bellmead Farm, Tennessee, where his record until his death in 1899 was fairly satisfactory, although he can hardly be said to have fulfilled the very high hopes that were held of him.

After Voluptuary's career over fences was finished, he was bought by an actor, Mr Leonard Boyne, who promptly put him in training for the stage. *The Prodigal Daughter* had a long run at the Drury Lane, and every night Voluptuary took the water-jump in the centre of the stage, while his unfortunate rider delighted the gallery by diving head first into the brook!

It was widely accepted that another American colt, Mr J. R. Keene's Foxhall, was an even better three-year-old than Iroquois, and that had he been entered for the classics, he would have carried off the Triple Crown. By Lexington, a descendant of the first Derby winner, Sir Charles Bunbury's Diomed, Foxhall first of all ran second to Bend Or in the City and Suburban. Then, with Fordham riding, he beat Archer's mount Tristan in a magnificent race for the Grand Prix. He won both the Cesarewitch and the Cambridgeshire, having nine stone on his back in the latter race, and the following year he carried off the Gold Cup at Ascot.

1881: Wednesday, 1 June . . . 242 Entries. £5,925.

MR P. LORILLARD's br.c. IROQUOIS by Leamington
out of Maggie B.B. — F. ARCHER — 1

MR GROSVENOR's br.c. PEREGRINE by Pero Gomez
out of Adelaide — F. WEBB — 2

LORD ROSEBERY's b.c. TOWN MOOR by Doncaster
out of Euxine — LEMAIRE — 3

Also ran:

Prince Soltykoff's Scobell (4th) (Rossiter); Mr F. Gretton's Geologist (T. Cannon); Mr J. R. Keene's Don Fulano (C. Wood); Mr Crawfurd's St Louis (Fordham); Lord Vivian's Fortissimo (Luke); Mr Lefevre's Tristan (J. Goater); Lord Bradford's Limestone (W. McDonald); Mr Mackintosh's Culloden (Gallon); Captain Machell's Cumberland (Morbey); Mr J. R. Keene's Marshal Macdonald (Morgan); Colonel Roden's Fortune's Favourite (Mordan); Lord Rosebery's Voluptuary (J. Osborne).

15 ran.

Betting:

6–5 Peregrine; 11–2 Iroquois; 100–15 Geologist; 100–8 St Louis; 20–1 Don Fulano and Scobell; 25–1 Town Moor and Voluptuary coupled; 33–1 Town Moor; 60–1 Fortissimo, Tristan, and Limestone; 100–1 Cumberland.

Won by half a length; two lengths between second and third. — 2 m. 50 s.
Winner trained by J. Pincus at Newmarket.

1882

When Robert Peck retired in 1881, the Duke of Westminster's horses were transferred in the late autumn to John Porter's stable at Kingsclere. Among them was a two-year-old filly called Shotover, by Hermit out of the Toxophilite mare Stray Shot, who had been bred by Sir Joseph Hawley and had proved herself quite a useful stayer on the racecourse. Shotover herself was bred by Mr Henry Chaplin, and Peck had bought her on the Duke's behalf for 1,400 guineas as a yearling. When the Duke first saw her he did not take to her at all and it was agreed that Peck should take her over for himself. Fortunately for the Duke, he changed his mind a little later and took the filly back.

Shotover was slow to come to hand and her two-year-old form held out little hope of her ever attaining classic standard. Starting at 50–1, she was unplaced in the Middle Park, and the following day was second to a moderate animal called Berwick in the Prendergast Stakes. At the Houghton Meeting she finished well down the course in a nursery. During the winter, however, her strength grew more in proportion to her generous frame, and in April it was decided to try her with a view to discovering what sort of a chance she might possess in the Two Thousand or One Thousand Guineas. She acquitted herself creditably in her trial, even if not with brilliance, and her trainer's view of her prospects in the classics could be described as hopeful rather than confident.

It was a very moderate field for the Two Thousand Guineas that year and Shotover, a 10–1 chance, won comfortably from Quicklime and Marden. Two days later, faced by only five opponents, she was a 4–1 on favourite for the One Thousand, but was beaten a neck by the handsome St Marguerite. Always a filly of delicate constitution, her exertions against the colts had taken far more out of her than had been supposed.

Shotover, however, picked up nicely in the period before Epsom, and the only horse that Porter feared in the Derby was Bruce, a colt by See Saw. Bruce had been bred at Morden Deer Park, Surrey and was bought for 1,100 guineas as a yearling by Mr H. Rymill. He won all his four races as a two-year-old and had beaten St Marguerite in the Criterion Stakes. He did not run as a three-year-old until Epsom, but he gave every satisfaction in his preparation on the Berkshire Downs and started a red-hot favourite. He looked a picture on Derby Day and as he cantered down past the grandstand he was heartily cheered.

Unfortunately for backers of Bruce, Mr Rymill, out of sheer loyalty, had entrusted the favourite to Sammy Mordan, who had ridden the colt as a two-year-old. A curious, lisping little man who habitually referred to himself in the third person, Mordan was a very moderate jockey and on this occasion he rode even worse than usual. Acting on orders, he forced the pace on Bruce and was in front approaching Tattenham Corner. At this point he appeared to lose control—it is said that the favourite shied at some paper that was blowing across the course—and went very wide at the bend. This left Pursebearer in front with Quicklime, Gareth, Dutch Oven, and Shotover hard on his heels, and Bruce and Mordan by no means out of it on the wide outside. Pursebearer and Dutch Oven, however, were in trouble two furlongs out and Bruce was done with at this stage as well. Quicklime then went on with Shotover in hot pursuit, but gamely as Quicklime struggled, the filly gradually mastered him and took the lead inside the final furlong to win by three parts of a length. Bruce would have finished a poor third, but Mordan rounded off a nice day's work by easing the colt close home so that he was passed on the post by Sachem. Many people thought Bruce should have won, and this view was reinforced a few days later when he won the Grand Prix de Paris with Fred Archer in the saddle. He then developed leg trouble and never ran in England again.

Although Mordan was never anything but an extremely indifferent rider, some well-informed persons were strongly of the opinion that he was downright dishonest in the Derby. A prominent bookmaker, not disposed to take a chance as a rule, persistently opposed Bruce in the market and laid him without hesitation to his clients at a point over the odds. He won so much money over Bruce's defeat that he built himself an enormous house in the worst of taste just outside London. Towards the end of his life he went insane, while an individual, hitherto much respected, who was said to be closely connected with him in the Bruce affair, found himself ostracized on the Turf and eventually reduced to beggary.

Born at Eton in 1846, Tom Cannon, who rode a beautiful race on Shotover, was one of the finest riders of his time. Imperturbable, a master of finesse and a superb judge of pace, he was gifted with the lightest of hands and was unequalled as a rider of a two-year-old. Slight of build and rather delicate in appearance, he was tougher than he looked both on a horse and off one, and was seldom the loser in a matter of business. He married a daughter of John Day and he trained at Danebury himself after deciding to retire from the saddle. He turned out a great many winners, over fences and hurdles as well as on the flat, but good as he was as a trainer of horses, he was even more successful as a trainer of jockeys. His sons Mornington and Kempton both reached the top of the tree and both won the Derby in their day, while Jack Watts was also under Tom Cannon's care as a boy.

Shotover was engaged in the Oaks, but it was decided not to take the risk of running her there, especially as her brilliant stable companion Geheimniss, owned by Lord Stamford, had shown herself at home to be clearly the better of the two. Geheimniss in fact won the Oaks quite easily from St Marguerite and Nellie. The Kingsclere stable's wonderful treble in the Two Thousand Guineas, the Derby, and the Oaks was celebrated by a huge picnic on the neighbouring Downs. Everyone in the village was entertained, air balloons in the colours of the Duke of Westminster and Lord Stamford were released, and there was a great display of fireworks in the evening.

Shotover won the Ascot Derby and the Triennial at the Royal Meeting and was then put by for the St Leger. It was widely believed by the public that Fred Archer would ride her at Doncaster, but at the last moment Lord Falmouth, who had first claim on his services, exercised his undoubted right and decreed that Archer should ride Dutch Oven. As a matter of fact if Lord Falmouth had waived his right, the Duke of Westminster, who had second claim on Archer, would probably have waived his own right as well and Archer would have ridden Geheimniss. Much to everyone's surprise Dutch Oven, starting at 40–1, beat the two Kingsclere fillies in the St Leger, largely because she was a more genuine stayer than they were.

Shotover won the Park Hill Stakes from some indifferent opponents on the Friday, but she was beginning to show signs of losing her enthusiasm for racing and at Newmarket she failed by a length in the Select Stakes to concede ten pounds to Kermesse and Nellie, who dead-heated. This was a wonderful year for fillies; not a classic was won by a colt, and fillies filled the first three places in the St Leger. But for splitting both pasterns in the autumn the previous year it is conceivable that Kermesse, who belonged to Lord Rosebery, would have been the best of them all.

As a four-year-old Shotover lost her form completely, and after losing at Ascot she was taken out of training and retired to the stud, where her best winners were Bullingdon and Orion. She is buried at Eaton between Ornament, dam of Sceptre, and Lily Agnes, the dam of Ormonde.

1882: Wednesday, 24 May . . . 197 Entries. £4,775.

DUKE OF WESTMINSTER's ch.f. SHOTOVER by Hermit
out of Stray Shot — T. CANNON — 1

LORD BRADFORD's b.c. QUICKLIME by Wenlock
out of Duvernay — C. WOOD — 2

MR P. LORILLARD's ch.c. SACHEM by War Dance
out of Sly Boots — F. WEBB — 3

Also ran:

Mr H. Rymill's Bruce (4th) (S. Mordan); Mr R. S. Evans's Marden (R. Wyatt); Lord Falmouth's Dutch Oven (F. Archer); Count F. de Lagrange's Executor (J. Goater); Count F. de Lagrange's Psycho (Groves); Mr P. Lorillard's Gerald (Morgan); General Randolph's Real Grit (Giles); Lord Rosebery's Gareth (Lemaire); Mr C. Perkins's Pursebearer (J. Osborne); Duke of Hamilton's Fénélon (J. Watts); Major Stapylton's Satrap (Morbey).

14 ran.

Betting:

9–4 Bruce; 11–2 Shotover; 6–1 Quicklime; 10–1 Dutch Oven; 100–8 Executor and Sachem; 100–7 Pursebearer and Fénélon; 25–1 Marden and Gerald; 66–1 Gareth.

Won by three-quarters of a length; a bad third.   2 m. 45$\frac{3}{5}$ s.
Winner trained by J. Porter at Kingsclere.

1883

One of the most successful racing 'confederacies' of the last century was that established between two well-known members of the Jockey Club, Lord Alington and Sir Frederick Johnstone. The partnership started in 1868 when they both had horses with William Day. In 1881 they transferred their patronage to John Porter's stable at Kingsclere, winning the Derby in 1883 with St Blaise and in 1891 with Common. Both betted heavily when the occasion offered; Lord Alington, born in 1825, appeared the more active partner, but their horses usually carried the colours of Sir Frederick, who was sixteen years the younger. Both were men of the world, rich, witty, and urbane, but the Turf was no light-hearted pastime for either and on the racecourse they neither gave nor expected any quarter. In many respects Lord Alington was typical of the English country gentleman of his day and he was certainly never happier than at his home at Crichel, in Dorset. When he died in 1904 he had been a member of the Jockey Club for fifty-four years.

St Blaise was bred by Lord Alington, by Hermit out of Fusee, by Marsyas, the mare having been mated with Hermit largely on the advice of Captain Machell, who was a strong adherent of the Orlando–Newminster cross. As a matter of fact St Blaise, a fine, big chesnut, was inclined to be coarse and had little trace of the Newminster delicacy about him.

As a two-year-old St Blaise gave scant indication of the successes that lay ahead. He made his début in the middle of the summer at Stockbridge, winning the Biennial, walking over for the Troy Stakes, and finishing second in the Hurstbourne Stakes. He dead-heated with Elzevir for the Molecomb Stakes at Goodwood, while at Newmarket in the autumn he was unplaced in the Dewhurst Stakes and won the Troy Stakes. It was the record of a useful horse rather than that of a potential winner of the Derby.

St Blaise put on a great deal of flesh in the winter and as the Kingsclere gallops got very heavy on account of an abnormally wet spring, it was found impossible to bring him to the peak of condition in time for the Two Thousand Guineas. In that event he started at 25–1 and finished down the course behind Lord Falmouth's colt Galliard, by Galopin. During the month that intervened before the Derby Porter was able to give St Blaise a lot of strong work and considerable improvement was anticipated in the colt's final trial, which took place over a mile and a half a week

277

before the race, the Prince of Wales being among the spectators present. The result of the trial was as follows:

St Blaise	three years	8 st. 6 lb.	1
Incendiary	six years	8 st. 2 lb.	2
Shotover	four years	8 st. 12 lb.	3
Geheimniss	four years	9 st. 5 lb.	4
Energy	three years	8 st. 5 lb.	5

Won by two lengths; four lengths between second and third; a head between third and fourth; a head between fourth and fifth.

Not unnaturally this trial gave considerable satisfaction to Porter and the two partners, who rightly considered that St Blaise would take a great deal of beating at Epsom.

Galliard, ridden by Archer, was favourite for the Derby, and other well-backed horses were Goldfield, runner-up in the Guineas, St Blaise, The Prince, who had recently been bought for £10,000, and Ladislas. In addition Highland Chief, a great, leggy, long-striding, split-up colt by Hampton that belonged to Lord Ellesmere, had been backed to win a very big stake by his trainer, Fred Archer's brother Charles. It was a perfect summer afternoon, the Prince and Princess of Wales were present, and a fire that broke out on the Downs before the race enabled many simple-minded spectators who connected 'blaze' with St Blaise to go home happy.

Bon Jour, who was acting as pacemaker for Ladislas, was the early leader, but he was done with at Tattenham Corner and so was Ladislas. The Prince did not last much longer, and St Blaise, partnered by Wood, took up the running, followed by Galliard and Goldfield, with Highland Chief beginning to make up ground in the centre of the course. St Blaise pressed on to make the best of his way home and set up what appeared to be a winning lead. Goldfield was beaten at the distance, but Highland Chief, hard-ridden by Webb, sustained his challenge unflinchingly. Stride by stride he cut down the leader's advantage; he swept past Galliard and a final tremendous effort in the last fifty yards seemed to land him in front in the last few yards. 'By God, we're done!' exclaimed Sir Frederick Johnstone as the horses passed the post, but the verdict of the judge was 'St Blaise'. Galliard was third and Goldfield fourth, thus confirming their form in the Two Thousand Guineas. A contemporary writer recorded that when the numbers went up Sir Frederick Johnstone was observed to smile, a rare event on the racecourse, while Lord Alington 'looked as if he had got all his rents paid a year in advance'.

After the race there were a number of unpleasant rumours, and it was freely stated that Fred Archer had pulled Galliard and had gone for a big win on Highland Chief. Certainly Lord Falmouth was dissatisfied with Archer's riding on this occasion,

Eleanor; by Edwin Cooper

and there was a story that immediately after the weigh-in he told Archer that his services were no longer required. Not long afterwards Lord Falmouth sold all his bloodstock, and it was alleged that this action was prompted by his disgust over the Galliard affair. It seems at least equally probable that his retirement from racing was primarily caused by advancing age and increasing ill-health. He was sixty-four years old at the time and died in 1889. Mr George Lambton in his book *Men and Horses I Have Known* discounted the allegations against Archer, and declared that in reality Archer had no fancy for his brother's colt at all. What is rather more certain is that Webb, a tall, long-limbed rider of the Archer type, left his effort on Highland Chief just a shade too late: in fact Webb himself agreed on that point. However, the following day Webb rode a brilliant race to win the Royal Stakes on Lord Ellesmere's Lowland Chief. This victory enabled Charles Archer to retrieve his Derby losses and a little bit more besides.

Charles Wood, rider of St Blaise, was a fine jockey, a good judge of form, and remarkably astute as far as his own interests were concerned. Unfortunately his integrity, at least during the first phase of his career, was strongly suspect. Sherrard's stable at Newmarket was really controlled by him and Sir George Chetwynd, and although Sir George was a member of the Jockey Club and had acted as Senior Steward, betting was really his livelihood. As far as racing was concerned there seems no doubt at all that he was 'sharp' and, despite his official position, disposed to overlook clear breaches of the Rules of Racing by Wood. The running of the horses in Sherrard's stable became something of a scandal and matters came to a head when another leading member of the Jockey Club, Lord Durham, made some scathing comments in a speech at the Gimcrack Club dinner. The sequel was a libel action brought by Sir George against Lord Durham. It was a protracted affair, involving much ill-feeling among the various partisans, and ultimately it resulted in the downfall of Sir George and his jockey. Sir George withdrew permanently from the Turf, and Wood lost his licence to ride. His licence was restored by the Jockey Club some years later and his first mount on his return was on a horse of Lord Durham's. He soon showed he had not lost his skill and he rode Galtee More to victory in the Derby of 1897. He lived to a ripe old age and died very comfortably off.

All too often owners had little mercy on their horses in those days, and despite his hard race at Epsom, St Blaise was despatched to Paris for the Grand Prix at Longchamps. He had another gruelling race and was narrowly beaten by Frontin, largely because the French jockeys made a dead set at Archer, who rode him on that occasion. Three days later St Blaise faced the starter in the Ascot Derby at the Royal Meeting, and not surprisingly under the circumstances was well and truly beaten by Ladislas and Ossian. Those three exacting efforts right on top of each other got to the bottom of St Blaise, and bar a couple of walk-overs, he never won a race again. He began to suffer from suspensory trouble, and after running down the course three times as a five-year-old, it was decided to take him out of training. He was bought by Mr August Belmont of New York and taken to America as a stallion. When Mr Belmont died, he was put up for sale by auction and fell to the only bid, one of 100,000 dollars by Mr Charles Read, a Tennessee breeder. 'I earthquaked 'em, that's all, just earthquaked 'em,' remarked Mr Read with a certain satisfaction afterwards. St Blaise got a good number of winners in America, but he was not an outstanding success as many of his stock failed to train on after showing precocious promise. At the age of twenty-nine the poor old horse was burnt to death in a fire at the Nursery Stud near Lexington.

Galliard won twice on hard ground at Ascot after the Derby, but those races stumped him up badly and he never saw a racecourse again. Highland Chief started favourite for the St Leger, but besides making a noise, he was not entirely sound and could not be given a proper preparation. Under the circumstances he did well to finish third to Ossian and Chislehurst, especially as he pulled up very lame.

1883: Wednesday, 23 May . . . 215 Entries. £5,150.

SIR F. JOHNSTONE's ch.c. ST BLAISE by Hermit
out of Fusee   C. WOOD   1
LORD ELLESMERE's b.c. HIGHLAND CHIEF by Hampton
out of Corrie   F. WEBB   2
LORD FALMOUTH's br.c. GALLIARD by Galopin
out of Mavis   F. ARCHER   3

Also ran:

Lord Cadogan's Goldfield (4th) (T. Cannon); Mr Adrian's The Prince (J. Osborne); Mr G. G. Stead's Splendor (J. Snowden); Lord Hastings's Beau Brummel (J. Watts); Mr Lefevre's Ladislas (G. Fordham); Lord Bradford's Laocoon (J. Goater); Mr T. Cannon's Sigmophone (S. Loates); Mr Lefevre's Bon Jour (C. Loates).

11 ran.

Betting:

100–30 Galliard; 5–1 Goldfield; 11–2 St Blaise, The Prince, and Ladislas; 100–6 Highland Chief; 25–1 Splendor; 40–1 Laocoon; 100–1 Sigmophone; 1,000–5 Bon Jour.

Won by a neck; half a length between second and third.   2 m. 48⅖ s.
Winner trained by J. Porter at Kingsclere.

1884

On Two Thousand Guineas day in 1883 Prince Batthyany was in a high state of excitement, as Galliard, a son of his much-loved Galopin, was expected to win the big race. Unfortunately, the strain proved too much for the old gentleman, who had a fatal heart seizure as he was walking up the short flight of stairs that led to the Jockey Club Luncheon Room. Prince Batthyany's death undoubtedly altered the course of racing history as the classic nominations of his colt St Simon were thereby rendered void according to the rule that then existed. St Simon proved one of the greatest racehorses and perhaps the greatest sire ever known to the English Turf, and would almost certainly have carried off the Triple Crown in 1884.

In St Simon's absence the Derby resulted in a dead-heat between Sir John Willoughby's Harvester and Mr John Hammond's St Gatien, the first dead-heat since that between Cadland and The Colonel in 1828. There was a considerable contrast in the social standing of the two respective owners. Sir John Willoughby, only twenty-five years of age at the time, was a young officer in the Royal Horse Guards more plentifully endowed, at any rate at that period, with money than sense. For a brief spell, as one of Captain Machell's young men, he cut a spectacular dash on the Turf, betting heavily and spending what was then accounted a regular fortune on bloodstock. In general he obtained a poorish return on his money. Later he went to South Africa and was a pioneer in the development of that country. He was a leader of that ill-fated fiasco, the Jameson Raid, but subsequently fought with some distinction in the South African War. Although well over fifty, he volunteered for service again in 1914 and was sent to South Africa, where he was killed. Jack Hammond, as he was usually called, had started life as a stable-boy in Captain Machell's establishment when Joe Cannon was the trainer, but he had brains and a flair for gambling that soon lifted him out of the rut. He owned a grand mare called Florence who won him the Cambridgeshire and a fortune in bets. He was a wonderfully astute judge of horses and form, and a shrewd, level-headed gambler. If the price was short, then his stake was small, but if he could obtain long odds about a horse that he fancied, he had his maximum on. He was an honourable man, extremely kind-hearted, and a great benefactor to the poor in Newmarket.

St Gatien was bred by Major E. Brace and was by Rotherhill or The Rover, presumably the latter, a son of Blair Athol, while his dam was St Editha, by Kingley

Vale. Besides being unfashionably bred, he was far from handsome as a yearling, having a long, curly coat better suited to a spaniel, and Major Brace had no intention of keeping him if he could possibly find a buyer. He asked his trainer Alfred Hayhoe to seek out a possible purchaser, but prospective clients took one look at the shaggy-haired colt and then departed. That season Robert Sherwood of Wild Dayrell fame took over the Exeter House stables from Hayhoe and was asked to train St Gatien by Major Brace. St Gatien soon showed that he was a good deal more useful than he looked, for he took part in three races as a two-year-old, the Teddington Plate at Kempton, the John O'Gaunt Plate at Manchester, and the Little John Plate at Nottingham, and won the lot. Major Brace then insisted on selling the colt and, at Sherwood's suggestion, disposed of him privately to Mr Hammond.

Harvester, by Sterling out of Wheat-ear, by Young Melbourne, was bred by Lord Falmouth, and Sir John Willoughby paid 8,600 guineas for him at the Falmouth dispersal sale. The colt had won two of his six races as a two-year-old, being successful in the Triennial Produce Stakes and the Clearwell Stakes at Newmarket in the autumn, but finishing unplaced in the Dewhurst Stakes behind Sir John's Hermit filly Queen Adelaide, whom he had bought as a yearling for 3,600 guineas. Incidentally, only two of the twenty-four horses in training that Lord Falmouth sold proved much of a success on the racecourse. These were Harvester and the filly Busybody, who cost Mr 'Abington' Baird 8,800 guineas. Busybody won the One Thousand Guineas and the Oaks, and when mated with St Gatien bred Meddler who, but for Baird's death, would in all probability have won the Derby.

As a three-year-old St Gatien did not run before the Derby, but Harvester took the field for the Two Thousand Guineas and so did his stable-companion, Mr Gerard's St Medard, by Hermit. St Medard beat Harvester by a head, but he himself was five lengths behind Mr Foy's Scot Free, who won the race in a canter. At the Newmarket Second Spring Meeting Scot Free and Harvester met again, this time in the Payne Stakes, run over a mile and a half. Scot Free, conceding seven pounds, was an odds-on favourite, but it was observed before the race that Sir John Willoughby and his friends were busy backing Harvester for the Derby. Their judgement was justified, as Harvester won comfortably by three parts of a length and promptly supplanted his owner's filly Queen Adelaide as Derby favourite.

Harvester, however, did not hold that position for long, as on the Saturday before Epsom he was slightly lame. It was generally assumed that Sir John would rely on his filly and scratch the colt, but he was anxious that Harvester's backers should have a run for their money if possible and delayed making a decision. On Wednesday morning Harvester pulled up perfectly sound after his exercise gallop and it was decided to run him. Thus the stable over which Captain Machell presided—J.

Jewitt was the actual trainer—had three candidates: Queen Adelaide, who was favourite at 5–2; St Medard, second favourite at 6–1, and Harvester, who had drifted to 100–7. After a rough gallop between the three ten days earlier Fred Archer had decided to ride St Medard, whom he believed to be best suited to the Epsom gradients; Webb was on Queen Adelaide, and Sam Loates on Harvester. Sam Loates was a first-rate rider, a wonderful judge of pace and fully capable of holding his own with the best. He and his brothers Tommy and Charles rode a lot of winners between them. They were all very small men, short in the leg and, at a time when jockeys rode with long leathers, they suffered as stylists in comparison with riders like Archer, Cannon, and Webb.

It was a typical English late spring day when the fifteen runners went to the post; the sky was dark grey, the temperature in the low fifties, and a searching east wind scudded across the Downs. As the field swept round Tattenham Corner and made for home, Loch Ranza was in front on the rails with Borneo and St Gatien on his heels. Waterford was close up in the centre, and then came Richmond, Harvester, Beauchamp, and Queen Adelaide. Two furlongs from home St Gatien went to the front but was immediately challenged by Harvester, who seemed to gain a fractional advantage. Almost immediately, however, Harvester faltered and changed his legs, thereby enabling St Gatien to recapture the lead, but Loates skilfully got Harvester balanced again and, driving him for all he was worth, drew level with Wood on St Gatien in the very last stride. The judge at once signalled a dead-heat, a verdict that the crowd received in silence. Queen Adelaide, badly hampered at a critical stage of the contest, was third and Waterford fourth.

It was taken for granted that there would be a deciding heat, but when Mr Hammond and Captain Machell met in the weighing room, Mr Hammond immediately expressed his willingness to agree with whatever course Sir John and his racing manager proposed; they could run or divide, whichever they pleased. 'Then we'll divide,' Machell immediately replied, a sensible decision in view of Harvester's doubtful leg. Moreover, subsequent form showed beyond question that St Gatien was the better horse of the two. In view of Mr Hammond's generous attitude, it was all the more regrettable that Sir John saw fit to lodge a somewhat frivolous objection to St Gatien the following day on the grounds that his entry was not correct. Quite rightly, this objection was subsequently withdrawn.

Queen Adelaide competed in the Oaks two days later, but could only finish third behind Busybody and Superba. There was a certain amount of local money in the Derby at very long odds for Mr Holdaway's The Hopeful Dutchman, who was trained on Banstead Downs. He was supposed to have recorded 2 m. 43 s. over the full mile and a half, but it subsequently transpired that someone had erred and the distance was only a mile and a quarter! He was hopelessly tailed off in the race.

St Gatien went from strength to strength. That season he won the Ascot Gold Vase, the Cesarewitch in a canter carrying 8 st. 10 lb., the Free Handicap, and the Jockey Club Cup. As a four-year-old he won the Gold Cup at Ascot, the Alexandra Plate, the King's Plate at Newmarket, and the Jockey Club Cup. He met with the first defeat of his career in the Cambridgeshire, finishing unplaced to Plaisanterie with 9 st. 10 lb. on his back. It was perhaps the best Cambridgeshire field there has ever been but, despite his weight and the formidable opposition, St Gatien started favourite.

As a five-year-old he was third to Bendigo and Candlemas in the very first race for the Eclipse Stakes at Sandown Park, and unplaced in the Cesarewitch carrying 9 st. 5 lb. On the other hand, he won the Rous Memorial Stakes at Ascot, the King's Plate at Newmarket, and the Jockey Club Cup for the third year running. Altogether he won sixteen races and was only beaten three times. He retired to the Heath Stud at Newmarket at a fee of fifty guineas, but was soon afterwards sold to the German Government, who re-sold him for export to America. After some years he returned to England again, was on offer for £1,500, and was in due course sent to America for the second time. His best son, Meddler, also went to America and was leading sire there in 1906.

Harvester ran four times in 1884 after the Derby, his one success being in the Gratwicke Stakes at Goodwood. In the St Leger he ran unplaced behind The Lambkin. At the end of the year he went to the stud at Newmarket at a fee of twenty-five guineas, but was eventually sold for 850 guineas for export to Austria.

1884: Wednesday, 28 May ... 189 Entries. £4,900.

MR J. HAMMOND's b.c. ST GATIEN by Rotherhill
  or The Rover out of St Editha   C. WOOD ⎫
SIR J. WILLOUGHBY's br.c. HARVESTER   ⎬ dead-heat
  by Sterling out of Wheat-ear   S. LOATES ⎭
SIR J. WILLOUGHBY's ch.f. QUEEN ADELAIDE
  by Hermit out of Adelaide   F. WEBB 3

Also ran:

Mr W. Stevenson's Waterford (4th) (J. Osborne); Mr Gerard's St Medard (F. Archer); Mr L. de Rothschild's Talisman (T. Cannon); Duke of Hamilton's Loch Ranza (Watts); Mr C. J. Lefevre's Brest (Wainwright); Mr R. Carington's Bedouin (R. Giles); Mr F. T. Walton's Richmond (C. Loates); Mr R. Jardine's Beauchamp (C. Bowman); Mr R. Jardine's Borneo (W. Platt); Mr W. A. Long's

Condor (Morgan); Mr L. de Rothschild's Woodstock (J. Goater); Mr Holdaway's The Hopeful Dutchman (G. Marks).

15 ran.

Betting:

5–2 Queen Adelaide; 6–1 St Medard; 7–1 Talisman; 9–1 Richmond; 100–9 Waterford; 100–8 St Gatien; 100–7 Beauchamp and Harvester; 100–6 Borneo; 25–1 Loch Ranza; 50–1 Condor; 1,000–15 Bedouin and Brest.

A dead-heat for first place; Queen Adelaide two lengths away third.　2 m. 46⅕ s. St Gatien trained by R. Sherwood at Newmarket; Harvester by J. Jewitt at New-market.

1885

The Derby of 1885 provided one of the most thrilling finishes in the history of the race, and Melton's victory by a head over Paradox was in no small measure due to the wonderful riding of Fred Archer.

Melton belonged to the twenty-eight-year-old Lord Hastings, whose home was at Melton Constable in Norfolk and who was in no way related to the Marquis of Hastings of unhappy memory. He succeeded his brother to the title in 1875, and three years later he began his racing career, like a good many other rich young men, under the guidance of Captain Machell. In 1879 Machell sold him a horse called Master Kildare, by Lord Ronald, that had finished third in the St Leger in Lord Lonsdale's colours. In 1880 Lord Hastings decided to transfer his horses to Matthew Dawson, who trained Master Kildare to win the City and Suburban. Dawson had a very high opinion of Master Kildare and advised Lord Hastings to retain him for the stud. Accordingly Master Kildare was retired to the Burghley Paddocks, Stamford, at a fee of twenty guineas, but so meagre was the patronage that he attracted that at the conclusion of his first season he was only credited with three foals, all of them the property of Lord Hastings.

One of the three was Melton, a colt of exceptional quality, a shade on the small side, perhaps, but very powerful, out of a mare called Violet Melrose, by Scottish Chief out of Violet, by Thormanby. From his very first days in training Melton showed quite exceptional promise. This promise was amply fulfilled as a two-year-old, since he won the Coventry Stakes, the New Stakes, and the Middle Park Stakes, in which he beat the French colt Xaintrailles by half a length. His one defeat was in the July Stakes at Newmarket when Luminary beat him.

Melton's rival Paradox was bred by the Graham brothers, who had bred Isonomy, at the Yardley Stud near Birmingham. He was a strong, good-looking colt by Sterling out of Casuistry, a mare that the Grahams had bought for 130 guineas, together with a colt foal called Graft, from Lord Rosebery, who disposed of her because she could barely stay five furlongs and was little more than a pony. As a yearling Paradox was bought for 700 guineas by John Porter of Kingsclere and his friend Captain Bowler, the latter afterwards taking over Porter's share as well. The colt was slow to come to hand, but early in October, before he had ever run, he did an exceptionally good trial and the Duke of Westminster bought him for £6,000.

Paradox had his first race a few days later in the Middle Park Plate and was greatly expected to win. Unfortunately he whipped round at the start and could only dead-heat for third place with Royal Hampton behind Melton, who was giving him seven pounds, and Xaintrailles. Some of the Duke of Westminster's friends chose to infer that 'he had been stuck with a brute', and he seems to have taken this allegation to heart, as a day or two later he ordered Porter to seek a purchaser for the colt forthwith. This instruction was rapidly accomplished and Paradox was bought for a new patron of the Kingsclere stable, the American, Mr Broderick Cloete. A fortnight later Paradox emphasized both the Duke's impulsiveness and the folly of his friends by winning the Dewhurst Plate in a canter by three lengths from Cora, with Xaintrailles four lengths away third.

The following year Paradox was very well tried before the Two Thousand Guineas, giving twenty-one pounds without any trouble at all to Ormonde's half-sister Farewell, who subsequently won the One Thousand Guineas. Ridden by Archer, he started a 3–1 on favourite for the Two Thousand, but gave his backers the fright of their lives and only scraped home by a head from Crafton, who was ridden by Tom Cannon. Paradox was very inclined to drop his bit when he found himself in front, and Tom Cannon's tactics in waiting just behind him and pouncing at the very last moment came near to succeeding. Melton did not run in the Guineas, but won the one and a half mile Payne Stakes at the Second Spring Meeting.

Unfortunately for Mr Cloete, Archer, who was fully aware of Paradox's weakness, was claimed by Matt Dawson to ride Melton. Fred Webb was thereupon engaged to ride the Kingsclere colt, who almost immediately began to travel suspiciously badly in the market. Some very ugly rumours, probably quite unfounded, were circulated, and when Webb weighed out before the Derby Mr Cloete told him to his face that he had heard that he was in the pay of certain bookmakers. 'But,' added Mr Cloete, 'whatever they have offered you, I'll pay you double if you win.'

The weather was perfect and the crowd enormous. Melton was favourite at 75–40, Xaintrailles stood at 4–1, and Paradox at 6–1. Rounding Tattenham Corner Xaintrailles led from Red Ruin, Paradox, Luminary, Royal Hampton, and Melton, but with three furlongs to go Paradox struck the front and headed for home with a clear lead over Melton, now the only member of the field with a hope of catching him. Knowing from experience how Paradox disliked racing in front, Archer was intent on delaying his challenge for as long as possible. At the distance it appeared to him that Paradox, bored with galloping on his own, was hanging fire. He began to move up, and with 150 yards to go, he made his challenge. The Kingsclere colt, finding an opponent to race with, immediately rallied and appeared to be getting the better of the desperate duel that then ensued. A few strides from the post he was still a head to the good, but at that point Archer went for his whip and hit Melton twice really hard. Melton at once bounded forward and his head was in front at the moment that mattered. Royal Hampton was a bad third and Xaintrailles fourth.

The crowd fully realized that the favourite's victory was largely due to Archer and gave him a wonderful reception. Poor Webb was extremely crestfallen, as not only had he come off second best in a battle of wits, but it was the fifth year in succession that he had been on a placed horse in the Derby.

Melton, an odds-on favourite, won the St Leger in a canter by half a dozen lengths, and in the autumn he won the Great Foal Stakes at Newmarket. His four-year-old career was less successful. He was no match for Ormonde in the Hardwicke Stakes at Ascot and after winning at Newmarket, Newcastle, and Leicester, he was unplaced in the Stewards Cup with 10 st. 6 lb. on his back, attempting to give thirty-seven pounds to the winner Crafton, who had so nearly won the Guineas the year before. He was beaten in the Chesterfield Cup, the Newmarket October Handicap, the Cambridgeshire, and the Jockey Club Cup in which he was second to St Gatien, but he finished his career with a creditable victory under 9 st. 3 lb. in the Liverpool Autumn Cup.

He retired to the stud at Newmarket at a fifty-guinea fee, but was soon afterwards sold to the Italian Government for £10,000. He did well there, and was subsequently repatriated to England by Mr J. Musker and stood at the Westerham Stud in Kent, where he got a number of very fast two-year-olds. He died at Mr Musker's estate at Thetford in 1906. Today he is perhaps best remembered as the sire of the late Mr J. B. Joel's mare Absurdity, dam of Black Jester, winner of the St Leger, and dam also of Jest, who not only won the One Thousand Guineas and the Oaks, but herself bred Humorist, winner of the Derby in 1921.

Paradox soon made up for his Derby defeat by winning the Grand Prix, ridden by Archer, in a canter by five lengths. He also won the Sussex Stakes at Goodwood, the Champion Stakes, and the Free Handicap. He was in the Cambridgeshire with 8 st. 12 lb. and had been heavily backed by certain Kingsclere patrons, who reckoned him a certainty, but Mr Cloete returned suddenly from Mexico to London and promptly scratched his horse without saying a word of his intention to John Porter. Mr Cloete explained that he only did this as he thought his colt had little chance at the weights, but in fact the act was probably done in a moment of extreme vexation on finding himself forestalled in the market. His horses left Kingsclere at the end of the season.

Paradox never ran after his three-year-old career. He went to the stud near Newbury at a fee of thirty guineas and died at the age of eight. According to some

1885

accounts, he had become extremely savage. The following not unwitty card was received by John Porter after the Cambridgeshire affair:

In Memoriam
PARADOX
Who took the inevitable
scratch
On Monday, October 5, 1885.
A select syndicate of bookmakers
sang his requiem, and the
British Public supplied the
money for his
burial.
'O thou, whatever title suit thee,
Auld Hornie, Satan, Nick or Clootie.'

1885: Wednesday, 3 June . . . 189 Entries. £4,525.

LORD HASTINGS's b.c. MELTON by Master Kildare out of Violet Melrose	F. ARCHER	1
MR BRODRICK CLOETE's b.c. PARADOX by Sterling out of Casuistry	F. WEBB	2
MR CHILDWICK's b.c. ROYAL HAMPTON by Hampton out of Princess	A. GILES	3

Also ran:

Mr A. Lupin's Xaintrailles (4th) (G. Barrett); General Pearson's Red Ruin (J. Snowden); Lord Bradford's Sheraton (Tomlinson); Mr W. H. Manser's Choubra (Morgan); Mr R. C. Vyner's Esterling (J. Osborne); Mr Gerard's Crafton (Watts); Lord Alington's Luminary (Platt); Lord Rosebery's Lynette colt by Macaroni (T. Cannon); Sir G. Chetwynd's Kingwood (C. Wood).

12 ran.

Betting:

75–40 Melton; 4–1 Xaintrailles; 6–1 Paradox; 100–15 Crafton; 10–1 Royal Hampton; 100–6 Kingwood; 1,000–35 Red Ruin; 1,000–30 Luminary; 66–1 Sheraton; 100–1 Esterling, Lynette colt, and Choubra.

Won by a head; a bad third. 2 m. 44$\frac{1}{5}$ s.
Winner trained by M. Dawson at Newmarket.

289

1886

This year's Derby was indeed a memorable one. The winner was Ormonde, one of the outstanding horses of the century, ridden by Archer, one of the greatest of riders. It was Archer's final victory in the Derby; in the autumn, in a moment of overwhelming depression after serious illness, he shot himself and plunged the English sporting world into mourning.

Ormonde, owned and bred by the Duke of Westminster, was one of Bend Or's first crop of runners and was out of Lily Agnes, by Macaroni. Thirty-nine years before Ormonde was foaled John Osborne, father of the much respected rider of that name, bought a Priam mare called Annette, together with her filly foal who was later given the name of Agnes, for fourteen pounds. A few years later Agnes was mated with Birdcatcher and produced a filly called Miss Agnes, who in 1863 was bought by Sir Tatton Sykes, then in the process of re-forming the Sledmere Stud. At Sledmere Miss Agnes was dam of a very weedy, unattractive filly foal, which Sir Tatton presented to his stud-groom, Snarry, on condition that the foal was removed from Sledmere forthwith.

The filly, subsequently named Polly Agnes, was sent off to Snarry's son, who had a farm near Malton, and in due course she was put to Macaroni. The produce, Lily Agnes, was a light-framed, lop-eared filly, unsound in her wind, but her ability was fortunately well in advance of her looks. In fact she was a stayer of great ability, and her twenty-one victories included the Doncaster Cup, the Ebor Handicap, and the Northumberland Plate.

Still owned by old Snarry, Lily Agnes was sent, after the conclusion of her racing career, to be mated with Doncaster at Eaton. Chapman, the Duke of Westminster's stud-groom, took a fancy to the mare and urged his employer to buy her. The Duke took a long time to make up his mind, but after the mare had returned to Malton, he bought her for £2,500, plus two free nominations to Bend Or, whose fee at the time was 200 guineas. When Lily Agnes was bought by the Duke, she was already the dam of two animals by Speculum, neither of which possessed any racing ability at all. Mated with Doncaster in 1880 she produced Rossington, who was exported to America; in 1881 she went to Doncaster again and this time bred Farewell, winner of the One Thousand Guineas in 1885. It was the custom at Eaton to mate, when possible, a mare who had produced a good foal to a given sire with the best son of that sire. That course, however, can hardly have been adopted with Lily Agnes in 1882, as Farewell's merits were at that time still undisclosed.

As a foal Ormonde was very much over at the knee and was slow to mature. The stud-groom described him as 'a three-cornered beggar, that might be anything or nothing', while the Duke expressed a preference for his contemporaries Kendal and Whitefriar. When sent to John Porter as a yearling he was still backward and over-grown; in addition he was troubled during the winter with splints underneath both knees.

It was not until the late summer of his two-year-old career that Porter judged Ormonde fit to do serious work. The colt then began to make rapid and continuous progress and in a trial on 7 October, conceding a pound, he finished only a length behind Kendal, a very useful two-year-old who had won five races in succession and whose victories included the Ham Stakes at Goodwood and the July Stakes at Newmarket. Kendal unfortunately broke down at the end of the season and it was never found possible to race him again. He sired the 1897 Derby winner Galtee More and later did well in the Argentine.

By this time Ormonde stood sixteen hands. His neck was perhaps a trifle short, but exceptionally powerful. He had good bone, beautifully laid shoulders, and rather straight hocks, while his head was of exceptional width between the ears. He was a splendid 'doer' and blessed with the most placid of dispositions. Some critics said that he was a poor mover in his slow paces, others crabbed him for being noticeably low in front of the saddle. In fact Archer himself always said that until Ormonde really extended himself, he always felt that he was sitting on his neck. When the horse was at the summit of his career the Duke himself rode him on the Downs in a couple of canters. 'I felt,' he said afterwards, 'every moment that I was going to be shot over his head, his propelling power is so terrific.'

Ormonde's first race as a two-year-old was a six-furlong Post Sweepstakes at Newmarket's Second October Meeting. There were only three runners, one of them being the Duke of Portland's game little filly Modwena, winner of eight of her ten races, including the Bretby Stakes earlier that afternoon. Although the going was heavy, and despite her previous exertions, Modwena started an odds-on favourite, but Ormonde was always going like a winner and beat her rather cleverly by a length. At the Houghton Meeting Ormonde won the Dewhurst Stakes and the Criterion Stakes, both with consummate ease. He then retired into winter quarters, in the opinion of many good judges the probable winner of next year's Derby.

There were, however, two other two-year-olds of outstanding merit, The Bard and Minting. The Bard, a beautifully made little chesnut by Petrarch, was trained by Martin Gurry for General Owen Williams and Robert Peck, who owned him in partnership. He won all his sixteen races as a two-year-old, and after winning the Tattersall Sales Stakes at Doncaster in September, General Williams declared that the colt would not run again before the Derby, and furthermore he would never be beaten! Minting was owned by Mr Robert Vyner, a great figure in north-country racing, and was a big, powerful colt by Lord Lyon. Trained by Matt Dawson, Minting's successes as a two-year-old included the Champagne Stakes and Middle Park Plate. His victory in the Middle Park, however, was only narrowly gained from Braw Lass and Saraband, as he became unbalanced racing into the dip and Archer had to ride him for all he was worth to secure the advantage in the final twenty yards. Archer afterwards stated that Minting hated racing downhill and would be singularly ill-suited to the Epsom gradients.

Ormonde wintered exceptionally well, and Porter's confidence in his ability to win the Two Thousand Guineas was only exceeded by Matt Dawson's confidence in Minting. There was a lot of support, too, for Saraband, for whom Fred Archer had been retained at considerable cost by Mr (later Sir) Blundell Maple, the London furniture dealer, who raced under the name of 'Mr Childwick'. Minting started favourite at 11–10. Saraband was at 3–1 and Ormonde, ridden by George Barrett, at 7–2. Barrett was a good rider at his best, but frequently erratic and sometimes unscrupulous. In later years his brain was affected and his conduct became totally unpredictable.

The race turned out to be a duel between Ormonde and Minting, whose riders set out to cut each other down from the start. Again Minting rolled and became unbalanced as he entered the Dip, and in the final furlong Ormonde drew clear to win quite comfortably by a couple of lengths. Matt Dawson took Minting's defeat very much to heart; the old man left the course immediately after the race, shut himself up in his bedroom, and there he remained for the rest of the meeting.

Neither Minting nor Saraband opposed Ormonde in the Derby, Minting being kept for the Grand Prix, which he won in a canter. Archer, released from Saraband, was able to take the mount on Ormonde, who started a 9–4 on favourite, the only horse seriously backed to beat him being The Bard at 7–2.

Just as the Guineas had been a match between Ormonde and Minting, so was the Derby in effect a match between Ormonde and The Bard, but whereas Wood was always having to push the little chesnut to hold his place, Archer was sitting quietly with a double handful on the favourite, who won unextended by a length and half, the judge declaring that he had never seen an easier winner. The Bard's subsequent career was proof of his conqueror's merit, as he was only beaten on one occasion again and that was when he failed to give Riversdale, a very smart performer, thirty-one pounds in the Manchester Cup. He won the Goodwood and Doncaster

Cups, and his name appears in the pedigree of Vatellor, sire of the Derby winners Pearl Diver (1947) and My Love (1948). Standing barely fifteen hands, The Bard had the heart of a lion and was good enough to have won the Derby in nine years out of ten.

Ormonde won the St James's Palace Stakes at Ascot, and also the Hardwicke Stakes, in which he trounced the previous year's Derby winner, Melton. He then rested until the St Leger, which he won in a canter from St Mirin. At the Newmarket First October Meeting he won the Great Foal Stakes and walked over for the Newmarket St Leger; a fortnight later he won the Champion Stakes and walked over for a Private Sweepstakes, the owners of Melton and The Bard preferring to fork out £500 forfeit. He finished the season by winning the Free Handicap by eight lengths carrying 9 st. 2 lb.

Amid the glittering triumphs of Ormonde's career, there was one cause for grievous disappointment. Just before the St Leger Porter discovered that Ormonde was wrong in his wind. During the winter Ormonde was given a course of 'the electric sponge', but derived no benefit at all, even though it was said he had been charged with sufficient electricity to illuminate the neighbouring town of Newbury. On foggy mornings up on the Downs, it was possible to hear him breathing a good half-mile away.

It was decided, however, to keep Ormonde in training for another season, but he did not appear until Ascot. On the third day of that meeting he won the Rous Memorial Stakes, giving twenty-five pounds to Kilwarlin, who subsequently won the St Leger. Kilwarlin was under the management of Captain Machell, who thought him unbeatable at the weights. The following day, ridden by Tom Cannon, Ormonde opposed Minting, Bendigo, winner of the first Eclipse Stakes, and a three-year-old called Phil in the Hardwicke Stakes. Matt Dawson refused to believe that Minting could be beaten over a mile and a half by a horse that had gone in his wind, but after a superb race Minting went under by a neck to the champion, with Bendigo three lengths away third. Ormonde's victory was all the more creditable because Barrett, who rode Phil, was furious at not having the mount on Ormonde, and indulged in some deliberately foul riding at the expense of the favourite on the final bend.

The excitement over the Hardwicke Stakes was tremendous and Ormonde's victory was greeted with prolonged cheering. After the 'all right' had been signalled, the Duke himself led Ormonde twice round the paddock and then walked him down on to the course and away to the stables. On the course Ormonde was cheered again and again until he finally disappeared from view. It was probably the greatest demonstration of admiration and affection for a great racehorse until Brown Jack's sixth and final victory in the Queen Alexandra Stakes at Ascot in 1934.

Ormonde's last racecourse appearance was in the six-furlong Imperial Gold Cup at Newmarket. In this he conceded six pounds to his former stable companion Whitefriar, a very useful sprinter, and won by two lengths. During the celebrations for Queen Victoria's Jubilee that took place that year, the Duke of Westminster held a reception at Grosvenor House, his London home in Park Lane. The Prince and Princess of Wales were there, four kings, two queens, and numerous Indian princes. The centre of attraction was Ormonde, who was paraded in the garden. The great horse seemed thoroughly at home in these surroundings and politely consumed the carnations offered him by the Queen of the Belgians and the geraniums that the Indian princes plucked and handed him.

Ormonde's stud-career was a sad anti-climax in view of his greatness as a race-horse. For his first year he stood at Eaton and among his first crop of foals was Orme, who would probably have won the Derby but for being poisoned either through malice or by a septic tooth, and who subsequently sired the Derby winners Flying Fox and Orby. For his second year Ormonde was leased to Lord Gerard and stood at Newmarket. There he caught a serious chill which was aggravated by lack of proper ventilation in his stable, and in consequence of this he only served one or two mares. He returned to Eaton a very sick horse, but as soon as he began to pick up the Duke decided to sell him and parted with him for £12,000 to the Argentine breeder, Señor Boucau. The sale caused a considerable commotion and not a few people expressed the opinion that the Duke had committed a grave disservice to racing and breeding in England by allowing Ormonde to leave the country. The Duke replied quite reasonably that Ormonde was a roarer and the descendant of roarers; that to retain him in this country might eventually prove detrimental to British bloodstock; and that furthermore, the warm, dry atmosphere of the Argentine might alleviate Ormonde's affliction. Ormonde was re-sold in 1894 for £30,000 to Mr Macdonough, a Californian breeder, but his procreative powers had been permanently impaired by his illness, and his foals in the United States, though good in quality, were few and far between. He was destroyed in 1904, his skeleton being returned to England and set up in the Natural History Museum at South Kensington.

1886: Wednesday, 26 May ... 199 Entries. £4,700.

DUKE OF WESTMINSTER's b.c. ORMONDE by Bend Or
  out of Lily Agnes   F. ARCHER   1
MR ROBERT PECK's ch.c. THE BARD by Petrarch
  out of Magdalene   C. WOOD   2
MR MANTON's br.c. ST MIRIN by Hermit
  out of Lady Paramount   T. CANNON   3

1886

Also ran:

Duke of Beaufort's Button Park (4th) (G. Barrett); Duke of Beaufort's Ariel (Wilton); Lord Calthorpe's Scherzo (J. Osborne); Duke of Westminster's Coracle (F. Webb); Lord Zetland's Grey Friars (J. Watts); Mr G. Lambert's Chelsea (J. Goater).

9 ran.

Betting:

9–4 on Ormonde; 7–2 The Bard; 25–1 Grey Friars; 40–1 Chelsea and St Mirin; 1,000–15 Scherzo and Button Park; 500–1 Ariel and Coracle.

Won by a length and a half; a bad third. 2 m. 45⅗ s.
Winner trained by J. Porter at Kingsclere.

1887

If 1886 was a vintage year for three-year-olds, the reverse was the case in 1887 when the winner was Mr 'Abington' Baird's Merry Hampton, trained by Martin Gurry and ridden by Jack Watts.

Bred by Mr Crowther Harrison in Yorkshire, Merry Hampton was bought as a yearling for 3,100 guineas by Mr George Baird, a rich young Scotsman who raced under the name of 'Mr Abington'. A rather long-backed bay standing sixteen hands, Merry Hampton was by Hampton out of Doll Tearsheet, by Broomielaw. He never saw a racecourse before the Derby, and for most of that period was trained by William Stevens at Compton in Berkshire, but a fortnight before Epsom he was transferred to Martin Gurry at Newmarket. Baird's horses had been with Gurry previously, but there had been a row—nothing unusual as far as Baird was concerned —and Gurry had ordered him to take his horses away.

Enterprise, winner of the Two Thousand Guineas, broke down not long after that race and an odds-on favourite for the Derby was The Baron, trained by Matt Dawson and nominated by a certain Mr Fern. Just who Mr Fern was never transpired but it was widely believed that Matt Dawson himself owned at least a share in the horse. A big, rather coarse colt by Xenophon, The Baron went to Epsom unbeaten, but in fact his record did not add up to much. The best that could be said of him was that he had successfully accomplished all that he had ever been asked to do.

The race proved to be a singularly uninspiring one. Merry Hampton took the lead early in the straight and never for one moment looked like being caught by The Baron, who had been noticeably sluggish beforehand. Tom Cannon, who partnered the favourite, seemed to accept the situation some way from the finish, much to the irritation of Matt Dawson. Merry Hampton and The Baron met again in the Grand Prix, the Baron, who was second, finishing a long way ahead of the Derby winner, who was fourth. In the St Leger Merry Hampton was beaten half a length by Lord Rodney's Kilwarlin, who dug his toes in at the start and lost twenty-five lengths but, thanks to the poor pace, was able to retrieve the lost ground without undue exertion. In the closing stages Merry Hampton met with considerable interference, otherwise he would probably have won.

The Baron gradually deteriorated and descended to plating company. Merry Hampton was unplaced the following season when favourite for the City and

Suburban and in 1889 was retired to the stud at a fee of thirty guineas. When Baird's stud was sold up in 1894, he was bought by George Barrett the jockey for 1,550 guineas, but he never did much good as a sire.

George Alexander Baird—commonly known as 'The Squire'—was born in 1861 and inherited two fortunes, one from his father, a Glasgow ironfounder, the second from his uncle, who had previously presented £200,000 to the Church of Scotland, a gift that prompted the comment that this was the biggest premium against fire ever paid.

Eton and Cambridge imparted no polish and little sense to 'The Squire'. He would probably have gone to the bad in any case, but after being 'warned off' the Turf for two years at the age of twenty-one for alleged foul riding in a flat-race at Fairoaks Park, he felt that the hand of the racing 'establishment' was against him, and he took to consorting with the riff-raff of the racecourse and the prize-ring. There is little doubt that the sentence was a harsh one and was probably inspired to a considerable extent by personal dislike. Baird was not without his good points—he was capable of acts of great kindness—but he had in him an unpleasant streak of the lout and the bully as well. He was apt to play unpleasant tricks on inoffensive strangers, who, if they had the spirit to retaliate, were dealt with by his prize-fighting hangers-on.

As a race-rider, thanks to tuition from Fred Archer and Tom Cannon, he was extremely competent. In addition his enthusiasm was unbounded, and it gave him far more pleasure to ride a winner at Worcester than to see a horse of his win a race at Ascot in the hands of a professional. Somewhat boorishly he refused to lead Merry Hampton into the winner's enclosure at Epsom, and the whole occasion seemed to leave him totally unmoved. All his adult life he was preyed on by his loathsome associates, of whom the females were if anything rather more rapacious than the males. The life he led inevitably undermined his health and he died in 1893 during a trip to America with some of the most repulsive members of his entourage. Much of his fortune, according to a leading Scottish newspaper, 'had been squandered in horse-racing, prize-fighting and harlotry'. What remained he left to his mother and his family, much to the disappointment, so it was said, of the reigning beauty of the time, whose name was linked not only with that of Baird, who had proved a most lucrative friend, but also with that of a person of the highest distinction.

Martin Gurry, who had trained the previous year's Derby second, The Bard, had learnt his trade as head-lad to Robert Peck. Capable, a shrewd judge though somewhat sceptical in outlook, he had a blunt way of expressing himself that was often extremely amusing.

Jack Watts, who also rode Sainfoin, Ladas, and Persimmon to victory in the

Derby, was one of the finest riders of the late Victorian era. He received his early schooling in his profession from Tom Cannon, and his style, quiet, cool-headed, and unspectacular, but at the same time highly effective, reflected the methods of his tutor. When he was seventeen he joined the Newmarket stable of Richard Marsh, with whom he enjoyed a long and successful association, culminating in his triumph on Persimmon.

The most loyal of servants, Watts was extremely reserved in manner and even after winning the Derby in the royal colours he hardly permitted himself the luxury of a smile. In the winter he sometimes hunted with the Pytchley and after being jumped on by a certain well-known lady, he contented himself with the observation that he wished to God she would go back to her ruddy paper-hoops! Towards the end of his career he had trouble with his weight, and the wasting he had to undergo caused him frequent phases of deep depression. His son trained Call Boy, winner of the Derby in 1927, and his grandson is Lord Derby's trainer today.

1887: Wednesday, 25 May . . . 190 Entries. £4,525.

MR 'ABINGTON'S' b.c. MERRY HAMPTON by Hampton		
out of Doll Tearsheet	J. WATTS	1
MR FERN'S b.c. THE BARON by Xenophon		
out of Tantrum	T. CANNON	2
MR F. DOUGLAS'S ch.c. MARTLEY by Doncaster		
out of Lady Margarette	F. BARRETT	3

Also ran:

Mr J. Hammond's Aintree (4th) (F. Webb); Lord Ellesmere's Grandison (G. Barrett); Lord Falmouth's Blanchland (E. Martin); Mr Manton's Eiridspord (Fagan); Duke of Westminster's Savile (Robinson); Mr C. Perkins's Porcelain (Bruckshaw); Mr C. J. Merry's Shannon colt by Doncaster (J. Osborne); Mr C. J. Lefevre's Consolidé (J. Goater).

11 ran.

Betting:

5–4 on The Baron; 100–14 Eiridspord; 10–1 Martley; 100–9 Merry Hampton; 100–8 Aintree; 1,000–45 Blanchland; 50–1 Grandison and Porcelain; 100–1 Savile; 200–1 Consolidé and the Shannon colt.

Won by four lengths; two lengths between second and third.   2 m. 43 s.
Winner trained by M. Gurry at Newmarket.

1888

The sixth Duke of Portland was an ensign in the Coldstream when he succeeded to the title and a fortune in 1879. Among his brother officers were Colonel Evelyn Boscawen, son of Lord Falmouth; Lord Lambton, who, as Lord Durham, was subsequently an outstanding Steward of the Jockey Club; and Mr Edgar Vincent, later Lord D'Abernon, breeder of that famous sprinter Diadem. Not surprisingly his interest in racing had been kindled, and once he possessed the means to do so, he decided to revive as far as he could the former glories of the Welbeck Stud.

Wisely he chose Matt Dawson as his trainer, and on Dawson's advice he bought St Simon for 1,600 guineas at the sale of Prince Batthyany's horses. Unbeaten on the Turf, St Simon proved the most successful sire in the history of English thoroughbred breeding; between 1889 and 1912, he sired the winners of 571 races of over half a million pounds in stakes, heading the list of winning sires on nine occasions, seven of them in succession. Seventeen classic races were won by his stock, which included the Derby winners Persimmon and Diamond Jubilee.

Nor did the Duke's good fortune end with St Simon, since between 1884 and 1902 he won fourteen classic races and two Ascot Gold Cups. He won the Two Thousand Guineas with Ayrshire (1888); the One Thousand Guineas with Semolina (1890) and Amiable (1894); the Derby with Ayrshire (1888) and Donovan (1889); the Oaks with Memoir (1890), Mrs Butterwick (1893), Amiable (1894), and La Roche (1900); the St Leger with Donovan (1889) and Memoir (1890); and the Gold Cup with St Simon (1884) and William the Third (1902).

With the turn of the century the Duke's luck began to deteriorate, and as he himself grew older, he lost much of his former enthusiasm. During the First World War his views on the continuance of racing brought him into sharp conflict with the majority of his fellow-members of the Jockey Club, and his colours were only rarely seen in the last twenty years of his life. A generous, friendly, straightforward man, he owned extensive estates in England and Scotland and represented the very best traditions as a landlord, while much of the stake money he won on the Turf he dispensed in charity. For many years he was Master of the Horse in the Royal Household. The little world that he knew and loved had vanished for ever when he died in his eighty-sixth year in 1942.

On account of increasing age, Matt Dawson had given up the tenancy of the

Heath House stables in 1886 and had gone to train privately for Lord Rosebery at Exning, where he turned out two Derby winners, Ladas (1894) and Sir Visto (1895). He was succeeded at Heath House by his nephew George Dawson, who had originally been apprenticed to a brewer, but whose enthusiasm for horses and an open-air life proved stronger than his liking for beer.

It was George Dawson, therefore, who had charge of Ayrshire, a medium-sized dark bay colt by Hampton out of Atalanta, a mare that the Duke had bought from Lord Rosslyn. Atalanta was by Galopin out of Feronia, by Thormanby, and her grand-dam was Honeysuckle, a sister to Newminster. As a two-year-old Ayrshire was third in his first two races, but then won all the next five including the Chesterfield Stakes at Newmarket, the Prince of Wales's Stakes at Goodwood, and the Champagne Stakes at Doncaster. Unfortunately he hurt himself at Doncaster and had to miss his later autumn engagements, but he recovered during the winter and cantered away the following spring from his solitary opponent in the Riddlesworth Stakes.

Ayrshire's chief opponent in the Two Thousand Guineas was Friar's Balsam, owned in partnership by Lord Alington and Sir Frederick Johnstone. This Hermit colt had won all his seven races as a two-year-old including the New Stakes, in which he defeated Ayrshire, the July Stakes, the Middle Park Stakes, and the Dewhurst Plate. There was only a field of six for the Two Thousand and the race was regarded as a mere formality for Friar's Balsam, who started at 3–1 on. The favourite looked well enough in the paddock, but just before 'the off' he burst an abscess on his gums and blood started oozing out of his mouth. Cannon decided to let him take his chance, but not surprisingly the colt ran badly, Ayrshire winning comfortably from the Duke of Portland's second string, Johnny Morgan. Friar's Balsam could not run again before the autumn and never really recovered his former brilliance although he did upset the odds laid on Minting in the Champion Stakes.

With Friar's Balsam out of the way, Ayrshire started a 6–5 on favourite for the Derby and, ridden by Fred Barrett, he won quite comfortably from Mr R. C. Vyner's Crowberry, who was subsequently second in the Grand Prix. There is little that needs to be said about an unexciting race except that Chillington bolted more than once and delayed the start for half an hour, while inside the final furlong Ayrshire suddenly took it into his head to swerve right across the course. Luckily he was well clear of Crowberry at the time. Apparently Barrett, excited at the prospect of winning his first Derby, had given his mount a sharp jab with his left spur with unfortunate results, having completely missed him with the right one!

A few days after the Derby Ayrshire was found to be lame, the cause being a splint just under the knee. He was unable to run again before the St Leger in which he started favourite at 2–1, but failed to stay, and finished unplaced behind Lord

Calthorpe's lovely chesnut filly Seabreeze. Lord Calthorpe, a prominent figure in racing and hunting circles, had a nice opinion of himself and firmly believed that he was the original of 'The Honourable Crasher' in Whyte Melville's novel *Market Harborough*. Ten days after the St Leger Ayrshire ran Seabreeze to three parts of a length in the seven-furlong Lancashire Plate at Manchester. Third in that event, which was then worth £10,000, was the handsome French grey Le Sancy. At the stud Le Sancy got Roi Hérode, a plodding stayer destined to sire The Tetrarch, the fastest horse ever seen on the English Turf.

Ayrshire, whose best distance was probably ten furlongs, ended the season by winning the Great Foal Plate at Newmarket from paltry opposition. As a four-year-old he had ample revenge on Seabreeze, as he beat her in the £10,000 Kempton Park Royal Stakes and again in the Eclipse Stakes at Sandown. In the Champion Stakes he broke down badly and was retired to the stud, having won eleven races and over £39,000 in stakes. As a sire he just missed reaching the very top rank, but he got plenty of winners, including Our Lassie and Airs and Graces, who both won the Oaks, and on several occasions he was in the first ten in the list of winning sires. He was eventually destroyed in 1910. His mares did well at the stud. Gas bred Cicero, winner of the Derby, and Airs and Graces bred Jardy, second to Cicero at Epsom and winner of the Middle Park Plate. In addition he bred the dam of Roseway, winner of the One Thousand Guineas, and the maternal grand-dams of the St Leger and Gold Cup winners, Prince Palatine and Solario.

It will be noted that for the first time since 1840 the value of the race fell below £4,000.

1888: Wednesday, 30 May . . . 169 Entries. £3,675.

DUKE OF PORTLAND's b.c. AYRSHIRE by Hampton out of Atalanta	F. BARRETT	I
MR R. C. VYNER's ch.c. CROWBERRY by Roseberry out of Lizzie Lindsay	J. OSBORNE	2
MR C. D. ROSE's ch.c. VAN DIEMAN'S LAND by Robert the Devil out of Distant Shore	J. WATTS	3

Also ran:

Mr N. Fenwick's Galore (4th) (F. Webb); Duke of Westminster's Orbit (T. Cannon); Lord Bradford's Chillington (S. Loates); Mr J. N. Astley's Netheravon (Robinson); Mr R. C. Vyner's Gautby (Elliot); Mr R. H. Combe's Simon Pure (Rickaby).

9 ran.

Betting :

6–5 on Ayrshire; 11–2 Orbit; 6–1 Crowberry; 100–14 Galore; 20–1 Van Dieman's Land; 40–1 Netheravon; 100–1 Chillington and Simon Pure; 250–1 Gautby.

Won by two lengths; five lengths between second and third.   2 m. 43 s. Winner trained by G. Dawson at Newmarket.

1889

The Duke of Portland won the Derby again in 1889 with Donovan, named after the hero of a novel by Edna Lyall that the Duke was reading when the colt was foaled.

A rather light-framed bay, all wire and whipcord, Donovan was by Galopin out of Mowerina, a mare that the Duke had bought in 1881 from Lord Rossmore for £1,400, the amount that Lord Rossmore had just lost at the Epsom Spring Meeting. Bred in Denmark by Mr Otto Scavenius, she was by Scottish Chief out of Stockings, by Stockwell out of Go Ahead, own sister to the Derby winner West Australian, who oddly enough was himself out of another mare called Mowerina. Mowerina, the dam of Donovan, was extremely fast and won the Portland Plate at Doncaster under 9 st. 3 lb. Her first foal, a full sister to Donovan, was Modwena, winner of nine races as a two-year-old and of the Portland Plate the following season. Mowerina also bred Semolina, winner of the One Thousand Guineas, and Raeburn, who was not only third in the Derby, but the only horse ever to beat Isinglass. This he accomplished, receiving ten pounds, in the Lancashire Plate.

The Brocklesby Stakes at Lincoln in the opening week of the season was then a far more significant affair than it is today, and it was the race selected for Donovan's first appearance. Although still backward he duly won, and shortly afterwards he won the £6,000 Portland Stakes at Leicester, among his defeated opponents being Chittabob, by Robert the Devil. In the Whitsuntide Plate at Manchester Donovan and Chittabob met again, but this time Chittabob, with a pull of thirteen pounds in the weights, was the winner.

Donovan's only other defeat that season was in the Prince of Wales's Stakes at Goodwood, when he was third to El Dorado and Gold. The course was like a snipe-bog after torrential rain, and George Dawson was heard to remark afterwards that unfortunately he had omitted to teach Donovan to swim. The remainder of Donovan's two-year-old career was one long triumph. In the summer he won the New Stakes at Ascot, the Bilbury Foal Stakes and Hurstbourne Stakes at Stockbridge, the July Stakes at Newmarket, and the Ham Stakes at Goodwood; in the autumn he won all his four races at Newmarket; the Buckenham Stakes, the Hopeful Stakes, the Middle Park Plate, and the Dewhurst Plate. Not surprisingly, he was winter favourite for the Derby.

Donovan wintered well, and towards the end of March he was galloped over the

Rowley Mile with Deschamps, a three-year-old carrying a very light weight to ensure a good pace, and the previous year's Derby winner, Ayrshire. Donovan carried one pound more than Ayrshire, and as he was going a good deal better than Ayrshire at the end of the gallop, it was clear that he was something approaching a racing certainty for the Two Thousand Guineas.

Donovan's first racecourse appearance of the season was at Leicester where he won the £12,000 Prince of Wales's Stakes—Leicester went in for big prizes for a very brief period—very comfortably from Pioneer, Minthe, and Enthusiast. In the Two Thousand Guineas he started at 85–20 on, but the form-book was turned upside down and Enthusiast beat him by a head. It was unquestionably a fluke result. To start with the pace was a false one, but the real reason for the favourite's downfall was that Fred Barrett thought Pioneer was the only danger, and having disposed of Pioneer he dropped his hands. Tom Cannon, on the far side of the course on Enthusiast, quickly seized the fleeting opportunity, and a strong late run landed Enthusiast in front at the winning-post before Barrett had the chance to get Donovan going again. Barrett was inclined to be conceited, but his reception from the Duke and George Dawson no doubt deflated him, for the time being at any rate. In the Newmarket Stakes Donovan, with The Turcophone acting as pacemaker, had no trouble in reversing the form with Enthusiast, who finished unplaced.

Just before the Derby Mr Leopold de Rothschild, who had first claim on Barrett, decided that he required that jockey to ride Morglay. The leading riders were all booked up and eventually it was decided to engage Tommy Loates to partner Donovan, despite the fact that Loates was very small and light and at a pinch could go to scale at 6 st. 7 lb. In fact, when Donovan was saddled at Epsom, there were three weight cloths under the saddle and Loates's legs were so widely straddled that he appeared to adopt what was shortly to be known as the American style of riding. Loates, who also won the Derby on Isinglass, was a good rider in many respects, but very short in the leg, and not at his best on big, strong, long-striding horses.

Donovan started at 11–8 on in the Derby, and after his pacemaker, The Turcophone, had dropped back beaten three furlongs out, he struck the front himself and went on to win with the maximum ease by a length and a half from Miguel, with El Dorado a bad third. The French Derby winner Clover broke down early in the race.

Donovan won the Prince of Wales's Stakes at Ascot and then had a rest until the St Leger, which he won very easily from Miguel. The fact that Donovan started at the remarkably generous price of 13–8 on was due to support for the Yorkshire colt Chittabob, who, however, was far from sound, and for that reason had not been given nearly as much work as he required.

Donovan finished the season by winning the Lancashire Plate at Manchester and the Royal Stakes at Newmarket. The following year he broke down during his preparation for the Ascot Gold Cup and was retired to the stud. He was undoubtedly a really good horse, and a desperately unlucky one not to have gained the 'Triple Crown'. Despite his unlucky defeat in the Guineas, he won £55,154 in stakes, a record sum at the time but surpassed in 1895 by Isinglass.

At the stud Donovan never got a horse within measurable distance of his own excellence, his best sons being Velasquez and Veronese, who were both placed in the Derby. He was also sire of Matchmaker, whose daughter Mother-in-Law was dam of the great stayer Son-in-Law. From Donovan's daughter Altoviscar are descended the Gold Cup winner Foxlaw, as well as Alcide and Parthia of recent memory. In addition, Feola, a great grand-daughter of Altoviscar, is largely responsible for the many triumphs of the Royal Stud in recent years, her descendants including Aureole, Hypericum, Kingstone, Above Board, Doutelle, and Above Suspicion. Another descendant of Altoviscar is Round Table, winner of well over a million dollars and voted 'Horse of the Year' in the United States in 1958.

Donovan was killed when he ran into a tree at the Worksop Manor Stud in 1905.

1889: Wednesday, 5 June . . . 169 Entries. £4,050.

DUKE OF PORTLAND's b.c. DONOVAN by Galopin
out of Mowerina   T. LOATES   I
MR J. GRETTON's bl.c. MIGUEL by Fernandez
out of Cream Cheese   G. BARRETT   2
MR DOUGLAS BAIRD's b.c. EL DORADO by Sterling
out of Palmflower   T. CANNON   3

Also ran:

Mr 'Abington's' Pioneer (4th) (J. Watts); Mr Douglas Baird's Enthusiast (Calder); Duke of Portland's The Turcophone (E. Martin); Mr J. Hammond's Laureate (Rickaby); Mr Rose's Gulliver (Liddiard); Mr L. de Rothschild's Morglay (F. Barrett); Mr W. Low's Gay Hampton (Robinson); Mr C. Perkins's Folengo (Fagan); M. E. Blanc's Clover (F. Webb); Mr T. Jennings, jun.'s Royal Star (J. Woodburn).

13 ran.

Betting:

11–8 on Donovan; 100–8 El Dorado; 100–6 Laureate and Pioneer; 20–1 Clover; 25–1 Morglay and Miguel; 1,000–35 Folengo; 33–1 Enthusiast; 50–1 Gulliver and The Turcophone; 66–1 Gay Hampton; 200–1 Royal Star.

Won by a length and a half; a bad third.   2 m. 44$\frac{2}{5}$ s.
Winner trained by G. Dawson at Newmarket.

1890

In the last century it was the custom to sneer at the yearlings bred at the Royal Stud at Hampton Court and to call them the 'Hampton Court Rats'. However, the fact remains that Sainfoin, winner of the Derby in 1890, and Memoir, winner of the Oaks and the St Leger that year, were both bred at Hampton Court.

Sainfoin was a beautifully made little chestnut colt by Springfield out of Sanda. Springfield was by St Albans, a son of Stockwell, while Sanda was by Wenlock out of Stockwell's daughter Sandal. John Porter and Sir Robert Jardine both took a fancy to Sainfoin at the Hampton Court Sale and bought him in partnership for 500 guineas.

Sainfoin only ran once as a two-year-old, winning the Astley Stakes at Lewes in August. He made excellent progress physically during the winter although he was barely fifteen hands two when fully grown. In the following April, after a very encouraging gallop the previous week, he won the Esher Stakes at Sandown, a handicap for three-year-olds and upwards, with 6 st. 11 lb. on his back. His style impressed quite a number of people, including a rich young subaltern in the 14th Hussars, Sir James Miller, who shortly afterwards made overtures with a view to buying him. Porter's own opinion was that Sainfoin was a good staying colt, but highly unlikely to beat the Two Thousand Guineas winner Surefoot at Epsom. Accordingly it was agreed to sell Sainfoin for £6,000, plus half the Derby stake as a contingency.

Sainfoin won the Dee Stakes at Chester from a solitary opponent and started at 100–15 in the Derby, for which Surefoot was an odds-on favourite. Surefoot, owned by Mr A. W. Merry, a quiet, reserved young officer in the Royal Horse Guards, was a big, massive bay, full of fire and dash. Despite looking as big as a bull and behaving with noticeable lack of decorum in the paddock beforehand, Surefoot had won the Two Thousand Guineas with considerable ease, and his trainer Jousiffe, a great burly, jovial man, was supremely confident of the outcome at Epsom.

For most of the spectators it was a thoroughly miserable Derby. The rain teemed down throughout the afternoon and the favourite was well and truly beaten. The crowd and the excitement were too much for Surefoot's temperament and he was thoroughly worked up before the start. He never settled down in the race, tried to savage the nearest of his opponents, and after pulling for all he was worth to Tattenham Corner, he began to yield ground. At that point Orwell, whom Porter trained for the Duke of Westminster, was in the lead, followed by Sainfoin, Rathbeal, and Surefoot. At the distance Rathbeal was beaten and Sainfoin went to the front. Surefoot rallied in astonishing fashion and came back right to the heels of the leaders, while a resolute challenge by Le Nord looked extremely dangerous. Sainfoin, how- ever, ran on valiantly in the hands of Jack Watts and passed the post three parts of a length ahead of Le Nord, with Orwell only a neck away third, and Surefoot missing a place by a matter of inches.

It was accepted that Surefoot's failure was due to lack of stamina and bad temper combined, but according to W. T. (Jack) Robinson, who rode Rathbeal, he was the victim of deliberate rough-riding by a number of jockeys. Some time previously Liddiard, who partnered Surefoot, had been instrumental in getting several riders 'stood down' for a month. In revenge Liddiard was filled up with gin before the Derby—no difficult task—and Surefoot was hampered and bustled throughout the race. Robinson later trained at Foxhill and had charge of Craganour, disqualified after winning the Derby in 1913.

The remainder of Sainfoin's career was undistinguished to say the least. He was second to Amphion in the Hardwicke Stakes, fourth to Memoir in the St Leger, and unplaced in the Free Handicap. As a four-year-old he was third in the Imperial Plate at Hurst Park and down the course in a minor event at Newmarket. The following year he failed in both the Lincoln and City and Suburban and was then retired to the stud at a fee of fifty guineas. A moderate Derby winner himself, he sired a far better one in Rock Sand, who won the 'Triple Crown' for Sir James Miller in 1903. Sir James himself became a member of the Jockey Club, served in the South African war, and in 1906 died from the effects of a chill caught out hunting. He was in his forty-seventh year and a Steward of the Jockey Club at the time. His other classic successes were the Oaks, won by Sagesse in 1895, and the One Thousand Guineas, won by Aida in 1901. After Sir James's death Sainfoin was sold to Lord Carnarvon for 700 guineas and stood at the Cloghran Stud in Ireland till his death in 1911.

Surefoot won a Biennial Stakes at Ascot, but was beaten in both the Hardwicke and Prince of Wales's Stakes. A fortnight later he won a £10,000 race at Leicester, beating Memoir. Hard racing was fining him down at last and getting him really fit, but unfortunately his temper was deteriorating and he ran indifferently both in the St Leger and the Free Handicap. The strain of looking after Surefoot was too much for poor Jousiffe, who died the following spring. The horse was then sent to Garrett Moore, who mastered him, but without breaking his spirit. In fact Surefoot was never better than the day he won the Eclipse Stakes, beating the Derby winner Common and Gouverneur.

Le Nord may have been an unlucky loser of the Derby. It was originally intended to keep him for Epsom and to run Heaume in the French Derby. Heaume went slightly amiss, however, and Le Nord was sent to Chantilly to take his place. Heaume, however, recovered in time to take the field and Le Nord returned to Newmarket. In view of this interruption to his preparation, Le Nord did remarkably well to finish as close as he did.

For some years previously the Derby had been declining in popularity with owners, if not with the general public. The reason was the parsimony of the Epsom authorities, who drew enormous benefit from staging the Derby without incurring the slightest liability in connexion therewith. Entries for some time past had been showing a marked decline, and under pressure from the Jockey Club, the Epsom authorities, who in addition were not a little alarmed at the success and prestige of the newly established Eclipse Stakes, agreed to alter the conditions. The race was now given the guaranteed value of £5,000, instead of being a Sweepstakes of fifty pounds, half forfeit, as heretofore. The minor forfeit of ten pounds (reduced two years later to five pounds) was instituted, while other changes were that the nominator of the winner henceforth received £500, and the owner of the third £200, instead of £150.

1890: Wednesday, 4 June . . . 233 Entries. £5,940.

SIR JAMES MILLER'S ch.c. SAINFOIN by Springfield out of Sanda	J. WATTS	1
BARON DE ROTHSCHILD'S ch.c. LE NORD by Tristan out of La Noce	F. BARRETT	2
DUKE OF WESTMINSTER'S b.c. ORWELL by Bend Or out of Lizzie Agnes	G. BARRETT	3

Also ran:

Mr A. W. Merry's Surefoot (4th) (Liddiard); Mr E. W. Baird's Golden Gate (T. Cannon); Mr James White's Kirkham (F. Webb); Captain Machell's Rathbeal (Robinson); Mr Douglas Baird's Martagon (J. Osborne).

8 ran.

Betting:

95–40 on Surefoot; 100–15 Sainfoin; 100–7 Le Nord and Rathbeal; 50–1 Golden Gate and Kirkham; 100–1 Orwell and Martagon.

Won by three parts of a length; a neck between second and third.　　2 m. 49⅘ s. Winner trained by J. Porter at Kingsclere.

1891

It was another victory for Kingsclere in 1891, the winner being Common, bred at Crichel by Lord Alington, and like St Blaise, the winner in 1883, owned by him in partnership with his friend Sir Frederick Johnstone.

Common was a great, lathy, sinewy colt by Isonomy out of Thistle, by Scottish Chief. Isonomy, who had the distinction of siring two 'Triple Crown' winners, Common and Isinglass, had been the outstanding three-year-old of his day, but his owner Mr Gretton had kept him for a gamble in the Cambridgeshire in preference to running him in the Derby. As a yearling Common was split-up, weedy, and thin, with extremely dubious joints. John Porter naturally decided that the only hope for the colt was time, and although Common made substantial progress as a two-year-old, he never saw a racecourse that season.

In the spring of 1891 Common began to shape like a really good horse, and his improvement was confirmed when he won a trial just about a week before the Guineas. He had never been in a horse-box before he travelled to Newmarket for the Two Thousand; he sweated up profusely, and the lime-wash from the walls of the box adhered to his coat. His appearance was, therefore, distinctly unprepossessing on arrival at Newmarket Station, where quite a crowd had collected to inspect the 'dark horse' from Kingsclere.

'He's very well named,' remarked Prince Soltykoff on seeing Common walking round the paddock before the Guineas, but to the surprise of the Prince and most of the Newmarket critics Common won in a canter from Gouverneur, owned by M. Edmond Blanc.

Not unnaturally Common started a short-priced favourite for the Derby, and in torrential rain that had begun about an hour before the race, he defeated Gouverneur by a comfortable two lengths, the pair having drawn well clear of the remainder in the straight. The riders were soaked to the skin, and most of them were at least two pounds overweight in consequence when they weighed in. Although the favourite had triumphed, conditions were too dismal for very much enthusiasm to be shown. The time was the slowest since 1879.

Common won the St James's Palace Stakes at Ascot from a single and moderate opponent, but in the Eclipse Stakes he was only third to Surefoot, winner of the Two Thousand Guineas the year before, and Gouverneur, to whom he conceded three pounds. Despite his success in the Guineas, he really needed a mile and a half to be seen at his best, and over the Sandown Park ten furlongs, Surefoot, who gave him twelve pounds, had a bit too much speed for him at the finish.

Common had run up very light by St Leger day and was probably stale. Starting at 5–4 on he duly won from Révérend and St Simon of the Rock, but he gave his backers some anxious moments and Barrett had his whip up with a good half-mile still to go. In fact only a very game horse would have run on under prolonged pressure the way that he did.

Just before the St Leger, the Austrian Government offered 14,000 guineas for Common, but this was refused. Two days after the race, the well-known furniture dealer Sir Blundell Maple offered 15,000 guineas, and this was accepted. The Austrians then increased their bid to 20,000 guineas, but Sir Blundell rather pompously wired back: 'THANKS FOR OFFER (stop) THE ENGLISH TURF REQUIRES COMMONS SERVICES (stop) MONEY WILL NOT TEMPT ME.' Sir Blundell wanted Common to remain in training with Porter for another season, but Porter either could not or would not have him as a patron of the Kingsclere stable. Common, therefore, retired to the stud forthwith at a fee of 200 guineas. He was a failure as a sire, and at one period before his death at Mr Boyce Barrow's stud near Chelmsford in 1912, his fee had dropped to nineteen guineas.

1891: Wednesday, 27 May . . . 203 Entries. £5,510.

SIR F. JOHNSTONE's br.c. COMMON by Isonomy out of Thistle	G. BARRETT	I
M. E. BLANC's ch.c. GOUVERNEUR by Energy out of Gladieuse	J. WOODBURN	2
SIR JAMES DUKE's b.c. MARTENHURST by Wenlock out of Hirondelle	FAGAN	3

Also ran:

Lord Bradford's Cuttlestone (4th) (Weldon); Mr J. B. Leigh's The Deemster (J. Watts); Lord Durham's Peter Flower (Rickaby); Colonel North's Old Boots (M. Cannon); Colonel North's Simonian (F. Barrett); Duke of Westminster's Orion (F. Webb); Mr Brydges Williams's Fitz Simon (J. Osborne); Mr Daniel Cooper's Dorcas (G. Chaloner).

11 ran.

Betting:

11–10 on Common; 10–1 Dorcas; 100–9 Gouverneur; 12–1 Orion; 100–6 The

Richard Marsh   Danny Maher

Diamond Jubilee (H. Jones up); by E. Adam

Minoru winning the
1909 Derby

King Edward VII leading in Minoru

Deemster; 20–1 Old Boots; 25–1 Fitz Simon; 1,000–35 Simonian; 33–1 Cuttlestone
and Peter Flower; 50–1 Martenhurst.

Won by two lengths; a bad third.   2 m. 56⅘ s.
Winner trained by J. Porter at Kingsclere.

1892

Surprise of surprises! A great shout arises,
  Proclaiming to all that the fav'rite is done—
Wisdom's chef d'œuvre, the son of Manœuvre,
  Lord Bradford's Sir Hugo the Derby has won.

The Kingsclere stable should have won again this year with Baron de Hirsch's great filly La Flèche, a half-sister by St Simon to Memoir, winner of the Oaks and St Leger, but due to the deplorable riding of George Barrett, she was beaten by the 40–1 outsider Sir Hugo. This was certainly not Kingsclere's lucky year as the Duke of Westminster's Orme, an outstanding two-year-old the previous season, was taken seriously ill—poisoned, according to his owner—just before the Two Thousand Guineas, and was unable to race before July.

Sir Hugo was bred and owned by the Earl of Bradford. A member of the Jockey Club and then in his seventy-fourth year, Lord Bradford had represented South Shropshire in the House of Commons for over twenty years, and at various times had held office as Lord Chamberlain and Master of the Horse. For many years he was prominent on the Turf, and his horses were trained by Tom Wadlow in his park at Weston in Shropshire and managed by his brother-in-law, Colonel Henry Forester, a famous man to hounds in Leicestershire in his day. Colonel Forester, generally known as 'The Lad', was a great character, full of minor eccentricities and super-stitions. Slight in build, with old-fashioned whiskers and a pair of spectacles on the end of his beak of a nose, he was said to resemble an old crow looking down a marrow bone. He was exceptionally shrewd on the Turf and was believed to do extremely well in most years out of his betting. He was blackballed for the Jockey Club time and again by the Earl of Glasgow, who made up for it by leaving him a handsome legacy when he died.

Sir Hugo, a fine, powerful colt though rather faulty in his hocks, was by Wisdom out of Manœuvre, by Lord Clifden. Wisdom was unplaced in the Derby of his year; in fact he never won a race of any description and at one time changed hands for fifty guineas. He was, however, a very successful sire, as besides Sir Hugo he got Surefoot, winner of the Two Thousand Guineas and Eclipse Stakes; Sagesse, winner of the Oaks; and Love Wisely, winner of the Gold Cup and sire of Fairway's grand-dam, Anchora. Wisdom himself was closely in-bred, his paternal grandsire, Rataplan, and his maternal grandsire, Stockwell, being full brothers.

As a two-year-old Sir Hugo was third in the Triennial Stakes at Ascot and then won the Rous Memorial Stakes at Goodwood. In the Champagne Stakes at Doncaster he was third to La Flèche and at Newmarket in October he won the Boscawen Stakes, but he was unplaced behind Orme in the Middle Park. There was little reason, therefore, to regard him as a classic hope, and his prospects were not improved the following spring when he finished unplaced behind Bona Vista in the Two Thousand Guineas.

An odds-on favourite for the Derby was La Flèche, who had been bought by Baron de Hirsch, the son of a Jewish banker in Munich, for 5,500 guineas as a yearling at the annual Hampton Court Sale. The price was considered enormous in those days and such was Mr Edmund Tattersall's emotion that he called at once for 'three cheers for Baron de Hirsch and success to the Royal Stud'. As a two-year-old La Flèche won all her four races, the Chesterfield Stakes at Newmarket, the Lavant and the Molecomb Stakes at Goodwood, and the Champagne Stakes at Doncaster. The opinion at Kingsclere was that there was very little indeed between Orme and La Flèche, the filly being perhaps a shade superior. The following spring La Flèche won the One Thousand Guineas in a canter, and as she made excellent progress between Newmarket and Epsom, her victory in the Derby was anticipated with the utmost confidence.

There is little doubt that poor George Barrett, who partnered La Flèche, was showing symptoms of incipient insanity. In the first part of the race he lay a long way out of his ground, shouting and gesticulating at the other riders. In consequence the filly was a long way behind the leaders at Tattenham Corner, and though Barrett then collected his wits and began to ride her in earnest, she had been left with just too much to do. Despite a most gallant effort, she failed by three parts of a length to reach Sir Hugo, who had taken the lead two furlongs out from Bucentaure. There had been rivalry carried to somewhat undesirable lengths by the Orme and La Flèche factions in Porter's stable, and some of the Orme partisans brought little credit on themselves by their openly expressed delight at La Flèche's defeat. La Flèche turned out for the Oaks two days later, but her hard race in the Derby had left its mark and she only won by a head from The Smew, whom she had beaten very easily in the One Thousand Guineas.

Sir Hugo was beaten into third place behind Angelo in the St James's Palace Stakes at Ascot and was then put by until the St Leger in which he was ridden by Tom Weldon in place of Allsopp, who had steered him to victory at Epsom. The Kingsclere pair, Orme and La Flèche, also took the field for the St Leger, Orme, ridden by George Barrett, being favourite at 11–10 on, while La Flèche, ridden by Watts, was at 7–2. Orme had made a successful and highly popular come-back in the Eclipse Stakes, in which, beautifully ridden by Barrett, he won by a neck from Orvieto, while after the race the Duke of Westminster, hat in hand, stood bowing to the crowd as they cheered him again and again. A fortnight later Orme won the Sussex Stakes at Goodwood, but not with the ease expected as he only beat his stable companion Watercress by a head. La Flèche had won the Nassau Stakes at Goodwood, and by Doncaster was reckoned to be back in her very best form.

Sir Hugo, who started at 10–1, gave his very best running in the St Leger but was no match for La Flèche, who had the better turn of speed at the finish and won quite comfortably by a couple of lengths. Orme was ridden into the ground by Barrett, who had taken offence, not surprisingly perhaps, at a suggestion by the Duke of Westminster that he had been 'got at' and that in consequence his riding would be observed with the closest attention. Orme might not have stayed the distance in any case, but he had little or no chance to do so ridden as he was.

After the St Leger Sir Hugo was unplaced behind La Flèche in the Lancashire Plate; second to El Diablo in the Lowther Stakes: and third to Orme and El Diablo in the Limekiln Stakes. The following year he won his only race, a Biennial Stakes at Newmarket, and then retired to the stud at a fee of 150 guineas. Ten years later he was transferred to the Athgarvan Lodge Stud in Ireland. He made little mark as a sire, but got Ravello, dam of the American-bred Two Thousand Guineas winner Sweeper II.

Orme, who won the Eclipse Stakes the following year, but broke down later in that season, sired two Derby winners, Flying Fox and Orby. La Flèche followed up her St Leger victory by winning the Lancashire Plate, the Grand Duke Michael Stakes at Newmarket, the Newmarket Oaks, and lastly the Cambridgeshire with the substantial burden for a three-year-old of 8 st. 10 lb. At the end of the year she went with the rest of her owner's horses to be trained by Richard Marsh. As a four-year-old she won the Lowther Stakes and also the Liverpool Autumn Cup in which she carried 9 st. 6 lb. As a five-year-old she won the Gold Cup at Ascot and the Champion Stakes. One of the greatest fillies in racing history, she won sixteen races and over £34,000 in stakes.

Soon after Baron de Hirsch's death in 1896 La Flèche was sold to Sir Tatton Sykes for 12,600 guineas. Her son John o' Gaunt, by Isinglass, was second in the Derby and sired the St Leger winner Swynford, who in his turn sired the Derby winner Sansovino. Baronesse La Flèche, her filly by Ladas, bred the One Thousand Guineas winner Cinna, dam of Beau Père and Mr Standfast, both by Son-in-Law. Neither of those two horses was of any account on the racecourse but both were brilliantly successful at the stud in New Zealand and Australia. Beau Père's stock did extremely well in the United States as well.

1892: Wednesday, 1 June . . . 259 Entries. £6,960.

LORD BRADFORD's ch.c. SIR HUGO by Wisdom out of Manœuvre	F. ALLSOPP	1
BARON DE HIRSCH's b.f. LA FLÈCHE by St Simon out of Quiver	G. BARRETT	2
M. CAMILLE BLANC's b.c. BUCENTAURE by Saxifrage out of Venise	CHESTERMAN	3

Also ran:

   Mr H. Wilner's St Angelo (4th) (F. Webb); Lord Penrhyn's Thessalian (Weldon); M. E. Blanc's Rueil (T. Lane); Duke of Hamilton's Persistive (J. Watts); Sir Blundell Maple's Hatfield (Rickaby); Colonel North's El Diablo (M. Cannon); Mr C. D. Rose's Bona Vista (Robinson); Mr C. D. Rose's St Damien (R. Chaloner); Sir R. Jardine's Llanthony (F. Barrett); Mr Fairie's Galeopsis (C. Loates).

13 ran.

Betting:

   11–10 La Flèche; 100–9 Rueil; 100–8 Bona Vista; 100–7 St Damien; 100–6 Thessalian, St Angelo, and Llanthony; 20–1 El Diablo; 25–1 Persistive; 40–1 Sir Hugo; 1,000–15 Hatfield: 100–1 Galeopsis and Bucentaure.

Won by three parts of a length; a length between second and third.   2 m. 44 s. Winner trained by T. Wadlow at Stanton.

1893

Isinglass, who gained the 'Triple Crown' in 1893, was one of the greatest of Derby winners. Only once was he beaten during the four seasons he was in training, and all told he won £57,455 in stakes, a sum that stood as a record in this country until surpassed by Tulyar in 1952.

He was a big, strong bay by Isonomy out of Deadlock, a mare by the St Leger winner Wenlock, a son of Lord Clifden, out of Malpractice by Chevalier d'Industrie. Deadlock originally belonged to Lord Alington and on a visit to the Crichel Stud Captain Machell had bought her for nineteen guineas. Mated with Trappist, she bred a colt called Gervas, who was quite a useful performer. Before Gervas had proved his merit, Machell had re-sold Deadlock, but believing that Wenlock mares 'nicked' with Isonomy, he decided to buy her back again if he could. For some time he was unable to trace her, but one day a farmer drove up in a trap to have a look at the cart stallion, Marvellous. Machell thought he recognized the animal pulling the trap and sure enough it was Deadlock. The farmer was delighted to swap her for a colt by Marvellous and she was put to Isonomy. The following year, with a colt foal named Islington at foot, she was sold to Mr Harry McCalmont for £500. In 1889 she returned to Isonomy and bred Isinglass.

Trained by James Jewitt, whose stable was managed by Machell, Isinglass made his first racecourse appearance at the Newmarket Second Spring Meeting in a maiden plate, which he duly won. Next time out he won the New Stakes at Ascot quite comfortably, and he then rested till the autumn when, starting at 10-1, he won the Middle Park Plate from Ravensbury, who was to become a persistent opponent of his the following season. The reason for the generous price about Isinglass was the gamble on Dame President, a filly owned by Sir Blundell Maple. Possibly the most brilliant two-year-old colt of the season was Mr 'Abington' Baird's unbeaten Meddler, by St Gatien out of Busybody, but Baird's death in America rendered all Meddler's classic engagements void.

The going was persistently hard throughout 1893 and it proved extremely difficult to train Isinglass properly, most of his work being done on the tan. In consequence, although he was only once defeated, he was rarely impressive and in almost every race the cry went up at one stage or another, 'The favourite's beat!' A contributory factor was the colt's own habitual laziness and the inability of Tom Loates, small and short-legged, to get the best out of a big, strong, indolent horse that was particularly broad in the back.

Before the Two Thousand Guineas the ground was like iron and Isinglass was sore after every gallop. Jewitt wanted to scratch him, but Machell refused and some heated disputes, nothing unusual between these two highly strung, hot-tempered men, took place. Eventually Machell ordered Isinglass to be taken out twice a day and cantered time and again up a short bit of hill on the Bury tan. Jewitt protested that no horse could win a classic race on a preparation like that, but Machell insisted that Isinglass could, as he had a stone in hand on any other horse in the race. Isinglass duly won, but he ran very sluggishly and at one point looked like being beaten by Ravensbury, whom he eventually defeated by three parts of a length, with the Duke of Portland's Raeburn third.

Better suited by the longer distance in the Newmarket Stakes, Isinglass won easily by three lengths from Phocion and Ravensbury. On that form it was difficult to see what could beat him in the Derby, for which he started favourite at 9–4 on. He duly won by a length and a half from Ravensbury, but there was a point two furlongs from home when Raeburn, who ultimately finished third, was alongside him and apparently going the better. In fact it was only when Loates set about him with all the vigour and strength at his command that the favourite asserted his superiority. It is perhaps worthy of note that the first three horses to finish had occupied similar positions in the Two Thousand Guineas.

The victory was a very popular one and was received with tremendous cheering. Mr (later Colonel) McCalmont, owner of the winner, was a thorough sportsman, straightforward, cheerful, and generous. As a subaltern in the Royal Warwickshire Regiment—he subsequently transferred to the Scots Guards—he inherited, somewhat unexpectedly it was said, an immense fortune from a rather eccentric uncle. Like many other rich young men with a hankering for the Turf, he placed his racing interests in the hands of Captain Machell, and in his own case he probably had no cause to regret his decision. He was largely instrumental in the introduction of steeplechasing to Newmarket, and he was responsible both for laying out the Links course and building the stand. The National Hunt Chase was run there in 1897, but jumping never thrived at the headquarters of flat-racing and was discontinued after 1899.

Colonel McCalmont served in the South African War, became a Member of Parliament, and died in 1902 in the prime of life from a heart attack. But for his death he might easily have won another Derby, as Zinfandel was a really good horse at his best, and trained by Major Charles Beatty, he won the Coronation Cup as a four-year-old, beating both Rock Sand and Sceptre.

1893

Mr C. D. Rose's Ravensbury, second to Isinglass in the Two Thousand Guineas, the Derby, and the St Leger, was trained by William Jarvis, whose sons William, Basil, and Jack all achieved fame in their profession. William trained Scuttle to win the One Thousand Guineas for King George V; Basil trained the 1923 Derby winner Papyrus, while Jack has so far trained two Derby winners in Blue Peter (1939) and Ocean Swell (1944). Ravensbury was a singularly unlucky three-year-old, as besides having Isinglass to contend with, he undoubtedly won the Grand Prix de Paris, only to have the judge, doubtless from motives of the highest patriotism, award the verdict to the French horse Rogotsky. However, Ravensbury did win a number of good races during his career, including the Manchester November Handicap with 9 st. 4 lb. on his back. At Epsom he was ridden by Harry Barker, a polished and versatile horseman, who ten weeks previously had finished second in the Grand National on Aesop.

Isinglass did not run again before the St Leger, which he won by a mere half-length from Ravensbury, but with any amount in hand. Ten days later he met with the one defeat of his career, being beaten half a length by Raeburn, to whom he gave ten pounds, in the Lancashire Plate, with La Flèche, who conceded him six pounds, third. Raeburn, a half-brother to Donovan by St Simon, was a pretty good horse as his running in the Derby showed, while a mile was too short a distance for Isinglass to exploit his tremendous reserves of stamina. In addition Isinglass was compelled to make all his own running, which he detested.

As a four-year-old Isinglass beat Bullingdon and the Derby winner Ladas in the Princess of Wales's Stakes at Newmarket, but the ground was very hard and he was all-out to scrape home by a head. That night it rained heavily, and it continued to rain every day until the Eclipse Stakes a fortnight later. For once Isinglass had conditions as he liked, and instead of frightening his backers to death as he had usually done, he dominated his opponents throughout to win easily from Ladas and his old rival, Ravensbury. In the autumn he had an easy task in the Jockey Club Stakes as his main opponent, the St Leger winner Throstle, ran out. As a five-year-old he had a single outing, the Ascot Gold Cup, which he won without difficulty from Reminder and Kilsallaghan. He then retired to his owner's stud at Cheveley, near Newmarket, and on Colonel McCalmont's death he was taken over, with the remainder of the Colonel's horses, by Lord Howard de Walden, who had just started racing.

It has been said that the tail-female line of Isinglass's dam Deadlock was weak, and this accounted for the fact that he hardly fulfilled expectations as a sire, considering the high quality of the mares he had sent to him. However, his stock won 320 races worth over £166,000 and included Cherry Lass (One Thousand Guineas

318

and Oaks); Glass Doll (Oaks); John o' Gaunt, second in the Two Thousand Guineas and the Derby, sire of Swynford (St Leger) and Kennymore (Two Thousand Guineas); Louvois (Two Thousand Guineas and sire of the Two Thousand Guineas winner St Louis); Star Shoot, a highly successful sire in the United States; Lady Lightfoot, dam of the St Leger and dual Gold Cup winner Prince Palatine; Corn-field, dam of the Oaks winner Love In Idleness; and Glasalt, dam of Canyon, who won the One Thousand Guineas and bred Colorado, winner of the Two Thousand Guineas and Eclipse Stakes.

1893: Wednesday, 31 May . . . 229 Entries. £5,515.

MR H. MCCALMONT's b.c. ISINGLASS by Isonomy
out of Deadlock   T. LOATES   1

MR C. D. ROSE's b.c. RAVENSBURY by Isonomy
out of Penitent   H. BARKER 2

DUKE OF PORTLAND's b.c. RAEBURN by St Simon
out of Mowerina   J. WATTS 3

Also ran:

Mr James Joicey's Peppercorn (4th) (Rickaby); Duke of Beaufort's Son of a Gun (Calder); Mr T. Cannon's Irish Wake (M. Cannon); Colonel North's Quickly Wise (R. Chaloner); Mr T. Jennings's Lord William (Mullen); Mr T. Jennings's William (F. Webb); Sir J. Blundell Maple's Dame President (G. Barrett); Colonel North's Royal Harry (Bradford).

11 ran.

Betting:

9–4 on Isinglass; 100–7 Irish Wake; 100–6 William; 20–1 Raeburn and Dame President; 25–1 Ravensbury; 28–1 Son of a Gun; 100–1 Royal Harry, Lord William, Quickly Wise, and Peppercorn.

Won by a length and a half; two lengths between second and third.   2 m. 43 s. Winner trained by James Jewitt at Newmarket.

1894

In boyhood the fifth Earl of Rosebery had expressed two outstanding ambitions: to become Prime Minister of England and to win the Derby. In March 1894 he took office as Prime Minister; a few weeks later he completed a remarkable 'double' when his handsome colt Ladas won the Derby amid scenes of unprecedented enthusiasm.

Born in 1848 and elected to the Jockey Club in 1870, Lord Rosebery was a patron of the Turf from early manhood. A colt of his, also called Ladas, ran last in the Derby in 1869 and his racing activities, which continued in defiance of the University authorities, resulted in his being 'sent down' from Oxford. As a matter of fact his career as an owner nearly came to an early and unhappy conclusion. Always unduly sensitive to criticism, he was hurt and offended by malicious insinuations in a sporting newspaper with respect to the running of one of his horses. He actually sold off his stud, but happily he repented of his decision not long afterwards. Between 1873 and 1883 he had many racing successes, including a victory in the Oaks with his filly Bonnie Jean. Between 1884 and 1889 his racing interests for a number of reasons diminished, but in 1890 he started off in earnest once again and Matt Dawson was appointed as his private trainer. Dawson in fact had been on the verge of retirement, and he always declared that only Lord Rosebery, then at the zenith of a brilliant career, could have induced him to change his mind.

Bred by his owner at Mentmore, Ladas was a bay colt standing just about sixteen hands, of outstanding quality and generally described by critics of the day as near perfection in make and shape. His sire was Hampton, his dam Illuminata, by Rosicrucian out of Paraffin. He was half-brother to Gas, dam of Lord Rosebery's third Derby winner, Cicero; and also to Chelandry, winner of the One Thousand Guineas and one of the great tap roots of modern bloodstock. Ladas was unbeaten as a two-year-old. He started off by winning the Woodcote Stakes at Epsom, upsetting a 3–1 on favourite in Sir Daniel Cooper's filly Glare, who was subsequently the dam of two brilliant fillies in Flair and Lesbia, and grand-dam of the St Leger and Gold Cup winner Prince Palatine. He followed up this success by winning the Coventry Stakes, the Champagne Stakes, and the Middle Park Plate, retiring into winter quarters as favourite for the Derby. His chief rival was reckoned to be the St Simon colt Matchbox, owned by Lord Alington and Sir Frederick Johnstone.

Matchbox had shown brilliant form in the autumn, winning in succession the Kempton Breeders Stakes, the Criterion Stakes, and the Dewhurst Plate.

Matt Dawson was well known for the exacting preparations that he gave to his classic candidates, but he made an exception in the case of Ladas, whom he considered better suited, by virtue of his breeding and constitution, to less strenuous methods. Ladas's lead horse was a good four stone inferior to Lord Rosebery's colt, but the pair invariably carried level weights at work. For the Two Thousand Guineas Ladas looked the very image of a high-class thoroughbred and, starting at 6–5 on, he beat Matchbox quite comfortably by a length and a half. He won the Newmarket Stakes with equal facility a fortnight later, and started at 9–2 on for the Derby in a field of seven, the smallest number of runners since 1803.

In front of a crowd that included the Prince and Princess of Wales and which was believed to be the biggest that had ever assembled on the Downs, Ladas, in the hands of Jack Watts, fully justified the confidence placed in him by beating Matchbox, who ran an extremely gallant race, by a length and a half, with Reminder six lengths away third. As soon as the winner passed the post, happy pandemonium broke out all over the course. The police were swept off their legs in their attempts to keep a ring in front of the weighing-room enclosure, and it was only with the greatest difficulty that Lord Rosebery was able to lead Ladas in. During the colt's return journey the cheering never stopped and was redoubled in volume when the 'all right' was finally signalled. Apart from his prestige as Prime Minister and one of the leading sportsmen in the country, Lord Rosebery was also acclaimed as a local man, having bought The Durdans estate adjoining the course from the Heathcote family. Everyone was happy, in fact, except the Nonconformist and radical members of the Liberal party, who judged that racing was sinful, particularly, of course, when the sinner happened to win.

The Derby was the apex of Ladas's career; unbeaten up till then, he never won another race of any description. He was given a rest after the Derby and missed Ascot, but it is no easy matter to let a horse down when he is thoroughly fit and then to produce him at the top of his form again a few weeks later. On 5 July Ladas was only third to Isinglass and Bullingdon in the Princess of Wales's Stakes at Newmarket. A fortnight later he ran considerably better in the Eclipse Stakes, but Isinglass was at the peak of his form on that occasion and beat him again.

Ladas was then put by for the St Leger, but he was becoming bad-tempered and had taken to pulling tremendously hard in his work at home. Unfortunately, Jack Watts was unavailable to ride him at Doncaster and little Tommy Loates, as he himself feared, proved unable to hold him. After fighting for his head for nearly a mile, Ladas overpowered Loates, forced his way to the front, and ran himself out.

Lord Alington's Throstle, a filly with defective sight that started at 50–1, had been a long way behind on the final bend, but she came with one long run in the straight to beat the favourite by three parts of a length, with Matchbox, who had been sold to Baron de Hirsch for £15,000 a few days after Epsom, third.

Ladas only ran once again and was then fourth in the Jockey Club Stakes as a four-year-old. He did not appear to be greatly fancied. He was a thoroughly genuine colt, but a rather delicate and highly strung one, and his races the previous year had got to the bottom of him. He lived until he was twenty-three and sired Troutbeck, winner of the St Leger, and Gorgos, winner of the Two Thousand Guineas, but he was hardly a success at the stud.

Lord Rosebery, who died in 1929, was allied to the Rothschild family by his marriage. His outstanding intellectual gifts were combined with charm, wit, and good looks. No doubt he would have achieved even more in the political sphere but for the fact that he was too sensitive and easily hurt to relish the coarse hurly-burly of party strife. He maintained his interest in racing to the end of his long life and his other classic victories, besides those of Ladas, were the Two Thousand Guineas with Neil Gow (1910) and Ellangowan (1923); the One Thousand Guineas with Chelandry (1897), Vaucluse (1915), and Plack (1924); the Derby with Sir Visto (1895) and Cicero (1905); the Oaks with Bonnie Jean (1883), and the St Leger with Sir Visto (1895).

After Lord Rosebery's death, his daughter, Lady Sybil Grant, lived at The Durdans, which is now the property of his granddaughter, Lady Irwin. The present Lord Rosebery, an outstanding Jockey Club personality during the past thirty years, has maintained the prestige of the Mentmore Stud and has bred two Derby winners there, Blue Peter (1939) and Ocean Swell (1944).

1894: Wednesday, 6 June . . . 224 Entries. £5,450.

LORD ROSEBERY'S b.c. LADAS by Hampton out of Illuminata	J. WATTS	1
LORD ALINGTON'S b.c. MATCHBOX by St Simon out of Match Girl	M. CANNON	2
MR T. CANNON'S b.c. REMINDER by Melanion out of Postscript	G. CHALONER	3

Also ran:

Lord Bradford's Hornbeam (4th) (Allsopp); Duke of Westminster's Bullingdon (T. Loates); Mr Douglas Baird's Galloping Dick (C. Loates); Mr Dobell's Clwyd (F. Finlay).

7 ran.

1894

Betting:

    9–2 on Ladas; 9–1 Matchbox; 100–6 Bullingdon; 33–1 Reminder; 40–1 Galloping Dick; 1,000–15 Hornbeam; 200–1 Clwyd.

Won by a length and a half; six lengths between second and third.   2 m. 45⅘ s. Winner trained by M. Dawson at Newmarket.

1895

Lord Rosebery won again in 1895 with Sir Visto, a colt greatly inferior to Ladas and merely the best of a very poor crop of staying three-year-olds. He was bred by his owner and was by Barcaldine out of Vista, by Macaroni, a mare that bred the Two Thousand Guineas winner Bonavista and traced back to Alice Hawthorn. Barcaldine, an unbeaten Irish horse that Fred Archer reckoned to be one of the best that he had ever ridden, was closely in-bred, his sire Solon being out of Darling's Dam, while his own grand-dam Bon Accord was out of the same mare. Through Marco, Hurry On, and Precipitation, Barcaldine is responsible for the continuance of the Matchem male line in England today. Sir Visto himself carried a great deal of Herod blood, there being no fewer than ten strains of Highflyer in his pedigree.

Sir Visto was long and plain, with sickle hocks. As a two-year-old he ran twice, finishing unplaced in the Woodcote Stakes and winning the Imperial Produce Stakes at Kempton in the autumn. The following season he was third to Kirkconnel and Laveno in a small field for the Two Thousand Guineas, beaten a length and two lengths. A fortnight later he was third in the Newmarket Stakes to The Owl and Solaro, but he finished in front of Kirkconnel, who failed to stay. The Owl, like Kirkconnel, belonged to Sir Blundell Maple and was completely unfancied. At a later stage of his life he was sold for ten guineas. Although he failed to win, Sir Visto was staying on stoutly at the finish, and for the very first time Matt Dawson had visions of his winning the Derby.

It was generally recognized as a sub-standard Derby field, and public interest was noticeably smaller than usual. Joint favourites at 5–1 were the Kingsclere colt Le Var and Mr McCalmont's Raconteur. Laveno was on offer at 100–15, The Owl at 7–1, and Sir Visto and Solaro at 9–1. As the field swept round Tattenham Corner, Beckhampton led from The Brook, with Sir Visto, ridden by Sam Loates, lying about eighth. Two furlongs out a half-bred gelding called Curzon went to the front, with Kirkconnel close up second and Sir Visto making significant headway on the outside. At the distance it looked very much as if a gelding was going to win the Derby, but with just under a furlong to go Curzon was mastered by Sir Visto, who ran on to beat him by three parts of a length, with Kirkconnel a mere half-length away third. Solaro, Beckhampton, Le Var, and Raconteur were all on the heels of the placed horses, and their proximity at the finish suggested that the runners were

324

as moderate as was generally believed. Lord Rosebery's victory was loudly cheered, but his reception did not match the wonderful spontaneous demonstration of the year before.

Sir Visto was unplaced to Le Var in the Princess of Wales's Stakes at Newmarket in July. Nevertheless he started a 9–4 favourite for the St Leger, and duly won by three parts of a length from Telescope, who won the Manchester November Handicap the following season. Sir Visto was unplaced to Laveno in the Jockey Club Stakes, and the following year he was beaten in all the five races that he contested. He retired to the Mentmore Stud at a fee of fifty guineas, but he was a failure as a sire, and in 1908 was transferred to the Knocknagarm Stud in Co. Kildare, where his fee was substantially reduced.

1895: Wednesday, 29 May . . . 222 Entries. £5,450.

LORD ROSEBERY's b.c. SIR VISTO by Barcaldine
out of Vista   S. LOATES   1
MR T. CANNON's br.g. CURZON by Ocean Wave
out of Tib   G. CHALONER   2
SIR J. BLUNDELL MAPLE's b.c. KIRKCONNEL
by Royal Hampton out of Sweet Sauce   W. BRADFORD   3

Also ran:

Mr 'Fairie's' Solaro (4th) (F. Pratt); Mr A. D. Cochrane's Beckhampton (F. Allsopp); Lord Ellesmere's Villiers (T. Calder); Mr G. Gregory's Chibiabos (C. Loates); Mr J. H. Houldsworth's Laveno (F. Rickaby); Sir F. Johnstone's Le Var (M. Cannon); Mr H. McCalmont's Raconteur (T. Loates); Sir J. B. Maple's The Owl (J. Watts); Colonel North's Galopian (J. Fagan); Mr G. A. Ralli's Salvington (H. Covey); General Randolph's The Brook (A. White); Mr Russell's Slow Step (F. Finlay).

15 ran.

Betting:

5–1 Le Var and Raconteur; 100–15 Laveno; 7–1 The Owl; 9–1 Sir Visto and Solaro; 100–8 Kirkconnel and Slow Step; 25–1 Beckhampton; 33–1 Curzon; 50–1 Villiers; 66–1 Galopian and The Brook; 100–1 Chibiabos and Salvington.

Won by three parts of a length; half a length between second and third. 2 m. 43⅖ s. Winner trained by M. Dawson at Newmarket.

1896

Albert Edward, Prince of Wales, subsequently King Edward VII, cannot be accused of having rushed headlong into the dangers and delights of ownership on the Turf. In 1875 he registered his colours—those adopted by the Prince Regent shortly before his accession—but it was two years before they were actually worn by a jockey. His first runner on the flat was an Arab called Alep, who was quite exceptionally slow and was beaten by thirty lengths in a four-mile Match at Newmarket, his conqueror being a singularly undistinguished animal by the name of Avowal.

After this unspectacular beginning, the Prince contented himself for some years with a few jumpers trained at Epsom by John Jones, father of Herbert Jones, who won the Derby for the Prince on Diamond Jubilee. In 1885, however, the Prince went to the Newmarket Sales to buy some fillies, with the object of founding a stud at Sandringham. In 1886 Lord Alington informed John Porter that the Prince would like to send him some horses, and Porter trained for him until the end of 1892. During that period Porter usually had about ten or a dozen horses belonging to the Prince in his stable. On the whole they were very unsuccessful, but races worth over £4,000 were won in 1891. In 1893 the Prince's horses were transferred to Richard Marsh at Newmarket. The ostensible reason for the change was that Newmarket was a great deal nearer Sandringham than Kingsclere was, but an underlying factor may well have been a clash of wills and temperaments between John Porter, cautious, inclined to be obstinate, and not really noted for his humour, and the Prince's racing manager, that witty and occasionally impetuous Irishman, Lord Marcus Beresford.

It was, however, John Porter that the Prince had to thank for many of the racing successes that subsequently came his way, as it was Porter who bought for him the mare Perdita II. Bred by Lord Cawdor in 1881, Perdita belonged to Mr Falconer, a jute merchant of Mark Lane, and was by Hampton out of Hermione, by Young Melbourne out of La Belle Helene. As a two-year-old she won a couple of selling races, but later on she won the Ayr Gold Cup and on two occasions the Great Cheshire Stakes. Her owner, despite these victories, regarded her as a jade, and was pleased enough to sell her for £900. When Sir Dighton Probyn handed over the cheque on the Prince's behalf, he remarked rather gloomily to Porter: 'You'll ruin the Prince if you go on buying these thoroughbreds.' No doubt racing cost the Prince a great deal of money in his time, but Perdita was a wonderful bargain. Before her death in 1889 her offspring, which included two Derby winners in Persimmon and Diamond Jubilee, won twenty-six races worth over £72,000 in stakes.

Persimmon, by St Simon out of Perdita, was an exceptionally handsome yearling when he entered Marsh's stable in August 1894. A lengthy bay slightly on the leg, he had a bold head, perfect shoulder, and wonderful power behind the saddle. A slight tendency towards lop ears was no doubt derived from the Melbourne blood in his pedigree. His temper was equable enough, although on one memorable occasion, as a three-year-old, he took it into his head to play up, and must have taken years off his trainer's life in so doing. As a two-year-old he continued to make good progress, and was already the picture of a high-class thoroughbred when he made his first racecourse appearance at Ascot in the Coventry Stakes, a race that he won with impressive ease. Before Goodwood he was highly tried at home and acquitted himself so well that there was complete confidence in his ability to win the Richmond Stakes. He duly won, but it was noticeable how he sweated up beforehand, and Marsh concluded that a colt with his exceptional high courage and nervous energy would need careful watching. It is perhaps worth mentioning that Ugly, the springer that Persimmon had beaten in his trial at level weights, won the Singleton Plate at Goodwood carrying 7 st. 7 lb.

Persimmon's only other race that season was the Middle Park Plate in which he was third, beaten half a length and five lengths, to St Frusquin and Omladina. He had been coughing for some time previously and Marsh was reluctant to run him, but after a rough gallop some three days before the race, Lord Marcus Beresford gave orders that the colt was to start. Fortunately the race did Persimmon no permanent harm, as Watts sensibly dropped his hands the moment he felt his mount was beaten.

St Frusquin, also by St Simon, was bred and owned by Mr Leopold de Rothschild and trained by Alfred Hayhoe. A high-class colt, he suffered intermittently from rheumatism and was slightly lame when beaten first time out at Kempton. He was beaten at Kempton again in October when he was short of a gallop and failed to concede twelve pounds to Teufel, but besides the Middle Park, he won the Sandringham Cup at Sandown, the Chesterfield Stakes, and the Dewhurst Plate. After the Middle Park had been run, a state of intense rivalry sprang up between the St Frusquin and Persimmon factions.

Marsh was the most patient of men and the ideal trainer for a highly strung colt. Hayhoe, more old-fashioned in his methods, could be hard on his horses, but when they did stand up to what he demanded of them, they reached the very summit of condition. Persimmon was slow to come to hand in the spring, and on Marsh's advice he was taken out of the Two Thousand Guineas, but St Frusquin, looking the picture of fitness, came out for the Column Produce Stakes at the Craven Meeting and won in admirable style. He followed that up by winning the Two Thousand Guineas from Love Wisely, a good horse that later in his career won the Gold Cup and the Jockey Club Stakes.

Towards the end of April Persimmon began to improve by leaps and bounds, but his first Derby gallop, some three weeks before the race, was a fiasco. To Marsh's dismay, he came labouring along with his tongue hanging out, a good four lengths behind a moderate animal called Safety Pin. 'A nice sort of Derby horse,' remarked Lord Marcus Beresford, who had been summoned to watch the display. Marsh was totally unable to account for Persimmon's deplorable exhibition, but fortunately four days later the colt was galloped again and this time went exceptionally well. The final gallop took place in front of the Prince and Princess of Wales and the Duke and Duchess of York. Persimmon did everything asked of him in the smoothest way possible, and it was clear that his chance in the Derby was second to none.

It had been arranged for Persimmon to be boxed from Dullingham Station to Epsom and that Marsh was to accompany him in the box. For some reason Persimmon, usually a most tractable traveller, declined to enter the box. Two horse specials had left Dullingham, and the third and final one was due to leave in fifteen minutes' time, but there was still not the slightest sign of Persimmon changing his mind. Any attempt to urge him on from behind he responded to by lashing out for all he was worth. Marsh, on the verge of apoplexy, finally enlisted twelve lusty volunteers, and between them they more or less carried Persimmon into the box. Once inside, his little game was over and he settled down quietly to enjoy his feed.

The late Mr George Lambton, who was staying with Lord Rosebery for Epsom, has recorded how he went out to see the morning work on the Downs. The going was hard and the weather sultry. Almost the first horse that Mr Lambton met was Persimmon, the sweat pouring off him, obviously irritable, and not looking at all like a prospective Derby winner. Marsh was sweating and irritable, too, and his hopes of winning had apparently almost vanished. Soon afterwards Mr Lambton came across St Frusquin and Alfred Hayhoe, St Frusquin looking beautiful but moving distinctly short, and Hayhoe, in a very bad temper, complaining about the state of the course. Mr de Rothschild was also there, beaming away as usual, but obviously hot and nervous. 'Such are the pleasures,' Mr Lambton wrote, 'of owning and training Derby favourites.'

There were eleven runners for the big race, which was regarded as virtually a match between St Frusquin, who started at 13–8 on, and Persimmon, a 5–1 chance. To the disappointment of all who went to the paddock St Frusquin was saddled in the grounds of The Durdans, Persimmon at Sherwood's stables close to the start. The preliminaries were far more free and easy in those days, and Persimmon took no part in the parade and canter in front of the stands.

There was no trouble at the start and Bay Ronald was the first to show in front, followed by Bradwardine, Tamarind, Earwig, and Gulistan, with Persimmon and St Frusquin the two backmarkers. With a mile to go the favourite joined the leaders, while Watts edged forward to within reasonable striking distance on the descent to Tattenham Corner.

Just over a quarter of a mile from home Bay Ronald was beaten, and from then on it was a thrilling duel between St Frusquin, ridden by Tommy Loates, who was just in front on the rails, and Persimmon. When Watts asked Persimmon for his effort the gap was gradually closed, but with just under a furlong to go Persimmon suddenly faltered. At this highly critical moment Watts kept his head and acted like the horseman that he was. He steadied Persimmon, balanced him, and then drove him to the front less than a hundred yards from the post to win one of the greatest of Derbys by a neck.

History has dealt harshly with King Edward VII, and a bleaker, more disillusioned age prefers to see him as a paunchy libertine with a guttural accent, forgetting his undoubted charm and his extraordinary popularity with the mass of his subjects. As Persimmon walked back towards the unsaddling enclosure, the Downs echoed from one end to another with cheers that were renewed again and again. Even the most dignified individuals in the stands for once really let themselves go, and it was a truly remarkable exhibition of spontaneous enthusiasm and delight. The only glum face on the course was that of Watts, who had been having a good deal of trouble with his weight. Wasting always brought on fits of depression, which he tried to relieve, according to Marsh, 'by indulging in an occasional stimulant'. However, even Watts at length permitted himself the luxury of a smile when Marsh, who had fought like a rugby forward to get to his horse, slapped him on the thigh and shouted, 'Don't you realize you've just won the Derby for the Prince of Wales?' The cheering reached its peak as the Prince came out to lead his horse in, and all in all it was a scene that could never be forgotten by those who saw it.

There can have been very little between St Frusquin and Persimmon, as in the Princess of Wales's Stakes at Newmarket St Frusquin, receiving three pounds, defeated his rival by half a length. St Frusquin then went on to win the Eclipse Stakes, but before the St Leger he broke down badly and was never able to race again. He became the sire of St Amant, winner of the Derby; Rosedrop, winner of the Oaks and dam of Gainsborough; and of Santa Fina, dam of the Grand Prix winner Galloper Light. He was leading sire twice, and second on two other occasions.

Though hard ground hampered Persimmon's St Leger preparation, he duly won the race quite comfortably from Labrador. His final appearance that season was in the Jockey Club Stakes, in which he defeated the previous year's Derby winner Sir Visto. As a four-year-old he was better than ever, winning the Gold Cup by eight lengths from Winkfields Pride and a number of other good stayers, and finally the Eclipse Stakes. This was a notable 'double' to bring off, the Gold Cup being over two miles four furlongs, and the Eclipse, only a few weeks later, over half that distance.

Persimmon then retired to the stud at a fee of 300 guineas and was an immediate success, among his first crop of runners being Sceptre, that superb filly that won every classic event of her year bar the Derby. Other good winners by Persimmon were Keystone II and Perola, who both won the Oaks, and Prince Palatine and Your Majesty, both winners of the St Leger. Prince Palatine and Zinfandel both won the Gold Cup at Ascot, and Zinfandel might well have won the Derby, too, but for the death of his nominator, Colonel McCalmont. Before he died from a fractured pelvis in his sixteenth year Persimmon had been Champion Sire twice and he was Champion on two subsequent occasions. He was equally successful as a sire of brood mares.

Bay Ronald, who ran unplaced behind Persimmon in the Derby, was only an average handicapper in point of merit, and not a particularly handsome one either. He retired to the stud at a fee of twenty-five guineas, and being scantily patronized, was exported to France where he died in 1907. Despite his few opportunities, he sired a really great racehorse in Bayardo, as well as Dark Ronald, sire of that fine stayer Son-in-Law. Dark Ronald was exported to Germany, and is reckoned the outstanding sire in the bloodstock annals of that country.

Richard Marsh, despite many changes of fortune, continued to hold the position of royal trainer till he retired in 1924. Born in 1851, he was the son of a Kentish hop-farmer. Sent into a Newmarket racing stable as a boy, he soon got too heavy for the flat, but became a very fine rider over hurdles and fences. His training reputation was first established with jumpers belonging to the Duke of Hamilton, but he won the St Leger in 1883 with Ossian, and the One Thousand Guineas and the Oaks three years later with Miss Jummy. His other Derby winners besides Persimmon were Jeddah (1898), Diamond Jubilee (1900), and Minoru (1909). Tall and beautifully dressed, he was the best of company and never spent much time in counting the pennies. He married a daughter of the famous trainer, Sam Darling, so his son Marcus, who has trained two outstanding Derby winners in Windsor Lad (1934) and Tulyar (1952), can be said to be bred for the job.

Lord Marcus Beresford, the King's racing manager, was the fourth son of the Marquis of Waterford, and was brother of Lord Charles Beresford, a distinguished sailor who conducted a vendetta against an indisputably greater one in Lord Fisher;

and of Lord William Beresford, v.c., for many years an outstanding figure in sporting and military circles in India. Lord Marcus was exceptionally witty, the most loyal of friends and an enemy to be respected. His remarkable charm enabled him to carry off situations and statements that would have undoubtedly been resented from others. A fine judge of a horse, he had been a first-class rider in his youth and won a great many races over fences. For a couple of seasons he acted as starter to the Jockey Club. He died in 1922.

1896: Wednesday, 3 June . . . 276 Entries. £5,450.

H.R.H. THE PRINCE OF WALES'S b.c. PERSIMMON by St Simon out of Perdita II	J. WATTS	1
MR LEOPOLD DE ROTHSCHILD'S br.c. ST FRUSQUIN by St Simon out of Isabel	T. LOATES	2
MR H. E. BEDDINGTON'S br.c. EARWIG by Hampton out of Wriggle	F. ALLSOPP	3

Also ran:

Mr B. S. Straus's br.c. Teufel (4th) (F. Pratt); Mr Leopold de Rothschild's Gulistan (Calder); Mr L. Brassey's Bay Ronald (Bradford); Mr L. Brassey's Tamarind (Grimshaw); Mr A. Calvert's Bradwardine (F. Rickaby); Mr J. Wallace's Spook (R. Colling); Mr E. Cassel's Toussaint (Woodburn); Mr H. McCalmont's Knight of the Thistle (M. Cannon).

11 ran.

Betting:

13–8 on St Frusquin; 5–1 Persimmon; 100–9 Teufel; 25–1 Bay Ronald and Knight of the Thistle; 33–1 Gulistan and Earwig; 40–1 Bradwardine; 100–1 Spook and Toussaint; 1,000–1 Tamarind.

Won by a neck; four lengths between second and third.　　　　2 m. 42 s.
Winner trained by R. Marsh at Newmarket.

1897

In the closing decades of the nineteenth century Ireland was making great strides as a centre of bloodstock breeding, and Galtee More, winner of the 'Triple Crown' in 1897, was bred by his owner, Mr John Gubbins, at Bruree in the famous Golden Vale of Limerick. Mr Gubbins, a martyr to gout in later life, had inherited a fortune from his uncle, whereupon he established two studs, installing Kendal and St Florian as stallions. Galtee More, named after a peak in the Galtee Mountains, was by Kendal out of Morganette, a mare that Mr Gubbins had bred himself; Ard Patrick, Mr Gubbins's second Derby winner, was by St Florian out of the same mare, and was named after a point in the Ballyhoura Hills. Morganette, who thus had the rare distinction of breeding two Derby winners, to say nothing of an Irish Derby winner as well, had been a mere selling plater and a roarer into the bargain. She had a good pedigree, though, being by Springfield out of Lady Morgan, a Thormanby mare that was half-sister to the Oaks and St Leger winner Marie Stuart.

Kendal was by Bend Or out of Windermere, a mare whose full sister Frivolity was grand-dam of Concertina, from whom such famous winners as Sir Gallahad III, Bull Dog, Admiral Drake, Bois Roussel, and Bahram are descended. Bred by the Duke of Westminster, Kendal was an extremely fast two-year-old, but after winning six races he broke down in the Rous Memorial Stakes at Newmarket and was never able to run again. At the stud he was successful not only in England and Ireland, but also in the Argentine, whither he was exported in his nineteenth year for £10,500. Over here he has exercised considerable influence through Tredennis and Tredennis's son Bachelors Double, both of whom sired a number of notable brood mares.

Almost faultless in conformation but for being rather high from the hocks to the ground, Galtee More was despatched to England to be trained by the famous Sam Darling of Beckhampton. As a two-year-old he was only once beaten and that was in the Lancashire Breeders Stakes at Liverpool, when he dead-heated for second place with Glencally, a short head behind the winner, Brig. His victories included the Molecombe Stakes at Goodwood, the Rous Plate at Doncaster, and finally the Middle Park Plate in which he defeated Lord Rosebery's Velasquez by six lengths. A son of Donovan, Velasquez was no mean performer, having won the New Stakes at Ascot, the July Stakes at Newmarket, the Prince of Wales's Stakes at Goodwood, and the Champagne Stakes at Doncaster.

The following season Galtee More was better than ever. He won the Two Thousand Guineas in a canter from Velasquez, and starting at 100–6 on, he made his opponents in the Newmarket Stakes look even more moderate than they were.

Not surprisingly Galtee More started a 4–1 on favourite for the Derby and, confidently ridden by Charles Wood, whose licence had recently been restored by the Jockey Club, he won very comfortably indeed by two lengths from the unlucky Velasquez, with History eight lengths away third. It all seemed remarkably tame after the drama of the previous year's race, but the Irish contingent did their best to liven things up with a display of uninhibited exuberance.

At Ascot, starting at 33–1 on, Galtee More won the Prince of Wales's Stakes. He then won the Sandringham Cup at Sandown, the St Leger, in which he started at 10–1 on, and the Sandown Park Foal Stakes. Finally, he competed for the Cambridgeshire with 9 st. 6 lb. on his back, but the task proved beyond his powers. Without question he was a very good horse indeed, and it was a pity that his mediocre contemporaries were incapable of providing sterner opposition.

At the end of the year Mr Gubbins, who never resisted a good offer, sold Galtee More, who had won him over £26,000 in stakes, to the Russian Government for £21,000. The horse did well as a sire in Russia and was eventually passed on to the Germans for £14,000. His sale was not without its humorous side. Among the Russian deputation was a certain General Arapoff, who claimed to own a vodka distillery. Before arriving at Beckhampton he fortified himself with a beaker of neat whisky at the Ailesbury Arms, Marlborough, and after seeing Galtee More move in a sharpish canter for nearly three furlongs, he was so overcome with enthusiasm that he rushed back to Sam Darling's house, removed a picture of Galtee More from the wall, and made off with it.

That night Mr Gubbins entertained the Russians in London at Princes Restaurant. General Arapoff was under the impression that the various ladies dining there had been provided for his particular gratification, and it was eventually found necessary to transfer him to the Empire, where he was able to accost such ladies as took his fancy without fear of unfortunate consequences, at any rate until very much later. In the meantime Mr Gubbins, whose gout was giving him twinges, turned sulky and declared that he refused to sell Galtee More after all. Luckily he proved more tractable the following morning and the deal was eventually completed.

Galtee More's trainer Sam Darling, father-in-law of Richard Marsh, was not only one of the finest trainers of his time, but an exceptionally popular man on the racecourse as well. Possessed of infinite patience, his horses, once he had got them really right, carried a bloom of health and vigour that seemed to distinguish them from all others. The professional association of the Darling family with the English Turf has been maintained for the best part of a hundred and fifty years. Sam Darling was grandson of the Darling who rode four Chester Cup winners and won the 1833 St Leger on Rockingham. Sam Darling's father was also a jockey, but never trained. Fred Darling, Sam's son, was of course one of the greatest trainers of this century and shared with John Porter the distinction of having prepared no fewer than seven winners of the Derby. Marcus Marsh, who trained two Derby winners in Windsor Lad and Tulyar, is Fred Darling's nephew and his former pupil as well.

1897: Wednesday, 2 June . . . 291 Entries. £5,450.

MR J. GUBBINS's b.c. GALTEE MORE by Kendal out of Morganette	C. WOOD	1
LORD ROSEBERY's b.c. VELASQUEZ by Donovan out of Vista	J. WATTS	2
SIR S. SCOTT's b.c. HISTORY by Hampton out of Isabella	M. CANNON	3

Also ran:

H.R.H. the Prince of Wales's Oakdene (4th) (O. Madden); Mr 'Fairie's' Eager (F. Rickaby); Mr C. D. Rose's Frisson (Calder); Mr Wallace Johnstone's Monterey (F. Allsopp); Mr J. G. Joicey's Silver Fox (S. Loates); Mr T. Wadlow's Prime Minister (W. Robinson); Mr J. R. Keene's St Cloud II (Bradford); Mr 'Jersey's' Angelos (F. Finlay).

11 ran.

Betting:

4–1 on Galtee More; 10–1 Velasquez; 25–1 History; 33–1 Silver Fox; 50–1 Monterey and Eager; 66–1 Oakdene; 100–1 St Cloud II, Frisson, and Prime Minister; 200–1 Angelos.

Won by two lengths; eight lengths between second and third.   2 m. 44 s.
Winner trained by S. Darling at Beckhampton.

1898

There can be little doubt that the best three-year-old in 1898 was Mr C. D. Rose's Cyllene, by Bend Or's son Bona Vista. Cyllene, however, was a very late foal and was so small and weedy in his early days that it was thought pointless to enter him for the classics. Nevertheless he turned out to be an exceptionally good horse and was equally successful as a sire. He got four Derby winners—Cicero, Minoru, Lemberg, and Tagalie—while his male line, through his grandson Phalaris, has proved immensely influential in modern racing. Exported to the Argentine for £25,000 at the age of thirteen, Cyllene rendered good service there until his death at the age of thirty.

In Cyllene's absence the Derby was won by Mr J. W. Larnach's Jeddah, the first successful 100–1 chance in the history of the race. Trained by Richard Marsh at Newmarket, Jeddah was bred by his owner and was by Janissary out of Pilgrimage. Janissary had an illustrious pedigree, being by Isonomy out of the Oaks and St Leger winner Jannette, by Lord Clifden, but he was useless on the racecourse and a failure as a sire with the notable exception of Jeddah. Pilgrimage, by The Earl or The Palmer, won both the Two Thousand and One Thousand Guineas for Lord Lonsdale in 1878. Mr Larnach bought her for a mere 160 guineas at the sale of the Duchess of Montrose's stock. The mare was then nineteen years of age and was believed to be not only barren but unlikely to breed again. In fact she was carrying Jeddah at the time, so what appeared to be a distinctly unpromising gamble on the part of Mr Larnach, paid off remarkably well. Apart from Jeddah, Pilgrimage bred Canterbury Pilgrim, winner of the Oaks, and dam both of the St Leger winner Swynford, and of Chaucer, sire of Scapa Flow, the dam of Fairway and Pharos. Canterbury Pilgrim was bought by Lord Stanley, later Earl of Derby, at the same sale for 1,600 guineas, while another filly disposed of was Roquebrune, subsequently the dam of the 1903 Derby winner, Rock Sand.

Jeddah was a big, leggy chesnut with a flaxen mane, standing sixteen hands three, with distinctly straight pasterns. Not surprisingly he took time to come to hand, and his first appearance as a two-year-old was in the Clearwell Stakes at the Second October Meeting. He ran considerably better than his trainer had expected and, starting at 10–1, was second to the odds-on favourite Orzil. A fortnight later he was second favourite for the Free Handicap, but was beaten a short head by Lord

335

1898

William Beresford's filly Meta II, on whom the American jockey Tod Sloan rode one of his very best races.

There was certainly nothing in Jeddah's two-year-old form to suggest that he was likely to win the Derby, but he made very good progress physically during the winter, and in a trial before the Newmarket Craven Meeting he finished in front of his stable companion, the Duke of Devonshire's Dieudonné, who had won the Middle Park Plate the previous winter, but was slightly touched in his wind. On the strength of this, and assisted by the maiden allowance, Jeddah started favourite for the Craven Stakes, which he duly won from Lord Stanley's Schonberg. This victory led to his being well backed for the Two Thousand Guineas, but in that event he could only finish fifth behind Mr Wallace Johnstone's Disraeli, whom Dieudonné had beaten by three lengths in the Middle Park Plate.

Jeddah next ran in the Newmarket Stakes, but although he finished in front of the Duke of Portland's Wantage, who had been second in the Two Thousand Guineas, he was nevertheless only fifth behind Cyllene. Shortly afterwards he was galloped again with Dieudonné, who this time defeated him comfortably. The result was that Jeddah drifted right out in the Derby market, while Dieudonné, despite not having seen a racecourse since the previous October, came in for substantial support. Mr Larnach, in fact, was very doubtful whether it was worth sending Jeddah to Epsom, but Marsh strongly advised him to do so, believing that Jeddah was a pretty useful colt that had unaccountably run below form in both his two previous races.

Disraeli, despite doubts about his stamina, started favourite for the Derby, while Dieudonné was second favourite. There was a good deal of money for Archduke II, a colt bred in South Africa, but hardly a penny for Jeddah, who was ridden by Otto Madden.

Approaching Tattenham Corner the leaders were Wantage and the Duke of Westminster's Batt, a half-brother to Flying Fox that had oddly enough been foaled at almost exactly the same time as Jeddah and in the very next box at Eaton. Close behind this pair came Disraeli, Hawfinch, Jeddah, and Heir Male, but Disraeli dropped back beaten as soon as the straight was reached, and with two and a half furlongs to go the issue appeared to lie between Batt, Wantage, and Jeddah. Below the distance Wantage was being shouted home, but as soon as he came under pressure he declined to exert himself further. From that point, although Dieudonné made a certain amount of headway on the outside, it was a duel between Batt and Jeddah. It was naturally assumed that the well-backed Batt would prove the winner, but to the general amazement it was the 100–1 outsider Jeddah who obtained the mastery, and striking the front a hundred yards from home, ran on like a true stayer to win by three parts of a length, with Dunlop, another 100–1 chance, a length and a half away third. The result, of course, gave the crowd little cause for satisfaction or rejoicing, but the bookmakers rallied in strength to give the winner a hero's reception.

Jeddah, whom the Eaton stud-groom had declared to be the largest and weakest foal he had ever seen, showed that his victory was no fluke by giving Batt six pounds in the Prince of Wales's Stakes at Ascot and beating him by a decisive five lengths. Not long before the St Leger he jarred a suspensory ligament in a gallop, but despite that ran a gallant race at Doncaster and finished second to Captain (later Sir Henry) Greer's Wildflower. As a four-year-old Jeddah only ran once and that was in the Jockey Club Stakes. He finished down the course behind Flying Fox, but he was patched up and only half-trained, and had no chance of winning whatsoever. His owner then retired him to the stud, but he made no mark as a sire.

Mr Larnach, a country squire, did not bet, but his tenants did and they gave the local bookmakers cause to remember Jeddah's year. He himself, having formed the ambition of winning the Derby when still at Eton, was for a long time an enthusiastic patron of the Turf, until he began to drift out of the sport about a dozen years after Jeddah's victory. The fact that he was permitted to have his horses in the same stable as those of the Prince of Wales is proof of his social standing.

Otto Madden, born in Germany in 1870, was of English parentage and his father had ridden the famous mare Kincsem in many of her victories. His own career was not without its vicissitudes—early in this century he forfeited his licence for a season for 'consorting with persons of known bad character'—but he was four times champion jockey, and besides riding Ard Patrick in that horse's famous Eclipse Stakes victory over Sceptre and Rock Sand, he won the Two Thousand Guineas on Norman III, the Oaks on Musa and Sunny Jane, and the St Leger on Challacombe. He retired in 1909 to take up training, but returned to the saddle during the First World War. Between the wars he kept a few mares and trained a horse or two for his own amusement at Newmarket, where he was a popular and respected figure, being churchwarden, together with Mr George Lambton, at St Agnes. He left close on £50,000 when he died in 1941.

1898: Wednesday, 25 May . . . 276 Entries. £5,450.

MR J. W. LARNACH's ch.c. JEDDAH by Janissary
out of Pilgrimage   O. MADDEN   1
DUKE OF WESTMINSTER's br.c. BATT by Sheen
out of Vampire   M. CANNON   2
MR W. WARD's b.c. DUNLOP by Ayrshire
out of Fortuna   F. C. PRATT   3

1898

Also ran:

Duke of Devonshire's Dieudonné (4th) (J. Watts); Duke of Portland's Wantage (F. Black); Mr J. S. Curtis's Archduke II (K. Cannon); Duke of Westminster's Calverly (Moreton); Mr Wallace Johnstone's Disraeli (S. Loates); Mr P. Lorillard's Elfin (C. Wood); Mr Horatio Bottomley's Hawfinch (F. Finlay); Sir M. Fitz-Gerald's Heir Male (N. Robinson); Mr T. R. Dewar's Perthshire (W. Bradford); Lord Ellesmere's Pheon (R. Colling); Lord Stanley's Schonberg (F. Rickaby); Mr J. B. Leigh's The Wyvern (C. Loates); Mr H. T. Barclay's Cherry-heart (Fagan); Mr Russell's The Virginian (F. Allsopp); Mr A. Belmont's Bridegroom II (T. Loates).

18 ran.

Betting:

2–1 Disraeli; 7–2 Dieudonné; 9–1 Archduke II; 10–1 Batt; 20–1 Perthshire; 1,000–45 The Virginian; 33–1 Heir Male and Wantage; 40–1 The Wyvern and Hawfinch; 50–1 Elfin and Bridegroom II; 100–1 Pheon, Jeddah, Schonberg, Cherry-heart and Dunlop; 300–1 Calverly.

Won by three parts of a length; a length and a half between second and third.

2 m. 47 s.

Winner trained by R. Marsh at Newmarket.

1899

In 1893 the Duke of Westminster asked John Porter to buy him a mare, and for 1,000 guineas Porter bought for him Vampire, a mare that had won a couple of races, by Galopin out of Irony, by Roseberry. When Vampire arrived at Eaton it soon became clear that she had a very vicious temper indeed, and after she had badly mauled a stud hand, the Duke decided to get rid of her. Porter said that he himself would be perfectly willing to take the mare, whereupon the Duke at once changed his mind and kept her. Her first foal she killed in a fit of temper. Then came Batt, second to Jeddah in the Derby, and in 1896 Flying Fox, by Orme. Vampire was only mated with Orme, who returned to her the Galopin blood with only one free generation, because her temper was so unreliable that it was thought inadvisable to send her away from Eaton, where the stud hands were accustomed to her peculiarities. But for that, the Duke would hardly have risked the results that might have ensued from in-breeding to the very 'hot' Galopin blood.

As soon as he was put into training Flying Fox, a spare, wiry bay with a beautiful action, not only showed signs of future greatness, but occasionally hints of a temper inherited from the dam. In fact Porter always thought it was just as well that events compelled the colt to be taken out of training as a three-year-old. Before the Royal Ascot meeting Flying Fox was very well galloped at home, and in consequence of what he had shown, he started a 5–4 favourite for the New Stakes, which he won by three parts of a length from Musa, winner of the Oaks the following season. He then won a small race at Stockbridge, but early in October he was beaten a head by Mr Leopold de Rothschild's St Gris in the Imperial Produce Stakes at Kempton. Porter reckoned that Flying Fox had been unlucky and was confident that the colt's reputation would be restored in the Middle Park Plate. In that event, however, Flying Fox was beaten a length and a half by Lord William Beresford's American-bred Caiman, ridden by Tod Sloan. It was a very slow-run race and according to Sloan, who was admittedly prone to exaggeration, the runners were almost walking as they came down the Dip. Sloan was emphatic that Caiman was greatly inferior to Flying Fox, and considered that he had stolen the race by getting first run with Caiman in the final furlong. A contributory factor may well have been the tremendous gale that was blowing, as Sloan, crouched over Caiman's neck, offered far less wind-resistance than did Mornington Cannon, who sat bolt upright on Flying Fox in the old English style that the American riders were beginning to make look so ridiculous. A fortnight after the Middle Park, Flying Fox won the Criterion Stakes at Newmarket and thereupon retired for the season.

Flying Fox wintered well, and in a trial on 15 April, receiving only three pounds he finished over two lengths in front of Batt, runner-up in the previous year's Derby. Calverly, a four-year-old to whom he conceded nine pounds and who was last of six in the trial, won the Esher Stakes at Sandown the following week. Not surprisingly Flying Fox started a short-priced favourite for the Guineas, which he won without difficulty from Caiman. He had given his backers some very uneasy moments, though, as at one point it looked as if he would never get off. Time and again, after the flag was up, he bolted away into the open country on the left. (This was before the starting-gate was introduced.) However, the starter showed wonderful patience and eventually got him away, and as the favourite sailed past the winning post, the Duke, normally the most reserved and dignified of men, relieved his feelings with an ear-splitting 'View Holloa' which re-echoed through the stands and deeply shocked the majority of his fellow patricians. In fact there was more talk afterwards about the Duke's yell of triumph than there was about Flying Fox's achievement.

Caiman was not engaged in the Derby, the last one to be started by flag, and the race was regarded as a match between Flying Fox, who started at 5–2 on, and the French horse Holocauste, a 6–1 chance. A big, powerful grey that some critics appeared to find coarse, Holocauste belonged to M. de Bremond and was ridden by Tod Sloan. There was a longish delay at the start, most of the trouble being caused by Desmond, always an excitable animal. Flying Fox and Beautiwick were the best away, but after a furlong Holocauste led from Flying Fox and from then on it was virtually a duel between the pair. Approaching Tattenham Corner the favourite moved up to the French colt, and there was little between the two of them, but with just over two furlongs to go it was noticeable that Cannon was distinctly uneasy on Flying Fox, whereas Sloan had not made a movement on the grey. Suddenly there was a noise like a pistol shot and Holocauste staggered and fell. The unfortunate animal had broken a fetlock, and according to Sloan, 'the stump was sticking into the ground'. After the race an attempt was made to get him to Sherwood's stables, but it was of no avail and he had to be shot on the course.

This unhappy accident ruined what might have been an extremely exciting race and Flying Fox was left to win at his leisure from Damocles, with Innocence third. Opinions of course differed as to whether Holocauste would have won. Sloan not unnaturally said that he had Flying Fox beaten when the disaster occurred, but the evidence of jockeys on occasions like that is usually valueless. Mr George Lambton, a really good judge, thought Holocauste would have won, and so did Mr Arthur

Coventry, the starter, but on the other hand there were plenty of people whose opinions commanded a certain respect, who took precisely the opposite view. At all events the result was immensely popular with the public, who gave Flying Fox and his owner a great reception. It was the fourth and final Derby victory of the Duke of Westminster, who died before the end of the year, and it was the seventh and last Derby success of John Porter, who retired from training in 1905. The Duke of Westminster remains to this day the only man who has owned and bred two winners of the 'Triple Crown'.

Lord Dunraven's Desmond, who ran unplaced in the Derby, was a black colt by St Simon out of L'Abbesse de Jouarre, who won the Oaks for Sir Winston Churchill's father, Lord Randolph Churchill. He was a good two-year-old, but then lost his appetite for racing. He did well as a sire, though, and headed the list in 1913 when his son Aboyeur was awarded the Derby on the disqualification of another of his sons, Craganour. He also sired the dual Gold Cup winner, The White Knight, and Charles O'Malley, winner of the Gold Vase and sire of Malva, the dam of Blenheim.

Mornington Cannon—usually known as 'Morny'—who rode Flying Fox, was born in 1873, the son of that great rider Tom Cannon, who had won the Derby for the Duke of Westminster on Shotover, and who named his elder son after a horse that won for him at Bath the day that his son was born. 'Morny' was a beautiful horseman, exceptionally strong and fit, and, like his father, he excelled in waiting tactics. He was in his heyday before the 'American invasion' caused races to be run at a faster pace and jockeys to pull up their leathers. He did adopt a modified form of the American style, but he was never very happy with it and gradually dropped out of racing. A man of the highest integrity, he deservedly enjoyed the affection and respect of the racing public.*

Flying Fox continued his successful career after the Derby, winning the Princess of Wales's Stakes at Newmarket, the Eclipse Stakes, and finally the St Leger, in which he beat Caiman by three lengths. All told, he won during his career just over £40,000 in stakes. Because of the Duke's death, he came up for sale in 1900 and was bought by M. Edmond Blanc for 37,500 guineas, a price which at the time was generally considered ridiculous. In actual fact M. Blanc obtained an excellent bargain, as Flying Fox was an outstanding success as a sire, his greatest successes, true to the custom of his forbears, coming at the start of his career. M. Blanc chose to apply the 'closed shop' principle to Flying Fox, whose services were never available to other French breeders, while foreign mares were only accepted on payment of a 600-guinea fee and on the understanding that they left France before they foaled. Teddy, by Ajax, a son of Flying Fox's that won the Grand Prix for M. Blanc, has

* A link with the great days of racing. Mornington Cannon is living in retirement at Brighton.

founded sire lines of powerful influence in France, Italy, and the United States, and among his best-known offspring are Sir Gallahad III, Asterus, Ortello, a great sire in Italy, and Bull Dog, sire of Bull Lea; to say nothing of Rose of England, winner of the Oaks and dam of the St Leger winner, Chulmleigh.

1899: Wednesday, 31 May . . . 264 Entries. £5,450.

DUKE OF WESTMINSTER's b.c. FLYING FOX by Orme
out of Vampire   M. CANNON   1
MR W. R. MARSHALL's ch.c. DAMOCLES by Suspender
out of Revelry   S. LOATES   2
MR J. A. MILLER's br.c. INNOCENCE by Simonian
out of La Vierge   W. HALSEY   3

Also ran:

Mr H. Barnato's My Boy (4th) (J. Watts); Lord Dunraven's Desmond (F. Pratt); M. de Bremond's Holocauste (T. Sloan); Mr T. L. Plunkett's Oppressor (T. Loates); Mr R. A. Oswald's Scintillant (O. Madden); Mr P. Pack's Jo I So I (W. Bradford); Mr 'Fairie's' Matoppo (F. Rickaby); Mr E. J. Fose's Sir Reginald (F. Allsopp); Mr Elliot Galer's Beautiwick (Palmer).

12 ran.

Betting:

5–2 on Flying Fox; 6–1 Holocauste; 15–1 Damocles; 20–1 Oppressor; 33–1 Desmond and My Boy; 50–1 Innocence; 66–1 Scintillant; 100–1 Sir Reginald; 200–1 Jo I So I, Matoppo, and Beautiwick.

Won by two lengths; a length between second and third.   2 m. $42\frac{4}{5}$ s.
Winner trained by J. Porter at Kingsclere.

*   *   *

A photograph taken just after Miss Davison had
brought down the King's colt Anmer

Derby Day, 1922

Steve Donoghue, Joe Childs, Fred Fox, Bernard Carslake

The turn of the century came rather more than half-way through the reign of the 'Dictator of Epsom', Henry Mayson Dorling, Clerk of the Course from 1873 until 1919. This unlovable official possessed great energy and no manners, so it was hardly surprising that he was continually in conflict with both the racing and the non-racing public. He was intensely unpopular and rejoiced in the fact: 'Everyone hates me,' he used to say, 'and I like it.' He was perpetually at loggerheads with the Stewards, and on three occasions was fined fifty pounds for alleged dereliction of duty, the last time when he was over eighty years of age.

By 1900 the Derby had recovered the prestige it was tending to lose some fifteen years previously through the parsimony of the Epsom Executive, but a gradual change was becoming perceptible in the attitude of the public to Derby Day itself. In the eighteen sixties and seventies, Derby Day above all else was a great national holiday. People went to Epsom less with the idea of seeing the race than of having a thoroughly good time. The Downs were converted into a gigantic fairground with merry-go-rounds, swing-boats, acrobats, clowns, and performing animals. Barnum's Show occupied a large space on the rails between the winning post and Tattenham Corner, and a popular feature for many years were the three world-famous dwarfs, 'General' Tom Thumb, 'Commodore' Nutt, and Minnie Warren. Another celebrated side-show was that provided by a supposedly 'wild man from the East'. He may not have been particularly wild, but he certainly came from the East, being a respectable citizen of Whitechapel made up for the occasion. Another regular Derby Day sight in the sixties was Sir John Bennett, a Cheapside clockmaker of venerable appearance, who rode down the course on a cob, pausing at frequent intervals to refresh himself and drink 'the health of the people'. Nor did the carnival on the Downs end when racing was over, as merrymaking went on without a pause far into the night. Whatever its failings as a work of art, Frith's picture of Derby Day is an accurate portrayal of Epsom Downs in the heyday of Queen Victoria.

At the close of the century, though, the festival spirit seemed gradually to be dying out, while the race itself assumed an ever-increasing importance. Derby Day was tending to become more and more a gathering of racing enthusiasts, less and less a 'beano' for the average man and woman.

The petrol age was approaching, and in a few more years the splendid coaches of 'the swells', the carriages, the waggonettes, the traps and decorated carts, the costers' barrows, would be but a memory of the past. Quite one of the best sights used to be the coaches galloping down the incline on the far side of the course to give impetus for the pull uphill to where they would stand for the day. Oddly enough, traffic jams on Derby Day were both more frequent and more serious in the era of horse-drawn vehicles than they are today when thousands of cars start heading for London as soon as the big race is over. It was nothing unusual to find a block of vehicles of every description that had been stationary at Mitcham Common for a good two hours, the road at that point being only twelve feet wide, and it was considered quite satisfactory for a carriage to reach its destination in central London by ten o'clock at night. There were plenty of diversions, though, on the way back, and there was dancing on the green till well on into the morning at all the favourite stopping places.

Another notable change at this period was in the style of jockeyship. The great English riders had sat erect, with long leathers and a long rein. Forcing the pace was unfashionable, and most events over a distance of ground were a dawdle followed by a sprint. The leading jockeys were nearly all superb horsemen and stylists, but they were made to look stilted and inept when the Americans, headed by Tod Sloan, 'Skeets' Martin, and the Reiff brothers, arrived with their crouched and unattractive seat and their almost indecent tendency to make the pace a cracking one from flagfall right to the finish. The Americans—'the monkeys up a stick'—were derided at first, but results soon showed that their methods, though apparently cruder and less artistic, represented a considerable advance in technique. English riders had to adapt themselves as best they could or drop out of the game.

The speed at which the Derby was run soon began to increase. Volodyovski broke the record in 1901, Cicero in 1905, Spearmint in 1906. Mahmoud in 1936 completed the Derby course in nearly twelve seconds faster time than Ormonde, and almost twenty-seven seconds faster than The Flying Dutchman. It is often said that the modern thoroughbred is less tough physically and temperamentally than his forbears, who used to turn out twice, or even three times, at Ascot and Goodwood, and who competed in the Grand Prix a mere four days after running in the Derby. The fierce pace, however, at which most modern races are run imposes a far greater strain on a horse than did the more elegant and leisurely methods of the past.

1900

In 1900 Diamond Jubilee, foaled in the sixtieth year of Queen Victoria's reign, won the 'Triple Crown' for the Prince of Wales. A bright bay whose conformation it was almost impossible to fault, he was by St Simon out of Perdita II, and thus a full brother of Persimmon. Perhaps because of his pedigree and high promise, he was undoubtedly 'spoilt' in his early days at Sandringham, and the over-indulgent treatment he received may well have accentuated a temperament that was naturally rebellious.

He proved by no means easy to break as a yearling, but later he seemed to settle down, giving his trainer Richard Marsh the impression that he combined outstanding ability with a reasonably equable disposition. However, when he made his first race-course appearance in the Coventry Stakes at Ascot he distinguished himself firstly by kicking an unfortunate bystander in the paddock, and then by a deplorable exhibition at the starting-post, in which he was either standing on his hind legs, or else twisting himself into knots in an attempt to savage Watts who rode him. Watts, least perturbable and most reticent of men, expressed himself with unusual freedom to Marsh after Diamond Jubilee had finished a moderate fourth. Mr Arthur Coventry, the starter, later stated that he had never seen a two-year-old behave quite so badly at the post.

At home every effort was made to curb Diamond Jubilee's temper without at the same time breaking his spirit, but before the start of the July Stakes at Newmarket he unshipped Watts and bolted away up the course. He was caught and remounted, but declined to race in earnest and finished an inglorious last. It was clear that he had taken a strong dislike to Watts, a sentiment that Watts reciprocated with interest, so at Goodwood he was partnered in the Prince of Wales's Stakes by 'Morny' Cannon. The ever-trusting public made him favourite once again and he certainly performed a great deal better, being beaten less than a length by Epsom Lad, who then belonged to Lord Rosebery. Ridden in a chifney and again partnered by Cannon, he won the £1,200 Boscawen Stakes at Newmarket early in October, but only scraped home by a head from a moderate animal called Paigle. Cannon was unable to ride him in the Middle Park Plate, but he went kindly enough for Watts and ran a good race to be beaten half a length by Democrat, who received a three-pound gelding allowance. A fortnight later the pair met again in the Dewhurst Plate, and this time Democrat conceded a pound and won by three parts of a length. Democrat was useless for racing after his two-year-old days, and ended his career as Lord Kitchener's charger in India.

Diamond Jubilee's two-year-old achievements hardly foreshadowed the triumphs to come, but he seemed to be settling down in the autumn. He was shaping like a stayer, while his brothers Persimmon and Florizel II had both improved with age. During the winter he was given plenty of work and was usually ridden by Herbert Jones, a lad whose father, Jack Jones, had formerly trained jumpers at Epsom for the Prince and Lord Marcus Beresford. Young Jones took immense pains in dealing with Diamond Jubilee, and certainly got on better with him than anyone else. In the spring, shortly before the Two Thousand Guineas, 'Morny' Cannon came down to ride Diamond Jubilee in a gallop. The gallop over, Cannon dismounted, whereupon Diamond Jubilee at once knocked him over and started to savage him. It was lucky indeed for Cannon that help was at hand, or else he might well have been killed. A few days later Cannon rode Diamond Jubilee again; not surprisingly he did not enjoy the experience, and when he got off he suggested that another jockey should be engaged for the Two Thousand Guineas. After Marsh had consulted the Prince and Lord Marcus Beresford, it was decided to give Herbert Jones his chance.

The change proved an eminently successful one, and Diamond Jubilee won the Guineas in convincing style by four lengths from Sir Ernest Cassel's Bonarosa. He followed that up by winning the Newmarket Stakes from Chevening, ridden by the redoubtable Sloan, but only by a matter of inches. On the home gallops his conduct remained unpredictable. Sometimes he amused himself by rearing continually on to his hind legs, on other occasions he stood stock still and refused to move. Some critics said that what he needed was a really good hiding, but Marsh never lost patience or temper, and never resorted to any measure that might conceivably have broken the spirit of a high-mettled colt.

The South African War was at its height when the Derby was run. Stung by a series of shaming defeats for which elderly and incompetent generals were largely responsible, the country was in the grip of a 'jingoistic' spirit that occasionally bordered on hysteria. A rumour reached Epsom during the afternoon that Lord Roberts's army had entered Pretoria; the report was false, but several thousand over-excited non-combatants sang 'God Save the Queen' in front of the Royal Stand.

Diamond Jubilee, with Jones again in the saddle, was favourite at 6–4 against. He would doubtless have started at shorter odds but for the narrow margin of his victory over Chevening. That race had shaken the confidence of many of his supporters, but in actual fact Chevening had been considerably flattered by his position, which was

346

largely due to some brilliant riding by Sloan. Mr Dewar's Forfarshire was second favourite at 100–30, and there was backing for Disguise II, Chevening, and Bonarosa.

The stress and tension of Derby Day can easily react on a highly strung horse, but Diamond Jubilee was on his very best behaviour, and his conduct throughout the preliminaries was faultless. Nor did he give a hint of trouble at the starting-gate, which was used for the first time in the history of the race. The start was a good one and Chevening was the first to show in front. At the mile post Chevening had lost ground, and the leader was Forfarshire, ridden by Sam Loates, with Disguise II and Diamond Jubilee not far behind. Coming down the hill Disguise II began to increase his pace and early in the straight he took the lead. In doing so, however, he galloped slap across Forfarshire, who had to be sharply checked. For this flagrant breach of the rules Tod Sloan was subsequently severely reprimanded by the Stewards.

Approaching the distance Disguise II was beginning to tire and was headed first by Diamond Jubilee and then by Simon Dale. At one point in the final two hundred yards it looked very much as if the Duke of Portland's colt was going to win, but the favourite stuck it out well and was still half a length to the good as he passed the post. Disguise II, a length away, was third, and Bonarosa fourth. The Prince, Diamond Jubilee, and Jones were of course afforded a wonderful reception, but somehow it lacked a little of the spontaneous warmth that had greeted the triumph of Persimmon four years previously. The unlucky horse of the race, of course, was Forfarshire. His trainer, Joe Day, had tried him over a mile and three-quarters to give the five-year-old Lord Provost four stone, and the younger horse had finished in front by almost a furlong.

In the Princess of Wales's Stakes at Newmarket Diamond Jubilee failed to give twenty pounds to Colonel Hall-Walker's good filly Merry Gal, subsequently the dam of the St Leger runner-up, White Eagle. However, he won the Eclipse Stakes, giving Chevening ten pounds and then the St Leger by a length from Elopement. At Doncaster he was in his most devilish mood. It took the perspiring Marsh nearly twenty minutes to get a saddle on his back, and on the way to the post the colt constantly reared up on to his hind legs. After that race he was never quite as good a horse again. In the autumn he was unplaced behind Disguise II in the Jockey Club Stakes. The following season he was second to Epsom Lad, who had been sold to Mr James Buchanan (later Lord Woolavington), in the Princess of Wales's Stakes; fourth to Epsom Lad in the Eclipse Stakes; and third to Pietermaritzburg and Epsom Lad in the Jockey Club Stakes. He was then retired to the Sandringham Stud at a 300-guinea fee, having won over £29,000 in stakes. To start with he proved a demon to manage at Sandringham, but gradually his conduct improved. In 1906 he was sold to a South American breeder for £31,500. He did extremely well in the Argentine, where he died at the age of twenty-six.

Herbert Jones was seventy years old when he was found dead in the kitchen of his home at Girton in 1951. He had been apprenticed to Richard Marsh at the tender age of ten, his first winner being Good News in 1896, his last one Erne, owned by King George V, in 1923. Diamond Jubilee, of course, provided him with his great chance, and he subsequently rode Vedas, Gorgos, and Minoru to victory in the Two Thousand Guineas; Minoru in the Derby; and Cherry Lass in the Oaks. Richard Marsh's description of him provides a suitable epitaph: 'He was, for a jockey, about the pluckiest and best rough-horseman I have ever seen, and with it all he was the cheeriest soul imaginable. The natural ready wit of Jones, and his gaiety, together with the absolute trust we had in him, appealed immensely to us all. A better servant no man ever had and a straighter jockey never got on a horse.'

1900: Wednesday, 30 May . . . 301 Entries. £5,450.

H.R.H. THE PRINCE OF WALES's b.c. DIAMOND JUBILEE
   by St Simon out of Perdita II   H. JONES   1
DUKE OF PORTLAND's b. or br.c. SIMON DALE
   by St Simon out of Ismay   M. CANNON   2
MR J. R. KEENE's b.c. DISGUISE II by Domino
   out of Bonnie Gal   T. SLOAN   3

Also ran:
   Sir E. Cassel's Bonarosa (4th) (L. Reiff); H.R.H. the Prince of Wales's Frontignan (R. Jones); Mr J. Musker's Chevening (O. Madden); Mr A. Stedall's Most Excellent (K. Cannon); Mr A. Stedall's First Principal (F. Rickaby); Mr T. R. Dewar's Forfarshire (S. Loates); Lord Rosebery's Sailor Lad (C. Wood); Lord Cadogan's Sidus (T. Loates); M. E. Blanc's Governor II (French); Lord William Beresford's Democrat (T. Weldon); Mr W. T. Jones's Dewi Sant (E. Jones).

14 ran.

Betting:
   6–4 Diamond Jubilee; 100–30 Forfarshire; 8–1 Disguise II; 10–1 Chevening and Bonarosa; 100–1 Simon Dale; 25–1 Sailor Lad; 33–1 Governor II; 40–1 Democrat; 50–1 Most Excellent; 66–1 First Principal and Sidus; 100–1 Frontignan; 200–1 Dewi Sant.

Won by half a length; a length between second and third.   2 m. 42 s.
Winner trained by R. Marsh at Newmarket.

1901

Up till this year women had played little or no part in the history of the Derby, but Volodyovski, winner in 1901, was bred by Lady Meux, who leased him as a yearling to Lord William Beresford, v.c. A bay or brown colt by Florizel II, full brother to Persimmon and Diamond Jubilee, out of La Reine, by Rosicrucian, Volodyovski was sent to Heath House, Newmarket, to be trained by John Huggins, a rubicund, thick-set American with a walrus moustache. As a two-year-old he was rather backward in the spring and made no show in his first two races, but displayed marked improvement at Ascot in running Good Morning to a head in the Coventry Stakes.

Once Huggins had him to his liking, Volodyovski—usually known as 'Voly' or 'Bottle o' Whisky'—ran up an impressive sequence of victories. Turning out for the second time at Ascot, he won the Windsor Castle Stakes in a canter by six lengths. At Newmarket in July he beat a good filly called Princess Melton by a neck in the Stud Produce Stakes, and he then won the Rous Memorial Stakes at Goodwood and a race of the same title at Newmarket early in October. Later that month he met with a reverse, failing by a length and a half to concede Aida thirteen pounds in the Imperial Produce Stakes at Kempton. The defeat was no disgrace, though, as Aida won the One Thousand Guineas the following season. 'Voly' ended the season by winning the Great Sapling Stakes at Sandown and retired for the winter as favourite for the Derby.

Unfortunately, Lord William Beresford died in December. Lilian, Duchess of Marlborough, his widow and executrix, maintained that the lease of the horse must continue; Lady Meux thought otherwise and a law-suit resulted, Lady Meux asking for an injunction to restrain Lilian, Duchess of Marlborough, from dealing with the horse, and in addition claiming its return. Mr Justice Grantham decided that the so-called 'lease' was only a personal agreement and terminated with the death of Lord William. Having won her case, Lady Meux leased her colt again, this time to the American sportsman Mr W. C. Whitney, who decided that the colt should continue to be trained by Huggins.

Volodyovski was not engaged in the Guineas, and Huggins made no attempt to hurry his preparation. In fact, the colt was still extremely backward when he ran for a Newmarket Biennial. He finished a poor third to St Maclou and Magic Mirror, both of whom received twelve pounds, but it was obvious that he had been in no condition to do himself full justice, and there was no recession in his Derby quotation of 7–1 as a result of his defeat. Huggins then proceeded to get to work on him in earnest, and the colt was a very different proposition when he was formally tried a fortnight before the Derby against the four-year-old Kilmarnock II, recently third in the Kempton Jubilee, and Prince Charles II, fifth in the Two Thousand Guineas. Volodyovski won the trial impressively, thereby encouraging Huggins to believe that he had a favourite's chance in the Derby.

There were twenty-five runners for the Derby, the biggest field since 1867. 'Voly', ridden by the American jockey Lester Reiff, was favourite at 5–2, with Floriform, Revenue, and Handicapper next in demand. The start was a good one and in the first half-mile the leaders were Olympian, Revenue, Lord Bobs, and Prince Charles II. Coming down the hill, though, Volodyovski and Floriform began to make noticeable improvement. Olympian and Prince Charles II were in front with three furlongs to go, but at that point both of them weakened and Reiff, hugging the rails in true American style, drove the favourite into the lead. William the Third, a little outpaced early on, was beginning to make up ground, but just below the distance 'Voly' was three lengths clear and his position appeared impregnable. Foolishly Reiff allowed himself to take things a little bit easily, but warning shouts from the crowd caused him to take a rapid glance over his shoulder. He saw the danger and began to ride for all he was worth, but the din from the spectators had made 'Voly' veer away from the rails, and through the gap that was left stormed Cannon on William the Third. For a few strides the result was in the balance, but the favourite rallied courageously and drew away to win by three-quarters of a length with Veronese a moderate third. The time, 2 m. 40⅘ s., set up a new record for the race. Although the victory was largely an American one, it was very well received by the crowd, and Mr Harry Payne Whitney, a famous polo player, deputizing for his father, was loudly cheered as he led the winner in.

The 'American Invasion' at the turn of the century landed some disreputable characters on the English Turf. On the whole, though, the invasion was beneficial, as apart from giving a much-needed shake to national complacency in the sport, it introduced new techniques in training, riding, and not least in plating. Huggins himself said that American plates were worth the best part of four lengths in a race. A very able man of complete integrity, Huggins was greatly liked at Newmarket and was one of the few American trainers over here who did not sometimes resort to doping, a practice which at that time had not been barred. He was once asked if there were very many crooks on the American Turf. 'Not a one,' he replied; 'they have all migrated over here!'

Another American trainer at Newmarket was Wishard, a likeable man in himself, but a confirmed and skilful doper of horses and the associate of some fairly desperate characters. He brought with him two jockeys, the brothers Lester and Johnny Reiff. Lester was tall and had continual trouble with his weight, but was an extremely able rider and a wonderful judge of pace. There is no doubt that he worked hand in glove with some of the big American gamblers who came over, and if certain of these gamblers did not back a short-priced favourite that he rode, then that favourite was sure to be beaten. It was no surprise when the Jockey Club imposed their ban on him. Johnny Reiff first appeared on English racecourses as an angel-faced boy in knicker-bockers and an Eton collar, but was rather less innocent than he looked. He was a brilliant light-weight in his youth and subsequently won the Derby on Orby in 1907 and Tagalie in 1912. He also rode Craganour, first past the post in 1913 but dis-qualified. He went over to France when the American millionaires started racing there and seldom appeared in England except to ride in a major event.

In John Porter's opinion William the Third had been unlucky in the Derby, but the form worked out accurately enough when the Duke of Portland's colt met Volodyovski in the one and a half mile Lennox Stakes at Hurst Park in August. Conceding three pounds, Volodyovski lost by a head, but was in front a stride past the post. It may be added that Volodyovski had been rested after Epsom and in August was midway through his St Leger preparation. William the Third was not engaged in the St Leger and may well have been the fitter of the two. The following season William the Third proved an outstanding stayer, winning the Ascot Gold Cup, the Alexandra Plate, and the Doncaster Cup. He subsequently sired Willonyx, winner of the Gold Cup and the Cesarewitch, and Winkipop, winner of the One Thousand Guineas and grand-dam of the Oaks winner Pennycomequick. Roseland, a rather undistinguished son of William the Third, sired Garron Lass, grand-dam of the Triple Crown winner Bahram.

In the St Leger Volodyovski started favourite, but was narrowly beaten by Mr Leopold de Rothschild's Doricles, like himself a son of Florizel II. It was an ugly race with a lot of bumping and barging, and there is little doubt that 'Voly' was des-perately unlucky to lose. An objection was lodged on his behalf, but it was overruled as the winner was not one of the horses that had hampered him. In his book *Memories of Men and Horses* Mr William Allison wrote: 'Volodyovski would have won the St Leger readily enough had not other jockeys made a dead set against Lester Reiff, who had scrupulously kept out of the Goudie machinations.' It may be remembered that a bank clerk called Goudie, who combined extreme simplicity with gross dis-honesty, robbed the Bank of Liverpool of £160,000. Most of this vast sum went into the pockets of a small gang emanating from the dregs of the racing world. Two members of the gang, purporting to be a bookmaker and a professional backer, pretended to place huge bets on certain horses on Goudie's behalf. Needless to say Goudie was never permitted to win, and when by some gross miscalculation a horse that he was supposed to have backed actually won, he was told that the bet had not been placed. Whatever the truth of Mr Allison's contention, there is no doubt that certain leading riders at that period were far from scrupulous, and in 1902, the year that Goudie and the gang that preyed on him were tried, certain jockeys were warned off for 'associating with persons of bad character'.

In October there was a very interesting race for the Kempton Park Stakes, Volodyovski, William the Third, and Doricles meeting on weight for age terms the four-year-olds Epsom Lad, Santoi, and Merry Gal. The result suggested that the three-year-olds were not an outstanding crop, Epsom Lad, a gelding by Ladas, winning by three parts of a length from Santoi, with Volodyovski a head away third. Epsom Lad, however, was a very good horse that season and had won the Princess of Wales's Stakes and the Eclipse Stakes, while Santoi had won the Kempton Jubilee and the Gold Cup, a somewhat unusual combination. The result did prove conclusively, though, that Volodyovski was the best of his age.

As a four-year-old Volodyovski deteriorated considerably and ran eleven times without winning a race. He was then retired to the stud at a fee of forty-eight pounds, but failed completely as a sire.

Mr Whitney, born in 1841, had held office as Secretary of the Navy in President Cleveland's administration. He only took seriously to racing in 1898, and it was in 1900 that he turned his attentions to the English Turf. In 1903 he decided to dispose of his horses in England, and to concentrate his energy and resources on racing in America. Unfortunately he died the following year, a grievous loss to the sport in the United States.

1901 : Wednesday, 5 June . . . 279 Entries. £5,670.

MR W. C. WHITNEY's b. or br.c. VOLODYOVSKI
  by Florizel II out of La Reine   L. REIFF   1
DUKE OF PORTLAND's b.c. WILLIAM THE THIRD
  by St Simon out of Gravity   M. CANNON   2
MR DOUGLAS BAIRD's ch.c. VERONESE by Donovan
  out of Maize   F. RICKABY   3

Also ran :

Mr T. Simpson Jay's Floriform (4th) (E. Watkins); Sir J. Duke's Wargrave (Clemson); Sir E. Cassel's Handicapper (J. H. Martin); Sir R. Waldie Griffith's

Veles (J. Reiff); Sir R. Waldie Griffith's Ian (O. Madden); Sir J. Blundell Maple's Lord Bobs (S. Loates); Mr Foxhall Keene's Olympian (M. Henry); Mr H. J. King's Orchid (F. Pratt); Lord Wolverton's Osboch (H. Jones); Mr J. Gubbins's Revenue (Halsey); Mr P. Lorillard's Tantalus (D. Maher); Colonel H. McCalmont's St Maclou (A. Nightingall); Mr G. Faber's Pietermaritzburg (Finlay); Mr C. Morbey's Royal Rouge (Fagan); Mr W. Raphael's Ruskin (W. Pratt); Sir W. Ingram's Cottager (Weldon); Mr L. de Rothschild's Doricles (K. Cannon); Mr Field's H.R.H. (W. H. Randall); Mr L. W. Humby's Royal George (J. Thompson); Sir E. Cassel's Sang Bleu (Anthony); Mr W. C. Whitney's Prince Charles II (Turner); Mr W. M. Singer's Claqueur (C. Jenkins).

25 ran.

Betting:

5–2 Volodyovski; 7–1 Floriform; 10–1 Handicapper and Revenue; 100–7 Ian and William the Third; 20–1 Doricles; 25–1 Pietermaritzburg; 33–1 Royal Rouge, Olympian, Tantalus, Orchid, and St Maclou; 40–1 Lord Bobs, Cottager, Veles, Veronese, and Wargrave; 50–1 Osboch; 66–1 H.R.H.; 100–1 Ruskin, Royal George, Prince Charles II, and Sang Bleu; 200–1 Claqueur.

Won by three parts of a length; four lengths between second and third. 2 m. 40⅘ s. Winner trained by J. Huggins at Newmarket.

1902

It was another Irish triumph in 1902 when Ard Patrick, bred at Bruree, Co. Limerick, gave his owner-breeder, Mr John Gubbins, a second Derby success. Good colt that Ard Patrick was, the outstanding three-year-old of the season was unquestionably Sceptre, winner of the Two Thousand and One Thousand Guineas, the Oaks, and the St Leger. Idolized by the racing public, she was perhaps the greatest filly in the history of English racing.

Ard Patrick was a brown colt, big, handsome, and imposing except for a rather unattractive neck, and hocks that were perhaps a shade away from him. A half-brother to his owner's 'Triple Crown' winner Galtee More, he was by St Florian, a son of St Simon that was a moderate racehorse, and with the notable exception of Ard Patrick, a moderate sire as well. St Florian's half-sister Musa won the Oaks, while his dam was a full sister to the Oaks winner Jenny Howlet. Morganette, dam of Ard Patrick, was a selling plater and a 'roarer' too, but her dam Lady Morgan was a half-sister to the Oaks and St Leger winner Marie Stuart.

Trained by Sam Darling, the most patient of men, Ard Patrick was given every chance to develop his strength, and his first racecourse appearance was in the Imperial Plate at Kempton in the autumn. He ran very green indeed and only scraped home by a head from Sir Blundell Maple's Royal Lancer, who was giving him thirteen pounds. Four days later the pair met again in the Clearwell Stakes at Newmarket, and although Ard Patrick only received three pounds on this occasion, he was again the winner. Ard Patrick's final appearance that season was in the Dewhurst Plate in which he ran a really good race, but failed by a neck to concede two pounds to Major Eustace Loder's Game Chick, who had beaten Sceptre in the Champagne Stakes at Doncaster.

Ard Patrick's great rival Sceptre was by Persimmon out of Ornament, a full sister to Ormonde. Bred by the Duke of Westminster, she was sold as a yearling after his death for the then unprecedented sum of 10,000 guineas to Mr Robert Sievier. Born in a hansom cab in 1860, Sievier, once an actor and later a journalist whose methods were occasionally not far short of blackmail, was involved throughout his life in a series of shady and discreditable episodes, and though devoid neither of charm nor courage, he can be described as an adventurer in the least complimentary sense of that word. He was a participant in some notorious law-suits, and after one in which his complete lack of moral scruples was thoroughly exposed, he was 'warned off' by the Stewards of the Jockey Club. He died in 1939.

As a two-year-old Sceptre ran three times, winning the Woodcote and July Stakes, and finishing third, when she had already gone in her coat, to Game Chick and Csardas in the Champagne Stakes. She was then trained by Charles Morton, who, at the end of the year, took up the position of private trainer to Mr J. B. Joel, for whom he won the Derby with Sunstar and Humorist. Unfortunately for Sceptre, Morton's American successor was a good deal less competent.

The following season Sceptre was trained for the Lincolnshire Handicap at the end of March. Carrying 6 st. 7 lb. she was beaten in the very last stride by St Maclou, a useful four-year-old that had run in the Derby the previous year and was conceding her nineteen pounds. There is little doubt that Sceptre should have won, and it will suffice to say that the day after the race Sievier took on the training of the filly himself. A month later she won the Two Thousand Guineas from Pistol and Ard Patrick, and then the One Thousand Guineas as well.

Ard Patrick was still very backward on Guineas day, and under the circumstances ran a highly satisfactory race. At Kempton the following week he failed by two lengths to concede twenty-one pounds to Royal Ivy over a mile and a quarter. His last race before the Derby was the Newmarket Stakes. Ridden by Mornington Cannon, he duly won from Fowling Piece, ridden by Jenkins. Jenkins promptly lodged an objection on the grounds of bumping and boring, while he also alleged that Cannon had dangled his whip in front of Fowling Piece's face. The Stewards awarded the race to Fowling Piece, but exonerated Cannon from the charge of deliberate misuse of his whip.

Sceptre, ridden by Herbert Randall, son of Sir Henry Randall, was made an even-money favourite for the Derby. Second favourite at 6–1 was a St Simon colt called Pekin, owned by Mr G. A. Prentice, who had some connexion with the Stock Exchange. Pekin had not run as a three-year-old, but had won twice in modest company the year before. Apparently he had done a wonderful gallop at home, and his owner and his owner's friends had gone for a mammoth win. There was a lot of sound backing at 100–14 for Ard Patrick, who was ridden by 'Skeets' Martin as Mornington Cannon was claimed for Friar Tuck. Martin came over with the 'American Invasion' and was one of the first American riders to make his home over here. He had the best of hands, was brilliant at the start, and particularly good on a two-year-old. Popular both with his employers and fellow-jockeys despite an uncertain temper, he might well have gone to the top of the tree but for a noticeable lack of self-confidence. Before a race he was very much inclined to be nervous and over-anxious, and if he was beaten on a well-backed horse, he took his defeat very hardly, whether the reverse was due to his own misjudgement or not. He was one of the first jockeys to take up winter sports seriously, and the latter part of his life was spent in Switzerland, where he died, completely destitute, in 1944.

Epsom was full of visitors for the Coronation, which had been postponed owing to the King's illness. Unfortunately it was a cold and rainy day, and some of the oriental princes looked very 'tucked up'. Sceptre did not accompany the other runners to the start, but by special permission went there the long way round via Tattenham Corner. Her rider elected to take her at a walk the entire way, a procedure which kept all the other horses waiting, and for which he and Sievier were subsequently reprimanded.

Mr Arthur Coventry got the field away to a very good start except that Sceptre dwelt a little, and Randall, naturally anxious on this great occasion, may have made up his ground a bit too quickly. At the mile post Csardas led from Ard Patrick, with Fowling Piece and Sceptre next. Approaching Tattenham Corner Ard Patrick went to the front and turned for home with a slight lead from Sceptre, Rising Glass, Csardas, and Pekin. At that point Sceptre was going so easily that it looked as if she could come away and win whenever she wanted. With two furlongs to go, though, she was in trouble and a cry went up, 'She's beaten!' Rising Glass passed her and so did Friar Tuck, but neither could make the slightest impression on Ard Patrick, who would probably have won by a dozen lengths if Martin had ridden him out. The cold and cheerless day, combined with Sceptre's defeat, had taken the heart from the crowd, and there was very little cheering for Ard Patrick, whose gout-stricken owner was not well enough to be able to lead his colt in.

Many theories were put forward to account for Sceptre's defeat. Some said that Sievier had never meant her to win. Others said she lacked stamina, but this latter notion was discounted by her easy victory in the Oaks two days later, and also by her St Leger success in September. It is true that Randall pushed her a bit too hard in the early stages to make up the ground she had lost at the start, but the real cause for her failure was probably a bruised foot, which interrupted her preparation at one stage. She was a filly that needed a great deal of work and may have been short of a gallop.

Ard Patrick was beaten in the Prince of Wales's Stakes at Ascot by Cupbearer, but won the race on an objection. He then developed leg trouble and was unable to run in the St Leger. In the Jockey Club Stakes, his only other outing that year, he was far from his best and finished a moderate third behind Rising Glass and Templemore.

As a four-year-old Ard Patrick completely recovered his form, and proved beyond doubt that he was a very good horse indeed. He won the Princess of Wales's Stakes in a canter from Royal Lancer, who received nine pounds, and then came his glorious victory in the Eclipse Stakes at Sandown Park.

By common consent the Eclipse Stakes in 1903 ranks as one of the finest races of the century. Two magnificent four-year-olds, Ard Patrick and Sceptre, were opposed by Sir James Miller's three-year-old Rock Sand, winner of the Two Thousand Guineas and the Derby. Rock Sand was favourite at 5–4; Sceptre, recently bought by Mr William Bass and now trained by Alec Taylor, was at 7–4, while backers of Ard Patrick could get 5–1 for their money. Ard Patrick had just been bought for £21,000 on behalf of the German Government, but ran in the name and colours of Mr Gubbins.

The excitement was tremendous as the field swept into the straight with Rock Sand, Ard Patrick, and Sceptre all in line. With two furlongs to go Rock Sand began to give ground and a great shout arose of 'Sceptre wins!' as the filly obtained a slender advantage. Ard Patrick, however, refused to give in, and when Otto Madden asked him for one final effort not more than a hundred yards from home, the big horse responded with the utmost courage and determination to win a wonderful race by a neck. It was the last race of Ard Patrick's career, for his leg went again soon afterwards, and unquestionably his greatest one. The crowd was too downcast, though, at Sceptre's defeat to give him the cheers he deserved.

Ard Patrick then retired to the stud in Germany, having won over £26,000 in stakes. He got Ariel, winner of the German Derby, but was not the success anticipated.

1902 : Wednesday, 4 June . . . 282 Entries. £5,450.

MR J. GUBBINS's br.c. ARD PATRICK by St Florian out of Morganette	J. H. MARTIN	1
COLONEL H. MCCALMONT's ch.c. RISING GLASS by Isinglass out of Hautesse	G. MCCALL	2
DUKE OF PORTLAND's br.c. FRIAR TUCK by Friar's Balsam out of Galopin Mare	M. CANNON	3

Also ran:

Mr R. Sievier's Sceptre (4th) (H. Randall); Duke of Devonshire's Cheers (D. Maher); Mr J. Barrow's Fowling Piece (C. Jenkins); Mr H. J. King's Prince Florizel (H. Jones); Sir J. Blundell Maple's Royal Lancer (C. Horan); Duke of Portland's Caro (Moreton); Mr G. A. Prentice's Pekin (Halsey); Mr Leopold de Rothschild's Royal Ivy (K. Cannon); Mr R. Forrest-Tod's Csardas (J. McCall); Mr W. C. Whitney's Intruder (Rigby); Mr J. R. Keene's Kearsage (Spencer); Mr G. Faber's Duke of Westminster (S. Loates); Mr 'Fairie's' Water Wheel (Clemson); Mr J. S. Curtis's Lancewood (C. Leader); Lord Carnarvon's Robert le Diable (Lewis).

18 ran.

Betting :

Evens Sceptre; 6–1 Pekin; 100–14 Ard Patrick; 100–8 Intruder and Fowling Piece; 100–7 Friar Tuck; 25–1 Cheers and Royal Ivy; 33–1 Duke of Westminster; 40–1 Csardas, Royal Lancer, and Rising Glass; 66–1 Robert le Diable; 100–1 Caro, Kearsage, and Prince Florizel; 200–1 Lancewood and Water Wheel.

Won by three lengths; same distance between second and third. 2 m. 42⅕ s. Winner trained by S. Darling at Beckhampton.

1903

Sir James Miller's Rock Sand, winner of the 'Triple Crown' in 1903, was a rather small, beautifully made colt by his owner's first Derby winner Sainfoin out of Roquebrune, a somewhat delicate mare by St Simon that had won the New Stakes at Ascot and was bought by Sir James at the disposal of the Duchess of Montrose's stock. Roquebrune was a half-sister to Seabreeze, winner of the Oaks and the St Leger, and also to Tredennis, a successful sire. Her dam, St Marguerite, by Hermit, won the One Thousand Guineas, while St Marguerite's sister Thebais won the One Thousand Guineas and the Oaks. It is perhaps worth mentioning that Stockwell's name appears three times in Rock Sand's pedigree at the fourth remove.

Rock Sand, the first foal of his dam, was trained at Newmarket by George Blackwell. On his first appearance he started at 10–1 in the Bedford Stakes at the Newmarket Second Spring Meeting and won in a canter by three lengths. He then won the Woodcote Stakes at Epsom, the Coventry Stakes at Ascot, the Chesterfield Stakes at Newmarket, and the Champagne Stakes at Doncaster. The one reverse in a spectacular two-year-old career occurred in the Middle Park Plate. In all his previous races he had been partnered by the great American jockey Danny Maher, but on this occasion he was ridden by W. Lane, while Maher was on his stable companion Flotsam, a colt of Sir Daniel Cooper's that had won the Imperial Produce Stakes at Kempton with the utmost ease. Rock Sand started favourite at evens, but was only third, beaten a head and two lengths, to Flotsam and Greatorex, a Carbine colt owned by the Duke of Portland. The racing public was not disposed to take this defeat very seriously, and no one was greatly surprised when Rock Sand beat Greatorex very easily in the Dewhurst Plate a fortnight later. Greatorex, incidentally, broke down in his Derby preparation the following year.

Rock Sand's first outing as a three-year-old was at the Craven Meeting, when he won a minor event very easily. He then won the Two Thousand Guineas quite comfortably from Flotsam, with the St Simon colt Rabelais third. A fortnight later Flotsam confirmed the form by beating Rabelais decisively in the Newmarket Stakes.

It had been generally assumed that Rock Sand's most formidable opponent at Epsom would be Vinicius, a French colt owned by M. Blanc. A big, powerful bay standing nearly seventeen hands, Vinicius had been heavily backed for the Derby before it was known that his owner intended to run him in the Prix du Jockey Club the Sunday before the Epsom meeting began. Vinicius started an odds-on favourite at Chantilly, but could only finish fifth. However, his jockey had ridden him with singular lack of judgement, and hope still remained that he would do considerably better on the Wednesday.

It was a perfect June day when the seven runners cantered down to the post, and the crowd was as big as ever even though the race was regarded as a certainty for Rock Sand, who started at 6–4 on. Nothing, however, went down worse than the favourite, who was always a desperately bad mover in his slower paces and seemed unable to extend himself until he was thoroughly warmed up. 'I suppose you know your horse is lame?' remarked an American owner to Blackwell as Rock Sand was scratching his way to the post. 'Oh, you've noticed that, have you?' replied Blackwell. 'I think he has a chance all the same.'

The starter this year was Mr Hugh Owen. A brother of that famous rider Captain 'Roddy' Owen, he was killed jumping a tiny fence out hunting five years later. The despatch was a good one and Rock Sand was the first to show in front, but after a furlong Maher took a pull at him and allowed Mead and Cerisier to lead. At the top of the hill Vinicius had dropped back last and the bookmakers were offering him at 20–1. Just before Tattenham Corner, Rock Sand came through on the rails and, heading Mead, was very soon out by himself with Flotsam, three lengths behind, his nearest attendant. Suddenly, however, Vinicius began to get going. One by one he passed his opponents, but he had been left with far too much to do, and gamely as he struggled, he was still two lengths behind the favourite when the winning post was reached. Vinicius had been forty yards behind Rock Sand with half a mile to go and it was a truly remarkable effort to finish as close to the winner as he did. Not surprisingly his rider, Thompson, was strongly criticized for lying quite so far out of his ground. Thompson, however, weighed less than seven stone and was quite the wrong partner for a big, powerful colt like Vinicius.

For the third year in succession the Derby winner had been ridden by an American. Danny Maher, who rode two other Derby winners in Cicero and Spearmint, had come to this country late in 1900 with a big reputation. He soon adapted his style to suit English courses and proved himself an artist of a very high order. Sometimes he overdid his waiting tactics, but in his prime he was second to none. A man of great charm and intelligence, he was liked and admired by men like Lord Rosebery and Lord Derby, but there was a strain of weakness in his character and some of his racing friends were no credit to a man in his position. No one could stop him from burning the candle at both ends, and to make matters worse he was tubercular. His health had gone by the time the Great War broke out and he died not long afterwards.

George Blackwell learnt the art of training from that master of the profession,

Matthew Dawson. He took out a licence in 1891 and soon made a reputation for himself, among his patrons being, besides Sir James Miller and Sir Daniel Cooper, Lord Cadogan, Mr P. Lorillard, Mr James R. Keene, Lord Rosebery, and Mr W. M. Cazalet. His notable winners included Aida and Flair, who both won the One Thousand Guineas, and Chaleureux, winner of the Cesarewitch and Manchester November Handicap, and subsequently sire of the Derby winner Signorinetta. In 1923 he prepared Sergeant Murphy, then thirteen years of age, to win the Grand National, and he shares with R. C. Dawson, J. Jewitt, and W. Stephenson the distinction of having trained the winners of both the Grand National Steeplechase and the Derby. Father-in-law of the well-known jockey Henri Jelliss, and brother-in-law of Bernard Carslake, he kept his money and was very well-off when he died in 1942.

At Ascot Rock Sand won the St James's Palace Stakes, and then came his defeat, already described in the account of Ard Patrick's career, in the Eclipse Stakes at Sandown Park. He won the St Leger very easily, but his limitations were again exposed when Sceptre gave him fifteen pounds and a decisive beating in the Jockey Club Stakes.

His first appearance as a four-year-old was in the Coronation Cup at Epsom. In this event both he and Sceptre were trounced by Lord Howard de Walden's Zinfandel, a Persimmon colt of outstanding ability, whose classic engagements the previous year, luckily perhaps for Rock Sand, had been rendered void by the death of his nominator, Colonel McCalmont. However, at Ascot Rock Sand won the Hardwicke Stakes, beating Santry and Sceptre, but there is little doubt that Sceptre was beginning to go downhill. He next won in rapid succession the Princess of Wales's Stakes, the Lingfield Park Stakes, and the First Foal Stakes at Newmarket. He then had a rest until competing in the Jockey Club Stakes in the autumn. Just before that event he had trouble with a suspensory ligament and his participation at one point looked extremely doubtful. He hobbled down to the post like a regular cripple, but it was a very different matter when it came to racing, and as he sailed past the post an easy winner, he was received with a storm of cheering, the like of which is rarely heard at Newmarket.

He then retired to his owner's stud, but not long afterwards Sir James Miller died and his stock was dispersed. Rock Sand was sold for £25,000 to Mr August Belmont, President of the New York Jockey Club, while his dam Roquebrune was sold for 4,500 guineas to a breeder in Belgium. In America Rock Sand sired Mahubah, dam of the famous American horse Man o' War, and Tracery, who came to England and won the St Leger. Tracery sired The Panther, winner of the Two Thousand Guineas; Papyrus, winner of the Derby; and Teresina, a great stayer that became one of the foundation mares of the Aga Khan's stud. Rock Sand was also sire of Needle Rock, dam of the Guineas winner Diolite, and of Epine Blanche, the dam of Epinard. He was eventually exported to France, where he died in 1914.

Rabelais, who ran fourth behind Rock Sand in the Derby, was provisionally sold to go to Russia, but the deal fell through owing to certain currency restrictions that came into force at the time of the Russo-Japanese war. He was then exported to France for £900 and sired Durbar II, winner of the 1914 Derby. He also sired Ranai, dam of the 1942 Derby winner Watling Street, and Havresac II, whose daughter Nogara was dam of Nearco.

The conditions for the Derby were slightly altered this year, the guaranteed value of the race being augmented to £6,500.

1903: Wednesday, 27 May . . . 295 Entries. £6,450.

SIR JAMES MILLER's br.c. ROCK SAND by Sainfoin out of Roquebrune	D. MAHER	1
M. E. BLANC's b.c. VINICIUS by Masque out of Wandora	J. THOMPSON	2
SIR D. COOPER's b.c. FLOTSAM by St Frusquin out of Float	HALSEY	3

Also ran:

Mr A. James's Rabelais (4th) (K. Cannon); H.M. King Edward VII's Mead (H. Jones); Mr H. B. Duryea's Acefull (J. H. Martin); Mr W. Brodrick Cloete's Cerisier (O. Madden).

7 ran.

Betting:

6–4 on Rock Sand; 11–2 Vinicius; 100–14 Flotsam; 9–1 Mead; 25–1 Rabelais; 33–1 Acefull; 100–1 Cerisier.

Won by two lengths; the same distance between second and third.   2 m. 42⅘ s. Winner trained by G. Blackwell at Newmarket.

1904

In the early part of the century there were no more popular colours than the blue jacket, yellow cap, of Mr Leopold de Rothschild, who had been a patron of the Turf since 1870. A thorough sportsman who loved his horses and usually exaggerated their virtues, he was really the kindest of men although his sudden outbursts of temper, which never lasted for long, could be intimidating. He had to wait a long time before he achieved his racing ambition of winning the Derby, but victory, when at length it came, was all the sweeter as St Amant was bred by himself at the Southcourt Stud near Leighton Buzzard, and was by his own sire St Frusquin, who had run second to Persimmon in a memorable race for the Derby. St Amant's dam, Lady Loverule by Muncaster, never ran, but her dam Nellie won seven races worth over £4,000 and was out of King Tom's daughter Hippia, who had won the Oaks for Baron Meyer de Rothschild.

As a two-year-old St Amant was overshadowed by Major Loder's brilliant filly Pretty Polly, but he was probably the best of his sex. He won the Coventry Stakes at Ascot and the Prince of Wales's Stakes at Goodwood, but ran a disappointing race in the Champagne Stakes at Doncaster, finishing a moderate third to Pretty Polly and Lancashire. There was an excuse, though, for his mediocre performance, as he had been badly pricked by the shoeing smith. He won the Rous Memorial Stakes at Newmarket in the autumn, but in the Middle Park Plate, although he finished in front of Lancashire this time, he was again no match for Pretty Polly.

His first appearance as a three-year-old was in the Newmarket Biennial at the Craven Meeting. Favourite at 7–2 on, he failed by three parts of a length to concede twelve pounds to His Majesty. Despite this reverse, though, he started favourite for the Two Thousand Guineas, which he won in faultless style from John o' Gaunt and Henry the First.

For some little time St Amant had been showing signs of temperament, and in the Newmarket Stakes he flatly declined to exert himself and was beaten by Henry the First and John o' Gaunt. With the home-trained colts either moderate or unreliable, a favourite for the Derby was found in the French colt Gouvernant, a son of Flying Fox, even though he was reputedly inferior to his stable companion Ajax, who had won the Prix du Jockey Club. Second favourite was John o' Gaunt, who had been unlucky in the Newmarket Stakes, and next in the betting came Henry the First and St Amant.

It was a dreadful Derby Day from the weather point of view and the rain came down in torrents. Just before the start a terrific thunderstorm swept across Epsom and anyone not under cover was soaked to the skin. As for the race itself there is little to be said. Lightning flashed as the tapes went up and away went St Amant as if the Devil himself was in hot pursuit. He led from start to finish, never looked like being caught, and won in a canter by three lengths from John o' Gaunt, with St Denis six lengths away third. Perhaps it was the lightning that did it, but Kempton Cannon, who rode St Amant in most of his races, used to tell the following story. When he got up on St Amant in the paddock and was being led round, the colt continually turned his head as if he wanted to catch his jockey by the leg. Cannon asked the lad leading him what on earth the horse was trying to do. 'I've been pinching him all morning,' the lad replied. 'He'll be fairly on his toes by now!'

Despite the weather, the crowd gave a great reception to Mr de Rothschild as, beaming with pleasure, he led his winner in. Mr de Rothschild had neither coat nor umbrella and had not watched the race from under cover. He was probably the wettest man on the course; he was almost certainly the happiest.

Walter Kempton Cannon was the son of Tom Cannon and brother of Mornington. A thoroughly sound and capable rider, he had a long association with Mr de Rothschild, for whom he also won the St Leger on Doricles. He gave up racing just before the First World War, in which he served in the Royal Flying Corps. He married Jack Watts's widow, and for a time conducted a garage at Newmarket. Finally he retired to Hove, where he lived happily in placid retirement until his death in 1951. He is survived by his brother, a wonderful link with the past, as Mornington rode in his first Derby in 1891.

It would have been better for St Amant's reputation if he had never run again. He failed ingloriously behind Pretty Polly in the St Leger, and ran six times without success in the autumn. At the end of the year, with a view to giving him a change of air and scenery, he was sent to young Tom Cannon at Stockbridge, and it was greatly to Cannon's credit that he trained St Amant to win the Jockey Club Stakes, the colt's only outing in 1905. As a five-year-old St Amant competed unsuccessfully in handicaps and was then retired to the Southcourt Stud, where he made little mark as a sire.

John o' Gaunt was ridden, as was then permitted, by an amateur, Mr George Thursby, half-brother of the colt's owner Sir John Thursby. Mr Thursby, who could stand comparison with all but the very best professionals, was also second on Picton two years later. John o' Gaunt, who only won one race in his whole career, was sire of the St Leger winner Swynford and the Two Thousand Guineas winner Kennymore.

1904: Wednesday, 1 June . . . 260 Entries. £6,500.

MR LEOPOLD DE ROTHSCHILD'S b.c. ST AMANT by St Frusquin out of Lady Loverule	K. CANNON	1
SIR J. THURSBY'S b.c. JOHN O' GAUNT by Isinglass out of La Flèche	MR G. THURSBY	2
MR S. B. JOEL'S b.c. ST DENIS by St Simon out of Brooch	HALSEY	3

Also ran:

Mr F. Alexander's Andover (4th) (W. Lane); M. E. Blanc's Gouvernant (M. Cannon); Mr J. Buchanan's Lancashire (E. Wheatley); Mr J. Musker's Henry the First (O. Madden); Mr D. J. Pullinger's Coxswain (Butchers).

8 ran.

Betting:

7–4 Gouvernant; 4–1 John o' Gaunt; 85–20 Henry the First; 5–1 St Amant; 100–9 Andover; 33–1 Lancashire; 50–1 St Denis; 100–1 Coxswain.

Won by three lengths; six lengths between second and third.   2 m. 45⅖ s.
Winner trained by A. Hayhoe at Newmarket.

1905

But for ill-fortune the Derby of 1905 would probably have been won by France. In the early spring M. Edmond Blanc was understood to have three outstanding colts, all by Flying Fox—Adam, Val d'Or, and Jardy. Hardly had the season started, though, than there was an exceptionally severe epidemic of coughing in the stable. Adam, the best of the three, and Val d'Or were both very ill indeed, but Jardy kept clear of the disease and was therefore detailed to represent his owner in the Derby. Unfortunately he started to cough soon after landing in England, but in spite of the illness he took the field and put up a really gallant fight. Had he been at his best, it is reasonable to suppose that he would have won.

The winner was Cicero, who beat Jardy by three parts of a length and won for Lord Rosebery that owner's third and final Derby. Bred by his owner, Cicero was by Cyllene out of Gas, a half-sister by Ayrshire to Ladas, winner of the Derby in 1894, and also to Chelandry, winner of the One Thousand Guineas. Cyllene, by Bona Vista, was a late-May foal and so undersized in his early days that it was thought pointless to enter him for the classics. However, he grew to full size in due course, became a top-class racehorse, and won the Ascot Gold Cup. As a sire he was extremely successful, getting four Derby winners—Cicero, Minoru, Lemberg, and Tagalie—before he was exported to the Argentine for £25,000 at the age of thirteen. Gas came from the famous Paradigm–Paraffin–Illuminata family, from which so many famous horses are descended, including the Derby winners Ocean Swell (1944) and Never Say Die (1954).

Cicero, a beautifully made little chesnut, full of quality, was quick to come to hand and won the Fitzwilliam Stakes at the Craven Meeting. He then won in succession the Woodcote Stakes at Epsom, the Coventry Stakes at Ascot, the July Stakes and the National Breeders Produce Stakes at Sandown. In the Coventry Stakes he beat Mr de Wend Fenton's Vedas, winner of his four previous races, while at Sandown he put up a remarkably good performance in carrying 9 st. 9 lb. to victory. He picked up a nail in the Sandown race and came in lame, but fortunately the injury did not prove serious. He did not race again that season after July. It had been intended to start him in the Imperial Produce Stakes at Kempton in October, but as the going was heavy and he would have had to concede weight to most of his opponents, it was thought wiser to keep him at home.

Cicero was not engaged in the Two Thousand Guineas which Vedas, whom he had beaten without difficulty the year before at Ascot, won decisively from Signorino and Llangibby. His first outing, which, incidentally, was his first racecourse appearance for ten months, was in the Newmarket Stakes, and he showed that he had at least maintained his form by beating Llangibby and Signorino as easily as Vedas had done in the Guineas. Vedas unfortunately met with a mishap just before the Derby and could not run, and with Jardy under the weather, Cicero, ridden by Danny Maher, started favourite at 11–4 on.

There is little that needs to be said about the race. Jardy and Cicero, fifth and sixth respectively approaching Tattenham Corner, swung wide on the bend and raced down the centre of the course. With two furlongs to go they were disputing the lead, but almost immediately they were joined by Signorino and for a few strides it was anyone's race. Cicero, however, responded gallantly when Maher called on him for a final effort, and he gradually pulled away to win by three parts of a length from Jardy, with Signorino a head away third. Lord Rosebery's victory was received with great enthusiasm, but there was sympathetic cheering, too, for Jardy, who had put up a magnificent fight under a very considerable handicap. The time, 2 m. 39⅖ s., established a new record for the race.

In the Eclipse Stakes Cicero started favourite at 13–8 on, but after an exciting struggle was beaten half a length by M. Blanc's Val d'Or, a result that suggested very strongly that he had been lucky to carry off the Derby. Shortly afterwards he developed leg trouble and was unable to run again that season. The following year he beat a solitary opponent in a Newmarket Biennial in the spring, but made no show in that famous race for the Ascot Gold Cup, in which Pretty Polly met with her first defeat on English soil and was beaten by Bachelor's Button. Cicero, however, was not at his best, and his trainer Percy Peck had had serious doubts about running him.

Cicero never ran again and retired to the Mentmore Stud at a fee of ninety-eight pounds. His best winner was Friar Marcus, a very fast horse that carried the colours of King George V and was unbeaten as a two-year-old. Friar Marcus sired a One Thousand Guineas winner in Brown Betty, and was also sire of Friars Daughter, dam of the Aga Khan's Bahram, winner of the 'Triple Crown' in 1935.

Jardy, second to Cicero at Epsom, was sold to the Argentine for £30,000; Signorino, a head behind him at Epsom, was exported to Italy for a tenth of that sum. Signorino was half-brother to the 1908 Derby and Oaks winner, Signorinetta.

Percy Peck, who trained Cicero, was a son of Robert Peck, an outstanding trainer of the previous century. Percy Peck had entered his profession at an unusually early age, and was only nineteen when he won the Chester Cup with Millstream. Later he became private trainer to Lord Durham and, after some years in that capacity, he became trainer to Lord Rosebery as well. In 1910 he won the Two Thousand Guineas with Lord Rosebery's good but very highly strung colt Neil Gow. He had lived in retirement for several years before his death in 1938.

1905: Wednesday, 31 May . . . 292 Entries. £6,450.

LORD ROSEBERY's ch.c. CICERO by Cyllene out of Gas	D. MAHER	1
M. E. BLANC's b.c. JARDY by Flying Fox out of Airs and Graces	G. STERN	2
CHEV. E. GINISTRELLI's b.c. SIGNORINO by Best Man out of Signorina	K. CANNON	3

Also ran:

Mr T. E. Liddiard's Silver Streak (4th) (B. Dillon); Mr J. Buchanan's Golden Measure (F. Rickaby); Mr A. Stedall's Leopold (J. Jarvis); Sir E. Vincent's Shah Jehan (O. Madden); Sir R. Waldie Griffith's Liao (W. Higgs); Mr R. H. Henning's Rouge Croix (M. Cannon).

9 ran.

Betting:

11–4 on Cicero; 4–1 Jardy; 33–1 Silver Streak; 50–1 Shah Jehan, Signorino, and Rouge Croix; 66–1 Liao; 100–1 Golden Measure; 200–1 Leopold.

Won by three parts of a length; a head between second and third.   2 m. 39⅖ s.
Winner trained by P. Peck at Exning.

1906

Spearmint, winner of the Derby in 1906, was a really good horse, and Danny Maher, who partnered him at Epsom, considered him the best that he ever rode with the possible exception of Bayardo.

Bred at the Sledmere Stud by Sir Tatton Sykes, Spearmint was a bay colt by Carbine out of Maid of the Mint, by Minting. Maid of the Mint, a half-sister to the Cesarewitch winner Wargrave, never ran. Carbine, a son of Musket, by Toxophilite, was bred in New Zealand and was one of the greatest horses ever to race in Australia, his finest performance being in the Melbourne Cup of 1890 which he won in record time from thirty-eight opponents, with 10 st. 5 lb. on his back and conceding fifty-three pounds to the runner-up! Carbine ran in forty-three races, and after a few seasons at the Stud in Australia, his owner, Mr Wallace, sold him for £13,000 to the Duke of Portland, who wanted a stallion at Welbeck that was unrelated to his own sires, St Simon, Ayrshire, Donovan, St Serf, and Raeburn. Mr Wallace was something of a character. Sitting at dinner next to Lady Hopetoun, wife of the Governor of Victoria, he suddenly exclaimed, 'Lady Hopetoun, I love you.' Lady Hopetoun was naturally slightly surprised, but Mr Wallace immediately added: 'I love you because you love old Carbine, and I love him, too.' Carbine got a lot of useful handicappers in England, but Spearmint was his only top-class winner. He lived to be twenty-nine.

A few weeks before the Doncaster Sales in 1904, Major Eustace Loder had visited the Sledmere Stud accompanied by his stud manager Mr Noble Johnson, a great expert on breeding matters and reputedly the finest judge of a horse in the whole of Ireland. Major Loder, not uncommonly known as 'Lucky Loder', was born in 1867 and served in the 12th Lancers for fifteen years. In his younger days he owned a number of useful jumpers, while his first important success on the flat was the Ascot Stakes, which Billow won for him in 1892. When Peter Purcell Gilpin moved his stable from Dorsetshire to Newmarket, Major Loder transferred his horses to that able Irishman's care, and it was Gilpin who trained for Major Loder the famous Pretty Polly, winner of the One Thousand Guineas, the Oaks, and the St Leger, and one of the outstanding fillies of this century. In 1913 Major Loder was Senior Steward at Epsom when Craganour was disqualified after winning the Derby on an objection lodged by the Stewards themselves. On his death his stud passed

369

to his nephew who, as Major Giles Loder of the Scots Guards, won the 1920 Derby with Spearmint's son Spion Kop.

Both Major Loder and Mr Noble Johnson took a very strong fancy to Spearmint and were determined to buy him. This they were able to do for a mere 300 guineas, Carbine's stock by then being in no great demand. No sooner had Spearmint reached Newmarket than the colt developed a fever that lasted for a good five months. Speaking of this illness after Spearmint's Derby victory, Gilpin remarked: 'The marvel is not that he should be worth thousands, but so much as half a sovereign.'

As a two-year-old Spearmint was nothing out of the ordinary. His first outing was the Great Foal Plate at the Lingfield Summer Meeting. The opposition was second-rate, but he ran very green and only won by a head from Succory. At Derby he was beaten three lengths by Colonel Hall-Walker's brilliant but unpredictable Black Arrow, and finally at Newmarket in the autumn he carried top weight into fourth place in the Richmond Nursery.

It is doubtful if many people at the end of 1905 gave Spearmint a moment's consideration as a prospective winner of the Derby. There were some pretty good two-year-olds that season, and in any case Spearmint was reckoned inferior to two others in his own stable—Major Loder's Admirable Crichton, a half-brother to Pretty Polly, and Sir Daniel Cooper's filly Flair, winner of the Middle Park Plate. As it happened Admirable Crichton failed to train on, but when Flair won the One Thousand Guineas with the utmost ease, it was decided that she alone was to represent the stable in the Derby, Spearmint being reserved for the Grand Prix at Longchamps. This plan, however, was shattered when Flair broke down badly a few days after her Guineas success. It was immediately decreed that Spearmint should run in the Derby, and so well did he work with Pretty Polly and the Cesarewitch winner Hammerkop, that within a few days his price came tumbling down from 20–1 to sixes.

The favourite for the Derby was Lally, owned by Captain W. Purefoy, the brains behind the famous Druids Lodge 'confederacy'. Lally, however, was by Amphion, whose stock were more noted for speed than stamina, and his ability to stay the distance was by no means certain. In the Newmarket Stakes Lally had only won by a short head from Malua with Gorgos, who had won the Two Thousand Guineas by inches from Sancy, a head away third. Spearmint was second favourite, while Malua, Sancy, and Gorgos were all well backed. At the time it was thought to be a moderate Derby field, but in fact it was well above the average standard. Among the losers, Troutbeck won the St Leger and every race he ran for that season bar the Derby; The White Knight won the Coronation Cup and two Gold Cups at Ascot;

Beppo won the Manchester Cup, while Radium won the Doncaster and Goodwood Cups and was a successful sire in France. His son Clarissimus sired the dams of two notable Grand Prix winners in Brantôme and Pharis, as well as the dam of Donatello II, the sire of Crepello.

The start was sensational as the favourite was very badly away and Dillon rode him so impetuously to make up the lost ground that the colt was beaten before half-way. Rounding the bend for home, Picton, ridden by Mr George Thursby, and Troutbeck were neck and neck, while Spearmint, prominent from the start, was close up third. Two furlongs out the three were virtually in line, but at the distance Picton held a fractional advantage and for a few strides it looked as if an amateur rider was going to win the Derby. However, as soon as Maher showed Spearmint the whip, Major Loder's colt immediately lengthened his stride and ran on to win in decisive style by a length and a half from Picton, with Troutbeck two lengths away third. The time, 2 m. 36⅘ s., easily beat the record established by Cicero.

Spearmint's only other race was the Grand Prix eleven days later. Cheered home by a strong English contingent, he won a thrilling race by a neck from Brisecoeur, thereby becoming the first English horse to win that event since his maternal grand-sire Minting won twenty years previously. There were great scenes of revelry that night, and in the Jardin de Paris a nephew of Major Loder danced a can-can with a senior member of the chorus, who was estimated to be well over fifty and to tip the scales at just over eighteen stone.

Shortly afterwards Spearmint developed leg trouble and retired to Major Loder's stud, Eyrefield Lodge, Co. Kildare, at a fee of 250 guineas. He was not an outstanding success, but besides the 1920 Derby winner Spion Kop, he got Royal Lancer, winner of the St Leger, and Zionist and Spelthorne, winners respectively of the Irish Derby and the Irish St Leger. He was also sire of that wonderful mare Plucky Liège, dam of Bois Roussel, winner of the Derby; Admiral Drake, winner of the Grand Prix; and also of Sir Gallahad III, a top-class racehorse and highly successful sire. Spearmint died in Ireland in 1924.

Peter Purcell Gilpin, trainer of Spearmint, was the son of a cavalry officer, Captain Peter Valentine Purcell, and he himself assumed the name of Gilpin when he married Miss Meux-Smith, who soon afterwards inherited the estate of her uncle, Sir Ralph Gilpin.

For some years Gilpin served in the 5th Lancers and was a successful amateur rider. After his marriage he started training a few miles from the Curragh and rapidly established his reputation. On moving to England he was equally successful and won the 1900 Cesarewitch with Clarehaven. Apart from Spearmint, Pretty

Polly, and Spion Kop, the most notable horse that he trained was Comrade, a twenty-five-guinea yearling that won the Grand Prix and the Prix de l'Arc de Triomphe. Always immaculately dressed, Gilpin was for years one of the most easily recognizable men on the racecourse. On his retirement in the nineteen twenties, the Clarehaven stable was carried on by his son Victor.

Sir George Thursby was born in 1870 and succeeded his half-brother in the baronetcy in 1920. Tall and slim, at any rate in his younger days he was 'the Fred Archer of the Amateurs', and is the only amateur to have ridden a placed horse in the Derby, a feat he achieved on two occasions. He was also second in the Two Thousand Guineas on Sir Archibald in 1908. By any standards he was a fine rider, and Danny Maher once remarked: 'It's lucky for some of us that Mr George doesn't turn pro.'

Thursby did not ride again after the First World War, his record on retirement being 202 winners from 827 mounts. He died in Scotland in 1941.

1906: Wednesday, 30 May . . . 284 Entries. £6,450.

MAJOR E. LODER's b.c. SPEARMINT by Carbine
out of Maid of the Mint   D. MAHER   I
MR J. L. DUGDALE's ch.c. PICTON by Orvieto
out of Hecuba   MR G. THURSBY   2
DUKE OF WESTMINSTER's b.c. TROUTBECK by Ladas
out of Rydal Mount   J. H. MARTIN   3

Also ran:

Mr Leopold de Rothschild's Radium (4th) (K. Cannon); H.M. King Edward VII's Nulli Secundus (H. Jones); Mr J. A. de Rothschild's Beppo (A. Templeman); Colonel W. Hall-Walker's Black Arrow (B. Lynham); Mr R. Dalgliesh's Buckminster (Wm Griggs); Mr Reid Walker's Dingwall (J. Rogers); Mr Arthur James's Gorgos (F. Rickaby); Lord Howard de Walden's His Eminence (M. Cannon); Captain W. B. Purefoy's Lally (B. Dillon); Mr E. L. Heinemann's Malua (H. Aylin); Mr Fairie's Plum Tree (W. Warne); Mr J. B. Joel's Prince William (H. Randall); Mr Leopold de Rothschild's Minos (C. Cannon); Mr W. Bass's Sancy (O. Madden); Mr E. A. Wigan's Sarcelle (W. Higgs); M. R. de Monbel's Storm (M. Henry); Mr G. Bird's Slipaway colt by Teufel (J. Markley); Colonel T. Y. L. Kirkwood's The White Knight (W. Halsey); Sir George Farrar's Frustrator (E. Wheatley).

22 ran.

Betting:

4–1 Lally; 6–1 Spearmint; 8–1 Malua and Sancy; 10–1 Gorgos; 100–7 Black Arrow; 18–1 Picton and His Eminence; 25–1 Beppo, The White Knight, Sarcelle, and Radium; 33–1 Troutbeck; 50–1 Nulli Secundus; 66–1 Storm, Buckminster, and Frustrator.

Won by a length and a half; two lengths between second and third.   2 m. 36⅘ s. Winner trained by P. P. Gilpin at Newmarket.

1907

Only two Irish-trained horses have won the Derby, Orby in 1907 and Hard Ridden in 1958. Orby was owned by Mr Richard Croker, who was born in Ireland in 1841 and emigrated to America as a child. Thick-set, rugged in features and more so in speech, self-opinionated and ruthless, he was a corrupt New York politician, 'the Boss of Tammany Hall', the decision to transfer himself and his ill-gotten fortune to England being made when matters at last got a bit too hot for him in the Land of the Free. Taking to the Turf, he entertained for some time the costly illusion that American horses must of necessity be greatly superior to the English thoroughbred, but eventually common sense prevailed and he founded the Glencairn Stud in Ireland where Orby was reared. Mrs Croker had social ambitions and used to give receptions at her house in Berkshire to which all the local nobility and gentry were invited. Mr Croker used to content himself on those occasions by poking his head round the drawing-room door, muttering 'How do, folks' without removing the in-evitable cigar from the corner of his mouth, then making himself scarce.

Orby, foaled at Wantage, was by Orme, sire of Flying Fox, out of Rhoda B., an American-bred mare by Hanover. Rhoda B. was imported as a yearling in 1896 and there were elements in her pedigree that would have rendered her ineligible for the Stud Book prior to a G.S.B. ruling of 1901. She was also the dam of Rhodora, winner of the One Thousand Guineas. At the stud Rhodora was incestuously mated with her half-brother Orby. The wretched object that resulted had to be cut away from her in pieces, and the unfortunate mare never really recovered from the ordeal.

A rangy, well-made chesnut colt with unusual length from hip to hock, Orby made his first racecourse appearance at Leopardstown in August. He had been very well galloped and started at 3–1 on, but could only finish third of six. On his second and final appearance of the season he was third of eight in the Railway Stakes at the Curragh, for which he again started favourite. As a three-year-old he had two outings before the Derby, the Earl of Sefton's Plate at Liverpool, and the Baldoyle Plate at Baldoyle. He won them both with considerable ease, and these two victories, coupled with persistent reports from Ireland that he was doing exceptionally well in his preparation, resulted in his being quite well backed for the Derby at 100–9. Few people, however, seriously entertained the idea that he could possibly beat Captain Greer's Gallinule colt Slieve Gallion, who had not only been a top-class two-year-old,

374

Sam winning the 1818 Derby; after H. Alken

but had won both the Craven Stakes and the Two Thousand Guineas very fluently. Slieve Gallion, ridden by Higgs, was favourite for the Derby at 13–8 on, second favourite being Major Loder's Galvani who had defeated Slieve Gallion in the Middle Park Plate the previous autumn.

Orby failed to impress the paddock critics at Epsom, who were inclined to find him rough compared to the best English standards, and lacking muscular development. Possibly the methods employed by his trainer were those best suited to the colt's constitution; a more orthodox preparation might have produced even better results.

The start was effected without incident. At the mile post the favourite went to the front, and at half-way he was two lengths clear of Bezonian, with Galvani, Orby, Earlston, and Wool Winder handily placed. Coming down the hill Wool Winder began to improve his position, but in doing so he collided sharply with another competitor. Madden virtually had to pull him up and he dropped back last.

Slieve Gallion was still in front when the straight was reached, but he did not stay the distance and two furlongs out he began to sprawl and veer to the right. Orby then took the lead, and coming to the distance the race seemed to be at his mercy, but then he, too, began to show signs of distress, changing his legs and hanging very badly to the right. Meanwhile Wool Winder was making up ground fast; he passed Slieve Gallion, who finished right under the stands, but gamely as he struggled he failed to get on terms with Orby, who won by a clear two lengths, with Slieve Gallion another half-length away third. There were scenes of uninhibited jubilation among the thousands of Irishmen present and raucous Hibernian revelry continued far on into the night. Johnny Reiff, Orby's rider, remarked with more truth than tact that the Derby competitors were a very moderate collection and there were several better three-year-olds in France. His comment was perhaps rather less dampening to enthusiasm than that of a jockey of more recent times, who, having won the Derby by a very considerable margin, observed to the beaming trainer: 'The others must be awful as ours ain't much!' Whether Orby really stayed a mile and a half is open to question: at any rate he had a bit more stamina than his opponents, with the exception of Wool Winder, who was distinctly unlucky.

Orby won the Irish Derby in a canter, but soon afterwards was last of four in a race at Liverpool. A veterinary surgeon examined him and prescribed rest. However, an attempt was made to train the colt for the St Leger, but he broke down completely and was retired to his owner's stud. The best horses he got were Grand Parade, winner of the 1919 Derby, and Diadem, winner of the One Thousand Guineas. Most of his stock were endowed with speed rather than stamina and the Orby male line exists today, not through Grand Parade, but through The Boss, who won six races worth £1,584. The Boss sired Sir Cosmo, who in turn sired that highly successful sprinting sire Panorama, while Golden Boss, another son of The Boss, sired Gold Bridge. Golden Boss was sold as a remount sire to America before Gold Bridge had proved himself the outstanding sprinter in Europe.

Croker's horses were originally trained by Charles Morton at Wantage, but when 'The Boss' transferred his racing and breeding interests to Ireland, he appointed Colonel Frederick McCabe as his trainer and racing manager.

Born in 1868, Colonel McCabe was a remarkable and versatile man, with original views on a great many subjects, including the training of racehorses. He had qualified as a doctor and in his youth he had attained some fame as a cross-country runner and cyclist. He gave up his practice in Dublin to serve as medical officer to the South Irish Horse in the South African War. On his return he began training a few horses at Sandyford, and had achieved a measure of success before Croker decided to employ him. In later years he had extensive commercial interests, and in addition owned and edited a number of publications in Ireland. He was eighty-six years of age when he died in 1954.

The colonel evidently continued his association with the South Irish Horse after the South African War was over. The regiment was in camp when Orby won the Derby, and the commanding officer received a telegram stating 'MEDICAL OFFICER AUTHORIZES THE ISSUE OF CHAMPAGNE TO ALL RANKS', a communication which resulted in some memorable scenes of celebration. On one occasion the colonel caused a sensation by lodging an objection after a horse of his had been beaten in a five-furlong race at Leopardstown, on the grounds that the course was not of the prescribed distance. It was then measured and found to be 111 yards short!

Wool Winder, who won the St Leger very easily, belonged to Colonel (later Brigadier) E. W. Baird of the 10th Hussars. A man of great personal charm and a fine all-round sportsman, Brigadier Baird had won the 1888 Grand National with his half-bred hunter Playfair. He had been a member of the Jockey Club for no fewer than sixty-four years when he died, aged ninety-two, in 1956. Slieve Gallion only ran once after the Derby, winning the St James's Palace Stakes at Ascot, and he was then exported to Austria for £15,000.

1907: Wednesday, 5 June . . . 278 Entries. £6,450.

MR R. CROKER's ch.c. ORBY by Orme
  out of Rhoda B.   J. REIFF   1
COLONEL E. W. BAIRD's b.c. WOOL WINDER by Martagon
  out of St Windeline   O. MADDEN   2
CAPTAIN GREER's bl.c. SLIEVE GALLION by Gallinule
  out of Reclusion   W. HIGGS   3

Also ran:

Lord Rosebery's Bezonian (4th) (D. Mahcr); Major E. Loder's Galvani (B. Dillon); Mr E. Dresden's Galleot (W. Halsey); Mr H. Bottomley's John Bull (J. Hare); Mr J. B. Joel's Earlston (H. Randall); Mr Abe Bailey's All Black (H. Blades).

9 ran.

Betting:

13–8 on Slieve Gallion; 7–1 Galvani; 9–1 Bezonian; 100–9 Orby and Wool Winder; 40–1 Earlston; 50–1 All Black and Galleot.

Won by two lengths; half a length between second and third.   2 m. 44 s.
Winner trained by Colonel McCabe at Glencairn, Co. Dublin.

1908

This year's Derby provided one of the most sensational results in the history of the race, the winner being the 100–1 outsider Signorinetta, a filly owned, bred, and trained by the Chevalier Ginistrelli. Furthermore, two days later Signorinetta won the Oaks, the first filly to bring off the double since Blink Bonny in 1857. These two victories administered a tremendous but by no means harmful shock to racing circles, and in particular to the professional element at Newmarket, where the Chevalier was regarded as a friendly, rather absurd little foreigner, whose activities were not to be taken too seriously.

The Chevalier had come to England from Italy in the eighteen eighties. He never quite absorbed the traditional local respect for Newmarket Heath, and on one occasion he had the immortal audacity to set up some posts for his own convenience. No sooner were they up than Mr Marriot, the Jockey Club's agent, had them down. They were up again the next day, and down they came the day after. 'Who does this Mr Marriot think he is?' asked the Chevalier in a very high state of indignation. 'Lord Durham, the Kaiser, and God Almighty rolled into one?'

On his arrival in England the Chevalier was accompanied by a mare called Star of Portici, by Heir at Law, a son of Newminster, out of Verbena, by the Flying Dutchman's half-brother De Ruyter. Rather surprisingly the Chevalier obtained for this unfashionably bred mare a nomination to St Simon, the resulting produce being a filly called Signorina. As a two-year-old Signorina won all her nine races, including the Middle Park Plate, and was the best of her age and sex that season. As a three-year-old she trailed off completely, but she found her form once again as a four-year-old, winning the Lancashire Plate, which was then a £10,000 race.

Signorina retired to the stud with the distinction of having won over £20,000 in stakes. For a long time afterwards, however, she was a sad disappointment to the Chevalier, as she was barren for her first ten seasons. At last she produced a colt by Best Man called Signorino, and the Chevalier's patience and his faith in the mare were fully justified, as Signorino proved a top-class colt, finishing second in the Two Thousand Guineas and third in the Derby in 1905. He was subsequently a very successful sire in Italy.

In 1904 Signorina was covered by Chaleureux, and the following spring, at eighteen years of age, she produced her second living foal, a bay or brown filly that was given the name of Signorinetta. Chaleureux by Goodfellow, a son of Barcaldine, out of a mare by John Davis, by Voltigeur, was an unfashionably bred nine-guinea sire that had started his career as a selling plater, later developing into a highly successful handicapper, his victories including the Cesarewitch, the Manchester November Handicap, and the Chesterfield Cup. It so happened that whenever Chaleureux was led out for his morning's exercise, he always passed the paddock where Signorina was grazing. The two seemed to form a warm attachment to each other, and the Chevalier, whose nomination to Cyllene that year had fallen through, decided to take a chance, based as he himself put it, 'on the boundless laws of sympathy and love'. Chaleureux, therefore, who was almost neglected by breeders, was selected as substitute for the great Cyllene. Chaleureux never got another top-class horse, and it says much for Signorina's quality that she was able to produce an outstanding filly by such a mediocre sire.

Signorinetta's two-year-old career was undistinguished. In her first five races she was unplaced on each occasion. Her sixth she won, beating five mediocre opponents in the Criterion Nursery at Newmarket. The following year she was well down the course in the One Thousand Guineas won by Mr Croker's Rhodora. Nor did she show to any better advantage in the Newmarket Stakes, in which she started at 25–1 and finished unplaced to St Wolf. The Chevalier, nevertheless, was undismayed, and determined to run her in the Derby. He continued to give her plenty of work over the full Derby distance, and although the touts, not surprisingly, continued to ignore her, he himself was sufficiently impressed by her progress to back her at 100–1, and he advised his somewhat sceptical friends at Newmarket to back her, too.

It was not a great Derby field by any means. Joint favourites were the American-bred Norman III, winner of the Two Thousand Guineas, and Mountain Apple, a good-looking and well tried colt by Persimmon. There was good money too, for the unattractively named French colt Sea Sick II, who had dead-heated for the Prix du Jockey Club, and also for Mr George Thursby's mount Sir Archibald, who had been second to Norman III in the Guineas.

Ridden with cool head and admirable judgement by W. Bullock, Signorinetta was sixth coming down the hill to Tattenham Corner. Half-way up the straight she took the lead from Mountain Apple, whose rider had made too much use of him. From that point the race was at her mercy and she won in the smoothest fashion possible by two lengths from the Duke of Portland's Primer, with Llangwm a neck away third. The time was considerably faster than that recorded by the 'Triple Crown' winner Rock Sand. For some little time the crowd was too dumbfounded to raise a cheer, but when the Chevalier, in a high state of excitement, which was excusable, and a panama hat, which was not, danced out on to the course to lead his filly in, he was given a reception that both he and the filly most thoroughly deserved.

Two days later, again ridden by Bullock, Signorinetta won the Oaks, a victory that was no doubt assisted by the fall of Rhodora. When the race was over the King sent for the Chevalier, congratulated him, and then led him to the front of the Royal Box, where they were both received with tumultuous cheering.

The rest of Signorinetta's racing career was a sad anti-climax. She was unplaced to Mr J. B. Joel's Your Majesty in the St Leger, and she was also unplaced in the Jockey Club Stakes and in a race at Newbury. Those three defeats completed her career. A rather mousy-coloured brown with length, scope, and liberty of action, she must have been a great staying mare at her best, and her victories at Epsom were all the more praiseworthy as the Chevalier had nothing else in his stable really suitable for her to work with. After her retirement from racing, she was bought for the stud by Lord Rosebery, but she made little lasting mark as a brood-mare. Her daughter Erycina, by Lemberg, bred four modest winners, the best of which was Clydesdale, winner of the Scottish Grand National as a six-year-old. Her colt by Son-in-Law, The Winter King, won four races on the flat and two over hurdles. Lord Rosebery retired him to the stud for a season or two at a fee of nineteen guineas and then sold him for a few hundred pounds. The Winter King then stood in Yorkshire, in France, and finally in Italy, and his fame, such as it is, rests solely on the one good horse that he got, Barneveldt, winner of the Grand Prix and sire of the war-time Derby winner Pont l'Evêque.

William Bullock was a member of a well-known sporting family in the north. His grandfather had been a trainer; his uncle rode Kettledrum to victory in the Derby of 1861; his brother Bertram was for many years a successful trainer, and another brother was a familiar figure in the coursing world up north. Signorinetta's great double may have brought William Bullock temporary fame, but the financial benefit was negligible, the Chevalier evidently holding the opinion that presents for jockeys were unnecessary. Bullock's last victory of note was on Leonard in the Northumberland Plate in 1933, but he rode work for Captain Elsey up till 1959.

1908: Wednesday, 3 June ... 291 Entries. £6,450.

CHEVALIER E. GINISTRELLI'S b. or br.f. SIGNORINETTA
    by Chaleureux out of Signorina   W. BULLOCK   1
DUKE OF PORTLAND'S b.c. PRIMER by St Simon
    out of Breviary   B. DILLON   2
MR BARCLAY WALKER'S b.c. LLANGWM by Missel Thrush
    out of Llangarren Lass   D. MAHER   3

Also ran:

Mr J. Buchanan's Mountain Apple (4th) (L. Lyne); H.M. King Edward VII's Perrier (H. Jones); Mr C. T. Pulley's Eaton Lad (Wm Griggs); Mr J. Byrne's Mercutio (W. Evans); Mr A. M. Simon's Moet (J. W. East); Mr A. Belmont's Norman III (O. Madden); Mr F. Gretton's Orphah (W. Higgs); Colonel W. Hall-Walker's Royal Realm (T. Price); Colonel W. Hall-Walker's White Eagle (H. Randall); Colonel W. Hall-Walker's Pom (L. Hewitt); Mr L. Robinson's Rushcutter (F. Wootton); Mr W. K. Vanderbilt's Sea Sick II (G. Stern); Mr A. F. Basset's Sir Archibald (Mr G. Thursby); Duke of Westminster's Vamose (W. Halsey); Mr J. R. Hatmaker's Azote (C. Maslin).

18 ran.

Betting:

11–2 Norman III and Mountain Apple; 7–1 Sea Sick II; 100–12 Sir Archibald; 100–9 White Eagle; 100–8 Perrier and Llangwm; 100–7 Vamose; 25–1 Mercutio and Orphah; 33–1 Pom; 40–1 Primer and Rushcutter; 50–1 Royal Realm and Eaton Lad; 66–1 Moet; 100–1 Signorinetta, 200–1 Azote.

Won by two lengths; a neck between second and third.   2 m. 39⅘ s.
Winner trained by the owner at Newmarket.

1909

After Diamond Jubilee's great victories in 1900, the Royal Stud went through a very unsuccessful phase. Winners were few and far between, and by 1907 things had come to such a pitch that the King agreed to lease half a dozen yearlings from Colonel Hall-Walker, owner of the Tully Stud, Co. Kildare. Colonel Hall-Walker, later Lord Wavertree, was a somewhat eccentric individual. A fervent astrologer, he observed the course of the stars with the closest attention, and all important decisions were based on what the stars appeared to foretell. Astrology, through the medium of the horoscope, was applied to the racing and mating of his horses, but the stars let him down badly when they advised him to sell Prince Palatine, subsequently winner of the St Leger and two Ascot Gold Cups, for 2,000 guineas. The Colonel eventually presented Tully—now the site of the Irish National Stud—to the British Government as a National Stud, while it was his flow of eloquent persuasiveness that induced the Aga Khan to take up racing on a princely scale.

The yearlings arrived at Marsh's stable at the end of August and Marsh at once selected Minoru as the pick. A bay with black points, Minoru was a trifle light about his middle piece and was possibly a little bit light of bone as well, but he was full of quality and vitality, with a beautiful head, perfect shoulders, and a fine length of rein. His sire was Cyllene, his dam Mother Siegel, by Hermit's son Friar's Balsam, who had been an exceptionally brilliant two-year-old, out of a Galopin mare. The great-grand-dam of Mother Siegel was a full sister to Hermit, while Grand Marnier, Mother Siegel's sister, was grand-dam of the 1919 Derby winner Grand Parade.

Minoru had the kindest of dispositions and was a pleasure to train, but his two-year-old career was somewhat disappointing. He began well enough by winning the Great Surrey Foal Stakes at Epsom, but he was beaten by Louviers in the Coventry Stakes and by Battle Axe in the July Stakes, while he could only finish third in both the Hopeful Stakes and the New Nursery at Newmarket. He certainly did not give the impression of being a future winner of the Derby, and there seemed little likelihood of his ever beating the Manton colt Bayardo, who had won all his seven races and was rated twenty-two pounds his superior in the Free Handicap.

At the end of 1908 Marsh decided that it was pointless to train Minoru for the classics, but the colt did so well during the winter that he began to change his opinion, and a splendid gallop just before the 1909 flat-racing season started showed beyond doubt that Minoru had improved to a quite remarkable extent. The colt's first appearance as a three-year-old was in the one-mile Greenham Stakes at Newbury. Lord Marcus Beresford came to see him before the race and was plainly somewhat sceptical of Marsh's enthusiasm. 'Well,' Lord Marcus said, 'he's certainly improved, but seven stone four in the Stewards Cup is more like his class.' Carrying 9 st. 10 lb., Minoru then proceeded to beat the odds-on favourite Valens and to demonstrate beyond doubt that he was a serious contender for the classics.

In the meantime Alec Taylor found it impossible to get Bayardo to his liking. It was a cold, dry spring and Bayardo, who suffered from shelly feet, hated the firm ground. He loathed, too, the searing east winds that blew day after day across the Wiltshire Downs. Taylor did not want to run him in the Guineas, but Mr 'Fairie'— the 'nom de course' of Mr A. W. Cox, who liked his own way and neither sought nor expected popularity—insisted that his colt should take the field.

Ridden by Herbert Jones, Minoru won the Guineas convincingly, while Bayardo finished unplaced. Some critics were convinced that Marsh had brought Minoru to his peak at too early a stage of the season, and Mr William Allison, the well-known racing correspondent, said outright that no man breathing could keep Minoru fit for the Derby after winning the Greenham with him so early in the spring. Marsh, however, fully realized that Minoru did not require an orthodox Derby preparation. He gave the colt a very easy time of it, and Minoru came to Epsom as well as he ever was in his life. Meanwhile Bayardo suddenly started to thrive about a fortnight before the race. Alec Taylor was hopeful, but in his heart of hearts he knew the time was too short for the colt to be really at his best.

Favourite for the Derby, but with no outstanding qualifications for that position, was the American-bred Sir Martin. He had been bought for 15,000 guineas by Mr Louis Winans specially to win the Derby and was trained by Joe Cannon, a charming and able man, but never one of fortune's favourites. Minoru was second favourite, while Bayardo and Valens were well backed, and so was Louviers, who had been third in the Two Thousand Guineas and had then won the Newmarket Stakes.

The morning was grey and wet, but the weather gradually improved and the crowd on the Downs looked bigger than ever. The race proved both sensational and desperately exciting. Coming down the hill, where Minoru was ideally placed, Sir Martin either struck into the horse in front or was galloped into from behind. At all events he fell, and in so doing he interfered with Bayardo, who was tracking him and who had to be snatched up. Once the straight was reached, there was a desperate struggle between Louviers and Minoru. Louviers, who held a narrow lead, came slightly away from the rails and Jones at once slipped Minoru through the gap.

Minoru led for a few strides, but Louviers drew level again and approaching the final furlong he led by the shortest of heads. With a hundred yards to go Minoru made a final supreme effort and seized the advantage, but Louviers would not give in. With wonderful courage he rallied again and was in front two strides past the post. It was Minoru's head, though, that had been in front at the one point that really mattered, and after an agonizing pause of a few seconds, a gigantic cheer went up when Minoru's number was hoisted into the frame. William the Fourth and Valens both ran splendidly and finished on the heels of the first two.

The scenes that followed rivalled the jubilations that followed Persimmon's victory. The crowd surged over the course, and it was with the greatest difficulty that Marsh reached Minoru to conduct him to the weighing-in enclosure, where the King, accompanied by the Prince of Wales, stood waiting to lead his colt in. As King Edward grasped the leading rein the cheering broke out once more, and when the 'All Right' was called, a well-known music-hall singer started up 'God Save the King', which was taken up first in all the enclosures and then by the thousands on the Downs. It was a great tribute to a King whose defects of character have been harshly emphasized by radical historians who choose to overlook the loyalty and affection in which he was held by the mass of the English people. Before the next Derby was run the King was dead.

Minoru won the St James's Palace Stakes at Ascot and the Sussex Stakes at Goodwood, but his action was beginning to go by the time the St Leger was run, and in that race he was no match for Bayardo, finishing a moderate fourth of seven. A bad bump he received at one stage of the contest did not really affect the ultimate result. He finished the season satisfactorily by winning the Free Handicap with top weight, but he was all out at the finish to beat Electra by a neck.

As a four-year-old Minoru developed eye trouble and he was retired after running unplaced in the City and Suburban. A fortnight after the Epsom Spring Meeting Edward VII died and Minoru was returned to Colonel Hall-Walker, who sent him to stand at Tully at a fee of ninety-eight pounds. He was exported to Russia two seasons later, but before he went he was mated with Gondolette, dam of Dolabella, who bred Big Game's dam Myrobella, and also of the 1924 Derby winner Sansovino. The produce of this union was the famous mare Serenissima, dam of the St Leger winner Tranquil, the Gold Cup winner Bosworth, and also of Selene, winner of over £14,000 and dam of Hyperion; of Sickle and Pharamond, both successful sires in America; and of All Moonshine, dam of Mossborough, the Champion Sire in 1958. Minoru disappeared during the Russian Revolution. There was a story that he and the 1913 Derby winner Aboyeur had been harnessed to a cart and driven from the suburbs of Moscow to Novorossiysk. There they are said to have been evacuated with the British Military Mission and sent to Serbia, where they ended their days. The identity of the two stallions taken, however, has never been satisfactorily confirmed.

The great piece of luck in Minoru's career was finding Bayardo below his best in both the Guineas and the Derby. After Epsom Bayardo went from strength to strength, and when he finally retired he had won twenty-two of his twenty-five races, including the St Leger and the Ascot Gold Cup. He was by that moderate racehorse and highly successful sire Bay Ronald, by Hampton, out of Galicia, dam of the 1910 Derby winner Lemberg. During his brief career at the stud he sired the Derby winners Gainsborough and Gay Crusader, as well as Bayuda, winner of the Oaks. It was a great loss to breeders when he died of thrombosis at the age of eleven.

Louviers, who put up such a gallant fight in the Derby, was not a success as a sire in this country and was eventually exported to Russia.

1909: Wednesday, 26 May . . . 299 Entries. £6,450.

H.M. KING EDWARD VII's b.c. MINORU by Cyllene out of Mother Siegel	H. JONES	1
MR W. RAPHAEL's b.c. LOUVIERS by Isinglass out of St Louvaine	G. STERN	2
LORD MICHELHAM's ch.c. WILLIAM THE FOURTH by William the Third out of Lady Sevington	W. HIGGS	3

Also ran:

Lord Carnarvon's Valens (4th) (F. Wootton); Mr C. S. Newtown's Sandbath (R. Keeble); Mr Mills's Prester Jack (W. Saxby); Mr W. Raphael's Brookland's (D. Blackburn); Mr J. Buchanan's Diamond Stud (W. Halsey); The Duke of Portland's Phaleron (W. Earl); Mr 'Fairie's' Bayardo (D. Maher); Mr J. Barrow's Strickland (Wm Griggs); Mr H. G. Fenwick's St Ninian (C. Trigg); Mr J. B. Joel's The Story (Walter Griggs); Mr A. H. Ledlie's Electric Boy (W. Bray); Mr L. Winan's Sir Martin (J. H. Martin).

15 ran.

Betting:

3–1 Sir Martin; 7–2 Minoru; 9–2 Bayardo; 8–1 Valens; 9–1 Louviers; 20–1 Phaleron and William the Fourth; 40–1 The Story; 50–1 Diamond Stud and Strickland; 66–1 Electric Boy, Sandbath, St Ninian, and Prester Jack.

Won by a short head; half a length between second and third.   2 m. 42⅖ s.
Winner trained by R. Marsh at Newmarket.

1910

Mr A. W. Cox, who raced as 'Mr Fairie', was an uncompromising Australian who had made a fortune in the Broken Hill Silver Mines. Brusque in manner and careless of public opinion, he was an exceptional judge of Havana cigars and old brandy. He was undoubtedly unlucky not to have won the Derby in 1909 with Bayardo, but recompense was soon forthcoming and he won the race the very next year with Lemberg, a half-brother to Bayardo by Cyllene. Galicia, who bred these two great horses in successive years, was by St Simon's sire Galopin, who was twenty-six years of age when she was foaled. She also bred Kwang-Su, second in the Two Thousand Guineas and the Derby, and Silesia, dam of the Oaks winner My Dear and grand-dam of the brilliant Picaroon, who won over £13,000 and unfortunately died when in training.

Lemberg, taller and leggier than Bayardo, was a brilliant two-year-old, winning six of his seven races, including the New Stakes, the Chesterfield Stakes, the Rous Memorial Stakes at both Goodwood and Newmarket, the Middle Park Plate, and the Dewhurst Plate. His only defeat was in the Champagne Stakes at Doncaster. He had been coughing beforehand, and could only finish third to Lord Rosebery's Neil Gow, who was to meet him in more than one stirring encounter in the future.

Lemberg's first race the following season was the Two Thousand Guineas. Ridden by Bernard Dillon, he was beaten a short head after a great battle by Neil Gow, on whom Danny Maher rode one of his finest races. He returned to Manton none the worse for his exertions and continued to please Alec Taylor. On 28 May he won his Derby trial comfortably, beating the three-year-old fillies Maid of Corinth and Rosedrop, who both received three pounds. Maid of Corinth, a daughter of Sceptre, was potentially brilliant, but too nervous to show her proper form on the racecourse. Rosedrop was to complete a fine double for the Manton stable by winning the Oaks the following week.

Neil Gow, by Marco out of Chelandry, was a beautiful colt except for rather weak hocks. His temperament, though, was unreliable, and he gave his trainer Percy Peck a good many anxious moments. Peck's stables at Exning belonged to Lord Durham and adjoined Lord Durham's place, Harraton House. That year a vast colony of rooks had established themselves in the elms that stood round Harraton House and the stables, and their chatter in the early hours of the morning was driving

Lord Durham to distraction. He gave the order, therefore, for their ruthless expulsion. Peck was extremely upset when he heard of this, believing that ill-fortune would descend on those responsible for forcing the rooks to desert their nests. The day that Lemberg won his gallop, Neil Gow sprang a curb. 'There you are, my lord,' said Peck. 'This comes of clearing out the rooks.' Neil Gow missed his final gallop and could only walk on Sunday and Monday. He was just short of his best, therefore, when he left for Epsom on Tuesday.

Despite the sunshine, it was rather a sombre Derby Day. Edward VII had died the previous month and the country was still in mourning. Black clothes predominated in the enclosures, the Royal Box was closed, there was no Royal Standard flying from the Private Stand. Above all, the usual air of gaiety was missing, even though the attendance seemed up to the usual standard. Lemberg, 7–4, and Neil Gow, 11–4, were backed almost to the exclusion of the other thirteen runners. Lord Derby's big colt Swynford had not yet reached his peak and was on offer at 50–1.

There was a fifteen-minute delay at the start, but both Lemberg and the highly strung Neil Gow were well away. Greenback was soon in front and close behind him came Charles O'Malley, Wildflower II, and Admiral Hawke. Greenback still led at Tattenham Corner, but Lemberg was making up ground very smoothly and appeared to be going the easier of the two. A quarter of a mile from home Lemberg delivered his challenge and went to the front. At that point it looked as if he was going to win with ease, but Greenback rallied in the gamest manner possible and drew level again. Lemberg was clearly tiring, but he still had a bit in reserve and, with Dillon riding him for all he was worth, he won by a neck. Charles O'Malley was two lengths away third, Neil Gow fourth, and Ulster King, who had lost a lot of ground at the start, close up fifth. There was, of course, a valid excuse for Neil Gow's failure, while Swynford was badly struck into and the skin was ripped off his leg from the hock to the fetlock joint. The time, 2 m. $35\frac{1}{5}$ s., established a new record for the race.

Lemberg won the St James's Palace Stakes at Ascot, but in heavy going was unplaced behind Nuage in the Grand Prix. That defeat, however, was excusable. He was clumsily shod by a French blacksmith, and in addition Maher, who partnered him on this occasion, notoriously detested both riding in France and the militant tactics of some of the leading French jockeys. In the Eclipse Stakes at Sandown Lemberg had another desperate battle with his old rival Neil Gow, who by then had fully recovered. The two ran wonderfully true to the Guineas form, and the result of a magnificent race was a dead-heat.

Neil Gow broke down in his St Leger preparation and never ran again, while Greenback, a small horse but a very game one, developed a fever and had to be scratched. The path, therefore, seemed nicely clear for Lemberg, but for once Maher rode an extremely bad race and got hopelessly shut in. The winner was Swynford, who had improved out of all knowledge since the Derby. Ridden by young Frank Wootton, who could go to scale without difficulty at 7 st. 4 lb., he hung very badly in the closing stages and was very nearly caught on the post by Mr J. de Rothschild's Bronzino, who came with a tremendous run in the final hundred yards. Lemberg, with Maher standing up in the stirrups, was a length and a half away third.

Lemberg showed not the slightest hint of staleness in the autumn and he finished the season in style, winning the Jockey Club, Champion, and Lowther Stakes at Newmarket, and the Sandown Park Foal Stakes. The following season he met Swynford on three occasions. He won a slow-run race for the Coronation Cup in which waiting tactics were mistakenly adopted on Lord Derby's colt. In both the Princess of Wales's Stakes and the Eclipse Stakes Swynford was permitted to stride out as freely as he pleased, and ridden like that he showed beyond doubt that he was the better four-year-old of the two.

Lemberg retired to the stud at a fee of 250 guineas. His record on the whole was satisfactory rather than brilliant, but he headed the list in 1922. The best of his stock were Lemonora (Grand Prix de Paris), Ellangowan (Two Thousand Guineas), and Taj Mah (One Thousand Guineas.) At one time his fee reached 400 guineas, but later it receded to half that sum.

Swynford broke a fetlock bone late in his four-year-old season, but luckily it was possible to save him for the stud. By John o' Gaunt out of the Oaks winner Canterbury Pilgrim he got the Derby winner Sansovino, two St Leger winners in Tranquil and Keysoe, and an Oaks winner in Saucy Sue. The most important of all his stock, though, was Blandford, a great sire, whose sons Trigo, Blenheim, Windsor Lad, and Bahram won the Derby.

Charles O'Malley, third in the Derby, was beaten a neck in the Gold Cup the following year. He was sire of Malva, dam of Blenheim, winner of the Derby in 1930, and dam also of King Salmon, runner-up to Hyperion in the Derby of 1933.

Alec Taylor, the 'Wizard of Manton', was one of the greatest trainers of this century. His grandfather had trained at Manton, and so had his father, 'Old Alec', who prepared Sefton there to win the Derby in 1878. When 'Old Alec' died in 1894, he left Manton to 'Young Alec' and his half-brother Tom. The two brothers worked in partnership, not altogether successfully, till 1902 when 'Young Alec' assumed entire charge of the Manton property.

Alec Taylor was the most patient of men and, regarding horses as mere babies until they were three, he was not nearly as hard on them as his father, who was always reputed to give the Manton yearlings a two-mile gallop before Christmas!

Most of Taylor's patrons were rich men who could well afford to wait, and it must be said that their patience was frequently and handsomely rewarded. The list of famous races that the Manton horses won is not only notable for its length, but also for the small proportion of two-year-old events that it includes.

Though Taylor never won the Epsom Derby again after Lemberg's victory, he won two war-time substitute Derbys with Gay Crusader and Gainsborough, while he had no fewer than five runners-up in the Derby after the First World War, four of them belonging to Lord Astor. A bachelor, dignified, frugal, and reserved, Alec Taylor left £595,790 when he died in 1943 in his eighty-first year.

Bernard Dillon, who rode Lemberg at Epsom, died penniless in 1941 at the age of fifty-four. Born in Ireland, he was brought to this country by Captain Purefoy and apprenticed to Jack Fallon at Druids Lodge. His first ride over here was in 1901, his last in 1911. Brilliant at his best, he was always liable to be erratic, particularly towards the close of his brief career. He won the One Thousand Guineas on Flair in 1906 and on Electra in 1909, but there is little doubt that the finest race he rode was to win the Grand Prix on Spearmint in 1906. He was associated with Pretty Polly in some of her races, and always said she was by far the best animal he ever rode. In 1913 he married Marie Lloyd, the famous music-hall artist. In later years he operated in a small way as a tipster, and it is probably kindest to employ that convenient old cliché 'his own worst enemy' and leave it at that.

1910: Wednesday, 1 June . . . 371 Entries. £6,450.

MR 'FAIRIE'S' b.c. LEMBERG by Cyllene
out of Galicia — B. DILLON — 1

LORD VILLIERS'S b.c. GREENBACK by St Frusquin
out of Evergreen — F. TEMPLEMAN — 2

MR A. P. CUNLIFFE'S b.c. CHARLES O'MALLEY
by Desmond out of Goody Twoshoes — S. DONOGHUE — 3

Also ran:

Lord Rosebery's Neil Gow (4th) (D. Maher); Mr W. M. Cazalet's San Antonio (H. Jones); Mr E. A. Wigan's Ulster King (G. Stern); Mr St Aubyn's Cardinal Beaufort (C. Trigg); Major E. Loder's Admiral Hawke (W. Saxby); Colonel W. Hall-Walker's Glazebrook (A. Templeman); Lord Derby's Swynford (B. Lynham); Mr J. J. Bell-Irving's Rokeby (Wm Griggs); Mr J. Wallis's General Botha (C. Foy); Mr D. McCalmont's Malpas (H. Randall); Mr J. B. Joel's Wildflower II (Walter Griggs); Mr H. S. Gray's Gog (F. Wells).

15 ran.

Betting :

7–4 Lemberg; 11–4 Neil Gow; 100–8 Admiral Hawke, Ulster King, and Green-back; 33–1 Charles O'Malley; 40–1 Rokeby; 50–1 Swynford and Cardinal Beaufort; 66–1 Glazebrook and Malpas.

Won by a neck; two lengths between second and third.   2 m. 35⅕ s.
Winner trained by A. Taylor at Manton.

1911

Mr J. B. Joel, an extremely shrewd man of humble origin who accumulated a vast fortune in South Africa towards the end of the last century, won the Derby on two occasions, with Sunstar in 1911 and with Humorist in 1921. Both Sunstar and Humorist were colts of exceptional courage that triumphed under grave physical disabilities. Neither ran again after Epsom.

Most Derby winners are by horses that have won or been placed in top-class races of a mile and a half or more. Sunstar was by a sprinter that had gone in his wind, while both his sire and his dam had competed in selling races. His sire Sundridge, by Amphion, rose from Selling Plates to become a really good sprinter, winning sixteen races worth over £6,000. He retired to the stud at a nine-guinea fee, but lived to become Champion Sire. Besides Sunstar he got Jest, winner of the One Thousand Guineas and the Oaks and dam of Humorist; Sun Worship, dam of the St Leger and Gold Cup winner Solario; and Sun Briar and Sunreigh, who both exercised considerable influence on bloodstock breeding in America. Sunstar's dam, Doris, was by Loved One, sire of the famous mare Gondolette, dam of Sansovino and great-grand-dam of Hyperion. Doris herself was little more than a pony and never rose above Selling Plates. She was originally owned by Mr 'Solly' Joel, who did not think very much of her and let his brother have her for nothing. Besides producing Sunstar, she also bred Princess Dorrie, winner of the One Thousand Guineas and the Oaks.

Charles Morton, private trainer to Mr Joel, took a great liking to Sunstar as soon as the colt entered his stable, but it was some little time before he realized that Sunstar had classic possibilities. As a two-year-old Sunstar's form was good rather than brilliant. He met with a number of reverses, but won the International Plate at Kempton Park and the Exeter Stakes at Newmarket, while in the autumn he put up his most promising performance by dead-heating for the Hopeful Stakes at Newmarket with Borrow, a very fast two-year-old that later won the Middle Park Plate.

Sunstar wintered exceptionally well and developed into a strikingly handsome colt. By the early spring Morton had come to believe that Sunstar was something out of the ordinary, and his opinion was confirmed on Good Friday morning when in Mr Joel's presence and over the severe Farringdon Road gallop, Sunstar came right away from a number of thoroughly reliable trial horses that included that wonderful old handicapper Dean Swift, as well as Lycaon, subsequently third in the Two Thousand Guineas. From this moment it was clear that it would take an exceptional horse to get the better of Sunstar in the classics.

Ridden by the very able French jockey George Stern, who had never set eyes on the colt till he rode him that afternoon, Sunstar won the Two Thousand Guineas very easily from Lord Derby's Stedfast and his own stable companion Lycaon. A fortnight later he won the Newmarket Stakes. Some critics were unimpressed by the manner in which this last victory was achieved, but Stern assured Morton that the colt had merely run lazily and in fact had a great deal in hand. Everything now seemed safely set for victory at Epsom.

It was a very dry spring and the Wantage gallops had become extremely hard, a fact that caused Morton considerable worry as Sunstar was a red-hot favourite for the Derby and Mr Joel and his friends had backed him to win a fortune. Eight days before the Epsom Meeting started the blow fell. Sunstar did a ten furlong gallop and pulled up so lame that he could hardly put a foot to the ground. He had strained a suspensory ligament. The other horses were some distance away and Morton at once got hold of the lad who was riding Sunstar, promising him a generous present if he kept his mouth shut, nothing, or worse than nothing, if he talked. He then rang up Mr Joel, the one crumb of comfort that he offered being the fact that Sunstar was exceptionally fit and might still run provided the actual lameness could be got rid of. Mr Joel, bearing in mind the public money on the horse and no doubt his own bets as well, decided that no effort must be spared to get Sunstar to the post. 'I'll do my best,' Morton said, 'but you must realize this will be his last race; he will never run again.'

By skilled treatment Morton succeeded in dispersing the lameness but inevitably news of the mishap had leaked out, and even when it was certain that Sunstar would run, the most extraordinary stories were in circulation. It was commonly said that he had been got at by bookmakers, who could not afford to let him win. There was also a rumour, which a number of normally intelligent persons affected to believe, of a plot to put George Stern over the rails on the descent to Tattenham Corner. Poor Morton was almost at his wits' end with worry and, to cap everything, he had a heavy fall on the way to the course and injured his shoulder so severely that he was unable to saddle his colt.

Despite his mishap and the stories, Sunstar was favourite at 13–8. Second favourite was Mr Leopold de Rothschild's Pietri, who had beaten Sunstar the year before in the Champagne Stakes, while Lord Derby's pair, King William and Stedfast, were well backed at 10–1 and 100–8 respectively. There was little between the two judging from their work at home, but Frank Wootton elected to ride King William.

It was a close, sultry day and there was a large, noisy, and somewhat unruly crowd round the starting-gate. Stedfast got thoroughly worked up and, as the tapes rose he whipped round, losing the better part of a hundred yards. Sunstar negotiated the first half-mile, run uphill, without mishap and from then on it was just a question of keeping him on his legs in order to win. There was one terrible moment when he faltered ominously below the distance, but Stern gave him a tap with the whip and he responded at once to win by two lengths from Stedfast, who had come on the wide outside and made up an immense amount of ground, with Royal Tender a good four lengths away third. Sunstar was dead lame when he pulled up and could hardly walk to the paddock. Morton had been quite right; the Derby winner never ran again. He must have been a horse of quite exceptional courage to have won as he did.

Sunstar retired to his owner's stud at Childwick Bury, St Albans, where his record was a good one although he was never Champion Sire. Altogether his stock won 440 races worth over £229,000. Among his notable winners were Buchan, second in the Derby in 1919 and Champion Sire in 1927; Craig an Eran, winner of the Two Thousand Guineas, second in the Derby, and sire of April the Fifth and Admiral Drake; Alan Breck, a very successful sire in the Argentine; and Galloper Light, who, like Admiral Drake, won the Grand Prix de Paris. He was twice Champion Sire of brood mares and died at the age of eighteen. At one stage in his career there was a rumpus among breeders about the very large number of mares he was permitted to cover. He was an exceptionally virile horse, though, and his exertions did him no harm.

It is arguable that Stedfast would have won the Derby had he got off on even terms. He was undoubtedly a really good three-year-old and won his next eight races in succession, including the St James's Palace Stakes and the Jockey Club Stakes. He did not run in the St Leger, which Prince Palatine won very easily from Lycaon. A big, slashing chesnut, Stedfast won twenty races and over £26,000 in stakes, but with the exception of the Oaks winner Brownhylda, his stud record was very mediocre.

George Stern was born in France of English parents and was bi-lingual. He was fully the equal of any rider of his day and no one rode a more powerful finish than he did. He could look after himself under any circumstances, and any militant tactics employed against him were liable to be repaid with considerable interest.

Mr Jack Barnato Joel was born in 1862 and died in 1940. He was a nephew of Mr Barney Barnato, who became a millionaire in South Africa in double-quick time, and when Barnato's interests got too big for him to manage on his own, he sent for Jack and 'Solly' Joel, who rapidly became millionaires, too.

At the close of the century Mr Joel returned to England and registered his colours, black jacket, scarlet cap, in 1900. The following year he engaged Charles Morton as his private trainer, and a very successful partnership it proved, Mr Joel winning eleven classic races between 1903 and 1921. In fact he won almost every important race in the *Calendar* bar the Gold Cup, which always eluded him. He was leading owner in 1908, leading owner and breeder in 1913, and in 1914 as well. He created a great sensation in racing circles by his purchase of Prince Palatine in 1913 for £45,000. It is probable that his final race, the Goodwood Cup, in which he was beaten by Magic, broke Prince Palatine's heart. Owing to foot trouble he was not really fit to run, and towards the finish he was staggering from utter exhaustion. He was a sad failure as a sire. In his younger days at least, Mr Joel betted very heavily and one of his biggest wins was when his hurdler Black Plum won the Imperial Cup at Sandown. Mr Joel's son, Mr H. J. Joel, has carried on the stud at Childwick Bury, which his father bought from Sir Blundell Maple, and today he is one of the best-liked and most respected members of the Jockey Club.

Charles Morton knew every aspect of the trainer's art. He learnt the business from Tom Parr, who had trained for Admiral Rous and who in Morton's opinion was the finest trainer and best judge of a horse he ever met. Before he was employed by Mr Joel, Morton had trained for Mr 'Abington' Baird and Mr 'Bob' Sievier among numerous other patrons. Neat in dress, quiet in speech and manner, he believed in personal supervision in his stable down to the smallest detail and no owner could have had a more loyal or conscientious servant. He retired in 1924 and was succeeded as Mr Joel's trainer by Charles Peck. He was over eighty years of age when he died at Brighton in 1936.

1911: Wednesday, 31 May . . . 363 Entries. £6,450.

MR J. B. JOEL's br.c. SUNSTAR by Sundridge out of Doris	G. STERN	1
LORD DERBY's ch.c. STEDFAST by Chaucer out of Be Sure	B. LYNHAM	2
CAPTAIN F. FORESTER's b.c. ROYAL TENDER by Persimmon out of Tender and True	S. DONOGHUE	3

Also ran:

Mr 'Fairie's' Phryxus (4th) (C. Trigg); Mr L. Winan's Adam Bede (B. Dillon); Mr J. Musker's Alan Melton (J. Thompson); Mr H. P. Whitney's All Gold (J. H. Martin); Mr J. A. de Rothschild's Atmah (F. Fox); Mr R. Mills's Chely colt by Ayrshire (E. Piper); Mr D. McCalmont's Bachelor's Hope (J. Musse); Mr J. F. Hallick's Bannockburn (F. Templeman); Lord Derby's Bridge of Allan (F. Winter); Mr L. Neumann's Cellini (Walter Griggs); Major H. Cumming's Duke of Lancaster

(W. Earl); Mr H. P. Nickalls's Eton Boy (W. Saxby); Sir R. Waldie Griffith's Helicon (F. Rickaby); Mr R. M. Dale's Kel d'Or (A. Templeman); Lord Derby's King William (F. Wootton); Mr H. J. King's Longboat (H. Jones); Mr F. Gretton's Maaz (W. Higgs); Mr G. Barclay's Normint (S. Walkington); Mr L. de Rothschild's Pietri (D. Maher); Mr W. M. G. Singer's Royal Eagle (J. Clark); Mr N. de Szemere's Sobieski (F. Taral); Lord Carnarvon's Sydmonton (H. Randall); Mr F. Alexander's Zorzal (Wm Griggs).

26 ran.

Betting:

13–8 Sunstar; 7–1 Pietri; 10–1 King William; 100–8 Stedfast; 100–7 Cellini; 100–6 Phryxus; 22–1 Bachelor's Hope; 25–1 Royal Tender and Sydmonton; 33–1 Eton Boy and Atmah; 40–1 Adam Bede; 50–1 Maaz and Bannockburn; 66–1 Royal Eagle, Sobieski, All Gold, Longboat, Helicon, and Zorzal; 100–1 Alan Melton; 300–1 Normint, Chely's colt, and Bridge of Allan.

Won by two lengths; four lengths between second and third.   2 m. 36⅘ s.
Winner trained by C. Morton at Wantage.

1912

Louviers, belonging to Mr Walter Raphael, a well-known and extremely rich London financier, was beaten a short head by King Edward VII's Minoru in the Derby of 1909. The judge's decision in favour of Minoru had been a controversial one, and backers of Louviers were not the only persons who felt very strongly that the verdict was incorrect. However, Mr Raphael did not have to wait long for compensation. Three years later he won the race with his grey filly Tagalie, ridden by Johnny Reiff and trained by Dawson Waugh.

Tagalie was the fifth filly to win the Derby since its inception and only the second grey of either sex, the previous grey winner being Gustavus in 1821. In the early part of this century greys were extremely rare on the English racecourse, but their number and quality increased tremendously following the importation in 1910 of the grey French-bred stayer Roi Hérode to the Straffan Stud, Co. Kildare. Roi Hérode sired The Tetrarch, the fastest horse ever seen on the English Turf, and although The Tetrarch's stud career was curtailed owing to his reluctance to fulfil his duties, his influence was considerable, while his son Tetratema, winner of the Two Thousand Guineas, proved a highly successful sire.

Bred by her owner, Tagalie was on the small side and noticeably back at the knee. Her sire was Cyllene—she was the last of his four Derby winners—and her dam a grey mare called Tagale, a daughter of Roi Hérode's grandsire Le Sancy. Tagale won two small races in France and was bought very cheaply on Mr Raphael's behalf. She bred six other winners beside Tagalie, but not one of them was of any particular importance. She was a full sister to Cypriote, whose descendants include three winners of the French Oaks, while her grand-dam Jenny Winkle was a half-sister to the Epsom Oaks winner Jenny Howlet.

Dawson Waugh, who at this period trained privately for Mr Raphael at Somerville Lodge, Newmarket, gave Tagalie every chance to develop her strength. She did not run till the Newmarket First October Meeting when she won the Boscawen Post Stakes. At the Second October Meeting she was third of five behind Lord Falmouth's Belleisle, the best two-year-old filly of the season. In her final race that autumn she was unplaced to Major Loder's Lance Chest at Sandown. On what she had shown, therefore, there was no reason to think that she would ever become the winner of a classic.

Tagalie's first race next season was the One Thousand Guineas. Starting at 20–1, she surprised everyone by leading from start to finish and winning comfortably from Alope, subsequently the dam of the Gold Cup winner Foxlaw. Her next race, the Newmarket Stakes, was a disappointment and she was beaten by Cylgad. Mr Raphael promptly announced that she would not run in the Derby but, fortunately for himself, he changed his mind.

It was not a good Derby field by any means. The American-bred Sweeper II was a very warm favourite at 2–1; Mr L. Neumann's Jaeger was second favourite at 8–1, while Mr J. B. Joel's White Star, a full brother to Sunstar, was substantially supported despite failures in both the Guineas and the Newmarket Stakes. Tagalie was bracketed at 100–8 with the King's colt Pintadeau. Undoubtedly the best horse in the race was the American-bred Tracery, by Rock Sand out of Topiary, a mare whose dam Plaisanterie had won both the Cambridgeshire and the Cesarewitch the same season. Tracery was still very backward at this period, but in due course he proved a great racehorse, winning the St Leger, the Eclipse Stakes, and the Champion Stakes. In the Gold Cup he was brought down by a lunatic who ran out on to the course. At the stud he sired the 1923 Derby winner Papyrus; Transvaal, winner of the Grand Prix; Cottage, a great sire of chasers; and Teresina, a foundation mare of the Aga Khan's stud.

There is little to be said about the race. Johnny Reiff gave the English jockeys an interesting example of the difficult art of waiting in front and Tagalie led from start to finish to win by four lengths from Jaeger, with Tracery, having his first outing in England, third. Two days later Tagalie started a 2–1 on favourite for the Oaks. George Stern rode her on this occasion, but he restrained her in the early stages and did not allow her to stride out in front from the start as she liked. She was in the lead at Tattenham Corner, but was in trouble soon after and eventually finished unplaced behind the outsider Mirska, who, like herself, was a descendant of Jenny Diver.

Tagalie was far from robust and she never produced her Derby form again. She was unplaced to Prince Palatine in the Eclipse, and in the St Leger, her final race-course appearance, she was well down the course behind Tracery. At the stud she bred four winners, the best of which were the sprinter Tagrag, by Chaucer, and Allenby, by Bayardo. Allenby won the Newmarket Stakes and was second to Tetratema in the Guineas, but like his dam he had not got the best of forelegs, and when he retired to the stud few of his offspring stood up to hard training. There are no descendants of Tagalie in this country today, but one of her great-great-granddaughters won the Chilean Derby.

Dawson Waugh, named after his godfather, the famous Matthew Dawson, was a member of a well-known Newmarket family. His father, James Waugh, had trained at Russley the previous century for Mr Merry. His brother Willie succeeded John Porter at Kingsclere, while two other brothers trained at Newmarket. A sister was mother of the Aga Khan's trainer Frank Butters.

Dawson Waugh himself learnt the elements of his profession from John Porter and then trained for three years in Hungary. In 1903 he was appointed private trainer to Mr Raphael, for whom he also won the Two Thousand Guineas in 1913 with Louvois. He eventually parted company with Mr Raphael, and after the war his chief patrons were Sir Edward Hulton, the newspaper proprietor, and Lord Howard de Walden. In 1924 he won the Oaks for Sir Edward Hulton with Straitlace, the only classic winner that Son-in-Law sired.

Little interested in betting, Waugh was a man of great kindliness and the utmost integrity. Probably he was never happier than when he could get away from Newmarket and go and watch the cricket at Cambridge. There was no stable where apprentices were better looked after, and among his protégés were H. F. Blackshaw, now a successful trainer, and Joe Sime, a leading jockey in the north. Waugh eventually retired to Bournemouth, where he died in 1955 in his eighty-fourth year.

1912: Wednesday, 5 June ... 353 Entries. £6,450.

MR W. RAPHAEL's gr.f. TAGALIE by Cyllene
out of Tagale — J. REIFF — 1

MR L. NEUMANN's b.c. JAEGER by Eager
out of Mesange — WALTER GRIGGS — 2

MR A. BELMONT's br.c. TRACERY by Rock Sand
out of Topiary — G. BELLHOUSE — 3

Also ran:

H.M. King George V's Pintadeau (4th) (J. Jones); Mr 'Fairie's' Aleppo (J. Clark); Mr C. Bower Ismay's Hall Cross (W. Saxby); Mr L. Brassey's Catmint (Wm Griggs); Mr P. Nelke's Cylba (F. Templeman); Lord Derby's Farman (F. Rickaby); Duke of Devonshire's Javelin (W. Higgs); Mr J. Buchanan's Jingling Geordie (F. Wootton); Mr N. de Szemere's Kosciusko (F. Winter); Mr L. de Rothschild's Lorenzo (F. O'Neill); Mr F. C. Stern's Mordred (E. Wheatley); Lord Michelham's Orchestration (M. Henry); Lord Ellesmere's Royal Mail (L. Hewitt); Mr H. B. Duryea's Sweeper II (D. Maher); Mr J. B. Joel's White Star (G. Stern); Mr F. H. Cripps's Wisemac (C. Trigg); Mr P. Raleigh's Chill October (A. Templeman).

20 ran.

Betting:

   2–1 Sweeper II; 8–1 Jaeger; 10–1 White Star; 100–8 Pintadeau and Tagalie; 100–7 Mordred and Catmint; 20–1 Jingling Geordie and Javelin; 33–1 Lorenzo; 50–1 Hall Cross, Kosciusko, and Farman; 66–1 Orchestration and Tracery.

Won by four lengths; two lengths between second and third.   2 m. 38⅘ s.
Winner trained by Dawson Waugh at Newmarket.

1913

The Derby of 1913 was the most sensational, the most tragic, and the most unsatisfactory in the history of the race. The King's colt Anmer was brought down by a militant suffragette, who herself received fatal injuries in so doing. The favourite Craganour was first past the post in a very rough race, but was disqualified after an objection lodged by the Stewards themselves, the prize being awarded to the runner-up, the 100–1 chance Aboyeur.

Craganour was by Desmond out of Pretty Polly's half-sister Veneration II, whom the Sledmere Stud had bought, together with her foal by Desmond, for £1,700 from Lord Dunraven in 1910. The foal, later named Craganour, a smallish, very light-coloured bay, was bought as a yearling by Mr C. Bower Ismay, who trained with W. T. (Jack) Robinson at Foxhill. Mr Ismay and his family were closely associated with the White Star Line and he himself had been a passenger in the *Titanic* on that fateful maiden voyage. In the bitter aftermath of the disaster, a number of unkind and unjustified stories in connexion with his survival on that terrible night were widely circulated. As regards his racing ventures, Mr Ismay was unfortunate, not only on the flat, but under National Hunt rules as well. He had a number of jumpers in training with the celebrated Tom Coulthwaite, and it was on account of the running of one of his horses that Coulthwaite was temporarily deprived of his licence. Mr Ismay always regarded this incident as a grave injustice to an innocent man. After Craganour's disqualification it was hinted that Major Eustace Loder, one of the Epsom Stewards, had strong personal reasons for disliking Mr Ismay. However, there is not a jot of evidence that Major Loder's actions were in any way influenced by his own feelings towards Mr Ismay.

'Jack' Robinson was a former jockey who had ridden in the Derby on several occasions himself. A somewhat bucolic individual, he had an explosive temper which at times made him the terror of his employees. His stable was essentially a betting one—Mr Ismay, who only betted in moderate sums, was an exception—and he specialized in carefully planned coups on handicaps.

Craganour proved a high-class two-year-old, winning five of his six races, including the New Stakes at Ascot, the Champagne Stakes at Doncaster, and the Middle Park Plate. He was officially rated the best of his age, seven pounds superior to the next best, Shogun.

Aboyeur was bred in Ireland by Mr T. K. Laidlaw, who later became a member of the Jockey Club and who at one time owned two future Grand National winners in Gregalach and Grakle, both of whom he sold before their triumphs at Aintree. Like Craganour, Aboyeur was by the St Simon horse Desmond, who had some brilliant form as a two-year-old but then lost his interest in racing. Pawky, dam of Aboyeur, never won a race herself or bred another winner of significance. She was by the Royal Hunt Cup and Gold Cup winner Morion, by Barcaldine. Morion had a very unpleasant temper and was not a successful sire.

As a foal Aboyeur was bought by Mr James Daly, who passed him on to Mr J. H. Peard, who was acting for his friend Mr A. P. Cunliffe. It was generally believed that Mr Cunliffe was the founder of a group of extremely shrewd, heavy betting owners, who were commonly known as 'the Netheravon Syndicate' or 'the Druids Lodge Confederacy', and included Captain Wilfred Purefoy, Mr J. H. Peard, Captain Frank Forester, and Mr E. A. Wigan. The trainers at Druids Lodge were firstly Jack Fallon and later Tom Lewis, but the parts they played in the many famous gambles that were successfully landed were essentially minor ones, the brains behind the planning being provided principally by Captain Purefoy, a man of exceptional astuteness who neither asked nor gave quarter as far as matters of the Turf were concerned.

As a two-year-old Aboyeur ran three times. In Lewis's name and colours he won the Champagne Stakes at the Bibury Club Meeting at Salisbury, but he then ran twice unplaced in the colours of Mr Cunliffe. His only outing before the Derby the following year was to run down the course in a race at the Kempton Easter Meeting. Ridden by E. Piper, an unfashionable jockey, it was hardly surprising that he figured among the 100–1 others at Epsom.

Craganour was backward when he turned out for the Union Jack Stakes at Liverpool in the opening week of the season and his trainer was little dismayed by his failure to win. His next race was the Two Thousand Guineas; ridden by W. Saxby he was beaten a head by Mr Walter Raphael's Louvois. The two finished wide apart and nearly everyone bar the judge thought that Craganour had won. Certainly Saxby did, as he rode throughout the final furlong with the easy confidence of one who is convinced beyond all measure of doubt that he has got the issue in safe keeping. The judge, Mr C. E. Robinson, later remarked: 'They are saying that Saxby won on Mr Ismay's horse. What they should say is that he ought to have won.' The upshot was that the unfortunate Saxby was taken off Craganour, who, ridden by Danny Maher, won the Newmarket Stakes very easily, with Louvois only third. It was hoped that Maher would be able to ride him at Epsom, but he was claimed for Lord Rosebery's Prue. Accordingly Mr Ismay sent over to France for Johnny Reiff.

The period between 1900 and 1914 was not a golden age for English jockeyship. In fact during that time only five winners of the Derby were ridden by English riders, and in races of importance owners were apt to call on George Stern or on one of the American jockeys who were at that time resident in France. This fact was strongly resented by English jockeys and bad feeling existed between them and their rivals from France, particularly as English riders were still apt to be given a rough passage in races like the Grand Prix, even though the Paris crowd was less blatantly hostile than in the previous century. In the particular case of Craganour, hostility towards Reiff was augmented by the fact that the English jockeys considered that Saxby had been unjustly treated. Saxby himself undoubtedly felt strongly that this was so, and it was unfortunate that he should have been called upon to give evidence during the hearing of the case against Craganour.

Derby Day was clear and fine. Craganour was a hot favourite at 6–4; Mr Edward Hulton's Shogun, ridden by Frank Wootton, was second favourite at 6–1, and there was plenty of money for Louvois, ridden by Saxby, and the French colt Nimbus, winner of the Prix Greffulhe. Aboyeur was soon in the lead, followed by Craganour and Aldegond, with Nimbus, Louvois, and Shogun all well placed. At Tattenham Corner Miss Emily Davison, well known as one of the most militant and fanatical members of the suffragette movement, darted out from under the rails and tried to grab the King's colt Anmer by the reins. Anmer, his jockey Herbert Jones, and Miss Davison came crashing to the ground. Fortunately Jones and the horse escaped serious injury, but Miss Davison sustained a fractured skull and died at Epsom Hospital on the following Sunday. Miss Davison's courage and devotion to her cause were beyond question, but it was an act of appalling recklessness, the effects of which might have been far more serious had Anmer been somewhere near the head of the field instead of lying almost at the tail.

In the straight a desperate race ensued. Craganour drew up alongside Aboyeur, while Nimbus, Great Sport, Louvois, Shogun, and Day Comet were all hard on the heels of the leaders. At one point Shogun appeared to be going better than anything else, but first of all he was involved in a scrimmage with Day Comet, and then, just as he was making rapid headway on the rails, Reiff deliberately barged into Aboyeur, who in turn veered left and baulked Shogun's passage. It had been a bumping, brawling, ugly race almost from the start, and when Aboyeur, flinching from the whip in Piper's left hand, came away from the rails inside the final furlong and collided with Craganour, Reiff, the last person to suffer interference with Christian resignation, at once retaliated. Possibly it was six of one and half a dozen of the other; as the pair passed the post virtually locked together, Aboyeur still seemed to be leaning on Craganour, but there can be little doubt that it was Reiff who had instigated the serious trouble in the straight. The present Lord Rosebery was watching the race from his father's box and as soon as it was over he turned to Mr J. A. de Rothschild and remarked: 'If there is an objection, the second is sure to get it.' When the objection flag was eventually hoisted, Mr de Rothschild went up and down the rails backing Aboyeur for all he was worth, while another supporter of Aboyeur at this stage was Jack Jarvis, who had observed the finish from the very top of the stand.

After a few seconds of fearful suspense, the favourite's number was placed in the frame and a great cheer went up from all over the Downs. Only a handful of experienced race-readers anticipated an objection and the bookmakers began to pay out. Piper never suggested to Mr Cunliffe that an objection should be lodged, and Mr Cunliffe, true to the Druids Lodge tradition, would have risked unpopularity without a qualm if he had thought that an objection might give him the race. There was, however, rather an ominous delay before the 'All Right' was called, and Robinson, crimson-faced and sweating as much as Craganour, began to show signs of uneasiness. At last, however, the shout of 'All Right' was heard in the unsaddling enclosure. 'Thank God!' said Robinson, mopping his brow. 'I was beginning to get very worried.'

Craganour was just being led away when Lord Durham, looking, in the words of that eminent journalist Mr Sidney Galtrey, 'rather fierce and terribly serious', ordered Craganour to be brought back and demanded to know by whose authority the 'All Right' had been given.

Gradually the news spread that the Stewards—Lord Rosebery, Lord Wolverton, and Major Eustace Loder—had themselves objected to the winner on the grounds that he had jostled the runner-up. Mr Ismay turned pale, and his jubilant friends fell suddenly silent; Robinson was frankly incredulous, while Piper was apprehensive that he would be called to account for failing to keep a straight course.

The evidence of various jockeys, including Saxby, was heard. No doubt the Stewards were fully aware of the undercurrent of hostility felt by the jockeys against the connexions of Craganour and took it into account when making their decision. It is said that the witness whose evidence was decisive from the prosecution's point of view was the Judge, Mr C. E. Robinson, an impartial and fair-minded man. At all events, after a long period of anxiety, frustration, and confusion, the Stewards sustained their own objection. The official announcement was given in these terms:

The Stewards objected to the winner on the grounds that he jostled the second horse. After hearing the evidence of the Judge and several of the jockeys riding in the race they found that Craganour, the winner, did not keep a straight course and interfered with Shogun, Day Comet, and Aboyeur. Having bumped and bored the second horse, they disqualified Craganour and awarded the race to Aboyeur.

The statement, rather a curious one, showed that the Stewards, having made the objection on the grounds of jostling, then added two other indictments, on both of which they found the winner guilty. Whether the verdict of the Stewards was the right one has always been a controversial question. Lord Rosebery did not sit on the objection, but Lord Wolverton and Major Loder were men of honour and integrity, very experienced in racing matters. Certainly they showed no lack of moral courage in carrying through their concept of their duty, and the whole distasteful business left its mark on Major Loder for the brief period of his life that remained.*

The critics of the Stewards, and there were many of them, based their disagreement with the decision on three points. Firstly, the Stewards were acting not only as prosecutors, but as judges as well. Secondly, Reiff was far from being the only offender in what was indubitably a very rough race. Thirdly, the connexions of Aboyeur, who were down-to-earth realists as far as racing was concerned and who stood to win £40,000 in bets, would certainly have lodged an objection if their jockey had advised them that there were reasonable grounds for so doing.

Mr Ismay gave notice of an appeal the following Sunday, but it could not be heard as it was not delivered within the forty-eight hours prescribed by Rule 166. He then applied to the Courts for an injunction to restrain the stakeholders from paying out, and an interim injunction was granted. In the meantime, however, Craganour was sold to Señor Martinez de Hoz for £30,000 and the protest was dropped. Craganour never ran in England again, but proved an outstanding success as a sire in the Argentine.

Mr Ismay had few illusions about human nature and his attitude throughout was one of cynicism rather than of bitterness. When the war broke out the following year he joined a cavalry regiment—he had served as a trooper in the South African War—and he died soon after its conclusion. The shock and disappointment over Craganour proved too much for poor Robinson. He was never the same man again and died two years later.

Aboyeur ran twice more, at Liverpool and Goodwood, being beaten on each occasion. He was then sold to the Imperial Racing Club of St Petersburg for £13,000. His ultimate fate during the Revolution is unknown, but there is a story that he and Minoru were evacuated to Serbia with the British Military Mission. Two stallions

---

* Lord Rosebery, who had had a runner in the race, did not sit on the objection, but he was in the room the whole time and subsequently stated that the evidence was clear and the Stewards had no option but to disqualify Craganour.

were certainly evacuated, but their identity was never satisfactorily confirmed. Piper lapsed into obscurity and had been forgotten by the racing world long before he died at Epsom in 1951. The same may be said of Tom Lewis, who was over eighty and had been in retirement for many years when he died in 1938. Mr Cunliffe, a director of Sandown Park, had his first winner in 1898, his last one in 1931. He won the Jubilee Handicap twice with Ypsilanti and the 1920 Oaks with Charlebelle, a filly that he bred himself. He died in 1942 within a few weeks of two other members of the 'confederacy', Captain Forester and Mr E. A. Wigan. Mr Cunliffe, who left over £150,000, was the poorest of the three. The fame of Druids Lodge was subsequently revived under the ownership firstly of Mr J. V. Rank and then of Mr Jack Olding, and many good winners were trained there by Noel Cannon. On Mr Olding's death, in 1958, the stables were sold and are never likely to be used for training purposes again.

Louvois, one of several horses in the Derby that their respective owners considered extremely unlucky not to have won, was a full brother to Louviers, beaten by inches by Minoru in 1909. He was sire of St Louis, winner of the Two Thousand Guineas in 1922. Shogun is best remembered as the sire of Verdict, winner of the Cambridgeshire and the Coronation Cup, and dam of the Oaks and Gold Cup winner Quashed.

Great Sport, a half-brother to the 1924 Derby winner Sansovino, was a failure as a sire. Hyperion and Big Game are among the many famous winners descended from his dam Gondolette.

1913: Wednesday, 4 June . . . 344 Entries. £6,450.

MR A. P. CUNLIFFE's b.c. ABOYEUR by Desmond
out of Pawky   E. PIPER   I
MR W. RAPHAEL's b.c. LOUVOIS by Isinglass
out of St Louvaine   W. SAXBY   2
COLONEL W. HALL-WALKER's b.c. GREAT SPORT
by Gallinule out of Gondolette   G. STERN   3

Also ran:

M. A. Aumont's Nimbus (4th) (M. Henry); Mr R. Bunsow's Agadir (W. Earl); Mr P. Broome's Aldegond (G. Bellhouse); Sir W. Nelson's Bachelor's Wedding (S. Donoghue); Mr L. de Rothschild's Day Comet (A. Whalley); Sir J. Willoughby's Jameson (E. Wheatley); Lord Rosebery's Prue (D. Maher); Mrs G. Foster Rawlin's Sandburr (H. Jelliss); Mr E. Hulton's Shogun (F. Wootton); Mr J. B. Joel's Sun

1913

Yat (W. Huxley); H.M. King George V's Anmer (H. Jones) (*fell*); Mr C. Bower Ismay's Craganour (J. Reiff) (*disqualified*).

15 ran.

Betting:

6–4 Craganour; 6–1 Shogun; 10–1 Louvois and Nimbus; 100–9 Day Comet; 100–7 Prue; 20–1 Great Sport; 25–1 Aldegond; 33–1 Bachelor's Wedding and Sun Yat; 50–1 Anmer; 100–1 others.

Craganour came in first, beating Aboyeur by a head, Louvois being a neck away third and Great Sport fourth. The Stewards objected to Craganour and he was disqualified. The race was awarded to Aboyeur.   2 m. 37⅗ s.
Winner trained by T. Lewis at Druids Lodge.

The Seventeenth Earl of Derby
and the Hon. George Lambton

Sir Henry Greer
and the Aga Khan

The Aga Khan leading in Blenheim
(H. Wragg up)

Bahram

1914

Mr H. B. Duryea's Durbar II, winner in 1914, was the first horse from France to win the Derby since Gladiateur's triumph in 1865.

After the passage of the Anti-Betting Bill, which had so dire an effect on American racing, Mr Duryea decided to ship his mares over to France and he established a stud at Neuvy, near Falaise in Normandy. His colours were not unknown in England, as he had won the Stewards Cup at Goodwood in 1909, while three years later he won the Two Thousand Guineas with Sweeper II.

Durbar II had no French blood in his veins. His sire Rabelais, a smallish horse by St Simon, had carried Mr Arthur James's colours to victory in the Goodwood Cup, besides running third in the Two Thousand Guineas and fourth in the Derby. Exported to France for £900, he proved an outstanding success as a sire there. Armenia, dam of Durbar, was bred in America by Mr W. C. Whitney and was by Meddler out of Urania, by Hanover out of Wanda, by Mortemer. Meddler, by St Gatien, was an outstanding two-year-old in England, but his classic engagements were rendered void by the death of his owner, Mr 'Abington' Baird, and he was exported to America where he did extremely well at the stud. Urania, a hardy mare who won thirty-five of her eighty-seven races, came from one of the best-known American racing families, but under the rules then in existence its members were ineligible for inclusion in the English Stud Book. Durbar, therefore, at the time of his Epsom victory, was not classified as a thoroughbred and his success was a painful blow to the purists. In 1949 Stud Book rules came into force that regularized his position and that of his descendants.

Durbar stood fifteen hands three and was a rather common-looking bay with a wonderful action when extended. He was his dam's third foal, both the other two having been winners, one of them, Blarney, a top-class two-year-old. Durbar's career during his first season was undistinguished, as he ran four times, finishing third in the Prix Partisan and unplaced on the other three occasions. As a matter of fact he was amiss after his second race and never really recovered his strength until he was a three-year-old. The following spring he won four races over a mile and a quarter, but ten days before the Derby he was only sixth in the French Two Thousand Guineas. There was an excuse for his failure, though, as he had been very badly away, and his owner thought he had run sufficiently well under the circumstances to back him substantially for the Derby. The very next day Durbar set off for Epsom, taking with him his own oats and hay, as well as special water in large containers. Everything was done to make his journey quick and comfortable, and he arrived at Epsom on the top of his form. Nominally he was trained by an American called Murphy, but in fact his preparation had been carried out under the personal supervision of his owner. His American rider, Matt MacGee, was a natural comedian who looked like a miniature prize-fighter.

It was not a vintage year for three-year-olds in England. A short-priced favourite for the Derby was Sir John Thursby's Two Thousand Guineas winner Kennymore, by John o' Gaunt. Second favourite was Mr J. B. Joel's Black Jester, ridden by George Stern, while Brakespear, Carancho, and Carrickfergus were all well backed. Durbar II caused little stir in the market and was on offer at 20–1. There was a long delay at the start caused by the antics of the King's colt Brakespear. Deservedly Brakespear was badly away, but an innocent sufferer was the favourite Kennymore. Durbar was nicely placed from the start and always seemed to be going well within himself. Early in the straight Black Jester looked very dangerous indeed, but he was a horse of moods and, suddenly dropping his bit, he declined to exert himself further. From then on it was all plain sailing for Durbar, who passed the post an easy three lengths clear of Hapsburg, with Peter the Hermit a further length and a half away third. Peter the Hermit was a surprise last-minute runner and his name was not even printed on the race-card. He subsequently won the Hardwicke Stakes, beating Corcyra, who had won the Newmarket Stakes but had not been entered for the Derby, and Black Jester, who later was to win the St Leger. Among the unplaced horses was My Prince, who in due course proved himself an outstanding sire of jumpers.

Durbar never raced in England again. He was fourth to Sardanapale in the Prix du Jockey Club, and third to Sardanapale and La Farina in the Grand Prix. The following month the world as the Edwardians knew it was up in flames and the German armies were virtually at the gates of Paris. There was to be no more racing in France for many a day.

As a sire Durbar is best remembered by his daughter Durban, who was out of the French One Thousand Guineas winner Banshee, by the American-bred Irish Lad out of Frizette. Also descended from Frizette are Jet Pilot, winner of the Kentucky Derby and a leading sire in America; and Black Tarquin, winner of the 1948 St Leger. Durban was a very good two-year-old and later did memorable service for M. Boussac's stud. Mated with Ksar, she produced Tourbillon, winner of the French Derby and an outstanding sire. Before his death in 1954 Tourbillon was four times Champion Sire in France, among his offspring being Djebel, winner of the Two

Thousand Guineas both in England and France and sire of the Derby winner Galcador; Caracalla II, unbeaten winner of the Grand Prix and the Gold Cup; and Goya II, a good winner and Champion Sire in France. For most of his stud career Tourbillon was not a thoroughbred according to English classification, but that stigma did not prevent him from being one of the most influential sires in the world. Durbar himself stood in France for ten seasons and was then taken to America, where he died in his twenty-first year.

Hapsburg, second to Durbar at Epsom, was the sire of a great stayer in Noble Star, winner of the Cesarewitch, Ascot Stakes, Goodwood Stakes, and Jockey Club Cup.

1914: Wednesday, 27 May . . . 372 Entries. £6,450.

MR H. B. DURYEA's b.c. DURBAR II by Rabelais out of Armenia	M. MACGEE	1
SIR E. CASSEL's br.c. HAPSBURG by Desmond out of Altesse	C. FOY	2
MR H. J. KING's ch.c. PETER THE HERMIT by St Petersburg out of Blare	R. WATSON	3

Also ran:

Lord Derby's Dan Russel (4th) (F. Rickaby*); H.M. King George V's Brakespear (H. Jones); Duke of Portland's Anglesea (L. Hewitt); Sir A. Bailey's Ambassador (W. Saxby); Mr J. B. Joel's Black Jester (G. Stern); Mr H. P. Nickalls's Best Boy (H. Randall); Mr E. Tanner's Carancho (S. Donoghue); Colonel W. Hall-Walker's Carrickfergus (F. Templeman); Mr W. N. McMillan's Cerval (F. Herbert); Mr J. W. Larnach's Conqueror (R. Stokes); Mr W. Clark's Courageous (F. Bullock); M. Aumont's Cupidon (M. Henry); Mr P. F. Heybourn's Desmond's Song (H. Robbins); Mr Kennedy Jones's Evansdale (W. Huxley); Mr G. Edwardes's Flying Orb (N. Spear); Sir J. Thursby's Kennymore (F. O'Neill); Mr. L. Neumann's Lanius (Walter Griggs); Mr J. Buchanan's Marten (E. Wheatley); Lord St David's My Prince (W. Earl); Mr W. Brodrick Cloete's Orebi (M. Wing); Mr. Russel's Polycrates (Wm Griggs); Mr F. Marsham-Townsend's Polygamist (A. Escott); Mr L. de Rothschild's St Guthlac (A. Whalley); Colonel E. W. Baird's Shepherd King (H. Jelliss); Mr W. J. Tatem's Southerndown (E. Piper); Mr E. Hulton's Woodwild (W. Smyth); Lord Carnarvon's Magyar (E. Huxley).

30 ran.

Betting:

9–4 Kennymore; 10–1 Black Jester; 100–8 Brakespear; 100–7 Carancho; 100–6

* F. Rickaby, father of the successful jockeys F. and W. Rickaby, was killed in action in France.

Carrickfergus; 20–1 Durbar II; 25–1 Evansdale and Dan Russel; 33–1 Ambassador, Hapsburg, and My Prince; 40–1 Lanius and Polycrates; 50–1 Flying Orb and Cupidon; 66–1 Courageous and Orebi.

Won by three lengths; a length and a half between second and third. 2 m. 38⅖ s. Winner trained by T. Murphy in France.

1915

By the end of 1914 it was all too clear that Lord Kitchener's unpopular prophecy of a long war was going to prove correct. Racing was greatly reduced in volume and Epsom was requisitioned by the military. In 1915, therefore, and in the following three years, a substitute race called the New Derby was run over a mile and a half over the July Course at Newmarket. In this particular year the £1,000 in added money was contributed by Lord Derby himself.

The winner of the first New Derby was Pommern, owned by Mr S. B. Joel, trained by Charles Peck, and ridden by Steve Donoghue. Bred by his owner, Pommern was by Polymelus out of Merry Agnes, by the St Simon horse St Hilaire. Polymelus, a very good middle-distance horse that was widely suspected of not being a genuine stayer, was by Cyllene, whose grand-dam Distant Shore, by Hermit, was also the dam of St Hilaire. Polymelus was an outstanding success at the stud and was five times Champion Sire. His great influence on thoroughbred breeding today comes not through his Derby winners Pommern and Humorist, but through the handicapper Phalaris, sire of Pharos and Fairway.

As a two-year-old Pommern won the Richmond Stakes at Goodwood and the Imperial Produce Stakes at Kempton, and it was after his Kempton victory that Donoghue was engaged to ride him in the Derby. The following spring he failed to concede fifteen pounds in the Craven Stakes to Rossendale, who was subsequently third in the Derby. However, he won the Two Thousand Guineas comfortably enough from Tournament and The Vizier, and started a short-priced favourite for the Derby. In that race he always had the situation comfortably in hand and won by an easy two lengths from Let Fly, a full brother to Big Game's grand-dam Dolabella, and Rossendale. There was only a meagre crowd to see Pommern win and the atmosphere was sombre. Gallipoli, Festubert, and the sinking of the *Lusitania* rather than sport were in most people's minds.

There was no St Leger at Doncaster, and the Doncaster Race Committee would not permit a substitute race of that title elsewhere. Pommern was therefore deprived of the honour of gaining the 'Triple Crown' that he undoubtedly deserved, but he did win the mile and three-quarter September Stakes at Newmarket, which was the nearest thing there was to a St Leger that season. He won another race as a three-year-old and the June Stakes at Newmarket, his only outing as a four-year-old.

He then retired to his owner's stud at a fee of 300 guineas which was subsequently raised to 400 guineas. He was not an outstanding success as a sire: Adams Apple, winner of the Two Thousand Guineas, Pondoland, second in the Two Thousand Guineas, and Glommen, winner of the Goodwood Cup, were about the best of his offspring.

Like his brother Mr J. B. Joel, Mr Solomon Barnato Joel—usually referred to as 'Solly' Joel—made an immense fortune as a young man in South Africa. He was an extremely forceful character and inclined to be self-assertive, but those who knew him best professed to find him kindly and genial. His stud at Maiden Erlegh and his stable at Moulton Paddocks were among the largest in the country, but he was far less successful on the Turf than his brother, and Pommern was his sole classic winner.

In 1906 Mr Joel made the most successful purchase of his racing career when he bought Polymelus for 4,200 guineas at the Newmarket October Sales. Before the season was over Polymelus had won firstly the Duke of York Stakes at Kempton and then the Cambridgeshire, in which he carried a ten-pound penalty, started a red-hot favourite, and won in a canter. Mr Joel and his friends won £100,000 in bets, and Mr Joel himself had a final bet of £6,000 to £5,000 when the horses were at the post. Polymelus not only was responsible for Pommern, but he also sired the next best horse that Mr Joel owned, Polyphontes, twice winner of the Eclipse Stakes. When Polymelus died in 1924, Mr Joel's racing fortunes soon started to decline.

Mr Joel made two other extremely lucky purchases. He bought Merry Agnes, who was carrying Pommern at the time, for £500, and for 500 guineas he bought Long Set out of a selling race at Lincoln. Long Set won for him the Doncaster Cup, the Cambridgeshire, the Hunt Cup, and the Lincoln.

Mr Joel's health began to fail when he was still comparatively young and he was only sixty-five when he died in 1931. His son Mr Stanhope Joel won the St Leger in 1945 with Chamossaire.

In the past hundred years there have been three jockeys who captured the imagination and affection of the racing public to a remarkable degree—Fred Archer, Stephen Donoghue, and Sir Gordon Richards.

'Steve' Donoghue was born in 1884, the son of an iron-worker in Warrington, one of the least attractive towns in the whole of England. He ran away from home more than once and had experience of a number of well-known stables before, at the age of eighteen, he accepted a post in France with the American trainer Edward Johnson. It was in France in 1904 that he rode the first winner of his career. In 1906 he left France and rode in Ireland for several seasons. His first English retainer was with 'Atty' Persse's stable in 1911.

Donoghue continued to ride until 1937, in which year, to everyone's delight, he won the One Thousand Guineas and the Oaks on Exhibitionist. The heyday of his career was undoubtedly the nineteen twenties, particularly the first six years of that decade, and it was then that the cry of 'Come on, Steve!' gradually became incorporated into the English language. It is a tribute to the fairness of his methods that not once in his thirty-three years as a rider was he summoned before the Stewards for an infringement of the rules.

Donoghue was first and foremost a superb horseman with beautiful hands. He loved horses, they went kindly for him, and it was a pleasure to watch him cantering down to the post on a highly strung two-year-old. He had sound judgement of pace, plenty of confidence, and an iron nerve that remained unimpaired to the end. He had some horrible falls in his career, and there can be no better illustration of his courage and toughness than the fact that after a shattering fall in the Derby in 1920 when he lay prone in the path of the oncoming field, he walked back to the weighing-room and, after a brief rest, rode two more winners that afternoon. He was always at his brilliant best at Epsom and that gallop down the hill to Tattenham Corner never caused him a second's anxiety even when he was over fifty years of age. He won the Epsom Derby on Humorist (1921), Captain Cuttle (1922), Papyrus (1923), and Manna (1925). He won war-time Derbys at Newmarket on Pommern and Gay Crusader, and altogether he had fourteen successes in English classic events. He won the Grand Prix on Kefalin (1922) and on Admiral Drake (1934). He won the Irish Derby four times, on the last occasion when he was fifty, and he was associated with two of the most famous horses of this century in The Tetrarch and Brown Jack.

Donoghue was a little short-legged man with a charming smile and a rather husky voice that the ladies found very attractive. He was the kindest and most generous of men, always ready to help others in any way that he could. At the peak of his career he might easily have been spoilt, particularly as he was too kind-hearted to rebuff some of the undesirable individuals who forced their attentions on him, but he never became swollen-headed or overbearing. Perhaps he was almost too generous and ready to accede to the many demands that were made on him; certainly hundreds of thousands of pounds must have passed through his hands, but there was very little left at the end. He lost a great deal of money at one point in an unsuccessful breeding venture, while his brief career as a trainer may have been costly, too. Sometimes he was deplorably casual towards those who employed him, but his charm could be relied on to extricate him from any predicament or to heal any temporary breach. The weaknesses in his character somehow seemed to add to his appeal, and everyone who followed racing in a greater or lesser degree felt that they had lost a delightful friend when he died suddenly in 1945.

Charles Peck, an extremely able man with a high sense of duty, was the son of Robert Peck, a famous trainer of the previous century, and brother of Percy Peck, who trained Cicero to win the Derby for Lord Rosebery. He trained his first winner in 1895, and after a period with the Imperial Light Horse in South Africa, he was appointed private trainer to Mr S. B. Joel. For Mr Joel he trained Bachelor's Button, who won two Gold Vases and the Gold Cup, Polymelus, and Pommern. He did not train Long Set, who was with J. H. Batho at Alfriston.

In 1916 Peck joined the Royal Horse Artillery, and his association with Mr Joel ceased, at any rate for the time being. For a brief period after demobilization he had a few horses near Winchester, but he then went to assist 'Atty' Persse at Stockbridge for a couple of years. In 1925 he was training for both the Joel brothers, and in 1926 he succeeded Charles Morton as private trainer to Mr J. B. Joel, firstly at Wantage and later at Foxhill, a property Mr Joel had bought after the suicide of Mr James White. The best horse he trained at Foxhill was Priory Park, winner of the Lincoln, the Stewards Cup, the City and Suburban, and the Hunt Cup. He himself only survived Mr Joel by a year, dying in 1941 at the age of sixty-eight. All told he trained 444 winners of just over £215,000 in stakes.

1915: The New Derby Stakes. Tuesday, 15 June . . . 18 Entries from those originally entered for the Epsom Derby. £2,440.

MR S. B. JOEL's b.c. POMMERN by Polymelus
out of Merry Agnes   S. DONOGHUE   1
COLONEL W. HALL-WALKER's b.c. LET FLY
by White Eagle out of Gondolette   J. CHILDS   2
SIR JOHN THURSBY's bl.c. ROSSENDALE
by St Frusquin out of Menda   J. CLARK   3

Also ran:

Mr Mortimer Singer's Achtoi (4th) (C. Trigg); Mr A. E. Barton's My Ronald (C. Foy); Mr A. Belmont's Danger Rock (A. Whalley); M. E. Blanc's Flormonde (H. Jelliss); M. E. Blanc's Le Melior (G. Stern); Lord Carnarvon's The Vizier (F. Bullock); Sir E. Cassel's Gadabout (F. O'Neill); Mr H. B. Duryea's Chickamaugwa (M. MacGee); Mr J. B. Joel's Sunfire (W. Huxley); Mr J. A. de Rothschild's Apothecary (R. Cooper); Mr E. Tanner's Rushford (M. Wing); Mr W. J. Tatem's The Revenge (E. Piper); Colonel W. Hall-Walker's Follow Up (E. Huxley); Mr G. H. Williamson's King Priam (C. Heckford).

17 ran.

Betting :

11–10 Pommern; 10–1 Danger Rock and Let Fly; 100–7 The Vizier; 100–6 My Ronald; 20–1 Gadabout, Sunfire, Le Melior, King Priam, and Chickamaugwa; 33–1 Achtoi; 40–1 Rossendale; 50–1 The Revenge.

Won by two lengths; three lengths between second and third. 2 m. 32⅗ s. Winner trained by C. Peck at Newmarket.

1916

Sir Edward Hulton is so far the only leading newspaper proprietor who has gone in for racing in a big way. Lord Beaverbrook launched out in great style in the late nineteen twenties, but he got bored almost before he had started and soon disposed of his horses. Hulton as a boy was delicate and studious; he was in fact being trained for the priesthood when his elder brother died and he was compelled to enter the newspaper world and help his father. At first he was very little interested in sport, but a taste in that direction rapidly developed through his close association with a number of sporting publications. At first he went in for coursing—he won the Waterloo Cup twice—but eventually racing became his chief hobby and relaxation. He studied the Turf very carefully before he became an owner and, unlike so many rich men, he entered the sport with an expert knowledge of every aspect of it. After his death in 1925 at the early age of fifty-three, his horses were sold and realized 288,380 guineas. His Oaks winner Straitlace was bought for the then record sum of 17,000 guineas by Mr E. Esmond.

Before the First World War Richard Wootton was Hulton's trainer; at the conclusion of hostilities he sent most of his horses to Dawson Waugh, but Fifinella, who won him the Derby and Oaks in 1916, was trained by Richard Dawson at Newmarket. Fifinella, bred by her owner, was by Polymelus out of Silver Fowl, by the St Leger winner Wildfowler, an indifferent sire that later in life changed hands for a tenner. Silver Fowl was bred in Ireland by Mr D. Shanahan, who raced her there and won three races with her including the National Produce Stakes. He then sold her to Hulton, who was just starting his racing career, for £1,500. Hulton transferred her to Wootton's stable, but she did not train on. She was sent to the stud as a four-year-old, but before she could be mated she got loose and injured herself so badly on some wire that her owner ordered her immediate destruction. Fortunately Wootton declined to carry out this instruction and in due course she completely recovered.

Just how lucky this reprieve was is shown by the fact that Silver Fowl bred eleven winners of over £27,000. These included, besides Fifinella, Silver Tag, winner of the Cambridgeshire and dam of Shrove, whose son Shred was a good winner in France; Silvern, winner of the Coronation Cup; and Soubriquet, second in both the One Thousand Guineas and the Oaks, grand-dam of the Two Thousand Guineas winner Pasch, and great grand-dam of the 1953 Derby winner Pinza.

Fifinella was mean and weakly as a yearling. She improved out of all knowledge in a physical sense during the winter, but unfortunately her manners grew less and less ladylike and throughout her racing career she was catty, peevish, and unreliable. Well galloped at home she won her first race, the Fulbourne Stakes at Newmarket, by five lengths. Next time out she was beaten a head by a fast filly of Mr J. B. Joel's called Telephone Girl, and on her final appearance as a two-year-old she was third in the Cheveley Park Stakes. In all these races she was partnered by Donoghue, an ideal jockey for a filly that needed a great deal of humouring.

The following year Fifinella was ridden by Joe Childs. In the One Thousand Guineas she played up at the start and Childs, who never possessed the sweetest of tempers himself, hit her hard. Because of this she sulked throughout the race and permitted herself to be beaten by Lord Derby's Canyon, subsequently the dam of the Two Thousand Guineas winner Colorado.

It was decided to allow Fifinella to take her chance in the Derby as the field for that race looked like being a long way below the usual standard. On the morning of the Derby she was in a vile temper, refused to be dressed over, and would not allow her lad to finish plaiting her mane. In the race itself she was slowly away, was badly bumped soon afterwards and only took hold of her bit close home. She then quickened in great style to dart through a narrow opening and win by a neck from Kwang-Su, half-brother of Lemberg and Bayardo, with Nassovian, a half-brother to Craganour, a head away third. Two days later she was on her very best behaviour and won the Oaks in a canter from Salamandra, afterwards the dam of Salmon Trout, winner of a sensational St Leger. She did not run in the September Stakes and, after finishing last of three behind Phalaris in a race at Newmarket in the autumn, she was retired to the stud. It was said that her trainer was by no means sorry to see her go. When in the mood she was a brilliant filly, but the best three-year-old that season was almost certainly Hurry On, who won the September Stakes, but did not compete in the Derby.

On her owner's death Fifinella, then twelve years old, with her foal by Tetratema at foot, was sold to Lord Woolavington for 12,000 guineas. She was not a great success at the stud and was inclined to transmit something of her own temperament to her offspring, the best of whom was the Hurry On colt Press Gang, winner of the Middle Park Stakes and the Princess of Wales's Stakes.

Richard Dawson was in his ninetieth year when he died in 1955. Born in Ireland, he trained in that country for some years after leaving Dublin University. In 1897 he moved to Whatcombe in Berkshire and the very next year he won the Grand National with Drogheda, a horse he had bought at the Dublin Show. To start with he concentrated chiefly on jumpers, ridden for the most part by Mr 'Atty' Persse, but before very long he transferred his interests to the flat, and in the early years of this century he won several important handicaps with horses belonging to Lord Carnarvon. One horse he trained, Mustapha, was second in the Cambridgeshire three years running.

During the war he moved to Newmarket and trained for Mr Hulton in 1915 but in the following year this association terminated when he stated that he could no longer go on training Hulton's horses for fifty shillings a week! He returned to Whatcombe in 1919 and won the Jubilee and Gold Cup with Tangiers in 1920. In 1921 he was appointed trainer to the Aga Khan, Mr George Lambton having previously declined that position. This association, a highly fruitful one for both parties, lasted for ten years, among the most notable winners in that period being Diophon (Two Thousand Guineas), Salmon Trout (St Leger), Blenheim (Derby), and Mumtaz Mahal, a grey filly of phenomenal speed that was the two-year-old champion of her season. During this same period Dawson won the Derby and St Leger for Mr W. Barnett with Trigo, and the Oaks for Vicomte de Fontarce with Brownhylda. Towards the end of 1931 there was serious disagreement between the Aga Khan and Dawson and, after a brief spell with J. Beary, the Aga Khan's horses were transferred to Frank Butters.

Dawson was leading trainer in 1916, 1924, and 1929, and he finally retired in 1945. In appearance he was hardly the typical trainer and in manner he was certainly not the Englishman's notion of an Irishman. With his drooping moustache, pince-nez, and almost sombre style of dress, he was more like the old-fashioned type of schoolmaster. He had singularly little sense of humour to help him meet the ups and downs of fortune that are inevitable in racing.

Joe Childs was born at Chantilly, one of five brothers who all became jockeys. Charles won the Grand Prix on Nuage and rode successfully in England during the war, while Albert and Arthur both subsequently did well as trainers in France. Joe was sent off to Newmarket to be apprenticed to Tom Jennings, junior, a noted trainer of young riders. He won his first race in 1900, and half-way through the following season he had done so well that he had lost the apprentice allowance. Once the allowance had gone he naturally got less riding, and in 1903 he returned to France to ride for M. Caillault. Particularly in his younger days he had an explosive temper that he was rarely able to control in face of criticism. His contract with M. Caillault was very soon terminated, nor did one with the Duc de Gramont last very much longer, while a spell in Italy proved equally unfruitful. In 1906 he returned to England, but only obtained a single ride throughout the season and went back to France at the end of the year. The tide turned in 1908 when, substituting for Bellhouse, who was ill, he won the Grand Prix on North East for Mr W. K. Vanderbilt.

The following year he rode for Prince Murat and did very well, but much wasting affected his health and he accepted a two-year contract to ride in Germany for the Weinberg brothers, with no stipulation about a minimum weight. The Weinberg's trainer was none other than Fred Darling, likewise strong-willed and inclined to irascibility. Not surprisingly there were many violent clashes of opinion between trainer and jockey. In 1912 Childs returned to France and that season he rode the Epsom Oaks winner Mirska, his first English classic success. When war broke out he was still in France. Leaving everything he owned behind him, he escaped by the last train from Chantilly before the Germans arrived, and on reaching England he was immediately befriended by Colledge Leader.

In 1916 Childs joined the Royal Flying Corps as a cadet, but his temper and disposition rendered him singularly unamenable to discipline. After a series of rows and a period with the Cavalry Reserve, he was drafted to the 4th Hussars. This regiment seldom refused him leave to ride, and in 1918, the year he rode Gainsborough to victory in the Derby, he gave all his riding fees to regimental funds.

His successes on Gainsborough were the start of a happy association with Alec Taylor, whom he described as 'the finest trainer in the world and the best master I ever had'. In the 1919 St Leger he was beaten on the odds-on favourite Buchan. Major Gerald Deane, Lord Astor's racing manager, made some biting comments afterwards, which Childs did not take lying down. He never rode for Lord Astor again.

Despite occasional rows—he had a serious one with Lord Lonsdale, then Senior Steward at Newmarket, who accused him of punishing a filly excessively at the starting-gate—he enjoyed almost unbroken success until he retired from riding in 1935. He rode fifteen English classic winners altogether, his third Derby winner being Coronach in 1926. He won another Grand Prix in 1921 on Lemonora, and the Gold Cup on Solario and on Trimdon twice. For the last ten years of his career he was first jockey to King George V, a post which afforded him considerable satisfaction and which he maintained with suitable dignity. In 1928 he won the One Thousand Guineas for the King on Scuttle, and probably the finest race he ever rode in his life was when he won the Hardwicke Stakes on His Majesty's colt Limelight.

As a rider Childs was extremely strong and wonderfully patient. He liked to come from behind and no one could ride a stronger finish. Tall for a jockey, lithe, with dark beetling brows, he mellowed considerably with age, but young jockeys always stood in considerable awe of him and it was a rash individual indeed who elected to take a liberty. After his retirement he acquired controlling interest in a greyhound racing track at Portsmouth, and occasionally he owned a horse in partnership with his friend George Digby. He was seventy-three when he died in 1958.

1916

1916: New Derby Stakes . . . 36 Entries. £2,900.

MR E. HULTON's ch.f. FIFINELLA by Polymelus
out of Silver Fowl   J. CHILDS   1
MR 'FAIRIE'S' b.c. KWANG-SU by Cicero
out of Galicia   F. TEMPLEMAN   2
MR J. SANFORD's b.c. NASSOVIAN by William the Third
out of Veneration II   F. O'NEILL   3

Also ran:

Mr W. M. G. Singer's Valais (4th) (J. Clark); Lord Derby's Canyon (F. Rickaby); Mr C. T. Garland's Polydamon (E. Lancaster); Mr C. E. Howard's Ferox (C. Childs); Mr J. B. Joel's Sirian (F. Bullock); Mr L. Neumann's Figaro (A. Whalley); Mr F. C. Stern's Flaming Fire (S. Donoghue).

10 ran.

Betting:

3–1 Kwang-Su; 11–2 Fifinella and Nassovian; 6–1 Figaro; 9–1 Flaming Fire; 10–1 Canyon; 33–1 Sirian and Ferox; 50–1 Polydamon and Valais.

Won by a neck; a head between second and third.   2 m. 36⅗ s.
Winner trained by R. C. Dawson at Newmarket.

1917

1917 was a sombre year. Casualties had been on an appalling scale and the Somme battle the previous summer had thrown half the nation into mourning. The shipping position was causing the gravest anxiety, the Russians were cracking, and the end of the war seemed a long way off. A question in the House of Commons on the propriety of feeding oats to racehorses in this time of crisis resulted in a Government decision to ban all racing after the First Spring Meeting at Newmarket.

The decision was fought by the Jockey Club and the Bloodstock Breeders Association, and early in July the Stewards of the Jockey Club were informed that racing could be resumed on a limited scale until the end of the season. The Derby, therefore, was not run until 31 July.

The winner of this overdue Derby was Gay Crusader, owned and bred by Mr 'Fairie'—the 'nom de course' of Mr A. W. Cox—who had won the race in 1910 with Lemberg. Gay Crusader was by Bayardo out of Gay Laura, by Beppo out of the One Thousand Guineas winner Galeottia. Gay Laura herself won once as a two-year-old and bred five other winners, including Sea Rover, who made a name for himself over fences.

When he arrived at Manton to be trained by Alec Taylor, Gay Crusader was on the small side, shelly, and distinctly mean in appearance. The following spring he suddenly began to improve by leaps and bounds, but unfortunately he developed sore shins in June and his introduction to the racecourse had to be delayed until the autumn. He was unplaced first time out. but then won the Criterion Stakes at the Houghton Meeting, beating Molly Desmond, who had been very badly away, and Grand Fleet in a tight finish.

The improvement in Gay Crusader was fully maintained during the winter, and by the following spring he was not only an exceptionally handsome colt, but a really good one, too. His first outing as a three-year-old was in the Column Produce Stakes at the Craven Meeting. The going was heavy, he had 9 st. 10 lb. to carry, and under the circumstances he did reasonably well to finish second to Lord Derby's Coq d'Or.

Before the Guineas, Gay Crusader did a very satisfactory trial at Manton, and so did another three-year-old of Alec Taylor's, Major (later Viscount) Astor's Magpie. Mr Cox, captious, critical, and exacting, declined to allow the two horses to be tried together, and it was difficult to separate them in point of merit. In the Guineas

Donoghue, who knew how to humour Mr Cox, rode Gay Crusader, while Otto Madden, who had just returned to race-riding after a long absence, was on Magpie. In the Dip the two Manton colts drew clear of the other twelve runners and raced home locked together neck and neck. Magpie was dead game but rather lazy. Donoghue cleverly kept Gay Crusader so close to Magpie on the whip hand that Madden was unable to bring his whip down to encourage his mount to produce that little bit extra that he probably had in reserve and Gay Crusader scraped home by a head. Magpie was exported soon afterwards to Australia where he not only won the Melbourne and Caulfield Cups, but proved a highly successful sire.

Gay Crusader continued to thrive and by Derby Day he had reached his peak. He started a short-priced favourite, and despite being baulked more than once when he tried to come through on the rails, he won very easily by four lengths from Dansellon, with Dark Legend a head away third. There were few spectators to witness his victory. The weather had been appalling, there was very little transport available, and the majority of spectators had been compelled to walk to the course from Newmarket Station.

Gay Crusader next proceeded to win the September Stakes, the Newmarket Gold Cup—a two and a half mile event finishing at the Rowley Mile winning post—the Champion Stakes, and the Lowther Stakes. The following year he seemed better than ever and there was every prospect of his winning a second Gold Cup. Quite early in the season, against Alec Taylor's advice, Mr Cox insisted on giving the horse a gallop, Donoghue up, that virtually amounted to a trial. Gay Crusader never went better than he did that morning; he pulled up well and he walked home sound. That evening he was found to be suffering from tendon trouble and his racing career was at an end. Donoghue thought him the best horse he ever rode during his long and distinguished career.

Gay Crusader retired to the stud at a 400-guinea fee and the best of mares were sent to him. He was not, however, the success anticipated, although he sired some good horses such as Hot Night (second in the Derby), Hurstwood (third in the Derby), Bright Knight, Kincardine, and Caissot. A good many of his stock were far from genuine although he had been the most generous of horses himself. Today he is best remembered through his mares: Loika was the dam of M. Boussac's great horse Djebel; Indolence was the dam of Prince Rose, a top-class horse and sire of Prince Chevalier, Prince Bio, and Princequillo; while Hellespont was the grand-dam of the 1946 Derby and St Leger winner Airborne.

Dark Legend, third to Gay Crusader in the Derby, was exported to India where he proved one of the best horses ever to race in that country. He came back to England as a six-year-old and was then exported to France where he did well as a sire. His daughter Rosy Legend bred Dante, winner of the 1945 Derby, and Saya-jirao, winner of the 1947 St Leger. `

1917: The New Derby Stakes. Tuesday, 31 July . . . 17 Entries. £2,050.

MR 'FAIRIE'S' b.c. GAY CRUSADER by Bayardo
  out of Gay Laura   S. DONOGHUE   1
SIR HEDWORTH MEUX'S br.c. DANSELLON by Chaucer
  out of Tortor   R. WATSON   2
SIR W. COOKE'S br.c. DARK LEGEND by Dark Ronald
  out of Golden Legend   J. CHILDS   3

Also ran:

  Mr Reid Walker's Invincible (4th) (V. Smyth); Mr J. Buchanan's Athdara (J. Evans); Mr D. Fraser's Brown Prince (F. Fox); Sir R. W. B. Jardine's Lord Archer (O. Madden); Duke of Portland's Colleger (W. Earl); Mr R. Sherwood's Sir Desmond (R. J. Colling); Colonel Hall-Walker's Kingston Black (T. Burns); Mr L. Winn's Planet (E. Lancaster); Lord D'Abernon's Diadem (F. Rickaby).

12 ran.

Betting:

  7–4 Gay Crusader; 5–1 Diadem; 100–15 Dark Legend; 7–1 Invincible and Dansellon; 100–7 Athdara; 100–6 Colleger; 20–1 Planet; 33–1 Kingston Black; 40–1 Brown Prince and Lord Archer; 100–1 Sir Desmond.

Won by four lengths; a head between second and third.   2 m. 40⅗ s.
Winner trained by Alec Taylor at Manton.

1918

This year the atmosphere at Newmarket was perceptibly brighter. Although the tide had not really turned yet on the Western Front, the impetus of the great German spring offensive had been spent and the American war effort was beginning to make itself felt. There were few, though, except the inveterate optimists, who dared believe in victory before Christmas.

As things turned out this was the last Derby to be run at Newmarket for twenty-two years. Gainsborough, who won, was, like Gay Crusader and Pommern, at least up to the average standard of peace-time winners of the race, probably considerably above it; unlike the other two, he proved an outstanding success at the stud.

Volodyovski was the first Derby winner bred by a woman; Gainsborough the first to be owned by one. Lady James Douglas, who was eighty-seven years old when she died in 1941, was born in France, the daughter of Mr F. Hennessy of the famous Anglo-French family of brandy distillers. Her first husband was another member of that family, Mr R. Hennessy of Bagnolet, Cognac, and after his death she married in 1888 the fourth son of the seventh Marquis of Queensberry, Lord James Douglas, who died in 1891. Her photograph taken side by side with Gainsborough depicts a short, erect, stoutly built lady attired in spats, a severely cut coat and skirt, a masculine bow-tie, and a hat totally devoid, perhaps intentionally so, of feminine allurement.

In 1910 Lady James Douglas bought the Harwood property near Newbury, and with John Porter to advise her she proceeded to establish a stud. One of her first purchases was Sir William Bass's Oaks winner Rosedrop, by St Frusquin out of the Trenton mare Rosaline, who had been held in such low esteem by Mr J. B. Joel that he gave her to the Fresh Air Fund to be sold for twenty-five guineas! Mated with Bayardo in 1914, Rosedrop foaled Gainsborough on 24 January the following year. Lady James Douglas nearly always sold her yearlings, and Gainsborough was despatched to the Newmarket Sales in 1916 with a reserve on him of 2,000 guineas. An offer of 200 guineas less was refused, and he was sent to Colledge Leader to be trained. Soon afterwards Leader joined the forces and the colt was transferred to Alec Taylor at Manton.

Gainsborough had much more of the Bayardo character than Gay Crusader, who was lighter-framed. He was not a big horse but he had exceptional power, fine bone, great quality, and, above all, a perfect racing temperament. As a two-year-old he was nothing out of the ordinary. On his first appearance, in a small race at Newmarket at the end of July, he was fourth. Next time out he was third, again in an event of negligible importance. He finished the season, though, by an impressive win in the Autumn Stakes over the six-furlong Bretby Course.

He was still a bit backward when he took the field for the first time as a three-year-old. The race chosen to sharpen him up was the five-furlong Severals Stakes at the Craven Meeting. Ridden by Joe Childs, he was unplaced behind Mr S. B. Joel's good sprinter Sicyon. On Guineas day, however, he looked a very different proposition and was fit to run for his life. He won that race from Somme Kiss and Blink, and Lady James Douglas became the first woman to win a classic race in her own colours.

It was not a strong Derby field and Gainsborough was favourite at 13–8 on. For the first four furlongs the leaders were his stable companions Air Raid, who won the Cesarewitch that autumn, and Blink. Heading for home King John went to the front with Gainsborough and Blink hard on his heels. With just over half a mile to go Gainsborough took the lead, and though Blink almost drew level at the distance, he responded immediately when Childs showed him the whip and ran on strongly to win by a length and a half. Blink was a gallant second and Sir W. J. Tatem's Treclare two lengths away third. Lady James Douglas was warmly applauded as she led her winner into the unsaddling enclosure. Two days later the Manton stable won the Oaks with Mr 'Fairie's' My Dear, by Beppo out of Bayardo's half-sister Silesia.

Gainsborough defeated his two older opponents in the Newmarket Gold Cup and in the autumn he won the September Stakes over the last mile and three-quarters of the Cesarewitch Course, beating his stable companions My Dear and Prince Chimay, the latter a colt owned by Mr W. M. Cazalet, father of Peter Cazalet, the well-known National Hunt trainer. In his final race, the Jockey Club Stakes, Gainsborough was beaten a length by Prince Chimay. Various reasons were advanced to account for this defeat, and it is possible that Joe Childs was outmanœuvred by Otto Madden on the winner. Prince Chimay, by Chaucer, became the sire of Vatout, whose son Bois Roussel won the 1938 Derby.

Gainsborough, who outlived his owner by four years, was one of the most successful stallions ever to stand in the country. He was Champion Sire in 1932 and 1933, second in 1931, third in 1930 and 1935, and fourth in 1925, 1926, and 1927. His colts were very much more effective than his fillies, and when he died at the age of thirty his colts had won eighty-three per cent of the stake money, totalling £340,144, earned by his stock. His most notable winners were Hyperion (Derby and St Leger), Orwell (Two Thousand Guineas), Singapore (St Leger and Doncaster Cup),

Solario (St Leger and Gold Cup), Costaki Pasha (Middle Park Stakes), and Goyescas (Middle Park Stakes and Hardwicke Stakes). His best filly was Gainsborough Lass, third in the One Thousand Guineas and winner of the Coronation Stakes. His most successful mares at the stud were Una Cameron, dam of the 1931 Derby winner Cameronian; Mah Mahal, dam of the 1936 Derby winner Mahmoud; and Imagery, dam of the Irish Derby winners Museum and Phideas.

It is perhaps worth mentioning that Trenton, who sired Gainsborough's grand-dam Rosaline, was bred in New Zealand and won eight races in that country and Australia. He did well as a sire in Australia and was exported to England at fifteen years of age. His name also appears in the pedigree of the dual Eclipse Stakes winner Buchan.

1918: The New Derby Stakes. Tuesday, 4 June . . . 55 Entries. £4,000.

LADY JAMES DOUGLAS's b.c. GAINSBOROUGH
by Bayardo out of Rosedrop   J. CHILDS   1
MAJOR W. ASTOR's br.c. BLINK by Sunstar
out of Winkipop   R. J. COLLING   2
SIR W. J. TATEM's ch.c. TRECLARE by Tredennis
out of Clare   W. LANGFORD   3

Also ran:

Captain G. Loder's King John (4th) (J. H. Martin); Mr J. P. Arkwright's McNeill (F. Fox); Mr W. M. Cazalet's Air Raid (O. Madden); Duc Decazes's Mont Saint Eloi (J. Hulme); Mr C. T. Garland's Somme Kiss (B. Carslake); Mr S. B. Joel's Rivershore (S. Donoghue); Mr J. W. Larnach's Arrowsmith (H. Jones); Mr Z. G. Michalinos's Zinovia (V. Smyth); Mr J. B. Thorneycroft's Thermogene (A. Whalley); Madame Varipati's Tricycle (J. McFadden).

13 ran.

Betting:

13–8 on Gainsborough; 8–1 Zinovia; 100–8 King John and Blink; 100–7 Somme Kiss and Air Raid; 100–6 Rivershore; 20–1 Tricycle; 33–1 Thermogene; 66–1 McNeill.

Won by a length and a half; two lengths between second and third.   2 m. 33⅕ s. Winner trained by Alec Taylor at Manton.

1919

At an appalling price in lives, 'the war to end wars' had been won and this year the Derby returned to Epsom once again. A lot of people had made a great deal of money during the past four years, while gratuities for those who had served and had the good fortune to survive were on a more generous scale than at the conclusion of the Second World War. There was, in consequence, a tremendous, if temporary, boom in racing, and the crowds in the Epsom enclosures and on the Downs were enormous. Luckily the carefree thousands who saw the victory of Lord Glanely's second string Grand Parade could not foretell that in just over twenty years England would be fighting for her existence again, and that Lord Glanely himself in his old age was to meet his death through enemy action.

Grand Parade was the second black horse to win the Derby, the first being Smolensko one hundred and six years previously. Bred in Ireland by Mr R. Croker, Grand Parade was by Mr Croker's Derby winner Orby out of Grand Geraldine, by Desmond. Grand Geraldine, who was rumoured to have pulled a cart at one stage of her career, never ran herself and bred nothing else of note. Her dam Grand Marnier by Friar's Balsam never ran either, but was a full sister to Mother Siegel, dam of the 1909 Derby winner Minoru.

Lord Glanely bought Grand Parade as a foal for 470 guineas. The colt came to hand nice and early as a two-year-old, and at the Craven Meeting he won the Fitzwilliam Stakes, for which he started a 3–1 favourite. He did not run again till the Second July Meeting when he won the Soltykoff Stakes. He was then sent to Ireland to fulfil a number of engagements there. He won a Biennial Stakes, the Anglesey Stakes, and the valuable National Produce Stakes. In this last event he showed signs of staleness and only scraped home by half a length from distinctly moderate opposition. As soon as that race was over he was sent to England and, despite a very rough crossing, was at once pulled out for the Moulton Stakes at the Houghton Meeting. Partnered by Donoghue, he could only finish third to another son of Orby, Glanmerin. Donoghue's riding came in for some acid criticism from 'interested parties', but as Glanmerin ran Grand Parade to three parts of a length at level weights the following season while on this occasion he was receiving fifteen pounds, it seems that the criticism was unjustified.

Lord Glanely owned another useful two-year-old in Dominion, by Polymelus.

Dominion only won once that season, but he was second to Buchan in the Chesterfield Stakes, beaten a head at level weights, and was third in the Coventry, Exeter, and Middle Park Stakes. The following year Dominion was third to Buchan in the Craven Stakes; third, beaten a neck and three parts of a length, to The Panther and Buchan in the Two Thousand Guineas; and won the Newmarket Stakes by five lengths, with Buchan's stable companion Lord Basil, an odds-on favourite, a moderate third.

In the meantime Grand Parade had not run, but he was thriving under Frank Barling's care at home. There was every indication that he was superior to Dominion, and in a gallop about a month before the Derby he had no difficulty in conceding a year and three pounds to He, beaten a head carrying 7 st. 10 lb. in the Cesarewitch the previous autumn. That spring He had won the Babraham Plate with 8 st. 7 lb. and the March Stakes with 9 st. 4 lb., successfully conceding sixteen pounds to Paper Money, subsequently third in the Derby. This gallop was a fine performance by Grand Parade, but just how good it was could only be fully realized the day after the Derby when He won the Coronation Cup.

Shortly before the Derby when hopes were running high Grand Parade began to show traces of lameness and had to be stopped in his work. The trouble abated, but it seemed inevitable that the colt's Derby prospects had been affected in some degree by this interruption to a carefully timed preparation. Under the circumstances the stable jockey Arthur Smith, who was offered the choice, elected to ride Dominion, so Fred Templeman was given the mount of Grand Parade. In the betting Grand Parade drifted to 33–1, while Dominion hardened to 100–9. In the race itself Smith wore the first colours, Templeman a distinguishing cap.

The course at Epsom was in very poor condition, very hard in places and with remarkably little grass. The public imagination had been captured by The Panther, who was a red-hot favourite at 6–5. The Panther was owned by Sir Alec Black, who had only just taken up racing, and was trained by George Manser. Quiet and reserved, Manser had been engaged in racing in various capacities most of his life. He had been on Ladas and Sir Visto in their pre-Derby gallops; he had ridden winners under both rules in England, Ireland, and Germany; he had trained in Austria, Belgium, France, Germany, South Africa, Ireland, and Spain; he had fought in the retreat from Mons. It was not his fault that a great deal of exaggerated nonsense was published in the newspapers about The Panther's capabilities. In 1918 Sir Alec Black had had the effrontery to send his colt to the Newmarket Sales with a reserve of £40,000 on him. 'This was to give a chance to all comers,' Sir Alec said. 'If he passes out of the ring unsold, there will be no further opportunity to buy the horse.'

The Panther, by Tracery out of the wayward mare Countess Zia, may not have been the world-beater that his owner was at pains to make out, but he was a beautiful mover. He headed the Free Handicap as a two-year-old and he won the Two Thousand Guineas. Unfortunately his temper on Derby Day was abominable. He showed signs of irritation on the way to the start, and when he got there he made a thorough nuisance of himself. He broke the tapes and then refused to line up. At the 'off' he threw up his head and lost lengths before Cooper could induce him to get going. Buchan, joint second favourite at 7–1 with Paper Money, was also badly away, but Paper Money, ridden by Donoghue, was smoothly into his stride and soon showed in front from Dominion and Grand Parade. Buchan was at the tail-end of the field in the early stages, but rapidly began to work his way forward.

At Tattenham Corner The Panther, who had made a short-lived flourish after half a mile, was hopelessly beaten and Paper Money led from Grand Parade with Buchan making steady progress on the outside. Brennan then decided to take Buchan over to the rails and tucked him in behind Paper Money, but soon afterwards, evidently fearing to get shut in, he tacked across to the outside again. Almost immediately Paper Money's stride began to shorten, so back went Buchan to the rails, this time at the rear of Grand Parade, who had taken the lead. There was an exciting tussle over the final furlong, but Grand Parade, faultlessly ridden by Templeman, stuck it out well to win by half a length. Paper Money was third two lengths behind Buchan and Sir Douglas fourth. Dominion stumbled on the hill and was never seen with a chance of any sort afterwards. It was a fine effort by Grand Parade to score without a previous race that season and after his preparation had been interrupted at a critical stage, but the general opinion was that Buchan had been desperately unlucky not to win.

At Ascot Lord Glanely had seven winners, all trained by Barling. One of the seven was Grand Parade, who beat his solitary opponent in the St James's Palace Stakes, Glanmerin, by three parts of a length. Foy, a notoriously erratic jockey, rode one of his less good races on the runner-up. Grand Parade was ridden by Arthur Smith, who also won the Prince of Wales's Stakes on Dominion, later in life a stud failure both in France and in Spain. Grand Parade never ran again and retired to the stud at a 400-guinea fee. He got a lot of moderate winners, but few good horses, the best one being Diophon, who gave the Aga Khan his first classic success by winning the Two Thousand Guineas in 1924. His mares did quite well, and his name appears in the pedigrees of the Derby and Grand Prix winner My Love and of the Oaks winner Ambiguity. Due to the Orby influence, most of his stock were noted for speed rather than stamina.

Buchan was a half-brother to Tamar, second in the Derby three years later. He was an unlucky horse, as he undoubtedly should have won the Derby and he was disqualified in 1920 after winning the Ascot Gold Cup. He did, however, win the Eclipse Stakes twice. He did well at the stud and was Champion Sire in 1927. His fillies were better than his colts and his best winners were Book Law (St Leger) and Short Story (Oaks). Rhodes Scholar (Eclipse Stakes), Pay Up (Two Thousand Guineas), Sun Castle (St Leger), and Airborne (Derby and St Leger) were all out of Buchan mares.

The Panther failed badly in the Irish Derby and the Champion Stakes. He was then exported to the Argentine, where he got a good many winners. Brought back to England, he died very suddenly and was found to have a badly diseased heart. This may have been the cause of his deterioration as a three-year-old.

Lord Glanely was seventy-five when he was killed in an air raid in 1942. Raised to the peerage in 1918, he was born William James Tatem at Appledore in Devonshire. His father died when he was seven, and after a brief period at sea, he went to work in a Cardiff shipping office. Shrewd, tireless, forceful, and forthright, he soon began to make his presence felt, and it was as a ship-owner that in due course he amassed an enormous fortune.

His first interest in horses lay with hackneys and hunters, but in 1908 he took up racing. He had his first winner in 1909 and at the time of his death he had won 552 races on the flat worth over £300,000. Between the wars he spent many hundreds of thousands of pounds on bloodstock. A lot of his most expensive purchases turned out to be useless, but he was leading owner twice and second in the list on four occasions. He was successful in all the classic races, but the victory that pleased him most was that of Chulmleigh in the 1937 St Leger. He bred Chulmleigh himself, and the colt was by his St Leger winner Singapore out of his Oaks winner Rose of England.

Stout, rubicund, and walrus-moustached, Lord Glanely was an easily recognized and respected figure on the racecourse. Staunchly patriotic, his colours included a red, white, and blue sash, while the names he gave his horses usually reflected either his pride in being an Englishman or his love for the county of his birth. It gave satisfaction to everyone connected with racing when he was made a member of the Jockey Club in 1929.

Fred Templeman was a very sound rider and became a successful trainer at Lambourn when he retired from the saddle. As a trainer he won the Two Thousand Guineas with Diolite, a grandson of Grand Parade, and the Hardwicke Stakes and Jubilee with Cotoneaster.

Frank Barling was originally a veterinary surgeon in Wales, and while in practice there, he assisted in running a stud of shire horses. He then took to training jumpers, but transferred after a few seasons to the flat. He became Lord Glanely's trainer at the end of the war, but his health was poor and he did not retain the appointment for long. He had been in retirement for a considerable time when he died in 1935. His son Geoffrey has for many years been a successful trainer at Newmarket.

1919: Wednesday, 4 June . . . 215 Entries. £6,450.

LORD GLANELY's bl.c. GRAND PARADE by Orby out of Grand Geraldine	F. TEMPLEMAN	1
MAJOR W. ASTOR's b.c. BUCHAN by Sunstar out of Hamoaze	J. BRENNAN	2
SIR W. GILBEY's b. or br.c. PAPER MONEY by Greenback out of Epping Rose	S. DONOGHUE	3

Also ran:

Admiral H. Meux's Sir Douglas (4th) (G. Hulme); Sir W. Nelson's Tangiers (E. Piper); Captain L. Montagu's White Heat (H. Jelliss); Lady Torrington's All Alone (F. Fox); Mr C. T. Garland's Milton (G. Colling); Lord Glanely's Dominion (A. Smith); Sir A. Black's The Panther (R. Cooper); Mr J. A. de Rothschild's Roamer (J. Childs); Mr F. Willey's Bay of Naples (W. Whalley); Sir G. Murray's Coriolanus (B. Carslake).

13 ran.

Betting:

6–5 The Panther; 7–1 Buchan and Paper Money; 100–9 Dominion; 20–1 Milton; 25–1 All Alone; 33–1 Grand Parade; 40–1 Tangiers; 50–1 Sir Douglas, Bay of Naples, Roamer, and Coriolanus; 100–1 White Heat.

Won by half a length; two lengths between second and third. 2 m. 35⅘ s.
Winner trained by F. Barling at Newmarket.

1920

Major G. Loder's Spion Kop was not one of the great Derby winners, but in a race that was run at a tremendous pace under extremely fast conditions, he succeeded in outstaying his opponents.

Bred by his owner, Spion Kop was a bay with a blaze face and four white pasterns, considerable depth, powerful quarters, and much better forelegs than most of his sire's stock. He was unquestionably bred to stay, being by the Derby and Grand Prix winner Spearmint out of Hammerkop, by Gallinule. Hammerkop raced for eight seasons and her victories included the Yorkshire Oaks, the Queen Alexandra Stakes, and the Cesarewitch. She only bred four foals and was seventeen years of age when she produced the last of them, Spion Kop, who was rather a weakly specimen in his early days.

Trained by Gilpin at Newmarket, Spion Kop lacked speed as a two-year-old. He ran six times, finishing third once and second on the other five occasions. In the Free Handicap he carried 7 st. 4 lb. and was beaten less than a length. There were certainly no grounds for regarding him as a likely candidate for the classics.

The following spring a rumour seeped through the City of London that Spion Kop, despite his unpromising public record, was a likely winner of the Derby and he was backed for that race at 33–1. On 8 May he won the mile and a half Spelthorne Stakes at Kempton in a canter and his price was immediately shortened to 9–1. As it happened, Gilpin had another Derby contender in Sir James Buchanan's grey colt Sarchedon, a full brother to Stefan the Great. Not long before the Derby Gilpin conducted a trial over a mile and a half at Newmarket with the following result: 1) Sarchedon; 2) Paragon; 3) Comrade; 4) Spion Kop. Paragon had finished third in the Two Thousand Guineas, while Comrade was destined to win the Grand Prix. As soon as the result of this trial was known, the public began to back the potentially brilliant but somewhat unreliable Sarchedon for the Derby, while Spion Kop on the other hand went out in the betting. Public opinion appeared to be confirmed when it was seen that Arthur Smith, the stable jockey, was on Sarchedon, while that very good American jockey Frank O'Neill had been summoned from France to partner Spion Kop, his terms being £200 for the ride and £1,000 if he won. As a matter of fact O'Neill, when he was engaged, was under the impression that he was due to ride Sarchedon and was not pleased to start with to find himself detailed for Spion Kop.

Whatever view the general public took about the trial, it is not unlikely that Gilpin, 'the Wizard of Clarehaven', and an extremely shrewd and experienced trainer, had his own views on the subject. He had trained Spearmint, and no doubt he realized that Spion Kop was more likely to stay the distance in a true-run race than Sarchedon, a son of that exceptionally fast horse The Tetrarch.

Favourite for the Derby was another Tetrarch colt, Tetratema, who had shown brilliant form as a two-year-old and had won the Two Thousand Guineas from Allenby, a son of the 1912 Derby winner, Tagalie. Allenby was second favourite, and next in the betting came Lord Derby's Archaic and Sarchedon, while there was a lot of good money for Spion Kop at 100–6. The going was firm and it was an exceptionally hot day for early June.

Right from the start Tetratema and Abbots Trace, Steve Donoghue's mount, went off at a tremendous pace, and by the mile post they were well clear of a field that was already becoming strung out. Racing flat out down the hill, Tetratema, whose stamina had always been suspect, suddenly cracked and dropped back beaten, while Allenby was in trouble soon afterwards. Once round Tattenham Corner Sarchedon and another grey, Poltava, set off in pursuit of Abbots Trace, and O'Neill, who had realized early on that the leaders could never maintain the terrific pace to the end, began to make rapid headway. With just under three furlongs to go Spion Kop swept past the tiring Abbots Trace and from then on the issue was never in doubt. He passed the post two lengths clear of Archaic, with Orpheus third and Sarchedon fourth. Near the finish Sarchedon swerved from exhaustion and collided with Abbots Trace, who almost immediately crossed his legs and fell. Donoghue crashed on to the hard ground right in the path of the oncoming horses and it looked inevitable that he was going to be seriously injured. To everyone's surprise and relief he got up, walked back to the weighing-room, and after a short rest rode two more winners that afternoon, a wonderful exhibition of nerve and toughness.

Spion Kop never won again. In the Grand Prix he was unplaced behind his stable companion Comrade, and after a rest he may not have been quite ready when Abbots Trace beat him at level weights over eleven furlongs in a two-horse race at Derby. Following a very good gallop with Comrade, he was made favourite for the St Leger, but ran unplaced and according to the *Bloodstock Breeders Review* 'that display was probably due to an attack of "bug disease"'. He was fourth to Orpheus in the Champion Stakes, and after twice failing as a four-year-old he was retired to his owner's stud in Co. Kildare. As a sire he was not really a great success but he did get Felstead, winner of the 1928 Derby. Other good winners by him were Kopi, who won the Irish Derby and did well as a sire in France; Bongrace, a really good staying filly; and The Bastard, who, under the rather more refined name of The Buzzard, made a great reputation as a sire in Australia. Spion Kop died in 1941 and is buried at Eyrefield beside Spearmint, Pretty Polly, and the Grand National winner Ambush II.

Major (later Colonel) Giles Loder, M.C., inherited the racing interests of his uncle, the late Major Eustace Loder. In 1920 he was still serving with the Scots Guards and whether the race will ever again be won by a serving soldier seems highly doubtful. Colonel Loder owned and bred many good winners after Spion Kop, most of them descendants of Pretty Polly, but he did not have the luck to win another classic race. A bachelor whose home was in Sussex, he was a member of the Jockey Club for many years before his death in 1966.

Archaic was exported to America for 17,000 guineas. Orpheus, who won the Champion Stakes, became notoriously ill-tempered and proved a moderate sire. Sarchedon was sent to Australia. Tetratema was a great success at the stud, being Champion Sire in 1929 and second on two other occasions.

Frank O'Neill was born in America and rode his first winner there at the age of fourteen. Like many other capable American riders, he came to Europe before the First World War and proceeded to make a great name for himself in France, where during his career he rode the winner of every important race. In 1910 he rode 156 winners, in 1911 his total was 163, a record for French racing at that time, while in 1913 he was at the top of the tree with 156. These were remarkable totals considering the limited opportunities available to a jockey in the Paris area. In England he won the St Leger and the Gold Cup on Prince Palatine, the Oaks on Straitlace, and the Lincoln on Sir Gallahad III. He was not a great stylist and was reckoned to be somewhat hard on his horses, but he was tough, strong, and at his best on the big occasion. On retirement he opened a bar in Paris, which became a rendezvous for members of the racing community. He returned to America in 1955 and died there in 1960 aged seventy-four.

1920: Wednesday, 2 June . . . 260 Entries. £6,450.

MAJOR G. LODER's b.c. SPION KOP by Spearmint
out of Hammerkop   F. O'NEILL   1
LORD DERBY's ch.c. ARCHAIC by Polymelus
out of Keystone II   G. BELLHOUSE   2
SIR H. CUNLIFFE-OWEN's b.c. ORPHEUS by Orby
out of Electra   F. LEACH   3

Also ran:

Sir J. Buchanan's Sarchedon (4th) (A. Smith); Mr W. Raphael's Poltava (H.

Jones); Mr A. de Rothschild's Daylight Patrol (J. Childs); Admiral Sir H. Meux's Torelore (A. Balding); Lord Londonderry's Polumetis (T. Burns); Captain H. Whitworth's He Goes (F. Templeman); Sir E. Hulton's Silvern (A. Whalley); Lord Penrhyn's Kerasos (J. Shatwell); Sir A. Bailey's All Prince (F. Fox); Lord Zetland's Dynamo (H. Robbins); Major D. McCalmont's Tetratema (B. Carslake); Sir W. Nelson's Attilius (W. Saxby); Lord Anglesey's Firework (E. Wheatley); Mr W. Williams's Marshal Neil (G. Hulme); Mr W. Raphael's Allenby (F. Slade); Lord Dewar's Abbots Trace (S. Donoghue) (*fell*).

19 ran.

Betting :

  3–1 Tetratema; 8–1 Allenby; 9–1 Sarchedon; 10–1 Archaic; 100–7 He Goes; 100–6 Spion Kop; 20–1 Polumetis; 25–1 Dynamo; 33–1 Abbots Trace, Attilius, and Daylight Patrol; 40–1 Silvern; 50–1 Orpheus and Poltava; 66–1 Torelore.
Mr Raphael declared to win with Allenby.

Won by two lengths; a length and a half between second and third.   2 m. 34$\frac{4}{5}$ s.
Winner trained by P. P. Gilpin at Newmarket.

1921

Mr J. B. Joel's Humorist, winner of the Derby in 1921, must have been the gamest of the game. Unknown to anyone, he was suffering from a tubercular lung condition; within a fortnight of his triumph at Epsom he was dead.

Bred by his owner, Humorist was by Polymelus out of the 1913 One Thousand Guineas and Oaks winner Jest, by Sundridge out of Absurdity, dam of the St Leger winner Black Jester. Jest, who went back to Lord Jersey's Oaks winner Cobweb, the dam of the Derby winner Bay Middleton, was disappointing in her early years at the stud. For her first three seasons she was barren and in the fourth she produced a dead foal. Then came Humorist to atone for all her previous shortcomings. She never bred another winner and died after producing a dead foal in 1921.

Humorist, together with twenty-four other yearlings, arrived at Charles Morton's stables at Wantage in the late summer of 1919, and that highly skilled and very experienced trainer at once took a fancy to him. The colt had the smoothest of temperaments and made excellent progress throughout the winter. In the spring Morton tried him several times and so well did he go that he was considered certain to win the Woodcote Stakes at Epsom, the event that was chosen for his first appearance. A day or two before the race, though, he was off his feed and his coat was staring. His short life was full of these physical vicissitudes, and there can be little doubt that the disease that ultimately killed him was rooted in his system from an early age. He ran in the Woodcote Stakes and won, but was fading fast in the sixth and final furlong after he had looked like winning easily at five.

Just before Ascot Humorist began to cough and it was some weeks before he was really right again. In fact he was unable to run until the Champagne Stakes at Doncaster in September. Before that race he was tried with a very useful two-year-old called Thunderer and finished nearly ten lengths ahead of him. On that form he was a certainty for the Champagne Stakes, but he failed to run up to expectations and was beaten by Lemonora. The following week Thunderer won the Newbury Foal Stakes in a canter with 9 st. 6 lb. on his back, conceding two stone to a smart filly of Sir Abe Bailey's called Herself.

In October Humorist won the Buckenham Stakes, beating Night Patrol, who later won over £20,000 in stakes in Australia; and then the Clearwell Stakes, in which he was faced by a single and moderate opponent. His last race as a two-year-old was the Middle Park Stakes, in which he was beaten a neck by the Tracery colt Monarch. Carslake, who rode him, was convinced it was a fluke result and prophesied that Humorist would win the Derby the following year.

Humorist wintered well, and in April he was so convincing in a gallop with Corn Sack, winner of the City and Suburban the year before, that Morton thought he was sure to win the Guineas. Ridden by Donoghue, he looked to have the race at his mercy a furlong out, but he suddenly faltered close home and was beaten by the Manton pair Craig an Eran and Lemonora. Donoghue said afterwards that the colt's failure was due to lack of stamina, but that was a view that Morton declined to accept.

Between the Guineas and the Derby Humorist was a constant source of worry. One day he would look the picture of health, the next he would be obviously off-colour. His lapses never lasted long, though, and when he recovered he seemed to be right at the top of his form once again. Donoghue was engaged to ride him at Epsom, but his services were not procured without difficulty. Lord Derby, who had Glorioso running in the race, had paid Donoghue a handsome retainer for the season and naturally expected him to ride his horse. Donoghue, however, was determined to ride Humorist and Lord Derby very kindly allowed him to do so in the end, but he had some pertinent comments to make on the subject to Morton. The whole business was very typical of Donoghue, who had a great deal of charm and nearly always got his own way in the end.

The Derby favourite was Leighton, a Roi Hérode colt owned by Mr W. E. Whineray, a Liverpool cotton broker. Leighton was thought to be unbeatable by his trainer Harry Cottrill, but Cottrill was inclined to be over-optimistic, an expensive failing on the racecourse. The Guineas winner Craig an Eran was second favourite, Humorist was well backed at 6–1, and there was a lot of money, too, for Lemonora.

Morton instructed Donoghue not to come to the front until he felt that he had the race won. 'He has such tremendous speed,' Morton said, 'that you can put him where you like any time.' Humorist was drawn on the outside of the field, but he was very quickly into his stride, and after a couple of furlongs Donoghue took him across to the rails. Coming to Tattenham Corner Alan Breck led from Leighton with Humorist close up third, but as soon as the straight was reached Alan Breck, one of whose legs was heavily bandaged, began to weaken and Leighton did not last much longer. At that point Craig an Eran began his challenge, but just as he started his run Donoghue drove Humorist into the lead on the rails. A great battle ensued and at one point Craig an Eran very nearly drew level, but Humorist ran on with the utmost courage to win by a neck. Lemonora was three lengths away third and Alan Breck fourth. Donoghue had ridden a beautiful race on the winner and was rightly given a tremendous reception by the crowd.

Humorist was very distressed indeed after the race and Morton decided to keep him at Epsom that night instead of sending him back home as he had intended. Next morning, however, the colt was right on his toes again and he seemed so well a day or two later at Wantage that it was decided to run him in the Hardwicke Stakes at Ascot. On the Monday of Ascot, preparatory to a gallop, he was given a canter during the course of which he broke a blood-vessel. The bleeding did not last long and he was sent back to his stable to rest. He recovered as usual quite quickly and looked as well as he had ever done when Mr (later Sir) Alfred Munnings came to make some sketches of him a few days later. It was Munnings's intention to have him out again that afternoon, but just after lunch, as the head-lad was walking through the yard, he saw blood trickling from under the door of Humorist's box. Inside lay the Derby winner, dead. He had had a hæmorrhage of the lungs and must have died within a very few minutes.

To have accomplished what he did with such a disability Humorist must have been not only a really good horse, but a wonderfully gallant one as well. Mr Joel accepted this stroke of ill-fortune with his customary stoicism and really seemed more concerned over Morton, who was heartbroken, than at his own loss. The blow that Mr Joel had received was nevertheless severe, as he had been looking to Humorist to replace Sunstar at his stud in due course. In fact, Mr Joel's racing fortunes declined from this point, and though he remained an owner for the best part of another twenty years, Humorist's victory was the last of his eleven classic successes. Humorist's dam Jest was a charming filly, full of quality, but with an extremely delicate constitution; some people were inclined to attribute Humorist's weakness to her, others to the three crosses of Hermit in his pedigree, Hermit being a 'bleeder' himself and a well-known transmitter of that infirmity.

Craig an Eran was by Sunstar out of Maid of the Mist, by Cyllene out of Sceptre. He went on to win the Eclipse Stakes, but failed as an odds-on favourite in the St Leger. He was disappointing at the stud in England, although he sired a Derby winner in April the Fifth. He did better in France where he got Admiral Drake, winner of the Grand Prix and sire of the Derby winner Phil Drake; and Mon Talisman, winner of the Prix du Jockey Club and sire of the Grand Prix winner Clairvoyant. Both Mon Talisman and Clairvoyant were seized by the Germans during the war and were never recovered.

Lemonora won the Grand Prix de Paris, but was probably very lucky to beat Ksar, a really good horse who had the misfortune to be ridden with conspicuous lack of judgement on this occasion. Ksar, sire of Tourbillon, was a great success at the stud; Lemonora, on the other hand, was an undoubted failure.

John Skeaping working on a sculpture of Hyperion

Miss Dorothy Paget and Gordon Richards

Fred Darling and Aly Khan

Charlie Smirke

1921

1921: Wednesday 1 June . . . 335 Entries. £6,450.

MR J. B. JOEL's ch.c. HUMORIST by Polymelus out of Jest	S. DONOGHUE	1
LORD ASTOR's b.c. CRAIG AN ERAN by Sunstar out of Maid of the Mist	J. BRENNAN	2
MR J. WATSON's ch.c. LEMONORA by Lemberg out of Honora	J. CHILDS	3

Also ran:

Sir James Buchanan's Alan Breck (4th) (A. Balding); Mr W. E. Whineray's Leighton (M. Beary); Mr A. de Rothschild's Roman Fiddle (F. Lane); Lord Derby's Glorioso (B. Carslake); Sir J. Arnott's Pucka Sahib (F. Winter); Mr F. Hardy's Beauregard (I. Strydom); Sir H. Cunliffe-Owen's Eaglehawk (F. Leach); Captain C. Hanbury's Highlander (G. Hulme); Lord Allendale's Goldendale (F. Bullock); Major A. B. Bayley-Worthington's Brinklow (H. Jelliss); Lord Glanely's Westward Ho (A. Smith); Mr G. E. D. Langley's Pride of Ulster (W. Barnett); Mr J. D. Cohn's Le Traquet (G. Garner); Mr S. M. Dennis's Euphrosynus (R. Cooper); Mr H. W. Rudd's Granite (A. Whalley); Major A. B. Bayley-Worthington's Bright Orb (T. Burns); Mr Z. G. Michalinos's Goldfinder (E. Gardner); Mr A. K. Macomber's The Bohemian (F. O'Neill); Mr F. Curzon's Our Prince (G. Walsh); Mr James White's Granely (V. Smyth).

23 ran.

Betting:

7–2 Leighton; 5–1 Craig an Eran; 6–1 Humorist; 8–1 Lemonora; 100–7 Alan Breck; 100–6 Highlander; 20–1 Pucka Sahib; 33–1 Granely; 40–1 Roman Fiddle, Goldendale, and Westward Ho; 50–1 Le Traquet; 66–1 Glorioso and The Bohemian.

Won by a neck; three lengths between second and third.   2 m. 36⅕ s.
Winner trained by C. Morton at Wantage.

1922

It is not unlikely that the best horse to race in England during the First World War was not Gainsborough or Gay Crusader but Hurry On, 'the best horse I have ever seen, the best I am ever likely to see' as he was described by his trainer Fred Darling, whose standards were exceptionally high.

By Marcovil, who was far from being a great racehorse and had very bad forelegs, out of the Sainfoin mare Toute Suite, a little pony that was too small to be put into training, Hurry On was bred by Mr W. Murland and foaled on 7 May. He was a magnificent great chesnut standing 17 hands, with a girth of 82½ inches and 9½ inches of bone below the knee. Bought as a yearling for 500 guineas by Mr James Buchanan, later Lord Woolavington, he only ran as a three-year-old, winning all his six races including the September Stakes and the Jockey Club Cup. At the stud he was Champion Sire in 1926 and head of the list of sires of successful brood mares on three occasions. He sired three Derby winners, Captain Cuttle, Coronach, and Call Boy, and at the age of twenty he got his most influential son, the Gold Cup winner Precipitation. Above all, he succeeded in reviving the Matchem male line that was almost extinct when he went to the stud.

The very first mare that Hurry On covered during his first season was his owner's Bellavista, by Cyllene out of Emotion, by Nunthorpe. She had been bred by Mr James Russel, and Lord Woolavington had bought her in 1915 for 1,950 guineas. She bred eight other winners, including Tom Pinch, a full brother to Captain Cuttle that was very useful as a two-year-old but turned 'doggy'.

The produce of this mating was a colt named Captain Cuttle, a great big massive chesnut with a white blaze. He was so heavy-topped that it was out of the question to train him seriously as a two-year-old, and throughout his career his great body imposed a considerable strain on his forelegs. His disposition was extremely amiable and he developed a warm affection for his trainer, whom he followed about like a dog. He only had one outing his first season, showing much promise, considering how backward he was, in finishing second to Collaborator in a minor event at Doncaster in September.

During the winter Darling rode Captain Cuttle a great deal himself. The colt was perfectly happy to play the part of trainer's hack, but he knew all right when it was his turn to work. He never set off without a few routine fly-kicks and bucks, and when

440

he did get moving he pulled extremely hard, although not quite so alarmingly as his sire had done. Darling was careful to give him as light a preparation as possible, as he always felt doubtful whether 'the Captain's' legs would stand the strain.

Ridden by Victor Smyth, Captain Cuttle reappeared at the Craven Meeting looking a picture and won the Wood Ditton Stakes by six lengths. He would probably have won the Two Thousand Guineas had he been at his best, but he was suffering from a slight digestive disorder and was beaten by St Louis and Pondoland. He very soon recovered from that little setback, but when Victor Smyth came down to Beckhampton on 24 May to ride him in a gallop, he did not go nearly as well as his trainer had hoped. Darling concluded that Smyth and the big chesnut were ill-suited to each other and, after a little wangling, the services of Donoghue were obtained. Donoghue flew to Beckhampton on the Saturday to make the acquaintance of his Derby mount, but owing to a misunderstanding an Irish jockey turned up under the impression that he had been selected to ride Captain Cuttle in the Derby. In the end, to save acrimonious argument, Darling rode the colt that morning himself and Donoghue did not get on Captain Cuttle's back until he rode work on him at Epsom on Monday morning. The colt then went so well that Donoghue was filled with the utmost confidence.

Donoghue's confidence was ultimately justified to the full, but there were some worrying moments first. To start with, Captain Cuttle had got loose in the yard when he was being boxed for Epsom and was trotting off briskly in the direction of the Bath Road when he heard his trainer calling him, whereupon he turned about and trotted docilely back. Far worse than this, though, was the crisis just before the race. Donoghue had mounted Captain Cuttle in the paddock and was forming up for the parade when he found that the horse was lame. He at once got off and discovered that the plate on one of Captain Cuttle's forefeet was broken. It was then a battle against time. Someone fetched Fred Darling, who was walking back towards the stand, someone else the blacksmith. In the now deserted paddock Captain Cuttle stood quiet as an old sheep while a new plate was fitted, but in the meanwhile rumours that he was lame had reached the betting rings and his price was extended to tens. The new plate was duly fitted but the next shock was that Captain Cuttle was still slightly lame when Donoghue remounted. This, however, was due to a temporary stiffness in the knee of the leg that had been held up while the plate was adjusted, and it soon wore off after the canter down to the post.

After some preliminary excitements the race proved remarkably uneventful. Captain Cuttle was going like a winner from the start and once he had taken the lead at Tattenham Corner, the result was never in doubt and he was cheered home an easy winner by four lengths from Tamar, with Craigangower a further three lengths away third. The time, 2 minutes 34⅗ seconds, set up a new record for the race. The unexpectedly long price at which the winner started was an unpleasant shock to bookmakers all over the country, but rendered Donoghue more popular than ever with the general public.

Captain Cuttle won the St James's Palace Stakes at Ascot, but tendon trouble prevented him from being trained for the St Leger. The following year it was hoped to run him in the Gold Cup, but his forelegs continued to give trouble and he was retired after winning a small race at Kempton. In his first season at the stud Captain Cuttle sired Scuttle, who won the One Thousand Guineas for King George V, while the following year he got Walter Gay, who was second in the 1929 Derby to Trigo. He also sired Glenabatrick, dam of the Gold Cup winner Tiberius. In 1927 he was sold for £50,000 to go to Italy and five years later he met with a fatal accident in that country when covering a mare. He was a grand stamp of horse, well above the average standard of Derby winners, and he might well have made a great name for himself as a sire had he stayed in this country.

Tamar was Lord Astor's third Derby runner-up in four years. A half-brother to Buchan, he was exported to Hungary where he died young. Craigangower was exported to the United States, where he was a stud failure, and he ended his days in Canada.

James Buchanan, first and last Lord Woolavington, was a self-made man. A shrewd, hardworking Scot with a prodigious memory and indifferent health, he amassed a tremendous fortune as a distiller of whisky and when he died in 1935 at the age of eighty-five, he left behind him something over £7,000,000. A generous donor to causes and institutions he deemed deserving, he received his peerage the year that Captain Cuttle won the Derby.

A visit to the Argentine towards the end of the last century stimulated his interest in horses and, returning to England with a trainer and a jockey from South America, he embarked on his racing career. For three years he raced under the 'nom de course' of 'Mr Kincaid', and the first good horse he owned was a gelding called Epsom Lad, whom he bought from the late Lord Rosebery for 1,050 guineas. The following season Epsom Lad won the Eclipse Stakes, ridden by Gomez, and over £18,000 in Stakes.

After a few seasons Sam Darling was appointed his trainer, and on Sam Darling's death his son Fred took his place. The turning-point of Lord Woolavington's racing career was his purchase of Hurry On, who sired not only his first Derby winner Captain Cuttle, but his second one, too, Coronach, who also won the St Leger and the Eclipse Stakes.

Lord Woolavington's stud, situated at the foot of the Sussex Downs, passed on his death to his daughter Mrs Macdonald-Buchanan, who won the Derby in 1941 with Owen Tudor.

Fred Darling died in 1953 at the age of sixty-nine, only three days after Pinza, a colt that he had bred, had won the Derby. He was beyond all argument one of the finest trainers in English racing history. He won nineteen classic races, one fewer than Alec Taylor, and was successful in the Derby on no fewer than seven occasions, thus equalling the record of John Porter. His Derby winners were Captain Cuttle (1922), Manna (1925), Coronach (1926), Cameronian (1931), Bois Roussel (1938), Pont l'Evêque (1940), and Owen Tudor (1941). The best colt he ever trained was Hurry On; the best filly Sun Chariot, who won the One Thousand Guineas, the Oaks, and the St Leger for King George VI in 1942.

The Darling family has been connected with racing for well over a century. Fred's father Sam trained two Derby winners, Galtee More and Ard Patrick; Sam's grandfather won the 1833 St Leger on Rockingham. Marcus Marsh, Fred's nephew and former pupil, has so far won the Derby with Windsor Lad and Tulyar.

Fred Darling rode a few winners as an apprentice, but never held a jockey's licence. He began training in 1907 and the following year he turned out twenty-seven winners. In 1909, however, he went to Germany and ran a stable there with notable success until returning to England shortly before the war to take over Beckhampton from his father.

Although grievously handicapped at times by ill-health, his record was one of remarkable success until he retired in 1947. As a man he was taciturn, secretive, and somewhat easily aroused to anger, although he mellowed a little with age. Bores, fools, and importunate members of the racing press were liable to be treated with a brusqueness that verged on hostility. Brought up in a hard school himself, he imposed an exacting standard of stable discipline, and in a clash of wills with a difficult patron or a recalcitrant horse, he rarely emerged second best. If on some occasions he overplayed the part of a martinet, the results he achieved were all that could be desired, and it was those who worked in the closest co-operation with him, like Sir Gordon Richards, who admired him the most.

It is impossible to say what exactly was the secret of Darling's success, but his methods, based on the conservation of vital energy for the racecourse rather than expending it on the gallops, were not for the imitator who lacked his apparently magic touch. The Beckhampton horses could be relied on almost without fail to produce their very best form on the one day that really mattered and, moreover, they carried an air of distinction and well-being that made them stand out from their rivals in the paddock. No doubt tireless attention to detail and the individual needs of each horse, faultless stable hygiene, the best of feeding and a determination that no horse should be overworked at home all contributed to the result, but Darling seemed to possess in an unusual degree the art of getting a horse fit to run for its life and building up condition simultaneously.

Ruthless in achieving his objectives and utterly indifferent to whether he was popular or not, Fred Darling may not have been the most lovable of characters, but the word 'genius' can be applied to him without reserve.

This year the Epsom Executive gave £3,000 in added money and for the first time in the history of the race there was a five-figure prize for the winner.

1922: Wednesday, 31 May . . . 361 Entries. £10,625.

LORD WOOLAVINGTON's ch.c. CAPTAIN CUTTLE
by Hurry On out of Bellavista   S. DONOGHUE   1
LORD ASTOR's b.c. TAMAR by Tracery
out of Hamoaze   F. BULLOCK   2
MR BARCLAY WALKER's ch.c. CRAIGANGOWER
by Polymelus out of Fortuna   M. BEARY   3

Also ran:

Lord Queenborough's St Louis (4th) (G. Archibald); Mr H. Salvin's Simon Pure (H. Jelliss); Mr W. Raphael's Villars (G. Bellhouse); Lord Jersey's Scamp (F. Lane); Sir E. Paget's Re-echo (E. Gardner); Mr S. B. Joel's Pondoland (F. O'Neill); Mr D. Fraser's Bucks Hussar (J. Childs); Lord Glanely's Great Star (V. Smyth); Mr F. Bibby's North End (H. Wragg); Sir G. Bullough's Satelles (E. C. Elliott); Mr A. W. Gordon's Jacquot (H. Blades); Mr G. Barclay's Galway Prince (W. Smyth); Captain F. Forrester's Psychology (H. Beasley); Mr H. C. Sutton's Lord Bilberry (J. Leach); Lord Lonsdale's Diligence (M. MacGee); Lord Wavertree's Baydon (J. Thwaites); Mr J. P. Arkwright's Dry Toast (B. Carslake); Sir P. Mostyn's Irish Battle (F. Fox); Mr G. Barclay's Lord of Burghley (A. Whalley); Mr James White's Norseman (W. Griggs); Major L. B. Holliday's Silpho (M. Wing); Lieutenant-Colonel G. W. Parkinson's Silvanus (E. Piper); Lord Wavertree's Rung Ho (J. Ledson); Lord Penrhyn's Doctor Quill (H. Jones); Mr A. Lowry's Double First (J. Patman); Major J. B. Paget's Lofox (F. Winter); Major A. Congreve's Moyode (G. Smith).

30 ran.

Betting:

4–1 St Louis; 11–2 Pondoland; 10–1 Tamar and Captain Cuttle; 100–9 Re-echo; 100–7 Psychology; 20–1 North End and Craigangower; 25–1 Bucks Hussar; 33–1

Lord of Burghley, Scamp, and Simon Pure; 40–1 Dry Toast and Great Star; 50–1 Villars and Diligence; 66–1 Irish Battle.

Won by four lengths; three lengths between second and third. 2 m. 34⅗ s. Winner trained by F. Darling at Beckhampton.

1923

Mr Ben Irish was a farmer from Sawtry, a small village not far from Newmarket. He made a bit of money in the course of the war and accordingly he asked Basil Jarvis to buy him a yearling. For 260 guineas Jarvis bought him Periosteum, who began by winning a £100 Maiden Plate at Folkestone and finished by winning the Gold Cup at Ascot. Mr Irish thereupon decided to play up his luck and at the Doncaster Sales in 1921 he bought Papyrus for 3,500 guineas.

Bred by Sir John Robinson at the Worksop Manor Stud, Papyrus was a brown colt by the American-bred St Leger winner Tracery out of Miss Matty, who never won a race herself but who bred eight other winners, including Bold Archer, subsequently quite a successful sire. Miss Matty was by Marcovil, sire of Hurry On, out of Simonrath, by St Simon. She was thus a half-sister to two good stayers, Bracket, winner of the Cesarewitch, and Flamboyant, winner of the Goodwood and Doncaster Cups.

Papyrus was if anything a shade on the small side and he came to hand readily enough as a two-year-old, winning six races and £3,835 in stakes. He failed disappointingly in the Champagne Stakes won by Drake, who also won the Middle Park Stakes, but at Newmarket in October he won the Criterion Stakes, beating Lord Woolavington's colt Town Guard, generally regarded as the leading two-year-old of the season. Papyrus's pedigree made it virtually certain that he would stay a mile and a half as a three-year-old and he was widely noted as a likely sort for the Derby.

No serious attempt was made to train Papyrus for the Two Thousand Guineas and he was still backward in condition when he competed in that event, his first outing of the season. He ran a very good race, though, finishing fourth to Lord Rosebery's Ellangowan and putting in all his best work at the finish. He then went to Chester, and ridden by Donoghue won the Chester Vase very comfortably by three lengths. 'And now,' said Basil Jarvis after that victory, 'we will get him ready for the Derby.'

Papyrus thrived in his preparation, and his final trial on the Saturday before Epsom was a brilliant success. This was witnessed by an appreciable concourse, including every tout in Newmarket, and no sooner was it over than the local bookmakers were swamped with money for Mr Irish's colt. The only worry was a certain amount of trouble over Donoghue, who had scant regard for owners who retained him when he wanted to ride a fancied horse in another stable. After Papyrus's victory over Town Guard the previous autumn, Donoghue had at once written to

446

offer his services for Mr Irish's colt in the Derby, entirely ignoring the fact that he was retained for that season by Lord Woolavington. As it happened, Lord Woolavington's two Derby candidates, Town Guard and Knockando, were not trained by Fred Darling but by Peter Gilpin, with whom he usually had a few horses. Gilpin's stable jockey Archibald was to ride the better fancied Town Guard, while Donoghue, to his intense disgust, found that he was required for the second string Knockando, who had finished close up second in the Guineas. Donoghue pleaded that he thought his retainer only applied to the horses trained by Fred Darling, and in the end he got his own way as usual.

The favourite for the Derby was Town Guard, whom the experts reckoned to have had an off-day when Papyrus beat him the previous autumn. He had not yet run as a three-year-old, but in gallops at home he was clearly superior to Knockando. Second favourite was Lord Derby's Pharos, winner of two races over a mile and a quarter, and there was good backing for Papyrus, Legality, and Ellangowan. Out on the Downs the crowd was on Papyrus to a man, and when Donoghue, who had a black eye as the result of a stone kicked up in the first race of the afternoon, went down to the paddock, the car he rode in was almost mobbed by admirers.

The real thrill of the race was provided by the tremendous duel in the straight between Papyrus and Pharos. Donoghue, confident of Papyrus's stamina, had sent him to the front rounding Tattenham Corner. With two and a half furlongs to go Pharos was at Papyrus's girths, and immediately afterwards he challenged in earnest. For a few strides he got his head in front, but as soon as Papyrus was shown the whip —Donoghue never actually hit him—he rallied in the gamest fashion possible to win by a length, with Parth, who had run a splendid race after losing ground at the start, a length and a half away third. Some backers of Pharos complained that Gardner had come too soon and that Lord Derby's colt would have won with riders reversed. No doubt Donoghue was a much more skilful rider than Gardner, but the fact was that Papyrus stayed every yard of the distance, whereas Pharos was really a very good ten-furlong horse. It was a wonderful achievement by Donoghue to win the race three years in succession, a feat that not even Fred Archer ever equalled.

After winning a race at York on an objection, Papyrus started a 13–8 favourite for the St Leger but was beaten by Lord Derby's big, raking filly Tranquil. Possibly the Derby winner was a shade unlucky. He was struck into at one point of the race, while in the straight he had a long and wearing battle with Parth, which left him with nothing in reserve when tackled by Tranquil.

Before the St Leger, Mr Irish had agreed to send Papyrus to New York to run in a match at Belmont Park in October against the American Champion, Zev. The race proved, as most people had anticipated, to be something of a farce. Papyrus, who was probably slightly stale by then, was not acclimatized and was totally unused to American conditions. To make matters worse heavy rain turned the track into a morass and Papyrus was not fitted with the American shoe which might have enabled him to get a grip on the ground. Inevitably he was well and truly beaten.

Mr Irish, who had enjoyed unparalleled good fortune in his brief racing career, was beginning to fail in health and at the end of the season he sold Papyrus for £25,000 to Mr J. P. Hornung, another patron of Basil Jarvis's stable. Papyrus never won for his new owner as a four-year-old but he was second, conceding fifteen pounds to Polyphontes, in the Eclipse, and second after a great race, conceding nine pounds to that fine staying mare Teresina, in the Jockey Club Stakes. He then retired to his owner's stud at West Grinstead at a 300-guinea fee. He got a fair number of winners, but not one approaching his own merit. Of his mares, Honey Buzzard bred Honey-way, a fine sprinter and successful sire, while Stella Polaris bred the Grand Prix winner Northern Light. Papyrus was found dead in his box at the Aislabie Stud, Stetchworth, in 1941.

Pharos was a good but not a great racehorse. He ran for four seasons, winning fourteen of his thirty races, his most important success being the Champion Stakes in 1924. He won the Duke of York Handicap at Kempton twice under top weight, and he also won the Liverpool Summer Cup with top weight. He never won over a longer distance than ten furlongs.

By Phalaris out of the Chaucer mare Scapa Flow, who competed in Selling Plates, Pharos was a full brother to the St Leger winner Fairway and the One Thousand Guineas winner Fair Isle. He was a tremendous success as a sire, firstly in England and later in France, where he died at the comparatively early age of seventeen. Cameronian, winner of the Two Thousand Guineas and the Derby, was among his second crop of foals and the following year he got the St Leger winner Firdaussi. Another good winner of his in England was Rhodes Scholar, who won the Eclipse and the St James's Palace Stakes. On the Continent his most famous winners were Nearco, bred in Italy, and Pharis, both unbeaten and both winners of the Grand Prix. Nearco will be referred to later when dealing with his Derby winners Dante and Nimbus; Pharis, exiled to Germany during the war, sired many good winners for M. Boussac on his return, including Scratch II and Talma, who both won the Doncaster St Leger. Pharos mares did extremely well and included the dams of the Derby winners Owen Tudor and Galcador. He himself was Champion Sire in England in 1931, and in France in 1935 and 1939.

Parth subsequently won the Prix de l'Arc de Triomphe and the Kempton Jubilee. He did well as sire in France without ever quite reaching the front rank.

Basil Jarvis, who died in 1957 aged seventy, was the son of an eminent trainer, and brother of the late William Jarvis, trainer to three kings, and of Jack Jarvis, who won the Derby with Blue Peter and Ocean Swell. He first took out a licence in 1909, but his heyday was the period between the wars when he numbered Mr J. P. Hornung, Major J. S. Courtauld, Lord Allendale, and M. Boussac among his owners. The best horse he trained for M. Boussac was Goyescas, who won the Chesham, Hardwicke, and Champion Stakes. In 1938 he took over most of Lord Glanely's horses and in 1939 he won four races at Goodwood, including the Goodwood Cup with Dubonnet. Devoted to sport of every kind, he was a friendly, cheerful, hospitable man and extremely popular at Newmarket. On the day he won the Derby with Papyrus, both his brothers won races at Epsom, too.

1923: Wednesday, 6 June . . . 344 Entries. £11,325.

MR B. IRISH's br.c. PAPYRUS by Tracery		
out of Miss Matty	S. DONOGHUE	1
LORD DERBY's b.c. PHAROS by Phalaris		
out of Scapa Flow	E. GARDNER	2
MR M. GOCULDAS's b.c. PARTH by Polymelus		
out of Willia	A. WALKER	3

Also ran :

Mr A. de Rothschild's Doric (4th) (J. Childs); Duke of Westminster's Twelve Pointer (B. Carslake); Lord Astor's Saltash (F. Bullock); Lord Astor's Bold and Bad (J. Brennan); Lord Rosebery's Ellangowan (E. C. Elliott); Duke of Westminster's Hurry Off (T. Burns); Lady Nunburnholme's Portumna (H. Beasley); Sir J. Robinson's Roger de Busli (H. Jelliss); Mr H. C. Sutton's Canova (J. Leach); Mr J. B. Joel's My Lord (V. Smyth); Sir Abe Bailey's Apron (W. Lister); Lord Woolavington's Town Guard (G. Archibald); Lord Woolavington's Knockando (H. Jones); Lord Furness's Legality (G. Hulme); Mr Foxhall Keene's Top Boot (F. Fox); Mr James White's Safety First (R. Stokes).

19 ran.

Betting :

5–1 Town Guard; 6–1 Pharos; 100–15 Papyrus; 9–1 Legality; 10–1 Ellangowan; 100–7 My Lord; 20–1 Knockando, Twelve Pointer, and Roger de Busli; 25–1 Saltash; 33–1 Parth and Doric; 50–1 Bold and Bad, Portumna, and Apron; 66–1 Hurry Off.

Won by a length; a length and a half between second and third.   2 m. 38 s.
Winner trained by B. Jarvis at Newmarket.

1924

After an interval of 137 years the race was once again won by an Earl of Derby. The great crowd fully appreciated the significance of the occasion and, forgetting the miseries of one of the wettest afternoons in a deplorable summer, gave Lord Derby and his colt Sansovino a reception reminiscent of that accorded to King Edward and Minoru in 1909.

Sansovino was a big, strong bay colt by his owner's St Leger winner Swynford out of Gondolette, by Loved One out of Dongola, by Doncaster. Lord Derby had bought Gondolette, then ten years of age, from Colonel Hall-Walker (later Lord Wavertree) in 1912. The chief reason for the purchase was that Loved One was by Sea Saw out of Pilgrimage and Lord Derby wished to try an experiment of mating Gondolette with either Chaucer or Swynford, both grandsons of Pilgrimage.

Gondolette had been bought as a yearling for seventy-five guineas by Mr George Edwardes of Gaiety Theatre fame, and he re-sold her as a three-year-old to Colonel Hall-Walker for 360 guineas. For the Colonel she bred Great Sport and Let Fly, both placed in the Derby, and Dolabella, dam of that very fast mare Myrobella, who bred the Two Thousand Guineas winner Big Game.

Gondolette bred six winners for Lord Derby, the most notable being Serenissima, Ferry (One Thousand Guineas), and Sansovino. Serenissima, by Minoru, bred eight winners of forty races worth over £47,000, including the Gold Cup winner Bosworth; Tranquil (One Thousand Guineas and St Leger); and Selene, winner of over £14,000. Selene bred Hyperion (Derby and St Leger); Sickle and Pharamond, both successful sires in America; and Hunter's Moon, a leading sire in the Argentine.

Sansovino ran twice as a two-year-old, winning the Ham Stakes at Goodwood and the Gimcrack Stakes at York. In both races the opposition was far from formidable. He was not entered for the Two Thousand Guineas, and his first race as a three-year-old was the Rugeley Stakes at Birmingham towards the end of April. A 5–1 on favourite, he only won by a head from the four-year-old Rugeley and the critics were not much impressed. However, he was still very backward and the form looked a good deal better when Rugeley won the Chester Cup three weeks later. In the Newmarket Stakes Sansovino was third, a neck and a head behind Hurstwood and Salmon Trout, with Bright Knight a head away fourth. Bright Knight, a stable companion of Hurstwood's, had been a very close second to Diophon in the Two

Thousand Guineas; in fact everyone—bar the judge—who saw the finish of the Guineas seemed convinced that Bright Knight had won.

Sansovino's performance in the Newmarket Stakes was satisfactory in view of the fact that the pace was too slow to suit such a genuine stayer, and in addition he had been hampered by Bright Knight at a critical stage. As Derby Day approached his very able trainer George Lambton grew more and more confident. Lambton had some wonderful trial tackle in his stable including the St Leger winner Tranquil, and Pharos, second in the Derby. When Sansovino, receiving a mere three pounds, beat these two good horses, pulling up by six lengths in his final gallop, he looked a certainty for the race. In fact one of the jockeys who rode in the gallop immediately went off, pawned his wife's jewellery and raised every penny he could to have a thumping good bet on Lord Derby's colt. Not surprisingly Sansovino's price soon began to shorten when news of his gallop leaked out and in the end he started favourite at 9–2. The Guineas winner Diophon, whose stamina was suspect, was at 8–1, and Captain Cuttle's unreliable brother Tom Pinch was at 10–1. There was a lot of money for Lord Astor's pair Bright Knight and St Germans, but the third Manton colt Hurstwood drifted to 20–1, the experts tending to regard his Newmarket victory as a fluke. Defiance was at 18–1 principally because he was ridden by Donoghue, who had been up to his old tricks again and had tried to obtain the mount on Tom Pinch, regardless of the fact that he was retained by Mr Joel and had had his contract with Lord Woolavington abruptly terminated the previous year.

On the Saturday and Sunday before the Derby it rained almost incessantly, and in some parts of the country four inches fell within thirty-six hours. The Epsom course became very heavy, a fact that was no disadvantage to Sansovino, who had the strength and substance to plough through the mud with a considerable weight on his back. On Derby Day itself the rain began to fall at midday and continued long into the night. The waterlogged track was unable to absorb this fresh downpour and by the time the big race was run it was in a deplorable condition. Buses on the Downs sank up to their axles and some were compelled to remain there all night before they could be dragged out. On Thursday part of the straight course near Tattenham Corner where traffic crossed it was in such a state that the two five-furlong races on the programme that afternoon could not be run. The Epsom executive was strongly criticized for lack of energy and initiative in coping with the situation, and at a subsequent Jockey Club meeting Mr Reid Walker declared that there were various matters at Epsom requiring investigation and a Committee of Inquiry was appointed.

Defiance, Tom Pinch, and Woodend all played up at the start and in the end both St Germans and Salmon Trout were slowly away. Dawson City made the running, but Sansovino, who ran rather sluggishly to begin with, soon began to improve and was second at the top of the hill down to Tattenham Corner. Third at this stage was Polyphontes, the biggest horse in the field, but he was soon passed by St Germans, who had swiftly recovered from his indifferent start.

Sansovino took the lead coming down the hill and entered the straight two lengths clear. From that point it was merely a question of by how far he won. He never showed the slightest sign of weakening and passed the post six lengths clear of St Germans, who was a neck in front of his stable companion, the fast-finishing Hurstwood. Parmenio was fourth, Polyphontes fifth, and Salmon Trout sixth. St Germans was the fifth horse to carry Lord Astor's colours into second place in seven years.

An hour after the Derby twenty-one-year-old Tommy Weston, who had ridden a confident and enterprising race on the winner, was sharing a wooden horse with his wife on a merry-go-round on the Downs. Brought up in a hard school, he had served his apprenticeship in a Yorkshire stable controlled by a bookmaker, and in all circumstances he was fully capable of taking care of himself. In his prime he had great dash and courage combined with the best of hands, but his form was always liable to be rather erratic. He rode for Lord Derby for many years, a tribute both to his character and to his ability, and his eleven classic successes included the Derby and the St Leger on Hyperion, and the St Leger on Fairway. A distinct personality, he had always been much liked by every section of the racing community and no jockey has possessed a livelier sense of humour. He served with much credit in the Royal Navy during the last war, and it is sad to hear that he has fallen on hard times in his retirement.

Sansovino won the Prince of Wales's Stakes at Ascot but in his second outing at that meeting he finished unplaced behind Chosroes in the Hardwicke Stakes. Not long before Doncaster he developed a cough. Lambton did not want to run him in the St Leger, but Lord Derby decided to give the public a run for their money and started him. He finished unplaced behind Salmon Trout in a sensational race, which brought disaster to a certain well-known bookmaker, who thought he had good reasons for assuming that whatever won, it would not be the Aga Khan's colt.

As a four-year-old Sansovino had leg trouble and never really found his best form. He was beaten by St Germans in the Coronation Cup and he failed in the City and Suburban—he was the last Derby winner to compete in that event—and the Jockey Club Cup. He did, however, prove his speed by beating Diophon at level weights over a mile at Lingfield. At the stud, considering his opportunities, he was a shade disappointing. His most notable winners were Sandwich, who won the St Leger but proved a stud failure; Jacopo, a leading two-year-old in this country and later a successful sire in America; Monument (Coronation Cup); Buckleigh (Jockey Club Cup); Sansonnet, the dam of Tudor Minstrel; Sans Peine (Goodwood Cup); and St Magnus and Portofino, both successful sires in Australia. When he died in 1940 he had sired the winners of 205 races worth over £113,000.

St Germans, like Sansovino, was by Swynford. His dam Hamoaze, by Torpoint out of Sceptre's daughter Maid of the Mist, bred two other Derby seconds in Buchan and Tamar, as well as Saltash, winner of the Eclipse Stakes and a leading sire in Australia. St Germans won the Coronation Cup and the Doncaster Cup before being exported to America, where he did well as a sire, his best winner being Twenty Grand, who unfortunately proved virtually sterile at the stud. Polyphontes won the Eclipse Stakes twice, but was a failure as a sire. Salmon Trout won the St Leger, being the third son of The Tetrarch to do so. He was a moderate sire, his best winner being King Salmon, who won the Eclipse Stakes and was second to Hyperion in the Derby. Obliterate is best remembered today as sire of the Oaks and Gold Cup winner Quashed. Donzelon in later life proved a highly successful three-mile 'chaser.

The seventeenth Earl of Derby, a great Englishman, was born in 1865 and died in 1948. His long life was largely devoted to the service of his country. Elected Member of Parliament in 1892, he was appointed Postmaster-General with a seat in the Cabinet in 1903. In the First World War he was Director-General of Recruiting and later Secretary of State for War. In 1918 he was appointed Ambassador in Paris, where he achieved immense popularity. He retired from active politics in 1926 and concentrated his energies for the rest of his life chiefly on interests in his native county of Lancashire. He was a man who combined outstanding ability and a high sense of duty with geniality, charm, and complete integrity.

Lord Derby had inherited a love of racing and bloodstock breeding from his father and he enjoyed remarkable success both as owner and breeder. His classic successes were as follows:

Two Thousand Guineas: Colorado (1926); Garden Path (1944).
One Thousand Guineas: Canyon (1916); Ferry (1918); Tranquil (1923); Fair Isle (1930); Tideway (1936); Herringbone (1943); Sun Stream (1945).
The Derby: Sansovino (1924); Hyperion (1933); Watling Street (1942).
The Oaks: Toboggan (1928); Sun Stream (1945).
St Leger: Swynford (1910); Keysoe (1919); Tranquil (1923); Fairway (1928); Hyperion (1933); Herringbone (1943).

A multitude of other important victories included the Gold Cup with Bosworth, and the Eclipse Stakes with Colorado, Fairway, and Caerleon. The last really good horse that he bred was Alycidon, who won the Ascot, Goodwood, and Doncaster Cups in 1948, and who is sire of the St Leger winners Meld and Alcide.

Probably no man has equalled Lord Derby's immense influence all over the world in bloodstock breeding, and it would require a volume on its own to deal adequately with the subject. It must suffice to say that among the great stallions he owned were Chaucer, Swynford, Phalaris, Pharos, Colorado, Fairway, and Hyperion, while there are few more famous mares in the Stud Book than Canterbury Pilgrim, Gondolette, Serenissima, Selene, Scapa Flow, and Aurora.

Lord Derby's eldest son, Lord Stanley, died in 1938 and the stud passed to Lord Stanley's eldest son, the present Lord Derby, who was born in 1918.

Sansovino's trainer, the Hon. George Lambton, fifth son of the second Earl of Durham, was born in 1860 and died in 1945. In his younger days he was a brilliant amateur rider and a fearless bettor. He rode in five Grand Nationals and on one occasion came very close to winning. His successes included the National Hunt Chase and the Grand Steeplechase de Paris.

After a bad fall at Sandown in 1892 he decided to take up training, a decision that caused considerable comment at the time as in those days 'gentlemen trainers' were few and far between. In 1893 the sixteenth Earl of Derby invited him to become his trainer; this was not only the turning-point in Lambton's life, but it was also an important date in the history of British racing as Lord Derby, his eldest son, and Lambton himself set about restoring the fortunes of the Stanley colours and laying anew the foundations of the Knowsley Stud.

Lambton loved and understood horses and was undoubtedly a trainer of the highest ability. He won almost every important event in the *Calendar*, including thirteen classic races, all of which were gained for the sixteenth and seventeenth Earls of Derby with the exception of the One Thousand Guineas won by Lord D'Abernon's Diadem. He was a marvellous judge of a yearling and it was he who bought the Aga Khan's first yearlings, thereby laying the foundations of a great and successful stud.

In 1933, when he trained Hyperion to win the Derby, Lambton was in his seventy-fourth year and at the conclusion of that season he was succeeded as Lord Derby's trainer by Colledge Leader. Lambton, however, continued to run a stable with marked success virtually up to his death.

Even in old age Lambton was slim, good-looking, and beautifully dressed, with a delightful smile and wonderful charm of manner. Everyone liked him and no Newmarket trainer commanded greater loyalty and affection from his staff. His reminiscences—*Men and Horses I Have Known*—remain one of the most entertaining books on racing ever written.

454

1924

1924: Wednesday, 4 June . . . 332 Entries. £11,755.

LORD DERBY's b.c. SANSOVINO by Swynford out of Gondolette	T. WESTON	I
LORD ASTOR's b.c. ST GERMANS by Swynford out of Hamoaze	F. BULLOCK	2
MR S. TATTERSALL's b.c. HURSTWOOD by Gay Crusader out of Bleasdale	V. SMYTH	3

Also ran:

Lord Rosebery's Parmenio (4th) (E. C. Elliott); Mr S. B. Joel's Polyphontes (W. McLachlan); H.H. Aga Khan's Salmon Trout (E. Gardner); Sir R. Jardine's Obliterate (T. Burns); Sir E. Hulton's Spalpeen (F. O'Neill); Lord Astor's Bright Knight (F. Lane); Lady Cunliffe-Owen's Corolet (E. J. Morris); Mrs A. Blain's Browside (H. Wragg); H.H. Aga Khan's Diophon (G. Hulme); Lord Glanely's Grand Joy (S. Ingham); H.M. King George V's Resinato (G. Archibald); Sir G. Bullough's Great Barrier (J. Leach); Mr A. K. Macomber's Thunder Cloud II (A. Esling); Lord Woolavington's Tom Pinch (H. Beasley); Admiral of the Fleet Sir H. Meux's Donzelon (B. Carslake); Mr A. C. Saunder's Skyflight (G. Richards); Mr M. L. Meyer's Canusa (W. Lister); Mr J. L. Replogle's Optimist II (M. MacGee); Mr B. Irish's Dawson City (H. Jelliss); Mr A. de Rothschild's Tippler (J. Childs); Mr A. B. Walker's Woodend (M. Beary); Mr J. B. Joel's Defiance (S. Donoghue); Mrs S. Whitburn's Arausio (R. A. Jones); Sir Abe Bailey's Bucks Yeoman (C. Smirke) (*fell*).

27 ran.

Betting:

9–2 Sansovino; 8–1 Diophon; 10–1 Tom Pinch; 100–7 St Germans and Bright Knight; 18–1 Defiance; 20–1 Salmon Trout, Dawson City, Parmenio, Woodend and Hurstwood; 33–1 Tippler; 50–1 Spalpeen, Optimist II, Grand Joy, Obliterate and Donzelon; 66–1 Thunder Cloud II and Polyphontes.

Won by six lengths; a neck between second and third.   2 m. 46⅗ s.
Winner trained by Hon. G. Lambton at Newmarket.

1925

In the late summer of 1923 Mr H. E. Morriss, a Shanghai bullion broker, sent a cable to Fred Darling asking him to buy on his behalf the best yearling at the coming Doncaster Sales. For 6,300 guineas Darling bought Manna, a bay colt by Phalaris out of Waffles, bred by Mr J. J. Maher at the famous Confey Stud in Ireland.

Phalaris, by Polymelus, had proved himself a very good middle-distance handicapper during the war. He was a great success as a sire and has exerted, particularly through his male-line descendants, a profound influence on modern bloodstock breeding. He was Champion Sire twice and leading sire of winning brood mares three times. Besides Manna his most important winners were Pharos (second in the Derby), Fairway (St Leger and Eclipse Stakes), Chatelaine (Oaks), Fair Isle (One Thousand Guineas), Colorado (Two Thousand Guineas and Eclipse Stakes), and Caerleon (Eclipse Stakes).

Waffles stood barely fifteen hands and was never trained. In-bred to St Simon on her dam's side, she was by Buckwheat, a useful handicapper, whose stud fee was only forty-eight pounds. Besides Manna she bred Sandwich, winner of the St Leger; Parwiz, winner of over £3,000 and sent to the Argentine; and Bunworry, a filly that won four times as a two-year-old and was then sent to India. Eventually Bunworry was acquired by the great Italian breeder Signor Tesio. For him she bred Bernina, winner of three Italian classics and grand-dam of the Gold Cup winner Botticelli; Bozzetto, three times Champion Sire in Italy; and Brueghel, a leading sire in Australia.

Manna was a medium-sized colt, beautifully made and full of the St Simon quality and vitality. When he went into training he was alarmingly high-spirited but never vicious; it amused him to scare people, and he was reputed to be the only Beckhampton horse that ever succeeded in kicking Fred Darling. On one occasion he threw his lad, jumped a five-foot hedge, then dropped down a steep bank and landed on the tarmac of the main Bath Road, fortunately with only minor injury to himself. Another time he bucked off a lad and succeeded in kicking him before he had reached the ground.

His first race was the National Breeders Produce Stakes at Sandown in which he finished a creditable third to Garden of Allah and Bucellas. He then won the Richmond Stakes at Goodwood, but was beaten in the Imperial Produce Stakes at Kempton by the Manton colt Picaroon. A brilliant but delicate colt by Beppo, Picaroon went on to win the Middle Park Stakes from Solario and Manna. Manna himself finished the season satisfactorily by beating Lord Astor's Cross Bow in the Moulton Stakes. Though plainly inferior to Picaroon, Manna had shown that he possessed considerable ability and, despite his habitual exuberance, a suitable temperament for racing.

The winter and spring were unusually wet and the Beckhampton gallops heavy in consequence. Manna was not quite ready when the Two Thousand Guineas took place but, ridden by Donoghue, he made every yard of the running and won by two lengths at 100–8. Between Newmarket and Epsom he improved with every gallop but nevertheless started at a longer price in the Derby than either Cross Bow, who had won the Newmarket Stakes from Zionist, or Lord Derby's Conquistador. The weather on Derby Day was dismal and the going heavy; a fear that Manna would not stay a mile and a half under those conditions caused him to ease perceptibly in the market. Picaroon, who died the following year, was unable to run at Epsom but he won the Champion Stakes later in the season.

Solario was caught by a loose tape at the starting-gate and lost several lengths in consequence. The early leaders were Priory Park and Dalmagarry, with Manna not far behind. Coming down the hill to Tattenham Corner Manna went to the front and he turned for home well clear of Zionist, Warminster, The Sirdar, and St Becan. None of these, however, ever looked like catching him and, increasing his advantage with every stride, he passed the post with his ears pricked, no fewer than eight lengths ahead of Zionist, with The Sirdar two lengths away third. Solario made up a lot of ground in the closing stages to finish fourth. Manna was Donoghue's final Derby winner and the first horse to win the Two Thousand Guineas and the Epsom Derby since Sunstar in 1911.

Some people reckoned that Solario would very nearly have won had he got off on level terms. This view was strengthened a fortnight later when Solario made mince-meat of Manna in the Ascot Derby. Solario beat him again in the St Leger, but Manna broke down badly in that race and was never able to run again. At the stud Manna did reasonably well; the most notable horses he got were Colombo (Two Thousand Guineas and over £26,000 in stakes); Miracle (Eclipse Stakes); Manitoba (winner of over £4,000 and later Champion Sire in Australia); Mannamead, who was unbeaten on the racecourse and died shortly after export to Hungary; and Pasca, dam of the Two Thousand Guineas winner Pasch and grand-dam of Pinza.

Of the other Derby competitors Zionist won the Irish Derby and was second in the Lincoln. Solario won the Gold Cup the following year and sired two Derby winners in Mid-day Sun (1937) and Straight Deal (1943). Cross Bow won the Hunt Cup as a four-year-old, while Priory Park proved a wonderfully successful handicapper, his victories including the Stewards Cup, the Lincoln, the Hunt Cup, and the City and Suburban. Pons Asinorum won the Doncaster, Manchester, and Newbury Summer Cups as well as the Ebor, while Ethnarch sired an extremely good filly in Eclair, dam of Khaled, a successful sire in America.

Mr Morriss died in Shanghai in 1951. After Manna's Derby victory he started a stud at Banstead Manor, near Newmarket. There he bred Pasch, winner of the Two Thousand Guineas and Eclipse Stakes in 1938, and Tai-Yang, a good but unsound horse that only ran twice, winning the Jockey Club Stakes in 1933 and the Chippenham Stakes in 1935. He also bred a useful horse in Artists Proof, whose daughter Art Paper was dam of Petition, the Champion Sire in 1960.

1925: Wednesday, 27 May . . . 325 Entries. £11,095.

MR H. E. MORRISS's b.c. MANNA by Phalaris
out of Waffles — S. DONOGHUE 1
H.H. AGA KHAN's b.c. ZIONIST by Spearmint
out of Judea — B. CARSLAKE 2
MR A. K. MACOMBER's br.c. THE SIRDAR by McKinley
out of Gibbs — A. ESLING 3

Also ran:

Sir J. Rutherford's Solario (4th) (M. Beary); Mrs W. Raphael's Warminster (V. Smyth); Sir G. Bullough's St Becan (E. C. Elliott); Lord Astor's Cross Bow (F. Bullock); H.M. King George V's Runnymede (J. Childs); Mr A. Lowry's Pons Asinorum (T. Burns); Capt. J. D. Cohn's Ptolemy II (G. Stern); Mr A. C. E. Howeson's Solitary (G. Richards); Mr W. M. G. Singer's Sparus (T. Pryor); Sir C. Hyde's Dignity (F. Dempsey); Lady Bullough's Ethnarch (J. Leach); Sir E. Tate's Roidore (G. Hulme); Mr V. Thompson's Dalmagarry (F. Winter); Mr T. F. Ryan's The Virginian (H. Beasley); Major A. Vigor's Vicot (F. Lane); Mr J. P. Hornung's Bucellas (H. Jelliss); Lord Derby's Conquistador (T. Weston); Mr S. B. Joel's St Napoleon (H. Wragg); Lord Glanely's Sunderland (C. Smirke); Mr H. C. Sutton's My Crackers (J. Thwaites); Mr C. Howard's Priory Park (F. Fox); Lord Rosebery's Tissaphernes (R. A. Jones); Mr R. W. Foster's Flying World (W. Maclachlan, jun.); Admiral of the Fleet Sir Hedworth Meux's Constantius (G. Archibald).

27 ran.

Betting:

9–2 Cross Bow; 8–1 Conquistador; 9–1 Manna; 10–1 Zionist and Solario; 100–7

Ptolemy II; 100–6 Runnymede; 20–1 St Becan; 25–1 Dignity; 40–1 Bucellas, Pons Asinorum, Sparus, and Vicot; 50–1 The Sirdar and Warminster; 66–1 Sunderland, Tissaphernes, and Constantius; 100–1 Priory Park, Roidore, and The Virginian; 200–1 others.

Won by eight lengths; two lengths between second and third. 2 m. $40\frac{3}{5}$ s.
Winner trained by F. Darling at Beckhampton.

1926

Lord Woolavington had his second Derby success in 1926 with Coronach, trained by Fred Darling and ridden by Joe Childs.

Bred by his owner, Coronach stood well over sixteen hands and was a light-coloured chesnut with flaxen mane and tail by Hurry On out of Wet Kiss, by Tredennis. Wet Kiss, whom Lord Woolavington bought for £3,000 from Mr W. Higgs in 1918, won three races and was a full sister to Soldennis, winner of the Irish Two Thousand Guineas and twenty-three other races as well. Tredennis was useless as a racehorse and never succeeded in winning during the three seasons he was in training. Sold for £100, he went to the stud in humble circumstances, serving chiefly half-bred mares. However, he managed to get winners from the few thorough-bred mares he was sent and gradually his reputation increased. When he died at the age of twenty-nine his stock had won 480 races worth over £147,000. His best offspring were Bachelors Double, a great sire of brood mares; and Golden Myth, winner of the Gold Cup and the Eclipse.

Coronach was high mettled, wilful, and loathed restraint both on the gallops and the racecourse. From the start, though, Darling recognized the colt's high promise and wisely did not hurry his preparation. A maiden race at Salisbury in July was chosen for Coronach's first racecourse appearance and he won that event with the ease expected. In the Rous Memorial Stakes at Goodwood he again toyed with the opposition, scoring by four lengths from the future One Thousand Guineas winner Pillion. He was expected to face a sterner battle in the Champagne Stakes at Doncaster where one of his rivals was the Gimcrack Stakes winner Lex, but again he won unchallenged. In the Middle Park Stakes he was opposed only by Lex and Tenacity and started at 100–15 on. It was a first-class sensation, therefore, when Lex beat him by a neck. The form was obviously all wrong and in fact he was found to have a temperature when he returned to Beckhampton. Nevertheless, a rumour began to circulate that he had gone in his wind. Before the season ended Darling gave Coronach a rough gallop to satisfy himself that the colt was none the worse for his race at Newmarket. Coronach went in his best form and, moreover, showed no trace of wind infirmity. The Jockey Club Handicapper evidently took the view that Coronach had not shown his true form in the Middle Park, as he rated him equal top with Legatee in the Free Handicap, the pair being four pounds in front of Lex.

Coronach made normal progress during the winter and it was decided to run him in the Two Thousand Guineas. Before that race he had an outing in the Column Produce Stakes at the Craven Meeting, winning with the utmost ease from Lancegaye although he was far from being fully wound up. Not unnaturally he started a red-hot favourite for the first of the classics. He gave Childs a certain amount of trouble at the start and was slowly away, but he soon pulled his way to the front. At the Bushes he held a clear lead and was going so easily that he looked certain to win, but when he was tackled going into the Dip by Lord Derby's Colorado, he found absolutely nothing and Colorado strode away from him to win as he pleased. The only excuse that could be advanced for Coronach was that he was a big, backward colt and perhaps not as fit as his trainer had thought.

Coronach did not run again before the Derby, but it was discovered at home that he was a vastly superior horse when no effort was made to restrain him and he was allowed to stride out as he pleased. In consequence it was decided that in the Derby he would be permitted to force the pace from the start. The plan was carried through with spectacular success. He made every yard of the running and had no difficulty in disposing of Colorado's challenge at an early point in the straight, passing the post a clear five lengths ahead of the Manton colt Lancegaye, with Colorado, eased near the finish, a short head away third. Lord Astor's Swift and Sure, who had started second favourite on the strength of a stylish win in the Chester Vase, was fourth. For the third year running it was a wet and miserable Derby Day. The going was heavy, and the exacting conditions no doubt suited the big powerful Coronach more than the smaller but beautifully proportioned Colorado. It was Weston's opinion, though, that Colorado would very nearly have won had he himself not been ordered by George Lambton to ride a waiting race. According to Weston, the pace that Coronach set was a moderate one, and Childs was able to get a decisive advantage by suddenly accelerating and slipping his field in the straight.

Coronach won the St James's Palace Stakes by twenty lengths, the Eclipse Stakes by six lengths, and then the St Leger from Caissot in record time. He gave Childs some uneasy moments at Doncaster, though, as he was virtually running away in the early stages of the race. Luckily his attention was distracted for a couple of seconds by a policeman who had stepped from under the rails, and in that brief space of time Childs was able to regain some semblance of control. Coronach's task in the St Leger had been eased by the fact that Colorado was under a cloud and unable to run, while Lancegaye had broken down.

As a four-year-old Coronach was a very handsome horse indeed, having let down considerably and noticeably darkened in colour. He won the Coronation Cup at Epsom, but he gave his backers a certain anxiety before he won and he might even have been beaten if Embargo's challenge had not been delayed for so long. He won the Hardwicke Stakes at Ascot easily enough, but by then the story that he had gone in his wind was circulating freely again.

Colorado was off the racecourse for a long time after the Derby. His spring form on his reappearance the following season was unconvincing and he was unplaced in the Newbury Spring Cup and the Jubilee. However, he showed signs of coming back to his best when he won the Rous Memorial Stakes at Ascot, and this effort was followed by a brilliant four-lengths victory under top weight in the Newbury Summer Cup. In the Princess of Wales's Stakes at Newmarket he renewed his rivalry with Coronach. In this race he never let Coronach get very far ahead, and when he challenged over two furlongs out, Coronach at once crumpled up. Colorado went on to win by no fewer than eight lengths. Much the same thing happened in the Eclipse Stakes a fortnight later. Coronach came into the straight with a lead of two lengths, but as soon as Colorado tackled him he compounded and eventually finished last in a field of three.

These two crushing defeats made an inglorious finish to Coronach's career. A good many people declared that he was soft and could only win when everything went his way. Possibly there was a streak of softness in Coronach's temperament, but there is little doubt that at this stage of his life he was seriously handicapped by his wind infirmity.

As a sire Coronach was a failure in England, the best horse he got being Montrose, winner of the City and Suburban and over £10,000 in stakes. On the Continent, though, his record was better. For M. Boussac he got a great filly in Corrida, twice winner of the Prix de l'Arc de Triomphe and over £47,000 in stakes. Unfortunately she was stolen by the Germans during the war and was never recovered. For Signor Tesio Coronach sired Niccolo Dell'Arca, a half-brother to Nearco that won the Italian Triple Crown and later became a successful sire in England. Coronach also sired a filly called Jacopo del Sellaio that won all five Italian classic races.

In 1940 Mrs Macdonald-Buchanan, Lord Woolavington's daughter, made a gift of Coronach to New Zealand. He spent the last nine years of his life in that country and his stud record there was extremely good.

Colorado met Coronach four times and beat him over a mile, a mile and a quarter, and a mile and a half, each time by a very wide margin. By Phalaris out of the One Thousand Guineas winner Canyon, he was a horse of outstanding quality and ability. It was a tragedy for breeders that he died in 1929 as few horses have made a greater mark at the stud within so brief a period. Among the more notable winners he got were Felicitation (Gold Cup); Loaningdale (Eclipse); Colorado Kid (Jubilee, Hunt Cup, and Doncaster Cup); Coroado (Wokingham Stakes and July Cup); Figaro

(Stewards Cup) ; and Riot (dam of the Oaks winner Commotion). With his combination of class, speed, and stamina, Colorado might well have become one of the greatest classic sires of this century.

Finglas, who ran unplaced behind Coronach in the Derby, developed into a very fine stayer and won the Queen Alexandra Stakes at Ascot on two occasions.

1926: Wednesday, 2 June . . . 305 Entries. £10,950.

LORD WOOLAVINGTON's ch.c. CORONACH by Hurry On out of Wet Kiss	J. CHILDS	1
MR W. M. G. SINGER's b.c. LANCEGAYE by Swynford out of Flying Spear	R. PERRYMAN	2
LORD DERBY's br.c. COLORADO by Phalaris out of Canyon	T. WESTON	3

Also ran:

Lord Astor's Swift and Sure (4th) (R. A. Jones) ; Lord Barnby's Review Order (H. Beasley) ; H.H. Aga Khan's Cimiez (C. Smirke) ; M. E. de St Alary's Finglas (G. Archibald) ; Mr S. B. Joel's Pantera (H. Wragg) ; Mr A. K. Macomber's War Mist (A. Esling) ; Lord Glanely's Tenacity (J. Thwaites) ; Mr F. Curzon's Comedy King (F. Dempsey) ; Sir G. Bullough's Harpagon (E. C. Elliott) ; Mr T. W. Bleniron's Le Gros (J. Kirby) ; Mr F. Gretton's Macanudo (F. Lane) ; Mr H. Shaw's Simon the Beggar (J. Leach) ; Mrs S. Whitburn's Bassoon (E. Quirke) ; Admiral of the Fleet Sir H. Meux's St Mary's Kirk (T. Burns) ; Sir A. Bailey's Lex (M. Beary) ; Mr J. P. Hornung's Apple Sammy (H. Jelliss).

19 ran.

Betting:

2–1 Colorado ; 9–2 Swift and Sure ; 11–2 Coronach ; 100–12 Lex ; 100–8 Finglas ; 20–1 Apple Sammy ; 33–1 Review Order and Cimiez ; 40–1 Lancegaye, Tenacity, and Harpagon ; 50–1 Comedy King ; 66–1 others.

Won by five lengths ; a short head between second and third.   2 m. 47⅘ s.
Winner trained by F. Darling at Beckhampton.

1927

The Derby of 1927 was in one respect at least a tragic one. Mr Frank Curzon, owner of the winner, Call Boy, was a dying man at the time and knew it. Nevertheless he bravely summoned his last reserves of strength to lead his colt in. Ghastly pale and half-dazed, he was a pathetic sight in his hour of triumph as he stumbled into the unsaddling ring clutching the white leading rein. A few weeks later he was dead.

Bred by his owner, Call Boy was Hurry On's last Derby winner and was out of Comedienne, whom Mr Curzon had bought as a yearling for 130 guineas. Comedienne was by Bachelors Double out of Altoviscar, by the Derby and St Leger winner Donovan. Altoviscar was the dam of Alope, who bred both the Gold Cup winner Foxlaw and also Aloe, from whom such good horses as Parthia (Derby), Alcide (St Leger), Hypericum (One Thousand Guineas), Aureole (King George VI and Queen Elizabeth Stakes), and Round Table, a top-class horse in the United States, are descended. Comedienne herself also bred Comedy King, winner of over £7,000, and Comedy Star, ancestress of Dancing Time (One Thousand Guineas) and Umberto (winner of over £8,000). It is perhaps worth mentioning that Bachelors Double, a good racehorse and successful stallion, was by a non-winning sire out of a non-winning dam, by a non-winning maternal grandsire out of a non-winning grand-dam.

Call Boy was a well-grown, well-made chesnut, and throughout his career he was trained at Newmarket by Jack Watts, whose father rode four Derby winners, including Persimmon, and whose son and grandson have both trained classic winners. The colt made his first appearance in the July Stakes at Newmarket, but over five furlongs he had not got the speed to cope with The Satrap, a brilliant full brother to Tetratema who met with an accident later in the season, and Sickle, a Phalaris colt of Lord Derby's. He did better over six furlongs in the Champagne Stakes in September, finishing second to Damon, a grey colt by Stefan the Great, with Sickle this time half a length behind him. He won the Linton Stakes at Newmarket in October and finished the season by beating Sickle and Birthright in a finish of heads for the Middle Park Stakes. He had made consistent improvement throughout the summer and autumn and was generally regarded as having excellent prospects for next year's classics. Moreover, from his breeding there seemed no reason why he should fail to stay a mile and a half.

Call Boy wintered satisfactorily and did all that was asked of him when formally tried at Newmarket early in April. He started a firm favourite for the Two Thousand Guineas, but in a most exciting finish he lost by inches to the outsider Adams Apple, who went wrong in his wind not long after. Call Boy was undoubtedly at a disadvantage in having to race by himself in the closing stages; in addition Elliott, who rode him, declared that he would have won had he used his whip, only he did not wish to jeopardize the colt's Derby prospects by punishing him in his first race of the season.

Call Boy continued to thrive and won the Newmarket Stakes by four lengths. Backers, however, were somewhat wary in supporting him as the state of Mr Curzon's health was generally known and his death would have rendered Call Boy's nomination void. There was in fact a strong rumour on the day that Call Boy won at Newmarket that his owner had just passed away. Fortunately this proved to be untrue and Mr Curzon rallied sufficiently to attend the Press Club Derby lunch, at which he stated that Call Boy would prove himself at Epsom to be five or seven pounds superior to any other three-year-old in the country, an assessment that the Derby proved to be correct.

After three dismal years, the weather was warm and sunny on Derby Day. The old grandstand had been demolished and replaced by the present more convenient but very much uglier structure. For the first time in its history the race was broadcast by the B.B.C. The start was a good one and Call Boy went straight to the front. Adams Apple was beaten before Tattenham Corner and Sickle was in trouble soon afterwards. The last two furlongs were in fact a duel between Call Boy and the second favourite Hot Night, who had run well in the Guineas and then won quite impressively at York. Below the distance Hot Night challenged resolutely and succeeded in getting his head in front. His backers, though, had hardly started to cheer him home when Call Boy rallied and, lengthening his stride like a true stayer, he drew away to win by a clear two lengths from Hot Night, with Shian Mor a very indifferent third. Sickle injured a pastern in the race and never ran again. He was exported to America where he became a top-class sire, Native Dancer being one of the most illustrious of his descendants.

Mr Curzon died on 2 July. His original name was Deeley, but he changed it to Curzon when he went on the stage as a young man. Later he made a fortune in theatrical ownership. Call Boy never ran again and was bought for £60,000 by Mr Curzon's brother, Sir Harry Mallaby-Deeley. Unfortunately, Sir Harry made a bad bargain as Call Boy, who died in 1940, proved virtually sterile at the stud. Hot Night was a stud failure, too, while Shian Mor was exported to Japan. Son and Heir never won a race and retired to the stud at a nine-guinea fee. He was just beginning to make a considerable name for himself when he met with a fatal accident. He sired Robin Goodfellow, second to Bahram in the 1935 Derby. It will be noted that Lord Beaverbrook had a runner in this year's Derby, but his interest in the Turf proved to be of singularly brief duration.

Charles Elliott was a leading rider for more than twenty-five years. He was still apprenticed to Jack Jarvis when he deposed Donoghue from the position of Champion Jockey in 1924, a position that Donoghue had occupied for the previous ten years. In 1923 he had shared the lead with Donoghue, both of them riding eighty-nine winners. A very polished and resourceful horseman, strong, self-confident, and intelligent, Elliott had fourteen successes in classic races, his other Derby victories being on Bois Roussel in 1938 and Nimbus in 1949. When he gave up riding he became trainer to M. Boussac in France for a number of years, but unfortunately he assumed that post just when the Boussac fortunes were starting to decline and in 1958 he returned to England. For a time he trained a few horses at Newmarket.

1927: Wednesday, 1 June ... 344 Entries. £12,615.

MR F. CURZON's ch.c. CALL BOY by Hurry On
out of Comedienne — E. C. ELLIOTT — 1
SIR VICTOR SASSOON's b.c. HOT NIGHT
by Gay Crusader out of Tubercurry — H. WRAGG — 2
MAJOR J. S. COURTAULD's b.c. SHIAN MOR
by Buchan out of Orlass — F. LANE — 3

Also ran:
Mr R. D. Cohen's Buckfast (4th) (J. Evans); Lord Derby's Sickle (T. Weston); Mrs C. Rich's Silverstead (F. Fox); Sir D. Broughton's Knight of the Grail (F. Winter); Sir Abe Bailey's Son and Heir (B. Carslake); H.H. Aga Khan's Hossan (C. Smirke); Mr A. de Rothschild's Tattoo (R. Perryman); Lord Woolavington's Applecross (J. Childs); Major J. B. Walker's Spiramonde (P. Donoghue); Mr F. W. Horlock's Adieu (J. Marshall); Lord Beaverbrook's Restigouche (C. Childs); Mr J. Philips's Jacks Son (A. Burns); Eleanor Lady Torrington's Lone Knight (S. Donoghue); Mr J. P. Arkwright's Treat (H. Beasley); Mr C. W. S. Whitburn's Adams Apple (J. Leach); Mr. D. L. Wilson's Flashing Star (R. Dick); Sir M. McAlpine's Birthright (A. Garnett); Mr C. Austin's Parker (L. Butchers); Mr C. Howard's Chichester Cross (G. Richards); Mary Lady Queensbury's Stampede (G. Bowden).

23 ran.

Betting:

4–1 Call Boy; 9–2 Hot Night; 6–1 Adams Apple; 7–1 Sickle; 100–8 Lone Knight; 22–1 Applecross and Shian Mor; 25–1 Tattoo; 33–1 Treat; 40–1 Hossan; 50–1 Birthright and Silverstead; 66–1 Knight of the Grail, Son and Heir, and Adieu; 100–1 Buckfast, Chichester Cross, Restigouche, and Spiramonde; 200–1 Jacks Son and Flashing Star; 1,000–1 Parker and Stampede.

Won by two lengths; eight lengths between second and third.   2 m. 34$\frac{2}{5}$ s.
Winner trained by J. Watts at Newmarket.

1928

There is little doubt that the best three-year-old in 1928 was Lord Derby's Fairway, by Phalaris out of Scapa Flow, and thus a full brother to Pharos. Fairway, however, was unplaced in the Derby, his one defeat of the season, that race being won decisively enough by the 33–1 outsider Felstead, owned by Sir Hugo Cunliffe-Owen and trained by Captain Bell at Lambourn.

Felstead was by the 1920 Derby winner Spion Kop out of Felkington, by Lemberg. Felkington had been bred at the Fort Union Stud in Ireland and as a foal she was sold, together with her dam Comparaison, by William the Third, to Mr J. Watts of Newcastle. Trained by Dobson Peacock she won over £1,900 in stakes and was then bought by Mr Watts's son, Mr A. T. Watts. At the Newmarket July Sales in 1924 she was bought, in foal to Spion Kop, for 2,100 guineas by Captain Bell on behalf of Sir Hugo Cunliffe-Owen. Captain Bell was an Australian and may well have been impressed by the fact that the produce of Spion Kop and Felkington would have three lines of Carbine blood in its pedigree. Felkington bred six other winners besides Felstead, including Finis who won a war-time Gold Cup and was later a successful sire in New Zealand. Carpathus, a half-brother to Felkington, won the Northumberland Plate in 1923.

Felstead's two-year-old career was undistinguished to say the least. He ran four times without winning and the nearest he came to success was to finish second in some minor event at Chepstow. Even allowing for the fact that his pedigree suggested staying power rather than speed, it was quite impossible to visualize his playing an important part in the next season's classics. The outstanding two-year-old was undoubtedly Fairway, who won the Coventry, July, and Champagne Stakes, and was placed top of the Free Handicap. The following spring it was intended to run Fairway in the Guineas, but for some little time before the day he had suffered from an abscess in his mouth. It burst the day before the Guineas, and under the circumstances it was judged wiser not to run him. The race was won by Sir L. Philipps's tough and courageous little colt Flamingo by a matter of inches from Royal Minstrel, a really handsome grey by Tetratema. O'Curry was third, Lord Derby's second string, Pharamond, fourth, and Felstead sixth. This was quite a creditable performance on Felstead's part and he was running on nicely at the finish. He had improved considerably during the winter and at the Newbury Spring Meeting at the beginning of April he had started favourite for a maiden race, which he won very smoothly. He was then third in a seven-furlong handicap at Epsom to a horse called Caballero, owned and trained by Mr Tom Walls; the distance was too sharp for him, but he appeared to act well on the course. After the Guineas he had one more race, winning the ten-furlong Davis Stakes at Hurst Park. The horses he beat, though, were too moderate to advertise his claims in the Derby.

Fairway won the Newmarket Stakes and was a 3–1 favourite for the Derby. Unfortunately he was beaten at Epsom before he had even reached the starting-gate. He had been as quiet as a lamb in the paddock, but when Weston walked him out on to the course before the parade in front of the stands, part of the crowd got completely out of control and he was hemmed in on every side by cheering admirers, some of whom, more idiotic than the others, proceeded to pluck hairs from his tail as souvenirs. In a trice the unfortunate favourite's tail was in rags and tatters and he himself was sweating and shaking with fright. Under the circumstances it is quite understandable that he failed to run within two stone of his proper form. Most unjustly he was criticized afterwards on the grounds that his temperament had failed to stand up to the stress and tension inseparable from Derby Day. He had in fact been subjected to treatment which was calculated to upset any high-mettled thoroughbred.

Both in 1926 and 1927 the Derby had been won by horses that had made almost every yard of the running, while Sansovino and Manna both had the race more or less at their mercy by the time Tattenham Corner was reached. Possibly the success that had attended such forcing tactics had impressed itself on the minds of certain jockeys and trainers and can account for what happened in this particular race. Right from the start Elliott on the second favourite Flamingo and Richards on the heavily backed Sunny Trace saw fit to indulge in a private duel of their own. Neck and neck they raced in front at a pace that seemed foolhardy in view of the distance to be covered. They were still in front at Tattenham Corner, but Felstead was not far behind them and was moving uncommonly well. With two furlongs to go Sunny Trace cracked and dropped back beaten. Flamingo struggled on gamely enough, but he had nothing in reserve when Felstead, ridden with admirable judgement by Harry Wragg, came up to challenge him below the distance. Felstead ran on strongly to win by a length and a half, while Flamingo was a clear six lengths in front of the third, Black Watch. No doubt luck was on Felstead's side in that Fairway was mobbed, while Flamingo and Sunny Trace were both ridden in such tearaway style. Nevertheless he proved that he was a good horse by his ability to keep in touch with the pacemakers and to come and win his race as soon as he was asked to. Stamina was undoubtedly his strong point and he would probably have been even better over longer distances, but unfortunately he developed splint trouble during his

St Leger preparation and never ran again. At the stud he never sired a colt anything like as good as himself, but he got a really good filly in Rockfel, winner of the One Thousand Guineas and the Oaks in 1938. She unfortunately died after foaling Rockefella, sire of the 1961 Two Thousand Guineas winner, Rockavon. Felstead also sired Steady Aim, who won the Oaks in 1946, the year that he died.

Flamingo was not a great success as a sire, but he got the 1939 Gold Cup winner Flyon as well as Flamenco, who won the St James's Palace Stakes and the Lincoln and was later a good sire of jumpers. Fairway won his three remaining races as a three-year-old, the Eclipse Stakes, the St Leger, and the Champion Stakes. The following year his victories included the Princess of Wales's Stakes, the Champion Stakes, and the two and a quarter mile Jockey Club Cup. He broke down in his Gold Cup preparation as a five-year-old. A great sire, his stock won almost £315,000 in stakes, a total that would have been very much larger but for the war. His two Derby winners were Blue Peter (1939) and Watling Street (1942).

Royal Minstrel won the St James's Palace Stakes and the following year he not only won the Victoria Cup, but trounced the mighty Fairway in the Eclipse Stakes. He was exported to America, but eventually returned to this country. Palais Royal II landed a big gamble when he won the Cambridgeshire with 7 st. 13 lb. at the end of the season. Bubbles II proved a very successful sire in France. Stolen by the Germans when he was fifteen, he was repatriated at the age of twenty-one and sired both Guersant and Ocarina. Pharamond became a leading sire in America.

Sir Hugo Cunliffe-Owen at the time of Felstead's success was chairman of the British American Tobacco Company and had numerous other business interests. His only other classic winner was Felstead's daughter Rockfel, but he was second in the 1933 Derby with King Salmon, whom he had bought very cheaply as a two-year-old from Lord Carnarvon. He gave £10,000 for the French sprinter Highborn II and probably got most of the purchase price back when Highborn won at Ascot a day or two later. He certainly wagered heavily at times and, like most betting owners, he preferred long prices rather than short ones about his winners and was all out to achieve them when possible. Those who knew him well said he introduced into his racing the same spirit with which he conducted his business affairs so profitably. He expended a great deal of breath and energy in the weeks following Felstead's success explaining to all who cared to listen that Felstead would still have won even if Fairway had not been mobbed and Flamingo had been ridden with some restraint. Although a lavish supporter of racing for a good many years, he never became a member of the Jockey Club. He died in 1947.

Captain 'Ossie' Bell was born in Australia in 1871, the son of Sir J. P. Bell of Queensland. He trained in India in the early part of the century, but had migrated

West Australian, ridden by Frank Butler; after A. F. de Prades

to England and set up at Epsom shortly before the outbreak of war in 1914. On demobilization he started a stable at Lambourn with little behind him but his war gratuity. He had, however, both a capacity for hard work and a flair for training, and it was not long before he established his reputation. Besides his classic victories with Felstead and Rockfel, he won the Eclipse Stakes with King Salmon and the Ebor Handicap twice with Flint Jack. Possessing a charming and modest personality, he was very much liked in the racing world. He died in 1949.

Harry Wragg, the eldest and most accomplished of three brothers, was without any doubt the coolest and most calculating rider of his time. Intelligent, thoughtful, and with unusual powers of concentration, his wonderful judgement of pace, combined with remarkable patience, enabled him to excel at waiting tactics. 'The Head Waiter' in fact was his racecourse nickname, but rarely did he ever wait too long. He won ten classic races, his second Derby victory being on Watling Street in 1942. In his opinion Felstead needed at least two miles and would have proved a very great stayer had he kept sound. Since retirement from the saddle, Wragg has trained with considerable success at Newmarket and won the Derby in 1961 with Mrs A. Plesch's Psidium.

1928: Wednesday, 6 June . . . 328 Entries. £11,605.

SIR HUGO CUNLIFFE-OWEN's b.c. FELSTEAD
    by Spion Kop out of Felkington   H. WRAGG   I
SIR LAURENCE PHILIPPS's b.c. FLAMINGO
    by Flamboyant out of Lady Peregrine   E. C. ELLIOTT   2
MR L. NEUMANN's b.c. BLACK WATCH
    by Black Gauntlet out of Punka III   C. SMIRKE   3

Also ran:

Lady Richardson's Fernkloof (4th) (R. Perryman); Mrs G. Drummond's Gang Warily (S. Donoghue); Lord Rosebery's Camelford (J. Leach); Mr C. W. S. Whitburn's Scintillation (J. Sirett); M. J. Wittouck's Palais Royal II (M. Allemand); Baron E. de Rothschild's Bubbles II (C. Bouillon); Lord Dewar's Sunny Trace (G. Richards); H.H. Aga Khan's Ranjit Singh (M. Beary); Sir A. Bailey's Advocate (J. Marshall); Lord Derby's Fairway (T. Weston); Mr S. B. Joel's Porthole (F. Winter); Captain G. P. Gough's Royal Minstrel (J. Childs); Mr W. J. Waldron's Grange View (H. Graves); Mr T. Davidson's Constant Son (B. Carslake); Mr H. R. Armitage's Yeomanstown (E. Gardner); Mr D. M. Gant's Royal Crusader (G. Hulme).

19 ran.

1928

Betting:

3–1 Fairway; 9–2 Flamingo; 5–1 Sunny Trace; 100–8 Ranjit Singh; 100–6 Royal Minstrel; 18–1 Gang Warily; 22–1 Bubbles II; 25–1 Camelford; 33–1 Black Watch, Felstead, and Fernkloof; 40–1 Porthole; 50–1 Palais Royal II; 200–1 others.

Won by a length and a half; six lengths between second and third.   2 m. 34⅘ s. Winner trained by Captain O. Bell at Lambourn.

1929

In the ten years' racing between 1929 and the outbreak of the war, the outstanding classic sire was Blandford. He sired four Derby winners, Trigo (1929), Blenheim (1930), Windsor Lad (1934), and Bahram (1935), while Blenheim's son Mahmoud won in 1936. It was a serious blow to British bloodstock breeding that the Aga Khan saw fit to export Blenheim, Bahram, and Mahmoud, particularly as Trigo was a stud failure, while Windsor Lad contracted a fatal disease and died young. There seems a strong possibility at present, though, that the Blandford male line will be revived to some purpose by Alycidon, Crepello, Alcide, and Parthia.

Blandford was bred at the National Stud and was by Swynford out of Blanche, a White Eagle mare who was half-sister to the One Thousand Guineas and Oaks winner Cherry Lass. As a foal Blandford was extremely delicate and when he came up for sale as a yearling the well-known trainer R. C. Dawson and his brother S. C. Dawson were able to buy him cheaply for 720 guineas. He was a heavy-topped colt and as he did not have the best of legs, he was by no means easy to train. In fact he only ran four times, winning on three occasions, his most important success being in the Princess of Wales's Stakes at Newmarket as a three-year-old. He then retired to the Dawson brothers' stud at Cloghran near Dublin, where he rapidly established a reputation. When he died at the early age of sixteen his stock had won over 300 races worth more than £327,000. In the year of his death, which took place in 1935, he was Champion Sire in France as well as in England.

It so happened that Mr William Barnett, a Belfast corn merchant with extensive business connexions in the Argentine, maintained a few mares at the Dawsons' stud. Among them was Athasi, by Farasi out of Athgreany, by His Majesty or Galloping Simon. Farasi, a son of Desmond, was a thirty-five-guinea yearling; in three seasons' racing he won three races worth £1,014, so not surprisingly there was little demand for his services as a sire. In fact at one point his stud fee was five pounds. Athgreany was also of precious little account on the racecourse, her three victories in seventeen attempts being worth only £542.

Bred by Mr Peter Murphy of Poulaphuca, Co. Wicklow, Athasi was bought as a yearling by a Mr Wallace for 270 guineas. As a three-year-old she was acquired by Mr Barnett's brother, Mr D. W. Barnett, who sent her to be trained by Burns in Scotland. Altogether she won five races worth £1,300 between the ages of two and six and at one time she was competing over hurdles without success. At her best she was little, if anything, above Selling Plate class. In 1924 Mr D. W. Barnett sent her to Cloghran to be mated with Blandford, and on his death soon afterwards Mr William Barnett took over both Athasi and her colt foal, subsequently named Athford. In due course Athford won the Jubilee and the Doncaster Cup and was then exported to Japan. Athasi continued to be mated with Blandford with wonderfully successful results, producing Harinero, who won the Irish Derby and Irish St Leger and went to Australia; Trigo, winner of the Derby, St Leger, and Irish St Leger; Primero, who dead-heated for the Irish Derby, won the Irish St Leger, and was exported to Japan; Centeno, winner of £961 and grandsire of the Grand National winner Quare Times; Harina, winner of £4,128 and grand-dam of Tulyar (Derby, St Leger, and King George VI and Queen Elizabeth Stakes) and also of St Crespin III (Eclipse Stakes and Prix de l'Arc de Triomphe); and finally Avena, a winner and dam of Oatflake, who won a war-time November Handicap and is herself dam of the good sprinter Milesian.

In all, Athasi's offspring won $28\frac{1}{2}$ races worth over £51,000 and in addition she became the great grand-dam of two outstanding horses in Tulyar and St Crespin, a remarkable effort by an ex-hurdling mare who was by a five pound sire, and whose own first mate was a Premium Sire.

As a two-year-old Trigo was trained in Ireland by J. T. Rogers. He won the Phoenix Plate, as his brother Athford had done, and also the Anglesey Stakes at the Curragh. Two days after the Anglesey Stakes he failed in very heavy going in the Railway Stakes at the Curragh to give fourteen pounds to Soloptic, who won the Irish One Thousand Guineas and the Irish Oaks the following year. At the end of the season Trigo was sent to join R. C. Dawson's stable in England. 'Take great care of him,' Jack Rogers said to Manuel, his travelling head-lad, who was escorting Trigo. 'He's the best colt that has ever left Ireland.'

Trigo started off well enough in England by winning a seven-furlong handicap from a big field very comfortably at the Newbury Spring Meeting. He continued to please at home afterwards and in consequence started third favourite for the Two Thousand Guineas. In that race, however, which Mr Jinks won by a head from Lord Astor's Cragadour, he ran deplorably and was never seen with the ghost of a chance at any stage of the proceedings.

It was a very dry spring and the gallops in every part of the country were bone-hard, a condition which hardly assisted the preparation of most of the Derby candidates. The Derby itself looked extremely open and Mr Jinks was made favourite despite the fact that his sire was Tetratema, who did not stay an inch beyond a mile; moreover, Mr Jinks had been narrowly beaten in the Newmarket Stakes by Hunters

Moon, who would undoubtedly have started at a shorter price had he not pulled up shin-sore after a gallop on 27 May. Cragadour was second favourite, despite having been temporarily under a cloud, while there was backing for Gay Day, third in the Guineas, Walter Gay, and Kopi. Trigo, neglected by backers since his abject failure in the Guineas, was on offer at 33–1. In general, the runners were considered as below the usual standard and that view was probably justified.

Rain fell steadily throughout Derby Day, dampening the spirits of the crowd without having any noticeable effect on the condition of the track. The race itself did little to cheer the spectators up; neither Mr Jinks nor Cragadour were ever seen with a chance, while Kopi, a popular each-way selection, got involved in a scrimmage coming down the hill and fell. As Kopi subsequently won the Irish Derby easily, it may have been just as well for Trigo that he was safely out of the way.

With half a mile to go Trigo, whose name is the Spanish for 'wheat', moved up to join Hunters Moon and they came round Tattenham Corner together. Trigo soon mastered Hunters Moon in the straight and in the last two furlongs he never for one instant looked like being beaten, although Walter Gay, hampered when Kopi fell, put in a very strong finish. Brienz was a moderate third and Hunters Moon fourth. The victory was received in bewildered and gloomy silence except for a few jubilant cheers from the Irishmen present. The bookmakers had a wonderful race except in Mr Barnett's home town of Belfast, where the inhabitants were on Trigo to a man and are estimated to have won over £100,000. Joe Marshall, a former apprentice of Stanley Wootton's, who rode the winner with admirable confidence, was twenty years of age at the time and lived with his parents at Brighton. This fine success did not in fact bring him lasting fame and fortune, although he rode a good many winners over hurdles up to the outbreak of the war. His first important victory had been on Lord Dewar's Abbot's Speed in the Jubilee three years previously.

Trigo did not run again before the St Leger. Ridden by the stable jockey Michael Beary, who had been on the better-fancied Le Voleur in the Derby, he won a desperate struggle by a short head from Lord Derby's Bosworth, winner of the Gold Cup the following year. The unplaced favourite was Lord Astor's Oaks winner Pennycomequick. Only a bare seven days after that gruelling battle, Trigo, carrying 9 st. 12 lb., won the Irish St Leger, the little horse showing the greatest possible courage to win by a short head from Visellus, to whom he conceded twelve pounds. That effort concluded Trigo's career and he was sent to the stud. Unfortunately, he signally failed to come up to expectations, and never succeeded in siring a winner of any particular importance. He died in 1946.

Of the other Derby competitors, Walter Gay won the Atlantic Cup at Aintree as a four-year-old and was second in the Hardwicke Stakes. He made no mark as a sire in the country and was exported to Russia before the war. Brienz was cut and eventually became one of the best steeplechasers in the country. He continued to win races until he was thirteen years of age. Hunters Moon, a half-brother to Hyperion by Hurry On, was exported to the Argentine later in the season and became a leading sire there. Kopi did quite well at the stud in France, but Mr Jinks disappointed as a sire after a very promising start.

1929: Wednesday, 5 June . . . 326 Entries. £11,965.

MR W. BARNETT'S b.c. TRIGO by Blandford out of Athasi	J. MARSHALL	1
LORD WOOLAVINGTON'S ch.c. WALTER GAY by Captain Cuttle out of William's Pride	F. FOX	2
MR S. TATTERSALL'S br.c. BRIENZ by Blink out of Blue Lake	R. A. JONES	3

Also ran:

Lord Derby's Hunters Moon (4th) (T. Weston); Lord Astor's Cragadour (H. Jelliss); Lord Astor's Cavendo (J. Brennan); Lord Woolavington's Rattlin the Reefer (J. Childs); Major J. S. Courtauld's Osiris (H. Leach); Lord Dewar's Aristotle (F. Lane); Sir F. Eley's N.P.B. (P. Donoghue); Lord Glanely's Grand Prince (G. Richards); Mrs C. Glorney's Posterity (J. Taylor); Lord Wyfold's Reedsmouth (E. Gardner); H.H. Aga Khan's Le Voleur (M. Beary); Lord Londonderry's Barbizon (H. Wragg); Major D. McCalmont's Mr Jinks (H. Beasley); Mr H. E. Morriss's Tom Peartree (J. Dines); Sir L. Philipps's Horus (E. C. Elliott); Duke of Portland's Leonard (J. Leach); Mr A. de Rothschild's Reflector (R. Perryman); Sir Victor Sassoon's Gay Day (S. Donoghue); Mr H. G. Selfridge's P.D.Q. (P. Beasley); Mr W. M. G. Singer's En Garde (C. Ray); Mr J. Tait's Roberto (J. Thwaites); Sir Mathew Wilson's Golden Rain (R. Dick); Mr S. B. Joel's Kopi (F. Winter) (*fell*).

26 ran.

Betting:

5–1 Mr Jinks; 15–2 Cragadour; 10–1 Hunters Moon and Gay Day; 100–8 Kopi and Walter Gay; 20–1 Le Voleur; 25–1 Posterity; 33–1 Trigo, Barbizon, Osiris, Rattlin the Reefer, En Garde, Reflector, and Reedsmouth; 40–1 Tom Peartree and Horus; 50–1 Cavendo, N.P.B., and Brienz; 66–1 Leonard; 100–1 others.

Won by a length and a half; two lengths between second and third.   2 m. 36⅖ s. Winner trained by R. C. Dawson at Whatcombe.

1930

From 1922, the year that he first raced in England, until his death in 1957, His Highness the Aga Khan was the outstanding figure on the Turf in Europe.

He was originally inspired to take up racing by Lord Wavertree during a visit to the latter's stud at Tully, Co. Kildare, in 1904. At that period, though, he considered he had neither sufficient time nor money to operate on the scale that he desired and it was not until 1921 that he at last felt able to put his long thought-out plans into action. That year he asked George Lambton, an outstanding judge of bloodstock, to buy him some yearlings that were to form the foundation of a stud. Lambton agreed to do so, and, his own stable being full, he advised that they should be trained by R. C. Dawson.

Among the more notable animals that Lambton bought were Diophon and Salmon Trout, two colts that won the Two Thousand Guineas and St Leger respectively, and three fillies, Mumtaz Mahal, Teresina, and Cos, who were not only highly successful on the racecourse, but became foundation mares of the stud as well. Eventually the Aga Khan, himself a fine judge of a pedigree, established a chain of studs in Ireland and France that enabled him to breed bloodstock and race on a scale unapproached by any other owner in England, and only by M. Boussac in France. In 1931 he had a bitter quarrel with Dawson and transferred his horses to Frank Butters. When Butters retired in 1949, he was succeeded by Marcus Marsh and Noel Murless. In 1954 the Aga Khan decided to move his racing interests to France, giving as the reason the lower costs to owners in that country compared with the prize money available. From then until his death, most of his Irish-bred yearlings were sent to Alec Head at Chantilly.

The Aga Khan enjoyed glittering success on the English Turf and shares with Lord Egremont the distinction of having won the Derby five times, the difference being that the Aga's winners were unquestionably three-year-olds, while Lord Egremont's in all probability were not! The winners in the chocolate and green hoops were Blenheim (1930), Bahram (1935), Mahmoud (1936), My Love (1948), and Tulyar (1952). The Aga bred Bahram, Mahmoud, and Tulyar himself; Blenheim he bought as a yearling and My Love he owned in partnership with that horse's breeder, M. Volterra.

In addition, the Aga Khan won the Two Thousand Guineas twice, the One

Thousand Guineas once, the Oaks three times, and the St Leger five times. He won the Eclipse Stakes three times, the Gold Cup twice, and the Middle Park Stakes on six occasions. In Ireland he won fourteen classic races, while in France he won the Grand Prix with My Love and the Prix de l'Arc de Triomphe with Migoli and Nuccio. He was leading owner thirteen times in England, leading breeder eight times. Altogether in Great Britain he won 741 flat races worth £1,043,934.

The Aga Khan was extremely conscious of the commercial aspects of racing and, despite his vast wealth, he never permitted the luxury of sentiment to interfere with business. He was in fact a dealer of exceptional shrewdness and that may well have been the side of racing that really appealed to him most. Popular enough with the racing public as a whole, for his horses were always run in the most open manner possible, he was strongly criticized in some quarters for selling Blenheim, Bahram, and Mahmoud for export. Tulyar, who eventually went to America, he sold to the Irish National Stud, while My Love, a stud failure, ended up in South America. In his later years the Aga Khan used to send batches of mares to be sold in the United States. By and large he can be said to have conferred great benefits on English racing, but those benefits would have been considerably greater had he been a little less commercially-minded.

Bred by Lord Carnarvon, Blenheim was a medium-sized colt of beautiful quality by Blandford out of Malva, by Charles O'Malley who was third in the Derby in 1910 and second in the Gold Cup the following season. Malva, who won three races worth £1,052 herself, was also dam of His Grace, by Blandford, and King Salmon, by Salmon Trout. His Grace dead-heated with Cecil for the Coronation Cup and won over £6,000 in stakes, while King Salmon won the Eclipse Stakes and was second to Hyperion in the Derby.

Bought as a yearling on behalf of the Aga Khan for 4,100 guineas at the Newmarket July Sales, Blenheim came to hand very early and on 13 April he started favourite for a £200 Plate at Newbury. He beat a big field very easily by three lengths, and on the strength of that performance was a 9–4 on favourite shortly afterwards for the Stud Produce Stakes at Sandown. He was beaten, however, by the Bridge of Bath filly to whom he conceded nine pounds. He won the Speedy Plate at Windsor on 1 June and then moved successfully into a higher class, winning the New Stakes at Ascot from Press Gang, a colt of Lord Woolavington's by Hurry On out of the war-time Derby winner Fifinella. In the Champagne Stakes at Doncaster Blenheim ran a very game race but was just beaten by Lord Woolavington's Fair Diana, while in the Middle Park Stakes Press Gang reversed the Ascot form and beat him rather more easily than a half-length verdict might suggest. Between those two defeats Blenheim won the Hopeful Stakes at Newmarket. Although not rated in the first three for the Two-Year-Old Free Handicap, the leaders in which were Diolite (9 st. 2 lb.) and Challenger (9 st. 1 lb.), there seemed a reasonable chance that he might prove a top-class three-year-old. He had never run a bad race, and on the occasions that he did meet with defeat, he showed admirable courage and resolution.

At the beginning of 1930 the plan was that Blenheim should represent the Aga Khan in the Guineas; Rustom Pasha, a colt by the stayer Son-in-Law out of the sprinter Cos, in the Derby; and Ut Majeur, by the French sire Ksar, in the St Leger. As it happened, to the Aga Khan's great good fortune, that scheme was not strictly adhered to.

Blenheim made his first appearance early in April in the one-mile Greenham Stakes at Newbury. Easy to back at 8–1, he was some little way from being really fit, and those who knew him best were neither surprised nor disappointed when he finished unplaced in a big field behind Colonel Loder's Christopher Robin. On the same day Ut Majeur won the seven-furlong Berkshire Maiden Plate by a head. Shortly afterwards Rustom Pasha won the one-mile Nonsuch Stakes at Epsom by four lengths, with Press Gang unplaced. Rustom Pasha's performance certainly looked impressive enough on paper, but the race had been run at a muddling pace throughout and was not in fact a reliable criterion of merit.

The Two Thousand Guineas took place on yielding ground. Caerleon, a full brother to Colorado, was favourite, with Blenheim and Diolite joint second favourites. Diolite had the race at his mercy a long way from home and won by an easy two lengths from Paradine, with Silver Flare third. The running of Paradine was a good advertisement for Rustom Pasha, who had given him seven pounds and a decisive beating at Epsom, while Iliad, who was fifth, just behind Blenheim, had finished some way behind Ut Majeur at Newbury. Ut Majeur, however, was beaten in the Newmarket Stakes by the American-bred The Scout II a fortnight later and it was eventually decided that Rustom Pasha should be accompanied to the post in the Derby by Blenheim in view of the creditable race that Blenheim had run in the Guineas. Michael Beary, the stable jockey, chose to ride Rustom Pasha and Harry Wragg was given the mount on Blenheim.

Diolite, owned by Sir Hugo Hirst and trained by Fred Templeman, who had won the 1919 Derby on Grand Parade, started favourite at Epsom at 11–4 despite serious doubts of his ability to stay the distance. Rustom Pasha was heavily supported at 9–2 and there was plenty of money for Silver Flare and the Manton colt Trews, the latter being said to have done an impressive gallop at home. The Scout II and Blenheim, 100–6 and 18–1 respectively, were both popular each-way selections.

Silver Flare, not unexpectedly, gave a lot of trouble at the start, refusing to line up and lashing out wildly in all directions, luckily without doing any harm. At long last he was induced to face the tapes and in the end the only horse badly away was Blenheim. Wragg wisely did not hurry to make up the lost ground and Blenheim was still last as the field passed the ten-furlong starting-gate.

Diolite was the first to show in front with Rustom Pasha second, but at the top of the hill Rustom Pasha took the lead and turned for home about a length in front of Diolite, with Ballyferis, Silver Flare, and Trews close up, and Iliad beginning to make noticeable progress. Almost as soon as the straight was reached Rustom Pasha's stamina gave out and he dropped back beaten. This left Diolite in the lead, but below the distance he, too, began to falter and was headed by Iliad, the 'Manton Neglected'. Blenheim in the meantime had been making steady headway on the outside and, coming to the final furlong, he delivered a perfectly timed challenge. Running on with the utmost determination he swept past Iliad close home to win a most exciting race by a length. Diolite was third, Silver Flare fourth, Trews fifth, and Seer sixth. The Aga Khan, who had given up hope when Rustom Pasha began to retreat, had been quite confused by the change in his fortunes in the final stages of the race and is traditionally supposed to have shouted 'Come on, Rustom Pasha!' just as the gallant Blenheim struck the front. Although Blenheim was only the stable second string his victory was well received and both he and his owner were loudly cheered. Harry Wragg, who had ridden a typical cool-headed race, remarked afterwards that the winner was 'a lovely little horse to ride and did everything I asked him in the most gentlemanly manner'. Dick Dawson, beaming through his pince-nez, had every reason to feel elated, as it was his second successive Derby victory and both winners were by Blandford, who was owned by his brother and himself.

The Derby was Blenheim's last race. He jarred a tendon during his preparation for the Eclipse Stakes and was sent to his owner's stud in France, where he proved extremely successful. Among his first crop of foals was Mumtaz Begum, dam of Nasrullah and grand-dam of Royal Charger, both good horses who became leading sires in America. In his second crop Blenheim got Mahmoud, winner of the 1936 Derby, and Wyndham, a very fast horse who sired an even faster one in Windy City.

For Signor Tesio Blenheim sired Donatello II, who ran second in the Grand Prix and later became a very influential sire in England, his offspring including the Derby and Two Thousand Guineas winner Crepello; the One Thousand Guineas winner Picture Play; the Gold Cup winners Alycidon and Supertello, of whom the former is a highly successful sire; and the dams of Pinza, winner of the Derby, and of Aureole, winner of the King George VI and Queen Elizabeth Stakes. In America Blenheim did equally well, getting winners such as Whirlaway and Jet Pilot, as well as the dams of the Kentucky Derby winners Hill Gail and Ponder. He died in 1958.

Of the other Derby competitors, Iliad retired from the Turf a maiden, and so did

Silver Flare and Trews, who were both running over hurdles as four-year-olds. Diolite deteriorated, and his only other win was in a Liverpool handicap as a four-year-old. He eventually was exported to Japan. Rustom Pasha, a far bigger horse than Blenheim but without Blenheim's quality, won the Eclipse and Champion Stakes later in the season and was third to Singapore in the St Leger. He was at the stud first in France and later in the Argentine; mated with Mumtaz Mahal, he got Rustom Mahal, the dam of that exceptionally fast horse Abernant. Sea Rover turned out to be a good chaser, while Noble Star, by Hapsburg out of a mare by Herodote, developed into a really good stayer, winning the Ascot and Goodwood Stakes, the Cesarewitch, and the Jockey Club Cup.

1930: Wednesday, 4 June ... 316 Entries. £10,036 5s.

H.H. AGA KHAN's br.c. BLENHEIM by Blandford out of Malva	H. WRAGG	1
MR S. TATTERSALL's ch.c. ILIAD by Swynford out of Pagan Sacrifice	R. A. JONES	2
SIR H. HIRST's b.c. DIOLITE by Diophon out of Needle Rock	C. RAY	3

Also ran:

Major J. S. Courtauld's Silver Flare (4th) (E. C. Elliott); Lord Astor's Trews (R. Dick); Mr G. G. H. Peek's Seer (H. Jelliss); Mr H. P. Nickall's Noble Star (H. Beasley); Major D. Dixon's Ballyferis (J. Canty); Lord Woolavington's Dick Swiveller (F. Fox); Mr J. M. Clayton's The Sponger (R. Perryman); H.H. Aga Khan's Rustom Pasha (M. Beary); Lord Glanely's Grand Salute (G. Richards); Lord Howard de Walden's Bargany (J. Dines); Mr A. R. Cox's Sea Rover (S. Donoghue); Mr T. Richards's Tetragem (F. Lane); Mr W. Woodward's The Scout II (J. Childs); Mr A. K. Macomber's Parthenon (E. Goldin).

17 ran.

Betting:

11–4 Diolite; 9–2 Rustom Pasha; 7–1 Silver Flare; 100–7 Trews; 100–6 The Scout II; 18–1 Blenheim; 20–1 Ballyferis; 22–1 Dick Swiveller and Noble Star; 25–1 Iliad; 40–1 Seer; 50–1 Sea Rover and The Sponger; 100–1 others.

Totalizator: (2s. unit). Win: 40s. 9d. Places: 10s. 6d., 10s. 3d., 4s. 6d.*

Won by a length; two lengths between second and third.　　　　2 m. 38⅕ s.
Winner trained by R. C. Dawson at Whatcombe.

* This was the first time the totalizator operated on Derby Day.

1931

For years the Jockey Club had been worried by the question of nominations rendered void by the death of an owner. Backed by the highest legal opinion, the Jockey Club had always acted on the assumption that fees and forfeits incurred for horses entered under Jockey Club rules could not be recovered under process of law, because if they were contracts, they were contracts by way of gaming and wagering, and therefore without legal sanction. If a living owner evaded his forfeit liabilities, his name was published in the forfeit list in the *Racing Calendar*. As that deterrent could hardly be inflicted with decency on a dead man or on his executors, the 'Void Nomination' rule came into existence, this rule stipulating that when an owner died, all entries for his horses ceased to exist.

The matter was under discussion in 1927 when Mr Edgar Wallace, the well-known author and journalist and a very keen racing man, suggested a 'friendly' action between the Jockey Club and himself. It was agreed that Mr Wallace should be sued in the High Court for the recovery of four pounds due in respect of a horse of his entered at Newmarket. In the Chancery Court the verdict was in favour of Mr Wallace, much to his disappointment, as while the action was pending he was unable to run any of his horses, since if he had won a race he would have had a credit balance at the office of the Jockey Club and the four pounds in dispute would have been appropriated. The case was then taken to the Court of Appeal, where the Master of the Rolls and Lords Justices Lawrence and Russell found in favour of the Jockey Club. All the expenses incurred by Mr Wallace during the case were paid by the Jockey Club.

The change in the rule made possible by this action and carried through in 1929, came just in time for Cameronian, whose owner-breeder Lord Dewar died in April 1930, and left the colt to his nephew, Mr J. A. Dewar. It is typical of the twists of fortune that so frequently occur in racing that Lord Dewar owned horses for thirty years and never won a classic; his nephew and heir succeeded in doing so at his very first attempt. Oddly enough, when Mr Wallace visited Lord Dewar's stud in 1928, Lord Dewar pointed to a colt-foal and remarked, 'He will win the Derby, but I may not live to see it.' The colt was Cameronian. It was a strange comment to make as at that time the 'Void Nominations' rule was still in force.

Cameronian was rather a small bay colt of superb quality and with a beautiful action, by Pharos out of Una Cameron, by Gainsborough. Una Cameron, dam of three other winners besides Cameronian, ran for two seasons herself but never won. She was out of Cherimoya, by Cherry Tree, by a son of Hampton. Cherry Tree never won a race; Cherimoya only ran once and that was in the Oaks, which she won. Lord Dewar bought her in 1915 for 2,300 guineas, her previous owner, Mr Broderick Cloete, having been drowned when the *Lusitania* was torpedoed by a German submarine.

Fred Darling soon recognized that Cameronian was a colt of high promise and decided to give him an easy time as a two-year-old. In fact, Cameronian's only outing during his first season was in a race of no importance at Salisbury, which he won with considerable ease. He started favourite for his first race as a three-year-old, the Craven Stakes, but was rather disappointing and only finished third to a second-class performer called Philae. Despite this set-back, it was considered worth while running him a fortnight later in the Two Thousand Guineas, in which, starting at 100–8, he was ridden by Childs, the stable jockey Fox being up on the second favourite, Lord Ellesmere's Lemnarchus. Neither Lemnarchus nor the favourite Portlaw stayed the mile, and Cameronian won by two lengths from M. Boussac's Goyescas, with Orpen third. Goyescas was unlucky in that he lost several lengths at the start, but Cameronian appeared to win with a bit in hand.

Cameronian did not run again before the Derby, but on 30 May he was tried over a mile and a half at Beckhampton with very satisfactory results, winning easily, receiving eight pounds from Parenthesis, second in the previous year's St Leger and destined to win the Coronation Cup the day after Cameronian won the Derby. Last to finish of the five horses that took part in the trial was Lord Ellesmere's filly Four Course, who received six pounds from Cameronian. She had won the One Thousand Guineas rather luckily, and was to go very close indeed to winning the Oaks.

Cameronian started a firm favourite for the Derby at 7–2; Sandwich, a half-brother to Manna, had been heavily supported since winning the Chester Vase and was second favourite at 8–1. Orpen was well-backed, being regarded as certain to stay the distance, and there was good money as well for Pomme d'Api, winner of the mile and a half Burwell Stakes, and for Doctor Dolittle, who had beaten Jacopo, joint head of the Free Handicap in 1930, in the one mile Londesborough Stakes at York.

The weather was perfect and Captain Allison's start gave the huge crowd nothing to complain about. Sandwich was rather slow to find his stride and, being drawn on the inside, was badly squeezed out in the initial furlong. He had improved a little by the time the mile and a quarter starting-gate was reached, but was still a good many lengths behind the leaders.

Coming to Tattenham Corner Gallini was a length in front of Armagnac, Zanoff, and Cameronian. Orpen was not yet in the first six and Sandwich was still behind Orpen. With three furlongs to go a shout went up as Cameronian moved to the front on a tight rein. Almost immediately, though, he was challenged by Orpen, who reduced the lead to a head. Cameronian, however, still had a bit in reserve, and as soon as Fox showed him the whip he rallied at once and increased his advantage to a length. Just when the race was almost over, Sandwich suddenly appeared from nowhere travelling very much faster than anything else. He swept past Goyescas, Gallini, who had lost a shoe in the straight, Pomme d'Api, and Jacopo, and was bearing down fast on the two leaders, but the winning post came just a few yards too soon, Cameronian winning by three parts of a length from Orpen, with Sandwich the same distance away third. Goyescas was fourth, Gallini fifth and Pomme d'Api sixth. The result was highly profitable to the general public and the winner was cheered to the echo. The bookmakers, on the other hand, were unanimous in describing the result as 'terrible'. 'It is possible,' said Harry Wragg, Sandwich's rider, after the race, 'that I was an unlucky loser.' Sandwich's backers considered this the most notable understatement of the century. There is no doubt that Sandwich was hampered at various stages, switched from one position to another, and never got a really clear run until it was all too late. No fancied horse had such ill-luck in the great race again until Shantung in 1959, and Shantung at least had a clear passage from Tattenham Corner.

Cameronian's only race before the St Leger was the St James's Palace Stakes, which he won as a Derby winner should. He started at 6–5 on favourite at Doncaster for the final classic and the complete débâcle that occurred has never been satisfactorily explained. Normally he was the most placid of individuals, but both before and during the St Leger he was in the wildest state of excitement. He kicked Orpen before the start, and when the tapes went up he fought for his head like a madman. Inevitably he ran himself right out, was stone cold by the final bend and finished last. He had a temperature two degrees above normal afterwards, but Fred Darling calmly refuted any suggestion that the colt had been 'got at', remarking, 'There are various causes for horses suddenly going wrong in this way and I put no sinister construction upon the occurrence.' The Stewards were apparently satisfied, though the racing public were not, and that was the end of the matter. It only remains to add that the St Leger was won easily by Sandwich from Orpen and the American-bred colt Sir Andrew, who had earlier in the season won the Newmarket Stakes.

It was a long time before Cameronian really recovered and for almost a year he ran a very slight but persistent temperature. As a four-year-old in consequence he never found his form until the late autumn, although he was far from disgraced when defeated in the Coronation Cup, the Ribblesdale Stakes, and the Jocket Club Stakes. In the Jockey Club Stakes he ran particularly well to finish close up third to the St Leger winner Firdaussi, to whom he conceded twelve pounds, and a fortnight later he won the Champion Stakes with all his old brilliance to complete his racing career. At the stud he was only a moderate success. His best winner was Mr J. V. Rank's Scottish Union, winner of the St Leger in 1938 and runner-up in both the Two Thousand Guineas and the Derby. He was also sire of Snowberry, dam of the 1945 St Leger winner Chamossaire. After eight seasons in England he was exported to the Argentine where he did not do well. He died in 1955.

Of the other Derby competitors it can be said that they were on their best behaviour at the subsequent Royal Ascot meeting, where besides Cameronian, Pomme d'Api, Sir Andrew, Grindleton, Abbots Worthy, Coldstream, Orpen, Sandwich, and Doctor Dolittle all won races. Orpen was a stud failure and so was Sandwich, whose only success as a four-year-old was a walk-over for 'The Whip', although he did finish third in the Cesarewitch with 9 st. 5 lb. Goyescas broke a pastern at St Cloud as a five-year-old and was destroyed. Jacopo did well as a sire in America, while Armagnac won a number of races over fences and hurdles. Shell Transport later in the season dead-heated with The Recorder for the Princess of Wales's Stakes and won the Jockey Club Stakes.

Mr John Dewar was just over forty when he inherited from his uncle a million pounds, plus a two-thirds interest in a £2,500,000 trust fund, as well as a stud and a string of racehorses that included a future winner of the Derby. He had little interest in the Turf before this sudden stroke of good fortune, but he very soon developed one and maintained it until his death in 1954. His other classic winners were Tudor Minstrel, a horse of exceptional speed that won the Two Thousand Guineas by eight lengths in 1947; Commotion, winner of the Oaks in 1941; and Festoon, who won the 1954 One Thousand Guineas. He also owned Fair Trial, a good racehorse and a brilliantly successful sire. Elected a member of the Jockey Club in 1941, Mr Dewar bought the Beckhampton establishment and gallops on Fred Darling's retirement for £60,000, but sold the property in 1952 when Noel Murless, Darling's successor there, announced his intention of moving to Newmarket. Mr Dewar left an estate valued at over £3,000,000, and when his horses in training, his mares, yearlings, and foals were sold, they realized the gigantic total of £398,595.

Fred Fox, who rode Cameronian in the Derby, was born in Wiltshire in 1888. At the age of eighteen he was apprenticed to Fred Pratt at Lambourn and soon made his name. He rode his first winner in 1907 and had his first important success the following season when he won the Cesarewitch on Yentoi, trained by Fred Darling. For two years before the First World War he rode for the von Weinberg stable with success both in Germany and Austria, but he had numerous pre-war victories in England, including the One Thousand Guineas on Atmah in 1911, and the Ascot Gold Cup on Bomba in 1909 and on Aleppo in 1914.

From 1914 until his retirement in 1936 he rode with consistent success in England. He won the Two Thousand Guineas on Diolite in 1930, the Two Thousand Guineas and Derby on Bahram in 1935, and the St Leger on Firdaussi in 1932. He would have won the St Leger on Bahram as well but for being incapacitated by a serious fall the day before. He rode five winners in a day at Sandown in 1929 and was Champion Jockey in 1930, defeating Gordon Richards by a single point. He was a thoroughly sound horseman—he rode regularly to hounds in the winter—and at home on every type of horse. To the end of his career he could go to scale without difficulty at 7 st. 7 lb.

When he retired he settled down in Berkshire, became a Justice of the Peace, and was affectionately known as 'The Mayor of Wantage'. A very kind-hearted, generous, and amusing little man, his closing years were saddened by the death of his only son Michael when serving in the R.A.F. He himself was killed in a car accident at Frilford in 1945.

1931: Wednesday, 3 June ... 404 Entries. £12,161 5s.

MR J. A. DEWAR's b.c. CAMERONIAN by Pharos out of Una Cameron	F. FOX	1
SIR J. RUTHERFORD's b.c. ORPEN by Solario out of Harpy	R. A. JONES	2
LORD ROSEBERY's b.c. SANDWICH by Sansovino out of Waffles	H. WRAGG	3

Also ran:

M. M. Boussac's Goyescas (4th) (E. C. Elliott); Sir E. Hanmer's Gallini (J. Taylor); H.H. Aga Khan's Pomme d'Api (M. Beary); Mr Marshall Field's Jacopo (J. Childs); Mr A. de Rothschild's Armagnac (R. Perryman); Lord Howard de Walden's Rose en Soleil (W. Turtle); Lt.-Col. W. Guinness's Estate Duty (T. Weston); Mr A. F. Basset's Doctor Dolittle (H. Beasley); Mr V. T. Thompson's Abbots Worthy (J. Canty); Mr W. M. Cazalet's Shell Transport (R. Dick); Mr J. P. Hornung's Apperley (B. Carslake); Mr E. M. Sykes's Lemonition (J. Leach); Mr J. B. Leigh's Lightning Star (J. Marshall); Mr T. W. Blenkiron's Cheery Lad (C. Ray); Mr B. Davis's Te Hau (T. Burns); Mr B. Davis's Te Ruru (F. Herbert); Lord Glanely's Coldstream (G. Richards); M. Robert Kahn's Knoloma (W.

Sibbritt); Mr Z. Michalinos's Zanoff (J. Sirett); Mr J. W. Sharples's Grindleton (L. Brown); Mr W. Woodward's Sir Andrew (P. Beasley); Sir G. Bullough's Reveillon (H. Jelliss); (M. M. Calmanor's Primitifo was withdrawn by order of the Stewards).

25 ran.

Betting:

7–2 Cameronian; 8–1 Sandwich; 9–1 Orpen; 10–1 Doctor Dolittle and Pomme d'Api; 100–6 Goyescas and Jacopo; 25–1 Sir Andrew and Coldstream; 33–1 Zanoff; 40–1 Reveillon, Lightning Star, Estate Duty, Gallini, and Rose en Soleil; 50–1 Cheery Lad, Shell Transport, Apperley and Abbots Worthy; 66–1 Armagnac; 100–1 others.

Totalizator: (2s. unit). Win: 8s. 7d. Places: 4s. 11d., 4s. 3d., 5s. 9d.

Won by three parts of a length; the same distance between second and third.

2 m. 36⅗ s.

Winner trained by F. Darling at Beckhampton.

1932

Mr Tom Walls, part-owner and trainer of the 1932 Derby winner April the Fifth, was a remarkably able, energetic, and versatile man. Born in 1883, the son of a Northamptonshire builder, he was educated at Northampton County School and for a brief spell served in the Metropolitan Police. As far as he was concerned, though, a policeman's life was not a happy one, and by 1905 he had transferred his attentions to the stage. In that profession he soon began to make good, but the real turning-point in his fortunes came in 1922 with his first managerial venture. With Mr Leslie Henson he produced a farce at the Shaftesbury Theatre called *Tons of Money* which ran for two years.

This was followed by a series of successful farces at the Aldwych Theatre which were written by Mr Ben Travers and in which Walls himself was the perfect foil to Messrs Ralph Lynn and Robertson Hare. He became one of the best-known and most popular figures on the lighter stage and also appeared in a number of films.

Walls had always loved every form of sport, and racing in particular, so as soon as his theatrical interests had earned him sufficient money, he took out a licence and started a stable at Epsom. In this capacity he enjoyed a fair measure of success, winning all told about a hundred and fifty races, mostly small handicaps and Selling Plates. April the Fifth, the first Epsom-trained Derby winner since Amato in 1838, was, of course, his greatest triumph, but a victory that gave him almost equal pleasure was that of Crafty Alice, owned and ridden by his son, an officer in the 5th Dragoon Guards, in the Grand Military Gold Cup at Sandown.

Tom Walls died in 1949. A most amusing, generous, and hospitable man, he must have made a fortune in his day, but he did not keep it and there was not a great deal left at the time of his death.

April the Fifth was bred in partnership by Mr Sidney McGregor of Leamington Spa and Mr G. S. L. Whitelaw, both well known in the steeplechasing world. His sire was Craig an Eran, winner of the Two Thousand Guineas and the Eclipse Stakes, his dam Sold Again, by Call o' the Wild out of Market, by Marcovil. There was precious little in the bottom half of his pedigree to suggest a Derby winner although his sixth dam was the 1856 Oaks winner Summerside, a half-sister to the Derby winner Ellington. Sold Again was useless on the racecourse and was given as a present to her trainer Sam Pickering, whose opinion of the value of the gift is clearly shown by the fact that he passed her on to a dealer for twenty guineas not long afterwards. Two years later Sold Again appeared at one of Messrs Tattersall's Monday Sales of Hunters at Knightsbridge; Mr McGregor took a fancy to her and bought her for 230 guineas. She ran once over hurdles the following season, broke down, and was sent to the stud. She was frequently barren, and her only other winner in England except for April the Fifth was his full sister Sybil, who won the Atalanta Stakes at Sandown. Call o' the Wild, by Polymelus, ran three times, winning the Payne Stakes at Newmarket. He then broke a leg but was saved for the stud. He made no great mark as a sire and was ultimately exported to the Argentine. Market won two small races and was the dam of a single minor winner.

April the Fifth was sold at Newmarket as a yearling 'to dissolve a partnership' and Mr McGregor bought him for 200 guineas. Mr McGregor kept the colt on grass till January 1931 and then sent him to Mr Walls to train on the understanding that Walls should race him and train him at his own expense, but that any stake money should be divided equally between owner and trainer. He was to race in Walls's name and colours and it was agreed that above all he was not to be hurried.

As a two-year-old April the Fifth ran at Gatwick, Wolverhampton, and Derby, and although the class of event he competed in was moderate, he did not succeed in reaching the leading three. He grew a good deal during the winter, but did not appear to have made any striking improvement when fourth in a small handicap at Birmingham at the end of March. However, he was not taken out of his classic engagements, possibly because Donoghue, who had ridden him once as a two-year-old, had apparently been impressed by his promise. In the Two Thousand Guineas the colt was not disgraced in finishing sixth of eleven behind Orwell, Dastur, and Hesperus, but at the same time there were no grounds yet for assuming that he might ever reach the top class.

April the Fifth's first success was in a one-mile maiden race, the Marlborough Plate, at Gatwick on 14 May. Ridden by Fred Lane, he started favourite at 11–8 and beat three very moderate opponents by six lengths. His next outing, the Lingfield Derby Trial, imposed a very much severer test. The favourite was the Manton colt Spenser, winner of the New Stakes at Ascot and the Richmond Stakes at Goodwood the year before. Other runners included Firdaussi, who had won the Dewhurst Stakes as a two-year-old and was destined to win the St Leger; Foxhunter, a future Gold Cup winner; and Silvermere, winner of the Gold Vase a few weeks later. Starting at 6–1 and again ridden by Lane, April the Fifth won decisively by two lengths from Firdaussi and was clearly a far more formidable proposition over a mile and a half than a mile. Nevertheless, comparatively few people were prepared to take his Derby chance very seriously. If he had been trained at Manton or

Beckhampton it would have been different, but the racing public had a picture in their minds of Walls in one of his typical Aldwych farce roles and found it impossible to take such an accomplished comedian quite seriously. They just could not visualize him training the winner of the Derby.

A 5–4 favourite for the Derby was Mr W. M. G. Singer's Gainsborough colt Orwell, trained by Alec Taylor's successor at Manton, Joe Lawson, and ridden by Bobby Jones, who had been on the runner-up in the Derby the two previous years. Orwell had been a brilliant two-year-old, his five victories including the Middle Park Stakes, while this season he had won first the Greenham Stakes at Newbury, and then the Two Thousand Guineas very comfortably. Some people doubted whether a horse with such brilliant speed could stay a mile and a half, but he had done everything asked of him in his final gallop, finishing a long way in front of Spenser, fifth in the Two Thousand Guineas. Second favourite was Lord Woolavington's big chesnut Buchan colt Cockpen, who subsequently turned out to be a sprinter, while a popular each-way selection was Miracle, a big colt by Manna that Lord Rosebery had bought from Lord Beaverbrook as a yearling for 170 guineas and who had won the Newmarket Stakes by four lengths. Hesperus, third in the Guineas, was offered at 100–8 and April the Fifth at 100–6. Dastur was at the surprisingly good price of 18–1 considering that he had been second in the Guineas and was bred to stay the distance. His stable companion Firdaussi, who was not yet at his best after a spring cough, figured at 22–1.

The weather and the start were both perfect. Bacchus, Cockpen, and Wyvern were the first to show in front, but Portofino took the lead after two furlongs and came to Tattenham Corner in front of Firdaussi, Miracle, and Dastur, with Orwell well enough placed if he was good enough and April the Fifth in quite a handy position as well. Portofino compounded early in the straight, Firdaussi could find no more, and with two furlongs to go Orwell was obviously beaten. At that point the race seemed to lie between Dastur, who led, and Miracle, who was slowly but surely reducing Dastur's advantage. Below the distance, however, Lane, who had ridden a very patient race, suddenly set April the Fifth alight. April the Fifth, so-named because he was foaled on that date which also happened to be Mr McGregor's birthday, immediately responded and came storming through in the final furlong to win by three parts of a length from Dastur, with Miracle a short head away third. Royal Dancer was fourth, Firdaussi fifth, and Celebrator sixth. It was a popular and well-deserved victory for a colt that, unlike most of his opponents, had no trouble in staying the distance. His one bit of luck was getting to the course just in time to take part, as his horse-box got stuck in a traffic-jam and he was compelled to get out and walk. Tom Walls, his friends, and theatrical circles in general won a great deal of money, although perhaps not quite as much as some newspapers suggested. Fred Lane, a sound if unspectacular rider, rode a perfectly judged race on the winner. He had a long career in the saddle and was at his best in long-distance events. This was his only success in a classic race. A quiet, reliable, and unassuming personality, even in late middle age he was much in demand to ride work at Newmarket.

April the Fifth was sent to a stable near Arundel for a rest, but unfortunately sustained a knee injury. He was a long way short of his best when he ran in the St Leger and performed by no means badly under the circumstances even though he ultimately finished thirteenth. Firdaussi won from Dastur and Silvermere, the Aga Khan owning four of the first five horses to finish. April the Fifth never ran again and retired to the stud where he was a complete failure. His best winner on the flat was Bright Lady, a useful stayer that won five races worth over £2,700. He was also sire of Lord Stalbridge's Red April, who won £12,900 under National Hunt rules, more than double the total amount won by his stock on the flat. He died at Mr McGregor's stud in 1954.

Dastur, second in all three classics, won the Irish Derby and as a four-year-old the Coronation Cup. A half-brother to Bahram, his stud career was slightly disappointing, but Darius (Two Thousand Guineas), Diabletta (£14,492), and The Cobbler (£17,011) are all out of Dastur mares. Miracle was surprisingly beaten in the Prince of Wales's Stakes at Ascot, but won the Eclipse Stakes in July easily enough. He never ran again after that and proved a sad disappointment at the stud. Orwell was unplaced in the St Leger, but won the ten-furlong Great Foal Stakes at Newmarket, his final racecourse appearance, in the autumn. He failed at the stud. Portofino was exported to Australia and so was Andrea, while Totaig, carrying 7 st. 3 lb., won the Royal Hunt Cup a fortnight after the Derby.

1932: Wednesday, 1 June . . . 342 Entries. £9,730 5s.

MR T. WALLS's br.c. APRIL THE FIFTH by Craig an Eran
   out of Sold Again   F. LANE   I
H.H. AGA KHAN's b.c. DASTUR by Solario
   out of Friars Daughter   M. BEARY   2
LORD ROSEBERY's b.c. MIRACLE by Manna
   out of Brodick Boy   H. WRAGG   3

Also ran:

   Mr E. Esmond's Royal Dancer (S. Wragg); H.H. Aga Khan's Firdaussi (S. Donoghue); Mr R. S. Croker's Celebrator (T. Burns); Mr R. S. Croker's Corcy

(E. Quirke); Mr J. G. Thompson's Portofino (W. Nevett); Mr W. M. G. Singer's Orwell (R. A. Jones); Mr S. Tattersall's Spenser (R. Dick); Mr P. Haldin's Buckle (T. Weston); M. M. Boussac's Hesperus (E. C. Elliott); Sir L. Philipps's Wyvern (H. Jelliss); Prince Aly Khan's Jackdaw the Second (J. Childs); Mr C. C. Hall's Bacchus (J. Marshall); Mr V. Emmanuel's Totaig (B. Carslake); Duke of Marlborough's Andrea (F. Fox); Lord Woolavington's Cockpen (G. Richards); Mr W. Littauer's Jiweh (J. Canty); Mr C. Gulliver's Summer Planet (F. Rickaby); Mrs C. Gulliver's Peter Planet (F. Herbert).

21 ran.

Betting:

5–4 Orwell; 9–1 Cockpen; 100–9 Miracle; 100–8 Hesperus; 100–6 April the Fifth; 18–1 Dastur; 20–1 Portofino; 22–1 Firdaussi; 33–1 Royal Dancer and Wyvern; 40–1 Andrea; 50–1 Jiweh and Spenser; 66–1 Celebrator; 100–1 others.

Totalizator: (2s. unit). Win: 48s. 3d. Places: 8s., 7s., 5s. 9d.

Won by three parts of a length; a short head between second and third.

2 m. 43$\frac{1}{5}$ s.

Winner trained by T. Walls at Epsom.

1933

Hyperion, who lived until 1960, was unquestionably one of the best and most influential Derby winners of the inter-war period. Moreover, he captured the affection of the racing public as few horses do, partly because he was only a little fellow and gave the impression of battling against physical odds; partly because he had always been something of a character, a horse with a distinct individuality of his own.

If April the Fifth's pedigree had been somewhat undistinguished on the dam's side, the same criticism could hardly be levelled at Hyperion's. Bred by the late Lord Derby, he was a chestnut by the 1918 Derby winner Gainsborough out of Selene, both of whom were bays. Selene was by Chaucer out of Serenissima, by Minoru out of Gondolette. Selene was rather on the small side, but a good race mare and a tough one, too, winning fifteen and a half races worth over £14,000. The ten winners she bred won thirty races worth £47,345 and included Pharamond and Sickle, both by Phalaris and both successful sires in America; Hunters Moon, by Hurry On, a successful sire in the Argentine; and All Moonshine, by Bobsleigh, dam of Mossborough, Champion Sire in 1958. Serenissima was dam of the dual classic winner Tranquil as well as of Bosworth, winner of the Ascot Gold Cup. Gondolette's winners included Lord Derby's previous Derby winner, Sansovino; Ferry (One Thousand Guineas); and Dolabella, dam of Myrobella and grand-dam of Big Game.

As a foal Hyperion was so small and weakly that there was talk of putting him down. His physique gradually improved, but when he was in training he only stood 15·1½, with a girth of 68 in. and 7¾ in. of bone below the knee. By comparison Hurry On stood 17 hands, had a girth of 82½ in. and 9¾ in. of bone. As a two-year-old Hyperion showed nothing at all on the gallops, and when he made his début at the end of May in the £162 Zetland Maiden Plate at Doncaster, he started at 25–1 and his trainer, George Lambton, did not even come up to see him run. However, he displayed a zest and vitality on the racecourse that he had never given a hint of at home and finished a creditable fourth in a big field behind the Aga Khan's filly Aidetta.

Despite the promise of this performance, Lambton was still inclined to be sceptical of Hyperion's merit, but at Ascot the little colt proved his ability beyond doubt in winning the New Stakes by three lengths from a field of twenty-two. At Goodwood he dead-heated for the Prince of Wales's Stakes with the Nancy Stair filly, who could go very fast when she happened to be in the mood, but at Newmarket in the autumn he was outpaced in the five-furlong Boscawen Stakes by Lord Woolavington's Manitoba, who finished a clear eight lengths in front of him. Manitoba next proceeded to win the Middle Park Stakes by three parts of a length from the Aga Khan's Felicitation, but was immediately disqualified for crossing. A fortnight later Hyperion won the seven-furlong Dewhurst Stakes very comfortably, with Felicitation, who certainly did not lack stamina, not in the leading three. In the Free Handicap Manitoba was given 9 st. 1 lb., Hyperion 9 st., and Felicitation 8 st. 11 lb. The three leaders in the Handicap were all fillies, Myrobella (9 st. 7 lb.), Betty (9 st. 4 lb.), and Brown Betty (9 st. 3 lb.).

Hyperion worked in singularly unimpressive manner at home the following spring, and in his first race of the season, the Chester Vase, he started off in such thoroughly sluggish fashion that Weston felt compelled to give him a sharp reminder in the hope of livening him up. The result was remarkable; Hyperion was immediately galvanized into activity and, taking the lead within the next twenty strides, he ran on to win with the utmost ease. This was his sole outing before the Derby for which he started a 6–1 favourite. The opposition was by no means outstanding in quality. Manitoba had faded out at the Bushes in the Guineas, and although he later won a ten-furlong event at Birmingham with 9 st. 9 lb. in the saddle, he swerved rather ominously near the finish. King Salmon had been second to the French colt Rodosto in the Guineas, but had then been beaten by Young Lover in the Newmarket Stakes. Tuppence's position in the market was inexplicable, as although he was a half-brother by Spion Kop to Manna and Sandwich, he had never shown the slightest sign of racing ability. On the Monday of Epsom Week he was quoted at 125–1, odds that were by no means over-generous in view of his mediocre record. On Tuesday he was supported in the market by a host of small backers who were probably attracted by his name, and a mild panic among a number of the lesser bookmakers, who began to be frightened of their commitments, resulted in this absurd animal becoming fourth favourite at 10–1. Scarlet Tiger, Young Lover, Felicitation, and Statesman were all popular each-way selections. Scarlet Tiger, a half-brother by Colorado to the 1934 Oaks winner Light Brocade, was a stable companion of Hyperion, whom he regularly trounced without difficulty on the gallops at home. Thrapston carried Lord Derby's second colours, and there was something rather pathetic in seeing Donoghue, the idol of the nineteen twenties, glad enough to take the mount on a stable second string.

There were no doubts on the score of Hyperion's stamina and the plan was for Thrapston to force the pace from the start. It was assumed that he would weaken somewhere near Tattenham Corner, at which point Hyperion was to dash to the front and win. The scheme worked out to perfection. At Tattenham Corner Thrapston led from Hyperion, with Light Sussex, King Salmon, Raymond, and Statesman not far behind. Early in the straight Thrapston had had enough and Hyperion at once took his place at the head of the field. From that moment the result was never in doubt and Hyperion ran on to win unchallenged by a margin that looked considerably larger than the judge's estimate of four lengths. King Salmon, who never for one instant had really looked like getting on terms with the winner, beat Statesman by a length for second place, and Scarlet Tiger was fourth. Neither Manitoba nor Tuppence was ever seen in the race with the ghost of a chance after the first half-mile. The victory was tremendously popular, except with the bookmakers, and Lord Derby and his gallant little colt were given a memorable reception. Unfortunately George Lambton, who ceased to be Lord Derby's trainer at the end of the year, was seriously ill and unable to see the race.

Hyperion won the Prince of Wales's Stakes at Ascot and then had a rest until Doncaster, where he completed his three-year-old campaign with a very easy victory in the St Leger after making the whole of the running. No horse could have been blessed with a better action and it was always a pleasure to observe the way that he moved.

Hyperion's third and final season in training was an anti-climax, to say the least, after the triumphs of the previous year. His main objective was the Gold Cup and he started off satisfactorily enough by winning the March Stakes and the Burwell Stakes at Newmarket. According to Weston, however, Colledge Leader, a man of much charm and ability who had succeeded George Lambton, did not fully appreciate what a stiff preparation a lazy worker like Hyperion really needed. It was only a bare three weeks before Ascot when Hyperion was given his first two-mile gallop and he then became so distressed that Weston was forced to pull him up. News of this fiasco inevitably circulated round Newmarket, and on Gold Cup Day Frank Butters instructed Gordon Richards, who was riding Felicitation, to set a cracking fast pace from the start in order to test Hyperion's stamina and fitness to the utmost. Felicitation made every yard of the running to win as he pleased by eight lengths, while poor Hyperion, to the intense disappointment of his owner and of his many admirers, laboured home a very exhausted third. Nor did Hyperion's final appearance on the racecourse afford any consolation for that defeat, as in the Dullingham Stakes at Newmarket he was beaten a short head by his solitary opponent, Caithness.

As a sire Hyperion proved an outstanding success and his record would no doubt have been even more impressive but for the war. He was Champion Sire on six occasions—1940, 1941, 1942, 1945, 1946, and 1954—a record only surpassed by St Simon, Stockwell, and Hermit. His classic winners were Godiva (One Thousand Guineas and Oaks), Sun Chariot (One Thousand Guineas, Oaks, and St Leger), Sun Stream (One Thousand Guineas and Oaks), Hypericum (One Thousand Guineas), Owen Tudor (Derby), Hycilla (Oaks), and Sun Castle (St Leger). In addition, Aureole was second in the Derby and won the King George VI and Queen Elizabeth Stakes. In general, Hyperion's fillies have been a bit better than his colts, and Sun Chariot is worthy to rank with Sceptre, Pretty Polly, and Petite Etoile.

In this country Aureole, Champion Sire in 1960 and 1961, seems likely to perpetuate the Hyperion male line. In America Alibhai, Khaled, and Heliopolis all did extremely well at the stud, while in New Zealand, Australia, the Argentine, and South Africa he has been worthily represented by Ruthless, Helio, Selim Hassan, and Deimos respectively.

By the end of 1960, when he died, Hyperion's stock in England and Ireland had won 752 races worth £633,520 12s. 2d. His mares have also been extremely successful and include the dams of Parthia (Derby), Alycidon (Gold Cup), Supertello (Gold Cup), Carrozza (Oaks), and Citation (winner of thirty-two races and over a million dollars in America).

Of the other Derby competitors King Salmon, a half-brother to Malva, won the Coronation Cup as a four-year-old and also beat Windsor Lad in a sensational race for the Eclipse Stakes. A son of Salmon Trout, by The Tetrarch, he might conceivably have sustained the fast-dying Herod male line in this country, but he was eventually exported to Brazil. His best winner was Herringbone, a filly of Lord Derby's that won the One Thousand Guineas and the St Leger in 1943. His daughter Chenille was dam of the 1958 St Leger winner Alcide and grand-dam of the 1959 Derby winner Parthia.

Scarlet Tiger won the Midsummer Stakes at Newmarket and the Gratwicke Produce Stakes at Goodwood. He ultimately went to the Argentine. Gino went to the United States, while Manitoba made up for disappointments on the racecourse by becoming Champion Sire in Australia. Felicitation, second in the St Leger, became an outstanding stayer, his victories including the Churchill Stakes at Ascot, the Gold Cup, the Yorkshire Cup, and the Jockey Club Cup. After a brief stud career over here he was exported to Brazil. Raymond won the Princess of Wales's Stakes and ended up in Japan. Harinero, a brother of Trigo, won the Irish Derby and was exported to Australia. Tuppence, who had been the most costly yearling of 1931, never won a race and was eventually deported to Russia.

1933

1933: Wednesday, 31 May . . . 304 Entries. £9,836 10s.

LORD DERBY's ch.c. HYPERION by Gainsborough out of Selene	T. WESTON	1
SIR H. CUNLIFFE-OWEN's b.c. KING SALMON by Salmon Trout out of Malva	H. WRAGG	2
MR V. EMMANUEL's br.c. STATESMAN by Blandford out of Dail	B. CARSLAKE	3

Also ran:

Lord Durham's Scarlet Tiger (4th) (A. Wragg); Lord Derby's Thrapston (S. Donoghue); Sir Abe Bailey's Raymond (G. Nicoll); Count McCormack's Franz Hals (T. Burns); Sir F. Eley's Solar Boy (J. Collins); Major C. Behren's Light Sussex (P. Donoghue); Mr E. Esmond's Interlace (E. Smith); Mr W. Barnett's Harinero (C. Ray); Mrs G. H. Drummond's Melfort (W. Johnstone); Sir A. Butt's Young Lover (R. Perryman); Mr E. J. Marshall's Happy Call (K. Gethin); H.H. Aga Khan's Gino (M. Beary); H.H. Aga Khan's Felicitation (E. C. Elliott); Lord Carnarvon's Madagascar (T. Bartlam); Mr W. H. Gull's Blue Grass (F. Fox); Mr H. E. Crum-Ewing's Caymanas (F. Lane); Miss D. Paget's Tuppence (H. Beasley); Mr D. Crossman's Lovers Walk (J. Childs); Lord Woolavington's Manitoba (G. Richards); Mr W. M. G. Singer's Myosotis (R. A. Jones); Colonel F. J. Lundgren's Coroado (D. McGuigan).

24 ran.

Betting:

6–1 Hyperion; 13–2 Manitoba; 7–1 King Salmon; 10–1 Tuppence; 100–8 Young Lover; 18–1 Scarlet Tiger; 20–1 Statesman and Felicitation; 22–1 Harinero and Light Sussex; 25–1 Thrapston, Gino, and Happy Call; 28–1 Franz Hals and Interlace; 33–1 Melfort and Raymond; 40–1 Caymanas; 50–1 Madagascar and Myosotis; 66–1 Lovers Walk; 100–1 others.

Totalizator: (2s. unit). Win: 17s. Places: 6s., 4s. 9d., 10s.

Won by four lengths; one length between second and third.   2 m. 34 s.
Winner trained by Hon. G. Lambton at Newmarket.

1934

Few owners have had the good fortune to win the Derby with their very first runner in that race. The Maharaja of Rajpipla was lucky enough to do so in 1934 with Windsor Lad, a colt that he had bought as a yearling for 1,300 guineas.

Bred in Ireland by Mr Dan Sullivan, Windsor Lad was a bay colt by Blandford out of Resplendent, by By George! out of Sunbridge, by Bridge of Earn. Resplendent was a really good mare, winning the Irish One Thousand Guineas and the Irish Oaks, as well as finishing second in the Epsom Oaks. Besides producing Windsor Lad she was dam of the Cheveley Park Stakes winner Lady Gabrial, and Radiant, second in the Oaks. By George!, a son of Lally, was a top-class two-year-old in 1913, but later proved difficult to train. In 1916 he retired to the stud in Ireland at a nine-guinea fee and most of the mares he served before his sale to Canada in 1925 were extremely moderate. Sunbridge won two small races herself, and in addition to Resplendent was dam of Soldumeno (Irish Two Thousand); Sol Speranza (Irish One Thousand and Irish Oaks); Ferrybridge (third in the One Thousand); and Queen Scotia, ancestress of King of the Tudors (Eclipse Stakes) and Our Babu (Two Thousand Guineas). Bridge of Earn was not more than a handicapper, but did quite well as a sire; his daughter Duccia di Buoninsegna was grand-dam of Donatello II.

Windsor Lad was nothing much to look at when he came up for sale as a yearling and his breeder took the view that a reserve of 1,000 guineas was sufficient. Mr H. S. Persse, who trained for him in England, advised him to raise the reserve to 2,000 guineas and this Mr Sullivan agreed to do, but at the very last minute he reverted to his original valuation, without, however, letting his trainer know. Mr Persse had been prepared to bid for the colt himself, but he had not opened his mouth when, greatly to his surprise, it was knocked down to young Marcus Marsh, acting on behalf of the Maharaja of Rajpipla, for 1,300 guineas.

Windsor Lad took a long time to furnish and was backward as a two-year-old. His first outing was the Two-Year-Old Sale Stakes at the Newmarket Second July Meeting. The class was only moderate, but he was not in the first eight of the fourteen runners. At Goodwood there was a marked improvement and he was far from disgraced in finishing fourth of eight in the Prince of Wales's Stakes behind Lord Glanely's brilliant colt Colombo. He then rested till the late autumn when, ridden by Lane and starting at 100–8, he won the six-furlong Criterion Stakes at

Newmarket by a short head from Lord Astor's Bright Bird. In the Free Handicap he was allotted 8 st. 3 lb., eighteen pounds below the top-weight Colombo. The most encouraging features of his two-year-old career were firstly that he had made steady improvement both in appearance and performance; secondly, he had shaped like a stayer.

Windsor Lad did exceptionally well during the winter and his appearance won him many admirers when he was saddled for the Chester Vase early in May. He won that event quite comfortably and followed it up by winning the Newmarket Stakes from Lord Rosebery's useful colt Flamenco. These two victories resulted in his being substantially supported for the Derby, although the majority of backers declined to look further than Colombo, who had won firstly the Craven Stakes, and then, as an odds-on favourite, the Two Thousand Guineas. Others well backed for the Derby were the Aga Khan's Blandford colt Umidwar, and Easton, a French-bred colt that Lord Woolavington had bought from Mr R. B. Strassburger after it had finished second in the Two Thousand Guineas. Leading English riders in Wragg, Richards, and Smirke were up on Umidwar, Easton, and Windsor Lad respectively, but Colombo was ridden by W. R. Johnstone, an Australian who had ridden in India and France and who had been retained by Lord Glanely for the season. He had no great experience of English racing and had only once previously ridden in the Derby. Donoghue, who had ridden Colombo to victory more than once the previous season and possibly thought that he ought to have been riding that colt again, was on Mr J. A. Dewar's Medieval Knight.

The race itself was destined to provoke an immense amount of controversy, rumour, and ill-feeling. Coming down the hill to Tattenham Corner, Colombo, who had been prominent on the inside from the start, got 'pocketed' on the rails behind Medieval Knight, whose rider, understandably enough, displayed no inclination at all to let him through, even though his own mount was palpably weakening. Medieval Knight, in fact, was stopping so fast that Colombo had to be sharply checked, thereby losing the impetus from his downhill run and becoming unbalanced as well. Windsor Lad, on the other hand, who had been racing wide of the favourite, had a perfectly clear run throughout. He turned for home several lengths ahead of Colombo, who had been pulled away from the rails and who came rather wide on the bend.

In the straight Colombo made a valiant effort to get on terms, but Windsor Lad was too good a horse and too stout a stayer to be given such a start. With a quarter of a mile to go Windsor Lad mastered Tiberius, who was unable to quicken, and though strongly challenged by Easton, found a little bit extra close home to win by a length. Colombo was third, a neck behind Easton, and Tiberius fourth. Colombo weakened just a little in the final stages of the race, but that was excusable in view of the task he had been set from the final bend and which he came so close to accomplishing.

The general view was that Johnstone had ridden a shocking race, had got himself into every sort of trouble, and that Colombo had been desperately unlucky not to win. Donoghue, a not unbiased commentator, subsequently wrote: 'Had I ridden him, he would have won on the bit by many lengths. Had any other English jockey, who knew the course, ridden him, he would have won comfortably.' Lord Glanely presumably held a similar opinion as Johnstone ceased to ride for him soon afterwards.

An alternative theory that a few people advanced was that Colombo did not stay, and that had he not been shut in, he would have run himself out sooner and been beaten by a wider margin. A satisfactory answer to the problem was not forthcoming as Colombo only ran once subsequently and that was in the one-mile St James's Palace Stakes at Ascot. His Derby exertions had left their mark on him and he was beaten in a sensational race by Flamenco. He injured a knee in his St Leger preparation and retired to the stud, where he was not an outstanding success although he sired two classic winners in Dancing Time (One Thousand Guineas) and Happy Knight (Two Thousand Guineas). His son British Empire was a brilliant two-year-old, but later became unmanageable. Exported to the Argentine, he did very well as a sire. In general, Colombo's stud career tended to support the view that he might not have been a genuine stayer.

Windsor Lad's next race was the Eclipse Stakes. Ridden by Smirke he started a heavily backed favourite, but had the misfortune to get badly shut in in the straight and was beaten two half-lengths by the four-year-old King Salmon, who was giving him nine pounds, and Umidwar, to whom he conceded ten pounds. With a clear run there is very little doubt he would have won and he was never defeated again. Soon afterwards some rather complicated negotiations took place and he became the property of a well-known bookmaker, Mr M. H. Benson, who is said to have written out a cheque for £50,000. It was in Mr Benson's colours that he won firstly the Great Yorkshire Stakes at York, and then the St Leger, his final race as a three-year-old. An odds-on favourite at Doncaster, he was by no means spectacular in beating Tiberius and Lo Zingaro, but nevertheless equalled the record time for the race set up by Coronach in 1926.

Windsor Lad made up into a magnificent stamp of four-year-old and had lost every trace of the angularity of his earlier days. There was considerable disappointment when it was learnt that he was not to be trained for the Gold Cup, but his new owner evidently considered that discretion would prove more profitable than valour, remarking, 'My main business now is to see that he is not beaten before he retires to the stud.' Windsor Lad started off by winning the Burwell Stakes at Newmarket, and then, in the Coronation Cup, he repeated his Derby victory over Easton, who had been greatly fancied to reverse the form. He next showed his speed by winning the seven-and-a-half-furlong Rous Memorial Stakes at Ascot and concluded his racing career by beating Theft and Fair Trial in the Eclipse. This was a slow-run race, which did not suit him at all, and when Fair Trial headed him in the straight, it looked as if he might easily be beaten, but his courage and stamina pulled him through successfully in the end. All told he won ten races worth £36,257.

Windsor Lad may have had luck on his side on Derby Day, but he was undoubtedly a great horse once he had developed his full powers, possessing first-class speed as well as stamina. Moreover, he kept on improving as he grew older and there is no telling what he might have accomplished had Mr Benson not decided on a somewhat cautious policy. His stud career was a tragedy. In 1938 he developed sinus trouble; a partial recovery was effected, but the disease soon reasserted itself and he was really a sick horse until he was ultimately destroyed in 1943. At one point Mr Benson had wanted to have him put down himself on the grounds of humanity, but there were difficulties over insurance and the underwriters would not agree to the proposal. Finally a compromise was reached; the underwriters paid over a certain sum of money and Windsor Lad ended his stud career as their property. The most notable horses he sired were Windsor Slipper, unbeaten winner of the Irish 'Triple Crown' and sire of The Cobbler and Solar Slipper; and Phase, dam of the Oaks winner Neasham Belle and the Coronation Cup winner Narrator.

Marcus Marsh, son of Richard Marsh, trainer to King Edward VII and King George V, trained Windsor Lad throughout his career and also takes credit for having spotted his promise as a yearling. He served in the Royal Air Force in the last war, was shot down early on, and remained a prisoner in Germany for nearly five years. On the retirement of Frank Butters he was appointed trainer to the Aga Khan, for whom he won the Derby in 1952 with Tulyar. He retired in 1965.

Like many another good rider, Charles Smirke was originally apprenticed to Stanley Wootton. His long career in the saddle had its ups and downs, and from 1928 until October 1933 he was banned by the Jockey Club after an incident at the start of a race at Gatwick. He rode in his first Derby in 1924, in his last one thirty-five years later, winning on Mahmoud (1936), Tulyar (1952), and Hard Ridden (1958). A great rider at his best, he was almost aggressively self-confident, and no matter how important the occasion, he never displayed the slightest sign of nerves. Perhaps he always appeared a bit too brash and cocky to earn the affection of the racing community as a whole, but he has won many admirers for his superb skill, his cheerfulness in bad times, and even for that distinctly impudent sense of humour that can never be entirely subdued.

Of the other Derby competitors, Easton was a stud failure and ended up in America. Tiberius won the Ascot and Goodwood Cups as a four-year-old, but made little mark as a sire. Umidwar won the Jockey Club Stakes and the Champion Stakes and was sire of Norseman, whose son Montaval won the King George VI and Queen Elizabeth Stakes in 1957. Admiral Drake, by Craig an Eran, won the Grand Prix and sired the 1955 Derby winner Phil Drake. Badruddin, by Blandford out of the famous Mumtaz Mahal, was third in the Guineas and sired Perfume II, dam of the Two Thousand Guineas winner My Babu and also of Marco Polo, a successful sire in New Zealand. Primero won the Irish St Leger and dead-heated with Patriot King in the Irish Derby. Bondsman was used as a hack by General Eisenhower during the war and was winning under National Hunt rules at the age of sixteen.

1934: Wednesday, 6 June . . . 309 Entries. £8,852.

H.H. MAHARAJA OF RAJPIPLA's b.c. WINDSOR LAD
  by Blandford out of Resplendent   C. SMIRKE   1
LORD WOOLAVINGTON's br.c. EASTON
  by Dark Legend out of Phaona   G. RICHARDS   2
LORD GLANELY's b.c. COLOMBO by Manna
  out of Lady Nairne   W. JOHNSTONE   3

Also ran:

Sir Abe Bailey's Tiberius (4th) (G. Nicoll); H.H. Aga Khan's Alishah (R. Perryman); Sir Abe Bailey's Valerius (R. A. Jones); Mr W. Barnett's Primero (C. Ray); M. L. Volterra's Admiral Drake (E. C. Elliott); Mr J. A. Dewar's Medieval Knight (S. Donoghue); H.H. Aga Khan's Badruddin (F. Fox); H.H. Aga Khan's Umidwar (H. Wragg); Mr V. P. Misa's On Top (J. Caldwell); Mr G. A. Monkhouse's Baron Munchausen (C. Richards); Mr V. H. Parr's Rathmore (M. Beary); Mrs W. Raphael's Fleetfoot (W. Wells); Mr W. Raphael's Hornsey Rise (J. Taylor); Mr J. A. de Rothschild's Patriot King (G. Bezant); Mr H. S. Lester's Pride of the Chilterns (F. Herbert); Mr W. Woodward's Bondsman (J. Childs).

19 ran.

Betting:

11–8 Colombo; 7–1 Umidwar; 15–2 Windsor Lad; 100–9 Easton; 18–1 Tiberius; 25–1 Admiral Drake and Medieval Knight; 30–1 Alishah; 33–1 Valerius, Badruddin, and Primero; 40–1 Bondsman; 66–1 On Top and Rathmore; 100–1 others.

Totalizator: (2s. unit). Win: 16s. 6d. Places: 4s., 4s. 9d., 5s.

Won by a length; a neck between second and third.   2 m. 34 s.
Winner trained by M. Marsh at Lambourn.

Tattenham Corner, 1953: Pinza is lying second

Sir Victor Sassoon's Pinza in the winner's enclosure (G. Richards up)

Captain Sir Cecil Boyd-Rochfort

Noel Murless

Vincent O'Brien

1935

Bahram, the Aga Khan's second Derby winner, was one of the greatest racehorses of the century. A brilliant two-year-old, he won the 'Triple Crown' the following season—the latest horse to do so—and retired to the stud both sound and unbeaten.

Bred in Ireland by his owner, Bahram was the fourth son of Blandford to win the Derby within seven years. His dam was Friars Daughter, by Friar Marcus, a very fast horse by Cicero that was bred and raced by King George V, out of Garron Lass, by Roseland out of Concertina. Friars Daughter was bred by Colonel F. Lort Philips who sold her to Mrs E. M. Plummer as a foal for 120 guineas. The Aga Khan bought her as a yearling for 240 guineas—an unusually cheap purchase for him—possibly being attracted by the fact that she was in-bred to St Simon.

Friars Daughter only ran as a two-year-old and won a single race worth £168. Besides Bahram, her seventh foal, she was dam of Dastur, runner-up in the Two Thousand Guineas, the Derby, and the St Leger; Fille de Salut, grand-dam of Sunny Boy, a leading sire in France; and Fille d'Amour, grand-dam of The Phoenix, winner of the Irish Two Thousand Guineas and the Irish Derby. Garron Lass never ran and died after producing two foals. She was out of the St Simon mare Concertina, whose daughter Plucky Liège bred Sir Gallahad III, Admiral Drake, and Bois Roussel. Great-grand-dam of Concertina was Miss Agnes, from whom Ormonde and Sceptre are descended.

As a foal Bahram was extremely good-looking, but for a time rather delicate as his lungs were affected by an attack of pneumonia. However, he was sound enough by the time he went into training, and from his earliest days in Frank Butters's stable he was regarded as highly promising. His first race was the National Breeders Produce Stakes at Sandown in July. He was still a little bit backward and was certainly not expected to beat the Aga Khan's other runner, Theft, a Tetratema colt that had won the Windsor Castle Stakes at Royal Ascot. Theft, who conceded Bahram nine pounds, was ridden by Gordon Richards and started second favourite at 5–2. Bahram, with Perryman up, was almost neglected in the market at 20–1. From half-way it was a match between the two stable companions, but Bahram ran on just the stronger in the final furlong to win rather cleverly by a neck. Ten days later Bahram won the Rous Memorial Stakes at Goodwood by a similar margin, but clearly with a good deal still in reserve. He next won the Gimcrack Stakes at York where he ran rather lazily in defeating Consequential by a length and had to be shown the whip. In the autumn he won the Boscawen Stakes at Newmarket and finally the Middle Park Stakes, in which he started at 7–2 on and won very comfortably from Godolphin and Consequential. He was placed top of the Free Handicap with 9 st. 7 lb., one pound above two other colts of the Aga Khan's, Theft and Hairan.

As a three-year-old Bahram was a handsome and powerful bay colt, his appearance being only slightly marred by a rather weak tail. His action was faultless, his disposition placid to the point of indolence. It had been intended to give him an outing at the Craven Meeting, but he was off his feed and running a temperature, and he forfeited, therefore, the advantage of a race before the Guineas. He looked extremely well, however, on Guineas day and came in for plenty of admiration in the paddock. He was a horse that seemed to enjoy being admired and would lean nonchalantly against a wall with his front legs crossed, looking extremely pleased with himself.

The favourite for the Guineas was Lord Derby's Gainsborough colt Bobsleigh, but he did not come down the hill any too well and the finish was fought out by the Aga Khan's pair, Bahram and Theft. At the Bushes Theft held a narrow advantage, but Bahram finished the stronger and drew clear of his stable companion in the final furlong to win by a length and a half, with Sea Bequest third and Bobsleigh fourth.

Bahram did not run again before the Derby for which, ridden by Freddy Fox, he started favourite at 5–4. Second favourite was the Aga Khan's Hairan, a half-brother by Fairway to the Eclipse Stakes winner Royal Minstrel. He had been soundly beaten by Bobsleigh in the Newmarket Stakes, but Lord Derby's colt went wrong shortly afterwards and had to be scratched. There was a certain amount of backing for Field Trial, winner of the Lingfield Derby Trial, Theft, and Sea Bequest, but in general the public were solidly behind the favourite.

The early leaders were First Son, St Botolph, and Theft. At the top of the hill Theft was still very nicely placed, but Bahram's position, behind him and on the inside, was none too happy. At this point Wragg, Theft's rider, heard a shout behind him and looking over his shoulder saw that Fox was trying to get through on the favourite. He at once pulled Theft out—he was wearing the second colours and Fox the first—and Bahram, a wonderfully handy colt to manœuvre, slipped smoothly into his stable companion's place. From that moment the race was as good as over. Bahram easily mastered the leader Field Trial more than two furlongs out, and the late effort by Robin Goodfellow never looked like causing him a moment's concern. It was an immensely popular victory, the cheering starting as soon as the winner had got the better of Field Trial and lasting until after the proud and smiling owner had led the victor in. Theft finished fourth and was almost certainly second best on merit. When the Bahram–Theft incident at the top of the hill became known to the Stewards, they at once sent for Wragg and drew his attention to Rule 139, which states that 'Every horse which runs in a race shall run on his merits, whether his owner runs another horse in the race or not'. Wragg was cautioned, and the Stewards added that any future offenders would be severely dealt with.

There is little that needs be said of the rest of Bahram's career. An 8–1 on favourite, he won the St James's Palace Stakes not altogether impressively by a length from Portfolio. His final race was the St Leger, which he won by five lengths from Solar Ray and Buckleigh, starting at 11–4 on and being ridden by Smirke, Fox having been hurt in a bad fall earlier at the meeting. Although Bahram was perfectly sound, the Aga Khan saw fit to retire him to the stud as a three-year-old. At the time he professed great admiration and affection for Bahram and declared he would never sell him, but he did, nevertheless, five years later.

Bahram won nine races worth over £43,000. He proved himself a great horse from five furlongs to a mile and three-quarters, and no doubt he would have crowned his career by winning the Gold Cup had he been given the opportunity to do so. His detractors complained that he had only had indifferent horses to beat but that, even if true, was scarcely his own fault, and he could hardly do more than keep on winning.

In England Bahram sired Big Game, who won the Two Thousand Guineas in the colours of King George VI and has since proved a successful sire, particularly of fillies. Other notable sons of Bahram are Turkhan, who won a war-time St Leger, and Persian Gulf, sire of the 1959 Derby winner Parthia. Elpenor (Gold Cup), Migoli (Eclipse Stakes and Prix de l'Arc de Triomphe), and Noor, a good winner in England and America, are all out of Bahram mares, while Mah Iran, dam of Migoli, is grand-dam of the brilliant Petite Etoile, winner of the One Thousand Guineas, the Oaks, the Champion Stakes, and the Coronation Cup.

In 1940 the Aga Khan sold Bahram for £40,000 to an American syndicate, an action that caused much surprise and a certain resentment among many bloodstock breeders in the United Kingdom, particularly in view of the Aga Khan's earlier declarations that he would never part with the horse. Bahram was not in the best of health when he landed in America and breeders in that country never really took to him. In 1946 he was exported to the Argentine, where he died ten years later. Considering what a great horse he was, his stud record was undoubtedly disappointing, but it might well have been a very different story had he been permitted to remain in England.

Of the other Derby runners Robin Goodfellow did well as a sire in New Zealand. Field Trial won the King Edward VII Stakes at Ascot, but his St Leger preparation was interrrupted and he ran poorly in that race. He was difficult to train as a four-year-old and was ultimately sent to Australia. It was Theft's misfortune to be born in the same year as Bahram, but for which he would have won the Two Thousand Guineas and probably the Derby as well. He won the Rosebery Stakes at Kempton as a four-year-old and was eventually exported to Japan. Hairan was sent to America, where he was not a success at the stud.

Frank Butters, who died in 1957 at the age of seventy-nine, is worthy to rank with the great masters of his profession. He trained over a thousand winners in Great Britain, and his fifteen successes in classic races included the Derby twice, the Oaks six times, and the St Leger five times.

Butters's father was a member of a well-known and respected Newmarket family and his mother was a daughter of James Waugh. In his early days he trained in Austria-Hungary and was interned in that country, together with other members of the English racing community, throughout the First World War. After the armistice he trained for some years in Italy, but in 1927 he was appointed trainer to Lord Derby, Mr George Lambton being employed as Lord Derby's racing manager. During the brief period that he was at Stanley House, Butters trained Beam (Oaks), Colorado (Two Thousand Guineas and Eclipse Stakes), Fairway (St Leger and Eclipse Stakes), Fair Isle (One Thousand Guineas), Toboggan (Oaks), and Bosworth (Gold Cup). In 1930, however, owing to the economic crisis, Lord Derby felt compelled to reduce his racing interests, and Butters's contract was not renewed. Thus at the age of fifty-two, just after appearing to be on the crest of the wave, he found himself without a job.

He immediately set up on his own at Fitzroy House and before the end of 1931 the Aga Khan, who had quarrelled bitterly with Dick Dawson, sent him his horses. He was leading trainer in 1932 and he continued to train with the utmost success for the Aga Khan until a serious road accident in 1949 forced him to retire. He considered Bahram the best horse he had ever trained, adding that 'as Bahram was very lazy, and never beaten, not even I ever knew how good he was'.

Butters did not believe in mollycoddling his horses, and by modern standards his training methods sometimes appeared severe, but he was abundantly justified by the consistently good results that he produced. He rarely betted, and his one big wager was on Fairway when that brilliant horse was unplaced in the Derby. A modest, friendly man of complete integrity, he devoted himself unsparingly to the interests of his patrons. The great grief of his life was the sudden death of his only son Victor, who assisted him and might well have succeeded him, while on holiday in Switzerland in 1939.

1935: Wednesday, 5 June . . . 292 Entries. £9,216.

H.H. AGA KHAN's b.c. BAHRAM by Blandford out of Friars Daughter	F. FOX	1
SIR ABE BAILEY's bl.c. ROBIN GOODFELLOW by Son and Heir out of Eppie Adair	T. WESTON	2
LORD ASTOR's b. or br.c. FIELD TRIAL by Felstead out of Popingaol	R. DICK	3

Also ran:

H.H. Aga Khan's Theft (4th) (H. Wragg); Lord Derby's Fairhaven (R. Perryman); Mr C. W. Gordon's Sea Bequest (E. Smith); H.H. Aga Khan's Hairan (G. Richards); Mr C. Glorney's Assignation (S. Donoghue); Lt.-Col. G. Loder's Fairbairn (C. Smirke); Mr C. Evans's First Son (R. A. Jones); Mr A. E. Berry's Peaceful Walter (D. Smith); Lord Glanely's Screamer (A. Wragg); Sir Abe Bailey's Japetus (F. Lane); Mr H. W. W. Simms's Pry II (M. Beary); Mr E. T. Thornton-Smith's Barberry (S. Smith); Mr F. W. Dennis's St Botolph (H. Beasley).

16 ran.

Betting:

5–4 Bahram; 5–1 Hairan; 9–1 Field Trial; 100–8 Sea Bequest and Theft; 100–6 Assignation; 25–1 Japetus, Fairhaven, and First Son; 40–1 Fairbairn; 50–1 Robin Goodfellow, Screamer, and Pry II; 100–1 Peaceful Walter; 200–1 others.

Totalizator: (2s. unit). Win: 6s. Places: 3s. 3d., 13s. 6d., 4s. 3d.

Won by two lengths; half a length between second and third.   2 m. 36 s.
Winner trained by F. Butters at Newmarket.

1936

The Aga Khan gained his third Derby victory in 1936, the winner being Mahmoud, who was only the second grey colt to score since the race's foundation, the first being Gustavus, who won in 1821. The only other grey winners have been the filly Tagalie, who won in 1912, and Airborne, who carried Mr J. E. Ferguson's colours to victory in 1946.

Mahmoud was bred by his owner in France and was by the 1930 Derby winner Blenheim out of Mah Mahal, by Gainsborough out of Mumtaz Mahal, by The Tetrarch. Mah Mahal, a grey, was herself a moderate sprinter and won 1½ races worth a mere £380. Besides Mahmoud, she bred five winners, including Pherozshah, who did quite well as a sire before being sent to New Zealand; Khan Bahadur, who sired a number of minor winners; and Mah Iran, winner of five races, the dam of Migoli and grand-dam of Petite Etoile.

Mumtaz Mahal, 'the Flying Filly', possessed remarkable speed and was the outstanding two-year-old of 1923. As a three-year-old she ran third in the One Thousand Guineas, although in fact she barely stayed six furlongs. The most notable of her offspring were Badruddin, third in the Two Thousand Guineas, Mirza II, a very fast two-year-old and winner of over £7,000; Rustom Mahal, the dam of Abernant; and Mumtaz Begum, the dam of Nasrullah, a highly successful sire first in England and later in America.

The Tetrarch, unbeaten as a two-year-old, was perhaps the fastest horse ever seen on the English Turf although his sire Roi Hérode was only a plodding long-distance handicapper. Unfortunately he met with an accident as a three-year-old and was unable to run. He started off well enough at the stud, but gradually grew more and more reluctant to fulfil his duties. He only got a hundred and thirty foals, but eighty of them won and four of them, Tetratema, Polemarch, Caligula, and Salmon Trout, won classic races. Lady Josephine, dam of Mumtaz Mahal, was by Sunbridge out of Americus Girl; she also bred Lady Juror, winner of £18,000 herself and dam of Fair Trial, who in due course became Champion Sire. In addition Lady Juror is ancestress of Tudor Minstrel (Two Thousand Guineas), Commotion (Oaks), and Faux Tirage, a successful sire in New Zealand.

The Aga Khan sent Mahmoud as a yearling to the Deauville Sales, but he failed to reach his reserve and was despatched to Frank Butters's stable at Newmarket instead. His first outing was at the Newmarket Second Spring Meeting, but the race proved a ludicrous fiasco. In a false start, thirteen of the sixteen runners completed the course. The race was then re-run, but of the original field only four took part. Mahmoud was one of those withdrawn.

At Royal Ascot Mahmoud finished third to Miss Paget's very fast Bossover colt, later named Wyndham, in the New Stakes. This was promising, and a fortnight later he was a convincing winner of the six-furlong Exeter Stakes at Newmarket. He then won the Richmond Stakes at Goodwood and the Champagne Stakes at Doncaster, in the latter event reversing the Ascot form with the Bossover colt, who was probably, however, not at his best, having only just recovered from a cough infection. Mahmoud's final appearance of the season was in the Middle Park Stakes. Unfortunately, he was badly away and lost several lengths. He rapidly made up the lost ground, but the effort took too much out of him and he weakened on the hill, eventually finishing third to M. Boussac's Abjer and the Bossover colt, both of whom he had beaten at Doncaster. In the Free Handicap he was rated equal with Abjer, a pound below the Aga Khan's Bala Hissar, who had won both his races, one of them being the Dewhurst Stakes.

Mahmoud did not grow very much during the winter and his appearance in the paddock before the one-mile Greenham Stakes at Newbury at the beginning of April was somewhat disappointing. Nor was his performance very encouraging, as in rather heavy going he finished down the course behind Noble King, to whom he was conceding a stone. He faded out so completely in the last two furlongs that many spectators wrote him off as a non-stayer, but he always disliked yielding ground, and in any case he probably needed the race.

In the Guineas Mahmoud, ridden by Donoghue, started at 100–8; his stable companion Bala Hissar, who had gone the better in a gallop some days previously, was ridden by Smirke and was on offer at 8–1. Mahmoud played up at the start and, entirely through his own misbehaviour, lost about a length. This, however did not greatly worry Donoghue, who had very little confidence in his mount's stamina and planned to tuck him in behind and come with a burst at the finish. Unfortunately Bala Hissar, who was in front of Mahmoud, faded out sooner than was anticipated and Mahmoud was 'uncovered' a good deal earlier than his rider really wanted. Soon after the Bushes, in fact, Mahmoud was in front, and in the Dip he led by half a length. In the final furlong it was a tremendous battle between him and Pay Up; neither colt flinched under pressure, but Pay Up, belonging to Lord Astor, found a little bit extra close home to win a thrilling race by a short head. Thankerton was third and Rhodes Scholar fourth.

There was more speed than stamina in the bottom half of Mahmoud's pedigree and it was generally accepted that he was unlikely to stay a mile and a half. Ridden by Smirke, he started at 100–8 in the Derby and was considerably less fancied than his stable companion Taj Akbar, who was ridden by Gordon Richards. A son of Fairway, Taj Akbar had proved he could act on the Epsom course when he won the Nonsuch Stakes in April, while he had demonstrated his stamina by winning the Chester Vase. Pay Up was favourite at 6–1, and there was good money both for Noble King, winner of the Dee Stakes at Chester, and for Boswell, by Bosworth, who was reckoned at least certain to stay the distance.

The start was delayed by the antics of Abjer, and during this period Thankerton was kicked on the knee and his jockey, Burns, received a blow in the mouth from another horse's head. Carioca was the first to show in front, but at the top of the hill he was headed by Bala Hissar. Almost at once, however, Bala Hissar was passed by Thankerton who then proceeded to gallop flat out for home as if the winning post was only a furlong away rather than five.

Thankerton turned into the straight a good six lengths clear of Bala Hissar, with Pay Up and Boswell both prominent and Mahmoud lying about sixth. The leader continued to gallop on so strongly that Smirke, who had planned to hold Mahmoud up for a late run, felt compelled to change his plans and set off in pursuit. With two and a half furlongs to go, he gave Mahmoud a tap with the whip; the grey bounded forward and simultaneously Thankerton began to shorten his stride. The result was that Mahmoud was in front with a quarter of a mile still to go. Smirke could not help wondering whether he had made his effort too soon, but Mahmoud showed not the slightest sign of weakening and won easily from his stable companion Taj Akbar, whose effort had come a bit too late to be effective. Thankerton, who had run most gallantly considering the tearaway tactics employed, was third, and Pay Up fourth. The time, 2 minutes 33⅘ seconds, set up a new record for the race. The Aga Khan shares the distinction of having owned both first and second horses in the Derby with the Duke of Bedford (1789), Lord Grosvenor (1790), Lord Jersey (1827), and Colonel Peel (1844).

Mahmoud's next race was the St James's Palace Stakes at Ascot. Probably he had not fully recovered from his Epsom exertions, and he was well and truly beaten by Rhodes Scholar, who was receiving seven pounds and who had been prevented by sore shins from running at Epsom. In the St Leger Mahmoud finished third to Boswell and Fearless Fox. This was a creditable performance, as he was only just recovering from an attack of heel-bug. Rhodes Scholar, whose preparation had been hampered by the hard ground, was unplaced.

Mahmoud, though perfectly sound still, was hustled away to the stud after Doncaster, his fee being fixed at 300 guineas as compared with 400 guineas charged for Blenheim and 500 guineas for Bahram. He was a smallish colt, standing only fifteen hands three, very light grey in colour, and with a typical Arab-like head. His quarters were extremely powerful and he had a beautiful light action. His great good fortune was finding the going on Derby Day extremely firm, which was exactly to his liking. In 1940 he was exported to America for £20,000. He made a great name for himself there and one year was Champion Sire. His daughters, more-over, have proved admirable brood mares. His most important winner before his departure was Majideh. She won the Irish One Thousand Guineas and the Irish Oaks, and was later the dam of the Oaks winner Masaka.

Taj Akbar was a stud failure and ended up in Hungary. Thankerton was a half-brother to the Oaks and Gold Cup winner Quashed; he was the only member of the Derby field to win at Ascot that year. Pay Up turned out to be a very moderate sire. His Grace, a full brother to Blenheim, dead-heated with Cecil for the Coronation Cup as a four-year-old. Couvert won the Hunt Cup as a five-year-old and Squadron Castle the Lincoln as a six-year-old. Boswell, a stud failure, won the Eclipse Stakes carrying 9 st. 10 lb. the following season. Midstream, a son of Blandford, became a leading sire in Australia and Raeburn won the Irish Derby. As four-year-olds, Fearless Fox won the Goodwood Cup and Haulfryn the Doncaster Cup.

1936: Wednesday, 27 May ... 287 Entries. £9,934 5s.

H.H. AGA KHAN's gr. or ro.c. MAHMOUD by Blenheim out of Mah Mahal	C. SMIRKE	I
H.H. AGA KHAN's b.c. TAJ AKBAR by Fairway out of Taj Shirin	G. RICHARDS	2
MRS J. SHAND's br.c. THANKERTON by Manna out of Verdict	T. BURNS	3

Also ran:

Lord Astor's Pay Up (4th) (R. Dick); Lord Carnarvon's His Grace (H. Wragg); Mrs W. P. Ahearn's Squadron Castle (J. Dines); Sir Abe Bailey's Mendicant Friar (T. Weston); Mr F. W. Shenstone's Barrystar (J. Marshall); Mr H. G. Blagrave's Couvert (M. Beary); M. M. Boussac's Abjer (E. C. Elliott); Sir A. Butt's Noble King (R. Perryman); Major J. S. Courtauld's Walvis Bay (T. Lowry); Lord Hirst's Magnet (B. Carslake); Mr S. D. Hollingsworth's Raeburn (J. Sirett); H.H. Aga Khan's Bala Hissar (R. A. Jones); Mr F. C. Minoprio's Haulfryn (F. Lane); H.H. Maharaja of Rajpipla's Carioca (A. Wragg); Mr J. Ramsden's Spinalot (H. Jelliss); Mr A. de Rothschild's Midstream (F. Fox); Mr A. G. Smith's Fearless Fox

(E. Smith); Duke of Norfolk's Bel Aethel (S. Donoghue); Mr W. Woodward's Boswell (P. Beasley).

22 ran.

Betting:

  5–1 Pay Up; 6–1 Taj Akbar; 9–1 Noble King and Boswell; 100–8 Abjer and Mahmoud; 100–6 Bala Hissar; 22–1 Carioca; 28–1 Barrystar, His Grace, and Midstream; 33–1 Couvert and Thankerton; 40–1 Magnet, Bel Aethel, and Fearless Fox; 45–1 Raeburn; 66–1 Haulfryn; 100–1 others.

Totalizator: (2s. unit). Win: 25s. Places: 8s. 3d., 7s., and 10s. 6d.

Won by three lengths; three parts of a length between second and third. Winner trained by F. Butters at Newmarket.   2 m. 33⅘ s. (record).

1937

Gainsborough had won the Derby for Lady James Douglas in 1918, but that was only a war-time substitute race at Newmarket. The first Epsom Derby winner to carry a woman's colours was Mid-day Sun, who ran in the name of Mrs G. B. Miller and was owned in partnership by that lady and her mother, Mrs Talbot. Curiously enough Sandsprite, who ran second to Mid-day Sun, was also owned by a woman, Mrs F. Nagle.

In 1933 Mrs Talbot, widow of Major J. A. W. Talbot of the Gloucestershire Hussars, and her daughter Miss L. M. Talbot, who the following year married Mr George Butt Miller, rented Heath House at Newmarket for part of the racing season from Mr G. D. Smith, a member of the Jockey Club, and his wife Lady Barbara Smith, the breeder of the Oaks and Gold Cup winner Quashed. Heath House adjoined the stables then occupied by the horses trained by Fred Butters, brother of the Aga Khan's trainer, Frank Butters. Quite early in the year Mrs Talbot and her daughter were going round the stables one evening when they suggested to Butters that he should buy a horse and train it for them. He accordingly bought a two-year-old from the Aga Khan, but it proved of little ability and was disposed of at the end of the season. However, during an evening session at the Newmarket July Sales he bought for his new patrons two fillies, both by Blandford and both bred at the National Stud. Both in due course won races, and Ankaret, the one out of Sister Stella, was only beaten in the very last stride in the 1935 Oaks by Quashed. Ankaret, who had only cost 580 guineas, won the Coronation Stakes at Ascot and over £6,000 in stakes and, encouraged by her successes, the two ladies asked Butters to buy them a yearling colt that might be good enough to run in the classics, the price limit being fixed at 2,000 guineas. Butters selected a colt bred by Mr W. T. Sears, by Solario out of Bridge of Allan, by Phalaris. The colt failed to reach the reserve placed on him by his breeder and was led from the ring unsold, but immediately afterwards Mr Sears agreed to accept Butters's offer of 2,000 guineas. The joint owners were delighted with their purchase and bestowed on him the name of Mid-day Sun.

As regards Mid-day Sun's pedigree, Solario, by Gainsborough, won the St Leger and the Gold Cup. He sired a second Derby winner in Straight Deal, who won in 1943, while he was Champion Sire in 1937, and second on the list in 1936 and 1943. Bridge of Allan, Mid-day Sun's dam, only ran twice, winning one small race. The only other winner she bred was a moderate animal called Thistle Bridge. Spean Bridge, dam of Bridge of Allan, won three small races and was by the Derby winner Spearmint out of the St Simon mare Santa Brigida. She also bred Knockando, second in the Two Thousand Guineas, and Brig of Ayr, grand-dam of the One Thousand Guineas winner Brown Betty. Santa Brigida, whose dam Bridget was a sister of the Derby winner Melton, won the Yorkshire Oaks and was for many years a treasured member of Lord Derby's stud. She bred Bridge of Canny, winner of over £14,000; Bridge of Earn, winner of the Newbury Cup and a successful sire; and Bridge of Sighs, dam of Light Brigade, who won over £11,000 and proved a highly successful sire in America. Santa Brigida is also the ancestress of Tideway (One Thousand Guineas), Heliopolis (£14,792 and Champion Sire in America), Shannon II (a big winner both in Australia and America); Sun Stream (One Thousand Guineas and Oaks); and Gulf Stream (Eclipse Stakes).

By the time that Mid-day Sun came to him Fred Butters had moved his stable to Kingsclere, where nine previous Derby winners had been trained. Mid-day Sun himself showed little early promise and for most of his two-year-old career seemed backward and sluggish. Altogether he ran eight times his first season, winning once. The first time he gave a hint of better things to come was in running sixth in the Richmond Stakes at Goodwood and he followed this up by a creditable effort, only just missing a place, in the one-mile Prince of Wales's Nursery at Doncaster. These two performances aroused hopes in Butters that the colt might eventually make a useful stayer and in October Mid-day Sun opened his account by winning the Ditch Mile Nursery at Newmarket from a second-class animal called Jupiter, who was conceding him thirteen pounds. A fortnight later he carried top weight in another mile nursery at Newmarket but was beaten by a filly to whom he was giving more than a stone. In the Free Handicap he was rated at 7 st. 1 lb., thirty-four pounds below the top weight Foray. In general, he looked the type of colt that if all went well with him might run prominently in the Cesarewitch with about 7 st. 6 lb.

During the winter Mid-day Sun discarded much of his sluggishness, becoming a masterful, high-spirited colt that bucked and kicked on the Downs every morning, but remained kindly and placid in the stable. In February he bruised a foot and had to be stopped in his work; in consequence he was still backward when he ran in the Free Handicap at the Craven Meeting. Nevertheless he won by three parts of a length from Sir Victor Sassoon's Solario filly Exhibitionist who was conceding him six pounds. In view of the low weights carried no one was disposed to take the form very seriously, at least as far as the classics were concerned, but the fact remains that the son and the daughter of Solario won three of the five classic races between them and Mid-day Sun was desperately unlucky not to have won the St Leger as well.

Although the distance was really too short for him Mid-day Sun, ridden by Lowrey, was third to the two French horses Le Ksar and Goya II in the Two Thousand Guineas, and on the strength of this highly satisfactory performance, Michael Beary was engaged to ride him in the Derby. With Beary up he won the Lingfield Derby Trial by a length and a half, but the absurdly slow pace—the time was 2 minutes 59 seconds for a mile and a half—rendered the race more or less useless as a guide to the future and there was no wild stampede afterwards to back him for the Derby itself, in which he started at 100–7.

The joint favourites were Cash Book, winner of the Newmarket Stakes, and Perifox, an American-bred colt that had been second in the Hastings Stakes when still backward and had then won the Payne Stakes. Le Ksar, who had been defeated on soft ground in the French Guineas, was bracketed at 9–1 with M. Boussac's Goya II. Solfo, another Solario colt, and The Hour, trained by Jack Jarvis, were both popular each-way selections. The general opinion was that the competitors were well below the average standard and that the race was exceptionally open.

It was the year of the Coronation of King George VI, and the perfect summer weather enabled the thousands of visitors from the Empire to see Epsom at its best and gayest. The King and Queen were present and were given an enthusiastic reception by a crowd that seemed even larger than usual. Goya II and Pascal caused a slight delay at the start and, when the tapes went up, Le Ksar lost a couple of lengths. Donoghue, riding in his last Derby, soon showed in front on Renardo, while Le Bambino, Solfo, Fairford, Le Grand Duc, and Gainsborough Lass were all well placed. Just behind this leading group came Cash Book and Mid-day Sun.

At the top of the hill Fairford took the lead and Perifox began to improve. As the field turned for home Fairford was just in front of Goya II, with Mid-day Sun and Solfo about a couple of lengths behind. With three furlongs to go the two leaders were joined by Le Grand Duc, Cash Book, and Perifox; Mid-day Sun and Solfo were hard on their heels and at that point any one of those seven might have won.

Fairford was the first to crack and his example was soon followed by Cash Book. Le Grand Duc, Goya II, and Perifox then had a tremendous battle with first Perifox and then Le Grand Duc appearing to hold the advantage. Below the distance Mid-day Sun delivered his challenge. As soon as Beary began to ride him in earnest he lengthened his stride impressively, and sweeping past Le Grand Duc he took the lead and ran on strongly to the finish, resisting by a length and a half an astonishing late run by the 100–1 outsider Sandsprite. Le Grand Duc was third, a similar distance behind the runner-up, and Perifox fourth. It had been a thrilling race from the final bend and there can have been few occasions when so many horses were shouted home by their supporters as the probable winner.

Mid-day Sun's victory was very well received and everyone seemed delighted at the success of two charming ladies, who were scarcely known in racing circles at all. Mid-day Sun was only the fourth horse they had ever owned and the only one they had in training at the time. The winner was greeted on his return to Kingsclere by a brass band and a large concourse of local admirers. He walked calmly to his box to the strains of 'See, the conquering hero comes' and apparently regarded the entire proceedings with considerable enjoyment.

Mid-day Sun won the Hardwicke Stakes at Ascot despite swerving rather abruptly when Beary used the whip. He was at his peak for the St Leger and would almost certainly have won but for meeting with considerable interference in the straight. As it was he finished close up third to Chulmleigh, owned by Lord Glanely, and Fair Copy. It was intended to keep him in training as a four-year-old with the Gold Cup as his objective, but he began to get so difficult temperamentally and showed so much resentment when asked to work on the Downs that it was reluctantly decided to send him to the stud. Circumstances were against him as a sire. The war broke out after his first season at the stud and his owner—Mrs Talbot died in 1938—did not possess a large stud with plenty of mares to tide him over a bad time. In 1941 he served only nineteen mares, in 1948 only seven. He was exported to New Zealand in 1950 and died there four years later. His best winner was Sterope, who won the Cambridge-shire twice and over £14,000 in stakes.

Sandsprite was a maiden when he ran second in the Derby and remained one throughout his career. In the Prince of Wales's Stakes at Ascot Cold Scent, another three-year-old, conceded him twelve pounds and beat him a head. His Derby effort may have been one of those queer flukes that sometimes happen in racing. Le Grand Duc was unplaced in the St James's Palace Stakes at Ascot and went to the stud in Belgium at the end of the year. Goya II won the St James's Palace Stakes at Ascot; a son of Tourbillon, he was Champion Sire in France in 1948 and was later exported to America. Solfo won the King Edward VII Stakes at Ascot and the Jockey Club Stakes. Full Sail was a full brother to the 1939 Derby winner Blue Peter and became a leading sire in the Argentine. Le Ksar was also sent to the Argentine.

Michael Beary was a voluble and engaging Irishman from Tipperary. He spent part of his apprenticeship in H. S. Persse's stable and it was on Donoghue's recommendation that he obtained his first ride in public. He was a beautiful rider in his prime, extremely stylish and particularly good with difficult horses. He rode four classic winners, the last one being Ridge Wood in the 1949 St Leger. It was his great misfortune that his own temperament was far from equable. His abundant self-confidence antagonized a good many people and too often he spoke without thought of the consequences. In addition, he was hopelessly impractical over matters of finance. Because of these defects of character, he went through periods of adversity, which he faced with courage and humour. He was granted a trainer's licence in 1951, but although he won the Two Thousand Guineas that year with Ki Ming, he was very soon faced by financial difficulties. He was a poor man when he died in 1956 at the age of sixty.

Fred Butters, like his brother Frank, was interned in Austria for the duration of the First World War. He assisted his father at Newmarket for some years afterwards before setting up on his own. His delightful and modest personality made his Derby triumph extremely popular in racing circles.

1937: Wednesday, 2 June . . . 315 Entries. £8,441 5s.

MRS G. B. MILLER's b.c. MID-DAY SUN by Solario
out of Bridge of Allan   M. BEARY   1
MRS F. NAGLE's b.c. SANDSPRITE by Sandwich
out of Wood Nymph   J. CROUCH   2
H.H. AGA KHAN's b.c. LE GRAND DUC by Blenheim
out of Douairiere   C. SMIRKE   3

Also ran:

Mr W. Woodward's Perifox (4th) (P. Beasley); Lord Derby's Snowfall (R. Perryman); Lord Astor's Cash Book (R. A. Jones); M. M. Boussac's Goya II (E. C. Elliott); Major J. S. Courtauld's Solfo (T. Lowrey); Mr B. D. Davis's Honquan (B. Carslake); Sir E. Eley's Winnebar (A. Richardson); Lord Glanely's Inglefield (P. Maher); Sir John Jarvis's Gainsborough Lass (H. Wragg); Mr R. McAlpine's Scarlet Plume (J. Sirett); Mr H. E. Morriss's Pascal (G. Richards); Mr W. Murray's Fairford (T. Weston); Sir L. Philipps's The Hour (E. Smith); Lord Rosebery's Full Sail (W. Nevett); Mr A. Sainsbury's Battle Royal (H. Packham); M. E. de St Alary's Le Ksar (C. Semblat); Sir V. Sassoon's Renardo (S. Donoghue); Mr R. B. Strassburger's Le Bambino.

21 ran.

Betting:

7–1 Cash Book and Perifox; 9–1 Le Ksar and Goya II; 10–1 Solfo and The Hour; 100–9 Le Grand Duc; 100–7 Mid-day Sun and Gainsborough Lass; 20–1 Renardo; 22–1 Pascal, Full Sail, and Fairford; 50–1 Inglefield and Le Bambino; 100–1 others,

Totalizator: (2s. unit). Win: 31s. Places: 8s. 9d., 43s. 9d., 6s. 9d.

Won by one and a half lengths; the same between second and third.   2 m. 37⅗ s.
Winner trained by F. S. Butters at Kingsclere.

1938

This year saw a welcome revival in the fortunes of the St Simon male line, which had once been so powerful in England. Between the victory of Durbar II in 1914 and that of Bois Roussel twenty-four years later, not a single male-line descendant of St Simon won the Derby and only three were placed.

Bois Roussel was bred in France by M. Léon Volterra and was by Vatout out of that famous mare Plucky Liège, by Spearmint out of Concertina, by St Simon. His dam was twenty-three years of age when he was foaled. Vatout won the French Two Thousand and ran second in the Cambridgeshire to Double Life. His sire Prince Chimay, by St Simon's son Chaucer, was raced by Mr W. M. Cazalet and created a sensation when he beat Gainsborough in the Jockey Club Stakes in 1918. He was exported to France in 1920, but with the exception of Vatout, made little mark as a sire. Vatout himself went to the stud in 1931 and died six years later. One of the most notable horses he got was Vatellor, sire of two Derby winners in Pearl Diver (1947) and My Love (1948).

Plucky Liège was bred by Lord Michelham and was originally called Lucky Liège, her name being changed owing to her breeder's admiration for the defenders of Liège in the opening weeks of the war. She won four races as a two-year-old and in 1915 was bought by Mr Jefferson Cohn and taken to France. She remained in Mr Cohn's possession until 1934 when he sold most of his bloodstock to M. Volterra. She had twelve foals, the most famous of which, excluding Bois Roussel, were Sir Gallahad III, Bull Dog, and Quatre Bras, all by Teddy, and Admiral Drake, by Craig an Eran. Sir Gallahad III won the French Guineas and the Lincoln, sired the Oaks and One Thousand Guineas winner Galatea II, and was four times Champion Sire in America; Bull Dog won races in France and was almost as successful a sire in America as Sir Gallahad. Quatre Bras won in France and America, and did fairly well as a sire in the latter country; Admiral Drake won the Grand Prix and sired the Derby winner Phil Drake (1955). Concertina never ran and was great-grand-dam of the unbeaten 'Triple Crown' winner Bahram. Plucky Liège is not the oldest mare to have bred a Derby winner, that distinction being held by Horatia, who was twenty-five years of age when she produced Paris, who won in 1806.

Bois Roussel, a short-legged, well-made, powerful brown colt standing fifteen hands three, never raced as a two-year-old. At Longchamp in April he won the Prix

Juigné, for three-year-olds that had never won before, by a neck from Mr Widener's Astrologer. Among the spectators was Mr Peter Beatty, the twenty-eight-year-old younger son of the late Admiral Lord Beatty. Mr Beatty, accompanied by his trainer Fred Darling, had gone to France in the hope of buying a horse that would win him some good races in England. He took a great liking to Bois Roussel and the Aly Khan negotiated the colt's purchase on his behalf for £8,000, a far greater sum than he had originally intended to spend.

Bois Roussel's arrival in England aroused no particular interest as it was well known that the classic hopes of the Beckhampton stable were centred on Pasch, a Blandford colt owned by Mr H. E. Morriss. At the end of April Pasch won the Two Thousand Guineas from Scottish Union and Mirza II, but Bois Roussel took time to settle down in his new quarters and it was only about a fortnight before the Epsom meeting that he began to reveal his true potentialities on the gallops. Both Darling and Gordon Richards formed a high opinion of his ability, but at the same time hardly considered him to be the equal of Pasch. Richards, therefore, rode Pasch, while Elliott was retained for Bois Roussel.

Pasch, who had never run as a two-year-old, was favourite for the Derby at 9–4, while joint second favourites were Scottish Union and Portmarnock, second and fourth in the Guineas respectively. Mirza II was well backed despite doubts of his ability to stay the distance, and there was plenty of money for Golden Sovereign, who had won a slow-run race for the Newmarket Stakes. Bois Roussel was the subject of a fair number of each-way bets at 20–1. For the first time in its history, the race was televised. At first the Epsom executive refused to grant the British Broadcasting Corporation the facilities they asked for, but there was such an outcry against the decision that it was reversed.

The sun had been shining during the parade, but rain began to fall as the race started and continued throughout the afternoon. The first horse to show in front was Licence, owned by H.M. King George VI, and he was followed by Halcyon Gift and Pasch. Bois Roussel began a bit slowly and was at the tail-end of the field. At the top of the hill Halcyon Gift took the lead, and at the half-way mark he showed clear of Scottish Union, Portmarnock, Pasch, Golden Sovereign, and Mirza II. At the turn for home, Halcyon Gift still held a two-lengths lead, and then came Scottish Union, Pasch, and Portmarnock. Bois Roussel was about a dozen lengths behind Portmarnock, and with only five horses behind him, his position appeared pretty hopeless.

Halcyon Gift suddenly weakened three furlongs out and was headed by Scottish Union and Pasch, both of whom were going very well indeed, Portmarnock, Golden Sovereign, Cave Man, and Mirza. With a quarter of a mile left, Pasch challenged Scottish Union and for a few strides it looked as if the favourite was going to win. Scottish Union, however, was the better stayer and when he had successfully beaten off Pasch, it appeared any odds on him winning. Suddenly, however, Bois Roussel dashed on to the scene, obviously travelling faster than any other horse in the race. Elliott had given him a 'reminder' coming down the hill and the electrifying response made him recall Fred Darling's words: 'Now don't forget, when you really get at him, he will find a bit.' Bois Roussel certainly found something when he really got going, and once in the straight he fairly flew. He passed horse after horse, and swooping on Scottish Union with just under a furlong to go, he finished so strongly that he had four lengths to spare when the winning post was reached. In another furlong he would probably have been a hundred yards clear, and it was certainly one of the most remarkable and spectacular victories in the history of the race. Scottish Union was second, two lengths ahead of Pasch, and then came Lord Astor's pair Pound Foolish and Cave Man.

Bois Roussel was not entered in the St Leger and his only other race was the Grand Prix in which he finished third behind the great Italian horse Nearco. He was entered for the Gold Cup as a four-year-old, but it was found impossible to train him and he retired to the stud at a 300-guinea fee. In 1946 Mr Beatty sold him to the Aly Khan, by whom he was syndicated later that year. Later in life he suffered much from laminitis and was destroyed in 1955. His stud career was reasonably successful—he was Champion Sire in 1949—but his popularity and prestige tended to diminish as so many of his stock proved unreliable and difficult to train. He got two St Leger winners in Tehran and Ridge Wood. The latter has proved a stud failure, and no doubt Tehran would be accounted one, too, but for Tulyar, the one brilliant flash in an otherwise very dim pan. Other notable winners by Bois Roussel were Migoli (Eclipse Stakes and Prix de l'Arc de Triomphe), Swallow Tail (third in the Derby and now in Brazil), Fraise du Bois II (Irish Derby), and Hindostan (Irish Derby and now in Japan). Several Bois Roussel horses have done well as sires in the Antipodes, and Delville Wood was Champion Sire in Australia. Bois Roussel mares have been highly successful; in 1959 they produced thirty-five winners, including Petite Etoile and Cantelo, of over £114,000 in stakes, while in 1960 their number included Edie Kelly, dam of St Paddy.

Mr Beatty suffered throughout his life from defective eyesight and he knew he was faced with total blindness when he fell to his death from a window in the Ritz Hotel in 1949. Despite his weakness, he had managed to secure a commission in the R.N.V.R. during the war and served with a Commando Brigade in the Middle East before being invalided out. The best horse he bred was My Babu, winner of the Two Thousand Guineas for the Maharaja of Baroda in 1948.

Scottish Union, a Cameronian colt bred at Sledmere, won the St James's Palace Stakes, the St Leger, and the Coronation Cup. At the stud he sired some well-known handicappers, including Strathspey, who won the Cesarewitch, Goodwood Stakes, and Queen Alexandra Stakes. Pasch won the Eclipse Stakes as a three-year-old and was third in the St Leger. He died after one season at the stud. Pound Foolish won the Princess of Wales's Stakes by inches from Cave Man and was exported to India. Golden Sovereign did fairly well as a sire in Australia. Mirza II went to the stud in France, was stolen by the Germans and repatriated after the war. Flyon, by Flamingo, won the Gold Cup in 1939, but failed as a sire.

1938: Wednesday, 1 June . . . 294 Entries. £8,728 15s.

MR P. BEATTY's br.c. BOIS ROUSSEL by Vatout
out of Plucky Liège · · · E. C. ELLIOTT · 1
MR J. V. RANK's b.c. SCOTTISH UNION
by Cameronian out of Trustful · · · B. CARSLAKE · 2
MR H. E. MORRISS's b.c. PASCH by Blandford
out of Pasca · · · G. RICHARDS · 3

Also ran:

Lord Astor's Pound Foolish (4th) (R. A. Jones); H.M. King George VI's Licence (J. Crouch); Lord Astor's Cave Man (M. Beary); Sir Abe Bailey's Golden Sovereign (T. Weston); Sir Abe Bailey's Caerloptic (F. Lane); Lord Derby's Farce (R. Perryman); Mr J. A. Dewar's Troon (S. Wragg); Lt.-Col. H. S. Follett's Malabar (J. Marshall); Mr P. Haldin's Chatsworth (T. Lowrey); Mr D. S. Kennedy's Manorite (P. Maher); H.H. Aga Khan's Tahir (C. Smirke); H.H. Aga Khan's Mirza II (H. Wragg); Mrs G. A. Monkhouse's Halcyon Gift (C. Richards); Captain L. Montagu's Slip On (W. Rickaby); Sir L. Philipps's Flyon (E. Smith); H.H. Maharaja of Rajpipla's Blandstar (H. Sprague); Sir H. de Trafford's Portmarnock (P. Beasley); Mr J. E. Widener's Unbreakable (W. Stephenson); Mr W. Woodward's Valerian III (J. Taylor).

22 ran.

Betting:

9–4 Pasch; 8–1 Scottish Union and Portmarnock; 100–7 Mirza II; 100–6 Golden Sovereign and Manorite; 20–1 Pound Foolish, Cave Man, Flyon, Bois Roussel, and Blandstar; 28–1 Faroe, Malabar, and Tahir; 40–1 Chatsworth, Unbreakable, and Valerian III; 50–1 Troon and Halcyon Gift; 100–1 others.

Totalizator: (2s. unit). Win: 91s. 7d. Places: 18s. 9d., 4s. 11d., 5s. 9d.

Won by four lengths; two lengths between second and third. · · · 2 m. 39⅕ s.
Winner trained by F. Darling at Beckhampton.

1939

On the surface Derby Day this year was as gay and as colourful as ever. By then, however, it had become all too clear that Hitler was determined on war. Many of the older spectators must have wondered sadly if they would ever see a Derby at Epsom again; the younger ones, mindful of the terrible casualty lists of the First World War, were intent on making the most of the few hours of sunshine that were left before the inevitable outbreak of the storm.

The winner in 1939 was Blue Peter, owned and bred by Lord Rosebery, whose father had won the Derby with Ladas, Sir Visto, and Cicero. A strong, handsome rangy chestnut, perhaps a shade long in the back and standing just over sixteen hands, Blue Peter was by Fairway out of Fancy Free, by Stefan the Great out of Celiba, by Bachelors Double out of Santa Maura. Fairway, own brother to Pharos, won thirteen of his sixteen races including the Eclipse Stakes, the St Leger, and the two and a quarter mile Jockey Club Cup. He was four times Champion Sire and sired six winners of classic races, his second Derby winner being Watling Street, who won in 1942.

Lord Rosebery bought Fancy Free, together with the remainder of Lord Wimborne's bloodstock, when Lord Wimborne decided to give up racing. She was a useful mare and a hardy one, too, running twenty-four times in three seasons and winning four races worth £2,477. At the stud she bred eight winners of which, apart from Blue Peter, the most notable were Tartan, a good middle-distance handicapper and later a highly successful sire of jumpers; Blue Peter's brother Full Sail, who won the National Breeders Produce Stakes at Sandown and did well as a sire in the Argentine; and Springtime, the dam of eight winners. In addition Fancy Free was dam of Flapper, who never won herself, but bred six winners of over £15,000 in stakes.

Stefan the Great, a grey by The Tetrarch, won the Middle Park Stakes in 1918. He was much fancied for the Two Thousand Guineas, but hit a joint in that race and never ran again. In 1922 he was exported to America, where he sired a fair number of winners; he returned to England in 1929, but failed to make very much mark. He died at the age of nineteen. He was sire of Tolgus, who got the Oaks winner Lovely Rosa, and also of Portree, dam of that extremely fast horse Portlaw. Celiba never ran herself, but bred six winners as well as a filly called Micmac, who never won but ran

522

third in the Oaks. Santa Maura, dam of six winners, was second in the One Thousand Guineas and a sister of St Florian, sire of the Derby winner Ard Patrick.

Blue Peter was trained for Lord Rosebery by Jack Jarvis, who had bought Fancy Free as a yearling for Lord Wimborne for 3,000 guineas and who had trained her for him as well. From his earliest days in Jarvis's stable Blue Peter possessed an attractive action and was quiet and easy to handle as well. It was very soon realized that he was a classic hope and he was given every possible chance to develop his strength; in fact it was not until the middle of September that he was given his first serious gallop. He shaped so impressively that it was decided to run him in the six-furlong Imperial Produce Stakes at Kempton on 1 October. He was still a long way from being really fit and 'Eph' Smith was told on no account to hit him; nevertheless, he ran an excellent race to finish fifth after being up with the leaders for four furlongs. Twelve days later he was second to the American-bred Foxborough II in the Middle Park Stakes, and when he retired into winter quarters, he was widely regarded as the probable winner of the 1939 Derby.

Blue Peter's first race as a three-year-old was the one-mile Blue Riband Trial Stakes at Epsom, this event being selected for him as his owner and trainer were anxious to see how he acted on the course. He gave a faultless performance and won with the utmost ease. He then won the Two Thousand Guineas, taking the lead at the Bushes and running on strongly to win by half a length and three parts of a length from his stable companion, Admiral's Walk, and Fairstone.

Blue Peter started favourite for the Derby at 7–2. Second favourite was the Hyperion colt Hypnotist, sixth in the Guineas and winner of the Lingfield Derby Trial, while well backed at 100–9 was another Hyperion colt, Heliopolis, winner of the Chester Vase. Next in the betting came Triguero, winner of the Dee Stakes, Admiral's Walk, and Casanova, a half-brother to the Gold Cup winner Precipitation by Hyperion. The weather was fine and the going good.

There is little that needs to be said about the race. Approaching Tattenham Corner Larchfield led from Heliopolis, with Blue Peter close up third and Fox Cub rapidly improving his position. Larchfield faded out early in the straight, and with three furlongs to go Blue Peter moved up to challenge Heliopolis. For a few moments they raced neck and neck and then Smith showed the whip to the favourite. The effect was instantaneous and conclusive, as Blue Peter at once accelerated and drew right away from his rivals to win in majestic style by a clear four lengths. Fox Cub ran on strongly to secure second place, three lengths ahead of Heliopolis, who weakened noticeably in the final two hundred yards. Casanova was fourth, Buxton fifth, and Hypnotist sixth. It was an extremely popular victory, not only because the best-backed horse had won like a champion, but also because Lord Rosebery, who was congratulated on every side as he led his colt in, was widely recognized as having worked extremely hard for the good of racing in many capacities.

Blue Peter, starting at 7–2 on, next won the Eclipse Stakes by a length and a half from Glen Loan, with Scottish Union, winner of the 1938 St Leger and the 1939 Coronation Cup, unplaced. Some disappointment was expressed that the victory had not been achieved in a more spectacular manner, but Blue Peter was inclined to be idle, and had Smith hit him—he only showed him the whip—no doubt the winning margin would have been greatly increased. The only other horses to have won the Two Thousand Guineas, the Derby, and the Eclipse are Flying Fox and Diamond Jubilee.

The racing world contemplated with the keenest interest the prospective meeting of Blue Peter and M. Boussac's unbeaten Grand Prix winner Pharis in the St Leger. Alas, the long-awaited storm broke on 3 September and the Doncaster meeting was abandoned. Lord Rosebery had hoped to keep Blue Peter in training as a four-year-old with a view to winning the Gold Cup, but owing to the uncertainty over racing's future he decided to retire his colt to the stud instead. There has been no more impressive Derby winner this century than Blue Peter, and there is no knowing what he might not have accomplished had his career not been unavoidably curtailed. In a gallop just before the St Leger should have taken place, he gave two stone with ease to Tutor, who later won the Manchester November Handicap with 8 st. 3 lb.

Blue Peter was far from being a failure as a sire—when he died in 1957 his stock had won 436 races worth over £265,000—but considering what a very good horse he was, his achievements were a little disappointing. He started off well enough by getting Ocean Swell, who won the Derby for Lord Rosebery in 1944 and the Gold Cup the following year, but that was the only classic winner that he sired. Other notable winners by him were the Italian-bred Botticelli (Gold Cup), Peter Flower (Hardwicke Stakes), and Blue Train, a very good but unsound horse out of the brilliant Sun Chariot. He was third in the list of winning sires in 1944 and fourth in 1950. His mares have done well and include the dam of the half-brothers King of the Tudors (Eclipse Stakes) and Our Babu (Two Thousand Guineas). He was the leading sire of brood mares in 1954.

The sixth Earl of Rosebery, K.T., D.S.O., M.C., succeeded his father, a former Prime Minister of England, in 1929. He has for many years been one of the most industrious and influential members of the Jockey Club. In his younger days he excelled in many fields of sport—he captained Surrey at cricket from 1905 to 1907, he was just about the best heavy-weight to hounds in the country, and was up to international standard at polo—while as a racing administrator his work has been marked by great shrewdness and determination, backed by up a remarkable memory and formidable powers of repartee. Like many other people who think quickly and dislike wasting time, he has never been widely noted for his tolerance of fools and bores. He has won the Derby twice with horses bred by himself, while he won the St Leger with Sandwich, whom he bought as a yearling. His knowledge of racing in all its aspects over the past seventy years is probably unequalled.

Jack Jarvis, who was knighted for his services to racing in 1967 and died aged eighty in 1968, was the son of a Newmarket trainer and brother of Basil Jarvis, who won the Derby with Papyrus, and of William Jarvis who trained for King George V and King George VI. He rode with success until he became too heavy and then became one of the most consistently successful trainers in the country. He won the Two Thousand Guineas three times, the One Thousand Guineas three times, the Derby twice, the St Leger once, the Eclipse Stakes three times and the Gold Cup four times. His explosive temper could be alarming at times but the eruptions never lasted long and in fact he was one of the most kindly and hospitable of men. He showed courage, too, in overcoming indifferent health in his later years. The appearance of his horses did not always please the paddock critics but they were trained to win races, not prizes in the show-ring, and when a fancied runner from the stable failed, it was never from lack of condition. He was a master at assessing a horse's capacity and placing it to the best advantage, while the best tribute to his character and ability is that most of his owners were loyal patrons of the stable for years.

Ephraim Smith, brother of Douglas Smith, had a successful career in the saddle for over thirty years. The son of a sporting farmer near Maidenhead, he was apprenticed to the Berkshire trainer, Major F. B. Sneyd. Sound in his methods and a strong finisher, he was never troubled by problems of weight and he overcame the handicap of being extremely hard of hearing. He won the 1953 St Leger on Premonition and the King George VI and Queen Elizabeth Stakes on the Queen's Aureole. In character he was quiet and unflamboyant. When he retired, he devoted himself to breeding gundogs. There was much sorrow when he was found drowned not far from his home in the summer of 1972.

Of the other Derby runners, Fox Cub was exported later in the year to the Argentine. Heliopolis won the Princess of Wales's Stakes; he was exported to America where he did extremely well, being Champion Sire in 1950 and 1954. Casanova proved a moderate sire and ended up in Norway. Dhoti, by Dastur, became a leading sire in Australia.

1939

1939: Wednesday, 29 May . . . 317 Entries. £10,625 10s.*

LORD ROSEBERY's ch.c. BLUE PETER by Fairway out of Fancy Free	E. SMITH	1
MR E. ESMOND's ch.c. FOX CUB by Foxhunter out of Dorinas	G. RICHARDS	2
LORD DERBY's b.c. HELIOPOLIS by Hyperion out of Drift	R. PERRYMAN	3

Also ran:

Lady Zia Wernher's Casanova (4th) (W. Nevett); Sir Abe Bailey's Fairstone (C. Richards); Mr W. Barnett's Triguero (T. Burns); Mr W. Barnett's Wheatland (J. Taylor); Sir G. Bullough's Vesperian (E. C. Elliott); Mr J. D. Cohn's Ortiz (F. Lane); Major R. B. Glover's Larchfield (H. Sprague); Princesse de Faucigny-Lucinge's Romeo II (R. Brethes); M. M. Goodchaux's Hastings (R. A. Jones); Sir Yeshwant Rao Holkar's Dil-Bharah (T. Bartlam); Sir John Jarvis's Admiral's Walk (H. Wragg); H.H. Aga Khan's Dhoti (C. Smirke); Prince Aly Khan's Pointis (D. Smith); Mr R. McAlpine's Mauna Kea (M. Beary); Mr R. Middlemas's Fairchance (W. Rickaby); Miss D. Paget's Fairfax (T. Lowrey); Mr J. A. Phillips's Major Brackey (J. Simpson); Mr J. V. Rank's King Legend (B. Carslake); Mr J. F. A. Harter's Buxton (W. Stephenson); Mr R. B. Strassburger's Solford II (F. Hervé); M. M. Boussac's Rogerstone Castle (J. Marshall); Mr H. G. Blagrave's Atout Maître (W. Sibbritt); Mr W. Woodward's Hypnotist (P. Beasley); Mr L. Corbett's Bellman (S. Wragg).

27 ran.

Betting:

7–2 Blue Peter; 5–1 Hypnotist; 100–9 Heliopolis; 100–7 Triguero, Admiral's Walk, and Casanova; 100–6 Fox Cub, Fairstone, and Dhoti; 25–1 Hastings; 28–1 Romeo II; 33–1 Vesperian and Buxton; 40–1 Wheatland; 50–1 King Legend, Atout Maître, and Mauna Kea; 66–1 Bellman, Solford II, and Rogerstone Castle; 100–1 others.

Totalizator: (2s. unit). Win: 8s. 7d. Places: 4s. 7d., 8s. 4d., 7s. 5d.

Won by four lengths; three lengths between second and third.   2 m. 36⅘ s.
Winner trained by J. Jarvis at Newmarket.

* This year the added money was increased by £200.

1940

The extraordinary thing about the 1940 Derby was the fact that it took place at all, coinciding as it did with the disintegration of French resistance and the evacuation, less arms and equipment, of the British Expeditionary Force from Dunkirk. Yet at this moment of national peril, some thousands of people had the time and the inclination to go racing, a tribute to national imperturbability in the face of crises or, alternatively, a deplorable example of sheer lack of imagination combined with a refusal to face unpleasant facts.

Epsom had been requisitioned for military purposes and on 24 January Weatherbys announced the abandonment of the Spring and Summer Meetings there. On 1 February the Stewards of the Jockey Club published a notice in *The Racing Calendar* stating that there would be a substitute Derby at Newbury on 12 June, entries to close on 27 February. The Newbury Meeting was not held and the race was transferred to the July Course at Newmarket. A mile and a half race on the July Course is considerably less exacting than at Epsom. There is no hill at the start, no steep descent later on, no Tattenham Corner; all it provides in the way of variety is a gradual right-hand bend at half-way and some wild undulations in the straight. It is certainly a less searching test than Epsom for a horse with indifferent conformation.

The winner was Pont l'Evêque, owned and trained by Fred Darling whose sixth Derby winner it was. A late May foal, Pont l'Evêque was bred by Mr H. E. Morriss, who won the Derby with Manna, at the Banstead Manor Stud and is by Barneveldt out of the grey mare Ponteba, by Belfonds out of Poets Star, by Chaucer. Barneveldt won the Grand Prix and was the best horse sired by The Winter King, by Son-in-Law out of the 100–1 Derby winner Signorinetta. The Winter King's career has been recorded as fully as it deserves in the section dealing with Signorinetta (see page 380).

Ponteba, carrying Pont l'Evêque, was imported from France by Mr Morriss in 1936. Mr Morriss's objective was to produce, by a reverse process, a second Fifinella. Winner of the Derby and the Oaks in 1916, Fifinella was by Polymelus out of Silver Fowl, the grand-dam of Mr Morriss's horse Tai-Yang; Lady Cynosure, grand-dam of Ponteba, was a sister of Polymelus, so Mr Morriss decided to mate Ponteba with Tai-Yang. The result of this experiment was a small late foal that was cut and then sold at the earliest opportunity.

Belfonds won the Prix du Jockey Club and was a grandson of Le Samaritain, who was also grandsire of The Tetrarch. Poets Star bred six winners including Priok, winner of the Hunt Cup, and Pervencheres, grand-dam of Perifox, joint favourite for the Derby in 1937.

Pont l'Evêque was small and mean when he went to Beckhampton to be trained. He ran twice as a two-year-old, on the second occasion finishing second in a field of twenty runners. Mrs Morriss, who was looking after her husband's racing interests while he was in Shanghai, desired, as a war-time expedient, to reduce the number of horses that Mr Morriss had in training and asked Fred Darling if he could find a buyer for Pont l'Evêque at £500. Darling offered the colt to several people without success, and finally bought it himself. As he remarked later, 'I felt I couldn't go far wrong at that price.'

During the winter Pont l'Evêque did extremely well physically, and when the entries for the New Derby were opened, Darling decided to take a chance and put him in the race. The colt's first outing as a three-year-old was the one-mile Spring Maiden Plate at Newbury, an event that he won from twenty-one opponents with the utmost ease. He was then expected to win the Newmarket Stakes, but was soundly beaten by Lord Derby's Lighthouse II. He was five lengths behind the winner at the finish, but that margin could have been considerably reduced had he not been eased when victory was out of the question. Before that race Darling, at Mrs Morriss's request, cabled to Mr Morriss offering him a half-share in Pont l'Evêque for 2,500 guineas. Perhaps not altogether surprisingly, no reply to this offer was received. Pont l'Evêque in the meantime completed his Derby preparation by winning a minor event at Salisbury by five lengths.

M. Boussac's good colt Djebel, who had won the Two Thousand Guineas, was unable to make the journey from France and the favourite was the Pharos colt Lighthouse II. Second favourite was the Aga Khan's Stardust, second in the Guineas, while Tant Mieux, third in the Guineas and winner of the Derby Trial Plate at Hurst Park, was well backed at 11–2. Gordon Richards was assigned by Darling to Tant Mieux, the stable first string, while Pont l'Evêque, a 10–1 chance, was ridden by Sam Wragg. Mr Morriss's Pâques, a 28–1 chance, had been sent, at Darling's suggestion, to complete his preparation with Mr George Lambton at Newmarket.

Pont l'Evêque was prominent from the start, and after five and a half furlongs, he was seen to be in front and going very easily indeed. Half a mile from home he was challenged by Lighthouse II and the Aga Khan's second string, Turkhan, while Tant Mieux looked a possible danger as well. The leader, however, showed not the slightest sign of weakening and ran on like a true stayer to win by three lengths from

Turkhan, with Tant Mieux a short head away third. It was a decisive victory in a somewhat dull and colourless race.

Pont l'Evêque, a strong, workmanlike bay, only ran once again and that was in the Champion Stakes in which he finished third behind Stardust, subsequently disqualified for crossing, and Hippius, his defeat being apparently due to his inability to quicken in the last two furlongs. At the end of the season he was retired to the Egerton Stud at a fee of ninety-eight guineas, but was soon afterwards sold for export to the Argentine and was shipped to that country in 1942. He did not prove an outstanding success there.

Turkhan, by Bahram out of Theresina, won the substitute St Leger from Stardust and Hippius in a field of six. The race was run at Thirsk over a mile and seven furlongs on 23 November. Exported to France in 1952, Turkhan sired no important winners but his mares have done reasonably well. Lighthouse II sired a number of useful handicappers and eventually went to Australia, where his son Sailors Guide proved an outstanding racehorse. Stardust, by Hyperion, proved quite a successful sire, chiefly of quick-maturing two-year-olds. His son Star King won over £11,000 and has done extremely well as a sire in Australia, where he has been re-named Star Kingdom. Hippius, by Hyperion, died at sea in very severe weather on the way to Brazil in 1941.

Sam Wragg is the younger brother of Harry Wragg, who won the Derby on Felstead, Blenheim, and Watling Street. Sam was never in quite the same class as Harry but he rode a lot of winners in his prime and won the Oaks on Chatelaine and the One Thousand Guineas on Rockfel. He was a publican for some time after his retirement, but later returned to ride work at Lambourn.

The added money for the war-time Derbys was £2,000 in 1940–41–42 and £3,000 in 1943–44–45.

1940: Run over the July Course, Newmarket, on Wednesday, 12 June ... 78 Entries. £5,892 10s.

MR F. DARLING's b.c. PONT L'EVÊQUE by Barneveldt
out of Ponteba — S. WRAGG — 1
H.H. AGA KHAN's b.c. TURKHAN by Bahram
out of Theresina — C. SMIRKE — 2
LORD DERBY's br.c. LIGHTHOUSE II by Pharos
out of Pyramid — R. PERRYMAN — 3

Also ran:
H.H. Maharaja of Kolhapur's Tant Mieux (4th) (G. Richards); Sir Abe Bailey's

Solway Firth (M. Beary); Lady Beatty's Black Toni (T. Lowrey); M. M. Boussac's Pharatis (E. C. Elliott); H.H. Aga Khan's Moradabad (D. Smith); H.H. Aga Khan's Stardust (H. Wragg); Mr H. E. Morriss's Pâques (T. Weston); Miss D. Paget's Romulus (A. Wragg); Miss D. Paget's Olidon (F. Lane); Lord Rosebery's Hippius (E. Smith); Sir H. de Trafford's Golden Tiger (P. Beasley); M. L. Volterra's King of Trumps II (W. Nevett); Captain G. H. Wilbraham's Ridley (J. Taylor).

16 ran.

Betting:

85–40 Lighthouse II; 7–2 Stardust; 11–2 Tant Mieux; 10–1 Pont l'Evêque; 100–7 Hippius and Turkhan; 20–1 Black Toni and Pharatis; 25–1 Golden Tiger; 28–1 Pâques; 33–1 Moradabad; 40–1 King of Trumps II; 50–1 Ridley and Solway Firth; 66–1 others.

Totalizator: (2s. unit). Win: 47s. 9d. Places: 12s. 3d., 7s., 4s. 9d.

Won by three lengths; a short head between second and third. 2 m. 30⅘ s. Winner trained by F. Darling at Beckhampton.

1941

The winner in 1941 was the Hon. Mrs (later Lady) Macdonald-Buchanan's Owen Tudor, trained by Fred Darling and ridden by Nevett. It was Darling's seventh and final Derby victory. He also trained the runner-up in the race, Morogoro, as well as Commotion, who won the Oaks the following day. Lady Macdonald-Buchanan, the third lady-owner to win the Derby, is the daughter of the late Lord Woolavington, who won the race with Captain Cuttle and Coronach, and whose stud she inherited on his death.

Bred by his owner, Owen Tudor is by Hyperion out of Mary Tudor II, by Pharos out of Anna Bolena, by Teddy. Lord Woolavington bought Mary Tudor shortly before he died, attracted, no doubt, not only by her racing record and her good looks, but also because she traced back on the female side to Queen Mary, dam of the Derby and Oaks winner Blink Bonny.

Mary Tudor was bred in France by Captain J. D. Cohn and was transferred to M. Léon Volterra when the latter took over the Bois Roussel Stud in Normandy. She won several races as a two-year-old, and the following season she won the French One Thousand Guineas and was second in the French Oaks. Before she died, in her twenty-fifth year in 1954, she bred six winners which included, besides Owen Tudor, Solar Princess, who was third in the Oaks; Edward Tudor, winner of £6,155; Tudor Maid, unbeaten as a two-year-old and dam of the 1949 Derby favourite Royal Forest, now a leading sire in Brazil; and King Hal, a highly successful sire of jumpers.

Anna Bolena, like Mary Tudor, won the French One Thousand Guineas; she was out of Queen Elizabeth II, whom Captain Cohn bought at Newmarket for 200 guineas and who never ran. Queen Elizabeth was by the Carbine horse Wargrave, who was closely related to Spearmint. Wargrave, raced by the notorious Horatio Bottomley, was a good staying handicapper, whose successes included the Ebor Handicap and the Cesarewitch. As a sire his record was mediocre.

Owen Tudor ran three times as a two-year-old; he won the Salisbury Stakes at Salisbury, while at Newmarket he was unplaced in the Criterion Stakes and beaten a head by City of Flint in the Boscawen Stakes. The following season he started off well by winning the Column Stakes at Newmarket in the spring, his stable companion Morogoro, a beautifully made little grey by Felicitation, having won the Craven

Stakes the previous day. Ridden by Gordon Richards, Owen Tudor started favourite for the Two Thousand Guineas, but the best he could do was to finish fifth, the race being won quite comfortably by the Duke of Westminster's Lambert Simnel from Morogoro and Lord Portal's Hyperion colt Sun Castle.

It had been intended to run the Derby at Epsom on 27 May, but in March the race was transferred to Newbury and the date altered to 6 June. The Newbury Town Council, however, backed by the Chief Constable, objected to this plan so eventually the race was run at Newmarket on 18 June. The day was fine and warm, the crowd extremely large. There were frustrating traffic jams on the London road, and many racegoers did not arrive in time to see the Derby, which was run at two o'clock. A small section of the crowd became impatient at the delay at the turnstiles and successfully stormed one of the gates. There was a good deal of criticism subsequently, both in Parliament and in the Press, on the score of wasted time, manpower, and petrol. Much of what was said and written was either wildly exaggerated or blatantly untrue, and it was conveniently overlooked that gatherings of comparable dimensions habitually frequented greyhound tracks and football grounds. Racing, though, in the minds of the more spiteful critics, was the sport of the rich and therefore a suitable target: 'the dogs' and football were the pastimes of 'the people' and therefore immune from attack.

Owen Tudor's failure in the Guineas was followed by another set-back, as in the Trial Stakes run over ten furlongs at Salisbury, he was well beaten, conceding ten pounds, by the moderate Fairy Prince, whose owner, Mr Francis Williams, was a prisoner of war in Germany. As a result Owen Tudor was not only less well backed for the Derby than his owner's other runner, Thoroughfare, but he was the least fancied of Darling's fleet of five runners in the race, attracting few friends in the market at 25–1.

The favourite was Lambert Simnel although, being by Fair Trial, his prospects of staying the distance were somewhat remote. Morogoro, the Beckhampton first string, was second favourite at 11–2; he was partnered by Harry Wragg, as Gordon Richards was in hospital with a broken leg. Sun Castle, who had won the mile and a half Melbourn Stakes, was heavily backed at 6–1, and there was a lot of money for the Beckhampton colt Château Larose who had won the Berkshire Trial Stakes at Newbury on 7 June. Popular each-way selections included Lord Glanely's Devonian, by Hyperion, and another Hyperion colt, Orthodox, who had won the Newmarket Stakes narrowly from Sunny Island and Starwort.

With two and a half furlongs only to go the field was closely bunched up and it looked anyone's race. Approaching the distance, though, Starwort, who had been prominent from the start, shook off his co-leader Annatom, and supporters of Mrs

Arthur James's colt began to shout him home. Almost immediately, however, he was headed by Morogoro, and coming into the Dip the stout-hearted little grey looked likely to win. Owen Tudor, meanwhile, had been making steady progress by himself on the wide outside and, lengthening his stride as he met the rising ground, he finished very fast indeed to win by a length and a half from Morogoro, with the outsider Firoze Din a further two lengths away third. 'I took it up from Morogoro coming out of the Dip,' Nevett said afterwards, 'but I had been going so well the whole way that I never had the slightest anxiety.'

The reason for Owen Tudor's failure at Salisbury has never been really explained, but undoubtedly there was a streak of inconsistency in his record. In the St Leger, which was run at Manchester early in September, he failed to finish in the first six behind Sun Castle, Château Larose, and Dancing Time, but he redeemed his reputation to some extent by beating Château Larose decisively at level weights in the Newmarket St Leger. Possibly he was a better horse at Newmarket than anywhere else, and the following season he completed his career by winning the two and a quarter mile substitute Gold Cup there by three lengths from the three-year-old filly Afterthought. He died in 1966.

In training Owen Tudor stood sixteen hands one and was a colt of superb quality, although some critics maintained that he was a little lacking in substance and perhaps a trifle light of bone as well. On his day he was unquestionably a good horse and the best of his generation. At the stud he has sired two horses of exceptional speed in Tudor Minstrel, winner of the Two Thousand Guineas and £24,629 in stakes; and Abernant, a superb sprinter who failed by a matter of inches in the Guineas, but nevertheless won over £26,000 in stakes. In addition Owen Tudor sired a Gold Cup winner in M. Boussac's Elpenor and the French colt Right Royal V who slammed St Paddy in the King George VI and Queen Elizabeth Stakes at Ascot.

Morogoro broke down later in the season and died the following year on a very stormy voyage to South America. Sun Castle won the St Leger, but died before taking up stud duties. Château Larose went to the Argentine. Lambert Simnel, sold for 2,500 guineas to Mrs Thurston at the end of the season, was a stud failure. Thoroughfare sired a Champion Hurdler in Fare Time, while Devonian sired Queen Elizabeth the Queen Mother's good chaser Devon Loch, who created a first-class racing sensation by collapsing on the flat in the Grand National within a stone's throw of the winning post and with the race at his mercy. Orthodox ended up in Denmark.

When he rode Owen Tudor to victory William Nevett was serving as a private in the Royal Army Ordnance Corps. Born in Lancashire, he was apprenticed to the late Dobson Peacock of Middleham in 1918 and in due course became the leading rider in the north. He rode his thousandth winner in 1940. He won the Derby in 1944 on Ocean Swell and again in 1945 on Dante. He trained for a short time at Ripon but found training less profitable than riding.

1941 : Run over the July Course, Newmarket, on Wednesday, 18 June . . . 65 Entries. £4,473.

HON. MRS MACDONALD-BUCHANAN'S br.c. OWEN TUDOR
  by Hyperion out of Mary Tudor II   W. NEVETT   1
H.H. SENIOR MAHARANI SAHIB OF KOLHAPUR'S
  gr.c. MOROGORO by Felicitation
    out of Moti Begum   H. WRAGG   2
SIR WILLIAM JURY'S b.c. FIROZE DIN by Fairway
  out of La Voulzie   W. STEPHENSON   3

Also ran:

Lord Glanely's Devonian (4th) (R. Perryman); Mrs Arthur James's Starwort (J. Taylor); Mr H. G. Blagrave's Royal Academy (C. Richards); Sir V. Sassoon's Camperdown (T. Lowrey); Mrs Macdonald-Buchanan's Thoroughfare (S. Wragg); Mr R. C. Dawson's Mazarin (T. Burns); Mr W. U. Goodbody's Selim Hassan (M. Beary); Mr J. A. Hirst's Valdavian (F. Herbert); Prince Aly Khan's Annatom (A. Wragg); Mr H. E. Morriss's Château Larose (G. Bridgland); Lord Portal's Sun Castle (P. Beasley); Mr J. V. Rank's Orthodox (D. Smith); Lord Rosebery's Ptolemy (E. Smith); Duke of Westminster's Lambert Simnel (E. C. Elliott); Duke of Westminster's Sunny Island (T. H. Carey); Mr F. T. Williams's Fairy Prince (F. Lane); Sir Richard Brooke's Cuerdley (R. A. Jones).

20 ran.

Betting:

4–1 Lambert Simnel; 11–2 Morogoro; 6–1 Sun Castle; 10–1 Château Larose; 100–9 Devonian; 100–8 Orthodox and Starwort; 100–6 Thoroughfare; 20–1 Ptolemy, Annatom, and Fairy Prince; 22–1 Cuerdley; 25–1 Owen Tudor, Mazarin, and Camperdown; 40–1 Sunny Island; 66–1 Selim Hassan and Valdavian; 100–1 others.

Totalizator: (2s. unit). Win: 57s. Places: 15s. 6d., 5s., 116s. 6d.

Won by a length and a half; two lengths between second and third.   2 m. 32 s. Winner trained by F. Darling at Beckhampton.

The old style: H. Grimshaw on Gladiateur

And the new: L. Piggott on St Paddy

The field of the 1961 Derby half a mile from the start: Psidium is lying last

A photograph taken by a spectator immediately after the fall in the 1962 Derby, as the jockeys scrambled for safety

1942

King George VI won four of the five classic races in 1942. Unfortunately the only one he did not win was the one that mattered most, the Derby. In this his brilliant colt Big Game started an odds-on favourite, but was unplaced behind Lord Derby's Watling Street.

Big Game, by Bahram out of the sprinter Myrobella, was bred at the National Stud and leased to the King for racing. He was the outstanding two-year-old colt of 1941, winning all his races including the Coventry Stakes at Newmarket and the Champagne Stakes at Newbury. It was significant, though, that whereas he beat Watling Street by four lengths in the five-furlong Coventry Stakes, he was all out to beat him by a short head in the Champagne Stakes which was run over a furlong further.

Bred by his owner, Watling Street was by Fairway out of Ranai, by Rabelais out of Dark Sedge, by Prestige out of Beattie. Ranai was bred in France by M. Couturié and was bought by Lord Derby at the Deauville Sales. She won twice for him in France, and in addition to Watling Street, she bred eight winners including Garden Path, also by Fairway, a filly that won the Two Thousand Guineas in 1944. Ruthless, a grandson of Ranai, never won a race, but was Champion Sire in New Zealand in 1954.

St Simon's son Rabelais was somewhat temperamental himself and so were many of his stock, but he was a great success as a sire in France and headed the list of winning sires there on three occasions. Dark Sedge never won herself, but bred six winners. Prestige, by Le Pompon, won sixteen races and sired a really good horse in the Grand Prix winner Sardanapale. Beattie was by the Derby winner Volodyovski and was a very moderate performer on the racecourse; nor had she been a stud success when exported to France in 1911.

Watling Street ran six times as a two-year-old, winning the Littleport Stakes and the Chesterfield Stakes, both at Newmarket. His gallant battle in the Champagne Stakes against Big Game made it apparent that he might well make a top-class stayer the following season, but his exertions in that race probably left their mark on him for the time being, as in the Middle Park Stakes won by the King's filly Sun Chariot he sweated up beforehand, was reluctant to start, and was never really galloping on an even keel throughout the contest. In the Free Handicap he was given 9 st. 4 lb., three pounds less than Sun Chariot, two pounds less than Big Game.

In the following season Watling Street won the one-mile Shelford Stakes at the Craven Meeting and then opposed Big Game in the Two Thousand Guineas. Over that distance he was no match for His Majesty's colt, who started at 11–8 on and beat him without the slightest trouble by a clear four lengths. Neither colt ran again before the Derby, which took place at Newmarket on Saturday, 13 June. Big Game, a mass of muscle, remarkably powerful and mature for his age, was favourite at 6–4 on. Second favourite was Lord Rosebery's Hyperion colt Hyperides, who had won the ten-furlong Fakenham Stakes at Newmarket on 27 May, while Watling Street was soundly backed at 6–1. Compared to the favourite, Watling Street, who possessed unusual length from hip to hock, looked leggy and narrow, while the expression in his eye was noted as being not altogether friendly. The crowd was small owing to the scarcity of transport, but there was a greeting of very genuine warmth for the King, wearing Field-Marshal's uniform, and the Queen. The going was on the firm side, the weather cool and showery.

The probability is that Big Game would have been beaten for lack of stamina however the race was run, but he contributed in no small measure to his own downfall by impetuosity. He fought for his head in the first half-mile, and though he then appeared to settle down for a bit, he pulled his way to the front over two furlongs out, only to drop back beaten soon afterwards, his reserves of energy expended. Harry Wragg had always taken the view that Big Game was a short-runner and Hyperides the horse he had to beat, so he decided to wait behind the latter. With three furlongs to go he began his effort, but at the top of the hill, where he administered one tap with the whip, he was still four lengths behind the leaders. With only a furlong left there were still two lengths to be made up on Hyperides and he did not want to risk using the whip again on a colt of Watling Street's temperament. Watling Street, however, lengthened his stride as he met the rising ground and, running on like a true stayer, he headed Hyperides fifty yards from the post to win rather cleverly by a neck. Ujiji and Shahpoor, both owned by Mr A. E. Allnatt, were third and fourth respectively. Lord Derby was not present to witness the victory of his colt, who was a chance ride for Wragg, Dick Perryman having been injured.

Watling Street did not run again until the St Leger in which he ran a thoroughly genuine race, but was no match for the King's Sun Chariot, who had already won the One Thousand Guineas and the Oaks. He was then retired to the stud, but he was not a success as a stallion, many of his offspring being highly strung and difficult to train. He was exported to America in 1952 and died there not long afterwards.

Hyperides won the Coronation Cup as a four-year-old and then was sold to Lady

Yule. He died a year or two later. Ujiji, bred by the Aga Khan and bought as a yearling for 400 guineas, won the substitute Gold Cup in 1943. He was a failure as a sire and was eventually sent to Sweden. Big Game won the Champion Stakes in the autumn, and then retired to the stud. When he died in 1963 his offspring had won over £256,000 in stakes. His classic winners were Queenpot (One Thousand Guineas) and Ambiguity (Oaks). His fillies did better than his colts.

Walter Earl, who trained Watling Street, was born in Bohemia of English parents, his father being a trainer in Austria-Hungary for forty years. At the age of fourteen he was sent to England to be apprenticed to Willie Waugh at Kingsclere, and he rode his first winner in 1906 at Goodwood. Before long he became too heavy for the flat, but rode with success for a number of years under National Hunt rules. In 1920 he took out a trainer's licence—Bob Sievier was one of his first clients—and in 1924 he became private trainer to Mr 'Solly' Joel, a position he held with success until Mr Joel's death seven years later. He was then a public trainer once again until 1939 when Lord Derby appointed him to succeed the late Colledge Leader. For Lord Derby he won each of the five classic races within the space of four seasons—the One Thousand Guineas with Herringbone (1943) and Sun Stream (1945); the Two Thousand Guineas with Garden Path (1944); the Derby with Watling Street (1942); the Oaks with Sun Stream (1945); and the St Leger with Herringbone (1943). He had to endure a lot of ill-health in his later years and his death at the age of sixty in 1955 came as no surprise. He was a first-class trainer, a brilliant judge of a yearling, and a very lively and well-liked personality.

1942: Run over the July Course, Newmarket, on Saturday, 13 June ... 56 Entries. £3,844.

LORD DERBY's b.c. WATLING STREET by Fairway
out of Ranai — H. WRAGG — 1
LORD ROSEBERY's ch.c. HYPERIDES by Hyperion
out of Priscilla — E. SMITH — 2
MR A. E. ALLNATT's b.c. UJIJI by Umidwar
out of Theresina — C. RICHARDS — 3

Also ran:

Mr A. E. Allnatt's Shahpoor (4th) (M. Beary); H.M. King George VI's Big Game (G. Richards); Miss P. Bullock's Solway (S. Ellis); Lord Londonderry's Tribonian (S. Wragg); Mr H. A. Jelliss's Gold Nib (R. A. Jones); Lord Rosebery's Seasick (G. Walsh); Lord Astor's Hasty Shot (W. Nevett); Mr F. O. Bezner's Canyonero

(T. H. Carey); Mr J. A. Hirst's Argon (F. Lane); Mr J. A. Hirst's Cavendish (K. Mullins).

13 ran.

Betting:

6–4 on Big Game; 9–2 Hyperides; 6–1 Watling Street; 18–1 Ujiji; 20–1 Shahpoor and Gold Nib; 33–1 Tribonian and Canyonero; 40–1 Hasty Shot and Solway; 200–1 others.

Totalizator: (2s. unit). Win: 21s. 6d. Places: 4s. 9d., 4s. 3d., 9s.

Won by a neck; two lengths between second and third.   2 m. 29⅗ s.
Winner trained by W. Earl at Newmarket.

1943

Considering the vast sums of money that she spent and the scale on which she raced, the Hon. Dorothy Paget's horses were not particularly successful, at any rate under Jockey Club rules. During the thirty years that her colours were carried, the 1943 Derby won by Straight Deal represented her sole classic success. She did, however, enjoy the rare distinction of owning both a Derby winner and a winner of the Grand National. The Prince of Wales, later King Edward VII, is the only person to have won both those events in the same year, a success he achieved in 1900.

Bred by his owner, Straight Deal was by the St Leger and Gold Cup winner Solario out of a rather unfashionably bred mare called Good Deal, who only produced four foals, none of which won except Straight Deal. Good Deal herself was a very useful mare, winning seven races worth over £4,000, and was by the Italian Derby winner Apelle out of Weeds, winner of eight minor races, by Arion out of Dandelion, by Rochester. Apelle, by Sardanapale, was imported to England, but proved somewhat disappointing and eventually went back to Italy. Among his first crop of runners was the Grand Prix winner Cappiello. Arion was a useful handicapper but a moderate sire, while Rochester, too, was only a handicapper.

Straight Deal, a medium-sized bay, compact and with plenty of depth, won six-furlong races at Salisbury and Windsor as a two-year-old. In addition he was second to Nasrullah, a good but temperamental colt, in the Coventry Stakes, and to Umiddad in the Dewhurst Stakes. In the Middle Park Stakes he charged the tapes, unseated his rider, and galloped off. He was eventually caught and remounted, but had expended his energy and was stone cold after a couple of furlongs. In the Free Handicap he was given 9 st. 1 lb., Lady Sybil being top with 9 st. 7 lb. and Nasrullah second with 9 st. 6 lb.

Straight Deal began his three-year-old career by winning a race at Windsor on Easter Monday, and then, starting at 17–2, he was sixth in the Two Thousand Guineas to the Manton colt Kingsway, who won a closely contested race from Pink Flower, Way In, and Nasrullah. Straight Deal did best when held up for a late run, but in the Guineas the horses in front of him faded too soon and in his rider's words: 'I was left with the whole course in front of me. I do not think Straight Deal knew what to do in such circumstances and he dropped out.' Nasrullah, who wore blinkers, was reluctant to go to the post, as he had been in his previous outing as well.

It was not a great Derby field by any means. Nasrullah looked the class horse of

539

the field, and there was a lot to like about Persian Gulf, though he still seemed a little bit backward. The favourite was Lord Astor's Fairway colt Way In, who had been third in the Guineas, and second favourite was High Chancellor, a fine big colt by Fair Trial. There were a fair number of spectators, who showed no resentment at numbers of military police being present for the purpose of checking identity cards.

The race proved an extremely exciting one. Persian Gulf made the running for nearly a mile and a quarter, but then weakened and was headed by Umiddad. Nasrullah challenged coming down to the Dip, but he hung to the right and hampered both Merchant Navy and Pink Flower. Gordon Richards, however, succeeded in balancing Nasrullah, who headed his stable companion Umiddad and looked very much like winning. Umiddad, however, refused to give in, and battling on with great resolution he succeeded in regaining the lead from Nasrullah. At that moment, though, Straight Deal, who had been tucked away behind a small group of horses, was asked for his effort. He accelerated smoothly, and a perfectly timed run took him to the front a few strides from the post. Nasrullah was third, half a length behind Umiddad, and Persian Gulf fourth. Miss Paget, wearing one of her familiar overcoats, led her winner in, while the breeding pundits pointed out that no other modern Derby winner contained the names of so many indifferent stallions close up in his pedigree.

Straight Deal won a mile and a half race at Ascot and started favourite for the St Leger, but he was outstayed by two good fillies in Herringbone and Ribbon, the former of whom won a desperate finish by a short head, with the Derby winner third. In the One Thousand Guineas Herringbone had beaten Ribbon by a neck, while in the Oaks the gallant but luckless Ribbon was second and Herringbone fourth.

Straight Deal, who lived till 1968, was then retired to the stud. Partly because of the unfashionable blood on his dam's side, he was rather neglected by breeders. He sired, though, three good fillies in Ark Royal, Kerkeb and Above Board. Ark Royal won £12,400 in stakes as a three-year-old despite the misfortune of being foaled the same year as the brilliant Meld. Kerkeb was second in the Oaks and probably ought to have won. Above Board won the Cesarewitch and bred two good winners in Doutelle and Above Suspicion. The best of Straight Deal's sons was Aldborough, winner of the Doncaster Cup and the Queen Alexandra Stakes. Silly Season, winner of over £61,000, is out of a Straight Deal mare and so is Dart Board, third in the Derby.

Of the other Derby runners, Umiddad won a war-time Gold Cup but was a stud failure. Nasrullah won the Champion Stakes later in the season. No doubt because of the colt's temperamental defects, the Aga Khan sold him quite cheaply to the

Irish breeder, Mr J. McGrath. He proved an outstanding success as a sire; in England his classic winners were Never Say Die (Derby and St Leger), Nearula (Two Thousand Guineas), Belle of All (One Thousand Guineas), and Musidora (One Thousand Guineas and Oaks). He was Champion Sire in 1951, and when exported to America he was as successful there as in England, being Champion Sire five times. Persian Gulf won the Coronation Cup as a four-year-old. A half-brother by Bahram to Precipitation, he sired the 1959 Derby winner Parthia. Kingsway was not a stud success over here and eventually went to America where some of his stock had done well. Way In, a half-brother to Court Martial, was sold at the end of the season for 5,500 guineas, but was not a stud success. Pink Flower sired Wilwyn, winner of the Laurel Park International. Wansford in later years was a well-known hunter-chaser.

The Hon. Dorothy Paget was a daughter of Lord Queenborough and grand-daughter of Mr W. C. Whitney, who won the 1901 Derby with Volodyovski. She inherited a great fortune at an early age and was a leading personality on the Turf, both jumping and on the flat, from 1930 till her death in 1960. A very heavy bettor, particularly at minor meetings, she was one of racing's eccentrics. Her concern for her personal appearance was exiguous and her clothes were roughly identical for a Kempton meeting in July and one on the same course in January. She was invariably accompanied by a platoon of female aides-de-camp and sometimes she held post-mortems, attended by her trainer and her retinue, on the running of her horses which took place on the racecourse and continued long hours after everyone else had gone home. She liked privacy and was wonderfully successful in keeping the Press at something a good deal further than arm's length away. In her younger days she was probably not an easy person to train for—her ex-trainers could have made up a couple of cricket elevens—but she mellowed as she grew older and her later trainers found her reasonable and considerate. She was liked and respected by the few who knew her at all well and was an extremely generous person in a great variety of ways. She must have spent hundreds of thousands of pounds on racing, and National Hunt sport in particular would have been a great deal duller without her patronage.

A member of a well-known Epsom family and nephew of Arthur Nightingall who rode three Grand National winners, Walter Nightingall was a very young man when he took over the stables on his father's death in 1926. He turned out over a thousand winners under both rules, up till his death in 1968. His second classic winner was Niksar, winner of the 1965 Two Thousand Guineas. He trained many winners for Sir Winston Churchill including Colonist II, High Hat and Vienna.

Tommy Carey was born in London and apprenticed to Walter Nightingall's father at the age of fourteen. He won a race over hurdles when he was sixteen, but established his reputation before the war as the outstanding rider under Pony Turf

Club rules. He won the Northolt Derby several times, once on Scottish Rifle for Miss Paget. He received a licence to ride under the Rules of Racing in 1941. He later trained for some years at Epsom.

1943: Run over the July Course, Newmarket, on Saturday, 19 June . . . 72 Entries. £4,388.

MISS D. PAGET's b.c. STRAIGHT DEAL by Solario
   out of Good Deal   T. H. CAREY   1
H.H. AGA KHAN's b.c. UMIDDAD by Dastur
   out of Udaipur   E. C. ELLIOTT   2
H.H. AGA KHAN's b.c. NASRULLAH by Nearco
   out of Mumtaz Begum   G. RICHARDS   3

Also ran:

Lady Zia Wernher's Persian Gulf (4th) (G. Bridgland); Mr A. E. Saunders's Kingsway (S. Wragg); Mr A. Hedley's Merchant Navy (W. Nevett); Captain A. Gillson's Pink Flower (T. Lowrey); Mr W. Woodward's Herald (D. Smith); Sir H. Cunliffe-Owen's Flight Commander (A. Wragg); Lord Astor's Way In (C. Richards); Lt.-Col. B. Hornung's High Chancellor (E. Smith); Mr J. S. Barrington's Brush Off (P. Evans); Mr H. G. Blagrave's Tippet (E. Gardner); Mr C. Wade's Anubis II (F. Payne); H.H. Aga Khan's Baman (A. Burns); Sir M. McAlpine's First Edition (J. Marshall); Mr R. F. Watson's Runway (J. Taylor); Duke of Norfolk's Victory Torch (M. Beary); Mr J. Olding's Wansford (K. Mullins); Mr J. Olding's Whirlaway (R. A. Jones); Mr A. J. Redman's Harroway (W. Stephenson); Lord Sefton's Deimos (P. Gomez); Lord Derby's Booby Trap (H. Wragg).

23 ran.

Betting:

6–1 Way In; 13–2 High Chancellor; 7–1 Merchant Navy; 8–1 Kingsway; 17–2 Pink Flower; 9–1 Nasrullah; 100–8 Umiddad; 100–6 Straight Deal; 18–1 Flight Commander; 28–1 Booby Trap; 50–1 Runway and Persian Gulf; 66–1 Tippet and Herald; 100–1 others.

Totalizator: (2s. unit). Win: 34s. 3d. Places: 10s. 9d., 10s. 3d., 8s.

Won by a head; half a length between second and third.   2 m. 30⅖ s.
Winner trained by W. Nightingall at Epsom.

1944

There was a noticeably more cheerful atmosphere at the 1944 Derby. The allied forces had successfully landed in Normandy and it was not only the unreasoning optimists and the inveterate wishful-thinkers who visualized a victorious conclusion to the war within the course of the next few months. The race was won by Lord Rosebery's Ocean Swell and later in the year, in his Presidential address to members of the Thoroughbred Breeders Association, Lord Rosebery related with justifiable pride that he himself, his father, and his maternal grandfather had between them bred six Derby winners at Mentmore—Favonius, Ladas, Sir Visto, Cicero, Blue Peter, and Ocean Swell.

Ocean Swell, a bay, was workmanlike and masculine rather than handsome. He never carried much flesh when he was hard-trained, and as a three-year-old, at any rate, there was a good deal of daylight under him. He was one of the first crop of runners by his owner's 1939 Derby winner Blue Peter, and was out of Jiffy, by Hurry On out of Juniata, by Junior out of Samphire, by Isinglass. Jiffy, bred by Lord Rosebery, never won a race but was placed on several occasions. The other eight winners she bred included Iona, by Hyperion, second in the Oaks; Parhelion, by Mid-day Sun, a very useful stayer who went to Australia; and Staffa, by Hyperion, winner of £2,728.

Juniata won one minor race herself and was dam of two minor winners. Junior, a top-class handicapper, was by Symington; a handsome horse that got a fair number of winners, he was at Mentmore on lease for a couple of seasons. Samphire was dam of Wrack, a good handicapper and a brilliant hurdler in England and later a successful sire in America. Samphire herself was out of a very famous mare in Chelandry, winner of the One Thousand Guineas and half-sister to Ladas. A whole chapter could be written about the Paraffin–Chelandry family; it must suffice to say that it has for many years now been a mainstay of the Mentmore Stud and famous with bloodstock breeders all over the world.

Ocean Swell was slow to develop as a two-year-old. In his first three races he was unplaced, but there were signs of improvement in the autumn as he finished second in the Isleham Plate at Newmarket and then won the six-furlong Alington Plate on the same course from nineteen opponents, among them Golden Cloud, a fine sprinter, and Tehran, who was destined to win the St Leger.

During the winter Ocean Swell came on nicely and won his first race, the Column Stakes at the Craven Meeting, by four lengths. At the Newmarket First Spring Meeting on 3 May, however, he could only finish third over ten furlongs to Lord Derby's Borealis, while in the Two Thousand Guineas a fortnight later the distance was all too short for him, and starting at 33-1 and ridden by Nevett, he was well down the course behind Lord Derby's filly Garden Path, who won by a short head from Major David Wills's Growing Confidence, with Tehran a creditable third. In that race E. Smith, who rode for Jack Jarvis's stable, had been up on Lord Milford's Honeyway. Afterwards Smith mentioned to Lord Rosebery that as Honeyway was not running in the Derby, he might get the ride on Growing Confidence, who in the Guineas had been partnered by Ken Mullins, later a successful rider under National Hunt rules. Lord Rosebery made no objection to Smith's suggestion, and turning to Nevett, he said: 'Then I engage you definitely to ride Ocean Swell in the Derby.' As it so happened Mullins again rode Growing Confidence in the Derby, and Smith got the ride instead on Tehran, Gordon Richards having been claimed to ride the Beckhampton candidate Mustang.

Growing Confidence, another son of Blue Peter, was favourite for the Derby at 9-2, Garden Path, Watling Street's sister, was almost as well backed at 5-1, while there was plenty of money for Mustang and Tehran. Ocean Swell, who certainly looked in the paddock as if he had been given plenty of work, was almost neglected at 28-1. The going was firm and it was a grey and chilly afternoon. It had been a cold, dry spring, and most of the runners looked as if they needed a few weeks' sunshine on their backs.

The pace was moderate in the early stages and when the field came into view His Excellency held a clear lead. At half-way he was joined by Tehran and Ocean Swell, while Garden Path, Growing Confidence, and Abbots Fell were all well in the picture. With three furlongs to go the favourite and Garden Path both came under pressure but could find no more; this left Ocean Swell and Tehran in front, with Happy Landing improving his position and challenging Abbots Fell on the far side of the course. Happy Landing did not enjoy the smoothest of runs down the hill, and entering the Dip the race was clearly between Lord Rosebery's colt and Tehran. Ocean Swell probably disliked the firm ground rather less than his rival and he succeeded in gaining a narrow advantage, to which he clung tenaciously to the end. He passed the post a neck in front of Tehran with Happy Landing, who had finished very fast indeed as soon as he met the rising ground, only a short head away third. Abbots Fell was fourth and the favourite, whose poor running mystified his trainer George Beeby, eleventh. Lord Rosebery said afterwards that he would have fancied the winner more but for the colt's moderate display in the Guineas. 'Had it not been for that race I might have thought very differently, as I knew he would stay every yard of the mile and a half.'

Ocean Swell did not run again before the St Leger. It was unfortunate that his lead horse Brush Off jarred his knee badly, and for the last three weeks of the Derby winner's preparation, Jack Jarvis was without a suitable animal to work with him. Nevertheless, it was generally agreed that Ocean Swell looked far better for the St Leger run at Newmarket on 16 September, than he had done on Derby Day. He ran a very genuine race, but found a couple too good for him in Tehran, who appreciated the better going, and Borealis, a half-brother by Brumeux to the great stayer Alycidon. However, he finished the season in great style by winning the two and a quarter mile Jockey Club Cup by three lengths from the five-year-old Historic, who was conceding him thirteen pounds. This victory stamped him as a really good stayer, and Lord Rosebery's decision to keep him in training for another year with the Gold Cup as his main objective gave general satisfaction in racing circles.

Ocean Swell began his final season by beating Borealis in the April Stakes, but Borealis turned the tables on him in a very fine finish for the Wood Ditton Stakes in May, and then beat him again in the Coronation Cup, in which the 1944 Oaks and Champion Stakes winner Hycilla was third and Abbots Fell fourth. The memory of these defeats, however, was obliterated on 7 July when Ocean Swell became the first Derby winner since Persimmon to win the Gold Cup at Ascot. Tehran, despite being unsuited to the distinctly firm ground, was a red-hot favourite at 7–4 on. Borealis was on offer at 5–1 and Ocean Swell, who did not appear to carry an ounce of superfluous flesh, was one point longer. The pace was hardly as good as Ocean Swell's supporters had hoped and when Tehran moved smoothly into the lead approaching the final bend, the race looked as good as over. In the straight, though, E. Smith brought Ocean Swell with one long run, and showing by far the better speed in the final furlong, the Derby winner won by a length and a half from Tehran, with Abbots Fell a similar distance away third. Sad to relate, since that day, only one Derby winner, Blakeney, has ventured to take part in the Gold Cup.

Ocean Swell was then retired to the stud at a fee of 300 guineas. Unfortunately, despite his many admirable qualities, he proved a failure as a sire, many of his stock inheriting his less attractive physical characteristics without his outstanding racing ability. When he was destroyed after an accident in 1954, his only notable winners had been Fastnet Rock (Victoria Cup and Rosebery Stakes), Sea Parrot (Yorkshire Oaks), and St Vincent, who won the Prince of Wales's Nursery at Doncaster and later did well in California.

Of the other Derby runners, Tehran was syndicated at the end of 1945, the forty shares costing £2,500 each. The brightest spot in his disappointing stud career was

Tulyar, winner of the Derby in 1952. Thanks to him, Tehran was Champion Sire in that year, the first member of the St Simon male line to occupy that position since 1913. He also sired Mystery IX, who won the Eclipse and later went to South Africa; and Tabriz, sire of the 1959 Two Thousand Guineas winner Taboun. Happy Landing, a half-brother by Windsor Lad to the 1946 Guineas winner Happy Knight, was a stud failure. Growing Confidence died from a broken blood-vessel as a four-year-old, while His Excellency did well as a sire in South Africa. The Solicitor sired one exceptionally fast two-year-old in The Pie King, while Mustang has got a fair number of moderate-class winners under both rules.

1944: Run over the July Course, Newmarket, on Saturday, 17 June . . . 95 Entries. £5,901.

LORD ROSEBERY's b.c. OCEAN SWELL by Blue Peter out of Jiffy	W. NEVETT	1
H.H. AGA KHAN's b.c. TEHRAN by Bois Roussel out of Stafaralla	E. SMITH	2
MR W. HUTCHINSON's br.c. HAPPY LANDING by Windsor Lad out of Happy Morn	R. A. JONES	3

Also ran:

Sir H. Cunliffe-Owen's Abbots Fell (4th) (A. Wragg); H.M. King George VI's Fair Glint (D. Smith); Sir M. McAlpine's Rameses (M. Beary); Miss D. Paget's Orestes (T. H. Carey); Mrs P. Hill's Mustang (G. Richards); Lord Astor's High Profit (C. Richards); Mr C. R. Harper's Treble Crown (P. Donoghue); Lord Derby's Garden Path (H. Wragg); Major D. H. Wills's Growing Confidence (K. Mullins); Mr C. Wade's Wood Cot (J. Marshall); Mr J. W. Boyle's The Solicitor (F. Lane); Mr L. Hyman's Blue Archer (W. Stephenson); Mr H. J. Joel's His Excellency (E. C. Elliott); H.H. Aga Khan's Hyder Ali (S. Wragg); Mr E. C. Nolan's Salver (P. Evans); Mr A. J. Thomas's St Athans (A. Richardson); Mr M. H. Benson's Lord Bobs (P. Maher).

20 ran.

Betting:

9–2 Growing Confidence; 5–1 Garden Path; 7–1 Mustang; 8–1 Tehran; 10–1 Fair Glint; 100–8 His Excellency; 100–7 High Profit; 18–1 Orestes; 22–1 Happy Landing; 28–1 Ocean Swell; 33–1 Lord Bobs, Abbots Fell, and Wood Cot; 50–1 Rameses and Salver; 66–1 others.

Totalizator: (2s. unit). Win: 52s. 6d. Places: 13s. 6d., 7s. 6d., 8s. 3d.

Won by a neck; a short head between second and third.   2 m. 31 s.
Winner trained by J. Jarvis at Newmarket.

1945

Although the war in Europe was over, the Derby was still run on the July Course at Newmarket in 1945. The race resulted in the first victory of a northern-trained colt since Pretender in 1869, the winner being Sir Eric Ohlson's Dante, trained by Matthew Peacock at Middleham and ridden by the leading north-country jockey, W. Nevett.

Bred by his owner, Dante was an exceptionally handsome brown colt by Nearco out of Rosy Legend, by Dark Legend. Nearco, by Pharos, was bred in Italy by Signor Tesio. He won all his fourteen races, and although possibly not a true stayer, his class and speed enabled him to win the 1938 Grand Prix de Paris, in which he defeated the Derby winner Bois Roussel. Bought as a stallion for £60,000 by Mr M. H. Benson, a bookmaker, he proved a brilliant success as a sire in England. He was twice Champion Sire, and between 1942 and 1956 he was never lower than eighth on the list. His second Derby winner was Nimbus, who won in 1949. He died at Newmarket in 1947, having exerted immense influence on bloodstock breeding and racing, not only in England, but also in America, where his son Nasrullah was twice Champion Sire, and another son, Royal Charger, has been very successful as well.

Rosy Legend was bred in France where she won four races, all over a mile and a half or more. She came to England as a five-year-old, and in 1941 Sir Eric Ohlson bought her, carrying Dante, for 3,500 guineas at the dispersal of the late Lord Furness's stud. She bred eight winners, the most important of which, excluding Dante, was Sayajirao, also by Nearco, winner of the 1947 St Leger and sire of the 1958 Gold Cup winner Gladness. Dark Legend was third to Gay Crusader in the Derby and then won most of the important races in India. A son of Dark Ronald, he did well as a sire in France, his winners including Easton, second in Windsor Lad's Derby, and Galatea II, winner of the One Thousand Guineas and the Oaks. Rosy Cheeks, dam of Rosy Legend, won four races and bred several useful winners. She was by St Just, a son of St Frusquin.

Dante, remarkably powerful and mature for his age, was the outstanding two-year-old of 1944, and headed the Free Handicap with 9 st. 7 lb., a pound in front of Lord Astor's Court Martial. The Free Handicap was in fact sharply criticized on the grounds that Dante was not separated from his contemporaries by the margin to which he was entitled. He had won all his six races, his most notable victories being in the Coventry Stakes, run at Newmarket, which he won by four lengths from Fordham; and the Middle Park Stakes, which he won by two lengths from Miss Paget's colt by Solario out of Tornadic, subsequently named Sun Storm.

Dante wintered exceptionally well. He was already the idol of north-country racegoers and there was a huge crowd at Stockton on 7 April when he made his first appearance of the season. Even the most grudging critics had to admit that he was a magnificent stamp of three-year-old, and he duly won his race, which was over a mile, without the slightest difficulty. On the same afternoon Miss Paget's Sun Storm beat Court Martial by a neck over seven furlongs at Salisbury, but most observers reckoned that Court Martial would just about have won had he been ridden out to the very final ounce.

Two days before the Guineas, it was learnt that Dante had suffered a minor injury to his eye. It was thought at the time that the inflammation was caused by a piece of grit, but there can be little doubt that it was the onset of the disease that finally rendered him blind. Despite this mishap, which no one seemed disposed to take very seriously, he started an even-money favourite for the Two Thousand. To the dismay of his many admirers who had travelled from Yorkshire to see him win, he was beaten a neck by Court Martial. At one point Court Martial looked like winning by a wider margin, but Dante stayed on gallantly up the hill and reduced the gap considerably. It was afterwards suggested that owing to defective vision, Dante had been unable to see Court Martial when the latter challenged him and passed him, but the strength of the favourite's finish somewhat reduced the validity of that excuse.

Neither Dante nor Court Martial ran again before the Derby for which Dante started favourite at 100–30. Lord Derby's Hyperion colt High Peak, said to have done extremely well in a trial at home on 2 June, was at 5–1, and Midas, a four-lengths winner of the Newmarket Stakes, at 6–1. Court Martial, being by Fair Trial, was not really expected to stay the distance and figured at 100–9. The crowd was enormous, and there were long queues of traffic on the London road. Uniform was still prevalent but there seemed fewer Americans than in previous years. It was extremely difficult to get a view of the horses in the paddock, and judging from the number of bodies stretched out in slumber, the bars had been doing an excellent trade. The going could hardly have been better.

Approaching Plantation Corner, Sun Storm led from High Peak, Rising Light, and Midas, with Chamossaire well placed and Dante and Court Martial both going nicely. Sun Storm was beaten soon afterwards, while although High Peak led momentarily coming down the hill, he was soon in trouble as well, and in the Dip it was Midas in front, with Dante, Court Martial, and Chamossaire, all pressing him hard. As Dante met the rising ground, Nevett gave him a reminder with the whip, and the favourite at once responded, lengthening his stride to sweep past Midas in the smoothest manner imaginable and win by a clear two lengths. Court Martial, who finished well, was only a head behind Midas, while Chamossaire, who did not enjoy the best of runs, was fourth. It was an extremely popular and impressive win by an exceptionally good-looking and indubitably high-class horse. The victory was naturally received with great rejoicing in Yorkshire; the famous Bell at Middleham was tolled, and later on there was a Dante Ball at which Nevett was carried shoulder-high in triumph.

For a long time Dante was an odds-on favourite for the St Leger, but from early August rumours about his well-being were in constant circulation and poor Matt Peacock had a harassing time from the Press. As late as 22 August, however, highly encouraging reports were emanating from Middleham, and despite the rumours, it came as a distinct shock to the public when Dante was scratched from the St Leger on the 25th. The final statement issued to the Press stated that 'Dante could not be got ready in time for the St Leger, but that he was perfectly sound'. In fact he never ran again and retired to the stud where in due course he became completely blind.

As a sire Dante was a qualified success. He got plenty of winners, but there was a not ill-founded suspicion with regard to the stoutness of many of his stock. His two classic winners were Darius, winner of the Two Thousand Guineas, and Carrozza, winner of the Oaks. Darius was third in the Derby, but he did not really quite stay a mile and a half. The best stayer that Dante got was the Italian horse Toulouse Lautrec; the most genuine performer Durante, a gelding that won fourteen races, many of them under a big weight, worth over £14,000. At the time of his death in 1956 Dante had sired the winners of 256 races worth over £189,000. He was third in the sires list in 1954 and 1955.

Midas never ran again after the Derby. He was an indifferent sire and was exported to America in 1956. Court Martial won the Champion Stakes in the autumn. He proved a brilliant sire, being particularly successful with his two-year-olds. He was twice Champion Sire before he was sold to America in 1958. Chamossaire won the St Leger run that year at York. He was Champion Sire in the year of his death, 1964, when his son Santa Claus won the Derby. He also sired the St Leger winner Cambremer and the Irish Derby winner Chamier. High Peak was exported at the end of the season to Australia, where he has sired a fair number of winners. Rising Light, by Hyperion, was second in the St Leger and won the Jockey Club Stakes. A mediocre sire, he went to Japan in 1954. Royal Charger, by Nearco, proved a top-class sprinter. As a four-year-old he won the Ayr Gold Cup and was second in the Stewards Cup. At the end of his racing days he was sold to the Irish National

Stud for 50,000 guineas. He proved a highly successful sire and was exported in 1953 to America where he was an outstanding success. Descended from him are the American-bred Derby winners Sir Ivor and Roberto. Here he sired Happy Laughter (One Thousand Guineas) and Gilles De Retz (Two Thousand Guineas). Preciptic was also bought in due course by the Irish National stud and has sired a number of useful handicappers.

Dante's trainer Matt Peacock had held a licence for sixteen years and before that had assisted his father, Dobson Peacock, at Middleham. He was a great character and one of the best-known personalities in racing circles in the north. Broad and rugged, he was forthright of manner and blunt of speech, sometimes disconcertingly so. Intolerant of humbug, indolence, and sharp practice, he was fundamentally an extremely kind and generous man. He never felt really at his ease except in Yorkshire, and when racing caused him to come down south, he always turned for home once again with an unconcealed sense of relief. His comments were brief and to the point. 'Aye, he goes a bit,' he remarked to a friend after Dante had won the Derby. He was desperately worried by the various uncertainties that surrounded Dante's St Leger preparation, and those who knew him best said he was never quite the same man afterwards. He was a dying man—and admitted as much in his own vernacular —when he saddled three winners at York on 7 June 1951. He died a few weeks later aged seventy-two.

1945: Run over the July Course at Newmarket, 9 June . . . 206 Entries. £8,339.

SIR E. OHLSON'S br.c. DANTE by Nearco		
out of Rosy Legend	W. NEVETT	1
LORD ROSEBERY'S b.c. MIDAS by Hyperion		
out of Coin of the Realm	E. SMITH	2
LORD ASTOR'S ch.c. COURT MARTIAL by Fair Trial		
out of Instantaneous	C. RICHARDS	3

Also ran:

Sqn.-Ldr. S. Joel's Chamossaire (4th) (T. Lowrey); H.M. King George VI's Rising Light (D. Smith); Lady Derby's High Peak (H. Wragg); H.H. Aga Khan's Fordham (E. C. Elliott); Mrs M. Harvey's Black Peter (S. Wragg); Colonel F. J. Lundgren's Rio Largo (P. Maher); Miss D. Paget's Sun Storm (T. H. Carey); Sir A. Butt's Paper Weight (A. Wragg); Maharaja of Baroda's Gaekwar's Pride (E. Britt); Mrs J. S. Barrington's Sapper (F. Lane); Mr J. S. Barrington's The Chiseller (G. Littlewood); Mr P. Bartholomew's Edenbridge (W. Stephenson); Mr P. Beatty's Wood Note (P. Evans); Mr F. Boxall's Audentes (P. Beasley); Mr M. Freed-

man's Avalanche (K. Mullins); Mr C. Gulliver's Prince Val (R. Hardwidge);
Sir John Jarvis's Royal Charger (R. A. Jones); Sqn.-Ldr. S. Joel's Sorrento (C.
Parker); H.H. Aga Khan's Manuchehr (G. Richards); Sir M. McAlpine's Con-
centration (M. Beary); Mr C. Wade's Train Bleu (T. Bartlam); Major J. B.
Walker's Vicinity (G. Bridgland); Captain A. S. Wills's Preciptic (P. Gomez); Mr
T. M. Horn's Prediction (E. Gardner).

27 ran.

Betting:

    100–30 Dante; 5–1 High Peak; 6–1 Midas; 8–1 Sun Storm; 100–9 Court Martial
and Chamossaire; 20–1 Rising Light, Paper Weight, and Manuchehr; 28–1 Fordham and Preciptic; 40–1 Vicinity; 50–1 Wood Note, Black Peter, Edenbridge,
Royal Charger, and Concentration; 66–1 Rio Largo; 100–1 others.

Totalizator: (2s. unit). Win: 7s. Places: 4s. 6d., 4s. 6d., 7s.

Won by two lengths; a head between second and third.   2 m. 26⅗ s.
Winner trained by M. Peacock at Middleham.

1946

At long last the Derby returned to its real home at Epsom after six years' exile at Newmarket. The stands and the course, to say nothing of the spectators, looked rather shabby and war-worn, and there was not a single top-hat to be seen in the Members Enclosure. Strict rationing was still in operation, and facilities for eating and drinking were depressingly spartan. The King and Queen were present and the attendance seemed well up to the best pre-war standards. The winner was Mr John Ferguson's Airborne, the fourth grey to win the Derby since its inception, the others being Gustavus, Tagalie, and Mahmoud. He was virtually unknown before the race, and as he started at 50–1, his victory brought little profit to backers except to former members of the Airborne forces, their relations, wives, and sweethearts, who had supported him for purely sentimental reasons.

Airborne was bred in Ireland by Colonel Harold Boyd-Rochfort, brother of the Newmarket trainer, and was bought as a yearling by Mr Ferguson for 3,300 guineas. A rangy, strongly made colt standing sixteen hands one and a very light grey in colour, he was by Precipitation out of Bouquet by Buchan. Precipitation, a half-brother by Hurry On to Persian Gulf, sire of the 1959 Derby winner Parthia, never ran as a two-year-old or competed in the classics, but was a top-class stayer and won the Ascot Gold Cup as a four-year-old. He was a successful sire, and his other classic winners were Chamossaire (St Leger), Premonition (St Leger), and Why Hurry (Oaks). He was also, in all probability, sire of Supreme Court, winner of the first race for the King George VI and Queen Elizabeth Stakes. It is largely due to Precipitation that the Matchem male line did not fade out completely in this country.

Bouquet was an unlikely sort of mare to breed a Derby winner. Bred by Major H. S. Cayzer, she was a distinctly undersized grey. She injured a stifle when in training at Newmarket and, being unable to race her, Major Cayzer decided to give the mare away. In due course she became the property of Mr J. Johnston Cooney, and on his death she was bought by Captain Arthur Boyd-Rochfort, v.c., for 400 guineas. For him she bred Fragrant View, a smart sprinter by Panorama, and when he died in 1940 she passed into the possession of his brother, Colonel Harold Boyd-Rochfort. Altogether she bred nine winners, but they were of small account bar Airborne and Fragrant View, the latter of whom was dam of Summer Rain, by Precipitation, winner of the Manchester November Handicap.

Bouquet's dam was Hellespont, a Gay Crusader mare that won one small race and bred nothing. Airborne's third dam, however, was Barrier, by Grey Leg, a grey horse that won the City and Suburban and at one time was a Queen's Premium Hunter Sire. Barrier produced five winners including Indolence, who bred a very successful sire in Prince Rose, whose stock included Prince Chevalier, Prince Bio, and Princequillo. Bouquet traces back to Blink Bonny's dam Queen Mary, one of the greatest mares in the Stud Book, while her grey coat colour derives from Grey Leg, a descendant in tail-male of Herod, through Wild Dayrell.

Like most of Precipitation's offspring, Airborne took plenty of time to come to hand and as a two-year-old he ran four times without success. He did well physically during the winter, but his first appearance as a three-year-old, when he ran third in a moderate field for the Hastings Stakes at the First Spring Meeting, did little to suggest classic possibilities. A fortnight later he won the mile and a half Maiden Stakes at Newmarket by three parts of a length in quite good time, but this success attracted no particular interest among the betting public.

Despite well-founded doubts in respect of his stamina, the favourite for the Derby was Happy Knight, a Colombo colt who had won the Two Thousand Guineas by four lengths from four sons of Hyperion—Khaled, Radiotherapy, Gulf Stream, and Edward Tudor. Joint second favourites were Khaled, Gulf Stream, and the winner of the Lingfield Derby Trial, Fast and Fair. Radiotherapy, who won the Newmarket Stakes, was well backed at 8–1 and so was Gordon Richards's mount Edward Tudor at 100–9. The start was a good one and before very long Gulf Stream was seen to be leading at a moderate pace from Peterborough, Happy Knight, and Khaled. Coming down the hill to Tattenham Corner, Khaled went to the front but he could not keep it up and was beaten early in the straight. Three furlongs out Gulf Stream, going very easily on the rails, led from Radiotherapy and looked all over a winner, this impression being strengthened a quarter of a mile from home when it was clear that Radiotherapy was making no impression, while neither Peterborough nor White Jacket could quicken sufficiently to offer a serious threat.

Just as Gulf Stream's supporters were beginning to cheer him home, Airborne suddenly descended from the clouds on the stand side of the course. Coming with one long, devastating run, he passed horse after horse, and despite veering to the right he finished full of running to win by a length from Gulf Stream, with Radiotherapy a further two lengths away third. There was no excuse for Gulf Stream, who had a wonderfully clear run throughout, but barely stayed the distance and weakened a little in the final hundred yards.

Dick Perryman, who trained the winner, had retired from race-riding not long previously because of a serious injury to an arm in a car accident. He had originally been apprenticed to the late Fred Leader and rapidly made his mark as a jockey, his first important success being on Winalot in the 1925 Manchester Cup. He won the Gold Cup on Quashed and Invershin, and three times rode the winner of the One Thousand Guineas. His previous success as a trainer in a classic event had been the year before, when he won the St Leger with Mr Stanhope Joel's Chamossaire. Tommy Lowrey, a sound and experienced rider, who rode a perfectly judged race on Airborne, was a close friend of Perryman's and, like him, had been one of Fred Leader's apprentices.

Airborne did not take the field at Ascot, but he won the Princess of Wales's Stakes, beating the much fancied Hardwicke Stakes winner Priam II. At Newmarket in August, however, he had a very narrow squeak in the mile and a half Stuntney Stakes, only dead-heating on level terms with Fast and Fair. Nevertheless he started a clear favourite for the St Leger and duly won in slowish time from his stable companion Murren, owned by Mr Joel. He was probably the only true stayer in the field. In the two-mile King George VI Stakes at Ascot on 12 October his limitations were somewhat drastically exposed and he could only finish third, beaten five lengths and a head behind the Grand Prix winner Souverain and the Irish Derby winner Bright News. As it turned out, this was his last race, it being found impossible to train him as a four-year-old. He proved a sad failure as a sire although a filly of his, Silken Glider, came very close indeed to winning the Oaks in 1957.

Mr John Ferguson was a close friend from his Eton days of Mr Stanhope Joel, who inspired his interest in racing. He registered his colours in 1936, his trainer then being Walter Earl, who also trained for Mr Joel. Apart from Airborne, the best horses to carry his colours were Arabian Night, second in the 1954 Derby, and that very fine sprinter Matador, who won the Stewards Cup just after Mr Ferguson's death, carrying 9 st. 2 lb., a record weight for a three-year-old in that event. Mr Ferguson was elected to the Jockey Club in 1954, and with his great business ability, enthusiasm, and charming personality there is little doubt that he would have made an outstanding racing administrator. His death in 1956 at the age of fifty-three was a serious loss to the Turf.

The 1946 Derby field was in all probability a pretty indifferent one and it was, perhaps, just as well for Airborne that there was not a challenger from France. Two of the other runners are perhaps worthy of brief mention. Gulf Stream won the Eclipse Stakes and has done well as a sire in the Argentine. Khaled was exported to America where he was a great success at the stud, among his offspring being Swaps, winner of the Kentucky Derby.

1946

1946: Wednesday, 5 June . . . 237 Entries. £7,915 10s.

MR J. E. FERGUSON's gr.c. AIRBORNE by Precipitation out of Bouquet	T. LOWREY	1
LORD DERBY's b.c. GULF STREAM by Hyperion out of Tide-way	H. WRAGG	2
MR T. LILLEY's ch.c. RADIOTHERAPY by Hyperion out of Belleva	T. H. CAREY	3

Also ran :

Lord Durham's White Jacket (4th) (W. Nevett); Sir R. Brooke's Peterborough (E. Britt); Mrs Macdonald-Buchanan's Edward Tudor (G. Richards); Duke of Norfolk's Royal Commission (E. Smith); H.H. Aga Khan's Khaled (R. A. Jones); Miss P. Bullock's Neapolitan (D. Smith); Lord Astor's Fast and Fair (C. Richards); Mr J. S. Barrington's Bridle Path (P. Evans); Sir H. Bruce's Friar Tuck (T. Burn); Sir W. Cooke's Happy Knight (T. Weston); Mr F. W. Dennis's Hispaniola (D. L. Jones); Mrs A. James's Sunstroke (J. Simpson); Mr P. Rose's Qui Va La (H. Packham); Mrs F. Nagle's Massif (M. Beary).

17 ran.

Betting :

5–1 Happy Knight; 7–1 Gulf Stream, Fast and Fair, and Khaled; 8–1 Radiotherapy; 100–9 Edward Tudor; 13–1 Neapolitan; 100–6 Peterborough; 20–1 White Jacket; 50–1 Airborne and Royal Commission; 66–1 Friar Tuck and Sunstroke; 100–1 others.

Totalizator : (2s. unit). Win: 77s. Places: 17s. 6d., 6s. 3d., 5s. 6d.

Winner won by a length; two lengths between second and third.   2 m. 44⅜ s.
Winner trained by R. Perryman at Newmarket.

1947

With the victory of Pearl Diver in 1947, a new phase opened in English racing, a phase in which the hitherto undisputed supremacy of the British thoroughbred was continually and successfully challenged, chiefly by horses bred in France, in a lesser degree by horses bred in Italy, and in the United States as well.

Up to 1946 only three French-bred horses had won the Derby; Gladiateur, Durbar II, and Bois Roussel. Between 1947 and 1959, the race was won five times by French horses, while Never Say Die, though trained in England, was American-bred. In the same period French horses won the Two Thousand Guineas twice, the One Thousand Guineas four times, the Oaks five times, the St Leger three times, the Gold Cup six times, the Eclipse Stakes five times (that does not include the French-trained but Irish-bred St Crespin III), and the King George VI and Queen Elizabeth Stakes three times. In addition, there were two American-bred winners of the St Leger, while Italian horses won the King George VI and Queen Elizabeth Stakes, the Gold Cup, and the Goodwood Cup.

The underlying cause of this situation (though others were given) was the structure of English racing. In this country there has been for years a high proportion of two-year-old events right from the start of the season. Many betting owners consider a smart two-year-old the most reliable medium for a gamble, and the biggest demand from commercial breeders has been for quick-maturing animals that are likely to win over five or six furlongs during their first season's racing. Except for potential classic colts and fillies, there has never been a brisk demand for animals that will probably win over a distance of ground in due course, given time to develop.

In 1960, spurred on by Mr Phil Bull who felt strongly that the Rules of Racing as they then existed gave undue advantage to the precocious type of two-year-old, the Jockey Club set up a committee under Lord Rosebery to examine the effect the Rules of Racing had on the production of middle-distance horses.

The most important feature of the report was the recommendation to increase the number of seven furlong and one mile races for two-year-olds and to permit seven furlong races as from 1 July, two months earlier than had previously been the case. In the meantime Mr Bull had himself initiated the one mile 'Timeform' Gold Cup to be run over a mile at Doncaster in October, as the counterpart to France's Grand Criterium. That race, now the 'Observer' Gold Cup, proved an outstanding success from the start. Certainly the changes that have taken place have swung the balance rather more in favour of two-year-olds likely to stay a mile or more at three.

In France, on the other hand, there have always been fewer rich prizes for two-year-olds, and in fact fewer opportunities of any sort for animals of that age. Furthermore, little is done to encourage the older sprinters and most of the big races tend to be of a mile and a quarter or more. Consequently there has been a far higher proportion of stayers on the French Turf, while at the stud there are many more stoutly bred mares capable of producing a top-class mile and a half horse even when mated with a fast sire that did not stay that distance himself. In addition, many of the best French horses, at least until quite recently, were required to prove their stoutness and soundness as four-year-olds, whereas in England the tendency increased after the war to hustle a good three-year-old off to the stud, before its toughness and constitution had been thoroughly tested.

It must be emphasized, though, that in the past few years French racing has had plenty of worries of its own to contend with, and many of the most valuable races are now being won by horses bred in England, Ireland or the United States. French victories in this country are now few and far between but it is fair to add that because of the vastly superior level of prize money in France, there is scant incentive to send the best French horses to run here.

The apparent deterioration in the French thoroughbred can be attributed to several factors. Firstly, French breeders have been unable to resist the temptation to sell many of their best stallions for export. Secondly, French bloodstock is in need of a strong infusion of sheer speed. Thirdly, the lavish watering of the main racecourses round Paris has tended both to blunt speed, and to reduce the value of soundness.

The outstanding two-year-old of 1946 was Mr J. A. Dewar's Tudor Minstrel, by Owen Tudor out of Sansonnet, by Sansovino. Unbeaten, he was placed at the head of the Free Handicap with 9 st. 7 lb., two pounds in front of Sir Alfred Butt's Fair Trial colt Petition. The following spring he won a small race at Bath, and then made mincemeat of his rivals in the Two Thousand Guineas, winning in the most brilliant style imaginable by a clear eight lengths from Saravan and Sayajirao.

Some of the more exuberant racing journalists at once began to write Tudor Minstrel up as 'the horse of the century', and public imagination was inflamed to such an extent that the colt started favourite at the absurd price of 7–4 on for the Derby. Tudor Minstrel was trained at Beckhampton by Fred Darling, and at one point it looked as if the stable would have another formidable candidate for the race in Blue Train, by Blue Peter out of the triple classic winner Sun Chariot. Blue Train, leased to the King by the National Stud, won the Newmarket Stakes by four lengths, but jarred himself severely on the firm going and never saw a racecourse again. Gordon Richards, the stable jockey, was therefore spared having to make the decision whether he would ride the dazzling Tudor Minstrel or alternatively Blue Train, who not only carried the royal colours, but looked the stouter stayer of the two.

Dante's brother Sayajirao, who had won the Lingfield Derby Trial, was almost the only Derby candidate seriously backed to beat the favourite. Very little interest was taken in the French colt Pearl Diver, who was trained by Percy Carter at Chantilly, but had come to Claud Halsey's stable at Newmarket for a few weeks to complete his preparation. A big, rich bay standing sixteen hands two and very strongly made, Pearl Diver was bred by the late Mr Edward Esmond and on his death became the property of his son-in-law, Baron G. de Waldner. He was by Vatellor who also sired the 1948 Derby winner My Love, out of Pearl Cap, by the French Derby winner, Le Capucin.

Vatellor, by Bois Roussel's sire Vatout, a grandson of Chaucer, was a good, hardy stayer whose chief success was the Prix du Président de la République. Pearl Cap was a great race mare; a top-class two-year-old, she subsequently won the French Oaks and the Prix de l'Arc de Triomphe. She was a stud failure, though, until, at the age of sixteen, she was mated with Vatellor. According to the French Stud Book, she was then owned by M. Paul Doboscq; that, however, was mere camouflage to mislead the Germans while France was occupied.

Pearl Maiden, dam of Pearl Cap, was by the beautifully bred but wayward Phaleron. She was sold by Mr H. Sidebottom at the Newmarket December Sales in 1924 to the Newmarket trainer Mr Harvey Leader, who subsequently re-sold her for 1,000 guineas to Mr Frank Carter, acting on behalf of Mr Esmond. In addition to Pearl Cap, she bred Bipearl, winner of the French One Thousand Guineas, and Pearlweed, winner of the French Derby. Seashell, dam of Pearl Maiden, was bred by the Duke of Westminster and was by Orme out of Rydal Fell, three parts sister to the St Leger winner Troutbeck. Seashell's career contained a number of vicissitudes, and on one occasion she was sold at Newmarket to an inn-keeper at Long Melford for five guineas.

Pearl Diver ran twice as a two-year-old, winning the seven-furlong Prix de Saint Patrick in September. The following spring he started off promisingly enough by finishing second over a mile at Le Tremblay to Imprudence, later the winner in England of the One Thousand Guineas and the Oaks. Subsequently, however, he was only third in the mile and a quarter Prix Jean Prat, and although he won the mile and a half Prix Matchem, it was only on the disqualification of a second-rate animal called Timor. His form, therefore, hardly suggested he was anything out of the ordinary, but Baron de Waldner had faith in him; he turned down a good offer from an English breeder and sent the colt to Claud Halsey at Newmarket to finish his Derby preparation. At Newmarket Pearl Diver singularly failed to impress the local touts, but Halsey himself at once realized he was a very good horse and, after seeing him work one morning, an experienced Newmarket trainer immediately went and backed him at long odds for the Derby.

As Tudor Minstrel was by a Derby and Gold Cup winner out of a mare by a Derby winner, there seemed, superficially at any rate, no reason why he should fail to stay the distance. A few sceptics, however, doubted whether a horse with such phenomenal speed could also stay, while others thought that the dominating influence in his pedigree might well be that of the non-staying Americus Girl, granddam of Mumtaz Mahal.

There is little that needs be said about the race. Tudor Minstrel never settled down at all. From the start he fought Gordon Richards for his head, and although he led coming into the straight, he was a spent force with three furlongs still to go. Sayajirao led a quarter of a mile out, but Pearl Diver, who had been travelling very smoothly throughout, finished full of running and won by a decisive four lengths from the grey Migoli, with Sayajirao third. There were some who thought that Tudor Minstrel would have won if only Richards had not sought to restrain him, but Tudor Minstrel's subsequent running in the Eclipse Stakes showed that a mile was clearly his limit.

In the Grand Prix de Paris Pearl Diver was a long way down the course behind Avenger. He returned to England for the St Leger, but the very hard ground was all against him and he was only fourth to Sayajirao, Arbar, and Migoli. As a four-year-old he ran five times; he won the Prix d'Harcourt, but was unplaced in the Coronation Cup and the Prix de l'Arc de Triomphe. He was then bought by Mr Clifford Nicholson and retired to the Limestone Stud at a fee of 300 guineas. He was a failure as a sire, and in 1957 was exported to Japan.

Baron de Waldner, who died in 1970, was a banker by profession. A comparatively young man at the time of Pearl Diver's victory, he had served in the United States Army during the war. George Bridgland is English-born, but has spent most of his racing career, both as rider and trainer, in France. During the war he returned to England and won the St Leger on Sun Castle and the Oaks on Hycilla. He trained Cambremer to win the St Leger for Mr R. B. Strassburger in 1956.

Migoli, second in the Derby, was a game and consistent horse. He beat Tudor Minstrel in the Eclipse Stakes and finished the season by winning the Champion Stakes and the Aintree Derby. As a four-year-old he won the Prix de l'Arc de Triomphe. He proved a disappointing sire, though he did get the Belmont Stakes winner Gallant Man. Sayajirao, who cost 28,000 guineas as a yearling, won the

Irish Derby and the St Leger. He sired an outstanding stayer in Gladness, winner of the Gold Cup and the Goodwood Cup, and the St Leger winner Indiana. Tudor Minstrel won the St James's Palace Stakes and the Knights Royal Stakes, but was beaten in the Eclipse. The best horses he sired were King of the Tudors (Eclipse Stakes) and Tomy Lee (Kentucky Derby), as well as the successful sire Tudor Melody. He was exported to America in 1959 and retired from stud duties in 1970.

In order to interfere as little as possible with industrial output the race was run on a Saturday for the first occasion in its history in peace-time.

1947: Saturday, 7 June ... 253 Entries. £9,101 4s.

BARON G. DE WALDNER's b.c. PEARL DIVER by Vatellor
out of Pearl Cap   G. BRIDGLAND   1
H.H. AGA KHAN's gr.c. MIGOLI by Bois Roussel
out of Mah Iran   D. SMITH   2
GAEKWAR OF BARODA's br.c. SAYAJIRAO by Nearco
out of Rosy Legend   E. BRITT   3

Also ran:

Mr J. A. Dewar's Tudor Minstrel (4th) (G. Richards); M. M. Boussac's Cadir (E. C. Elliott); Mr Y. J. Kirkpatrick's Grand Weather (T. Burns); Lord Rosebery's Firemaster (E. Smith); Mr J. V. Rank's Merry Quip (T. Weston); M. L. Volterra's Parisien (R. Brethes); Princess Aly Khan's Saravan (C. Smirke); Sir O. Goonetilleke's Castle Street (T. Burn); Executors of the late Lord Harewood's Tite Street (W. Evans); Mr J. W. Boyle's Richard the Third (C. Richards); Gaekwar of Baroda's Bhisma (P. Khade); Mr W. Hutchinson's Blue Coral (W. Carr).

15 ran.

Betting:

7–4 on Tudor Minstrel; 13–2 Sayajirao; 100–6 Grand Weather; 20–1 Migoli; 22–1 Merry Quip; 28–1 Saravan; 40–1 Tite Street, Pearl Diver, and Cadir; 50–1 Firemaster and Parisien; 100–1 Castle Street; 200–1 others.

Totalizator: (2s. unit). Win: 67s. 3d. Places: 13s. 3d., 6s. 6d., 4s. 6d.

Won by four lengths; three-quarters of a length between second and third.

2 m. 38⅖ s.

Winner trained by P. Carter in France. (For three weeks before the race the winner was with C. Halsey at Newmarket.)

1948

There were thirty-two runners for the Derby in 1948, the biggest field for eighty-six years. The race proved a humiliating one for British bloodstock as both the first two horses to finish were French, and there were four French-bred horses in the first six.

My Love, the winner, was owned in partnership by the Aga Khan, whose colours he carried, and M. L. Volterra. He was bred by M. Volterra and was by Pearl Diver's sire, Vatellor, whom M. Volterra had acquired when in 1933 he bought all Captain Jefferson Cohn's bloodstock. My Love's dam, For My Love, was bred by M. Volterra in 1936 and won twice as a two-year-old. My Love was her second foal, and before producing My Love she had been barren to Vatellor the three previous years. She subsequently bred one other winner in Mon Chéri, who, however, only won one race. For My Love was by Amfortas, by Ksar, out of Najmi, by Grand Parade. Amfortas, second in the Ascot Gold Vase, was not more than a goodish staying handicapper and not particularly successful as a sire. Najmi, bred in Ireland, was at one time owned by Colonel Loder, for whom she bred three winners. He sold her to M. Volterra for 165 guineas at the Newmarket December Sales in 1933.

Trained by Richard Carver, My Love ran twice as a two-year-old, being beaten by only a head on his first appearance. In his first outing the following spring he was beaten a neck over ten and a half furlongs at Longchamp by Flush Royal, a good, tough horse that subsequently won sixteen races in England, including the Cesarewitch as a seven-year-old. In the Prix Greffulhe, over the same course and distance, My Love was only third to Rigolo and Flush Royal, but stamina was his strongest point and in the important Prix Hocquart run over the Derby distance at Longchamp in May, he showed impressive improvement to win by a length and a half from Turmoil with Flush Royal third. This success stamped him as a stayer of high promise, and after the Aly Khan had watched him work at Chantilly on 23 May, it was announced that the Aga Khan had purchased a half-share. The price was rumoured to be £15,000.

Favourite for the Derby was the French-bred My Babu, by Djebel. In winning the Two Thousand Guineas, though, he had sustained an overreach, and an anti-tetanus injection had caused stiffness and swelling, which resulted in an interruption to the colt's preparation. Joint second favourites were M. Boussac's Djeddah, who had been unplaced in the Guineas, and the Bois Roussel colt Valognes, winner of the Chester Vase. The Cobbler, narrowly beaten in the Guineas but reckoned unlikely to stay a mile and a half, was easy to back at 10–1, while My Love and the American-bred Black Tarquin, the latter of whom had been decisively beaten in the Newmarket Stakes, were on offer at 100–9. Solar Slipper would have been a fancied competitor, but he got cast in his box, and an hour and a half before the race was due to start, it was announced that he was unable to run. He was reckoned considerably superior to his stable companion Straight Play, who finished fifth. It was not a particularly good-looking field. My Babu, a colt of great quality, and The Cobbler were probably the pick, but the former became a little upset by the preliminaries, although not to the same extent as Valognes, who had sweated his chance away long before the 'off'. My Love, a strongly made colt standing roughly sixteen hands, was certainly more attractive than his stable companion Royal Drake, who looked leggy and narrow, and who had not run since finishing sixth in the Two Thousand Guineas. The going was good, the crowd one of the largest in the history of the race.

The start was a satisfactory one. The hooded Henley-in-Arden led for five furlongs, by which time Valognes was already in a hopeless position. Coming down the hill Tormie was in front, followed by Royal Drake, Ottoman, Djeddah, and Straight Play. Black Tarquin, lying seventh at the time, swung wide at Tattenham Corner, colliding with My Babu and carrying the favourite out with him. At this point My Love, who had gradually been improving his position, was a good eight lengths behind the leaders.

In the straight Tormie was done with and Doyasbère sent Royal Drake into a clear lead of several lengths. My Babu, cleverly balanced again by Smirke, set off in pursuit; with two furlongs to go he was second and looked dangerous, but as soon as his rider really got at him he began to falter, and he was clearly in trouble at the distance. Meanwhile My Love's stamina was beginning to tell and from three furlongs out he made rapid and unimpeded headway. He hung to the left a little bit from the distance, but nevertheless caught his stable companion a hundred yards from the post to win by a length and a half, with Noor, who was putting in all his best work at the finish, a further four lengths away third. My Babu was fourth, Straight Play fifth, and Djeddah sixth. Smirke was of the opinion that My Babu would have won but for being bumped, but the probability is that the favourite did not quite stay a mile and a half.

This was the fourth time the Aga Khan's colours had been first past the post in the Derby. M. Volterra, who had the distinction of breeding both first and second, also bred Bois Roussel, winner in 1938, and Amour Drake, beaten a head by Nimbus in 1949. The day after Amour Drake's defeat, M. Volterra, whose health had suffered greatly during internment by the Germans towards the end of the war, died from heart trouble. A most amusing and witty man, he made his own way in life without the initial advantages of education or money, but intelligence and hard work earned him a fortune as 'King' of the theatre and the music-hall in Paris. The turning-point in his racing career came in 1933 when he took over all Captain J. D. Cohn's bloodstock, together with the lease of the Bois Roussel Stud, William Hayton agreeing to remain as manager. In 1934 he won the Prix du Jockey Club with Duplex and the Grand Prix with Admiral Drake, while among the notable horses he bred besides those previously mentioned were Le Ksar, winner of the Two Thousand Guineas; Mary Tudor, dam of the Derby winner Owen Tudor; and Quick Arrow, dam of the Oaks winner Steady Aim. His widow won the 1955 Derby and Grand Prix with Phil Drake.

Richard Carver, sixty-four years of age at the time, was in fact a British subject though born in Chantilly. Though for many years one of the foremost trainers in France, he had never been to Epsom before and had never saddled a horse for an English classic event until Royal Drake ran in the Two Thousand Guineas. 'Rae' Johnstone, who rode a beautiful race on the winner, was born in Australia in 1905. For most of his career he rode in France, but in 1934 he came to England to ride for Lord Glanely. He won the Two Thousand Guineas that year on Colombo, but his handling of Colombo in the Derby was sharply criticized and he returned to France before the summer was over. No doubt this well-earned victory did much to obliterate any unhappy memories of that earlier occasion. Johnstone, a smooth, sophisticated, cosmopolitan character, was a very polished rider at his best. He won twelve English classic races, his subsequent Derby successes being on Galcador (1950) and Lavandin (1956). He trained in France until his death in 1964.

My Love completed a great double by winning the Grand Prix from Flush Royal and Bey, but in the St Leger, apart from being unsuited to the hard ground, he was probably stale and was only sixth behind Black Tarquin, Alycidon, and Solar Slipper. He never ran again after that and began his stud career in France the following year. He had shown little sign of being a success when, after five seasons, he was sold to the Argentine Government. Put up for auction in Buenos Aires, he fetched the equivalent of £46,250. He was not a success there.

Royal Drake twice won the March Stakes at Newmarket, was second in the Coronation Cup and Princess of Wales's Stakes, and third in the Queen Elizabeth Stakes. He went to the stud in France in 1951. Noor was third in the Eclipse Stakes; sent to America, he won eight races, including the Hollywood Gold Cup. My Babu won the Victoria Cup at Hurst Park as a four-year-old. He sired a Two Thousand Guineas winner in Our Babu and was exported to America in 1956 where he died in 1970. Djeddah won six races in France and the Eclipse and Champion Stakes in England; he went to the stud in America. Ottoman and Valognes have both got plenty of winners in Australia, while The Cobbler, who, as a four-year-old, won the Wokingham Stakes, was sent to New Zealand in 1958. Black Tarquin won the St Leger, but the following year was trounced by Alycidon in a famous race for the Gold Cup. He sired a great stayer in Trelawny but was chiefly noted as a sire of jumpers.

Added money for the Derby this year was increased by £250 to £3,250, and the winning owner also received a trophy valued at £250.

1948: Saturday, 5 June . . . 386 Entries. £13,059 5s.

H.H. AGA KHAN's b.c. MY LOVE by Vatellor
out of For My Love   W. JOHNSTONE   1
M LÉON VOLTERRA's b.c. ROYAL DRAKE
by Admiral Drake out of Hurrylor   J. DOYASBÈRE   2
H.H. AGA KHAN's br.c. NOOR by Nasrullah
out of Queen of Baghdad   T. WESTON   3

Also ran:

H.H. Maharaja of Baroda's My Babu (4th) (C. Smirke); Mr R. J. Sainsbury's Straight Play (H. Packham); M. M. Boussac's Djeddah (E. C. Elliott); Mr A. Lyon's Tory II (T. Burn); Mrs E. Cockerline's Prince Hardi (C. Rowley); Mr N. P. Donaldson's Hope Street (W. T. Evans); Mrs M. Freedman's Julian (J. Gilbert); Captain P. G. A. Harvey's Speciality (W. Rickaby); Mr J. Hetherton's Black Pampas (D. L. Jones); Mr W. Hutchinson's Valdavian (H. Blackshaw); Mr W. Hutchinson's Valignus (W. Marland); Lord Irwin's Ottoman (T. Lowrey); Mr H. J. Joel's Pride of India (J. Sime); Mrs G. Kohn's Henley-in-Arden (T. Hawcroft); Lt.-Col. Giles Loder's The Cobbler (G. Richards); Sir Malcolm McAlpine's Rubaiyat (M. Molony); Sir Malcolm McAlpine's Native Heath (M. Beary); Lt.-Col. R. Macdonald-Buchanan's Valognes (E. Britt); Mr M. L. Meyer's Millwall (P. Gomez); Mr R. Middlemas's Ravenswood (G. Bridgland); Mrs Lionel Montagu's Usher (C. Richards); Mr M. Ostrer's Tormie (W. Nevett); Mr D. Robinson's Mallowry (K. Gethin); Mr E. R. Charles's Jacobite (E. Smith); Captain T. E. Thorpe's Blue Mickie (J. Marshall); Mr W. Woodward's Black Tarquin (W. H. Carr); Mr W. Woodward's The Senator II (T. Gosling); Mrs M. Glenister's Tarka (W. Lister); Mr W. Harvey's Blue Falls (S. Wragg).

32 ran.

Betting:

4–1 My Babu; 8–1 Djeddah and Valognes; 10–1 The Cobbler; 100–9 My Love and Black Tarquin; 100–6 Tormie; 22–1 Noor; 25–1 Native Heath and Royal Drake; 40–1 Ottoman; 50–1 Hope Street, Pride of India, and Blue Mickie; 66–1 Julian, Blue Falls, Black Pampas, Usher, Mallowry, Straight Play, The Senator II, and Henley-in-Arden; 100–1 others.

Totalizator: (2s. unit). Win: 18s. 3d. Places: 7s., 13s., 9s. 6d.

Won by a length and a half; four lengths between second and third.   2 m. 40 s. Winner trained by R. Carver in France.

1949

For the first time in its history, the racecourse camera decided the result of the Derby. The judge, Mr Malcolm Hancock, called for a photograph which revealed that Nimbus had won by a head from the French colt Amour Drake, with Swallow Tail a further head away third.

Nimbus was bred by the well-known bookmaker William Hill and was by the Italian-bred Nearco, sire of the 1945 Derby winner Dante, out of the grey mare Kong, by Baytown out of Clang. Whenever Nimbus's Derby chances were being assessed, it was invariably asserted in disparagement that he was far from classically bred on his dam's side. There may well have been some truth in that opinion; however, the 'rough' but undeniably stout blood in Kong's pedigree undoubtedly blended well with the quality and vitality imparted by Nearco.

Kong's sire Baytown was a good, hardy grey who raced for four seasons, winning ten events including the Irish Two Thousand Guineas and the Irish Derby. He was also runner-up in the Cambridgeshire. He retired to the stud at the age of six, but his record as a sire was indifferent. Achtoi, sire of Baytown, was third in the 1915 St Leger; he sired a lot of tough, staying handicappers, including two Cesarewitch winners, as well as a number of good horses under National Hunt rules. He was by Santoi, a bad-tempered horse but a good stayer, who won the Ascot Gold Cup.

Kong's dam Clang was by Hainault, a half-brother by Swynford to Phalaris. Bought as a yearling by Sir Charles Hyde for 2,000 guineas, she won one race. Besides Kong she bred four other winners, one of which won over fences at Aintree.

Kong herself was a useful sprinter and won the six-furlong Wokingham Stakes at Ascot as a four-year-old. She bred four other winners besides Nimbus, including the very fast Grey Sovereign, by Nearco's son Nasrullah. Grey Sovereign was inclined to be somewhat awkward temperamentally but proved an extremely successful sire. Congo, a mare by Bellacose out of Kong, has done well at the stud, her offspring including the sprinter Byland, winner of over £5,000.

Mr William Hill had bought the Whitsbury Manor Stud in 1942 after the death of the previous owner, Sir Charles Hyde, and when the Whitsbury yearlings came up for sale in 1947, George Colling, the Newmarket trainer, gave 5,000 guineas for Nimbus, acting on behalf of Mr H. A. Glenister, a salaried official of the Midland Bank, who gave the colt to his wife as a birthday present. Nimbus began his racing

Ormonde, ridden by Fred Archer, with John Porter; by Emil Adam

career by running a promising third in the Spring Stakes at Newmarket on 12 May. He followed this up by winning the Redfern Stakes at Kempton by a neck after losing a little ground at the start. The form hardly looked up to Royal Ascot standard, but Nimbus was steadily improving and in the Coventry Stakes he only lost by a head to Royal Forest after a desperate struggle. Next time out he won the July Stakes at Newmarket by a length. This victory was all the more creditable as he was badly baulked at the start and appeared in a hopeless position at half-way. The manner in which he responded to some hard driving by Elliott in the last two furlongs was proof of his courage and resolution. He only ran once again as a two-year-old and that was in the Champagne Stakes at Doncaster. He was a long way short of his best on that occasion and never saw the way that the Beckhampton colt Abernant went. In the Free Handicap he was given 8 st. 11 lb., ten pounds less than Abernant and six pounds less than his Ascot conqueror Royal Forest.

Nimbus thrived during the winter and grew into a fine, big, handsome colt although his hocks were a trifle away from him. His first appearance was in the one-mile Classic Trial Stakes at Thirsk, and although still a bit backward, he won rather cleverly by a length. In the Two Thousand Guineas he started at 10–1, the flying grey, Abernant, being a hot favourite at 5–4, while there was good money for Star King, winner of the Greenham Stakes, and for the French colt Amour Drake. Abernant led from the start and looked sure to win coming down the hill, but he faltered in the final hundred yards, and Nimbus, who had been outpaced early on, ran on in the most determined fashion from the Dip to catch the favourite in the very last stride. A photograph was called for, and this showed that Nimbus had won by a short head. Barnes Park was a moderate third and Amour Drake fourth.

Nimbus did not run again before the Derby, but his final gallop at home thoroughly satisfied his connexions. His preparation had not been helped by the fact that Colling was ill—he was too ill, in fact, to go to Epsom—and much responsibility devolved, therefore, on the head-lad, Dick Jones, and on Elliott, the stable jockey. Favourite for the Derby was Royal Forest, an impressive winner of the Sandown Park Trial Stakes. Nimbus was second favourite, while Amour Drake, who had won the French Two Thousand and had improved immensely in appearance since Newmarket, was at 10–1. Lord Derby's Swallow Tail who, like Royal Forest, was a son of Bois Roussel, had been backed at 4–1 after winning the Chester Vase, but he had drifted out to 100–8 after a puzzling defeat when a 9–2 on favourite for a minor event at Liverpool.

The going was good, the weather perfect after morning showers, and the crowd enormous. Nimbus, inclined to be a bit obstreperous at home, was ridden in the paddock by a boy, but on this great occasion his conduct was suitably decorous.

Royal Forest sweated up a little, but had cooled off before he reached the start. As soon as the tapes went up off went Nimbus, into the lead, followed by Grani, Highlander III, Val Drake, Swallow Tail, and the favourite. Grani and Val Drake were done with coming down the hill and at this stage Nimbus led from Swallow Tail, while Amour Drake was a good ten lengths behind the leaders.

With three furlongs to go Nimbus and Swallow Tail were both being ridden and it looked like being a punishing duel between the two. Just below the distance Swallow Tail, a powerful, short-legged, close-coupled colt, got his head in front, but Nimbus, with typical gameness, fought back and regained the advantage. Just inside the final furlong Nimbus, resolute but tiring, began to veer over to the right and in so doing came very close indeed to Swallow Tail, who became unbalanced and hung to the right as well. At this point Amour Drake, who had been making up ground very fast, was just behind the leaders and on the outside. Johnstone obviously thought that with Swallow Tail coming over to the right, he would inevitably find himself baulked. He made a split-second decision and switched Amour Drake to the inside. This manœuvre very nearly succeeded, and as the three horses swept past the post in a great finish, it was impossible to say which had won. A photograph was called for, and there was an interval of almost unbearable tension before it was announced that Nimbus had won by a head, with Swallow Tail a head away third. The strain during those moments of waiting must have been appalling not only for Mr and Mrs Glenister, who had undergone the same dreadful ordeal at Newmarket, but also for George Colling, who was listening in to the race in his bedroom at home.

Elliott, who was riding his third Derby winner, had shown daring confidence in Nimbus's stamina in electing to force the pace from the start; if Nimbus had cracked, his rider's tactics would inevitably have been blamed. Johnstone was widely criticized for making his last-minute switch to the rails, but it must be remembered that he had only a fraction of a second in which to make up his mind and that he only lost the race by a matter of inches. If the leaders had kept straight, there would almost certainly have been a French triumph, for the third year in succession. The following day Amour Drake's owner, M. Léon Volterra, who had been lying for some days at death's door in Paris, died.

Nimbus never raced again. He was not entered for the St Leger, so the Prix de l'Arc de Triomphe was made his objective. He received a walk-over for a small event at Haydock in August, but rapped himself soon afterwards and was taken out of training. He was retired to the stud forthwith, a syndicate with shares totalling £140,000 being formed. He cannot be said to have fulfilled expectations as a sire, but he got a good horse in Nucleus, who was second in the St Leger and before his death as a four-year-old, won over £14,000 in stakes. Another of Nimbus's sons, Nagami, was placed in the Two Thousand Guineas, Derby, and St Leger, besides winning valuable races in France and Italy. Nimbus was exported to Japan in 1962.

George Colling was the son of 'Bob' Colling, formerly a well-known trainer, and brother of 'Jack' Colling, who has been a leading trainer now for thirty years. George Colling was a capable rider until he got too heavy and he then assisted his brother for a number of years. Shortly before the war he started up on his own, but just as he was making a name for himself, his career was interrupted by service in the Royal Artillery. He was never a strong man, though, and in 1941 he was invalided out of the Army. Professionally this was lucky for him, and his stable was fully established again when racing started up in earnest once more in 1945. After the death of Walter Earl he was for a time private trainer to Lord Derby, but he was never really happy in that position and a few seasons later he decided to return once again to his own stables at Hurworth House.

A very fine trainer, whose one objective was to serve the interests of his employers, George Colling was a man of considerable charm, a good golfer and a first-class shot. Unfortunately he was dogged throughout life by indifferent health and the fact that he never really felt well accounted for a marked streak of pessimism in his nature. However, with great courage he carried on for as long as his strength held out; by the winter of 1958 he was desperately ill and he died the following spring. His stable jockey, 'Manny' Mercer, of whom he was very fond and whom he trusted implicitly, was killed at Ascot a few months later.

Amour Drake won the Coronation Cup as a four-year-old. He went to the stud in Ireland in 1951, but was not a success and was in due course exported to Peru. Swallow Tail won the King Edward VII Stakes at Ascot and was fourth in the St Leger; he has done well as a sire in Brazil, and Royal Forest has been a success there as well. Barnes Park won the Lincoln as a five-year-old, while Marco Polo II, a half-brother of My Babu, has been a stud success in New Zealand. Hindostan, winner of the Irish Derby, went to Japan in 1956. Val Drake won the Goodwood Cup as a four-year-old and was second in the Queen Alexandra Stakes at Ascot.

Added money this year was increased by £1,000 to £4,250.

1949: Saturday, 4 June ... 417 Entries. £14,245.

MRS GLENISTER's b.c. NIMBUS by Nearco
out of Kong   E. C. ELLIOTT   I
M. LÉON VOLTERRA's b.c. AMOUR DRAKE
by Admiral Drake out of Vers l'Aurore   W. JOHNSTONE   2
LORD DERBY's b.c. SWALLOW TAIL by Bois Roussel
out of Schiaparelli   .   D. SMITH   3

1949

Also ran:

Major R. Macdonald-Buchanan's Royal Forest (4th) (G. Richards); Mr H. Lane's Barnes Park (W. Cook); Mr F. W. Dennis's Normanton (M. Molony); H.H. Maharaja of Baroda's Jai Hind (C. Smirke); Mr J. S. Barrington's Grani (T. Burn); Mr P. Beatty's Marco Polo II (T. Gosling); M. M. Bernier's High-lander III (M. Lollierou); Mr T. H. Bletsoe's Scottish Meridian (E. Smith); M. M. Boussac's Targui (R. Poincelet); Colonel G. C. Buxton's Xerxes (W. T. Evans); Mr J. F. Duff's Button Boy (C. Bentick); Mr J. E. Ferguson's Courier (T. Lowrey); Mr E. H. Hammond's Big Wig (A. P. Taylor); Mr W. Hutchinson's Happy Mick (T. Hawcroft); Mrs A. Johnston's Prionium (F. Lane); H.H. Aga Khan's Hindostan (W. Nevett); Prince Aly Khan's Iran (P. Blanc); Mrs J. D. Kyle's Enver Pasha (W. H. Carr); Mr J. Luttmer's Le Troubadour (F. Emanuelli); Mr J. V. Rank's Conservative (W. Rickaby); Mr R. B. Strassburger's Gades (J. Doyasbère); Mr G. A. Tachmindmi's Boisson (J. Marshall); Mr Jack Hylton's Lord Drake (K. Gethin); Mr Jack Hylton's Royal Empire (M. Beary); M. L. Volterra's Val Drake (C. Bouillon); Mr O. J. Jackson's Mon Chatelain (S. Wragg); Mr W. Woodward's Brown Rover (E. Britt); Mr H. F. Hartley's Willoughton (C. Richards); Miss H. Groves's Neapolitan Star (F. Durr).

32 ran.

Betting:

9–2 Royal Forest; 7–1 Nimbus; 10–1 Amour Drake; 100–9 Hindostan; 100–8 Swallow Tail; 100–7 Brown Rover; 100–6 Val Drake; 20–1 Scottish Meridian; 22–1 Barnes Park; 25–1 Jai Hind; 28–1 Courier and Gades; 33–1 Targui and Xerxes; 66–1 Grani, Willoughton, Conservative, and Royal Empire; 100–1 others.

Totalizator: (2s. unit). Win: 15s. 3d. Places: 6s., 7s. 9d., 12s.

Won by a head; a head between second and third.   2 m. 42 s.
Winner trained by G. Colling at Newmarket.

1950

This was a dismal year indeed for British bloodstock. A French colt and an American-bred colt fought out the finish of the Derby, and French colts were first and second in the St. Leger. French fillies won the One Thousand Guineas and the Oaks, and there were French triumphs, too, in the Eclipse Stakes, the Coronation Cup, and the Goodwood Cup. All told, French-bred horses won over £200,000 in stakes during the season, while M. Boussac headed the lists of successful owners and breeders, the second Frenchman to achieve that distinction, Count F. de Lagrange having accomplished it in 1865.

Before the season began it was widely known that Captain Cecil Boyd-Rochfort trained a three-year-old of outstanding promise in Prince Simon, an American-bred colt belonging to Mr William Woodward, for many years Chairman of the New York Jockey Club. Prince Simon, a fine big colt by Princequillo, had not run as a two-year-old and his first racecourse appearance was in the Wood Ditton Stakes at the Craven Meeting. Starting at 3–1 on, he won with the utmost ease. He was made favourite for the Two Thousand Guineas, but failed by a short head to catch the Aga Khan's grey Fair Trial colt Palestine, who obtained first run on him and just lasted home after being the best part of three lengths clear coming into the Dip.

Palestine had no pretensions to being a stayer and was not engaged in the Derby, for which Prince Simon started a 2–1 favourite after a highly impressive six lengths victory in the Newmarket Stakes. Second favourite was Mme Volterra's Admiral Drake colt, L'Amiral, while another French colt, Vieux Manoir, was on offer at 7–1, despite the fact that many of the best French judges reckoned that he was still very green and that his high action was singularly ill-suited to the Epsom gradients. Lord Rosebery's Castle Rock, winner of the Chester Vase, was a popular each-way choice at 9–1, and there was plenty of money at 100–9 for the Aga Khan's Khorassan, winner of the Dee Stakes at Chester, and also for M. Boussac's Galcador. It had originally been planned that Pardal should carry M. Boussac's colours, but he was sore after the Prix Hocquart in which he finished a moderate third, L'Amiral winning that event after a very hard battle with Lacaduv. Galcador, therefore, was chosen to represent the strongest stable in Europe in his place.

Bred by his owner, Galcador was a chestnut, full of quality, standing about fifteen hands three, and with the Arab head so typical of the stock of his sire Djebel, a really

571

good little horse and a tough one, too, his fifteen victories including the English and the French Two Thousand Guineas and the Prix de l'Arc de Triomphe. The more he raced the better Djebel became, and he probably reached his zenith as a five-year-old. By Tourbillon out of a Gay Crusader mare, Djebel was a great success at the stud and was four times Champion Sire in France. His notable winners in England included My Babu (Two Thousand Guineas), Arbar (Gold Cup), Hugh Lupus (Champion Stakes), and Djeddah (Eclipse Stakes and Champion Stakes). He died in 1958, having been in no small way responsible for the many remarkable successes gained by the Boussac horses in the nineteen forties and early nineteen fifties.

Pharyva, Galcador's dam, was by Pharos out of Souryva, by Gainsborough. She never won herself but bred eight winners. Souryva was a non-winner, too, but her grand-dam was the celebrated Zariba, by Sardanapale, dam of Goyescas, Abjer, Corrida, and Goya II. The line traces to the Bend Or mare Fairy Gold, who bred the great American horse Fair Play.

Galcador ran only once as a two-year-old, winning the five-furlong Prix St Firmin at Longchamp in October very easily. The following spring he won a mile race at Le Tremblay in the spring and then ran Tantième, a very good horse indeed, to half a length in the French Two Thousand Guineas. There was never any doubt about his speed; the questionable point was whether he would stay a mile and a half in a true-run race.

In the paddock Prince Simon and Galcador stood out in an otherwise undistinguished field. Prince Simon, tall, and built in proportion to his height, was the more commanding colt of the two, but some critics thought he was straight in the shoulder and he was certainly an unattractive walker. He was quite unaffected by the occasion and his demeanour could hardly have been more placid. Galcador, smaller but full of quality and standing over a lot of ground for his size, looked trained to the minute and was as hard as a cricket ball. After a good start Pewter Platter was the leader from Prince Simon, L'Amiral, Telegram II, Galcador, and Vieux Manoir. Coming down the hill Carr, confident of Prince Simon's stamina, took him to the front and he entered the straight ahead of Pewter Platter, L'Amiral, Khorassan, Galcador, and Vieux Manoir. L'Amiral and Khorassan were beaten soon after, and Prince Simon, cheered on by the shouts of thousands of his supporters, headed for home apparently full of running.

Meanwhile Johnstone had been holding up Galcador for a short, sharp run, and with a furlong to go he asked his mount for his effort. Beautifully balanced, Galcador at once accelerated to such effect that he swept past the favourite and with a hundred yards to go he was nearly a length in front. His stride began to shorten, though, in the final fifty yards, and Prince Simon, running on gallantly under pressure, was only a head behind when the winning post was reached. Double Eclipse, a stable companion of the favourite's, was a moderate third and another French colt, Telegram II, fourth. There was a tendency to criticize Carr for Prince Simon's defeat, apparently on the grounds that he should have driven the American colt, who had little power of acceleration, for all he was worth from Tattenham Corner. Johnstone, on the other hand, was judged to have ridden a brilliant race. A minority view—and a rather more sensible one—was that Carr had done everything within his power and that he could hardly be blamed if his best fell a little bit short of the standards of Fred Archer, Steve Donoghue, and Gordon Richards; furthermore, that Galcador would have won by a wider margin if Johnstone had been a bit more patient and had not made his effort quite so soon on a horse that barely stayed a mile and a half.

Galcador never ran again and he was eventually exported to Japan. Prince Simon's career ended ingloriously when, as an 8–1 on favourite, he was beaten by Babu's Pet in the King Edward VII Stakes at Ascot. He never ran again and later in the year went back to America where his stud career proved a fiasco. Double Eclipse, by Hyperion out of a half-sister to Precipitation, won the Jersey Stakes at Ascot and then the Princess of Wales's Stakes. He was exported to South Africa, but after a few seasons there he was re-sold and sent to America. Babu's Pet, a Hyperion colt that cost 13,500 guineas as a yearling, has sired a fair number of winners in France. Vieux Manoir, by Brantôme, won the Grand Prix de Paris, but was beaten by M. Boussac's Scratch II in the St Leger. He was leading sire in France in 1958.

The great French industrialist M. Marcel Boussac, who had won the Oaks two days previously with Asmena, has been a leading European figure both as owner and breeder for more than forty years. In 1918 he purchased the bloodstock of Mr H. B. Duryea, who had won the 1914 Derby with Durbar II, and he has gradually increased the scope of his activities so that in Europe only the Aga Khan, and more recently the Aly Khan, can be said to have raised thoroughbreds and raced them on a comparable scale.

M. Boussac's policy has been based on the accumulation of mares possessing the best blood-lines of Great Britain, France, and America and then mating them, for the most part, with his own sires. He had many outstanding successes in France and England before the war, but he reached the peak of his achievements on the race-course between 1945 and 1951, thanks in no small measure to the fact that he possessed two outstanding stallions in Djebel and Pharis, whose services were only rarely made available to other breeders.

In 1950 it looked as if M. Boussac might continue to dominate European racing for an indefinite period, but fortune on the Turf is notoriously fickle and quite suddenly the Boussac luck began to change. Today the once dreaded orange jacket and grey cap are seldom seen in England, and even in France it has become a rarity for a Boussac horse to win a race of primary importance. Various theories have been advanced for this remarkable reversal of luck. Some attribute it to the comparative failure of the successors of Djebel and Pharis; others to too much in-breeding or too little attention to conformation. Perhaps the wheel of fortune will turn again, but M. Boussac's experiences show that unlimited financial resources backed by first-class brains and the most up-to-date methods are insufficient to command consistent success on the Turf.

C. H. Semblat was a leading rider in France before he took up training. He never came to England to saddle M. Boussac's runners, and this season he achieved the unique feat of being the leading trainer in English racing without once setting foot on English soil. He died in 1971.

1950: Saturday, 27 May ... 372 Entries. £17,010 10s.

M. M. BOUSSAC'S ch.c. GALCADOR by Djebel out of Pharyva	W. JOHNSTONE	1
MR W. WOODWARD'S b.c. PRINCE SIMON by Princequillo out of Dancing Dora	W. H. CARR	2
LADY ZIA WERNHER'S ch.c. DOUBLE ECLIPSE by Hyperion out of Doubleton	E. SMITH	3

Also ran:

M. F. Dupré's Telegram II (A. Breasley) (4th); Lord Allendale's Rising Flame (E. Britt); Lord Rosebery's Castle Rock (W. Rickaby); Mr. L. A. Abelson's Bright Society (K. Gethin); H.H. Maharaja of Baroda's Babu's Pet (T. Burn); Lt.-Col. W. A. G. Burns's Welsh View (E. C. Elliott); Mr. F. W. Dennis's Stenigot (M. Molony); Mme V. Esmond's Peter Fox II (F. Palmer); Commander D. Lycett Green's Bilbrough (J. Caldwell); Mr C. R. Harper's Tramper (T. Hawcroft); Mr J. Ismay's New Pioneer (F. Barlow); H.H. Aga Khan's Khorassan (C. Smirke); Miss B. Locker Lampson's Pewter Platter (T. Lowrey); Mr C. C. Matthew's Port o' Light (T. Gosling); Mrs A. G. Samuel's Napolcon Bonapartc (G. Richards); Mr P. Bartholomew's Main Road (D. Smith); Lord Rosebery's Paradiso (T. Weston); Baron Guy de Rothschild's Vieux Manoir (J. Laumain); Mr S. R. Single's Billiter Street (J. Marshall); Mrs P. T. Dodd's Persia (T. Thompson); Mme Volterra's L'Amiral (R. Poincelet); Baron de Montalbo's Mattygainmal (A. Roberts).

25 ran.

Betting:

2–1 Prince Simon; 11–2 L'Amiral; 7–1 Vieux Manoir; 9–1 Castle Rock; 100–9 Galcador and Khorassan; 25–1 Telegram II; 28–1 Napoleon Bonaparte; 40–1 Persia and Double Eclipse; 50–1 Rising Flame and Port o' Light; 66–1 Welsh View, Tramper, Billiter Street, and Babu's Pet; 100–1 others.

Totalizator: (2s. unit). Win: 25s. 3d. Places: 7s. 9d., 3s. 9d., 25s. 3d.

Won by a head; four lengths between second and third.   2 m. 36⅘ s.
Winner trained by C. H. Semblat in France.

1951

There was a National Hunt flavour about the 1951 Derby. The winner, Arctic Prince, was ridden by C. Spares, better known as a hurdle race rider, while the third horse to finish, Signal Box, was partnered by the great Irish steeplechase jockey, Martin Molony.

Arctic Prince was bred in Ireland by his owner, Mr Joseph McGrath, and was a brown horse by the French-bred Prince Chevalier out of Arctic Sun, by the Italian-bred Nearco. Prince Chevalier, by Prince Rose, was a top-class performer in France, winning the Prix du Jockey Club and finishing second in the Grand Prix and the Prix de l'Arc de Triomphe. He was exported to England in 1947 and Arctic Prince was one of his first crop of foals. He also sired Charlottesville, winner of the 1960 Prix du Jockey Club and Grand Prix. He died in 1961.

Arctic Sun was the best two-year-old filly in Ireland in 1943. She bred two other winners besides Arctic Prince and died in 1956. Her dam Solar Flower, by Solario out of the Winalot mare Serena, was a top-class filly, winning over £10,000 in stakes besides being placed in the One Thousand Guineas and the Oaks. She was dam of Peter Flower, winner of over £11,000 in stakes, and also of Solar Slipper, third in the St Leger and sire of the 1955 Derby runner-up, Panaslipper.

Mr McGrath sent Arctic Prince to be trained by W. Stephenson at Royston. The colt made his first appearance in a £207 Maiden Plate at Redcar in August and out-classing the moderate opposition, won on the bit by six lengths. The following month he was well backed to win the Gimcrack Stakes at York, but faded out in the final stages after being there with a chance at the distance. There seemed no particular reason to regard him as the prospective winner of a classic race.

As a three-year-old Arctic Prince was a nice quality, well-proportioned, medium-sized colt, but perhaps rather lacking in scope. He did not run before the Two Thousand Guineas in which he started at 40–1 and finished a creditable seventh behind Ki Ming, Stokes, and Malka's Boy. A few people noticed how well he was running on at the finish, but in general his performance attracted a minimum of attention. He was not seen out again before Epsom.

There were thirty-three runners for the Derby, most of them extremely moderate. There was no single candidate with outstanding credentials, and this fact no doubt encouraged optimistic owners to take a chance with some very forlorn hopes. The favourite was the Guineas winner Ki Ming, trained by Michael Beary and owned by a Chinese restaurant-owner, Mr Ley On. Being by the sprinter Ballyogan, though, Ki Ming's hopes of staying the trip were somewhat remote. Second favourite was M. Boussac's Nyangal, who had won the Gainsborough Stakes at Hurst Park the previous autumn, but who was destined to prove an extremely disappointing three-year-old. Arcot, by Nearco, was well-backed on the strength of having won the ten-furlong Royal Standard Stakes at Manchester, and there was fair support for Le Vent, Malka's Boy, and Fraise du Bois II. Arctic Prince attracted little attention at 28–1. Ki Ming and Crocodile were the pick of a very plain field; both Nyangal and Stokes sweated up considerably in the preliminaries.

There is little to be said about the race. Malka's Boy and the favourite were both well beaten before Tattenham Corner, where Mystery IX led from Raincheck, Le Tyrol, Arctic Prince, and Sybil's Nephew. Once in the straight, Spares pulled his mount out and round the leaders and from that point the contest was over. Arctic Prince drew clear of his rivals in the smoothest style imaginable, and showing not the slightest sign of weakening, went on to win by a clear six lengths from Sybil's Nephew, with Signal Box a head away third. It was quite one of the easiest victories in the history of the race. Unfortunately it was never proved whether the winner was something more than by far the best of a mediocre lot, as in his next race, the King George VI and Queen Elizabeth Stakes, he broke down badly and was never able to run again. The best horse he sired before export to America in 1956 was the Eclipse Stakes winner, Arctic Explorer. He is also the sire of Exar (Gran Premio d'Italia, Gran Premio di Milano, Goodwood and Doncaster Cups), and of Nellie Park, dam of that great mare Park Top.

Mr McGrath, as a patriotic Irishman, served in the Irish Republican Army during 'the troubles'. He was a minister in the Irish Free State and played a leading part in the development of the Irish Hospitals Sweepstakes. His stud in Co. Kildare became one of the most powerful in Europe and would no doubt have been even more successful had Mr McGrath not sold Nasrullah, whom he bought cheaply from the Aga Khan, to America. Mr McGrath died in 1966.

William Stephenson was apprenticed as a lad to the late Major W. V. Beatty and became an extremely competent jockey on the flat. He is a good horseman, too, and in his younger days went boldly to hounds. For some years he has conducted a 'mixed' stable at Royston with conspicuous success, and in 1959 he completed a rare double by training the Grand National winner Oxo.

'Charlie' Spares, originally apprenticed to L. Cundell, was a useful, hardy all-round rider but never in the first flight on the flat, or anywhere near it. In fact his best season was in 1952 when he rode twenty-one winners under Jockey Club rules.

He had never had a ride in the Derby before he won on Arctic Prince. His association with Stephenson ended in 1953, and he soon faded out of the picture after that. He was only forty when he died in 1958.

Of the other Derby competitors Sybil's Nephew won the Newmarket St Leger and the following year the Manchester Cup. He did well as a sire in South Africa. Signal Box won the Irish Two Thousand Guineas and was second in the Irish Derby; he died after a few years at stud. Medway won the Queen Alexandra Stakes and the Goodwood Cup and was third in the St Leger. Fraise du Bois II won the Irish Derby, was second to Talma in the St Leger, and died as a four-year-old. Mystery IX, by Tehran, won the Eclipse Stakes. Ki Ming won the six-furlong Diadem Stakes from a single opponent at Ascot in the autumn. He failed as a sire. Malka's Boy won the six-furlong Wokingham Stakes as a four-year-old. Stokes became very unreliable temperamentally and was exported to Australia. Zucchero was a good but highly strung horse that not infrequently gave trouble at the start. Before he retired to the stud, though, he won the Coronation Cup, the Princess of Wales's Stakes, the Rose of York Stakes (twice), and a total of £14,837 in stakes. He was exported to Japan.

1951: Wednesday, 31 May . . . 448 Entries. £19,386 5s.

MR J. MCGRATH's br.c. ARCTIC PRINCE
by Prince Chevalier out of Arctic Sun   C. SPARES   1
LORD MILFORD's b.c. SYBIL'S NEPHEW by Honeyway
or Midas out of Sybil's Sister   E. MERCER   2
MR F. W. DENNIS's ch.c. SIGNAL BOX by Signal Light
out of Mashaq   M. MOLONY   3

Also ran:

Mr R. B. Strassburger's Le Tyrol (4th) (W. Snaith); Mr J. Olding's Crocodile (N. Sellwood); Mme Volterra's Le Vent (R. Poincelet); Lord Allendale's Paradise Street (E. Britt); Mr P. Bartholomew's Medway (D. Smith); M. M. Boussac's Nyangal (W. Johnstone); Mrs Warwick Bryant's Claudius (D. Page); Mrs J. F. C. Bryce's North Carolina (E. Smith); Mr H. E. Elvin's Malka's Boy (W. Cook); Madame V. Esmond's Mystery IX (F. Palmer); Mrs R. Foster's Faux Pas (D. L. Jones); Mr C. W. Gordon's Sun Compass (W. Rickaby); Major L. B. Holliday's Wateringbury (S. Clayton); Captain A. M. Keith's Sashcord (W. Nevett); Mr Ley On's Ki Ming (T. Gosling); Mr J. McGrath's Clare Hill (A Brabazon); Mr D. W. Molin's Part du Lyon (K. Gethin); Mrs F. C. W. Newman's Woodcote Inn (T. Hawcroft); Miss D. Paget's Ardent Hope (C. Richards); Miss D. Paget's Straight Quill (F. Durr); Mr W. F. Phillips's Nourreddin (T. Lowrey); Mr J. V.

Rank's Expeditious (A. Breasley); Sir V. Sassoon's Stokes (G. Richards); Mr H. D. Waddington's Bokara (W. T. Evans); Mr. F. T. Williams's Raincheck (C. Bouillon); Mr W. Woodward's Turco II (W. H. Carr); Mr F. Wright's Turk's Reliance (J. Sime); H.H. Aga Khan's Fraise du Bois II (C. Smirke); Mr G. Rolls's Zucchero (L. Piggott); Mrs M. Glenister's Arcot (E. C. Elliott).

33 ran.

Betting:

9–1 Ki Ming; 100–9 Nyangal; 100–8 Arcot; 100–7 Le Vent; 100–6 Malka's Boy and Fraise du Bois II; 20–1 Paradise Street, Stokes, Raincheck, and Signal Box; 22–1 Expeditious; 25–1 Sun Compass; 28–1 North Carolina, Arctic Prince, Crocodile, Zucchero, and Turco II; 40–1 Le Tyrol; 50–1 Wateringbury, Sybil's Nephew, and Straight Quill; 66–1 Medway, Mystery IX, and Faux Pas; 100–1 others.

Totalizator: (2s. unit). Win: 106s. 9d. Places: 29s. 9d., 25s. 9d., 11s.

Won by six lengths; a head between second and third.   2 m. $39\frac{2}{5}$ s.
Winner trained by W. Stephenson at Royston.

1952

In 1952 the Aga Khan's colours were for the fifth and last time first past the post in the Derby. Like Blenheim, Bahram, Mahmoud, and My Love, Tulyar never ran as a four-year-old and was in due course sold by his owner, a great horse-dealer who wisely never permitted sentiment to interfere with business.

Tulyar was bred at his owner's stud in Co. Kildare and is by Tehran out of Neocracy, by Nearco. Tehran, by Bois Roussel, won the 1944 St Leger and was second to Ocean Swell in both the Derby and the Gold Cup. On the whole he was a disappointing sire, although thanks almost entirely to Tulyar he was Champion in 1952 with the then record total of £86,072 17s. 6d., the previous best being Blandford's £75,707 in 1934. Without Tulyar's efforts, Tehran would not have been in the leading thirty.

Neocracy is out of Harina, by Blandford out of the late Mr W. Barnett's famous mare Athasi and is thus a full sister to the 1929 Derby winner Trigo. The history of Athasi has been given in the section dealing with Trigo, and it must suffice to say here that Harina won the Imperial Produce Stakes at Kempton and was sold by Mr Barnett to Mr Peter Beatty, who had her covered by Nearco and sold the filly foal Neocracy to the Aga Khan. Neocracy, the only winner Harina bred, won two races worth £2,562 as a two-year-old. Tehran was her first foal and she is also dam of Cobetto, by Migoli, winner of the Princess of Wales's Stakes, and of St Crespin III, by Aureole, winner of the Eclipse Stakes and the Prix de l'Arc de Triomphe.

Tulyar was a May foal and as a yearling he was small and backward. In fact it was decided to keep him in Ireland for a further six weeks after the rest of the Aga Khan's yearlings had been sent off to Marcus Marsh's stable at Newmarket. As a two-year-old he showed little sign of future greatness. He was unplaced in the Spring Stakes at Newmarket in May, third in the Virginia Water Stakes at Ascot in July, and unplaced in the Acomb Stakes at York in August. However, in the autumn he gave proof of his stamina by winning a couple of mile races in succession, the Buggins Farm Nursery at Haydock Park and the Kineton Nursery at Birmingham. He concluded the season by finishing second in the seven-furlong Horris Hill Stakes at Newbury. In the Free Handicap he was rated at 8 st. 2 lb., nineteen pounds below the top-weight Windy City, and the general impression he gave was that if all went well he might train on into a useful staying handicapper.

As a three-year-old Tulyar stood fifteen hands three, and although not a dominating individual, he was a difficult one to fault and was blessed with a perfect racing temperament. He very soon demonstrated how much he had improved by winning the seven-furlong Henry VIII Stakes at Hurst Park on 5 April, defeating with considerable ease King's Bench, who had been placed ten pounds above him in the Free Handicap and who was subsequently second to the French colt Thunderhead II in the Two Thousand Guineas. At this stage of his career it was thought that Tulyar was unsuited to firm ground, and it was for that reason that the colt did not compete in the first of the classics.

Tulyar's next appearance was in the mile and three-quarters Ormonde Stakes at Chester, where the going, after several days of heavy rain, was distinctly heavy. Carrying 7 st. 9 lb., he won by half a length from the three-year-old Nikiforos, the pair finishing ten lengths ahead of the two very moderate four-year-olds who comprised the remainder of the field. Tulyar can be said to have shown his stamina in this victory, but critics pointed out quite rightly that the form in fact amounted to very little. Indeed Nikiforos, who later became a useful long-distance hurdler, never won a race that season.

A good deal more convincing was Tulyar's success in the Lingfield Derby Trial eight days later. Starting favourite at 4–1 and ridden by Smirke, he won by a comfortable two lengths and was staying on strongly at the finish. Even that performance, though, left a good many backers dubious of his true ability and early on Derby Day it was possible to support him at double the odds at which he finally started. Like many other good horses Tulyar was disinclined to pull out more than necessity demanded, and the manner of his victories was workmanlike rather than brilliant.

The going had been good when Tulyar won at Lingfield but it was undoubtedly hard at Epsom. Tulyar started favourite at 11–2, an immense volume of late money forcing his price down rapidly from initial offers of 100–8. Joint second favourites were Silnet, third to Auriban and Worden II in the Prix Hocquart, and Argur, third in the Two Thousand Guineas, while there was plenty of support as well for the Guineas winner Thunderhead II, Worden II, and Faubourg II. Lack of public confidence in the English runners was shown by the fact that of the first six horses in the betting, Tulyar alone was trained in this country.

The field got away to a good start and at the top of the hill Chavey Down, who had won the Newmarket Stakes, led from Monarch More, Caerlaverock, Bob Major, Thunderhead, and Tulyar. Approaching Tattenham Corner, however, Gordon Richards drove Monarch More into the lead, while H.V.C. began to improve and Thunderhead dropped back beaten.

Turning into the straight Monarch More still led with Bob Major, Tulyar, Chavey

Down, and H.V.C. in line abreast not more than a length behind. It was not long before Monarch More cracked and Chavey Down went to the front. With two furlongs to go, though, Chavey Down's stride began to shorten and he was headed by Tulyar, who soon had a two-lengths lead. Lester Piggott's mount Gay Time, however, had been making rapid headway from Tattenham Corner and at the distance he was second to Tulyar. A final challenge brought him to Tulyar's quarters and for a few strides he looked very dangerous, but in the last hundred yards he hung to the left as tiring horses so often do at Epsom, and with Tulyar running on valiantly, he was still three parts of a length behind when the winning post was reached. Faubourg II, who had been sixth at Tattenham Corner and who stayed on at one pace afterwards, was a length away third, and Bob Major, prominent throughout, close up fourth. Considering the fast conditions, the time was not a particularly good one.

After passing the post Gay Time slipped up, unseated Piggott, and galloped away. Piggott returned to the weighing-room without the horse, who was eventually arrested by a mounted policeman down at The Durdans and, ridden by a stable-lad, entered the unsaddling enclosure some twenty minutes after the race was over. Piggott then proceeded to weigh-in. That was not the only excitement, however, as Piggott alleged that Tulyar had leant on Gay Time in the closing stages and wanted to object, but Mrs Rank, after consulting her trainer, Noel Cannon, wisely decided to take no action.

Tulyar was led in by the Aly Khan as the Aga Khan was not well enough to be present. It was the third of Smirke's four Derby victories and Marcus Marsh's second training success in the race. In the opinion of a number of experienced riders, it was a very rough Derby indeed. Marsyad broke a fetlock after going a mile and had to be destroyed.

Tulyar went from strength to strength after the Derby. Starting at 3–1 on, he won the Eclipse Stakes at Sandown by three lengths and the following week, ridden with superb confidence by Smirke, he won the King George VI and Queen Elizabeth Stakes at Ascot very cleverly by a neck and a length and a half from Gay Time and Worden II, to both of whom he conceded two pounds. He was an odds-on favourite for the St Leger and won by three lengths from Kingsfold, despite having to be checked and switched to the outside at the distance. That race concluded his three-year-old campaign and there was general satisfaction when Marsh announced that the colt would remain in training for a further season. All the same, few people were greatly surprised when it became known in the winter that the Aga Khan had changed his mind and had sold Tulyar to the Irish National Stud for a sum rumoured to be something like a quarter of a million pounds.

In two seasons Tulyar won £76,417 10s. in stakes, thereby beating the record of

£57,455 established by Isinglass, who raced until he was five. As a three-year-old Tulyar won over distances from seven furlongs to a mile and three-quarters on going that varied from rock-hard to mud. He may seldom have been spectacular, but no opponent ever succeeded in getting to the bottom of him and there can be no doubt that he was a very great racehorse indeed. In 1955 he was sold by the Irish National Stud to an American syndicate headed by the Claiborne Farm, Kentucky. He left Ireland after the covering season of 1956, but his career as a stallion was impaired by a grave illness and at one time his life was despaired of. He recovered, without, though, making his mark as a sire. Most of his runners in England and Ireland were disappointing, but his daughter Ginetta won the French One Thousand Guineas in 1959.

Just before Goodwood, Gay Time, runner-up to Tulyar in the Derby and the King George VI and Queen Elizabeth Stakes, was bought by the National Stud for £50,000. Unfortunately he proved a bad bargain. His form deteriorated, he was found to be suffering from respiratory trouble, and it was deemed expedient to export him forthwith to Japan. Faubourg II, who won over three million francs in stakes in France, was exported to Australia in 1960, after siring some useful winners in England. Argur won the Eclipse Stakes in 1954, while Worden II, winner of the Laurel Park International as a four-year-old, has been a notable sire.

1952: Wednesday, 28 May . . . 483 Entries. £20,487.

H.H. AGA KHAN's br.c. TULYAR by Tehran
out of Neocracy · · · C. SMIRKE · · · 1
MRS J. V. RANK's b.c. GAY TIME by Rockefella
out of Daring Miss · · · L. PIGGOTT · · · 2
M. F. DUPRÉ's b.c. FAUBOURG II by Vatellor
out of Fast Lady · · · J. DOYASBÈRE · · · 3

Also ran:

Lord Rosebery's Bob Major (4th) (W. Rickaby); Mr R. S. Belasco's Bold Buccaneer (W. Snaith); M. P. Duboscq's Silnet (R. Poincelet); Mrs H. V. Cozens's H.V.C. (A. P. Taylor); Sir Bracewell Smith's Trim Curry (H. Packham); Baron de Zuylen de Nyevelt's La Varende (C. Maire); Mr R. B. Strassburger's Worden II (M. Lollierou); Mr R. W. Sharples's Chavey Down (W. H. Carr); Lord Milford's Summer Rain (D. Smith); Duke of Norfolk's Caerlaverock (F. Durr); Mr B. A. Abbott's Rego (M. Lynn); Mr C. W. Bell's Hasty Prince (E. Smith); M. M. Boussac's Argur (E. C. Elliott); M. E. Constant's Thunderhead II (E. Fordyce); Mr I. Guise's Shahcrenda (P. Evans); Major L. B. Holliday's Neath (S. Clayton); Lord

Howard de Walden's Silver Wraith (J. Sime); Lady Irwin's Serpenyoe (G. Younger);
Mr L. L. Lawrence's Ararat II (F. Palmer); Major D. McCalmont's Speechmaker
(F. Barlow); Mr E. C. R. Sheffield's Postman's Path (C. Spares); Mr H. J. Simms's
Merry Minstrel (P. Maher); Mrs R. Straker's Torcross (W. Nevett); Mr S. T.
Tate's Khor-Mousa (K. Gethin); Mr G. M. Bell's Indian Hemp (J. Marshall);
Mr. F. T. Williams's Nick la Rocca (E. Britt); Captain A. S. Wills's Monarch More
(G. Richards); Mr F. G. Robinson's Kara Tepe (E. Mercer); Mr R. S. Clark's
Fiery Torch (G. Littlewood); M. M. Boussac's Marsyad (W. Johnstone).

33 ran.

Betting:

11–2 Tulyar; 7–1 Silnet and Argur; 100–9 Thunderhead II; 100–7 Worden II;
100–6 Faubourg II; 20–1 Indian Hemp; 22–1 Torcross, Marsyad, and Postman's
Path; 25–1 Gay Time, Bob Major, and Monarch More; 33–1 La Varende and
Ararat II; 40–1 H.V.C. and Chavey Down; 50–1 Kara Tepe, Speechmaker, Summer Rain, and Khor-Mousa; 66–1 Rego; 100–1 others.

Totalizator: (2s. unit). Win: 14s. 5d. Places: 5s. 10d., 10s. 11d., 17s. 4d.

Won by three-quarters of a length; a length between second and third. 2 m. $36\frac{2}{5}$ s.
Winner trained by M. Marsh at Newmarket.

1953

The 1953 Derby was indeed a memorable one and seldom can the sympathies of those present have been so equally divided between the two horses that fought out the finish. On the one hand there was the eventual winner Pinza, partnered by Gordon Richards, who, to the great delight of all followers of racing, had just been awarded a knighthood, and whose wonderful career lacked only a victory in the greatest race of the year. On the other hand there was the runner-up Aureole, carrying the colours of the young and greatly loved Queen, who, on a day of national rejoicing, had earlier that week been crowned in Westminster Abbey.

Pinza was bred by that great trainer Mr Fred Darling, who lived just long enough to hear of Pinza's success—he died, in fact, three days later. By the French-bred Chanteur II out of Pasqua, by the Italian-bred Donatello II, Pinza was bought as a yearling by Sir Victor Sassoon for 1,500 guineas. Chanteur, by the French Derby winner Château Bouscaut, was a good tough stayer. He won seven races in France and was second in the Grand Prix; in England he won three races worth over £9,000, including the Coronation Cup, and was twice second in the Gold Cup. He was imported into England as a stallion and his many winners include Cantelo (St Leger) and Only For Life (Two Thousand Guineas).

Pasqua was out of Pasca, by Manna out of Soubriquet. She never won herself and her only winner besides Pinza was a moderate performer called Petros. In 1949 Mrs Morriss, whose husband, Mr 'Manna' Morriss, owned the Banstead Manor Stud, put Pasqua to Chanteur, who was then standing at Banstead, and being disappointed at the moderate quality of her first five foals, sent her off at the end of that year to the December Sales. Mr Darling, then in South Africa, saw her name in the catalogue, liked her blood-lines, and asked Mr Dewar to buy her for him. This Mr Dewar did for 2,000 guineas. When Mr Darling came back to England and actually saw Pasqua, he did not much care for her and in December she was back again at the Sales, where she was bought on behalf of a breeder in the Argentine for 525 guineas.

Pasca, winner of two races, bred Pasch, winner of the Two Thousand Guineas and the Eclipse Stakes, and Château Larose, second in the St Leger. Soubriquet, dam of that good but unsound horse Tai-Yang, was second in the One Thousand Guineas and the Oaks and a half-sister of the 1916 Derby and Oaks winner Fifinella.

Pinza stood over sixteen hands and was a powerful, massive bay, a trifle lacking in quality according to some of the critics. He undoubtedly had a plainish head and his forelegs were not all they might have been, but he possessed great depth, tremendously strong quarters, and a perfect hind leg. Trained at Newmarket by Norman Bertie, for many years head-lad to Darling at Beckhampton, he was still backward when he made his first racecourse appearance at Hurst Park in July. He was obviously not much fancied, but he ran with considerable promise for the future and his next outing was awaited with considerable interest. This was the Tattersall Sale Stakes run over seven furlongs at the St Leger meeting. He started at 2–1 and won in a canter by half a dozen lengths. Later that month he was a 5–2 on favourite for the one-mile Royal Lodge Stakes at Ascot, but after taking the lead three furlongs out he was beaten for speed close home by the Aga Khan's Neemah, who defeated him by a length and a half. There were only four runners and no doubt Pinza would have been seen to better advantage in a more strongly run race. Neemah was a lovely filly of great quality, but unfortunately she went wrong early the following year. Pinza completed the season and redeemed his reputation by winning the Dewhurst Stakes by five lengths after making every yard of the running. In the Free Handicap he was given 9 st. 2 lb., five pounds less than the leader, Nearula.

During the winter Pinza, always inclined to be high-spirited, got rid of his rider at exercise one morning, galloped off, and came down on a gravel path, gashing his forearm. He seemed to recover well enough but later became lame and it was found that a small piece of gravel had not been extracted. This was only a minor mishap, but it interrupted his preparation and he was not judged to be sufficiently well forward to compete in the Two Thousand Guineas, which was won convincingly by Nearula, a very good-looking colt by Nasrullah.

Pinza in fact did not run until the Newmarket Stakes in the middle of May, at which period his Derby price was 33–1. It was rumoured that he was still very backward and he looked on the big side when he was led into the paddock, ridden by a boy. He certainly did not seem fit enough to do himself full justice, and for that reason he drifted in the betting to 3–1, Polynesian being favourite at 7–4. However, fit or not, Pinza put up a very impressive performance, taking the lead three furlongs out and winning in a canter by four lengths, a margin that he could have doubled without difficulty had Richards not eased him on the hill. His Derby price contracted forthwith to 8–1.

Pinza continued to thrive and there was considerable confidence behind him on Derby Day. At 5–1 he was joint favourite with Premonition, a good-looking Precipitation colt from Boyd-Rochfort's stable. Premonition had won the Blue Riband Stakes at Epsom in fine style, but was then beaten in a falsely run race at Sandown Park. He came back to favour, though, after a smooth victory in the Great Northern

Stakes at York. Aureole, a stable companion of Premonition's, was well backed at 9–1 following a win in the Lingfield Derby Trial, but Nearula had drifted from favouritism to 10–1 on account of a minor accident that held up his preparation for a week at a critical stage. For once in a way there was no seriously fancied candidate from France. In the paddock Pinza, who had fined down considerably since Newmarket, dominated his rivals although Premonition and Nearula were both much admired. Aureole, always highly strung, played up in the preliminaries and began to sweat. The crowd, which included many Coronation visitors from overseas, was enormous, the going slightly on the firm side.

The outsider City Scandal was the first to show in front, but after a quarter of a mile the Aga Khan's Shikampur took the lead, followed by Jaffa II, Star of the Forest, Mountain King, Victory Roll, Nearula, and Pinza. Shikampur continued to set a strong gallop, and coming down the hill, he was a good four lengths clear of Victory Roll and Mountain King, with Good Brandy, Pinza, and Nearula all well in the picture.

Racing down the hill to Tattenham Corner, Richards had the good luck to find an opening on the rails and moved up second to Shikampur who still led by several lengths on the turn for home. Mountain King was third, Good Brandy fourth, Pharel fifth, and Aureole sixth. Premonition was badly placed at this point and was never seen with the ghost of a chance in the straight. Shikampur continued to battle on gallantly, but two furlongs out Pinza swept past him and soon opened up a clear lead. Aureole, who had begun to make progress with three furlongs to go, strove valiantly to get on terms, but he had too much to do and Pinza stormed home amid tremendous cheering to win unchallenged by four lengths. The French colt Pink Horse, ninth into the straight, made up a lot of ground in the closing stages to finish third with Shikampur a very tired fourth. Thus at his twenty-eighth attempt the newly knighted Gordon Richards won the Derby and the wonderful reception he was given when he rode Pinza back to the unsaddling enclosure was proof of the place he had held for so long in the hearts of the racing public. When he had weighed-in, the Queen sent for him and congratulated him on his success.

It is typical of racing that Sir Victor Sassoon, who over a long period of years had spent hundreds of thousands of pounds in endeavouring to purchase top-class horses, should attain his objective and win the Derby with a colt that cost, by his standards at any rate, such a modest sum. Before Pinza's victory, his only English classic winner had been Exhibittionist, who won the One Thousand Guineas and the Oaks in 1937. However, Sir Victor won the Derby again in 1957 with Crepello, whom he bred himself; in 1958 with the Irish-trained Hard Ridden, who cost a mere 270 guineas as a yearling; and in 1960 with St Paddy.

1953

The career of Sir Gordon Richards is too recent and too well known to require much elaboration here. Born in Shropshire in 1904, he was apprenticed to the late Mr Martin Hartigan. He rode his first winner in 1921 and progressed so rapidly that he was Champion Jockey in 1925. In 1926 a serious illness necessitated long convalescence in Switzerland, but luckily he made a complete recovery and was Champion again in 1927. From that point his career never looked back, and when he eventually retired after a bad accident at Sandown in 1954, he had been Champion Jockey on no fewer than twenty-six occasions. Altogether he rode 4,870 winners, a record unapproached by any other rider, while the 269 winners he rode in 1947 form another record. He won the Two Thousand Guineas three times, the One Thousand Guineas three times, the Derby once, the Oaks twice, and the St Leger five times.

Small, sturdy, and short in the leg, Richards was never such a polished horseman as Donoghue, and his style, a dangerous one for lesser men to copy, was unorthodox. In a close finish he seemed to ride not only rather upright, but often sideways, and with a completely loose rein, yet he managed to retain perfect control and his horses rarely became unbalanced. He was uncannily good at the start, invariably in the right place at the critical stage of the contest, and above all he possessed an overwhelming determination to win. He used the whip a good deal, but to encourage rather than chastise, and in fact he very seldom hit a horse. Success combined with adulation both from the Press and the racing public never changed his pleasant and unassuming personality: his way of life was as modest as himself, and no leading jockey has ever better represented the highest tradition of the Turf. When he gave up riding he trained with success until 1970; on his retirement he was elected an honorary member of the Jockey Club.

Pinza's next race was the King George VI and Queen Elizabeth Stakes at Ascot. Starting favourite, he won with decisive ease by three lengths from Aureole, with Worden II third. It was intended to run him in the St Leger and the Prix de l'Arc de Triomphe, but unfortunately he broke down and had to be retired to the stud. There is no doubt that he was a great horse and one of the outstanding Derby winners of this century. Unfortunately, with few exceptions, he proved a disappointing sire.

Aureole failed to stay in the St Leger and was only third to Premonition and Northern Light. He did extremely well as a four-year-old, though, winning the Coronation Cup, Hardwicke Stakes, and the King George VI and Queen Elizabeth Stakes. Like Pinza he is out of a Donatello mare. He sired the outstanding St Crespin III, and was Champion Sire in 1960 when his son St Paddy won the Derby and the St Leger, and again in 1961. Premonition was disqualified after winning the Irish Derby and the race awarded to Chamier; he was, however, a clear-cut winner of the St Leger. As a four-year-old he won the Yorkshire Cup and a sensational race for the

Winston Churchill Stakes at Hurst Park, but failed in the Gold Cup. He proved an indifferent sire. Nearula won the St James's Palace Stakes and the Champion Stakes as a three-year-old. He died suddenly when covering a mare in 1960. Prince Charlemagne, ridden by Piggott, won the Triumph Hurdle in 1954. Chatsworth won the Kempton Jubilee and sired many winners in Australia.

1953: Saturday, 6 June . . . 446 Entries. £19,118 10s.

SIR VICTOR SASSOON's b.c. PINZA by Chanteur II out of Pasca	G. RICHARDS	1
H.M. QUEEN ELIZABETH II's ch.c. AUREOLE by Hyperion out of Angelola	W. H. CARR	2
PRINCE SAID TOUSSOUN's b.c. PINK HORSE by Admiral Drake out of Khora	W. JOHNSTONE	3

Also ran:

H.H. Aga Khan's Shikampur (4th) (C. Smirke); Lord Antrim's City Scandal (A. P. Taylor); M. M. Boussac's Pharel (J. Doyasbère); Mr N. W. Purvis's Barrowby Court (T. Carter); Lady Bullough's Prince Canarina (E. C. Elliott); Mr R. S. Clark's Good Brandy (D. Smith); Mr F. W. Dennis's Durham Castle (A. Roberts); Mr F. W. Dennis's Timberland (G. Littlewood); Mr C. Wijesinghe's Jaffa II (J. Egan); Mr J. E. Ferguson's Mountain King (T. Gosling); Major L. B. Holliday's Chatsworth (S. Clayton); Mr W. Humble's Nearula (E. Britt); Mr H. S. Lester's Gala Performance (E. Mercer); Mr Ley On's Fe Shaing (S. Wragg); Mr L. Lipton's Prince Charlemagne (L. Piggott); Lord Londonderry's Scipio (J. Lindley); Mr J. McGrath's Novarullah (C. Spares); Lord Milford's Empire Honey (W. Rickaby); Mr J. Olding's Victory Roll (M. Beary); Mr J. G. Morrison's Fellermelad (A. Breasley); Mr C. H. Rodwell's Peter-So-Gay (P. Evans); Mrs G. Alderman's Windy (F. Barlow); Mr W. Preston's Star of the Forest (K. Gethin); Brigadier W. P. Wyatt's Premonition (E. Smith).

27 ran.

Betting:

5–1 Pinza and Premonition; 9–1 Aureole; 10–1 Nearula; 100–8 Good Brandy and Novarullah; 100–6 Chatsworth and Shikampur; 22–1 Pharel, Fellermelad, and Star of the Forest; 33–1 Pink Horse and Mountain King; 40–1 Empire Honey; 50–1 Prince Canarina and Victory Roll; 66–1 Prince Charlemagne; 100–1 others.

Won by four lengths; one and a half lengths between second and third. 2 m. 35⅜ s. Winner trained by N. Bertie at Newmarket.

1954

This year the Derby was a triumph for America, the winner being Never Say Die, bred and owned by a much-liked American, Mr Robert Sterling Clark, and trained at Newmarket by Joe Lawson. Never Say Die was actually conceived in Ireland, but his dam was then sent to America, where she foaled.

Never Say Die is a medium-sized, strongly made chesnut by Nasrullah, a good but temperamental horse that ran third in the Derby in 1943. An outstanding success at the stud, Nasrullah was Champion Sire in England in 1961, and five times Champion in the United States, whither he had been exported in 1950. Singing Grass, dam of Never Say Die, was by War Admiral, a great American horse that stood only fifteen hands two high, out of Boreale, by Vatout. Singing Grass raced in England and won seven minor races worth £1,875. Boreale, bred in France, won one race in America; her best winner is Blow Wind Blow, who won six races in England worth £2,196 as a two-year-old. Boreale herself is a half-sister to Galatea II, who won the One Thousand Guineas and Oaks for Mr Clark in 1939, being out of Galaday II, by Sir Gallahad III out of the Sunstar mare Sunstep, who was bred in England but exported to America as a foal.

As a two-year-old Never Say Die was no better than second class and in the Free Handicap was given 8 st. 3 lb., eighteen pounds below the top-weight, the Irish colt The Pie King. Altogether he ran six times, his sole success being in the six-furlong Rosslyn Stakes at Ascot in July. He was third in the Richmond Stakes at Goodwood, and third as well in the Dewhurst Stakes in October behind Infatuation and Let Fly, both of whom were giving him weight. Lawson always had great hopes of Never Say Die and in view of the Nasrullah blood, had been careful to bring him along by very easy stages, but he was somewhat disappointed by the colt's apparent lack of progress after winning at Ascot. As for the members of the racing public, they did not connect Never Say Die with next year's classics at all.

Never Say Die did well during the winter but was still distinctly backward when he turned out for the Union Jack Stakes at Aintree in the first week of the flat-racing season. He ran quite creditably, but was beaten by Tudor Honey, who was conceding him five pounds. This outing was thought to have brought him along nicely and he started favourite for the Free Handicap at the Craven Meeting. The distance was too sharp for him, though, and he was never really in the picture and finished out of the leading six. He did not run in the Guineas, and his only other race before the Derby was the ten-furlong Newmarket Stakes. This race was run at a very poor pace and the time was nine seconds slower than when Pinza won in a canter the year before. The short-priced favourite, Arabian Night, who had been fourth in the Two Thousand Guineas, finished unplaced and the winner was Elopement, a full brother to the 1952 Derby runner-up Gay Time. Golden God, beaten half a length, was second, with Never Say Die a head away third. The slow pace gave Never Say Die no chance to exploit his stamina. Furthermore his rider, E. Mercer, overdid his waiting tactics. He was last at the Bushes, and then made up his ground so fast that he led leaving the Dip. Unfortunately, Never Say Die got unbalanced in the process and was caught close home. It is at least conceivable that in a true-run race Never Say Die, who started at 20–1, would have won, perhaps decisively, and become one of the most fancied runners in the Derby. As it was, the racing public remained unimpressed.

The Derby was generally regarded as an extremely open race. Joint favourites were the north-country colt Rowston Manor, a son of Pearl Diver who had won the Lingfield Derby Trial; and the French colt Ferriol, by Fastnet. Darius, by Dante, the winner of the Two Thousand Guineas, was well backed at 7–1 despite doubts of his ability to stay the distance. Elopement was soundly supported and so was Valerullah, a full brother of the Oaks winner Musidora; he had beaten the One Thousand Guineas winner Festoon in a small race at Salisbury in May, but as he was receiving sixteen pounds, the value of the performance could easily be exaggerated. Never Say Die had few serious backers at 33–1, and on the same mark was the Newmarket Stakes failure Arabian Night.

The weather was cold and grey for Derby Day, the going perfect. Arabian Night and Rowston Manor, both big handsome colts, took the eye in the paddocks, little attention being paid to Never Say Die although one or two critics noted favourably both the strength of his back and loins and his apparently placid temperament.

There was no delay at the start and after a furlong Rowston Manor, running rather too freely, pulled his way to the front. The big chestnut strode out in great style and at Tattenham Corner he led from the Queen's colt Landau, Darius, Blue Sail, ridden by the famous American jockey Johnny Longden, Never Say Die, and Elopement. Three furlongs from home Rowston Manor suddenly compounded, leaving Landau at the head of the field. A great cheer went up the moment the royal colours struck the front, but Landau, by Big Game out of that wonderful mare Sun Chariot, did not stay the trip and a furlong later 'blew up' as quickly and completely as Rowston Manor had done.

Meanwhile young Lester Piggott, perfectly placed throughout, brought Never

Say Die with an admirably judged run and the issue was now between the American-bred colt and Darius. Darius fought on gamely, but he did not really stay a mile and a half and was unable to quicken in the closing stages, whereas Never Say Die lengthened his stride impressively and drew away to win by a distinctly comfortable two lengths. Arabian Night finished strongly to beat Darius by a neck for second place, while Elopement was fourth and the Nearco colt Narrator, one of the more backward members of the field, fifth. The time was the good one of 2 minutes 35¼ seconds. Unfortunately Mr Clark was ill in New York and unable to witness his colt's decisive victory. The big bookmakers had a very good race, but some of the small firms were hard hit by the many inveterate followers of Lester Piggott, re-inforced by a host of minor punters who had backed the horse because they liked its name.

Joe Lawson, one of the most respected men in the training profession, was in his seventy-fourth year when Never Say Die won. For many years he assisted the great Alec Taylor and in 1928 he succeeded him. In 1931 he established what was then a record by winning £93,900 in stakes for his patrons. He was then training at Manton, but moved to Newmarket after the war. This was his thirteenth classic success, but he had never won the Derby before. He died in 1964.

Lester Piggott was then eighteen years of age and is the youngest rider of a Derby winner this century. Racing is in his blood as his father Keith Piggott, once a shrewd trainer with a small but successful stable, was a tough and capable jumping jockey, while his grandfather, Ernest Piggott, rode two Grand National winners and married Miss Cannon, sister of Mornington and Kempton Cannon, who each rode a winner of the Derby. As regards the bottom half of his pedigree, Lester's mother was before her marriage a Miss Rickaby, and is a member of a famous racing family.

Lester Piggott rode his first winner at the age of thirteen. Precociously brilliant as a boy, he managed to survive more or less unscathed a period of rather nauseating adulation by the popular Press, but sometimes his fearlessness, coupled with sheer determination to win, degenerated into recklessness and brought him into conflict with the Stewards. A few weeks after his Derby victory he was suspended for the remainder of the season because of an incident at Ascot. He thus missed riding Never Say Die in the St Leger.

Piggott's brushes with authority never affected adversely his nerve or his confidence, nor did they diminish his great popularity with the racing public, who readily forgave his indiscretions, partly on account of his youth, but chiefly because his sins were the result of his burning determination to win whatever the cost. Not without good reason, thousands of small punters felt strongly he was essentially on their side. In recent years Piggott has learnt to temper boldness with due regard for the Rules of Racing and also for the necks of his fellow-riders. Furthermore, he places far less reliance on the whip than he used to. Tall for a jockey, he rides very short indeed, and with his behind stuck up in the air his style is easily recognizable if not unduly elegant. Unimaginative and singularly unmoved by the importance of the occasion —the Derby, except in cash value, probably means little more to him than a seller at Windsor—he was brilliant at the gate before stalls were introduced, always seems to have his mount in just the right position throughout the race, and is a very powerful finisher indeed. He is unquestionably the finest Epsom jockey of our time and has equalled Robinson's and Donoghue's record of six Derby victories, winning again on Crepello (1957), St Paddy (1960), Sir Ivor (1968), Nijinsky (1970) and Roberto (1972)

Never Say Die was none the worse for his exertions at Epsom and turned out for the King Edward VII Stakes at Ascot a fortnight later. The race proved sensational to say the least. Never Say Die and Arabian Night, first and second in the Derby, were both unplaced. The Stewards objected to the winner Rashleigh and then withdrew their objection. Piggott was suspended for the rest of the meeting and reported to the Stewards of the Jockey Club.

The Times described the race as follows:

> The King Edward VII Stakes caused the crowd to gasp twice. As the horses came round the turn into the straight, Rashleigh and Garter received bumps that nearly put them on to the floor. Never Say Die, with L. Piggott up, had been pocketed on the inside of these two. Half-way up the straight Blue Prince II and Arabian Night were racing together in front. Arabian Night crossed rather quickly from the outside position to the rails, and a moment later swerved right out towards Blue Prince again. Meanwhile, Sir Gordon Richards on Rashleigh, pursued by Tulyar's brother Tarjoman, came up on the outside to win.

In due course the Stewards of the Jockey Club informed Piggott that 'they had taken notice of his dangerous and erratic riding both this season and in previous seasons, and that in spite of continuous warnings, he continued to show complete disregard for the Rules of Racing and for the safety of other jockeys'.

A statement was then issued that before any application for a renewal of Piggott's licence could be entertained, he must be attached to some trainer other than his father for a period of six months. Many people thought at the time that the Stewards had made Piggott the scapegoat for an affair in which others were at least partially to blame, but the suspension in fact proved a blessing in the long run and a turning-point for the better in his career.

Never Say Die did not run again before the St Leger in which, ridden by that irrepressible veteran Charlie Smirke, he started favourite at 100–30. He proved beyond doubt what a great horse he was over a mile and a half or more by winning in a canter by a clear twelve lengths and treating his fifteen opponents as if they were moderate platers. Mr Clark was present to see his colt's wonderful victory and showed not a little emotion when overwhelmed with congratulations afterwards.

Mr Clark, a thorough sportsman with no interest in the betting side of racing, had been a patron of the British Turf since 1930, and following a dispute with the New York Jockey Club in 1946, he transferred all his racing interests, bar his stud, to this country. He at one time owned a stud in France, but all the buildings there were destroyed during the battle for Normandy in 1944. A brother of Mr Ambrose Clark, for many years a popular figure in hunting and steeplechasing circles in England, he died in 1956 aged seventy-nine. Earlier that year, as a token of his regard for the English Turf, he most generously presented Never Say Die, who had been retired from racing after the St Leger, to the National Stud. In appreciation of this splendid gift, he was elected an honorary member of the Jockey Club.

Never Say Die was a great horse, possessing in no small degree that rare combination of speed and stamina. The further he went the better he went and he might have been a wonderful Cup horse had he been kept in training as a four-year-old. After a good start Never Say Die has hardly fulfilled expectations as a sire. Among his winners have been Larkspur (Derby) and Never Too Late (One Thousand Guineas).

Perhaps it can be added that Mr R. S. Clark's English-trained yearlings were divided between Lawson and Harry Peacock. In 1952 Peacock won the toss for first pick. Never Say Die was outstanding in looks but Peacock declined to have him as he did not care for Nasrullah's stock.

Of the other competitors in the 1954 Derby, Arabian Night was exported to South America, while Darius won the Eclipse Stakes as a four-year-old. Elopement, now at the National Stud, won the Hardwicke Stakes as a four-year-old, and Narrator won both the Champion Stakes and the Coronation Cup. Rowston Manor never ran again after the Derby.

1954: Wednesday, 2 June . . . 400 Entries. £16,959 10s.

MR R. S. CLARK's ch.c. NEVER SAY DIE
by Nasrullah out of Singing Grass — L. PIGGOTT 1
MR J. E. FERGUSON's b.c. ARABIAN NIGHT
by Persian Gulf out of Faerie Lore — T. GOSLING 2
SIR PERCY LORAINE's b.c. DARIUS by Dante
out of Yasna — E. MERCER 3

Also ran:

Sir V. Sassoon's Elopement (4th) (C. Smirke); Major L. B. Holliday's Narrator (F. Barlow); Mr W. M. Jefford's Blue Prince II (W. Carr); Mr F. W. Dennis's Rowston Manor (D. Smith); H.M. Queen Elizabeth II's Landau (W. Snaith); Mr H. J. Joel's L'Avengro (E. Smith); Mr G. M. Bell's Blue Sail (J. Longden); Comte de Chambure's Ferriol (W. Johnstone); Mr A. L. Hawkins's Moonlight Express (J. Mercer); Mr D. de Rougement's Blue Rod (F. Durr); Mrs L. W. Smith's Kingsloe (W. Anderson); Mr T. Lilley's Court Splendour (W. Nevett); Mr C. W. Bell's Alpenhorn (M. Beary); Mrs I. Gilmore's Hylas (F. Payne); Mr J. M. Abbot's Dark Corsair (J. Marshall); Mr J. McGrath's Valerullah (K. Gethin); Captain A. M. Keith's Ruwenzori (E. Britt); Mr G. A. Tachmindji's Rokimos (J. Egan); Mr J. McGrath's Cloonroughan (W. Rickaby) (*pulled up*).

22 ran.

Betting:

5–1 Rowston Manor and Ferriol; 7–1 Darius; 9–1 Elopement; 100–9 Valerullah; 100–7 Landau; 100–6 Blue Sail; 25–1 L'Avengro; 28–1 Court Splendour; 33–1 Never Say Die, Blue Rod, Blue Prince II, and Arabian Night; 40–1 Alpenhorn; 50–1 Cloonroughan and Moonlight Express; 66–1 Narrator and Ruwenzori; 100–1 others.

Totalizator: (2s. unit). Win: 77s. 1d. Places: 19s. 3d., 23s. 5d., 7s. 6d.

Won by two lengths; a neck between second and third.   2 m. 35$\frac{4}{5}$ s.
Winner trained by J. Lawson at Newmarket.

1955

This year saw the fourth French victory since the war, the winner being Phil Drake, owned and bred by that charming and attractive lady, Mme Léon Volterra.

Phil Drake was by the Craig An Eran horse Admiral Drake, who finished last in the 1934 Derby but, ridden by Steve Donoghue, won the Grand Prix de Paris shortly afterwards. Philippa, Phil Drake's dam, was by Vatellor, sire of the Derby winners Pearl Diver and My Love, out of Philippa of Hainault, by Teddy. Bred by the late M. Volterra, Philippa was a winner herself, while her first foal Bozet won the important Prix Morny at Deauville. Her second foal, a filly by Hyperion, won a small race, and her third and final foal, as she died after a malpresentation the following year, was Phil Drake. Pride of Hainault, grand-dam of Philippa, had been bought for 450 guineas on Captain J. D. Cohn's behalf in 1929 at the Newmarket December Sales and she passed into M. Volterra's possession four years later.

Trained by F. Mathet, a former cavalry officer who had been a first-class rider himself, Phil Drake was so big and backward as a two-year-old that he never ran. He still appeared to need plenty of time when he turned out for the Prix Juigné the following April, but he ran very well nevertheless, finishing very fast and only failing by a head to catch his stable companion Datour. Thirteen days before the Derby Phil Drake won the Prix La Rochette over eleven furlongs at Longchamp; that evening the well-known jockey 'Rae' Johnstone spoke from Paris to an English owner on the telephone and told him how impressed he had been by Phil Drake's performance, adding that the colt might well prove good enough to win the Derby. The owner in question repeated this conversation to a number of friends, and in consequence Phil Drake was quietly backed on the course at Lingfield the following day at 50–1. Up till then he had been virtually unknown and unmentioned as a Derby factor.

England's chief hope for the Derby was Acropolis, bred by Lady Irwin and leased to her grandmother, Alice, Lady Derby, who was well over eighty years of age at the time. Acropolis, a beautifully made liver chesnut of outstanding quality, is a full brother of that great stayer Alycidon. As a two-year-old he had run three times, winning the Acomb Stakes at York and a seven-furlong event of little significance at Stockton. The following season he won the one-mile Classic Trial Stakes at Thirsk in April and a month later the Newmarket Stakes. At Newmarket his solitary opponent elected to run out soon after the start, but Acropolis, compelled to gallop entirely on his own, strode out magnificently and his smooth, flowing action made a great impression on all who saw him that day. As soon as it became known that he had covered the ten furlongs in 5·46 seconds less than the average time for the course and distance, he was substantially backed for the Derby. Unfortunately, though, he had jarred himself a little on the firm ground; he had to be eased in his work and when the great day arrived he was, in the opinion of George Colling, his trainer, just short of a gallop.

Other fancied competitors were the Irish colt Daemon, winner by eight lengths of the Chester Vase; Our Babu, who had followed up a brilliant two-year-old career by winning the Two Thousand Guineas; and Hafiz II, the Aga Khan's big, handsome chestnut colt by Nearco. There was quite a lot of money for Phil Drake during the week before the race and he eventually started at 100–8. Hugh Lupus, winner of the Irish Two Thousand Guineas, bruised a foot at exercise the day before the Derby and was unable to run.

The weather was fine, the going good, and the crowd for some reason considerably smaller than usual. Acropolis stood out in the paddock, with Our Babu next best in a field that was far from outstanding in point of looks. Phil Drake, tall, lanky, un-furnished, and with his hocks a shade too far away from him, gave the impression that he was still rather backward in a physical sense.

Mr Marsh got them nicely away at the first attempt and Noble Chieftain showed in front of True Cavalier, Starlit II, and Daemon. Noble Chieftain was still in front at the top of the hill, but on the descent he was headed by Cardington King. Acropolis and Our Babu were nicely placed at half-way, but soon afterwards Our Babu started to sprawl and lose ground. Phil Drake in the meantime was last but five; he was running very green and was hopelessly at sea in the gallop downhill.

At Tattenham Corner Daemon was beaten and Cardington King led from Praetorian, Noble Chieftain, Acropolis, True Cavalier, and National Anthem. Panaslipper was only tenth at this point but was clearly going very well indeed, while Phil Drake was not yet in the picture at all. Once in the straight, Eddery decided to wait no longer and shook the reins at Panaslipper, who immediately quickened and headed Cardington King with just over a quarter of a mile to go. Acropolis in the meantime was plugging on gamely enough, but failing to show a hint of acceleration, and even though Panaslipper began to tire from the distance and hang on to the right, it looked as if the 100–1 outsider from Ireland could not possibly be caught.

Once round the final bend, however, Phil Drake had really begun to get going, but three furlongs from the winning post he still had fifteen horses in front of him. He weaved his way through the field, though, like an errand boy on a bicycle steering his course through more cumbersome traffic. By the distance he had made splendid headway, mostly on the outside, but there were still five horses in front of him and despite the pace at which he was travelling, it looked long odds on his being a bit too late.

At this critical moment Palmer, in a bold split-second decision, switched him to the inside to take advantage of the slope towards the rails. Phil Drake sustained his run superbly, and collaring the weakening Panaslipper a hundred yards from the post, he finished so strongly that he won by a length and a half. Acropolis stayed on at one pace to finish third, three lengths behind the gallant Panaslipper, and Cardington King was fourth. The time, 2 minutes 39⅘ seconds, was a poor one, but Phil Drake's astonishing run in the straight had transformed what might have been rather a humdrum Derby into a really thrilling and memorable one. Panaslipper ran a fine race, too, particularly as Eddery (the father of the successful jockey Pat Eddery) seemed to make his effort a good deal sooner than was either wise or necessary.

To Mme Volterra this victory no doubt atoned for the narrow defeat of her late husband's horse Amour Drake in 1949. Fred Palmer, who rode the winner with dash and resource, is of French nationality although his father was British. He served his apprenticeship in France with Claud Halsey and has ridden many winners in cross-country racing as well. Before this year he had ridden three Grand Prix winners, and in 1956 he won the Oaks on Sicarelle and the St Leger on Cambremer. He is now training at Chantilly.

Phil Drake's victory was all the more creditable as a minor leg injury a month previously had interfered with his programme. Any lingering doubts about his merit were dispelled a month later when he won the Grand Prix de Paris, a double only previously achieved this century by Spearmint and My Love. Not surprisingly those two races took a lot out of him and he had obviously passed his peak when, as an odds-on favourite, he finished unplaced behind Vimy and Acropolis in the King George VI and Queen Elizabeth Stakes at Ascot. It proved impossible to get him ready for the Prix de l'Arc de Triomphe and he was accordingly retired to the stud. Among his offspring was Dicta Drake, second in the Derby.

Panaslipper won the Irish Derby and stood at the Irish National stud prior to export to Japan. Acropolis, beaten a head by Vimy at Ascot, won the Commonwealth Stakes at Sandown and the Great Voltigeur Stakes at York, the latter on an objection. The coughing epidemic prevented him from running in the St Leger. He won one of his three races—the John Porter Stakes at Newbury—as a four-year-old, but it was found advisable to take him out of training quite early in the season. He sired plenty of winners until his death in 1970. Our Babu went to America before ending his life in Japan, while Hafiz II won the Queen Elizabeth II Stakes and the Cham-

Tattenham Corner, 1965: Sea Bird II is lying behind the third horse

Sea Bird II in the winner's enclosure

Sir Ivor

Nijinsky

pion Stakes later in the season. As a four-year-old, he ran a wonderful race in the Cambridgeshire to finish second with 9 st. 7 lb., to a horse receiving twenty-seven pounds. He was exported to America.

1955: Wednesday, 25 May . . . 459 Entries. £18,702.

MME LÉON VOLTERRA's b.c. PHIL DRAKE		
by Admiral Drake out of Philippa	F. PALMER	1
MR J. MCGRATH's ch.c. PANASLIPPER		
by Solar Slipper out of Panastrid	J. EDDERY	2
ALICE, LADY DERBY's ch.c. ACROPOLIS		
by Donatello II out of Aurora	D. SMITH	3

Also ran:

Mr C. R. Rawlin's Cardington King (4th) (W. Nevett); Mr S. Niarchos's True Cavalier (R. Fawdon); Mr R. B. Strassburger's Bryn (W. Rickaby); Mr Godfrey Davis's National Anthem (A. Breasley); Mr C. W. Bell's Kookaburra (E. Cracknell); Mr D. Robinson's Our Babu (E. Mercer); Captain D. FitzGerald's Praetorian (K. Gethin); H.H. Aga Khan's Hafiz II (R. Poincelet); Major L. B. Holliday's Noble Chieftain (F. Barlow); Mr J. McGrath's Windsor Sun (L. Piggott); Mr L. A. Abelson's National Holiday (J. Wilson); Mr C. W. Bell's Marwari (P. Canty); Mr C. W. C. Elsey's Tippecanoe (E. Britt); Mr M. Kingsley's Starlit II (J. Mercer); Mr H. J. Joel's State Trumpeter (E. Smith); M. M. Fabiani's Point Gamma (J. Deforge); Mr B. Mavroleon's Daemon (C. Smirke); Mr G. Albertini's Solarium (W. Snaith); Mrs D. Robinson's My Smokey (T. Gosling); Mr C. R. Harper's Bicester (W. H. Carr).

23 ran.

Betting:

11–4 Acropolis; 15–2 Daemon; 8–1 Our Babu; 100–8 Hafiz II, True Cavalier, and Phil Drake; 25–1 Tippecanoe, State Trumpeter, and My Smokey; 28–1 Solarium; 33–1 Praetorian, Point Gamma, and Windsor Sun; 50–1 Bryn, National Anthem, and Kookaburra; 66–1 Noble Chieftain; 100–1 others.

Totalizator: (2s. unit). Win: 28s. Places: 8s. 3d., 110s. 1d., 4s. 9d.

Won by a length and a half; three lengths between second and third.   2 m. 39⅘ s. Winner trained by F. Mathet at Chantilly.

1956

This was a black year for English racing. French horses were first and second in the Derby, first in the St Leger, and first, second, and third in the Oaks. In addition they won the Gold Cup, Coronation Cup, and the Eclipse Stakes, while the Italian champion Ribot won the King George VI and Queen Elizabeth Stakes. To make matters more depressing still, there was a strong feeling that the Derby winner Lavandin was by no means an outstanding performer, and his victory served to emphasize the mediocrity of the English colts.

Lavandin, by no means classically bred on his dam's side, was bred by his owner, M. P. Wertheimer, and is by Verso II, a son of the Grand Prix runner-up Pinceau, out of Lavande, by the Eclipse Stakes winner Rustom Pasha, whose sire was that great stayer Son-in-Law. Verso II was a good horse and his successes included the Prix du Jockey Club, Prix Royal Oak, and the Prix de l'Arc de Triomphe. He retired to the stud in 1945 and died ten years later. Among his more notable offspring were Lavandin's brother Lavarède, runner-up in the 1951 Grand Prix; Vice Versa, third in the Oaks; and Osborne, winner of the Goodwood Stakes under 9 st. 7 lb. and the Doncaster Cup.

Lavande won three races in France, and besides Lavandin and Lavarède, she bred Le Lavandou, who won the Portland Handicap and was doing well as a sire but who unfortunately died young. Lavande was barren four seasons running from 1949 and M. Wertheimer decided to put her down, but Verso's owner, the Comte de Chambure, implored him to give her one more chance and to try her with Verso once again. The result of this mating was Lavandin.

Lavande's dam was Lividia, by the brilliant Epinard; she never won, but bred four winners. Lady Kroon, Lavande's third dam, was a half-sister to the Two Thousand Guineas winner Diolite, but she could not win a seller herself. Her sire Kroonstad was a tough old horse that ran ninety-one times and whose victories included the Ascot Derby as well as some Selling Plates. He was the sire of Querquidella, dam of that famous stayer Brown Jack.

Lavandin ran once as a two-year-old, being beaten a short head in a minor event over six furlongs at Maisons-Laffitte in November. The following April he won the nine-furlong Prix de Boulogne at Longchamp and a month later was third in the far more important Prix Hocquart of a mile and a half. He undoubtedly ought to have won that race as he was last on the final bend and was travelling far faster than the first two, Floriados and Yellowstone, at the finish. The Stewards held an inquiry afterwards and Poincelet admitted riding an ill-judged race. In consequence of this, Johnstone was engaged to ride Lavandin at Epsom, Poincelet taking the mount on Buisson Ardent. It was M. Wertheimer who was largely responsible for inducing Johnstone to leave Australia to come and ride in France in the nineteen thirties.

Lavandin's running in the Prix Hocquart resulted in his starting favourite for the Derby, which in itself was hardly a compliment to the English competitors. The most fancied English runners were Pirate King, a Prince Chevalier colt that had won the Newmarket Stakes on very firm ground; and Induna, a colt by Migoli that had won the Lingfield Derby Trial very smoothly. It was in that race that the Two Thousand Guineas winner Gilles de Retz dismayed his supporters by a singularly lifeless display. He was lame when he got home—a spasmodic partial slipping of the stifle joint was the diagnosis—but he recovered sufficiently to be able to take the field at Epsom. Mr J. McGrath's Articulate was a popular each-way selection, and there was plenty of money, too, for Lavandin's stable companion Buisson Ardent, third in the Two Thousand Guineas, and also for Mr H. J. Joel's Full Measure, a Pardal colt that had won the Wood Ditton and the Raynor Stakes. In general it was regarded as an open race and a sub-standard field. Quite apart from any question of racing ability, it was, for a Derby field, an unusually plain one. Pirate King, well muscled up and fit to run for his life, was the pick, and not far behind him was Induna. Lavandin, heavily bandaged in front because of a 'doubtful' leg, was strong and workmanlike but a shade lacking in quality, a remark that also applied to Roistar. Full Measure seemed to have run up light since winning at Newbury, while Cash and Courage looked thoroughly tucked up in the driving rain.

Conditions, in fact, could hardly have been less pleasant as the wind swept the rain across the Downs and into the stands. Induna was obviously not enjoying himself and in Smirke's words he was 'moody, unhappy, and not his real self'.

When the gate went up Idle Rocks and Induna both lost ground, and Monterey, who had won the Blue Riband Trial Stakes over the course in April, went on from Stoney Ley, Pirate King, and Pearl Orama, with Lavandin in a handy position not far from the leaders.

Approaching Tattenham Corner, Monterey was a good four lengths clear, and he swept round the final bend pursued by Pirate King, King David II, Tenareze, Roistar, Pearl Orama, Lavandin, and Induna. Soon afterwards King David II and Pearl Orama were in trouble, while Pirate King and Tenareze did not last much longer. At the distance Monterey was still in front, but he was obviously tiring, whereas Lavandin was close behind him and apparently full of running. Inside the final furlong Lavandin moved smoothly into the lead and a somewhat tame race looked as good as over.

Suddenly, however, another French colt, Montaval, appeared on the scene. He had had a rough passage coming down the hill and was only twelfth at Tattenham Corner. He made up ground rapidly in the straight, though, and finished so strongly that he was only beaten a neck. If he had not stumbled fifty yards from the post he conceivably might have got up, but it must in fairness be added that Johnstone never looked unduly perturbed on the winner. Roistar, staying on at one pace, was third, while Hornbeam and Atlas ran on stoutly in the last two furlongs to finish fourth and fifth respectively. Monterey was sixth.

M. Wertheimer, who died in 1965, had long been known in European racing circles; it was in 1923 that he won the Stewards Cup at Goodwood with Epinard. In 1935 he won the One Thousand Guineas with Mesa and in 1955 the King George VI and Queen Elizabeth Stakes with Vimy. Lavandin, Johnstone's third Derby winner, was M. Wertheimer's very first runner in that race. Alec Head, trainer of the winner, was thirty-one years old at the time. A member of a well-known Anglo-French racing family, he rode with success on the flat and over jumps until he started training in 1947. That year he rode Le Paillon into second place at Cheltenham in the Champion Hurdle. His grandfather, who was English born, trained successfully in France and his father, who served with the British forces in the First World War, still does so. Alec Head himself soon made his mark as a trainer and that shrewd judge of men and horses, the late Aga Khan, became his patron in 1951. Since then Head has never looked back and can boast of a fine record of success both in France and England.

Lavandin only ran once again and that was in the Grand Prix, in which he finished well down the course behind Vattel. In the course of that race he sustained a badly cut knee and his owner decided to retire him to the stud forthwith. He was not a success and was exported to Japan in 1963.

Of the other competitors in the Derby, Montaval won the King George VI and Queen Elizabeth Stakes at Ascot as a four-year-old. Roistar paid no compliment to the Epsom form when Talgo beat him by six lengths in the Irish Derby. Hornbeam, a hardy, courageous Hyperion colt, won eleven races and over £10,000 in stakes. In 1966 he was exported to Sweden. His son Intermezzo won the 1969 St Leger and his daughter Windmill Girl bred the 1969 and 1973 Derby winners Blakeney and Morston. Atlas won the Doncaster Cup as a three-year-old. Induna was long regarded as a persistent rogue. Eventually he was cut, and that operation, combined with the patience and forbearance of the late Noel Cannon, transformed his character. He became a very genuine and consistent performer with over a dozen victories to his credit. Pirate King was sent to Australia in 1957, returning in 1963. He sired many winners before his death in 1969. Gilles de Retz was exported to Japan in 1965.

1956

1956: Wednesday, 6 June ... 382 Entries. £17,282 10s.

M. P. WERTHEIMER's b.c. LAVANDIN by Verso II out of Lavande	W. JOHNSTONE	1
MR R. B. STRASSBURGER's b.c. MONTAVAL by Norseman out of Ballynash	F. PALMER	2
MR J. MCGRATH's br.c. ROISTAR by Arctic Star out of Roisin	J. EDDERY	3

Also ran :

Lord Astor's Hornbeam (4th) (J. Mercer); Queen Elizabeth II's Atlas (W. H. Carr); Mr C. Leigh's Monterey (W. Snaith); M. P. Duboscq's Tenareze (L. Flavien); Mr T. West's Cash and Courage (W. Rickaby); Mr S. Jacobson's Pearl Orama (A. Breasley); Major R. Macdonald-Buchanan's Induna (C. Smirke); Mr J. McGrath's Articulate (D. Smith); Mrs J. S. Barrington's Sacré Bleu (R. Fawdon); Mr E. Y. Birkett's Birso Boy (H. Sprague); Mr H. T. Clifton's Al-Mojannah (T. M. Burns); Mrs T. Hanbury's Nimrod IV (J. Doyasbère); Major L. B. Holliday's Pirate King (G. Littlewood); Mr H. J. Joel's Full Measure (E. Smith); H.H. Aga Khan's Buisson Ardent (R. Poincelet); Mrs G. Kohn's Royal Splendour (E. Cracknell); Mr A. Plesch's Stephanotis (K. Gethin); Mr D. Robinson's Idle Rocks (S. Clayton); Mr A. Rye's Thunderbolt (F. Durr); Mr A. G. Samuel's Gilles de Retz (F. Barlow); Mr J. Skeffington's Chilham (G. Lewis); Mrs A. Thelwall's Affiliation Order (L. Piggott); M. C. Victor-Thomas's King David II (J. Massard); Lady Durham's Stoney Ley (E. Mercer).

27 ran.

Betting :

7–1 Lavandin; 9–1 Pirate King and Induna; 10–1 Articulate; 100–7 Buisson Ardent and Full Measure; 18–1 Cash and Courage; 20–1 Tenareze and King David II; 22–1 Roistar; 28–1 Gilles de Retz; 33–1 Affiliation Order, Sacré Bleu, Stephanotis, and Hornbeam; 40–1 Montaval; 50–1 Idle Rocks, Atlas, Monterey, and Pearl Orama; 100–1 others.

Totalizator : (2s. unit). Win: 22s. 7d. Places: 9s. 5d., 58s. 5d., 15s. 2d.

Won by a neck; two lengths between second and third.   2 m. 36⅘ s.
Winner trained in France by A. Head.

1957

This was a vintage year for three-year-old colts. Crepello is perhaps the best horse to have won the Derby since the war, while the runner-up, Ballymoss, had a brilliant career, too, and was certainly good enough to have won the 'Blue Riband' in nine years out of ten.

Crepello was bred by his owner, Sir Victor Sassoon, and, like most modern winners of the Derby, has imported blood close up in his pedigree, his sire being the Italian-bred Donatello II, a son of the 1930 Derby winner Blenheim, while his dam Crepuscule is by Mieuxcé, winner of the Prix du Jockey Club and the Grand Prix. Donatello II was never beaten in Italy and he ought to have won the Grand Prix, in which he was narrowly and unluckily beaten by Clairvoyant. After that race Mr E. Esmond bought him for £47,000 and sent him to the Brickfields Stud at Newmarket. Donatello had some lean periods at the stud and the proportion of his living foals that in fact won races was not high, but in addition to Crepello he sired Alycidon, a great stayer and a highly successful sire; Picture Play, winner of the One Thousand Guineas; Acropolis, third in the Derby and second in the King George VI and Queen Elizabeth Stakes; and Supertello, winner, like Alycidon, of the Ascot Gold Cup. His mares have done well and include the dams of both Pinza and Aureole.

Crepuscule was a moderate racehorse herself—her solitary success was in a maiden race at Hurst Park—but her first two foals were both classic winners. Honeylight, by Honeyway, won the One Thousand Guineas; her second foal was Crepello. She also foaled the Gold Cup winner Twilight Alley. Crepuscule is out of Red Sunset, by Solario out of Dulce II, by Asterus. Red Sunset only won one minor race but has bred seven winners. Dulce II was own sister of Astrophel, a good winner himself and sire of the Grand Prix winner Bagheera; she was also half-sister to the 1939 Derby runner-up, Fox Cub, being out of Dorina, the best French two-year-old of 1923.

A big, strong, handsome chesnut standing just over sixteen hands, Crepello was full of quality and notable in particular for his great depth and for his length from hip to hock. Bred to stay two miles or more, he very soon showed that he had plenty of speed, as on his first racecourse appearance, the five-furlong Windsor Castle Stakes at Royal Ascot, despite being physically backward still, he only failed by inches to catch Fulfer, who was a good performer at the time although later he descended to Selling Plates. After that effort Crepello was put away until the autumn when, obviously needing a race, he ran a fair fourth behind Pipe of Peace in the Middle Park Stakes. A fortnight later he toyed with the opposition in the Dewhurst Stakes, his victory by three parts of a length giving no indication of overwhelming superiority. Many people who saw him that day went home satisfied that they had seen the winner of next year's Derby. In the Free Handicap he was given nine stone, seven pounds less than the brilliant filly Sarcelle, and five pounds less than Pipe of Peace, the leading colt.

It was a very dry spring and the going was firm. It had been hoped to run Crepello in the Blue Riband Trial Stakes at Epsom, but at the last moment Noel Murless decided not to risk him. The colt, however, was on view in the paddock; he gave the impression of having done extremely well physically during the winter, but his conformation, quite apart from his pedigree, suggested that he would be far better suited to the St Leger than the Two Thousand Guineas. On the Saturday before the Guineas he was galloped over a mile and afforded his trainer every satisfaction.

It was asking a lot of a big colt like Crepello to win the Guineas on hard ground and without a previous outing that spring to sharpen him up, particularly as the distance was probably shorter than he liked, but there was plenty of confidence behind him and he started favourite at 7–2. Ridden by Lester Piggott, he ran on strongly up the hill to win by half a length from the north-country grey, Quorum, who had won the Free Handicap, with Pipe of Peace a head away third. From that moment there seemed no need to look elsewhere for the winner of the Derby.

Crepello did not run again before Epsom and was a heavily backed favourite for the big race at 6–4. Second favourite was the Aga Khan's Prince Bio colt Prince Taj, who had run on strongly to finish third in the French Two Thousand, while another French colt Royaumont, also by Prince Bio, had plenty of support at 100–9. Pipe of Peace was soundly backed, despite doubts of his ability to stay the distance, while there was a fair amount of Irish money at 33–1 for the then little-known Irish colt Ballymoss from Vincent O'Brien's stable. A few days previously Ballymoss had been quoted at 100–1. At Sandown a week or two earlier there had been a strong rumour that the favourite had gone wrong and for a brief period as much as 4–1 was available before the truth, that the colt had gone exceptionally well with Piggott up that morning, became generally known.

The going was firm on Derby Day. In the paddock Crepello stood out head and shoulders above his rivals, although Ballymoss, a well-made medium-sized chesnut with the best of limbs, attracted some favourable attention. The field got off at the second attempt, London Cry, a leggy Pardal colt, losing ground but not as much as Prince Taj, who whipped round at the last moment and forfeited half a dozen lengths. Crepello, drawn No. 2, had the pace to secure a good place early on. After two furlongs he was on the rails and lying sixth, a position he retained until he delivered his challenge in the straight.

At Tattenham Corner Brioche led from Chevastrid, with Eudaemon, Palor, Ballymoss, and Crepello, the whole field being closely bunched up at this point with the exception of Chippendale and Bois de Miel. With a quarter of a mile to go Ballymoss struck the front, but in a few strides later Piggott brought Crepello into the centre of the course and made his challenge. The favourite swept past Ballymoss in majestic style, and despite being eased in the final fifty yards, he had a length and a half to spare when the winning post was reached. Ballymoss was a length clear of Pipe of Peace, who finished full of running to deprive Tempest of third place in the last two strides. Royaumont was fifth and Apostol sixth. Smirke declared afterwards that it was the slowest Derby he had ever ridden in; in fact the time was the fastest since Mahmoud established the record for the race twenty-one years previously.

Crepello's next race was to have been the King George VI and Queen Elizabeth Stakes at Ascot in July. He was listed as a probable runner on the morning of that event and thousands of people travelled to Ascot to see him perform. An hour before the race was due to start, though, the decision was taken not to run him. There had been a considerable amount of rain that week and the going, which was really by no means bad, was the excuse given for his withdrawal. Not unnaturally the crowd was bitterly disappointed and a good deal of resentment was expressed. Possibly Murless had always entertained doubts of the wisdom of running a colt whose soundness, unfortunately, did not match his outstanding racing ability. Crepello, in fact, never ran again. Early in August he broke down on his off foreleg and Sir Victor thereupon decided to send him to the stud forthwith. Among his winners have been Busted (Eclipse Stakes, King George VI and Queen Elizabeth Stakes), Caergwrle (One Thousand Guineas), Celina (Irish Oaks), Crepellana (French Oaks), Lucy-rowe (Coronation Stakes, Ebbersham Stakes) and Linden Tree (second in the Derby); he was the leading sire in 1969.

The subsequent career of Ballymoss emphasized the excellence of Crepello, who had beaten him fairly and squarely in the Derby. As a three-year-old Ballymoss went on to win the Irish Derby and the Doncaster St Leger. The following season he was the best four-year-old in Europe, his victories including the Coronation Cup, Eclipse Stakes, King George VI and Queen Elizabeth Stakes, and finally the Prix de l'Arc de Triomphe. Altogether this son of Mossborough, who was not quite a top-class horse himself, won £107,165 in stakes for his American owner. He sired the 1967 Two Thousand Guineas and Derby winner Royal Palace.

Of the other Derby competitors it is perhaps worth noting that Pipe of Peace was exported to Australia; London Cry won the Cambridgeshire as a four-year-old carrying 9 st. 5 lb.; and Albergo has proved a hurdler of much ability and remarkable toughness. Doutelle proved a high-class horse and was making a fine name for himself as a sire when he met with a fatal accident. Prince Taj did well as a sire in France before being exported to America.

Noel Murless, who has now trained three winners of the Derby, was born in Cheshire. Before the war he was attached to Frank Hartigan's stable and rode with scant success under National Hunt rules, firstly as an amateur and later as a professional. Subsequently he assisted Hubert Hartigan, at Penrith and in Ireland, and no doubt he learnt every aspect of the trainer's art from that remarkably astute Irishman. Eventually Murless set up on his own at Hambleton in Yorkshire. He soon established his reputation and, on Fred Darling's retirement, was invited to succeed him at Beckhampton. He was never really happy there, however, and a few years later moved to Newmarket. Besides his Derby successes he has won the Two Thousand Guineas twice, the One Thousand Guineas five times, the Oaks five times and the St Leger three times.

A tall, thin, rather anxious-looking man, who gives the impression of taking his responsibilities very seriously indeed, Murless has remarkable patience and nothing would induce him to hurry the preparation of his horses, to whose interests he is genuinely devoted. Extremely conscientious, he is quite prepared to make an unpopular decision if he thinks it would benefit one of his horses to do so; hence, no doubt, the unfortunate Crepello affair at Ascot.

1957: Wednesday, 5 June . . . 414 Entries. £18,659 10s.

SIR V. SASSOON's ch.c. CREPELLO by Donatello II
out of Crepuscule   L. PIGGOTT   1
MR J. MCSHAIN's ch.c. BALLYMOSS by Mossborough
out of Indian Call   T. BURNS   2
MR S. NIARCHOS's br.c. PIPE OF PEACE
by Supreme Court out of Red Briar   A. BREASLEY   3

Also ran:

Mrs E. Graham's Tempest (4th) (W. Rickaby); Mrs G. Ohrstrom's Royaumont (J. Deforge); Lord Milford's Messmate (E. Mercer); M. F. Dupré's Apostol (J. Doyasbère); Lord Astor's Albergo (J. Mercer); H.H. Aga Khan's Prince Taj (J. Massard); H.M. Queen Elizabeth II's Doutelle (W. H. Carr); Mr W. Humble's Brioche; Mr J. McGrath's Chevastrid; Mr R. A. L. Cohen's Palor; Mr T. H. Lawley's Lightehran (W. Snaith); Mr R. F. Watson's London Cry (D. Smith); Mr P. Winstone's Mystic Prince (B. Swift); Mr C. W. Bell's Alcastus (C. Smirke);

Mr F. Sykes's Hedonist (K. Gethin); Mr J. M. Abbot's Barred Rock (D. Ryan); Mr E. Foster's Eudaemon (E. Britt); M. P. Wertheimer's Chippendale (W. Johnstone); Mr P. King's Bois de Miel (E. J. Cracknell).

22 ran.

Betting:

6–4 Crepello; 10–1 Prince Taj; 100–9 Royaumont; 100–8 Pipe of Peace; 100–7 Chippendale; 100–6 Doutelle; 18–1 London Cry and Apostol; 25–1 Messmate; 28–1 Tempest; 33–1 Alcastus, Palor, and Ballymoss; 45–1 Albergo and Eudaemon; 50–1 Brioche, Lightehran, and Chevastrid; 100–1 others.

Totalizator: (2s. unit). Win: 5s. 10d. Places: 3s. 7d., 17s. 2d., 7s. 5d.

Won by a length and a half; a length between second and third. 2 m. $35\frac{2}{5}$ s. Winner trained by N. Murless at Newmarket.

1958

Ireland had its second Derby triumph this year—the first was Orby's in 1907—when Sir Victor Sassoon's Hard Ridden, trained by J. M. Rogers at the Curragh, passed the winning post five lengths ahead of another Irish colt, Paddy's Point.

The result came as a shock to many of the breeding pundits, as the great majority of Derby winners are sired by horses that have won or been placed in top-class races of a mile and a half or more. Hard Ridden, a lean, rangy bay bred in Ireland by Sir Oliver Lambart, is one of the rare exceptions to this rule—Sunstar was another—his sire being Sir Victor Sassoon's sprinter Hard Sauce, whose victories included the July Cup and the Challenge Stakes. Hard Sauce, who had a curious action in which he splayed out his forelegs, never ran beyond six furlongs nor was he tried beyond that distance. It was felt that his conformation and action were more suited to sprinting, and in any case it was feared his speed might be blunted if an attempt was made to test his potentiality as a stayer. He undoubtedly carried a certain amount of stamina in his pedigree, his sire Ardan, by Pharis, having won the Prix du Jockey Club and the Prix de l'Arc de Triomphe; in addition Ardan finished first in the Grand Prix but was disqualified.

The probability is that Hard Ridden got most of his stamina from his dam Toute Belle II, who was bred in France by the late M. Léon Volterra. Weeded out by her breeder, she was bought for 460 guineas by Lady Lambart, acting on behalf of her son, the owner of the Beau Parc Stud. Toute Belle II, who only ran once, is by the Grand Prix winner Admiral Drake out of Chatelaine, by Casterari, a horse that was second in both the Prix de l'Arc de Triomphe and the Prix du Cadran. Chatelaine was a half-sister to a tough stayer called Vatelys, who won the Prix Gladiateur and the Grande Course de Haies, besides being second in the Champion Hurdle. Chatelaine's best winner before she was exported to Canada was Le Bourgeois, a useful stayer who won long-distance races on both sides of the Channel. Toute Belle II certainly came from a stout enough line, but it was necessary, before the advent of Hard Ridden, to go back nearly a hundred and fifty years to find the last classic winner that line had produced.

Toute Belle herself proved a disappointment at Beau Parc and in 1953 she was sent to the Newmarket December Sales, but as no reasonable offer was forthcoming, she was left there to be covered by Hard Sauce. Thus was the 1958 Derby winner produced. In 1955 Toute Belle was sent to the December Sales again and was bought for 160 guineas by Colonel Sir William Rowley. The following year, in foal to Patton, she was sold for £700 to the Anglo-Irish Agency, who passed her on to a breeder in Peru.

Hard Ridden came up for sale as a yearling at Ballsbridge, Dublin, and was bought for 270 guineas by Sir Victor Sassoon, who sent him off to be trained by 'Mickey' Rogers at the Curragh. No doubt Sir Victor hazarded a bid for him because he was by his own stallion Hard Sauce. As a two-year-old Hard Ridden only ran once, finishing second. The following spring, receiving eight pounds, he was second to a very useful colt called Tharp in the Tetrarch Stakes at the Curragh. He followed up that effort by winning the Irish Two Thousand Guineas by four lengths from Sindon, who later won the Irish Derby, with Paddy's Point third. It was an impressive performance, especially as the going was heavy, but the general view was that no son of Hard Sauce could possibly win the Epsom Derby, and even when Smirke was engaged to partner Hard Ridden, he attracted little attention in the ante-post market.

The best three-year-old in England by a long way was Sir Humphrey de Trafford's Alycidon colt Alcide. He won the Chester Vase and then finished no fewer than twelve lengths ahead of his nearest opponent in the Lingfield Derby Trial. Not surprisingly he was made a warm favourite for the Derby itself, but a week before the race he met with a mishap—a strained stomach muscle it was thought—and had to be scratched. In fact he was almost certainly 'got at'. Later in the season he won the Voltigeur Stakes at York by fifteen lengths and the St Leger by eight lengths.

In Alcide's absence the French colt Wallaby II, winner of the mile and a half Prix la Rochette, became favourite. Another French colt, Noelor II, winner of the Prix Juigné and Prix Noailles, was joint second favourite with the American-bred Nasrullah colt Bald Eagle, who had won the Dante Stakes at York after disappointing in the Two Thousand Guineas. Guersillus, winner of the Newmarket Stakes, and Nagami, third in the Guineas, were both well backed, but there was little inspired money for Hard Ridden, who started at 18–1. It was not a particularly good-looking field. The favourite pleased and looked a mass of muscle, but Noelor had run up light behind the saddle. Bald Eagle and Amerigo were both sweating, while Nagami, a big Nimbus colt, hardly looked the ideal Epsom type. Hard Ridden, tall and lean, was the very opposite in conformation to his compatriot Paddy's Point, who was short-backed and compact. Boccaccio sweated up badly and wore a hood.

Usually the Derby is run at a cracking pace right from the start but on this occasion it was a very modest gallop in the early stages. As a result the field was still pretty closely bunched approaching Tattenham Corner where Guersillus led from

Amerigo, Arctic Gittell, Bald Eagle, Boccaccio, and Nagami. At this point Hard Ridden was lying tenth, but early in the straight the watchful Smirke spotted a fine wide opening on the rails. Without a second's hesitation he drove Hard Ridden through it. Accelerating in fine style, the Irish colt made rapid headway; and from then on was never in danger of being caught, passing the post five lengths clear of Paddy's Point, who finished strongly and can be said to have run an excellent race considering he lost ground at the start and did not have nearly as smooth a passage as the winner in the straight. Nagami ran on stoutly to take third place a head in front of Baroco II, but never got close enouth to Hard Ridden to make an effective challenge. Guersillus, whose rider made a lot of use of him, was fifth, and the Queen's Miner's Lamp sixth. Wallaby was never seen with a chance in the straight; he really needed a longer distance, and he was badly hampered coming down the hill.

The race was a triumph for Smirke, who, at the age of fifty-one, proved that he still retained his skill and dash, and was second to none on the big occasion. George Robinson, who rode the runner-up, flew back to Ireland that evening to ride in a small steeplechase at Naas the following day. He won the 1964 Grand National on Team Spirit. Hard Ridden was the first horse that thirty-three-year-old 'Micky' Rogers had saddled in the Derby. Rogers comes from an Anglo-Irish family that has made a great contribution to Irish racing this century. He also trained the 1964 Derby winner Santa Claus.

There has always been a tendency, possibly unjust, to regard Hard Ridden's victory as a fluke. Certainly he had two pieces of luck: the absence of Alcide and the slow pace at which the race was run, for whether he really stayed the distance is by no means certain. He did not appear to stay when unplaced behind Ballymoss in the King George VI and Queen Elizabeth Stakes the following month, but he may have trained off by then. He did not run again that year, and though it was intended to keep him in training as a four-year-old, his Ascot failure in fact was his final appearance and in 1959 he was retired to the stud. He was exported to Japan in 1967.

Paddy's Point was beaten a short head by Sindon in the Irish Derby. Nagami was third in the St Leger and won the Italian Premio del Jockey Club as a three-year-old. The following season he won the Coronation Cup and the Grand Prix du Printemps at St Cloud. Wallaby II, who ended up in Japan, won the Ascot Gold Cup the following year by inches from Alcide, whose preparation had been interrupted and who was short of a gallop. Alcide had his revenge the following month in the King George VI and Queen Elizabeth Stakes. Bald Eagle and Amerigo earned the reputation in England of being potentially brilliant but extremely 'dodgy' customers. Both were sent to America where they did remarkably well,

1958

Bald Eagle twice won the Washington International at Laurel Park and sired San San, winner of the 1972 Prix de l'Arc de Triomphe. Amerigo won good races in America and sired Fort Marcy, twice winner of the Washington International.

1958: Wednesday, 4 June . . . 471 Entries. £20,036 10s.

SIR V. SASSOON's b.c. HARD RIDDEN by Hard Sauce out of Toute Belle II	C. SMIRKE	1
MR F. N. SHANE's b.c. PADDY'S POINT by Mieuxcé out of Birthday Wood	G. W. ROBINSON	2
MRS A. PLESCH's ch.c. NAGAMI by Nimbus out of Jennifer	J. MERCER	3

Also ran:

Mr R. Simpson's Baroco II (4th) (A. Breasley); Mr P. Bull's Guersillus (E. Hide); H.M. Queen Elizabeth II's Miner's Lamp (W. Rickaby); Mr G. Bell's Alberta Blue (J. Longden); Mme Volterra's Noelor II (M. Garcia); Marquise du Vivier's Currito (R. Poincelet); Lord Howard de Walden's Amerigo (E. Smith); Mr R. B. Strassburger's Mahu (G. Thiboeuf); Mr H. F. Guggenheim's Bald Eagle (W. H. Carr); Mr M. Kingsley's Arctic Gittell (D. Ryan); Baron G. de Waldner's Wallaby II (F. Palmer); Sir G. Tennyson d'Eyncourt's Elisha (E. Mercer); Major L. B. Holliday's Trimmer (S. Clayton); Mr G. Bell's Alberta Pride (W. Swinburn); Sir V. Sassoon's Boccaccio (L. Piggott); Mr L. A. Hordern's Crystal Bay (J. Lindley); Mr S. Mercer's Midlander (A. Rawlinson).

20 ran.

Betting:

4–1 Wallaby II; 7–1 Noelor II and Bald Eagle; 9–1 Guersillus; 10–1 Nagami; 100–7 Amerigo; 100–6 Miner's Lamp; 18–1 Alberta Blue and Hard Ridden; 20–1 Boccaccio; 33–1 Currito and Mahu; 40–1 Baroco II; 50–1 Arctic Gittell; 100–1 others.

Totalizator: (4s. unit). Win: 50s. 10d. Places: 16s. 10d., 80s. 10d., 12s.

Won by five lengths; a length and a half between second and third.   2 m. 41⅕ s. Winner trained by J. Rogers in Ireland.

1959

Sir Humphrey de Trafford had atrocious luck in 1958 when his colt Alcide, without question the best three-year-old stayer in the country, met with a mishap a week before the Derby and was unable to run. The Fates seldom relent in racing, but on this occasion they do and the very next year Sir Humphrey achieved one of his life's ambitions and won the Derby with Parthia.

Bred by his owner, Parthia was by Persian Gulf, out of Lightning, by Hyperion. A representative of the Blandford male line, Persian Gulf was a half-brother to the Gold Cup winner Precipitation by Bahram. He was in training during the war and his only success of note was in the substitute Coronation Cup. His best winners before Parthia were Zabara (One Thousand Guineas) and Zarathustra (Irish Derby and Gold Cup).

Lightning won the Sandwich Stakes at Ascot as a two-year-old and was out of Alcide's dam Chenille, by King Salmon. Chenille, who never ran, was bought at the December Sales in 1948 by Marcus Marsh, acting for Sir Humphrey de Trafford, who had asked him to buy a suitable mare as he had a nomination to Hyperion. Chenille was in foal to Borealis when Marsh bought her, the produce being Papillio, winner of the Goodwood Stakes. Grand-dam of Chenille was the Gold Cup winner Foxlaw's half-sister Aloe, from whom are descended Aureole (King George VI and Queen Elizabeth Stakes and sire of St Paddy); Hypericum (One Thousand Guineas); Above Board (Cesarewitch and dam of Doutelle and Above Suspicion); and Round Table, who was named as 'Horse of the Year' in the United States in 1958.

Parthia, a handsome rangy bay, was backward his first season and his trainer, Captain Cecil Boyd-Rochfort, gave him plenty of time as a two-year-old. He did not see a racecourse until October when he was sixth of nine behind High Perch in the one-mile Gainsborough Stakes at Hurst Park. At the Houghton Meeting shortly afterwards he ran very much better and made an extremely good impression when third in the Dewhurst Stakes.

The following season Parthia reappeared in April and won the ten-furlong White Rose Stakes at Hurst Park very smoothly. Moreover the form worked out well as My Aladdin, third, went on to win the Blue Riband Trial Stakes, while Fidalgo, fifth, won the Chester Vase by six lengths. Parthia missed the Two Thousand Guineas, for which it was thought he did not possess sufficient pace, and his next

outing was the Dee Stakes at Chester. He won, but it was not a convincing performance and it was only very close home that he got into top gear to overhaul the leader
on the post. One well-known racing correspondent saw fit to assert afterwards:
'Parthia is no more an authentic Derby colt than I am a clergyman.'

Parthia's last race before Epsom was the Derby Trial at Lingfield. Again he made
heavy weather of his task and it was by only three parts of a length that he defeated
the moderate Casque. A good many of his supporters deserted him after this effort,
and there was a feeling that the Newmarket touts who, because of the sluggish way
Parthia worked at home, rarely had anything good to say of him, might perhaps be
right after all. It was noticeable, though, that Harry Carr appeared supremely
confident throughout the race and he was inclined to ascribe the unconvincing manner of Parthia's victory to sheer indolence. For a time afterwards, Parthia wore
blinkers when he worked at home and it was believed he might wear them at
Epsom, but eventually it was decided there was no necessity for such a step.

Favourite for the richest Derby yet run was the French colt Shantung, by Sicambre
out of a mare by Hyperion. He had proved his ability to stay the distance when he
won the Prix La Rochette, but his position in the market—he was backed down from
8–1 shortly before the 'off'—was largely due to reports of a brilliant gallop he was
alleged to have done. Princillon, second to the outstanding French three-year-old
Herbager in the Prix Hocquart, was second favourite at 7–1, and well-backed at tens
were Parthia; the French Two Thousand Guineas winner Thymus; Fidalgo;
Tulyar's half-brother St Crespin III, who was rumoured to be short of his best after
intestinal trouble; and the somewhat unpredictable Dante colt Carnoustie, who had
been third to Taboun in the Two Thousand Guineas. Parthia, handsome, deep-
bodied, and powerful, was generally admired in the paddock and so was Shantung,
a nice-quality colt of medium size. On the other hand St Crespin had run up light,
and neither the bandaged Thymus nor the rugged Princillon quite looked the part
of a prospective Derby winner. Perhaps the best-looking competitor was the Queen's
Court Martial colt Above Suspicion.

In the early stages of the race an incident occurred that had significant bearing
on the final result. Princillon, after two furlongs, jumped a track that crossed the
course and in so doing slipped down on his knees. Shantung, who was tracking him,
collided with such force that Palmer thought the favourite might have broken a leg.
Accordingly he eased him back last preparatory to pulling him up. In fact he found
Shantung was uninjured and permitted him to race on again, but he was by then
tailed off and in an apparently hopeless position. Coming down the hill he was still
tailed off, and at Tattenham Corner he was a good four lengths behind the last horse
but one.

On the turn for home the very moderate Rousseau's Dream led from Lindrick, Josephus, Arvak, Fidalgo, Parthia, and St Crespin. Josephus, Lindrick, and Arvak were beaten almost immediately, and Rousseau's Dream was in trouble soon afterwards. With just under three furlongs to go Joe Mercer dashed Fidalgo to the front and in very quick time he was just about two lengths clear. Carr, however, at once sent Parthia in pursuit and, running on with the utmost determination, Parthia mastered Fidalgo inside the final furlong and stayed on stoutly to win by a length and a half.

Only Parthia and Fidalgo were really concerned with the finish, but meanwhile a desperate battle was in progress for third place. Once in the straight Shantung had begun a tremendous run, and passing horse after horse he made up at least twenty lengths to rob St Crespin of third place in the last two strides. It was a wonderful effort, and not surprisingly the favourite's backers reckoned they were desperately unlucky to have lost their money. St Crespin, who ran extremely well considering he was a bit below par, was a length and a half in front of Parthia's stable companion Above Suspicion, who had had a very bad run down the hill, but had then made up ground at a great rate in the straight; a bit too quickly, possibly, as he failed to maintain the headway in the final furlong. It is interesting to note that Parthia, who still had a bit in hand at the finish, was over thirty lengths in front of Casque, whom he had beaten by under a length at Lingfield.

It was an exceptionally popular victory and everyone seemed delighted to see Sir Humphrey win after his ill-luck, philosophically borne, with Alcide the year before. Sir Humphrey originally joined the Royal Navy, but life at sea did not suit him and he sensibly transferred to the Coldstream Guards, with which regiment he went to France in August 1914, being later awarded the Military Cross. He was closely connected with racing for nearly fifty years, firstly as a rider under National Hunt Rules, and later as owner, breeder, and administrator. A participator at one time or another in nearly every branch of sport, Sir Humphrey was one of the best-liked men in racing and thoroughly deserved his success. He died aged seventy-nine in 1971.

It was a first Derby victory for Harry Carr, who was born in Cumberland and was apprenticed to R. W. Armstrong, whom his father served as head-lad. Carr had ridden his first winner nearly thirty years previously at the age of thirteen, and for many years past he had enjoyed a reputation for soundness, reliability, and common sense as well as for loyalty to those who employed him. He had enjoyed a long and mutually fruitful association with Captain Boyd-Rochfort's stable—among his most notable successes being the classic victories of Alcide and Meld. He is the father-in-law of Joe Mercer, who partnered the Derby runner-up, Fidalgo.

In modern racing there have been few more easily recognized figures than Captain Cecil Boyd-Rochfort, tall, erect, dignified, impeccably dressed, and looking a good deal younger than his age, which was in fact over seventy when Parthia won. An Irishman by birth, he served in the Scots Guards in the First World War and was a leading trainer with an amazingly consistent record of success from the nineteen twenties. Envious rivals were inclined to say that he never had to establish himself 'the hard way', but always had the luck to train top-class horses for patrons who paid their bills regularly and could afford to be patient. It is, of course, an advantage to be patronized by rich Americans, but the fact is that no man gets sent top-class horses year after year unless he has proved himself beyond question a top-class trainer. Boyd-Rochfort was not only unsurpassed in training stayers, but he also had a formidable record of success in important handicaps. This was his one Derby victory among thirteen classic successes. He succeeded the late W. R. Jarvis as trainer to King George VI, and continued to train the royal horses on the accession of the Queen. He was knighted before his retirement in 1968, when his stable was taken over by his stepson Henry Cecil, who is married to Noel Murless's daughter.

To revert to Parthia, his preparation for the St Leger was interrupted by coughing. He had to miss the Voltigeur Stakes at York in consequence, and when he took the field at Doncaster, he had not been out since Epsom. This was a grave disadvantage to such a lazy worker at home; he failed to give his true running and was unplaced behind Cantelo, Fidalgo, and Pindari. In the closing stages he was barged into by Pindari and sustained a nasty cut that prevented him from running in the Champion Stakes as had been intended.

Unlike so many modern owners, who like to bundle a classic winner off to the stud before there is any possible chance of the laurels becoming a bit faded, Sir Humphrey decided to keep Parthia in training as a four-year-old. Unfortunately, his bold policy failed to meet with the reward that it deserved. Parthia started off well enough by winning the mile and a half Jockey Club Cup at Newmarket at the end of April and he then won the Paradise Stakes at Hurst Park. A failure to cope with the brilliant grey filly Petite Etoile in the Coronation Cup was readily forgiven, but far more disappointing was his failure to concede six pounds to Aggressor in the Hardwicke Stakes. In the King George VI and Queen Elizabeth Stakes he fared even worse and finished out of the leading six behind Aggressor, Petite Etoile, and Kythnos. On this occasion he gave the impression of having lost all his zest for racing and it was wisely decided to retire him. There is no doubt, unfortunately, that his reputation had suffered a considerable depreciation. At his best, though, there is no reason to think that he was not up to the average standard of Derby winners over the past thirty years. Before being exported in 1968 to Japan where he died, Parthia sired the Oaks winner Sleeping Partner and Parthian Glance, winner of the Yorkshire Oaks and the Park Hill Stakes.

Fidalgo won the Irish Derby in a trot, disappointed in the Eclipse Stakes, where he was probably stale, but ran a good race to finish second in the St Leger. He was exported to Japan in 1966. Shantung ran Herbager to a head in the Grand Prix de Saint Cloud, but went wrong afterwards and never ran again. He sired Full Dress II (One Thousand Guineas) and Ginevra (Oaks). St Crespin subsequently showed what a good horse he was by winning the Eclipse Stakes and the Prix de l'Arc de Triomphe. Unfortunately he had trouble with a joint and could not race as a four-year-old. He sired Altesse Royale (One Thousand Guineas, Oaks, Irish Oaks) before being sent to Japan in 1970. Above Suspicion won the St James's Palace Stakes at Ascot and the Gordon Stakes at Goodwood, but his career as a four-year-old brought nothing but disappointment. Dan Cupid, beaten a neck by Herbager in the Prix du Jockey Club, sired a great Derby winner in Sea Bird II.

The conditions for the Derby this year were £200 each, £100 if declared by 26 May 1959; £10 if declared by 1 July 1958, with £10,000 added (including a gold trophy, value £500). The prize to the winner, therefore, was over £36,000, which brought the race into line financially with leading events in France. The runner-up received £4,268, the third £2,134.

1959: Wednesday, 3 June . . . 442 Entries. £36,078.

SIR H. DE TRAFFORD's b.c. PARTHIA by Persian Gulf
out of Lightning — W. H. CARR — 1
MR G. A. OLDHAM's b.c. FIDALGO by Arctic Star
out of Miss France — J. MERCER — 2
BARON G. DE ROTHSCHILD's b.c. SHANTUNG by Sicambre
out of Barleycorn — F. PALMER — 3

Also ran:

Prince Aly Khan's St Crespin III (4th) (A. Breasley); H.M. Queen Elizabeth II's Above Suspicion (D. Smith); Lt.-Col. G. Loder's Carnoustie (L. Piggott); Mr A. M. Bird's Amourrou (E. Mercer); Prince Aly Khan's Princillon (G. Moore); M. F. Dupré's Regent II (M. Garcia); Mme P. Widener's Dan Cupid (R. Poincelet); Mr J. Lewis's Rousseau's Dream (G. Lewis); Mrs A. Plesch's Thymus (C. Smirke); Mrs J. Paul's Arvak (J. Lindley); Mr A. K. Kirk's Beau Tudor (S. Smith); Mr F. H. Bowcher's Josephus (W. Rickaby); Mr J. Kennedy's New Brig (R. Fawdon); Mr F. Ellison's Reactor (G. Littlewood); Miss B. C. Bentinck's Barbary Pirate

(E. Hide); Mr H. G. Blagrave's Casque (E. J. Cracknell); Mr A. Dormer's Lindrick (S. Clayton).

20 ran.

Betting:

11–2 Shantung; 7–1 Princillon; 10–1 Parthia, Thymus, Fidalgo, St Crespin III, and Carnoustie; 100–6 Above Suspicion; 18–1 Dan Cupid; 20–1 Regent II: 25–1 Amourrou; 28–1 New Brig; 33–1 Reactor and Casque; 40–1 Arvak and Josephus; 66–1 Lindrick; 100–1 others.

Totalizator: (4s. unit). Win: 28s. 4d. Places: 11s., 12s. 2d., 10s. 2d.

Won by a length and a half; the same between second and third.   2 m. 36 s. Winner trained by Captain C. Boyd-Rochfort at Newmarket.

1960

In 1960 Sir Victor Sassoon, who died the following year, won his fourth Derby in eight years with St Paddy, whom he had bred himself and who, like Crepello, was trained by Noel Murless and ridden by Lester Piggott.

In the dark days of the war Colonel Giles Loder sold a seven-year-old uncovered mare called Caerlissa for fifty-five guineas to Mr Hubert Hartigan, who was acting on behalf of his patron, Mr J. McLean. By the Eclipse winner Caerleon out of Sister Sarah, by Abbots Trace, she traced back, through Molly Desmond, to Pretty Polly. She never won herself but was half-sister to eight winners, including Lady Sybil, the leading two-year-old in 1942; Black Peter, winner of the Jockey Club Stakes; and the brilliant sprinter Welsh Abbot, who won the 1958 Portland Handicap for Sir Winston Churchill under 9 st. 2 lb. as a three-year-old.

Caerlissa proved a wonderful bargain as she bred eight winners, the most distinguished of which was The Web, who was a leading two-year-old in Ireland and subsequently won races in the United States. One of Caerlissa's daughters was Edie Kelly, by the 1938 Derby winner Bois Roussel. She was of no great account on the racecourse and her sole victory in fourteen outings was in an apprentice plate at The Curragh. In 1953 she came up for sale and was bought for 1,750 guineas by Mrs Hubert Hartigan, who re-sold her after her husband's death in 1955 to Sir Victor Sassoon for 3,500 guineas. She has bred six other winners, including Parmelia who won the Ribblesdale Stakes.

St Paddy ran twice as a two-year-old. He was made favourite for the Acomb Stakes at York in August, but was still backward and finished unplaced. The following month he was very much straighter in condition when he turned out for the one-mile Royal Lodge Stakes at Ascot. He outclassed the opposition to win with the greatest possible ease by five lengths. Admittedly his rivals were not of great account, but the manner of his victory convinced a good many people that they had seen the winner of next year's Derby.

St Paddy's first outing as a three-year-old was the Two Thousand Guineas. His real objective, however, was the Derby, and though he looked well in the paddock, it was clear that Murless still had plenty left to work on. He ran quite well until the fact that he was not one hundred per cent ready began to tell on him; he started to hang badly coming down the hill and he weakened perceptibly in the final furlong.

Taking everything into account, it was quite a satisfactory performance, although a majority of critics expressed a certain disappointment. His only other race before the Derby was the ten-furlong Dante Stakes at York. This he won with great ease from opposition that was not unduly formidable.

Favourite for the Derby was the French colt Angers, by Worden II. He had proved the best of his age in France the previous season, and in May he had been an impressive winner of the mile and a half Prix Hocquart. It was not in his favour, though, that he was inclined to pull very hard and to hang to the left; in an attempt to correct this latter fault, he was equipped with a 'pricker'. Second favourite was the Irish colt Die Hard, by Never Say Die, the winner of all his three previous races, while strongly supported at sevens were Kythnos, winner of the Irish Two Thousand; Tulyartos, an Irish colt that had been fourth in the English Two Thousand; and St Paddy. Other fancied competitors were Marengo, who was alleged to have accomplished a most impressive final gallop, and yet another Irish colt, Alcaeus. A late May foal, Alcaeus was just beginning to come to hand and had won the Dee Stakes at Chester very smoothly. It was not a particularly good-looking field and the pick in that respect were the big workmanlike Angers and St Paddy, a powerful, well-proportioned bay. There was a lot to like about Kythnos, but his joints suggested he might not care for the going, which was firm, or for the downhill gallop to Tattenham Corner.

The race proved a tragedy as far as Angers was concerned. He had cantered crabwise down to the post with his head twisted round, as if anxious to inspect his rider's left boot. From the 'off' he was never going well and was in the rear division when six furlongs out he broke a fetlock and had to be destroyed. Owing to the buses and cars on the Downs, this mishap to the favourite was more or less hidden from the stands and not one spectator in a hundred knew what had happened as the field swung round Tattenham Corner. Much sympathy was felt for Angers's eighty-year-old owner, who was watching the race from a box. However, she accepted this grievous misfortune in the same philosophical manner as she accepted the head defeat of her filly Paimpont in the Oaks two days later.

In some respects this was certainly an ill-fated Derby; the Irish colt Exchange Student broke a leg at exercise on the Downs, while Sir Winston Churchill's much-fancied Vienna was pricked by the blacksmith while being plated and was unable to run. On home form he was better than his stable companion Auroy, who finished fourth.

Coming to Tattenham Corner, Die Hard and Tudor Period were the leaders, with Auroy, Tulyartos, St Paddy, and Kythnos all handily placed. Tudor Period was soon beaten and Die Hard went on with Auroy in hot pursuit, with both St Paddy and Kythnos looking dangerous. With two and a half furlongs to go Die Hard was in trouble and was headed by Auroy, but no sooner had Auroy struck the front than St Paddy swooped on him and, lengthening his stride in great style, ran on to win by an easy three lengths from the fast-finishing Alcaeus, with Kythnos half a length away third. St Paddy had been beautifully placed throughout, and as soon as Piggott asked him for his effort, the race was virtually over. Seldom indeed does a Derby winner gallop past the post with so much in hand.

Alcaeus did not have nearly as good a run as the winner and had a lot to do from the final bend, but he battled on like a true stayer in the last two furlongs to secure second place close home. Kythnos, as expected, loathed the downhill gallop, but he rallied bravely in the straight and was there with every chance two furlongs from the finish. From that point, however, he could find no more but just kept going at one pace. Auroy was fourth, Proud Chieftain, who made good late headway, fifth, and Die Hard sixth. The victory was a popular one, not least among the thousands of faithful followers of Lester Piggott, who rode a supremely confident and skilful race. As a Derby field it was probably a poor one, and though St Paddy, according to his trainer, was not in the same high category as Crepello, he could scarcely have asserted his superiority in more convincing fashion.

St Paddy was let down after the Derby and did not appear again until Goodwood, where he competed in the Gordon Stakes, run over a distance just short of a mile and a half. Judging from the way he blew when it was all over, he was a long way short of his best, and after taking the lead two furlongs from home, he was worried out of his advantage by Lord Sefton's Kipling, who was receiving five pounds, and beat him by half a length.

It was disappointing to see the Derby winner beaten like this, but it was felt with some confidence that he would be a very different horse at Doncaster. At York he won the Voltigeur Stakes from a useful Blue Peter colt, Apostle, and, fit to run for his life on St Leger day, he won the final classic on the bit by three lengths from Die Hard and Vienna, thereby proving beyond doubt that he was head and shoulders above his admittedly mediocre contemporaries. Being by the high-mettled Aureole out of a mare by Bois Roussel, many of whose descendants proved a bit 'funny', St Paddy always needed very careful handling, and it says much for Murless's patience and skill that he produced St Paddy at the peak of condition on the two days that really mattered.

A hard race in the Derby took the edge off Alcaeus and in the Irish Derby he was beaten amid remarkable scenes of excitement and jubilation by Chamour. The cause of this extraordinary exhibition was that earlier in the season Chamour was found to have been 'doped' after winning a minor event at The Curragh, and Chamour's trainer, Vincent O'Brien, the idol of the Irish racing crowd, had to forfeit his licence temporarily, although there was not the slightest implication that he was personally responsible for what had occurred. Kythnos was sore after the Derby, but was fit to run in the King George VI and Queen Elizabeth Stakes at Ascot, in which he finished third to Aggressor and Petite Etoile. Tulyartos was second, beaten half a length, to Javelot in the Eclipse Stakes.

St Paddy began his four-year-old career by winning the Coombe Stakes at Sandown, the Hardwicke Stakes at Ascot, and the Eclipse Stakes. So masterful were his victories that he was generally regarded as a great racehorse and his meeting in the King George VI and Queen Elizabeth Stakes with the leading French three-year-old, Right Royal V, who, like St Paddy, was a grandson of Hyperion, aroused the liveliest interest.

What was expected to prove the race of the year in fact turned out a bitter disappointment. St Paddy, who appeared in somewhat irritable mood in the paddock, was not only beaten, but put up singularly little resistance when Right Royal tackled him in the straight. Rested until the autumn he won the Jockey Club Stakes, in which his task was simplified by the unintelligent riding tactics adopted on his chief rival, High Hat. A fortnight later he started an odds-on favourite for the final race of his career, the ten-furlong Champion Stakes, but was fairly and squarely beaten by a supposedly not quite top-class French three-year-old, Bobar II. These two defeats, coupled with the one inflicted by Kipling the year before, inevitably caused the comment that St Paddy never won a race in which he really had to fight hard for victory. In all he won over £97,000 in stakes, a total only second to that achieved by Ballymoss. He has sired Connaught (Eclipse Stakes, King Edward VII Stakes and second in the Derby), St Chad (Wills Mile), Sucaryl (News of the World Stakes) and St Pauls Girl (second in the One Thousand Guineas and the Oaks).

1960: Wednesday, 1 June . . . 444 Entries. £33,052.

SIR V. SASSOON's b.c. ST PADDY by Aureole
out of Edie Kelly   L. PIGGOTT   I
SIR R. BROOKE's ch.c. ALCAEUS by Court Martial
out of Martcline   A. BREASLEY   2
MR E. R. MORE O'FERRALL's b.c. KYTHNOS by Nearula
out of Capital Issue   R. HUTCHINSON   3

Also ran:
Mr A. Kennedy's Auroy (4th) (G. Lewis); Major L. B. Holliday's Proud Chieftain (S. Clayton); Mr J. McShain's Die Hard (G. Bougoure); Mr J. McGrath's Tulyartos (W. Williamson); Major H. P. Holt's Marengo (R. Fawdon); Duke of

Norfolk's Tudor Period (W. Rickaby); Mr E. W. Beechey's Oak Ridge (E. Hide); Mr G. M. Bell's Lustrous Hope (G. Moore); Mr M. P. Davis's Ides of March (E. Eldin); Sir A. Jarvis's Chrysler III (J. Mercer); Mr P. Winstone's Mr Higgins (D. Smith); Mr B. Gilmore's Port St Anne (S. Millbanks); Mr R. Shaw's Picture Goer (W. Elliot); Mme R. B. Strassburger's Angers (G. Thiboeuf) (*broke fetlock; destroyed*).

17 ran.

Betting:

2–1 Angers; 9–2 Die Hard; 7–1 St Paddy, Tulyartos, and Kythnos; 9–1 Marengo; 10–1 Alcaeus; 28–1 Lustrous Hope; 33–1 Auroy; 45–1 Chrysler III; 50–1 Ides of March and Mr Higgins; 66–1 Oak Ridge, Proud Chieftain, and Tudor Period; 200–1 others.

Totalizator: (4s. unit). Win: 30s. Places: 10s. 10d., 15s., 15s. 8d.

Won by three lengths; half a length between second and third.   2 m. $35\frac{3}{5}$ s.
Winner trained by N. Murless at Newmarket.

1961

The 1961 Derby, which produced the most surprising result since Airborne won in 1946, was a remarkable example of the international character of modern racing. Psidium, the 66–1 winner, was bred in Ireland by his owner Mrs Arpad Plesch, the wife of a Hungarian financier. Ridden by the French jockey Roger Poincelet and trained at Newmarket by Harry Wragg, Psidium is by the French-bred sire Pardal out of the Italian-bred mare Dinarella.

The two-year-old colts in 1960 had been rather a humdrum collection, markedly inferior to the fillies. The only one that had looked a possible Derby winner was Sir Adrian Jarvis's Test Case, who had won the Gimcrack Stakes, but unfortunately Test Case failed to train on. All through the winter, though, there were rumours that Noel Murless trained an outstanding colt called Pinturischio for Sir Victor Sassoon. Pinturischio, better-looking than most of Pinza's stock but with rather rough joints, had his first outing in the one-mile Wood Ditton Stakes at the Craven Meeting. He won in a canter from Nicomedus and Sagacity, but as the race was confined to horses that had never run before, it was impossible to assess the precise merit of the form.

Noel Murless, however, made no secret of the fact that Pinturischio was far superior to his other three-year-olds, which included Aurelius, subsequent winner of the St Leger, and Pinturischio started a 7–4 favourite for the Two Thousand Guineas. When Pinturischio struck the front just over a furlong out he looked all over a winner, but he was then challenged by the 66–1 outsider from Scotland, Rockavon, and Piggott was compelled to ride him in earnest. At this point the favourite's lack of experience began to tell; he became unbalanced, was quite unable to quicken up the hill, and eventually finished fourth, two lengths and two short heads behind Rockavon, Prince Tudor, and the Irish colt Time Greine. He himself was only inches in front of Bally Vimy and L'Epinay.

Rockavon presented no problem for the Derby as he was not engaged in the race, while Prince Tudor's breeding made it highly improbable that he would stay a mile and a half. Time Greine, who was putting in some good work near the finish, obviously came into the reckoning, but did not appear to hold very much scope for improvement. It was disappointing that Pinturischio had failed to reach the leading three, but his defeat could be partially attributed to lack of racecourse experience. He had certainly run at least as well as St Paddy had done in the corresponding event the year before and it was generally recognized that Noel Murless was timing his preparation for Epsom.

Pinturischio continued to thrive and was a firm favourite in the ante-post market for the Derby. It was planned to run him at York on 16 May in the Dante Stakes, the race that St Paddy had won the year before. On 15 May some miscreants succeeded in 'getting at' Pinturischio. He rallied quickly but was then 'got at' again. Not only could he not run in the Derby; his racing career was finished for good. Certain people made a lot of money from this incident, as Pinturischio was the one horse that had been strongly supported in the ante-post market. It was strongly rumoured that an individual very well-known in the betting world was the organizer of the crime.

The weather for most of May was cool and dry and the going on Derby Day was distinctly firm. Favourite at 5–1 was the French colt Moutiers, belonging to Mme Strassburger who had owned Angers, the ill-fated Derby favourite of 1960. A half-brother by Sicambre to the 1956 Derby runner-up Montaval, Moutiers had won the mile and a half Prix Hocquart at Longchamp quite impressively. Second favourite was Pardao, trained by Captain Boyd-Rochfort. A rather long-backed chesnut by Pardal, Pardao was known to like firm ground and had won the Lingfield Derby Trial very smoothly. Just Great, a tall long-striding colt by Worden II, was a popular each-way choice; he had not only won the Brighton Derby Trial, but was reputed to have been very well galloped with Apostle, a four-year-old that had recently won the Jockey Club Cup. There was good support, too, for Time Greine, who had not had a race since the Two Thousand Guineas, Dicta Drake, and Sovrango. Dicta Drake, by Phil Drake, was, like his sire, a late developer but was just coming nicely to hand and had recently won in France in attractive style. Sovrango, closely related to the dual classic winner Musidora, had won the Chester Vase very easily, but that success was achieved when the ground was soft. Tall and rather straight in front, he hardly looked the ideal type for the course; furthermore, he was known to dislike firm ground and in recent work at home was reported to have moved less well than his stable companion Psidium.

Psidium, an attractive, well-made half-brother to Thymus, winner of the French Two Thousand Guineas, had some fair form as a two-year-old. He ran seven times, winning the six-furlong Duke of Edinburgh Stakes (run at Kempton as the Ascot stand was being rebuilt) and finishing second in two seven-furlong events, the Horris Hill Stakes at Newbury and the Dewhurst Stakes at Newmarket. In the Dewhurst Stakes he was beaten less than a length by Bounteous, who was receiving four pounds and who finished second in the St Leger the following year. In the Free Handicap Psidium was given 8 st. 4 lb., seventeen pounds less than the French filly Opaline II.

He began his three-year-old career by finishing third in the Two Thousand Guineas Trial at Kempton to Dual and Good Old Days. Considering that the distance was too short for him, that he was last of the nine runners with just over two furlongs to go and had obviously been left with far too much to do, his performance was by no means unsatisfactory. He next ran in the Two Thousand Guineas in which, ridden by W. Snaith, he started at 50–1 and was never seen with a chance. His form could hardly have been less inspiring and it is difficult to find a photograph of the finish that extends sufficiently far down the course to include him. He was next sent to France for the Prix Daru, but could only finish fourth behind Moutiers. Piggott, who rode him on that occasion, took the view that the colt did not really stay. There was, therefore, singularly little inducement to support Psidium in the Derby. Incidentally, with the scratching of Pinturischio and the decision not to run his stable companion Aurelius, Lester Piggott, the best Epsom jockey of the day, was left without a mount in the Derby.

The start was a good one and the early leaders were Time Greine, Patrick's Choice, and Supreme Verdict. Psidium, who had sweated up in the paddock, was conspicuous right at the tail-end of the field, while Dicta Drake was poorly placed as well. Time Greine was done with before Tattenham Corner, where Supreme Verdict, Patrick's Choice, and Dual were in front, closely followed by Bounteous, Cipriani, and Pinzon, while Pardao, Moutiers, and Sovrango were all in a handy position. At this point Psidium was still a back-marker and Dicta Drake's chances looked anything but hopeful, too.

The last two furlongs proved extremely exciting with the situation changing with bewildering rapidity. Patrick's Choice soon began to falter and with just over a quarter of a mile to go Dual seized the lead from the tiring Supreme Verdict. No sooner had Dual's name been shouted by his supporters than he in his turn was headed by the Irish outsider Cipriani. Furthermore, Pardao and Dicta Drake were both improving rapidly, while Moutiers, Sovrango, Bounteous, and Latin Lover were all in the race with a chance.

Cipriani battled on bravely, but a furlong out he was headed by Pardao. A few strides later Pardao was challenged by Dicta Drake, who produced the better turn of foot and, gaining a neck advantage, looked all over a winner. All of a sudden, though, Psidium appeared on the scene, full of running and obviously travelling much faster than anything else in the race. He swept past horse after horse, and although there were only fifty yards left when he headed Dicta Drake, he was two lengths clear at the post. Pardao was a neck behind Dicta Drake and then came Sovrango, who had run a gallant race under conditions that he loathed, Cipriani, and Latin Lover. Just Great was making up ground at the finish, but never got sufficiently close to the leaders to make an effective challenge.

Psidium's victory seemed to stun the crowd and the winner returned to the un-saddling enclosure in a silence that was positively embarrassing. In fact almost the only smiling faces besides those of Mr and Mrs Plesch belonged to members of the Pardal syndicate. The first three horses to pass the post all belonged to women, a performance that was repeated in the St Leger. It was Harry Wragg's first Derby success as a trainer and two days later he was second in the Oaks with Ambergris. Roger Poincelet, for several years a leading jockey in France, was riding his first Derby winner, but had previously won the One Thousand Guineas and the Oaks on Never Too Late and the Two Thousand Guineas on Thunderhead. Later in the season he won the Prix du Jockey Club and the King George VI and Queen Elizabeth Stakes on Right Royal.

Pardal, sire of both Psidium and Pardao, was owned and bred by M. Boussac and was by the Grand Prix winner Pharis out of Adargatis, by Asterus. He never won till he was four years old. but then he proved a good horse although he may just have missed the top class. His victories included the Prince of Wales's Stakes, Great Yorkshire Stakes, Jockey Club Stakes and Lowther Stakes. Hearing that he was for sale, Lord Manton and his brother Mr R. F. Watson bought him at Newmarket one afternoon for £50,000. He has proved a remarkably good bargain and sired two Gold Cup winners, Pardallo and Parbury, before he died in 1969. Dinarella, Psidium's dam, was bred at the Razza Dormello and is by Nearco's half-brother Niccolo Dell'Arca. She goes back to Pretty Polly through Delleana, dam of Donatello II.

Not long after the Derby Psidium injured a tendon in training and never ran again. Perhaps he was a great racehorse; perhaps his victory was one of those strange flukes that sometimes happen in racing. Certainly Poincelet would never have dared to drop a fancied horse right out of the race as he did in the early stages of the Derby on Psidium. Psidium subsequently sired the Irish Derby and St Leger winner Sodium before being exported to the Argentine. Dicta Drake won the Grand Prix de Saint Cloud and the following year's Coronation Cup, but failed in the St Leger. He was sent to Japan in 1968. Pardao won the Gordon Stakes at Goodwood, but was third to Just Great in the Voltigeur Stakes at York, and fourth to Aurelius in the St Leger. He won the Jockey Club Stakes at four and was sent to America where he won two races. He returned to England and sired many winners before his death in 1971. Sovrango was badly jarred by his race on the hard ground at Epsom and his subsequent form was disappointing. Latin Lover has done well as a sire in Australia.

1961

1961 : Wednesday, 31 May . . . 490 Entries. £34,548.

MRS A. PLESCH'S ch.c. PSIDIUM by Pardal out of Dinarella	R. POINCELET	1
MME LÉON VOLTERRA'S b.c. DICTA DRAKE by Phil Drake out of Dictature	M. GARCIA	2
MRS C. O. ISELIN'S ch.c. PARDAO by Pardal out of Three Weeks	W. H. CARR	3

Also ran:

Mr G. Oldham's Sovrango (4th) (G. Moore); Lady Honor Svejdar's Cipriani (R. Hutchinson); Lord Derby's Latin Lover (D. Smith); Sir H. Wernher's Dual (J. Lindley); Mme R. B. Strassburger's Moutiers (G. Thiboeuf); Mrs H. Leggat's Bounteous (J. Sime); Mrs J. Audain's Supreme Verdict (P. Powell); Mr T. R. Gordon's Patrick's Choice (J. Uttley); Mr J. P. Philipps's Pinzon (E. Larkin); Miss H. Jacobson's Just Great (N. Sellwood); Mr J. W. Weston-Evans's Prince Tudor (W. Rickaby); Mme H. Herbaux's Belliqueux II (F. Palmer); Mr J. McGrath's Time Greine (W. Williamson); Mr J. B. Joel's Gallant Knight (E. Smith); Lt.-Col. E. J. H. Merry's Perfect Knight (G. Lewis); Mrs R. Evans's Nicomedus (A. Breasley); Mr C. M. Kline's Neanderthal (G. Bougoure); M. J. de Atucha's Ploermel (J. Massard); Mr J. J. Astor's Scatter (J. Mercer); Mr E. W. Beechey's Oakville (E. Hide); Sir Francis Cassel's Fontana di Trevi (B. Swift); Mr C. H. Dracoulis's Polyktor (D. Keith); Mr G. C. Judd's Owen Davis (S. Smith); Baronne A. de Rothschild's Aliosha (L. Flavien); Mr A. Kennedy's Hot Brandy (T. Gosling).

28 ran.

Betting:

5–1 Moutiers; 13–2 Pardao; 9–1 Just Great; 100–9 Time Griene; 100–8 Dicta Drake and Dual; 100–7 Sovrango; 20–1 Neanderthal and Latin Lover; 25–1 Belliqueux II and Nicomedus; 30–1 Aliosha; 33–1 Perfect Knight; 40–1 Supreme Verdict; 50–1 Bounteous, Gallant Knight, Scatter, and Owen Davis; 66–1 Psidium and others.

Totalizator: (4s. unit). Win: £18 3s. 4d. Places: £5 6s., £1 1s. 8d., 12s. 2d.

Won by two lengths, a neck between second and third.   2 m. 36½ s.
Winner trained by H. Wragg at Newmarket.

1962

1962 will be remembered as the year in which seven Derby runners, among them the favourite Hethersett, fell during the descent to Tattenham Corner. The winner, possibly a fortunate one, was Mr Raymond Guest's Larkspur, trained in Ireland by Vincent O'Brien. He was the third Irish-trained colt to win the Derby this century. Mr Guest, who for some years served as United States Ambassador to Ireland, has been a singularly fortunate owner as he won the Derby again in 1968 with Sir Ivor, undoubtedly a better horse than Larkspur, while in 1970 he won the coveted Cheltenham Gold Cup with L'Escargot, trained by Dan Moore.

Born in 1917, Vincent O'Brien is hardly the Englishman's notion of the typical Irishman, being quiet, dapper, immensely shrewd and thorough, and with a marked flair for administrative detail. He first took out a licence to train in 1944 and swiftly made a name for himself as a highly successful trainer of jumpers. He won the Cheltenham Gold Cup four times, the Champion Hurdle three times and the Grand National three years in succession.

He then turned his attention to the flat. His first three important winners were Chamier, Ballymoss and Gladness. Chamier won the Irish Derby. Ballymoss, after finishing second to Crepello in the Derby, won the Irish Derby, the St Leger, the Coronation Cup, the Eclipse Stakes, the King George VI and Queen Elizabeth Stakes and Prix de l'Arc de Triomphe. Gladness, a fine staying mare, numbered the Ascot Gold Cup, the Goodwood Cup, and the Ebor Handicap with 9 st. 7 lb. among her successes. Other good horses trained by O'Brien include Glad Rags (One Thousand Guineas); Valoris (Irish One Thousand Guineas and the Oaks); El Toro (Irish Two Thousand Guineas); Long Look (The Oaks); Ancasta (Irish Oaks); Aurabella (Irish Oaks); Gaia (Irish Oaks); Barclay (Irish St Leger); White Gloves (Irish St Leger); and Pieces of Eight (Eclipse Stakes and Champion Stakes). The triumphs of Sir Ivor, Nijinsky and Roberto will be recorded later. O'Brien's career for all its glittering successes, has not been without temporary setbacks, but he is now freely acknowledged to be one of the outstanding trainers of this century.

Bred at the Marlay House Stud, Rathfarnham, Co. Dublin by Mr Philip Love, Larkspur was a January foal and is a chestnut by the Derby and St Leger winner Never Say Die, out of Skylarking, by the Gold Cup winner Precipitation out of Woodlark, a half-sister to Alycidon, Acropolis and Borealis by the Derby winner

Bois Roussel. He is therefore a member of the highly successful Marchetta family and that family's first winner of the Derby.

Skylarking, foaled in 1950, carried Lord Derby's colours and as a three-year-old she won three races up to a mile and three-quarters and was third in the Park Hill Stakes. At the end of that season she was one of four fillies in training from Stanley House Stables that were sent up to the December Sales. The first of the four, Barley Corn, was sold for 4,100 guineas and became the dam of Shantung. The last was Skylarking whom Mr Love purchased for 4,000 guineas. In view of her racing record and her superb pedigree, she was cheap at the price. Besides Larkspur, she has bred seven other winners, including Ballymarais who won the Dante Stakes and £7,900.

Larkspur came up for sale at Ballsbridge as a yearling and O'Brien bought him on Mr Guest's behalf for 12,200 guineas. His first racecourse appearance was in the Barrow Maiden Plate at the Curragh the following year. Obviously backward and neglected in the market, he finished down the course. Clearly he needed time and he did not run again till September when he showed greatly improved form to win the Laragh Maiden Stakes, run over seven furlongs at Leopardstown, by three lengths. He evidently took his trainer somewhat by surprise as his starting price was 100–8.

On the strength of that performance he started joint favourite with Arctic Storm for Ireland's most important two-year-old event, the seven-furlong National Stakes at the Curragh. He ran well, and it was certainly encouraging that he was putting in his best work at the finish, but he was beaten a short head and three parts of a length by Mystery and Richmond. His final appearance that season was in the one mile 'Timeform' Gold Cup at Doncaster, worth £21,000 to the winner. He seemed rather out of his depth here and in a field of thirteen he was never conspicuous, finishing out of the first six behind Miralgo. On his breeding, brilliance could hardly have been expected of him as a two-year-old. He had, however, shown undeniable promise of making a very useful stayer even if no evidence existed to suggest that he was likely to play a prominent part in the classics.

Larkspur had two outings before the Derby in 1962. In April he was unplaced in the seven-furlong Madrid Free Handicap at the Curragh. A month later he was a much fitter colt and brought himself into the Derby reckoning by winning the mile and a half Wills Gold Flake Stakes at Leopardstown by a length from Sicilian Prince, who later that year won the French St Leger.

O'Brien trained a second Derby candidate in Mr Townsend B. Martin's Sebring, an Aureole colt that had cost 13,000 guineas as a yearling. After Sebring had won the Players Navy Cut Stakes at Phoenix Park, Pat Glennon, the talented Australian then riding for O'Brien's stable, elected to ride Sebring at Epsom. Several jockeys were offered the mount on Larkspur but were unable to accept and in the end

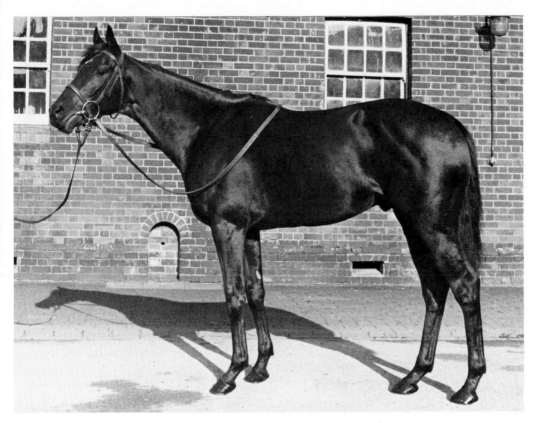

Mill Reef

Lester Piggott

Morston being led in after winning the 1973 Derby (E. Hide up)

O'Brien engaged Neville Sellwood, an Australian then riding in France for Alec Head. In the following November Sellwood, aged thirty-nine, was killed when his mount, ironically named Lucky Seven, fell at Maisons-Laffitte. At the time of his death he was leading jockey in France with 102 winners. Typical of the best Australian riders, he sat very close to his horse, rode with short leathers and rein, and was a wonderful judge of pace. Cool, modest and with charming manners, he was deservedly popular wherever he rode.

There was a time when it looked as if Larkspur would be unable to compete in the Derby. A week before the race a swelling appeared on his hock and Sellwood, who had flown from Paris to partner him in some work, was able to do no more than ride him around at a walk. O'Brien at once informed the Press that Larkspur might not be able to run and it was only on 1 June that O'Brien was able to issue a further statement saying that the colt had recovered and was a certain starter.

It had been a typical English May with sour grey skies and a searing and persistent wind from the east. Happily the weather changed just before Epsom and the meeting took place in almost unbroken sunshine. The going was firm but at least there was a good covering of grass.

It was widely considered to be a sub-standard Derby field and certainly there was no runner with outstanding qualifications. Favourite at 9–2 was the undeniably handsome Hugh Lupus colt Hethersett, bred and owned by Major Lionel Holliday, trained by Dick Hern and ridden by Harry Carr. As a two-year-old he had won the Duke of Edinburgh Stakes at Ascot and though unplaced to Miralgo in the 'Timeform' Gold Cup, there had been excuses for his failure as he had been struck into and cut. Before Epsom he had trounced the useful River Chanter in that now defunct event, the Brighton Derby Trial.

Joint second favourites at 8–1 were Miralgo, who had been third to Silver Cloud in the Chester Vase and had then been narrowly beaten in the Lingfield Derby Trial, and Madame Volterra's Le Cantilien, runner-up to Montfleur in the Prix Lupin. There was substantial support, too, for Silver Cloud, like Miralgo and Sebring a son of Aureole; the northern colt High Noon; Sebring, despite the disappointing lack of acceleration he had shown when an unsuccessful favourite for the Irish Two Thousand Guineas; and also for Pindaric, winner of the Lingfield Derby Trial. Larkspur failed to attract much money and started at 22–1.

In the paddock Hethersett stood out on looks. Larkspur was one of the smallest horses in the field and seemed lacking in scope, but at least he was well-proportioned and looked fit to run for his life. The crowd was enormous and rated one of the largest ever seen. Owing to a cold, the Queen was unable to be present.

The start was a good one and after a furlong a tubed horse called Romancero dashed to the front followed by Valentine, Escort, Ribobo, Miralgo and Sebring. At halfway, as the runners began that steep descent to Tattenham Corner, Romancero was two lengths clear of Valentine, River Chanter and Silver Cloud, while hard on the heels of this leading group came Escort, Ribobo, Miralgo, Sebring and Hethersett. At this point Larkspur had improved his position and was tracking the favourite.

Halfway down the hill occurred the disaster, the precise details of which are not known for certain to this day as it was all over in a couple of seconds and took place at a point where the race is not clearly visible from the stands. Moreover the patrol cameras did not cover that particular stage. The cause of the trouble, though, is not disputed. At this phase of the race, five furlongs from home, the mediocre competitors are beginning to drop back while the better ones are striving to improve their position. Inevitably crowding and jostling take place. When this happens with a field of twenty-six horses galloping flat-out downhill, it is not altogether surprising if an accident occurs.

One of the first horses down was Romulus, who fell right in the path of Hethersett. Both Carr on Hethersett and Sellwood on Larkspur pulled their horses violently away from the rails but Hethersett's legs caught those of Romulus and down went the favourite, too. Sellwood for his part was just able to keep Larkspur on his feet.

In the winking of an eye Crossen, Pindaric, Persian Fantasy, Changing Times and King Canute II were all brought down too, King Canute II breaking a leg and having to be destroyed. R. P. Elliott, who rode Pindaric, miraculously escaped injury but all the other riders were taken to hospital. Carr could not ride again until the end of July and Stan Smith was out of action even longer. The horses, except for King Canute II, were not seriously hurt.

As the field turned for home, Valentine held a clear lead from River Chanter, Romancero and Silver Cloud, while Escort and Le Cantilien were both going strongly on the rails, as were Sebring and Larkspur on the outside. Valentine, never a battler, had soon had enough and Silver Cloud dropped back suddenly, having swallowed his tongue. This left River Chanter in the lead but Sebring and Larkspur were moving up steadily to challenge. With two furlongs to go Sebring seemed poised for victory but from this point he simply could not quicken. Not so, however, Larkspur who lengthened his stride like a true stayer and swept past River Chanter at the distance. From then on he was never in danger and he passed the post two lengths clear of the fast-finishing Arcor with Le Cantilien half a length away third. Escort, the first English-trained horse to finish, was fourth, Sebring fifth and Prince d'Amour sixth.

The scene at the close of the race was far quieter and less animated than usual.

Loose horses were pulling up in the straight and anxious spectators were trying to identify them. No one in the stands knew at that time what had happened. Not surprisingly the gallant Larkspur received far less attention than usually accorded to the winner of the Derby. There was in fact one more sensation, albeit a minor one, still to come. Before the 'all-clear' signal had been given it was announced peremptorily over the public address system that O'Brien was to report to the Weighing Room immediately. Apparently the Stewards wished to question him about Larkspur's injury the week before. As O'Brien in this moment of triumph, was still standing in the unsaddling enclosure a few yards from the Weighing Room, a more tactful method of summoning him could surely have been devised. 'Public Relations', though, has never been a strong point with the English racing 'Establishment'.

Naturally a thorough investigation was made into the accident on the hill and in due course the following statement was issued:

'Derby Stakes. The Epsom Stewards enquired into the running of this race where seven horses fell. They interviewed several jockeys who had ridden in the race, and had reports from the jockeys who were still in hospital, of whom Carr was unable to make a statement on account of his injuries. The Stewards also saw films.

'The Stewards were satisfied that no individual was to blame. There was no evidence of rough riding.

'The general opinion of the jockeys was that too many horses were falling back after six furlongs, and the remainder closed up, and in the general scrimmage some horse was brought down, the rest falling over that horse.

'The Stewards accepted that view and regret that such a large number of horses not up to classic standard were allowed by their owners and trainers to start.

'The Stewards wish to record their gratitude to the amateur photographers who lent them the film taken near the scene of the accident.'

It only remains to add that Larkspur was at that time the highest-priced yearling ever to win the Derby and that his victory enabled Never Say Die to become the first American-bred horse to top the list of sires of winners.

The rest of Larkspur's career was an anti-climax. Favourite for the first running of the immensely valuable Irish Sweeps Derby, he could do no better than finish fourth behind the French colt Tambourine II, Arctic Storm and Sebring, being nearly eight lengths behind the winner passing the post. At the Curragh in September he was 2–1 on favourite for the mile and a half Blandford Stakes but lost by inches to Sicilian Prince, to whom he was giving three pounds. In fact, in view of Sicilian Prince's French St Leger victory later in the month, this was a creditable performance on the part of Larkspur.

The Italian colt Antelami was a firm favourite for the Doncaster St Leger and Larkspur was second favourite. They were not, however, concerned with the finish. Hethersett, who started at 100–8, won very easily by four lengths from Monterrico with Miralgo third. Larkspur ran an undistinguished race and finished a moderate sixth. Naturally it was a common conclusion that Hethersett would have won the Derby had he not been brought down.

Larkspur never ran again. He was syndicated for stud purposes and stood at Ballygoran Park, Maynooth, Co. Kildare. However in 1967 an offer for him from Japan was accepted and he became one of the seven post-war Derby winners to be exported to that country. There is no evidence to suggest that his sale represented a serious deprivation to bloodstock breeders in England and Ireland.

Of the other competitors in the 1962 Derby, Hethersett unfortunately died young. He sired the 1969 Derby winner, Blakeney. Pindaric was destroyed after a fall in the John Porter Stakes at Newbury the following year. Miralgo, Escort and River Chanter were exported to Japan, South Africa and Poland respectively. Spartan General became a successful hurdler and Silver Cloud has made a fair start to his stud career in this country. Romulus a fine miler, won the Sussex Stakes, Queen Elizabeth II Stakes and the Prix du Moulin de Longchamp. He made only a slow start as a sire and so off he went, too, to Japan in 1969.

1961: Wednesday, 6 June ... 509 entries. £34,786.

MR R. R. GUEST's ch.c. LARKSPUR by Never Say Die
   out of Skylarking   N. SELLWOOD   1
M.M. BOUSSAC's b.c. ARCOR by Arbar
   out of Corejada   R. POINCELET   2
MADAME L. VOLTERRA's b.c. LE CANTILIEN
   by Norseman out of La Perie   Y. SAINT-MARTIN   3

Also ran:

Mr J. J. Astor's Escort (4th) (J. Mercer); Mr Townsend B. Martin's Sebring (T. P. Glennon); Mr M. Bell's Prince d'Amour (A. Breasley); Mrs S. Joel's Triborough (E. Smith); Mr R. J. Sigtia's River Chanter (J. Lindley); Mr Clare Vyner's High Noon (E. Hide); Mr F. A. Laker's Spartan General (G. Ramshaw); Mr G. A. Oldham's Miralgo (W. Williamson); Mr F. More O'Ferrall's Pavot (G. Bougoure); Mr S. J. Hughes's Tannhills (W. Rickaby); Major D. McCalmont's Valentine (D. Smith); Mrs J. Phelps's Song of Pan (T. Masters); Lady Sassoon's Young Lochinvar (W. Snaith); Mr F. C. Thrush's Romancero (D. Keith); Mr R. D. Crossman's Ribobo (D. Ryan); Mr T. F. Blackwell's Silver Cloud (R. Hutchinson);

1962

Mr M. L. Gelb's Changing Times (T. Gosling) (fell); Comte G. D'Ornano's Crossen (M. Laurraun) (fell); Major L. B. Holliday's Hethersett (W. Carr) (fell); Miss E. Chanelle's King Canute II (G. Lewis) (fell); Mr C. Leigh's Persian Fantasy (S. Smith) (fell); Mr A. B. Askew's Pindaric (R. P. Elliott) (fell); Mr C. W. Engelhard's Romulus (W. Swinburn) (fell).

26 ran.

Betting:

9–2 Hethersett; 8–1 Miralgo, Le Cantilien; 100–7 Silver Cloud, High Noon; 100–6 Sebring, Pindaric; 20–1 Escort, Valentine; 22–1 Larkspur, Crossen, River Chanter, Prince d'Amour; 28–1 Young Lochinvar, Triborough; 40–1 Arcor; 50–1 Romulus; 100–1 others.

Totalizator: (4s. unit). Win: £4 10s. Places: £1 11s. 8d., £2 5s. 2d., £1 2s. 2d.

Won by two lengths; half a length between second and third. 2 m. 37·3 s.
Winner trained by M. V. O'Brien at Cashel, Co. Tipperary, Ireland.

1963

There was another French victory in 1963, the sixth since the war, the winner being M. F. Dupré's Relko, trained by François Mathet and ridden by Yves Saint-Martin. As was the case in 1962, only one English-trained horse, in this instance Merchant Venturer, finished in the leading four.

Bred by his owner, Relko is a bay by the Grand Prix de Saint-Cloud winner Tanerko, a son of Tantième, out of that famous mare Relance III, by Relic out of Polaric, by Volcan. Relance III herself won six races. Apart from Relko, she is the dam of two other high class horses in Match III and Reliance, both by Tantieme. Match III, who unfortunately died young just as he was making a name for himself as a sire, won seven races including the Prix Royal Oak (French St Leger), the Grand Prix de Saint-Cloud, the King George VI and Queen Elizabeth Stakes and the Washington International at Laurel Park. Reliance won the Prix du Jockey Club, the Grand Prix de Paris and the Prix Royal Oak. He was second to the brilliant Sea Bird in the Prix de l'Arc de Triomphe. Relance III traces back to the famous Sceptre who won every English classic bar the Derby.

Relko started off in great style as a two-year-old by winning the five and a half furlong Prix Gladiator at Le Tremblay and then over the same distance the Prix Isard at Maisons-Laffitte, defeating the very useful Quiqui by four lengths. On the strength of those performances he was confidently expected to win the valuable Criterium de Maisons-Laffitte but was surprisingly beaten by a filly well removed from the top class. In the Grand Criterium at Longchamp he was completely outpaced by the brilliant grey filly Hula Dancer and could only finish fourth. He ended the season by running second in the Prix Thomas Byron at Saint-Cloud. In the French Free Handicap he was given fifth position below Hula Dancer, Le Mesnil, Quiqui and Spy Well. He had done well, but not quite as well as had been anticipated after his first two races.

Relko thrived during the winter and as a three-year-old he was a fine big colt standing 16·1½ hands and girthing 73 inches. He started off in satisfactory fashion by winning the nine and three-quarter furlong Prix de Guiche at Longchamp. His next race was the Poule d'Essai des Poulaine, the French equivalent of the Two Thousand Guineas. This he won most impressively by two and a half lengths from the hitherto unbeaten Manderley. Up till then little thought had been given to sending Relko to Epsom, but when Mathet announced that Relko's next target would be Epsom Derby, the colt was at once made favourite for the race and never lost that position subsequently.

There were twenty-six runners for the Derby and bar the favourite and Ragusa, the latter of whom subsequently proved himself a great racehorse, they can hardly be described as a scintillating collection. The second favourite, Duplication, by Vimy, had been trained by Boyd-Rochfort as a two-year-old but inherited the wayward temperament of his dam Duplicity and became extremely wilful. He was sent for a spell to a rough-rider and then to Gosden's stable at Lewes. He was a maiden until he won the Lingfield Derby Trial by three lengths.

Fighting Ship, a Doutelle colt that carried Lord Rosebery's colours, had won the Greenham Stakes in very heavy going, defeating Only For Life who went on to win the Two Thousand Guineas. Portofino and Merchant Venturer had won respectively the Brighton Derby Trial and the Dante Stakes, but neither had made many new friends in so doing. Not much thought was given to the Irish-trained Ribot colt Ragusa who had been defeated by My Myosotis in the Dee Stakes at Chester.

The course at Epsom was fortunately in rather better condition than at the Spring Meeting when it came in for some well-merited adverse criticism. Thanks to heavy rain the day before, it was just possible to describe the going as good. The weather was atrociously cold and because of this the attendance was noticeably sparser than usual. Happy Omen was rated the pick of the runners on looks. Some critics claimed that Relko had run up rather light since he last ran. He certainly sweated up in the paddock, despite the cold, but had cooled off by the time the field paraded in front of the stands.

There was an extremely tedious delay of some fourteen minutes at the start due to the antics of an equine nonentity called Hullabaloo who backed away from the gate and kept on backing till the boards prevented him reversing any further. Eventually Mr Alec Marsh's generous quota of patience came to an end and he decided that Hullabaloo must be left where he was. In the meantime, though, Duplication had got bored and sulky hanging around in the cold. The only hint of animation he showed subsequently was when he stirred himself sufficiently to make quite a determined attempt to bite Singer.

The early leaders were Iron Peg and Hyacinthe, followed by Relko, Happy Omen, The Willies, Credo, Corpora and Merchant Venturer. There was little change at the top of the hill but soon afterwards Hyacinthe and The Willies began to drop back.

In the meantime Tarqogan, who had been poorly placed early on, was making swift headway and turning for home he was alongside Iron Peg with Corpora, Happy Omen, Relko, Credo, Merchant Venturer and Portofino close up behind. Iron Peg was in full retreat soon afterwards and with three furlongs to go Tarqogan looked a very likely winner.

Happy Omen raised the hopes of his supporters for a few strides only to falter from lack of stamina, while Merchant Venturer was starting a promising run on the extreme outside. All hopes, though, of an English or an Irish victory were shattered as soon as Yves Saint-Martin asked Relko for his effort. The favourite immediately lengthened his stride and accelerated to such purpose that he passed the post no fewer than six lengths in front of Merchant Venturer. The runner-up was himself three lengths in front of Ragusa who had stayed on stoutly in the straight. Tarqogan was fourth, Corpora fifth and Portofino sixth. M. Dupré was too ill to be present and Madame Dupré led in the winner amid the cheers invariably accorded to a winning Derby favourite.

There was a distasteful and disturbing sequel to Relko's victory. Six weeks after the Derby, the Stewards of the Jockey Club and of the National Hunt Committee issued a statement, the main paragraphs of which were as follows:

'The Stewards are seriously concerned that a number of routine tests have recently shown positive evidence of doping.

'There are seven such cases—two under N.H. Rules—covering a period from mid-April to the end of May.

'The local Stewards, having received positive confirmation of doping from the analysts, will now investigate each case, and after their enquiries will refer the cases to the Stewards of the Jockey Club and of the National Hunt Committee.

'Until the Stewards' enquiries have been completed, no details can be given as the cases are, of course, subjudice.'

This statement was perhaps not altogether a wise one since it gave no positive information but merely afforded grounds for wide speculation and sensational rumours. It was not long before it became generally known that Relko was one of the seven horses concerned and tension thereby was considerably heightened. Three weeks later the authorities held a press conference at which the names of the horses were given as well as other details such as the fact that the saliva tests had proved negative, the urine tests positive. It was furthermore announced that a reward of £2,000 had been offered for information leading to the conviction of persons engaged in doping.

The affair dragged on and not surprisingly considerable resentment was felt in racing circles in France. Eventually on 29 August the following statement appeared in the Racing Calendar:

'The Stewards of the Epsom Summer Meeting referred to the Stewards of the Jockey Club the reports which they had received from the Club's analysts on the examination ordered to be made of Relko after running in the Derby Stakes on 29 May.

'The Stewards of the Jockey Club held their enquiry at the Registry Office on 28 August, when they heard evidence from the trainer and other parties concerned, including technical witnesses called on their behalf. They also took evidence from the Stewards' Advisory Committee.

'The Stewards were satisfied that a substance other than a normal nutrient was present in the horse.

'From the technical evidence they were not satisfied that it was administered with the intention of increasing its speed or improving its stamina, conduct or courage in the race.

'They adjourned the case for further enquiry in conjunction with the Police.'

It was not until 3 October that the matter was finally settled with the following notice in the Racing Calendar:

'The Stewards of the Jockey Club, having considered the report on their further enquiries, are satisfied that the trainer and his employees have no case to answer under Rule 102(ii).

'They found no evidence that would justify a disqualification of Relko under Rule 66(c).'

The rumours that surrounded Relko for so long were undoubtedly intensified by the fiasco that concerned him in the Irish Sweeps Derby on 29 June. On that occasion he appeared perfectly sound in the paddock but nevertheless Saint-Martin saw fit to walk him for most of the way down to the start. At the gate he was obviously lame and after Saint-Martin had dismounted, the colt was examined by a veterinary surgeon. Following telephonic communication with Mathet, it was announced over the loud speaker system that Relko had been withdrawn from the race. On returning to the enclosures he was again examined and the lameness, the source of which remained uncertain, was confirmed. A routine dope test proved negative.

Relko did not run again till the Prix Royal Oak, the French equivalent of the St Leger, in September. He proved once more what a really good horse he was in winning by three lengths, among those he defeated being Sanctus, winner of the Prix du Jockey Club and the Grand Prix.

It would perhaps be an exaggeration to say that M. Dupré was ever one of the most popular members of the French racing world and there have been many trainers held in warmer public affection than Mathet. However in the Prix Royal Oak Relko was cheered from the final bend to the unsaddling enclosure, the applause being given not only for the horse, but for his owner and trainer, too. This decisive victory was considered a rebuttal of the doubts publicly cast on those most closely connected with the horse by the Jockey Club's action.

On the strength of his win in the Prix Royal Oak, Relko started favourite for the Prix de l'Arc de Triomphe, but he sweated up profusely before the race and ran far below his true form, finishing unplaced behind Exbury, Le Mesnil and Misti.

He remained in training as a four-year-old, a half share in him having been purchased by Lord Sefton, one of the Jockey Club's most able administrators but not, on the whole, a particularly fortunate owner. The first race chosen for Relko in 1964 was the £18,000 Prix Ganay run over ten furlongs at Longchamp and this he won in fine style by three lengths. He was distinctly less impressive in winning the Coronation Cup at Epsom by a neck from Khalkis, but he obviously resented the heavy going. He concluded a fine career by winning the £41,000 Grand Prix de Saint-Cloud.

Relko, who won nine races and £149,136, now stands in England at the Lavington Stud in Sussex. The best of his offspring so far is Breton, who won the Grand Criterium and the Prix de la Salamandre in 1969.

M. Dupré died in Jamaica in 1966, the day after his colt Danseur had won the Grand Prix de Paris. He first registered his colours in 1921, the year in which he became the partner of Duc Decazes in the Haras d'Ouilly. He owned many famous winners of whom Tanerko, Reliance and Match III were mentioned earlier. Tantième, later a highly successful sire, twice won the Prix de l'Arc de Triomphe, while Bella Paola won the Grand Criterium, One Thousand Guineas, Oaks, Prix Vermeille and Champion Stakes.

Among other competitors, distinguished in greater or lesser degree, in the 1963 Derby were Ragusa, Tarqogan and Fighting Ship. Ragusa, trained by P. J. Prendergast, went from strength to strength. He won the Irish Derby, the St Leger, the Eclipse Stakes and the King George VI and Queen Elizabeth Stakes. Altogether he earned £148,960 in prize money. Tarqogan, by Black Tarquin, won the Chesterfield Cup with 9 st. 1 lb. and the Cambridgeshire with 9 st. 3 lb. Fighting Ship won the Jockey Club Stakes and the Henry II Stakes. He looked like making a really good stayer but unfortunately went wrong shortly before the Ascot Gold Cup. Credo won the Chester Cup the following year.

Merchant Venturer never won a race after the Derby and in due course was exported to the Antipodes.

1963

1963 : Wednesday, 29 May . . . 497 Entries. £35,338 10s. 0d.

M. F. DUPRÉ's b.c. RELKO by Tanerko
out of Relance III   Y. SAINT-MARTIN   1

SIR FOSTER ROBINSON's ch.c., MERCHANT VENTURER
by Hornbeam, out of Martinhoe   G. STARKEY   2

MR J. R. MULLION's b.c. RAGUSA by Ribot
out of Fantan III   G. BOUGOURE   3

Also ran:

Mr J. McGrath's Tarqogan (4th) (W. Snaith); Mr R. F. Scully's Corpora (L. Piggott); Mr P. Winstone's Portofino (W. Rickaby); Lord Rosebery's Fighting Ship (S. Smith); Major L. B. Holliday's Happy Omen (F. Durr); Captain A. M. Keith's Coliseum (E. Hide); Mr J. McShain's Deep Gulf (T. P. Glennon); Mr B. Sunley's Singer (J. Uttley); Mr A. Plesch's Fern (A. Breasley); Lady Zia Wernher's Duplication (J. Lindley); Mr H. Guggenheim's Iron Peg (W. H. Carr); Mr L. M. Gelb's Credo (P. Matthews); Mr G. M. Bell's Count Albany (F. Palmer); Mrs J. Thursby's Final Move (W. Williamson); Mr A. J. Allen's Neverlone (D. Keith); Mr K. O. Boardman's African Drum (D. Smith); Mrs J. F. C. Bryce's Doudance (J. Mercer); Mr C. Leigh's Hanassi (R. P. Elliott); Mr J. Meacock's Vakil-ul-Mulk (A. Harrison); Mrs A. Plesch's Hyacinthe (S. Clayton); Mr R. N. Richmond-Watson's The Willies (R. Hutchinson); Mr E. Thornton-Smith's Fair Decision (W. Swinburn); Mr R. N. Richmond-Watson's Hullabaloo (E. Smith) (left).

26 ran.

Betting:

5–1 Relko; 6–1 Duplication; 8–1 Fighting Ship; 100–8 Corpora; 100–7 Final Move; 100–6 Portofino, Happy Omen, Fern; 18–1 Merchant Venturer; 25–1 Ragusa; 28–1 African Drum; 30–1 Iron Peg; 33–1 Deep Gulf; 50–1 Doudance, Neverlone; 66–1 Credo, Fair Decision, The Willies; 100–1 others.

Totalizator: (4s. unit) Win: £1 5s. 4d. Places: 15s. 8d., 19s., £1 13s. 10d.

Won by six lengths; three lengths between second and third.   2 m. 39.4 s.
Winner trained by F. Mathet at Chantilly, France.

1964

To produce a Derby winner is every bloodstock breeder's dream. Great, and on the whole extremely successful, owner-breeders like the late Lord Astor and the late Major Lionel Holliday failed in this particular objective. Needless to say the chance that a small scale hobby-breeder has of bringing it off is infinitesimal. The fact remains, though, that Santa Claus, who won the Derby in 1964, was bred by a Warwickshire medical practitioner, Dr F. Smorfitt, who owned one other mare at the time.

Santa Claus was by the 1945 St Leger winner Chamossaire out of Aunt Clara, by the Derby winner Arctic Prince out of Sister Clara, a half-sister by Scarlet Tiger to the brilliant but temperamental Sun Chariot, winner of the One Thousand Guineas, Oaks, and St Leger.

Chamossaire was by the Gold Cup winner Precipitation out of Snowberry, a half-sister by the Derby winner Cameronian to Big Game, Snowberry's dam being the brilliant grey Myrobella, by Tetratema. He was eighteen years old when he covered Sister Clara and had never really acquired a fashionable reputation although he had sired a St Leger winner in Cambremer and two Irish Derby winners in Chamier and Your Highness. Up till 1964 he had only once been in the first ten in the sires' list—he was sixth in 1956—but in 1964, thanks to Santa Claus, he was leading sire. He died that year aged twenty-two.

The history of Santa Claus can really be said to begin in 1937 when the National Stud, then sited at Tully, Co. Kildare, sent Clarence, an unraced three year old by Diligence out of Nun's Veil, to visit Scarlet Tiger, a stallion who stood in the vicinity at a fee of £48. Scarlet Tiger, a half-brother by the Two Thousand Guineas winner Colorado to the Oaks winner Light Brocade, had run third in the Middle Park Stakes and third in the St Leger. He made little mark at the stud.

The result of this mating was Sister Clara, a filly with very bad forelegs who was sold as a yearling to the late Major E. C. Doyle for 20 guineas. She never ran but she suddenly acquired considerable value when in 1942 her half-sister Sun Chariot won three classic races in the Royal colours. In 1944 Sister Clara was in foal to the Derby runner-up Dastur and Major Doyle reckoned the time was opportune to cash her in. Accordingly she was sent to the Newmarket Sales, where the late Miss Dorothy Paget bought her for 11,000 guineas. She did in fact produce seven winners but not one of them was of any particular account.

When she was fifteen, Sister Clara produced her ninth foal, Aunt Clara, who, as an unraced two-year-old, formed member of a draft sent by Miss Paget to the December Sales. There she was bought for 130 guineas by Dr F. Smorfitt, who raced her three times without any success at all before retiring her to his small stud.

Aunt Clara's first foal, by Neron, was Clara Rebecca who was placed four times. Then came Millden, by Dumbarnie, who won one small race.

Santa Claus was the third foal, and as a foal he was sent to the December Sales where the Irish breeder Mr A. N. G. Reynolds bought him for 800 guineas. At the Newmarket September Sales the following year he was re-sold for 1,200 guineas to the Dublin branch of the BBA, then under the aegis of T. Vigors & Co. As for Aunt Clara, she was sold privately, before Santa Claus won the Irish Two Thousand Guineas, to Mr Tim Rogers, owner of the Airlie Stud and brother of Mick Rogers who trained Santa Claus at the Curragh for the joint owners, his mother Mrs Darby Rogers, and the octogenarian Mr John Ismay. Aunt Clara was in foal to Aureole when she was sold. The produce, a colt named Saint Christopher, was sold as a yearling for 25,000 guineas but failed to make much mark on the racecourse.

Mick Rogers gave Santa Claus plenty of time to develop his strength as a two-year-old and did not run him until August. Santa Claus was then unplaced, starting at 100–8 and ridden by W. Burke, in the six-furlong Anglesey Stakes at the Curragh. Also unplaced was Scissors, who subsequently won the 'Timeform' Gold Cup at Doncaster, only to be relegated to second place following an objection by the Stewards themselves.

In September Santa Claus turned out for Ireland's premier two-year-old event, the seven-furlong National Stakes run at the Curragh and that year worth £2,562 to the winner. Mesopotamia, who had won the Chesham Stakes at Royal Ascot and the Railway Stakes at the Curragh, was a hot favourite at 5–4 on. With a furlong to go she was disputing the lead with Victoria Quay when Santa Claus, who started at 4–1 and was again ridden by Burke, swept past them as if they had agreeably consented to mark time for his personal convenience. His power of acceleration was devastating and he was eight lengths clear when he passed the post. It was a most impressive performance and not surprisingly he was installed as winter favourite for the Derby. He did not run again as a two-year-old.

Conditions underfoot the following spring were far from ideal and Santa Claus did not appear in public until the Irish Two Thousand Guineas on 16 May. His presence proved an enormous attraction and the enclosures were packed. Ridden by Burke and starting at evens, he gave his admirers plenty to enthuse about, a tremendous burst of speed in the final hundred yards landing him a winner by three lengths from the English colt Young Christopher. His victory was greeted by prolonged applause, and every Irishman who saw him that day went home convinced he had seen the winner of the Derby. Indeed Santa Claus had again appeared to be that rare but eminently desirable type, a colt with a stayer's pedigree and top class speed.

The Derby this year carried an added incentive, namely the £40,000 added to the prize money by the Levy Board. Thus the race became worth over £70,000 to the winner, more than double the value of any previous Derby.

Derby Day was warm and bright, the going distinctly on the soft side. Santa Claus, for whom the famous Australian 'Scobie' Breasley had been engaged, was a firm favourite at 15–8, second favourite being Lord Howard de Walden's handsome Alcide colt Oncidium, who had won the Lingfield Derby Trial by five lengths. There was plenty of money too, for two French-trained candidates—the American-bred Baldric II who had won the Two Thousand Guineas, and Corah IV, a rather flashy chesnut that had been placed in the French Two Thousand Guineas and the Prix Noailles.

Santa Claus, a bay standing 16·1¾ hands, came in for plenty of adverse criticism in the paddock, it being claimed that he was lean and lanky, straight in the shoulder, and with joints that looked as if they had been causing Rogers a certain degree of anxiety. His bold, intelligent outlook, though, was generally admired. Oncidium, a compact, beautifully-proportioned colt, was widely rated the pick on looks.

The seventeen runners were off to a first-time start. Oncidium seemed to be fighting hard for his head and after a furlong had been covered his backers were slightly concerned to see him disputing the lead with Balustrade and Hotroy with Baldric II and Indiana not far behind.

There was little change at the top of the hill, at which point the patient Breasley, a specialist in waiting tactics, was content to be last but three. However on the down-hill run, which Santa Claus negotiated smoothly, the favourite improved his position considerably. He was handily placed close behind the leaders at Tattenham Corner, where Oncidium led from Baldric II, Hotroy, Dilettante II and Indiana.

Hotroy was done with at the furlong pole and a furlong later the all too impetuous Oncidium had shot his bolt. This left Baldric II in the lead but his stamina gave out at the distance and Indiana ridden by that admirable jockey Jimmy Lindley, struck the front.

Entering the final furlong Indiana looked all over a winner but Santa Claus had been making steady progress up the centre of the course and was moving up to deliver his challenge. Breasley, with two hundred yards to go, gave him a reminder with the whip. The response was less spectacular than Santa Claus's admirers hoped and desired, but he did find a little extra pace and some seventy yards from the line he headed the gallant Indiana and won by a length. Dilettante II, a 100–1 outsider having the second race of his career, was two lengths away third in front of Anselmo, Baldric II and Crete. Indiana and Anselmo, the latter the property of Mr Billy Fury, a 'pop-singer', were the only English-trained horses in the leading six.

It was a second Derby victory for Mick Rogers as he had won with Hard Ridden in 1958. It is perhaps worth noting that his two Derby winners cost less than a total of 1,500 guineas as yearlings. It was a first Derby success for Breasley, who was fifty years old and for the thirteenth time riding in the race.

The next race for Santa Claus was the Irish Sweeps Derby at the Curragh, worth £53,725 to the winner. Ridden by W. Burke and starting at 7–4 on, Santa Claus won with dignified ease by four lengths from Lionhearted, a maiden that had pulled up lame in the Derby. Sunseeker was third and down the course was Dilettante II who had run so well at Epsom. It was a second Irish classic success for Mr Ismay as in 1945 he had won the Irish St Leger with Spam, trained by Mick Rogers's father, Captain Darby Rogers.

The reputation of Santa Claus now stood extremely high and in his next race, the King George VI and Queen Elizabeth Stakes at Ascot, he started at 13–2 on in a field of four. The going however, was extremely firm and this did not suit him at all. Ridden by Burke, he was totally unable to produce his ability to accelerate and quite early in the straight it was painfully clear that he was not going to catch the American-bred, French-trained Nasram II who had bowled along merrily in front from the start.

Nasram II, a half-brother by Nasrullah to the Irish Derby winner Tambourine II, won comfortably by two lengths. He was conceding Santa Claus a stone and it was disappointing to say the least to see the favourite humbled in this manner by a horse not rated near the top of his generation.

Despite the Ascot defeat and despite rumours that he had been sore when he returned home, Santa Claus remained an odds-on favourite for the final classic. The bookmakers, though, with their brilliant intelligence service, knew that something was wrong. They began to ease him in the market and a week before the St Leger odds of 2–1 were freely available. The bookmakers, of course, were right even though the stable remained silent. In fact it was only five days before the race that Rogers finally admitted that Santa Claus was uncertain to run. On the Monday of Doncaster week a statement was issued saying that owing to the firm ground it had been impossible to give Santa Claus a proper preparation and accordingly he would not take part. Many people felt that the horse's connections might have been rather franker with the racing public and in fact ought to have informed them of the true situation a good deal earlier than they did. In Santa Claus's absence the St Leger was won by Indiana by a head from Patti.

Santa Claus's final appearance was in the Prix de l'Arc de Triomphe at Long-champ. Ridden by Lindley, he ran a great race but was beaten three parts of a length by the Ribot colt Prince Royal. La Bamba was a head away third. Among those unplaced were Nasram and Ragusa as well as White Label, winner of the Grand Prix; Le Fabuleux, winner of the Prix du Jockey Club; Barbieri, winner of the Prix Royal Oak; Belle Sicambre, winner of the Prix de Diane; and Astaria, winner of the Prix Vermeille.

Santa Claus, who was voted 'Horse of the Year' for 1964, had won £132,103 that season and in addition he had won over £2,000 as a two-year-old. He retired to the Airlie Stud, Lucan, Co. Dublin and it was a shock to breeders when he died of a thrombosis early in 1970. The best horses he had sired at the time of his death were Reindeer, who was third in the Irish Sweeps Derby and won the Irish St Leger by six lengths, and Santa Tina, winner of the Irish Guinness Oaks.

Of the other 1964 Derby competitors, Indiana won the Great Voltigeur Stakes and the St Leger. As a four-year-old he won the Ormonde Stakes and was otherwise disappointing. There was no marked demand by breeders for his stud services and he was exported to Japan in 1966. Dilettante II won the Warren Stakes at Good-wood but the rest of his career was uneventful. Baldric II won the Champion Stakes and sired the 1971 Irish Sweeps Derby winner Irish Ball. Oncidium remained a good horse on his day, but unpredictable. He had been trained by Jack Waugh for the Derby but he was with George Todd when he won the Jockey Club Cup and the Coronation Cup. He was in due course exported to Australia. The victories of Sweet Moss included the Dee Stakes, Dante Stakes and the City and Suburban.

1964: Wednesday, 3 June ... 565 Entries. £72,067

MR J. ISMAY's b.c. SANTA CLAUS by Chamossaire
out of Aunt Clara   A. BREASLEY 1

MR C. W. ENGELHARD's b.c. INDIANA by Sayajirao
out of Willow Ann   J. LINDLEY 2

MR L. M. GELB's b.c. DILETTANTE II by Sicambre
out of Barbizonette   P. MATTHEWS 3

Also ran:

Mr B. Fury's Anselmo (P. Cook) (4th); Mrs H. E. Jackson's Baldric II (W. Pyers); Lady Honor Svejdar's Crete (G. Bougoure); Lady Marks's Penny Stall (R. Poincelet); Lord Howard de Walden's Oncidium (E. Smith); Mr R. B. Moller's Balustrade (W. Williamson); Lady Sassoon's Sweet Moss (L. Piggott); Mr. A. Kennedy's Hotroy (G. Lewis); Mr J. McGrath's Cold Slipper (J. Roe); Mrs J. F. C.

Bryce's Con Brio (R. Hutchinson); Mr H. A. J. Silley's Roquefeuil (D. Ryan); Baron G. de Rothschild's Corah IV (J. Deforge); Mr C. R. Harper's Dromoland (J. Mercer); Sir Humphrey de Trafford's Lionhearted (W. H. Carr).

17 ran.

Betting:

15–8 Santa Claus; 9–2 Oncidium; 9–1 Baldric II, Corah IV; 100–8 Sweet Moss; 18–1 Lionhearted; 22–1 Crete; 25–1 Balustrade; 30–1 Indiana; 33–1 Hotroy; 40–1 Con Brio, Penny Stall; 50–1 Cold Slipper; 100–1 others.

Totalizator: (4s. unit). Win: 15s. 8d. Places: 9s. 8d., £1 0s. 2d., £4 0s. 8d.

Won by a length; two lengths between second and third.   2 m. 41·98 s.
Winner trained by J. M. Rogers at the Curragh, Ireland.

1965

The seventh, and undoubtedly the best, of the post-war French winners of the Derby was M. Jean Ternynck's Sea Bird II, who won with singular ease in 1965. He was in fact one of the outstanding Derby winners of this century and a horse worthy of comparison with the mighty Ribot.

He was bred by his owner, a French textile manufacturer who had gained his first English classic success in 1950 when Camaree trained by A. Lieux, won the One Thousand Guineas. In 1963 Sanctus had won for him the Prix du Jockey Club and the Grand Prix. Trainer of Sea Bird II was Etienne Pollet, a master of his profession. In addition to his many triumphs in France, Pollet has won the Two Thousand Guineas with Thunderhead II; the One Thousand Guineas and the Oaks with Never Too Late; the One Thousand Guineas and the Champion Stakes with Hula Dancer; the Irish Sweeps Derby with Tambourine II and Prince Regent; and the King George VI and Queen Elizabeth Stakes with Right Royal V.

The most striking point about Sea Bird II's pedigree is that not one of his five immediate dams won a race under the rules of a Jockey Club in any country. The fifth dam was Lady Disdain, by Hurry On. The property of Major J. S. Courtauld, she ran twice. The pick of her offspring was the Tetratema filly Crosspatch who won the Molecombe Stakes at Goodwood.

Colour Bar, Sea Bird's fourth dam, was by the Two Thousand Guineas winner Colorado. She ran without success in selling races but did manage to win under Pony Turf Club Rules. Major D. McCalmont bought her for 750 guineas and for him she bred the Tetratema colt Quarteroon who won the Woodcote Stakes at Epsom. After a time Major McCalmont disposed of Colour Bar to M. S. Guthmann and she moved to France. For M. Guthmann she bred the Tetratema colt Tetrabar, who won three races as a two-year-old. She was in Normandy at the time of the allied invasion and is presumed to have been killed in the fighting there as all trace of her was lost.

In 1939 Colour Bar had produced a filly named Couleur by the Prix Royal Oak winner Biribi. Couleur failed to win on the flat but won a hurdle race at Nice and was placed over fences. In due course she was bought by A. Lieux, who then trained for M. Ternynck. In 1946 she was purchased by M. Ternynck in foal to the Prix du Cadran winner Maurepas and with a filly foal by the same sire.

The foal, Camargue, won the Prix de Malleret at Longchamp while her younger sister Camaree won the One Thousand Guineas in very fast time. Couleur, however, did not live up to this early promise as a brood mare and she had only one other winner on the flat before she died in 1957. In 1948 she had been covered again by Maurepas, the produce being Marmelade, a filly who only ran once and was then unplaced. Marmelade was retired to the stud and her second foal was the Sicambre filly Sicalade, whose best effort was to dead-heat for second place in a race at Maisons-Laffitte. Sicalade's first foal never ran; her second was Sea Bird II.

Sire of Sea Bird II is the American-bred Dan Cupid, one of the first crop of runners of that famous American horse Native Dancer. A powerful, close-coupled chesnut that looked a typical sprinter, Dan Cupid won three races in France as a two-year-old, and coming to England for the Middle Park Stakes, was only beaten a length by Masham. The following season he was unplaced in the Two Thousand Guineas and the Derby. Many critics thought he was being raced well beyond his proper distance but this theory was jolted out of existence when he ran a great race for the Prix du Jockey Club in which he lost by a matter of inches to Herbager. That was the apex of his career and he apparently trained off afterwards.

Sea Bird II ran three times as a two-year-old. After a smooth victory in the Prix de Blaison, he faced a far stiffer test in the seven-furlong Criterium de Maisons-Laffitte, in which one of his rivals was Carvin, second in the Prix Morny. However he won this race convincingly too.

Pollet decided to run both Grey Dawn and Sea Bird II in the one-mile Grand Criterium at Longchamp, that year worth over £24,000 to the winner. Grey Dawn belonged to Madame Widener and was a grey Herbager colt that had won the Prix Morny and the Prix de la Salamandre. Ridden by Glennon, he started favourite, while Sea Bird II, partnered by Larraun, was second favourite.

Grey Dawn was quickly into his stride and won without ever being headed by a couple of lengths. Sea Bird II had been less favourably drawn. Moreover he was rather slowly away and did not negotiate the bend very cleverly. In the straight, though, he ran on really well to finish second in a field of thirteen. It was the one defeat of his career. Many who saw him that day reckoned that if he ever met Grey Dawn again, there would be a very different result.

1965 was a vintage year for French three-year-olds with colts such as Sea Bird II, Reliance and Diatome. Both Sea Bird II and Reliance had staunch partisans to claim superiority for their respective idols but that question was answered for good and all when the pair met in the Prix de l'Arc de Triomphe in October.

Sea Bird II's first race as a three-year-old was the Prix Greffulhe at Longchamp in April. He proceeded to win in a canter and it was clear that it would require a horse of quite exceptional ability to extend him, let alone beat him. The following month he won the £24,000 Prix Lupin at Longchamp by six lengths from the hitherto unbeaten Diatome who had won the Prix Noailles and was later to win the Washington International at Laurel Park. Third in the Prix Lupin at Longchamp was Cambremont, winner of the French Two Thousand Guineas. When Pollet announced after the Prix Lupin that Sea Bird II would go for the Derby, the chesnut was at once made favourite for the race. Soon afterwards it was decided that the target for Reliance would be the Prix du Jockey Club, a race he duly won by three parts of a length from Diatome.

Derby Day was bright and warm and the going was good. Sea Bird II not surprisingly was a hot favourite at 7–4 and second favourite was the Irish colt Meadow Court, one of the part-owners of whom was Mr Bing Crosby. There was a deal of money for the Two Thousand Guineas winner Niksar and for Mr J. H. Whitney's Chester Vase winner Gulf Pearl. In the paddock Sea Bird II was naturally the centre of attraction. A bright chesnut with a white blaze and two stockings behind, he stood just over 16 hands. He had exceptionally powerful and well-muscled quarters and a fine bold outlook, but as he walked round, though, it was observable that he 'dished' with his off-fore. There had been persistent rumours that he was very highly-strung and likely to be upset by the long drawn out Epsom preliminaries. However, he remained gratifyingly calm.

There is frankly little that needs be said about the race, the only dramatic quality in which was the winner's electrifying acceleration in the closing stages. Many experienced race-goers declared they had never seen a Derby more easily won.

The outsider Sunacelli led round Tattenham Corner from Niksar, Meadow Court, Gulf Pearl and I Say and Sea Bird II. With a quarter of a mile still to go Sunacelli, Gulf Pearl and Niksar were all in trouble and I Say moved into a clear lead. Backers of the favourite, though, felt not the slightest twinge of anxiety, so smoothly was he travelling on the bit. Just below the distance Pat Glennon asked Sea Bird II for his effort and the chesnut sailed contemptuously past I Say as if I Say had been some stationary object. With victory assured, Glennon eased Sea Bird II in the final fifty yards or the margin of two lengths that separated him from Meadow Court, who had run on stoutly without ever offering a serious threat, would have been considerably wider. I Say was a length and a half away third and then came Niksar, Convamore and Cambridge. It was Pat Glennon's first English classic success and he can seldom have had an easier ride.

English reaction to Sea Bird II's victory was intense admiration for him coupled with some surprise that Dan Cupid should be capable of siring so superlative a horse.

Reliance went for the Grand Prix which he won by a length from Diatome, while the next target for Sea Bird II was the £41,000 Grand Prix de Saint-Cloud on 4 July which he won with his customary facility. It was then decided that he would have one more race, Europe's richest prize, the one and a half mile Prix de l'Arc de Triomphe on 3 October.

The 'Arc' that year was worth £85,727 to the winner. The field was a powerful one and included Reliance, who had added the Prix Royal Oak to earlier successes; Diatome; the Russian champion Anilin; Tom Rolfe, winner of the Preakness Stakes and the American Derby; Demi-Deuil, winner of the Grosser Preis von Baden; Meadow Court, who had been second in the Derby and the St Leger and had won the Irish Sweeps Derby and the King George VI and Queen Elizabeth Stakes; and Oncidium, winner of the Coronation Cup.

With two furlongs to go the issue, as had been anticipated, lay between Sea Bird II and Reliance and the excitement was intense. In half a dozen strides, though, the duel was over. When Glennon asked Sea Bird to go, he simply flew and the unfortunate Reliance, a great racehorse by any standard, was made to look like a second-class handicapper. Despite a tendency to veer towards the stands, Sea Bird II won by six lengths while Reliance emphasized his superiority over the others by finishing five lengths in front of Diatome. For those lucky enough to see the race it was an unforgettable experience, and the result, with French horses occupying the leading places, was rightly regarded as a particular triumph for French bloodstock, a triumph to be repeated shortly afterwards when Diatome and Carvin were first and second in the Washington International.

The stud services of this great horse were not made available for European breeders. The American breeder Mr John Galbreath succeeded in leasing Sea Bird II, who had won £225,000 in stakes, to stand at his Derby Dan Stud in Kentucky. Mr Galbreath had previously leased Ribot, who was intended to return to Europe, but who was still in Kentucky when he died in 1972. Sea Bird returned to France shortly before his death early in 1973. He may not have been an unmixed loss to European breeding. His son Gyr was second in the 1970 Derby and won the Grand Prix de Saint Cloud, but his stock in general has seemed to suffer from defects of temperament.

Of the other Derby competitors Meadow Court won the Irish Sweeps Derby and the King George VI and Queen Elizabeth Stakes while he was second to Provoke in the St Leger. Unfortunately at the Stud his fertility record has been a source of concern. I Say won the Coronation Cup as a four-year-old and Niksar was exported to Australia. Silly Season won the St James's Palace Stakes, Champion Stakes and the Lockinge Stakes. He has made quite a good start as a sire.

1965: Wednesday, 2 June ... 620 Entries. £65,301.

M. J. TERNYNCKS' ch.c. SEA BIRD II by Dan Cupid		
out of Sicalade	T. P. GLENNON	1
MR G. M. BELL's ch.c. MEADOW COURT by Court Harwell		
out of Meadow Music	L. PIGGOTT	2
MR L. FREEDMAN's br.c. I SAY by Sayajirao		
out of Isetta	R. POINCELET	3

Also ran:

Mr W. Harvey's Niksar (W. Rickaby) (4th); Mr E. R. More O'Ferrall's Convamore (E. Hide); Mr D. Robinson's Cambridge (A. Breasley); Mr W. T. Stoker's Ballymarais (W. Pyers); Baron Thierry de Zuylen de Nyefelt's Vieuten (J. Deforge); Mr C. W. Engelhard's Solstice (W. Williamson); Lord Derby's Look Sharp (J. Roe); Mr B. van Cutsem's Alcalde (D. Smith); Mr J. H. Whitney's Gulf Pearl (J. Lindley); Mr P. Mellon's Silly Season (G. Lewis); Dr B. N. Pajgar's Billionaire (G. Bougoure); Mr W. H. D. Riley-Smith's King Log (R. Hutchinson); Lord Rosebery's Bucentaur (S. Smith); Mr W. T. Stoker's Sunacelli (B. Connorton); Mr T. E. S. Egerton's Foothill (J. Mercer); Mrs J. F. C. Bryce's Bam Royal (P. Matthews); Lord Rosebery's Creosote (P. Robinson); Major L. B. Holliday's As Before (G. Starkey); Mr J. H. Kartz's Sovereign Edition (R. Maddock).

22 ran.

Betting:

7–4 Sea Bird II; 10–1 Meadow Court; 100–8 Niksar; Gulf Pearl; 20–1 Foothill; 25–1 Look Sharp, Cambridge, Alcalde, Ballymarais, Vieuten; 28–1 I Say; 33–1 As Before; 40–1 Convamore, Solstice; 50–1 Silly Season, Buccenteur, Ling Log; 66–1 others.

Totalizator: (4s. unit). Win: 11s. 4d. Places: 7s. 6d., 10s. 2d., 17s. 10d.

Won by two lengths; a length and a half between second and third.   2 m. 38·41 s. Winner trained by E. Pollet at Chantilly, France.

1966

Lady Zia Wernher's Charlottown, who won in 1966, may have lacked the rare brilliance of Sea Bird II but he was a thoroughly genuine colt who, during the three seasons he was in training, only ran one indifferent race.

Sea Bird II's pedigree had caused the purists to raise their eyebrows just a little, but there could be no denying that Charlottown was superbly bred. His sire Charlottesville, by Prince Chevalier, had won the Prix du Jockey Club and the Grand Prix and was a half-brother to Sheshoon, winner of the Ascot Gold Cup, the Grand Prix de Saint-Cloud and the Grosser Preis von Baden. After the 1966 Derby in which Prince Chevalier was the paternal grandsire of the first three horses to finish, a bid of £750,000 was made from America for Charlottesville but it was turned down.

Dam of Charlottown was Meld, a great race-mare that had not only won the One Thousand Guineas, Oaks and St Leger but had been famous when in training for her magnificent appearance as well. Meld is by Alycidon out of Daily Double, by Fair Trial, and goes back to Double Life, the foundation mare of the Someries Stud.

Charlottown was Meld's fifth foal and until the time that he began to win races she had been a sad disappointment as a brood mare, her solitary winner having been Intaglio, a Tenerani filly that won a small race at the Curragh. Her first foal Lysander, by Nearco, possessed latent ability but was resolutely declined to employ it. He was ultimately shipped to Australia still a maiden.

For many years Lady Zia Wernher's horses had been trained with great success by Captain (later Sir) Cecil Boyd-Rochfort at Newmarket but she decided to send Charlottown to Jack Gosden who for a considerable time had trained certain of Sir Harold Wernher's horses, more particularly those that aimed to win the lesser prizes that the Turf has to offer. Gosden, the son of a Sussex farmer, was commonly known as 'Towser' and in his younger days he had been a capable amateur rider. For a time he assisted George Poole at Lewes and in 1928 he started training at Lewes himself. Up till the war he concentrated on jumpers and was extremely successful. After the war his stable was first of all a 'mixed' one but eventually he concentrated on the flat. His first really important success was to win the King George VI and Queen Elizabeth Stakes in 1960 with Sir Harold Wernher's Aggressor.

A dedicated professional, he was a true master of the trainer's craft and was remarkably adept at preparing a horse for an important handicap. Unfortunately by the time that Charlottown came to him his health was in decline. He had in fact been invalided out of the R.A.F. in the war.

Bred as he is, Charlottown was unlikely to shine over short distances against sprinter-bred types in the early part of the season and Gosden did not run him till the autumn. His first outing was the seven-furlong Solario Stakes at Sandown on 3 September. Starting favourite at 3–1, he made mincemeat of some rather second-rate opponents to win by eight lengths. This was all very encouraging but in fact the form did not add up to very much. Three weeks later he ran in the seven-furlong Blackwood Hodges Stakes at Ascot and was made favourite at 3–1 on. This time he was less impressive and he had to be bustled up to win by half a length from Gyropolis, a filly that had won a small event at Brighton on her previous appearance.

His final appearance that season was in the seven-furlong Horris Hill Stakes at Newbury on 23 October. Favourite at 11–10 he had quite a lot to do from three furlongs out but he responded gamely to Lindley's pressure and took the lead close home to win from Red Rumour and Bright Will. Again it was a performance more workmanlike than brilliant, and again the opposition was not of a particularly formidable character. At all events he retired in winter quarters unbeaten and was given third place in the Free Handicap with 9 st. 9 lb. The two rated above him were the speedy Young Emperor (10 stone) and Pretendre (9 st. 10 lb.), the latter a stayer of high promise that had won the Dewhurst Stakes and the 'Observer' Gold Cup.

At the close of the season Gosden, a sick man indeed—he died in 1967—retired and his Lewes stable was taken over by Gordon Smyth, a member of a famous English racing family. Smyth had been conducting the Duke of Norfolk's Arundel stable with marked success, having succeeded his father there in 1961 after acting for fifteen years as his father's assistant.

Pretendre was made winter favourite for the Derby, Charlottown second favourite. Charlottown did not compete in the Two Thousand Guineas, for which his talents were clearly unsuited, but Pretendre did and actually started favourite following a most impressive win in the Blue Riband Trial Stakes at Epsom. In the Guineas Pretendre found the pace too hot for him and never looked like winning, the victor being the Irish-bred, French-trained Kashmir II who won by about an inch from Pretendre's little-fancied stable-companion Great Nephew. The Irish colts Celtic Song, Young Emperor and Ambericos were respectively third, fourth and fifth and the French-trained Village Square sixth.

Following this failure, Pretendre's Derby price eased from 3–1 to 6–1 and a new favourite was found for that race in the Irish colt Right Noble who had won the

White Rose Stakes by a wide margin. Right Noble, by Right Royal V, was not a noticeably attractive colt and would not have looked grotesquely out of place with a trombonist on his back in the Household Cavalry Mounted Band.

The English-trained colts had fared so poorly in the Guineas that the French quite reasonably entertained high hopes of winning the Derby. Unfortunately for them, there was an outbreak of swamp fever in France and on Friday 13 May the Ministry of Agriculture imposed a ban, to begin to take effect on Sunday 15 May on all horses from the continent. This effectively destroyed the chances of the horses such as Nelcius, Barbare, Premier Violon and Village Square. Efforts were made to fly some of the French candidates in before Sunday, but clearances could not be obtained in time. The ban was received very badly in France and in racing circles the 'entente cordiale' was strained to snapping point. Indeed some French trainers made the ill-natured suggestion that the ban had really been imposed to protect the moderate English Derby competitors from their clearly superior French rivals.

In the meantime it had been planned to run Charlottown in the Brighton Derby Trial on 9 May and he was declared a runner for that race. A large crowd came to see him perform but on arrival swiftly learnt that Charlottown had bruised a foot and was unable to take the field. This was grave news with the Derby only sixteen days away. In Charlottown's absence Sodium, trained by George Todd, won the Brighton Trial from Crisp and Even.

Hermes won the Dante Stakes at York but as he finished with his ears back and his tail swishing it was not a particularly attractive performance. Finally there was the Lingfield Derby Trial in which Charlottown was judged fit to take his chance. For once in a way Ron Hutchinson, partnering Charlottown for the first and last time, seemed to ride a very indifferent race. Possibly anxious to spare Charlottown a severe ordeal on the heavy ground, he held him back to the extent that he was soon virtually tailed off in last place. Five furlongs from home Brian Taylor sent Black Prince II into the lead and he entered the straight twenty lengths clear of Charlottown. In the last two furlongs Charlottown made a valiant effort and despite a marked tendency to hang to the left at one stage, he was only three lengths behind Black Prince II at the winning post. The general opinion was that had he been ridden with better judgement, he would certainly have won and comfortably at that. All the same, the way he had hung to the left when he came under pressure was a little disturbing.

The following week the fifty-two-year-old 'Scobie' Breasley was engaged to ride Charlottown at Epsom. Just before the Epsom meeting began Breasley had a nasty fall at Windsor in a race and was badly shaken. However this tough and courageous veteran soon recovered and rode two winners on Epsom's opening day.

1966

There were twenty-five runners for the Derby, seven of them from Ireland. There was some very close betting before the race and at one time or another Pretendre, Right Noble and Charlottown all held the position of favourite. At the 'off', though, Right Noble and Pretendre were co-favourites at 9–2 while Charlottown figured at 5–1. A feature of the betting exchanges was the volume of money that poured in for the Irish colt Grey Moss who had devastated his rivals at Chester. His price came tumbling down from 100–7 to 8–1.

Just as Charlottown was being mounted by Breasley, he trod on his own off-fore and the plate was torn off. For fifteen minutes the start was delayed while Gordon Smyth's own blacksmith replated the colt, a delicate operation since Charlottown suffered from thin-soled feet. All went well, though, and eventually Charlottown joined the others at the start, leaving his owner, his trainer and those who had backed the horse heavily in anything but a placid frame of mind.

From the very start the leaders were Right Noble and St Puckle. After half a mile Pretendre was not in the first fifteen, while Charlottown had only three horses behind him one of them being Grey Moss who was well on the way to becoming tailed off. At the top of the hill Breasley was pushing Charlottown hard. Like most Australian jockeys, Breasley always hankered to be on the inside and though he was so far behind the leaders he boldly decided to make his run right up against the rails. Nine times out of ten he would not have obtained a clear run, but on this occasion luck was on his side. Charlottown never had to be checked and furthermore he had no chance to hang to the left. Some critics praised Breasley for the brilliance of his tactics; others reckoned he had taken an impermissible risk. The important thing, though, was that the tactics succeeded.

Right Noble and St Puckle had both had enough early in the straight, their place at the head of affairs being taken by Black Prince II and Sodium. Sodium was beaten at the two furlong pole and at that point it seemed that Black Prince II was going to win. Pretendre and Charlottown, though, were both rapidly improving their position and Pretendre, on whom young Paul Cook had ridden a perfectly judged race, headed Black Prince II at the distance. The only danger now was Charlottown who had enjoyed a piece of immense good fortune when the tiring Right Noble came away from the rails and let him through. This good fortune was repeated when Black Prince II, also, left a gap through which Charlottown was adroitly slipped.

Entering the final furlong Pretendre led Charlottown by about a neck. For a few strides Charlottown faltered but Breasley balanced him beautifully and then gave him two taps with the whip. Charlottown responded with courage and in a great finish he got his head in front close home to win a thrilling race by a neck. In later times Sir Jack Jarvis, trainer of Pretendre, always used to say that he wished Cook had given his mount just one sharp reminder with the whip. 'I don't like seeing a game horse hit,' he used to say, 'but after all, this was the Derby.'

Black Prince II was five lengths away third and then came Sodium, Crisp and Even and Ambericos. Charlottown was loudly applauded as he returned to the unsaddling enclosure and there is no doubt that happy memories of his dam Meld added to the generous warmth of his reception. It was highly satisfactory, too, that the finish had been fought out by the two top-rated English colts of 1965. Gordon Smyth was overwhelmed with congratulations for his feat in training a Derby winner in his first season as a public trainer, and congratulations, too, were showered on Jack Gosden, deprived by ill-health of the greatest triumph of his career.

Dope tests were made after the race on Grey Moss, who ran deplorably throughout, and on Sodium, who had been reported by his rider, Frank Durr, as choking and gurgling at the entrance to the straight. Both tests proved negative.

Breasley retired at the end of 1968 and is now training at Epsom. He was one of the best Australian jockeys to ride in this country. Cool, shrewd, business-like, and with a considerable charm of manner, he was a wonderful judge of pace and excelled in split-second timing. He was a master, too, at winning on two-year-olds without subjecting them to a severe race. He was perhaps rather less flexible in his methods than most of the best English jockeys and his liking for the rails sometimes led him to getting boxed in. He was champion jockey four times and besides winning the Derby on Santa Claus and Charlottown, he won the Two Thousand Guineas on Ki Ming; the One Thousand Guineas on Festoon; and the Prix de l'Arc de Triomphe on Ballymoss.

Charlottown ran on three more occasions that season and each time he was opposed by Sodium. In the Irish Sweeps Derby he started favourite at 11–8 on, but Sodium beat him a length. Breasley was blamed for lagging too far behind in the early stages, but he had been just as far behind at a similar stage in the Derby. Charlottown certainly had every chance in the last two furlongs at the Curragh, but could not quicken sufficiently at the finish.

In the Oxfordshire Stakes at Newbury, Sodium, who in July had been narrowly beaten by Aunt Edith in the King George VI and Queen Elizabeth Stakes, was the odds-on favourite, but he ran a lamentable race and finished thirteen lengths behind Charlottown who won from Desert Call II. A dope test on Sodium proved negative but soon after reaching home he displayed symptoms of kidney trouble which no doubt accounted for his failure. In this race Charlottown was ridden by Lindley as in an earlier event Breasley had had a very bad fall that put him out of action for the rest of the season.

1966

In the St Leger Charlottown, Lindley up, was favourite at 11–10. At 3–1 was Pretendre who had won the King Edward VII Stakes. Sodium, whom few punters seemed disposed to trust, was on offer at 7–1 in this field of nine. It proved a wonderfully exciting race. Charlottown took the lead from David Jack just inside the distance. He ran on courageously enough but was strongly challenged in the final furlong by Sodium who got his head in front to win by a head.

Charlottown ran three times in 1968. He began by winning the John Porter Stakes at Newbury by inches from Salvo, a good horse that was only just beaten in the autumn in the Prix de l'Arc de Triomphe. In June Charlottown won the Coronation Cup by two lengths, among his defeated rivals being Nelcius, winner of the Prix du Jockey Club in 1966, and Sodium, whose career as a four-year-old proved disappointing.

Charlottown's final race was the Grand Prix de Saint-Cloud in July. This was the only poor performance of his career and he finished sixth of eight behind Taneb, Nelcius and Taj Dewan. It was a pity he was not given an opportunity to retrieve his reputation. He had won seven races and £116,863. In 1966 he had been voted 'Horse of the Year'. He now stands at the Someries Stud, Newmarket. He may not have been one of the really great winners of the Derby, certainly not one of the most handsome ones, but he was a thoroughly genuine horse that won good races at two, three and four years of age. With his record and his pedigree, he ought to make a most successful sire.

Of the other Derby horses of 1966, Sodium is now at the stud in France. Black Prince II was sold for 29,000 guineas and exported to Australia. Pretendre was sold for a sum in the region of £150,000 before the St Leger for export to America. After his son Canonero II had won the Kentucky Derby Pretendre returned to England and it was the intention of his owner, Mr N. Bunker Hunt, to give him two mating seasons each year, one in the Northern Hemisphere, one in the Southern. Pretendre had just arrived back in New Zealand in 1972 when he died from heart failure. Hermes and St Puckle were both exported to New Zealand. Right Noble was killed in a hurdle race at Sandown, while Permit and Bermondsey went on to compete as steeplechasers. Crisp and Even is at the stud in France, Mehari in Poland.

1966: Wednesday, 25 May ... 552 Entries. £74,489 10s. 0d.

LADY ZIA WERNHER's b.c. CHARLOTTOWN
  by Charlottesville out of Meld   A. BREASLEY   1
MR J. A. C. LILLEY's ch.c PRETENDRE by Doutelle
  out of Limicola   P. COOK   2

658

1966

MR E. B. BENJAMIN'S BLACK PRINCE II
by Arctic Prince out of Rose II   J. LINDLEY   3

Also ran:

Mr R. J. Sigtia's Sodium (F. Durr) (4th); Mr J. S. M. Pearson-Gregory's Crisp and Even (G. Bougoure); Mrs A. Ford's Ambericos (J. Mercer); Mr E. R. More O'Ferrall's Khalekan (D. Lake); Lady Sassoon's Radbrook (W. Williamson); Mr C. W. Engelhard's Right Noble (L. Piggott); Lord Rosebery's St Puckle (W. Rickaby); Lord Allendale's Allenheads (E. Hide); Mrs H. Bamberg's Bermondsey (R. Maddock); Mr R. D. Hollingsworth's Hermes (G. Starkey); Mr K. Dodson's One For You (G. Lewis); Col A. C. R. Waites's Nous Esperons (E. Eldin); Mr R. Brown's Borodino (S. Clayton); Mrs A. Johnson's Dream Man (B. Taylor); Mrs T. Hartman's Splice the Mainbrace (R. Hutchinson); Mr W. G. Reynold's Baylanx (P. Sullivan); Mr D. Prenn's Mehari (D. Smith); Mrs F. Maxwell's Drevno (B. Raymond); Mr W. Harvey's Raket II (D. Keith); Mr E. Cousins's Permit (G. Cadwaladr); Mr C. W. Engelhard's Grey Moss (L. Ward); Brig C. M. Stewart's Northern Union (J. Roe) (pulled up).

25 ran.

Betting:

9–2 Right Noble, Pretendre; 5–1 Charlottown; 8–1 Grey Moss; 100–8 Hermes; 13–1 Sodium; 18–1 Ambericos; 20–1 Khalekan, Black Prince II; 33–1 Mehari, Northern Union; 40–1 St Puckle; 50–1 Raket II, Allenheads, Radbrook; 66–1 Crisp and Even, Splice the Mainbrace; 100–1 others.

Totalizator: (4s. unit). Win: £1 4s. 10d. Places: 11s., 9s. 4d., 17s. 6d.

Won by a neck; five lengths between second and third.   2 m. 37·63 s.
Winner trained by G. Smyth at Lewes.

1967

Like Charlottown, Mr Jim Joel's Royal Palace won good races at two, three and four years of age. Had he been able to run in the St Leger, he might well have been the first horse to win the 'Triple Crown' since Bahram in 1935.

Bred by his owner, Royal Palace is a bay by Ballymoss, a sire whose career needs no further elaboration, out of Crystal Palace, by Solar Slipper out of Queen of Light. Crystal Palace was a very useful filly up to ten furlongs, her successes including the Falmouth Stakes at Newmarket and the Nassau Stakes at Goodwood. Queen of Light was by Borealis out of the One Thousand Guineas winner Picture Play, by Donatello II. Like Crystal Palace, she included the Falmouth Stakes among her successes. One of her off-spring is Chandelier, dam of that good winner and successful sire Crocket. She herself traces back to the famous mare Absurdity, by Melton, whose descendants have won every classic for the famous black and red colours of Mr Jim Joel and of his father, the late Mr J. B. Joel.

Trained by Noel Murless, Royal Palace made his first racecourse appearance in the six-furlong Coventry Stakes at Royal Ascot. He was still rather backward and was not expected to beat some of the sprinter-bred, quick maturing types in that event. In fact he ran an extremely promising race to hold his own for rather more than four furlongs. The winner was the powerful American-bred colt Bold Lad who went on to win the Champagne Stakes and the Middle Park Stakes. Royal Palace did not run again until the York August meeting when he was a smooth winner of the six-furlong Acomb Stakes.

His final appearance as a two-year old was in the Royal Lodge Stakes at Ascot in September, a race run over a mile—The Old Mile—and worth £5,500 to the winner. Ridden by Piggott, he handicapped himself by a slow start and was still last on the final bend. In the straight, though, he accelerated to such purpose that he led two furlongs out and won by a length and a half from Slip Stitch. He had gone rather close to Slip Stitch and because of that he had to survive an enquiry by the Stewards.

In general he had given the impression of being a high-class colt that would surely come into serious consideration for the Derby. In the Free Handicap he was given second place, three pounds below Bold Lad.

Most thoroughbreds of today tend to be specialists over matters of distance, and few modern winners of the Derby have had the speed to cope with specialist milers in the Two Thousand Guineas. Royal Palace, however, proved an exception, as did Sir Ivor the following year.

Royal Palace was given no preliminary outing before the Two Thousand Guineas in which he was ridden by that gifted but rather highly-strung Australian, George Moore, Piggott having decided at the close of the previous season to sever his long and successful connection with Murless's stable and to ride 'free-lance' instead. Royal Palace started joint favourite with Bold Lad, while there was a lot of money for the French colt Taj Dewan, by Prince Taj.

A good many people reckoned that the sheer speed of Bold Lad who had no pretension of staying a mile and a half, would be decisive. Fortunately perhaps for Royal Palace, Bold Lad was badly hampered when right up with the leaders just over a furlong from home. He had to be snatched up and to change his position; he could never get going again afterwards.

Golden Horus led at the Bushes but at the distance he was passed by Taj Dewan. In the meantime, though, Royal Palace was making swift headway, and running on with the utmost determination, he headed the French colt coming up the hill. Taj Dewan, though, was no less courageous. He simply refused to give in and in fact he staged such a gallant final rally that Royal Palace had only inches to spare at the finish. Missile was a good third and Golden Horus fourth. It was exactly fifty-six years since Mr Joel's father had won the Two Thousand Guineas with Sunstar who then went on to win the Derby.

Royal Palace had shown that although bred to stay, he possessed first-class speed as well and it was evident that it was going to require a really good colt to vanquish him in the Derby. In the paddock at Newmarket, though, the critics had been somewhat sparing in their praise. A medium-sized bay, he had given the impression of being rather long in the back and short in the neck. He had sweated over his loins, and his whole bearing had seemed to convey an air of strain and nervous tension. However, no colt could have run his race with greater resolution.

Royal Palace thoroughly satisfied Murless in his Derby preparation and he started favourite at 7–4. Next in the betting came two Irish candidates, Royal Sword and Dominion Day. Ribocco, from whom so much had been expected at the start of the season, had failed to thrive in the cold weather and after successive defeats at Newmarket, Chester and Lingfield he had drifted to 22–1 despite the fact that he was ridden by Lester Piggott.

The going was good and so was the start from the stalls. Royal Palace was always going well within himself and coming to Tattenham Corner he was travelling smoothly in fifth position behind El Mighty, Privy Seal, Belted and Kiss of Life. In the straight it was clear that Moore could take the lead whenever he felt inclined to do so and riding with supreme confidence, he moved the favourite to the front with well over a quarter of a mile to go. Royal Sword pursued him doggedly but with no noticeable prospect of success.

Meanwhile Piggott had deliberately taken Ribocco very wide to keep him well clear of other competitors and was making rapid progress down the centre of the course, so rapid in fact that with a furlong to go he had almost drawn level with Royal Palace. Moore, though, was completely unperturbed even if the excitement in the stands was rising fast. He knew he still had a comfortable amount in reserve so he gave the favourite a couple of taps with the whip. The response was immediate; Royal Palace lengthened his stride to draw clear and win by two and a half lengths. Dart Board, who had stayed on stoutly in the straight, was third, two lengths behind Ribocco, and Royal Sword fourth.

Thus Murless and Moore had won all the first three classics as they were associated, too, with Fleet, winner of the One Thousand Guineas. It was Murless's third Derby success. The winner was given a hero's welcome not merely because he was a successful favourite, but because his owner is one of the kindest and most unassuming members of the racing world. He has always tried to breed the best type of horse at his Childwick Bury Stud, near St Albans, and his horses are invariably out to win. He celebrated this major triumph of his racing career at a small, entirely informal dinner party given for him at Whites by Mr Tom Blackwell, with a little bridge afterwards.

A somewhat unenterprising policy was pursued with Royal Palace after the Derby and he missed all the big mid-summer events. Possibly Murless at that time feared that Royal Palace's temperament might not stand up to much hard racing. At all events, everything was concentrated on winning the 'Triple Crown'.

Unfortunately, though, Royal Palace rapped himself in his work at home and had to miss the Great Voltigeur Stakes at York, his warming-up race before Doncaster. The injury seemed to clear up but the situation was hardly improved when he managed to contract a slight chill. The sad upshot was that after a final gallop on the Saturday before Doncaster, he blew so hard that both his trainer and his jockey doubted if he was fit enough to do himself justice in the St Leger. Accordingly he was taken out of that race which Ribocco won from the Queen's Hopeful Venture.

Royal Palace's final appearance as a three-year-old was in the ten-furlong Champion Stakes at Newmarket, in October. He was by then only a dim shadow of his true self and finished a rather moderate third to Reform, a really good colt up to ten furlongs, and Taj Dewan.

Royal Palace was kept in training for a third season, a decision that Mr Joel never had cause to regret as Royal Palace emerged undefeated at the end of it and many people thought him a little unlucky not to have been voted 'Racehorse of the

Royal Palace; by Richard Stone Reeves

Year'. George Moore was no longer riding in England and his place was taken most successfully by young Sandy Barclay.

Royal Palace's first three wins in 1968 were the Coronation Stakes at Sandown, the Coronation Cup, and the Prince of Wales's Stakes at Ascot. These successes did not in fact add up to a great deal as the opposition was anything but formidable. The Eclipse Stakes at Sandown in July, however, was a very different matter as in this famous ten-furlong race he had to meet the 1968 Derby winner Sir Ivor, as well as Taj Dewan who had beaten him in the Champion Stakes.

It was a magnificent race. Taj Dewan took the lead early in the straight and headed for home as hard as he could. Royal Palace, though, slowly but surely closed the gap and got up in the last two strides to win by a very short head. The odds-on favourite Sir Ivor was three parts of a length away third. He had not really been happy on the firm ground and failed to produce his characteristic acceleration.

Connections of Taj Dewan were supremely confident their colt had won, indeed to such an extent that they were reluctant to believe the evidence supplied by the camera. It was undoubtedly one of those races in which the photo-finish proves of the utmost benefit. Without it, there would surely have been doubt, arguments and possibly ill-feeling too.

Royal Palace's final race was the King George VI and Queen Elizabeth Stakes at Ascot, which he duly won by half a length from Felicio II with Topyo close up third. It was noticeable that Royal Palace failed to quicken in his best style in the closing stages while he was rather inclined to hang away from the rails as well. The reason for this was explained when he returned very lame to the unsaddling enclosure, having torn a suspensory ligament. He was a very game horse to have struggled on as he did and the courage he showed in those last two furlongs represented, so to speak, the finest hour of his entire racing career.

Royal Palace, who is now standing at the Egerton Stud, Newmarket, had won the record total for an English-trained horse of £166,063. Among the horses he had vanquished were Sir Ivor (Grand Criterium, Two Thousand Guineas, Derby, Champion Stakes and Washington International); Ribocco (St Leger, and Irish Derby); Topyo (Prix de l'Arc de Triomphe); Felicio II (Grand Prix de Saint-Cloud) and Taj Dewan (winner of £93,524).

Of the other horses in the 1967 Derby, Ribocco won the races mentioned in the preceding paragraph and was close up third in the Prix de l'Arc de Triomphe. He failed in the Washington International and is now at stud in America. Dart Board was exported to the Argentine. Royal Sword broke a leg in the Irish Sweeps Derby and had to be destroyed. Sloop went on to the Argentine and Dominion Day to Canada. Privy Seal was third in the Champion Hurdle in 1969.

1967

1967: Wednesday, 7 June . . . 584 Entries. £61,918.

MR H. J. JOEL's b.c. ROYAL PALACE by Ballymoss out of Crystal Palace	G. MOORE	1
MR C. W. ENGELHARD's b.c. RIBOCCO by Ribot out of Libra	L. PIGGOTT	2
MR M. SOBELL's ch.c. DART BOARD by Darius out of Shrubswood	A. BREASLEY	3

Also ran:

General R. K. Mellon's Royal Sword (J. Lindley) (4th); Mr A. H. Penn's Helluvafella (A. Barclay); Mrs A. Kalmanson's Landigou (C. Barends); Mr R. D. Hollingsworth's Sloop (G. Starkey); Mr D. Drewery's Dancing Moss (P. Boothman); Mr D. Robinson's Starry Halo (F. Durr); Mrs R. Sangster's Hang On (G. Cadwaladr); Mr G. M. Bell's Dominion Day (D. Lake); Mr H. S. Alper's Hambleden (J. Mercer); Mr L. M. Gelb's Great Host (Y. St-Martin); Mr A. J. Allen's Acroplier (D. Keith); Mr J. Ismay's Belted (A. Murray); Mr S. Terry's Persian Genius (E. Eldin); Mr S. Tsiatalo's El Mighty (P. Cook); Mr R. G. Angus's Kiss of Life (E. Larkin); Major G. Glover's Privy Seal (B. Raymond); Mr A. J. Struthers's Scottish Sinbad (V. Faggotter); Mr A. J. Richards's Tapis Rose (R. Hutchinson); Mr D. Morris's Great Pleasure (G. Lewis).

22 ran.

Betting:

7–4 Royal Palace; 15–2 Royal Sword; 8–1 Dominion Day; 10–1 Dart Board; 100–9 Great Host; 22–1 Ribocco, Starry Halo, El Mighty; 28–1 Tapis Rose; 33–1 Sloop; 66–1 Hambleden, Acroplier, Great Pleasure; 100–1 Dancing Moss; 150–1 Hang On; 200–1 others.

Totalizator: (4s. unit). Win 9s. 8d. Places: 6s., 13s. 4d., 10s. 1d.

Won by two and a half lengths; two lengths between second and third. 2 m. 38·3 s. Winner trained by N. Murless at Newmarket.

1968

It was America's year in 1968 when with a devastating late burst of speed that will never be forgotten by all who saw it, the brilliant and courageous Sir Ivor won for Mr Raymond Guest.

Sir Ivor has a completely American pedigree and was bred by Mrs Alice Headley Bell at Mill Ridge Farm, Kentucky. He is by Gaylord out of Attica, by Mr Trouble. Sir Gaylord was a good, fast two-year-old that won six races from five to six furlongs. As a three-year-old he won all his four races, the longest being nine furlongs, before he unfortunately broke down and had to be taken out of training. He was favourite for the Kentucky Derby at the time.

Sir Gaylord, who also is sire of that fine miler, Habitat, is by Turn-to, a son of Royal Charger. Turn-to was one of the best horses in America up to a mile but his career ended early on on account of injury to a tendon. Royal Charger was trained in England by the late Sir Jack Jarvis. Although bred to stay, being by the Grand Prix winner Nearco out of a mare by the St Leger and Gold Cup winner Solario, speed was his essential characteristic and his best performance was to win the six-furlong Ayr Gold Cup with top weight. It was on account of their recollection of Royal Charger, that many English followers of racing doubted Sir Ivor's ability to stay the full Derby distance.

Mr Trouble, sire of Sir Ivor's dam Attica, was by the grey Derby winner Mahmoud. Attica herself won five races at three and four years of age. Her dam Athenia, by Pharamond II, a half-brother to Hyperion by Phalaris, was a very good handicapper whose ten victories earned her 105,170 dollars. In addition she was second in the Kentucky Oaks. At the stud she produced eleven foals, nine of which won. The next dam Salaminia, by Man o'War, was a half-sister to Menow, sire of that good horse Tom Fool.

It only remains to add that the line had originally been introduced into America from England by Mrs Bell's father, the late Mr Hal Price Headley, who bought the two-year-old filly Regal Roman, by Roi Herode, for 560 guineas in 1923. Regal Roman bred Alcibiades, winner of the Kentucky Oaks and fourth dam of Sir Ivor.

As a yearling Sir Ivor was sent to the Keeneland Sales where he was bought for 42,000 dollars by Mr 'Bull' Hancock acting on behalf of Mr Raymond Guest. He was then packed off to be trained by Vincent O'Brien in Ireland, where Mr Guest held office as United States Ambassador.

Sir Ivor's introduction to racing was the Tyros Stakes at the Curragh on Irish Derby Day. Such was his reputation that he started joint favourite at 3–1 but he still needed time and though he performed with promise for the future, he ended up sixth behind Mistigo. A month later he turned out for the seven-furlong Probationers Stakes at the Curragh. By then he was straighter in condition, and in receipt of five pounds he defeated Mistigo by a neck with Candy Cane, who had not run before, third. In the £4,400 National Stakes run over seven furlongs at the Curragh on 16 September, Candy Cane was installed as favourite to beat Sir Ivor on level terms but Sir Ivor was improving in leaps and bounds and he slammed Candy Cane in the most impressive manner by three lengths with Society four lengths away third.

By now it was clear that Sir Ivor was a very good colt indeed and it was decided to run him in the one-mile Grand Criterium at Longchamp, a race that on this occasion was worth £30,108 to the winner. There were thirteen runners and the heavy going made it a true test of stamina. With Piggott riding, though, the issue was never in doubt and Sir Ivor fairly made the French sit up by going clear in the final furlong and winning with the utmost ease by three lengths from Pola Bella with Timmy My Boy third. The manner in which Sir Ivor had won substantially reinforced the hopes of those who had always regarded him as a potential winner of the Derby.

To avoid the worst of the Irish climate, Sir Ivor was sent for the winter to Italy. He thrived physically and as a three-year-old he was an exceptionally handsome individual, a bright bay, big, strong and muscular, but perfectly proportioned and giving an appearance of quality combined with high-powered activity. It was clear that his main opponent in the Two Thousand Guineas, his first major target, would be Captain Marcus Lemos's unbeaten Petition colt Petingo. Lester Piggott had been offered the ride on both Sir Ivor and Petingo and he had to come to a decision before the season began. He rode both colts in their work at home and finally opted for Sir Ivor. Joe Mercer was accordingly engaged for Petingo.

Sir Ivor won the Two Thousand Guineas Trial at Ascot, Petingo the Craven Stakes at Newmarket. They were the only two seriously backed for the Two Thousand Guineas, Sir Ivor starting at 11–8 while Petingo was on offer at 9–4. The running was made at a fierce pace by So Blessed, a very fast colt that later became a leading sprinter. Petingo kept in close touch and by so doing he may have taken more out of himself than was desirable. Sir Ivor on the other hand was permitted to take matters far more easily in the early stages and Piggott, riding with ice-cold confidence, was clearly not intending to hurry.

With three furlongs to go Sir Ivor began to make headway. Petingo, already under some pressure, went to the front with over a furlong to go but he had nothing left in reserve when Sir Ivor challenged him and the favourite went on to win in the smoothest and most effortless manner imaginable by a length and a half. Jimmy Reppin, later to prove himself an outstanding miler, was two and a half lengths away third. It was a most impressive victory by a high-class colt with superb power of acceleration. Worried indeed must have been that well-known bookmaker Mr William Hill who the previous summer had laid Mr Guest £50,000 to £500 against Sir Ivor winning the Derby and £12,500 to £500 against Sir Ivor being placed.

Sir Ivor did not run again before the Derby for which he started at 5–4 on. His appearance in the paddock delighted his supporters as he had clearly gained condition and put on weight since Newmarket. He looked in fact fit to run for his life. It had been anticipated that his most formidable rival would be Mr J. J. Astor's unbeaten Alcide colt Remand, winner of the Chester Vase that season. Backers of Remand, though, were mortified to find that he had run up light, was very fidgety, and clearly not at all on good terms with himself. He was in fact sickening for a virus infection that kept him off the course for the rest of the year. There was a fair amount of each-way money for Connaught, a big, burly, rather coarse St Paddy colt that carried Mr H. J. Joel's colours. The going and the weather alike were perfect.

It was widely anticipated that Piggott would wait on Sir Ivor for as long as he could, partly to make the best possible use of Sir Ivor's finishing speed, partly because a slight doubt existed of Sir Ivor's stamina to stay the distance in a fast-run race. No doubt it was with these points in mind that Sanday Barclay shot Connaught into the lead five furlongs out and headed for home as hard as he could. Piggott, though, was too experienced and too cool a hand to be rattled by such tactics and Sir Ivor was still only eighth on the final bend.

In the straight Sir Ivor and Remand both began to make solid progress but Connaught showed not the slightest sign of weakening and at one point must have been every bit of five lengths clear. Below the distance Remand, who had run a brave race considering his condition, had given everything he had and the only danger to Connaught was Sir Ivor.

Entering the final furlong it really looked as if Connaught, a maiden, could not be beaten but at that point Piggott pulled Sir Ivor to the outside, balanced him and asked him to go. For a fraction of a second Sir Ivor seemed to hesitate and then came his electrifying response. In a matter of seconds a turn of speed that had to be seen to be believed had swept him past Connaught, who certainly did not falter in the closing stages of the struggle, and had landed him the winner by a length and a half, with the fast-finishing Mount Athos third. That final furlong provided one of the most thrilling and spectacular Derby episodes within living memory and can never be forgotten by those who had the good luck to be there to see it. It was sad indeed that a grave duty in Ireland prevented Mr Guest from being present to see the race and in his absence the winner was led in by his wife. It was Piggott's fourth Derby winner and never had he ridden a better judged race. Piggott, in the exuberance of success, declared that Sir Ivor was superior to his earlier Derby winners, Never Say Die, Crepello and St Paddy, while O'Brien judged Sir Ivor an even better horse than Ballymoss.

Sir Ivor's reputation was accordingly now extremely high and in general he was regarded as one of the best Derby winners of the century. Yet the fact remains that he was defeated in his next four races.

In the Irish Sweeps Derby, starting at 3–1 on, he caused a sensation of no little magnitude in being defeated decisively by two lengths by Mr Engelhard's Ribero, a brother of Ribocco. Piggott was required for Ribero so Liam Ward rode Sir Ivor. No fault could be found with Ward's riding and Sir Ivor just faded in the final furlong. 'He simply died in my hands,' said Ward afterwards. Possibly Sir Ivor's Epsom exertions had taken more out of him than was thought at the time.

Much to his credit, Mr Guest declined to play safe and in fact adopted a fighting policy that formed a pleasing contrast to the all too cautious strategy adopted by so many modern owners. A week after his Curragh failure Sir Ivor took the field in the ten-furlong Eclipse Stakes at Sandown. The going was rather firmer than he liked and down the far side of the track he was never striding out with quite his customary zest and freedom. The result was that in the straight he had a lot of ground to make up on two top-class four-year-olds in Royal Palace and Taj Dewan. He ran on bravely and narrowed the gap considerably but he had taken too much out of himself and his characteristic acceleration was lacking. All the same, he was only beaten a short head and three parts of a length by Royal Palace, like himself a dual classic winner, and Taj Dewan.

Sir Ivor now deserved a rest and in any case had to be given one as he was distinctly sore after Sandown. His autumn target was the Prix de l'Arc de Triomphe rather than the St Leger, the distance of which would probably have been beyond his scope. Because of the firm ground, his preparation for the big Paris race got slightly behind schedule and it was deemed necessary to send him to Longchamp for a warming-up race only a week before the 'Arc'. The race chosen was the eleven-furlong Prix Henri Delamarre. In this he was beaten by Prince Sao, a three-year-old to whom he was conceding 9 lb. Since he badly needed this outing, his defeat was not taken too seriously.

As O'Brien had hoped, that race brought Sir Ivor on nicely and he was back at his best for the 'Arc', this time worth over £96,000 to the winner. He certainly ran up to his peak form but found one too good for him in the British-bred Vaguely Noble, who had been bought for 136,000 guineas at Newmarket the previous December. Vaguely Noble went clear three furlongs out and though Sir Ivor chased him home with his customary courage he could make no impression and Vaguely Noble, a three-year-old by Vienna, won by three lengths.

It was Sir Ivor's good fortune to possess a robust constitution allied to a perfect racing temperament. None the worse for his defeat in Paris he turned out at Newmarket on 19 October for the mile and a quarter Champion Stakes worth over £14,000 to the winner. Favourite at 11–8 on, he won very easily from Locris and Candy Cane with Taj Dewan a moderate fifth.

Sir Ivor's final race was the Washington International at Laurel Park. This he won by three-quarters of a length from the British-bred Czar Alexander, who was originally trained by Harvey Leader at Newmarket and since then has won over £150,000 in prize money in America. On this occasion Piggott may have been a shade over-confident with the result that Sir Ivor won by rather a narrower margin than he might have done. All the same, Piggott hardly deserved the sour comments at his expense in the American press.

Voted 'Horse of the Year' in 1968, Sir Ivor had run thirteen times altogether, winning eight times and being placed on four other occasions. His earnings were £116,787 in England and Ireland; in France 876,100 francs; in the United States 100,000 dollars. Probably a mile and a quarter was really his ideal distance but he was so easy to settle down that with judicious riding he could stay a mile and a half. His class was evident; his courage was never questioned; and not once did he run a bad race. It will be surprising indeed if he fails to prove an immensely successful sire. He stood for one season at the Ballygoran Stud in Ireland at a fee of 8,000 guineas, five thousand guineas more than the fee then charged for Royal Palace. It was planned for him to return to America in 1970. Foals by Sir Ivor realized big prices at the 1970 Newmarket December Sales.

Of the other horses in Sir Ivor's Derby, Connaught, unpredictable till then, reached his peak as a five-year-old when he won the Eclipse Stakes. Mount Athos won seven races worth over £13,000 but his temperament got the better of him as a four-year-old. Remand won twice as a four-year-old and was then exported to Japan. Society as a four-year-old was exported to Japan, while Torpid ran second in the 1969 Ascot Gold Cup. Laureate was exported to South Africa. Myrtus has won over hurdles and Royal Rocket won his first race in 1970.

1968

1968 : Wednesday, 29 May . . . 59 Entries. £58,525 10s 0d.

MR R. GUEST's SIR IVOR by Sir Gaylord
   out of Attica   L. PIGGOTT   1

MR H. J. JOEL's b.c. CONNAUGHT by St Paddy
   out of Nagaika   A. BARCLAY   2

MR A. J. STRUTHER's b.c. MOUNT ATHOS by Sunny Way
   out of Rosie Wings   R. HUTCHINSON 3

Also ran:

Mr J. J. Astor's Remand (J. Mercer) (4th); Mr F. MacMahon's Society (W. Williamson); Mr R. D. Hollingsworth's Torpid (G. Starkey); Mr R. N. Richmond-Watson's Atopolis (J. Lindley); Mr R. J. Sigtia's Royal Rocket (F. Durr); Mr N. Cohen's Myrtus (A. Murray); Mrs D. Langton's Floriana (W. Rickaby); Lord Derby's Laureate (W. Carson); Mr A. J. Kennedy's Benroy (D. Keith); Mr B. Fury's First Rate Pirate (P. Cook).

13 ran.

Betting:

4–5 Sir Ivor; 4–1 Remand; 100–9 Connaught; 100–8 Laureate; 25–1 Torpid; 28–1 Society; 40–1 Atopolis, Mount Athos; 66–1 Royal Rocket; 150–1 Myrtus, Benroy; 200–1 others.

Totalizator: (4s. unit). Win 8s. 2d. Places: 6s. 8d., 9s. 10d., 13s. 2d.

Won by a length and a half; two and a half lengths between second and third.

                                                  2 m. 38·7 s.

Winner trained by M. V. O'Brien at Cashel, Co. Tipperary, Ireland.

1969

Blakeney, winner in 1969, was of a very different calibre to Sir Ivor. In fact all the evidence, notably his subsequent form, suggests that he was a distinctly sub-standard Derby winner.

Blakeney was bred by the Whatcombe trainer Arthur Budgett and is by the St Leger winner Hethersett, who would very likely have become a great sire but for his early death, out of Windmill Girl, by Hornbeam. A good, honest stayer by Hyperion, Hornbeam found little favour with breeder's over here and in 1966 was exported to Sweden. He sired the 1969 St Leger winner Intermezzo. Windmill Girl herself was a good race-mare, finishing second in the Oaks and winning the Ribblesdale Stakes. Her dam, Chorus Beauty, by Chanteur II, was third in the Ribblesdale Stakes and fourth in the Cesarewitch. She goes back to the late Major L. B. Holliday's foundation mare Springtime, a half-sister to the 1939 Derby winner Blue Peter.

As a yearling Blakeney was sent up to the Newmarket Sales but failed to reach a modest reserve of 5,000 guineas. Accordingly Budgett decided to keep him and train him himself. He later sold shares in the colt to Mrs H. H. Renshaw and Mrs J. M. Carnegie but Blakeney ran in his name and carried his colours.

As a two-year-old Blakeney did not run until the autumn. At the end of September he ran an encouraging race to finish fourth to Caliban in the Clarence House Stakes at Ascot. Three weeks later he won the seven-furlong Houghton Stakes at Newmarket by half a length from Prince de Galles who was to land a tremendous coup in the Cambridgeshire the following year. That race concluded Blakeney's two-year-old career. He had looked a good stayer in the making but obviously had a long way to go before he could hope to reach the top of the tree.

Training conditions were difficult in the spring of 1969 and there were water-logged gallops all over the country. Blakeney did not run till 16 May when he took part in the Lingfield Derby Trial ridden be Geoff Lewis. Unfortunately Lewis rode one of his less admirable races and landed Blakeney in considerable trouble three furlongs from home. Once Blakeney got clear he ran on really well but could not quite catch The Elk who had won the 'Observer' Gold Cup the year before. There is no doubt at all that Blakeney ought to have won, and bearing in mind, too, that it was his first race since October, he was reckoned to have run a highly satisfactory Derby Trial.

In the Derby Blakeney was partnered by young Ernest Johnson who had been promised the mount after riding Blakeney to victory in the Houghton Stakes. Originally apprenticed to Ian Balding, Johnson was top apprentice in 1967 and in 1968 rode 62 winners, proving himself one of the strongest and most capable light-weights in the country. Success has never turned his head and he has always been receptive to advice from more experienced riders and shown a marked willingness to study his profession and to learn.

Favourite for the Derby at 7–2 was Lester Piggott's mount Ribofilio despite the mystery, that has never been satisfactorily explained, of Ribofilio's lamentable display in the Two Thousand Guineas in which he was unable to raise a gallop and was eventually pulled up. Second favourite was Mr H. J. Joel's Paddy's Progress, a tall St Paddy colt that had won the Craven Stakes with some ease. There was a lot of money for the French-trained Right Royal colt Prince Regent, who had beaten Caliban by inches in the £48,000 Prix Lupin, while Blakeney was a popular each-way choice at 15–2. The going was good.

There is little doubt that Prince Regent ought to have won but unfortunately his rider seemed to take him on a conducted tour of the lesser known portions of the Surrey countryside. With four furlongs to go, Prince Regent's position appeared quite hopeless but in the straight he made a valiant and determined effort, passing horse after horse to eventually gain third place only two lengths behind the winner. He was the unluckiest loser of the Derby since Shantung in 1959. Another unlucky horse behind Blakeney was the subsequent St Leger winner Intermezzo who was very badly hampered coming down the hill.

Johnson did not hurry Blakeney in the early stages and in fact was very nearly last. From halfway he began to improve his position, and like Breasley on Charlottown in 1966, he had the immense good fortune to find a trouble-free passage on the inside right to the finish of the race. It is much to Blakeney's credit, though, that when a narrow opening appeared on the rails close home, he went through it without a second's hesitation.

From the very start the running was made by the Irish-trained Moon Mountain, who, like Prince Regent, carried the colours of the Comtesse de la Valdene. Considering the use that Yves Saint-Martin made of him, Moon Mountain ran a marvellous race and he was only headed a furlong from home, eventually losing third place by a neck. It would be interesting to know the Comtesse's opinion of the jockeyship displayed on her two horses that day. Moon Mountain certainly had a very hard race and lost his form afterwards but Prince Regent found compensation in the Irish Sweeps Derby.

It was Shoemaker who headed Moon Mountain and he in turn was headed by

1969

the strong-finishing Blakeney well inside the final furlong. The victory was a popular one as apart from the fact that Blakeney was a well-backed, English-bred, English-trained winner, Arthur Budgett is one of racing's most modest and friendly personalities. An Old Etonian, the third one to train a Derby winner this century, he is a member of a well-known hunting and polo-playing family. He first took out a licence to train in 1939 but his career was then interrupted by six years' service in the army. In 1973, with Morston, he became the second man, after Mr I'Anson, to breed, own and train two Derby winners.

Blakeney's three remaining races last season brought a steady decline in his newly acquired reputation. In the Irish Sweeps Derby he could never work his way into a challenging position and finished a rather dim fourth behind Prince Regent, Ribofilio and Reindeer. He was sore after the Curragh and had to miss his engagement in the Great Voltigeur Stakes at York. He turned out for the St Leger, though, but could only finish fifth behind Intermezzo, Ribofilio, and Prince Consort. It is fair to emphasize that he had anything but a clear run in the straight and that excuses offered on his behalf appeared valid. Finally he was a modest ninth to Levmoss, Park Top and Grandier in the Prix de l'Arc de Triomphe. At four he won the Ormonde Stakes at Chester and was second in the Ascot Gold Cup and the King George VI and Queen Elizabeth Stakes. He was fifth in the Prix de l'Arc de Triomphe. He is now standing at the National Stud. Shoemaker won two races in France in 1970 worth over £28,000, the Prix Jean de Chaudenay and the Prix Gontaut-Biron. The previous year he had won the Prix Henry Delamare.

1969 : Wednesday, 4 June . . . 653 Entries. £63,108 6s. od.

MR A. M. BUDGETT's b.c. BLAKENEY by Hethersett
out of Windmill — E. JOHNSON — 1
MR P. G. GOULANDRIS's ch.c. SHOEMAKER
by Saint Crespin III out of Whipcord — B. TAYLOR — 2
COMTESSE DE LA VALDENE's br.c. PRINCE REGENT
by Right Royal V out of Noduleuse — J. DEFORGE — 3

Also ran:

Comtesse de la Valdene's Moon Mountain (Y. Saint-Martin) (4th); Mr C. W. Engelhard's Ribofilio (L. Piggott); Mr N. Hetherton's Tantivy (J. Seagrave); Mr H. J. Joel's Paddy Progress (A. Barclay); Mr G. A. Oldham's Intermezzo (R. Hutchinson); Madame L. Volterra's Belbury (R. Poincelot); Mr D. Van Clief's Stoned (D. Keith); Mr J. B. Harvey's Hard Slipper (G. Starkey); Major V. McCalmont's Agricultore (G. Lewis); Major H. P. Holt's Ribomar (J. Mercer);

Mr G. J. Van der Ploeg's Dutch Bells (A. Murray); Mr. S McGrath's Santomoss (E. Hide); Mr D. Baxter's Pardigras (D. Ryan); Lord Rosebery's Timon (J. Gorton), Miss M. Sheriffe's The Elk (J. Lindley); Mr J. Hanson's Sylvago (W. Bentley); Mr J. R. Mullion's Agustus (W. Williamson); Mrs D. Solomon's Silence d'Or (T. Burns); Mrs B. P. Gourdeau's Mitsouko (D. Richardson); Mr H. S. Alper's Chadwick Stone (B. Jago); Mrs J. Gilbert's Backing Britain (W. Carson); Captain M. D. Lemos's Soroco (E. Eldin); and Sir F. Cassel's Dieudonne (D. Yates).

26 ran.

Betting:

7–2 Ribofilio, 11–2 Paddy's Progress, 13–2 Prince Regent, 15–2 Blakeney, 100–9 Belbury and The Elk, 15–1 Intermezzo, 18–1 Agricultore and Stoned, 25–1 Agustus and Shoemaker; 28–1 Moon Mountain; 50–1 Timon, Sylvalgo, Pardigras and Ribomar; 75–1 Santamoss; 100–1 Backing Britain, Tantivy, Soroco and Dutch Bells; 200–1 others.

Totalizator: (4s. unit). Win: £1 9s. Places 10s. 10d., 17s. 4d., 10s. 4d.

Won by a length; same between second and third.   2 m. 40·3 s.
Winner trained by A. M. Budgett at Wantage.

1970

Nijinsky, the first Canadian-bred horse to win the Derby, was bred in Ontario by Mr Edgar P. Taylor, a man who has done much to raise the standard of the Canadian thoroughbred. A big, powerful, handsome bay with a magnificent head, Nijinsky is by Northern Dancer out of Flaming Page, by Bull Page. Northern Dancer, by Nearco's son Nearctic, stands only 15 hands 2 inches but is perfectly proportioned and full of quality. In 1964 he was the best three-year-old in the continent of North America. He won the Kentucky Derby and the Preakness Stakes and was third in the Belmont Stakes. He also won Canada's most important race, the ten furlong Queen's Plate at Woodbine.

Flaming Page is a big, rangey mare with an uncertain temper. She, too, won the Queen's Plate and was second in the Coaching Club American Oaks.

It is Mr Taylor's custom to sell all his yearlings if he can find a buyer to pay his price. If he does not, he races the animal himself. On the advice of the great Irish trainer Vincent O'Brien, Mr Charles Engelhard bought Nijinsky for 84,000 dollars at the Woodbine Sale in Toronto. Soon afterwards Nijinsky joined O'Brien's stable in Co. Tipperary.

Nijinsky proved by no means a placid colt when in training and excitability and impatience were among his characteristics. He would frequently play up on his way to the gallops and he was liable to become upset if he did not work first of the whole string. Although he stood 16 hands 3 inches, he did not take long to fill out and develop his strength. By July 1969 he was ready to race.

On 12 July Nijinsky, favourite at 11–4 on, took the field in the six furlong Erne Maiden Stakes at the Curragh. He won by half a length from Everyday. He followed up that modest success with consecutive victories in three far more important races, all at the Curragh, namely the Railway, Anglesey and Beresford Stakes. In the Beresford Stakes he had to fight hard to vanquish Decies, who won the Irish Two Thousand Guineas the following year.

In all those Irish races Nijinsky was ridden by L. Ward. When, however, he went over to Newmarket in October to run in the seven furlong Dewhurst Stakes, he was partnered by L. Piggott. He won the Dewhurst Stakes most impressively and was placed top of the English Free Handicap. He was, of course, top of the Irish one, too.

In 1970 Nijinsky was soon in action, winning the seven furlong Gladness Stakes at the Curragh, Ward up, on 4 April. He started at 7–4 on in the Two Thousand Guineas and in the hands of Piggott won by two and a half lengths from Yellow God with Roi Soleil the same distance away third. It was a majestic performance that stamped him as a three-year-old of the highest class.

Nijinsky did not run again before the Derby in which, ridden by Piggott, he was a firm favourite at 11–8. There was, however, a lot of support for Gyr, a big, awkward, gangling, highly-strung American-bred colt by Sea Bird trained in France by Etienne Pollet. Pollet held such a high opinion of Gyr that he had postponed his retirement for a year. Gyr started at 100–30 despite the fact that many people thought his conformation was ill-suited to the downhill gallop to Tattenham Corner. A popular each way choice was the Alcide colt Approval, winner of the 'Observer' Gold Cup and the Dante Stakes, and a good many paddock critics rated him better-looking even than Nijinsky.

Gyr negotiated the hill in splendid style and was fifth into the straight, just ahead of Nijinsky. A great shout went up from Gyr's supporters when he headed the outsider Great Wall just over a quarter of a mile from home and at that point he looked very much like winning. All this time, though, Piggott was sitting very comfortably on Nijinsky. With two furlongs to go he shook Nijinsky up and delivered his challenge. Nijinsky responded as only a great horse can and swept past Gyr, who was beginning to hang to the left, to win in masterful fashion by two lengths and a half. The French-trained Stintino, winner of the Prix Lupin, was third, three lengths behind Gyr. Great Wall, fourth, was the first English-trained horse to finish. Nijinsky's time was 2 minutes 34·6 seconds. This was the fastest since Mahmoud won in 1936 on very firm ground and with the course noticeably short of grass in places. Nijinsky's victory was achieved on good going with a lush coverage of grass.

It was Mr Engelhard's first Derby success and also his last one as he died the following March at the early age of fifty-four. He had lived his life to the full and looked very much older than he was. Chairman of the Engelhard Minerals and Chemicals Corporation, he took up racing at the age of forty and built up a vast racing empire with horses in America, England, Ireland and South Africa. His horses in England and Ireland were managed by Mr David McCall and his trainers were Vincent O'Brien, Jeremy Tree, Jack Watts, Bill Watts and Fulke Johnson Houghton. He won the St Leger with Indiana, who was second in the Derby, and Ribocco and Ribero. Ribocco and Ribero, full brothers, both won the Irish Sweeps Derby as well. A good sportsman and an honorary member of the Jockey Club, he derived immense pleasure from the racing of high-class horses and his death was a great loss to the Turf.

This was the third Derby triumph gained by Vincent O'Brien and the fifth by Lester Piggott.

Nijinsky's next race was the Irish Sweeps Derby. The opposition was far from formidable and, ridden by Ward, he won in a canter from Meadowville. A month later, ridden by Piggott, he took the field in the King George VI and Queen Elizabeth Stakes at Ascot. Here he was opposed by some notable four-year-olds. These were Blakeney (Derby), Crepellana (French Oaks), Caliban (Coronation Cup), Karabas (Washington D.C. International) and Hogarth (Italian Derby). Nijinsky simply outclassed them and won, pulling up, by two lengths from Blakeney. The following month, with his racing career uncompleted, Nijinsky was syndicated for £2,266,666 to stand at the Claiborne Farm, Paris, Kentucky.

It had not originally been the intention to run Nijinsky in the St Leger but the glitter of the 'Triple Crown' proved tempting, particularly as that honour had not been achieved since the victories of Bahram in 1935. Unfortunately Nijinsky suffered during August from an extremely severe attack of ringworm. He lost all the hair from one flank and he missed much work in consequence. Although he won the St Leger without difficulty, his affliction probably took a good deal more out of him than was thought at the time.

It was generally taken for granted that Nijinsky would win the Prix de l'Arc de Triomphe and it came as a severe shock when he was beaten a head by the French Derby winner Sassafras. Piggott was sharply criticized on the grounds that he had left Nijinsky with far too much to do. The film of the race, though, showed that Nijinsky was nicely placed on the final bend and was not more than three lengths behind Sassafras when he made his challenge. A hundred and fifty yards from home he was level with Sassafras and he would undoubtedly have won had he maintained his run, but he faltered and in the last few strides veered to the left as Piggott wielded the whip with his right hand.

It was natural to wish Nijinsky to end his career with a victory and accordingly he ran in the ten furlong Champion Stakes at Newmarket thirteen days after his defeat at Longchamp. A huge crowd gathered in the confident expectation of seeing a great horse win. To the mortification of those present, Nijinsky was beaten by Lorenzaccio, a five-year-old just on the outer fringe of the top class.

There is no doubt that in the autumn Nijinsky had deteriorated. The skin disease had undoubtedly affected him. Furthermore, he had won his first race that season early in April and for a highly-strung horse he had done a great deal of travelling. Before the Champion Stakes it was clear he was suffering from nervous tension. The pitcher had been taken to the well a bit too often.

A great horse, at his best one of the greatest of this century, Nijinsky won eleven of his thirteen races. He earned £246,132 in England and Ireland, 480,000 francs in France.

Of the other Derby competitors Gyr, whose victories included the Prix Daru, the Prix Hocquart and the Grand Prix de Saint Cloud, was syndicated for the stud and stands in England. Stintino looked an unlucky loser of the Coronation Cup the following year. Great Wall, always a difficult horse to ride, became wayward and unreliable, while Approval seemed to lose all interest in racing. Mon Plaisir became a top-class handicapper, winning the Victoria Cup at Ascot with 9 st. 8 lb. and the Newbury Spring Cup with 9 st. 10 lb. Meadowville was second to Nijinsky in the Irish Sweeps Derby and the St Leger. He won the Great Voltigeur Stakes at York and as a four-year-old the John Porter Stakes at Newbury and the Jockey Club Stakes at Newmarket.

1970: Wednesday, 3 June . . . 667 Entries. £62,311.

MR C. W. ENGELHARD's b.c. NIJINSKY
    by Northern Dancer out of Flaming Page   L. PIGGOTT   I
MR W. F. C. GUEST's ch.c. GYR by Sea Bird II
    out of Feria   W. WILLIAMSON   2
MR G. A. OLDHAM's b.c. STINTINO
    by Sheshoon out of Cynara   G. THIBOEUF   3

Also ran:

Executors of the late Mr Dato D. Sung's Great Wall (4th) (J. Mercer); Mr D. Robinson's Meadowville (G. Lewis); Mrs D. Riley-Smith's The Swell (R. Hutchinson); Sir H. de Trafford's Approval (G. Starkey); Lady St Johnston's Long Till (D. Keith); Lady Sassoon's Cry Baby (A. Barclay); Mr C. D. Alexander's Tambourine Man (A. Murray); Mrs O. Turner's Mon Plaisir (J. Lindley).

11 ran.

Betting:

11–8 Nijinsky; 100–30 Gyr; 13–2 Approval; 7–1 Stintino; 22–1 Meadowville; 33–1 Mon Plaisir; 40–1 Cry Baby; 50–1 The Swell; 80–1 Great Wall and Long Till; 200–1 Tambourine Man.

Totalizator: (4s. unit). Win: 11s. Places: 6s., 7s. 6d., 8s.

Won by two and a half lengths; three lengths between second and third.

                                                    2 m. 34·6 s.

Winner trained by M. V. O'Brien at Cashel, Co. Tipperary, Ireland.

1971

Mill Reef was bred in America by his owner Mr Paul Mellon and is a medium-sized bay, perfectly proportioned and of beautiful quality, by Never Bend out of Milan Mill, by Princequillo out of Virginia Water, by Count Fleet. Never Bend, by Nasrullah, was the top American two-year-old of 1962. The following year he was second in the Kentucky Derby and third in the Preakness Stakes.

Milan Mill, who failed to win a race, is a half-sister to Berkeley Springs, winner of the Cheveley Park Stakes and second in both the One Thousand Guineas and the Oaks. Red Ray, dam of Virginia Water, was by Hyperion out of Infra Red and in 1949 was bought as a two-year-old by Mr Mellon for 12,000 guineas at the dispersal of Lord Portal's bloodstock. A grand-daughter of that celebrated mare Black Ray, Red Ray never raced. She produced only two living foals before her death in 1953.

Mr Mellon has long been a supporter of English racing both on the flat and under National Hunt Rules. He originally had his horses with the Hon. Aubrey Hastings, and on Hastings's sudden death he became a patron of Ivor Anthony who took over the stable. He remained a patron when Aubrey Hastings's son, Captain Peter Hastings, succeeded Ivor Anthony. Peter Hastings died in the prime of life and the Kingsclere stable came under the control of his assistant Ian Balding, who subsequently married his daughter, and who was thirty years of age when Mill Reef arrived at Kingsclere as a yearling.

Mill Reef proved a brilliant two-year-old. His one defeat came when he was narrowly defeated, perhaps a shade unluckily, in the five and a half furlong Prix Robert Papin at Maisons-Laffitte by Mr David Robinson's My Swallow, a colt of exceptional maturity and speed that went on to win the Prix Morny and the Grand Criterium. Mill Reef won the five furlong Salisbury Stakes at Salisbury by five lengths; the six furlong Coventry Stakes at Royal Ascot by eight lengths; the six furlong Gimcrack Stakes at York on very heavy ground by ten lengths; the six furlong Imperial Stakes at Kempton by one length, his least impressive performance; and the seven furlong Dewhurst Stakes at Newmarket by four lengths. In the Free Handicap he was given 9 st. 6 lb., one pound less than My Swallow, one pound more than Brigadier Gerard, unbeaten winner of the Middle Park Stakes.

Mill Reef started off in 1971 with a highly satisfactory win by four lengths in the seven furlong Greenham Stakes at Newbury. There were only six runners for the

679

Two Thousand Guineas and the race was widely regarded as a match between himself and My Swallow who had won the seven furlong Usher Stakes at Kempton. Mill Reef was favourite at 6–4 while My Swallow was on offer at 2–1. There was a certain amount of support for Brigadier Gerard who had not had the benefit of a previous race that season. My Swallow (F. Durr) set off in front at a fierce pace with Mill Reef (G. Lewis) hard on his heels. With two furlongs to go, both horses were under pressure but neither could find any more. At this point along came Brigadier Gerard (J. Mercer) who sailed past them both as if they were standing still to win by the convincing margin of three lengths. Mill Reef defeated My Swallow by three parts of a length for second place. It was a widely-held view after the race that My Swallow and Mill Reef had cut each other's throat and had thereby presented the race to Brigadier Gerard. It was certainly not fully realized at that time just how good a horse Brigadier Gerard was.

Brigadier Gerard did not compete in the Derby and it was generally reckoned that Mill Reef was the class horse in that race and would win provided he stayed the distance. His sire Never Bend had apparently been beaten for lack of stamina in the Kentucky Derby and the Preakness Stakes, but he had been a tearaway front-runner whereas Mill Reef was amenable to being settled down. However there were a good many people in American racing circles who disparaged the notion of Never Bend siring a top-class mile and a half horse.

The going was good at Epsom on Derby day and Mill Reef, who had satisfied his trainer at home that he could stay, was favourite at 100–30. Second favourite was the French colt Bourbon, winner of the Prix Hocquart, and there was plenty of money, too, for the Irish colt Lombardo and the French-trained Aureole colt Millenium. A popular each-way choice was Linden Tree from Peter Walwyn's stable. He had won the 'Observer' Gold Cup the previous year and early in May he had won the Chester Vase, though not in particularly convincing style.

In the paddock Bourbon started to sweat and became fractious. During the parade in front of the stands, he reared up and plunged in such violent fashion that his bridle (an English one, as his trainer Alec Head was quick to point out) snapped in two places. A new bridle was fitted but Bourbon only consented to go down to the start with the encouragement of a mounted policeman. Not surprisingly he made no show in the race.

Duncan Keith had no doubts on the score of Linden Tree's stamina and sent him to the front after three furlongs had been covered. Linden Tree bowled down the hill in great style and turned for home with a clear lead over Homeric, who had won the Lingfield Derby Trial, Lombardo and Mill Reef. Backers of Mill Reef were able to note with satisfaction how comfortably Lewis was sitting on the favourite.

Linden Tree showed no hint of weakening and headed for home as hard as he could go. With two furlongs left Homeric could find no more and Lombardo's stamina gave out a furlong later. It was at the two furlong pole that Lewis initiated his challenge. Mill Reef at once accelerated in the smoothest manner possible and he swept past the gallant Linden Tree to lead just inside the distance. From that point the race was all over bar the cheering. Mill Reef passed the winning post two lengths in front of Linden Tree while the French colt Irish Ball, who, despite hanging to the right, had made up a lot of ground in the last three furlongs, was third, two and a half lengths behind the runner-up. Lombardo yielded third place to Irish Ball in the final fifty yards.

Mill Reef's success was an extremely popular one—those of Derby favourites usually are—and above all it was a triumph for Ian Balding who, at the age of thirty-two, achieved the summit of every trainer's ambition. The younger son of that great polo player the late Gerald Balding, he is a brother of 'Toby' Balding who trained the Grand National winner Highland Wedding. He himself is a man of many talents and wide interests. He won a 'blue' for Rugby football and was a highly competent amateur rider over fences, winning the coveted National Hunt Chase at Cheltenham in 1963.

It was a first Derby success for Geoff Lewis who was born in 1935 and was a page-boy in a London hotel before being apprenticed to Ron Smyth at Epsom. A cheerful character with a jaunty and confident manner, he enjoyed his first classic victory when Right Tack won the Two Thousand Guineas in 1969. At one time there was a tendency not to regard him as the ideal big-race jockey, but he finally demolished that view at this particular Epsom meeting when, apart from winning the Derby, he won the Oaks on Altesse Royale and the Coronation Cup on Lupe.

After the Derby Mill Reef went from strength to strength. In the Eclipse Stakes he trounced the much-fancied French four-year-old Caro by four lengths. He followed that up by winning the King George VI and Queen Elizabeth Stakes at Ascot by six lengths from the Italian horse Ortis. His greatest triumph, though, came in October when he won Europe's richest prize, the Prix de l'Arc de Triomphe, by three lengths from that fine filly Pistol Packer who had been handicapped by a bad position in the draw. Mill Reef was voted 'Horse of the Year' in England. It was a popular choice though a minority reckoned the honour ought to have been awarded to Brigadier Gerard, who had retained his unbeaten record and who had defeated Mill Reef fairly and squarely the only time they met.

Mill Reef remained in training at four and everyone looked forward to a possible meeting between him, Brigadier Gerard and Pistol Packer in the Eclipse Stakes. 'The Race of the Century', though, never came off. Pistol Packer was severely injured when another horse struck into her as she was pulling up after winning the Prix d'Harcourt at Longchamp early in April. Mill Reef started off in splendid style with a ten lengths victory in the ten furlong Prix Ganay at Longchamp on 30 April. His next race was the Coronation Cup at Epsom. He did not altogether please the paddock critics and he gave his backers some distinctly uncomfortable moments before winning by a neck from Homeric.

The reason for this far from scintillating performance was soon apparent as he went down immediately afterwards with the virus that swept through so many stables in the first half of the season, disrupting the plans for the summer campaign. Mill Reef had to miss the Eclipse and a minor mishap later on prevented him from taking on Brigadier Gerard and Roberto in the Benson and Hedges Gold Cup at York, the race in which Brigadier Gerard's great winning run was brought to a close.

It was hoped that Mill Reef would be fit to compete in the Prix de l'Arc de Triomphe again but at the end of August the racing world was shocked to hear that he had broken a leg while exercising at Kingsclere. Fortunately skilled veterinary treatment enabled this great horse, who, apart from his ability, was blessed with a perfect racing temperament, to be saved for the stud. He had won over £172,000 in England while his two victories in France earned him over £135,000. He was syndicated for £2,000,000, a British record, and stands at the National Stud.

Of the other runners in the 1971 Derby, Linden Tree became temperamental. He whipped away to the left after leaving his stall in the Irish Derby and had no chance in the race. He never saw a racecourse again and was retired to the stud in France. Irish Ball won the Irish Sweeps Derby and was second to Run the Gauntlet in the Washington International at Laurel Park. Athens Wood won the Gordon Stakes at Goodwood, the Great Voltigeur Stakes at York and the St Leger. Game and consistent at three, he proved disappointing at four. Homeric ran second in the St Leger. At four he was second to Mill Reef in the Coronation Cup and won two races in France, both worth over £11,000 to the winner, the Prix Maurice de Nieuil at Saint Cloud and the Prix Kergorlay at Deauville. Bourbon atoned for his Epsom fiasco by winning the French St Leger.

1971: Wednesday, 2 June . . . 664 Entries. £61,625.25.

MR P. MELLON's b.c. MILL REEF by Never Bend
 out of Milan Mill   G. LEWIS   1
MRS D. MCCALMONT's ch.c. LINDEN TREE
 by Crepello out of Verbena   D. KEITH   2
MR E. LITTLER's b.c. IRISH BALL by Baldric II
 out of Irish Lass   A. GIBERT   3

Also ran:

Mrs J. R. Mullion's Lombardo (4th) (W. Williamson); Mrs J. Rogerson's Athens Wood (G. Starkey); Mr G. Weston's The Parson (L. Piggott); Mr M. Sobell's Homeric (J. Mercer); Mr M. W. R. Hawn's Zug (J. C. Desaint); Mr F. H. Sasse's Meaden (W. Carson); Mrs R. Hue-Williams's Millenium (M. Philipperon); Mr S. Threadwell's L'Apache (E. Eldin); Mr H. J. Joel's Frascati (A. Murray); Mme P. Wertheimer's Bourbon (F. Head); Lord Vestey's Juggernaut (B. Taylor); Mr W. Elliott's Beaming Lee (T. Ives); Mr C. F. Sparrowhawk's Tucan (G. Ramshaw); Lady Beaverbrook's Seaepic (E. Hide); Mr J. Hardy's Coffee Royal (D. Maitland); Mr D. Morris's Dapper Dan (B. Jago); Mr W. J. Tustin's Joe's Dream (J. Lynch); Mr L. M. Gelb's Credit Man (Y. Saint Martin).

21 ran.

Betting:

100–30 Mill Reef; 8–1 Bourbon; 10–1 Lombardo and Millenium; 12–1 Linden Tree; 14–1 Athens Wood; 16–1 The Parson; 20–1 Zug; 25–1 Homeric, Frascati, Irish Ball, Credit Man and L'Apache; 30–1 Seaepic; 66–1 Juggernaut; 80–1 Dapper Dan; 100–1 others.

Totalizator: (10p unit). Win: 44p. Places: 29p, 27p, £1.55.

Won by two lengths; two and a half lengths between second and third.

2 m. 37·14 s.

Winner trained by I. Balding at Kingsclere.

1972

Roberto, the fourth North-American-bred winner of the Derby in five years, was bred by his owner Mr J. W. Galbreath at the Darby Dan Farm, Lexington, Kentucky. He is a bay horse, well made but by no means imposing, by Hail to Reason out of Bramalea, by Nasrullah's son Nashua. Hail to Reason, like Sir Gaylord who sired Sir Ivor, is by Turn-to, whose sire Royal Charger was a very fast son of Nearco that included the six furlong Ayr Gold Cup among his victories when trained by Sir Jack Jarvis. Hail to Reason only raced at two when he won nine of his eighteen races. Bramalea was a very good race-mare that won the eleven furlong Coaching Club American Oaks. Her grand-dam Bleebok was a half-sister to the Kentucky Derby winner Broker's Tip.

Sent to Vincent O'Brien's stable in Co. Tipperary, Roberto won his first three races in 1971 in such facile style that there was talk of him proving a second Nijinsky. His first race was the six furlong Lagan Maiden Stakes at the Curragh in July and starting favourite at evens, he won by three lengths. The following month he won the six furlong Anglesey Stakes at the Curragh by six lengths and in September the seven furlong National Stakes at the Curragh, worth £3,837 to the winner, by five lengths. His admirers could not visualise his defeat when in October he lined up for the one mile Grand Criterium at Longchamp. They hardly believed their eyes when he finished unplaced behind Hard to Beat, an Irish-bred colt that had cost 920 guineas as a yearling. Racecourse rumour suggested an adequate excuse for this disaster but the rumour was not substantiated by any statement from the horse's connections. Certainly on that form Roberto had been overrated.

Roberto was out early in 1972 and on 1 April, in very heavy going, he won the seven furlong Vauxhall Trial Stakes at Phoenix Park with no apparent difficulty. On 29 April, partnered by W. Williamson, he started second favourite for the Two Thousand Guineas, the favourite being Sir J. Thorn's High Top, who a fortnight earlier had slammed Waterloo by seven lengths in a mile race at Thirsk. On 27 April Waterloo had won the One Thousand Guineas.

It proved a great battle between High Top and Roberto. High Top set off in front right from the start and to begin with Roberto seemed outpaced. From the Bushes, though, Roberto made rapid headway and with a furlong to go he looked poised to win. He could not quite close the gap, though, and High Top, displaying admirable courage, held on to win by half a length. Sun Prince was six lengths away third.

Roberto did not run again before the Derby. The fast going was thought likely to suit him and he started favourite at 3–1. Williamson had been injured in May but he made a good recovery and was fit to ride at Epsom. To his surprise and distress, however, he was told that the decision had been taken to stand him down and that the ride had been given to Piggott. This was not a popular move in racing circles and there was in consequence an under-current of resentment against Mr Galbreath, O'Brien and Piggott. It is true that Williamson had at once been informed that he would not lose financially if Roberto won, but there are more things in racing than mere money, though doubtless some people would not agree. After the race it was said the decision to put Piggott up had been justified by the result. On the other hand if owners and trainers do not stand by their jockeys, they can hardly expect loyalty in return. One of the troubles with modern racing is that very large sums of money are involved, and what was once primarily a sport and a pastime has tended, to its detriment, to become more and more a ruthlessly conducted business.

Joint second favourites at 4–1 were the American-bred, French-trained Lyphard, and Yaroslav, a half-brother by Santa Claus to Altesse Royale, winner of the One Thousand Guineas and the Oaks the previous year. Lyphard, by no means an easy horse to ride, had been unlucky, at least in the view of most people who saw the race, when fourth in the Prix Lupin behind Hard to Beat. He had previously won the Prix Daru. Yaroslav, unbeaten at two, had not had the advantage of a previous outing in 1972. It was known, though, that Noel Murless, not an easy man to satisfy, held him in high esteem. The sturdy Steel Pulse, fourth in the Two Thousand Guineas, was on offer at 9–1 and the Chester Vase winner Ormindo at 14–1. One of the more popular outsiders was Rheingold from Barry Hills's stable. In April he had seemed ill-suited to the Epsom gradients when failing in the Blue Riband Trial Stakes and the decision to run him in the Derby was only taken after he had won the Dante Stakes at York quite impressively.

The leader after two furlongs was Pentland Firth, one of the better-looking members of a notably undistinguished Derby field. He had declined to start in the Ladbroke Derby Trial at Lingfield and was subsequently defeated by Scottish Rifle in the Predominate Stakes at Goodwood. He was still in front at Tattenham Corner where he was followed by Meadow Mint, Ormindo, Manitoulin, Palladium and Mercia Boy. It was at this point that Freddy Head, who rides so short that he looks to be standing on the horse's withers, was unable to control Lyphard who went so wide that he appeared desirous of visiting relatives in Putney.

In the straight Rheingold and Roberto began to make significant headway.

Piggott did not wish to deliver his challenge too soon as it was by no means certain that Roberto was really a stayer, but on the other hand there seemed a distinct danger of the gap between Pentland Firth, hard ridden from three out, and Rheingold being closed. Pentland Firth, obviously tiring, was inclined to hang away from the rails while Johnson was finding it difficult to balance Rheingold who was veering away to the left.

With a furlong to go, Piggott successfully squeezed Roberto through the narrow gap. At this point it looked as if Pentland Firth was slightly hampered but he was a beaten horse at the time and the result was in no way affected. The final two hundred yards was a thrilling duel between Rheingold, who had headed Pentland Firth inside the distance, and Roberto. Piggott really got to work on Roberto and seldom can this great jockey have ridden a more telling finish. On the other hand Johnson had his hands full trying to keep Rheingold on an even keel and therefore could not assist his mount in a manner comparable to the way that Piggott assisted Roberto. From the stands it looked as if Roberto had secured the lead close home and the camera confirmed he had won by a short head. Pentland Firth was three lengths away third and Our Mirage, a stable companion of Rheingold, fourth. The excitement was not all over, though, as, not unexpectedly, there came the announcement of a Stewards' inquiry. A considerable time elapsed before it was made known that the placings would remain unchanged.

Although Roberto had started favourite, his victory could hardly be described as a popular one. Piggott, who had ridden a magnificent race, was hardly given a cheer on his return to the unsaddling enclosure. This frigid reception was in embarrassing contrast to the storm of cheering that broke out when half an hour later Williamson rode the winner of the Woodcote Stakes.

Most people reckoned that Roberto had had an exceptionally hard race at Epsom, but O'Brien did not agree with that view. Be that as it may, Roberto gave a singularly lifeless display in the Irish Sweeps Derby, finishing unplaced behind Steel Pulse who had only been eighth at Epsom.

That defeat caused Roberto's stock to slump badly. In the ten and a half furlong Benson and Hedges Gold Cup at York in August, Piggott deserted him for Rheingold and he was accordingly partnered by the crack American rider, B. Baeza. The favourite at 3–1 on was the great Brigadier Gerard, the unbeaten winner of fifteen consecutive races. Rheingold, who had defeated Hard to Beat in the Grand Prix de Saint Cloud, was on offer at 7–2, while Roberto was more or less friendless at 12–1, an insulting price for a winner of the Derby.

Roberto answered this insult in striking fashion. He was in front with six furlongs to go, and maintaining a tremendous gallop, he had Brigadier Gerard stone cold a long way from home, having three lengths to spare over him at the finish. Gold Rod was ten lengths away third. The time established a new course record.

The result of the Benson and Hedges Gold Cup was the racing sensation of the season and it was the only defeat ever inflicted on Brigadier Gerard. Certainly Roberto's form that day seemed vastly superior to anything he had shown previously or showed subsequently. There was no question of Brigadier Gerard having deteriorated as he won the Queen Elizabeth II Stakes at Ascot in splendid style a month later and in October he won the Champion Stakes for the second time. Many interesting theories were advanced to explain Roberto's brilliant running at York. 'He must have been stung by a bee', observed Brigadier Gerard's owner, Mrs Hislop.

In his next race, the eleven furlong Prix Niel at Longchamp, Roberto, Baeza up, was beaten a comfortable length by Hard to Beat, partnered by Piggott. In his last race of the season, the Prix de l'Arc de Triomphe, Baeza rode him as if the distance was six furlongs rather than a mile and a half. Roberto did well to keep it up for nearly a mile and a quarter. The fierce gallop may well have accounted, partially at least, for the failure of the well-backed horses and the success of the little-fancied filly San San. Roberto went on to win the Coronation Cup in 1973, but failed badly in the King George VI and Queen Elizabeth Stakes.

Of the other Derby competitors, Rheingold went on to win the Grand Prix de Saint Cloud and was an even better horse at four years, with four consecutive victories before his startling defeat by the French filly Dahlia in the King George VI and Queen Elizabeth Stakes. Pentland Firth was beaten by Falkland in the Princess of Wales's Stakes at Newmarket. An injury prevented him running again that season. Our Mirage won the Great Voltigeur Stakes and lost the St Leger by half a length to Boucher. Moulton won the £11,000 Prix Henry Delamarre at Longchamp. Meadow Mint was a costly failure when favourite for the Cambridgeshire. Lyphard won the £19,000 Prix Jacques Le Marois at Deauville, beating High Top by a couple of inches. Yaroslav was injured in a rough race for the King Edward VII Stakes at Ascot and unable to run again for the rest of the season. After a promising first race in 1973, he disappointed in the Prince of Wales Stakes at Ascot.

1972: Wednesday, 7 June . . . 646 Entries. £63,735.75.

MR J. W. GALBREATH's b.c. ROBERTO
by Hail to Reason out of Bramalea — L. PIGGOTT — 1

MR H. ZEISEL's b.c. RHEINGOLD by Faberge II
out of Athene — E. JOHNSON — 2

MR V. HARDY's b.c. PENTLAND FIRTH
by Crepello out of Free for All — P. EDDERY — 3

Also ran:

Mr N. Cohen's Our Mirage (4th) (F. Durr); Mr J. R. Mullion's Gombos (C. Roche); Mr A. J. Struthers's Scottish Rifle (R. Hutchinson); Mr G. A. Oldham's Ormindo (B. Taylor); Mr R. N. Tikko's Steel Pulse (W. Pyers); Mr R. Moller's Moulton (E. Hide); Mr R. N. Webster's Meadow Mint (W. Carson); Mrs J. W. Galbreath's Manitoulin (W. Swinburn); Lady Zia Wernher's Charling (J. Lindley); M. D. Wildenstein's Sukawa (Y. Saint-Martin); Countess Margit Batthyany's Palladium (J. Higgins); Mme P. Wertheimer's Lyphard (F. Head); Mr G. van der Ploeg's Mercia Boy (R. Marshall); Mrs V. Hue-Williams's Yaroslav (G. Lewis); Lord Rosebery's Paper Cap (J. Gorton); Lady Beaverbrook's Donello (J. Mercer); Mr R. A. Woods's Young Arthur (A. Murray); Mrs J. MacDougald's Mezzanine (P. Waldron); Mme J. Coturié's Neptunium (A. Barclay).

22 ran.

Betting:

3–1 Roberto; 4–1 Lyphard and Yaroslav; 9–1 Steel Pulse; 20–1 Ormindo; 22–1 Rheingold and Scottish Rifle; 25–1 Charling; 35–1 Neptunium; 45–1 Moulton; 50–1 Gombos, Meadow Mint and Pentland Firth; 66–1 Sukawa, Manitoulin and Palladium; 100–1 Our Mirage; 200–1 others.

Totalizator: (10p unit). Win: 45p. Places: 23p, 45p, 85p.

Won by a short head; three lengths between second and third.   2 m. 36·09 s.
Winner trained by M. V. O'Brien at Cashel, Co. Tipperary, Ireland.

1973

The sequence of Derby successes by American-bred horses was checked in 1973 when the victor was the 25–1 outsider Morston, bred and owned by Mr Arthur Budgett and trained by him at Whatcombe as well. Budgett had also bred, owned (or at least part-owned) and trained the 1969 Derby winner Blakeney so he equalled the achievement of Mr William I'Anson who, in the last century, bred, owned and trained two Derby winners, the filly Blink Bonny in 1857 and Blink Bonny's son Blair Athol in 1864.

Morston is a well-grown, well-made chestnut by Ribot's son Ragusa out of Windmill Girl, by the St Leger runner-up Hornbeam. Ragusa was small and unprepossessing as a yearling and Sir Cecil Boyd-Rochfort politely declined to have him in his stable. Accordingly Ragusa's breeder, Captain H. F. Guggenheim, sent him up for sale in Dublin where the Irish trainer P. J. Prendergast bought him for 3,800 guineas on behalf of Mr J. R. Mullion. Ragusa's victories included the Irish Sweeps Derby, the St Leger, the Eclipse Stakes and the King George VI and Queen Elizabeth Stakes. All told he won over £146,000. He unfortunately died shortly before Morston's triumph.

Windmill Girl had died the previous winter. She fell heavily when galloping in her paddock and fractured her skull. She was also the dam of Blakeney and thus became the ninth mare to produce two winners of the Derby and the first one to achieve both winners this century. Morganette bred the 1902 winner Ard Patrick but her first winner, Galtee More, came in 1897.

Morston was slow to develop and never ran in 1972. His first appearance at three was in the ten furlong Godstone Maiden Plate at Lingfield on 11 May. Starting at 14–1, he won quite impressively from thirteen admittedly mediocre opponents. Some shrewd judges reckoned he might have to be reckoned with in the St Leger but there was no disposition whatsoever to connect him with the Derby. Budgett's stable already had a Derby candidate in Colonel Percy Wright's Projector, who was only narrowly beaten by Ksar in the Ladbroke Derby Trial Stakes at Lingfield the following day.

Budgett himself was in doubt as to the wisdom of running Morston in the Derby but as it looked an unusually open race and as Morston continued to thrive, he eventually decided to allow the colt to take his chance. The stable jockey Baxter was needed for Projector and it was only on the Sunday before the Epsom meeting began that Budgett engaged the experienced Edward Hide, who had never set eyes on Morston before he met him in the paddock at Epsom.

There appeared to be no horse of outstanding merit in the Derby field. During the spring there had been a succession of favourites but one after another these had fallen from grace. The favourite at the 'off' was Lady Rotherwick's Ksar, a good-looking Kalydon colt trained by Bernard van Cutsem. Ksar had won both his races at three but in neither had he given proof of ability to accelerate. Second favourite was Mon Fils trained by Richard Hannon. A tall, lanky colt, Mon Fils, after running third in the Greenham Stakes at Newbury, had surprised everyone bar his owner and trainer by winning the Two Thousand Guineas. In that race he was never out of the leading pair from start to finish. His success gave a painful jolt to the breeding pundits as he is by the Gold Cup winner Sheshoon, by the Gold Cup winner Precipitation, out of a mare by Precipitation's son Premonition, winner of the St Leger. Thus he is clearly bred to stay extreme distances but in fact he had been able to win a valuable six furlong event at two. It was reasonable to suppose that he would prove even more effective over distances greater than a mile.

There was a good deal of money for Noble Decree who had won the 'Observer' Gold Cup the previous autumn and had only lost the Two Thousand Guineas by a narrow margin. It was perhaps significant, though, that the stable jockey, Carson, had elected to ride Ksar while Piggott, a sound judge both of form and of his own interests, had preferred to partner the Sir Ivor colt Cavo Doro, trained by O'Brien in Ireland and bred by Piggott himself. Cavo Doro did not appear to be highly rated in Ireland. The best backed of the French runners was Bally Game, a Ballymoss colt that had run second to Kalamoun in the French Two Thousand Guineas.

The sun shone from a cloudless sky, the going was fast and the crowd enormous. The police estimated that 700,000 people were present of whom 30,000 paid for admission, the rest roaming free on the Downs. The gates had to be closed in two enclosures as they were full to bursting point.

After a delay caused by Princely Review, a 117,000-guinea yearling, spreading a plate, a smooth start was effected. Mon Fils and Romoke were the first to show in front and others prominent were Freefoot, Honey Crepe, Balompie, Natsun and Satingo. Morston was some way behind at this stage but began to improve his position from half-way.

Those backers of Mon Fils who had felt a certain apprehension in seeing him permitted to force the pace from the start found their fears fully justified when he began to weaken soon after Tattenham Corner. With three furlongs left, Freefoot struck the front but almost immediately a big cheer went up as he was headed by the favourite, Ksar. Ksar battled on courageously enough but he just could not find a bit of extra pace in the closing stages. Morston still had plenty to do from two out but despite his lack of experience he got down to his task in splendid style and raced home as straight as a gun barrel. Below the distance he swept past Ksar and from then on the one danger was Cavo Doro, who had been making steady progress from Tattenham Corner. Piggott rode him for all he was worth and Cavo Doro responded courageously but Morston refused to give in and won an exciting race entirely on his merits by half a length. Freefoot was third, two and a half lengths behind Cavo Doro, and Ksar fourth. The Two Thousand Guineas form suffered a sad collapse. Mon Fils finished eighteenth and Noble Decree had only Satingo behind him. The victory was a popular one, unlike that of Roberto the year before, as Budgett is the most modest and courteous of men while his stable, patronized for the most part by the old-fashioned type of owner who are genuinely fond of horses, has always been run in a thoroughly open and sporting manner.

Edward Hide was born in 1937 and served a seven-year apprenticeship with his father, a Shropshire trainer. A thoroughly sound jockey, he has ridden for the most part in the north and had a long association with the late Captain Charles Elsey and with Bill Elsey. He won the St Leger for the former on Cantelo and the Oaks on Pia for the latter. In 1957 he rode 131 winners.

1973: Wednesday, 6 June . . . 719 Entries. £66,348.75.

MR A. M. BUDGETT's ch.c. MORSTON by Ragusa
   out of Windmill Girl   E. HIDE   1
CAPTAIN M. LEMOS's b.c. CAVO DORO by Sir Ivor
   out of Limuru   L. PIGGOTT   2
MR R. B. MOLLER's b.c. FREEFOOT b.c. by Relko
   out of Close Up   P. EDDERY   3

Also ran:

Lady Rotherwick's Ksar (4th) (W. Carson); Mme L. Volterra's Bally Game (Y. Saint-Martin); Countess Margit Batthyany's Balompie (J. Cruguet); Sir M. Sobell's Club House (J. Mercer); Mr P. Mellon's Draw The Line (P. Waldron); Lord Rosebery's Duke of Ragusa (J. Gorton); Mr A. R. Perry's Flintstone (R. F. Parnell); Mr J. P. Philipps's Honey Crepe (P. Cook); Mrs A. Manning's Knock Out (A. Barclay); Mrs B. M. L. Davis's Mon Fils (F. Durr); Mr N. Cohen's Natsun (G. Lewis); Mr N. B. Hunt's Noble Decree (B. Taylor); Colonel Sir D. Clague's Princely Review (G. Moore); Mrs W. Jones's Proboscis (E. Eldin); Colonel P. L. M.

Wright's Projector (G. Baxter); Lt-Col J. Chandos-Pole's Proverb (E. Johnson); Mr F. O'Sullivan's Ragapan (W. Williamson); Sir Reginald Macdonald-Buchanan's Relay Race (G. Starkey); Mr V. Matthews's Romoke (M. L. Thomas); Mme P. Wertheimer's Satingo (F. Head); Mr J. H. Whitney's Sea Pigeon (A. Murray); Mrs C. Magnier's Solar Wind (T. Murphy).

25 ran.

Betting:

5–1 Ksar; 11–2 Mon Fils; 9–1 Noble Decree; 10–1 Bally Game; 11–1 Natsun; 12–1 Cavo Doro; 20–1 Relay Race; 22–1 Satingo and Club House; 25–1 Morston and Duke of Ragusa; 28–1 Projector and Ragapan; 33–1 Knock Out and Freefoot; 40–1 Proverb; 45–1 Draw The Line; 50–1 Balompie and Sea Pigeon; 66–1 Solar Wind; 100–1 Flintstone; 200–1 others.

Totalizator: (10p unit). Win: £1.75. Places: 51p, 36p, 90p.

Won by half a length; two and a half lengths between second and third.

2 m. 35·92 s.

Winner trained by A. M. Budgett at Whatcombe.

APPENDIX I

The Derby Results (1780–1961)

Year	Winner	Second	Third
1780	Sir Charles Bunbury's Diomed	Budrow	Spitfire
1781	Major O'Kelly's Young Eclipse	Crop	Prince of Orange
1782	Lord Egremont's Assassin	Sweet Robin	Fortunio
1783	Mr Parker's Saltram	Dungannon	Parlington
1784	Colonel O'Kelly's Sergeant	Carlo Khan	Dancer
1785	Lord Clermont's Aimwell	Grantham	Verjuice
1786	Mr Panton's Noble	Meteor	Clarter
1787	Lord Derby's Sir Peter Teazle	Gunpowder	Bustler
1788	H.R.H. Prince of Wales's Sir Thomas	Aurelius	Feenow
1789	Duke of Bedford's Skyscraper	Sir George	Brother to Skylark
1790	Lord Grosvenor's Rhadamanthus	Asparagus	Lee Boo
1791	Duke of Bedford's Eager	Vermin	Proteus
1792	Lord Grosvenor's John Bull	Speculator	Bustard
1793	Sir F. Poole's Waxy	Gohanna	Triptolemus
1794	Lord Grosvenor's Daedalus	Colt by Highflyer	Leon
1795	Sir F. Standish's Spread Eagle	Caustic	Pelter
1796	Sir F. Standish's Didelot	Stickler	Leviathan
1797	Duke of Bedford's Fidget colt	Esculus	Plaistow
1798	Mr J. Cookson's Sir Harry	Telegraph	Young Spear
1799	Sir F. Standish's Archduke	Gislebert	Eagle
1800	Mr C. Wilson's Champion	Colt by Precipitate	Mystery
1801	Sir C. Bunbury's Eleanor	Colt by Fidget	Remnant
1802	Duke of Grafton's Tyrant	Colt by Young Eclipse	Orlando
1803	Sir H. Williamson's Ditto	Sir Oliver	Brother to Stamford
1804	Lord Egremont's Hannibal	Pavilion	Hippocampus
1805	Lord Egremont's Cardinal Beaufort	Plantagenet	Goth
1806	Lord Foley's Paris	Trafalgar	Hector
1807	Lord Egremont's Election	Giles Scroggins	Coriolanus
1808	Sir H. Williamson's Pan	Vandyke	Chester
1809	Duke of Grafton's Pope	Wizard	Salvator
1810	Duke of Grafton's Whalebone	The Dandy	Eccleston

Jockey	Trainer	Value to Winner	Runners	Time	Starting Price
S. Arnull		£1,065 15s.	9		6–4
Hindley		£1,312 10s.	15		10–1
S. Arnull		£1,155	13		5–1
Hindley		£945	6		5–2
J. Arnull		£1,076 5s.	11		3–1
Hindley		£1,023 15s.	10		7–1
J. White		£1,155	15		30–1
S. Arnull		£1,050	7		2–1
W. South		£971 15s.	11		5–6
S. Chifney, sen.		£1,076 5s.	11		4–7
J. Arnull		£1,102 10s.	10		5–4
Stephenson		£1,076 5s.	9		5–2
F. Buckle		£834 15s.	7		4–6
W. Clift	Robson	£1,653 15s.	13		12–1
F. Buckle		£1,391 5s.	4		6–1
A. Wheatley		£1,470	11		3–1
J. Arnull		£1,470	11		Not recorded
J. Singleton		£1,155	7		10–1
S. Arnull		£1,233 15s.	10		7–4
J. Arnull		£1,155	11		12–1
W. Clift		£1,207 10s.	13		7–4
Saunders		£1,102 10s.	12		5–4
F. Buckle	Robson	£1,024 16s.	9		7–1
W. Clift		£929 5s.	6		7–2
W. Arnull		£1,076 5s.	8		3–1
D. Fitzpatrick		£1,338 15s.	15		20–1
J. Shepherd		£1,348 15s.	12		5–1
J. Arnull		£1,333 10s.	13		3–1
F. Collinson		£1,260	10		25–1
T. Goodisson	Robson	£1,443 15s.	10		20–1
W. Clift	Robson	£1,365	11		2–1

Year	Winner	Second	Third
1811	Sir J. Shelley's Phantom	Magic	No horse officially placed third
1812	Mr R. Ladbroke's Octavius	Sweep	Comus
1813	Sir C. Bunbury's Smolensko	Caterpillar	Illusion
1814	Lord Stawell's Blücher	Perchance	No horse officially placed third
1815	Duke of Grafton's Whisker	Raphael	Busto
1816	Mr Lake's Prince Leopold	Nectar	Pandour
1817	Mr J. Payne's Azor	Young Wizard	No horse officially placed third
1818	Mr T. Thornhill's Sam	Raby	Prince Paul
1819	Duke of Portland's Tiresias	Sultan	No horse officially placed third
1820	Mr T. Thornhill's Sailor	Abjer	Tiger
1821	Mr J. Hunter's Gustavus	Reginald	Sir Huldibrand
1822	Duke of York's Moses	Figaro	Hampden
1823	Mr J. R. Udney's Emilius	Tancred	No horse officially placed third
1824	Sir J. Shelley's Cedric	Osmond	No horse officially placed third
1825	Lord Jersey's Middleton	Rufus	Hogarth
1826	Lord Egremont's Lapdog	Shakespeare	No horse officially placed third
1827	Lord Jersey's Mameluke	Glenartney	Edmund
1828	Duke of Rutland's Cadland*	The Colonel*	No horse officially placed third
1829	Mr Gratwicke's Frederick	The Exquisite	No horse officially placed third
1830	Mr W. Chifney's Priam	Little Red Rover	Mahmoud
1831	Lord Lowther's Spaniel	Riddlesworth	Incubus
1832	Mr R. Ridsdale's St Giles	Perion	Trustee
1833	Mr Sadler's Dangerous	Connoisseur	Revenge
1834	Mr S. Batson's Plenipotentiary	Shilelagh	Glencoe

* Cadland won the run-off after a dead-heat.

Jockey	Trainer	Value to Winner	Runners	Time	Starting Price
F. Buckle		£1,680	16		5–1
W. Arnull		£1,601 5s.	14		7–1
T. Goodisson		£1,653 15s.	12		Evens
W. Arnull		£1,706 5s.	14		5–2
T. Goodisson	Robson	£1,680	13		8–1
Wheatley		£1,653 15s.	11		20–1
J. Robinson	Robson	£1,811 5s.	13		50–1
S. Chifney, jun.	W. Chifney	£1,890	16		7–2
W. Clift		£1,837 10s.	16		5–2
S. Chifney, jun.	W. Chifney	£1,758 15s.	15		4–1
S. Day		£1,758 15s.	13		2–1
T. Goodisson		£1,706 5s.	12		6–1
F. Buckle	Robson	£1,863 15s.	11		11–8
J. Robinson		£1,968 15s.	16		9–2
J. Robinson	Edwards	£1,995	18		7–4
G. Dockeray	Bird	£1,800	19		50–1
J. Robinson	Edwards	£2,800	23		9–1
J. Robinson		£2,600	15		4–1*
					(5–4 in the run-off)
J. Forth	J. Forth	£2,650	17		40–1
S. Day	W. Chifney	£2,800	22		4–1
W. Wheatley		£3,000	23		50–1
W. Scott		£3,075	22		3–1
J. Chapple		£3,725	25		30–1
P. Conolly		£3,625	22		9–4

Year	*Winner*	*Second*	*Third*
1835	Mr J. Bowes's Mündig	Ascot	No horse officially placed third
1836	Lord Jersey's Bay Middleton	Gladiator	No horse officially placed third
1837	Lord Berners's Phosphorus	Caravan	No horse officially placed third
1838	Sir G. Heathcote's Amato	Ion	Grey Momus
1839	Mr W. Ridsdale's Bloomsbury	Deception	No horse officially placed third
1840	Mr D. Robertson's Little Wonder	Launcelot	Colt by Mulatto out of Melody
1841	Mr A. T. Rawlinson's Coronation	Van Amburgh	No horse officially placed third
1842	Colonel Anson's Attila	Robert de Gorham	Belcoeur
1843	Mr J. Bowes's Cotherstone	Gorhambury	Sirikol
1844	Colonel Peel's Orlando	Ionian	Bay Momus
1845	Mr Gratwicke's The Merry Monarch	Annandale	Old England
1846	Mr J. Gully's Pyrrhus the First	Sir Tatton Sykes	Brocardo
1847	Mr Pedley's Cossack	War Eagle	Van Tromp
1848	Lord Clifden's Surplice	Springy Jack	Glendower
1849	Lord Eglinton's The Flying Dutchman	Hotspur	Tadmor
1850	Lord Zetland's Voltigeur	Pitsford	Clincher
1851	Sir J. Hawley's Teddington	Marlborough Buck	Neasham
1852	Mr J. Bowes's Daniel O'Rourke	Barbarian	Chief Baron Nicholson
1853	Mr J. Bowes's West Australian	Sittingbourne	Cineas
1854	Mr J. Gully's Andover	King Tom	Hermit
1855	Mr F. L. Popham's Wild Dayrell	Kingstown	Lord of the Isles
1856	Admiral Harcourt's Ellington	Yellow Jack	Cannobie
1857	Mr W. I'Anson's Blink Bonny	Black Tommy	Adamas
1858	Sir J. Hawley's Beadsman	Toxophilite	The Hadji
1859	Sir J. Hawley's Musjid	Marionette	Trumpeter

Jockey	Trainer	Value to Winner	Runners	Time m. s.	Starting Price
W. Scott	John Scott	£3,550	14		6–1
J. Robinson		£3,725	21		7–4
G. Edwards		£3,700	17		40–1
J. Chapple	R. Sherwood	£4,005	23		30–1
S. Templeman	W. Ridsdale	£4,100	21		25–1
W. Macdonald	W. Forth	£3,775	17		50–1
P. Conolly		£4,275	29		5–2
W. Scott	John Scott	£4,900	24		5–1
W. Scott	John Scott	£4,225	23		13–8
N. Flatman	Cooper	£4,450	29		20–1
F. Bell	J. Forth	£4,225	31		15–1 was offered 'Forth's lot'
S. Day	John Day	£5,500	27	2 55	8–1
S. Templeman	John Day	£5,500	32	2 52	5–1
S. Templeman	J. Kent	£5,800	17	2 48	Evens
C. Marlow	Fobert	£6,575	26	3	2–1
J. Marson	R. Hill	£4,975	24	2 50	16–1
J. Marson	A. Taylor	£5,325	33	2 51	3–1
F. Butler	John Scott	£5,200	27	3 2	25–1
F. Butler	John Scott	£4,450	28	2 55½	6–4
A. Day	John Day	£6,100	27	2 52	7–2
R. Sherwood	Rickaby	£5,075	12	2 54	Evens
Aldcroft	T. Dawson	£5,875	24	3 4	20–1
Charlton	W. I'Anson	£5,700	30	2 45	20–1
J. Wells	G. Manning	£5,575	23	2 54	10–1
J. Wells	G. Manning	£5,400	30	2 59	9–4

Year	Winner	Second	Third
1860	Mr J. Merry's Thormanby	The Wizard	Horror
1861	Colonel Towneley's Kettledrum	Dundee	Diophantes
1862	Mr C. Snewing's Caractacus	The Marquis	Buckstone
1863	Mr R. C. Naylor's Macaroni	Lord Clifden	Rapid Rhone
1864	Mr W. I'Anson's Blair Athol	General Peel	Scottish Chief
1865	Count F. de Lagrange's Gladiateur	Christmas Carol	Eltham
1866	Mr Sutton's Lord Lyon	Savernake	Rustic
1867	Mr H. Chaplin's Hermit	Marksman	Vauban
1868	Sir J. Hawley's Blue Gown	King Alfred	Speculum
1869	Mr J. Johnstone's Pretender	Pero Gomez	The Drummer
1870	Lord Falmouth's Kingcraft	Palmerston	Muster
1871	Baron Rothschild's Favonius	Albert Victor ⎫ dead-heat King of the Forest ⎭ for second place	
1872	Mr H. Savile's Cremorne	Pell Mell	Queens Messenger
1873	Mr J. Merry's Doncaster	Gang Forward ⎫ dead-heat Kaiser ⎭ for second place	
1874	Mr Cartwright's George Frederick	Couronne de Fer	Atlantic
1875	Prince Batthyany's Galopin	Claremont	Repentance colt
1876	Mr A. Baltazzi's Kisber	Forerunner	Julius Caesar
1877	Lord Falmouth's Silvio	Glen Arthur	Rob Roy
1878	Mr W. S. Crawfurd's Sefton	Insulaire	Childeric
1879	'Mr Acton's' Sir Bevys	Palmbearer	Visconti
1880	Duke of Westminster's Bend Or	Robert the Devil	Mask
1881	Mr P. Lorillard's Iroquois	Peregrine	Town Moor
1882	Duke of Westminster's Shotover	Quicklime	Sachem
1883	Sir F. Johnstone's St Blaise	Highland Chief	Galliard
1884	Mr J. Hammond's St Gatien ⎫ dead- Sir J. Willoughby's Harvester ⎭ heat		Queen Adelaide
1885	Lord Hastings's Melton	Paradox	Royal Hampton
1886	Duke of Westminster's Ormonde	The Bard	St Mirin
1887	'Mr Abington's' Merry Hampton	The Baron	Martley
1888	Duke of Portland's Ayrshire	Crowberry	Van Dieman's Land
1889	Duke of Portland's Donovan	Miguel	El Dorado

Jockey	Trainer	Value to Winner	Runners	Time m. s.	Starting Price
H. Custance	M. Dawson	£6,350	30	2 55	4–1
Bullock	Oates	£6,350	18	2 45	12–1
J. Parsons	Zachary	£6,675	34	2 45½	40–1
T. Chaloner	Godding	£7,100	31	2 50½	10–1
J. Snowden	W. I'Anson	£6,450	30	2 43	14–1
H. Grimshaw	T. Jennings	£6,875	30	2 46	5–2
H. Custance	J. Dover	£7,350	26	2 50	5–6
J. Daley	Bloss	£7,000	30	2 52	1,000–15
J. Wells	J. Porter	£6,800	18	2 43½	7–2
J. Osborne	T. Dawson	£6,225	22	2 52½	11–8
T. French	M. Dawson	£6,175	15	2 45	20–1
T. French	J. Hayhoe	£5,125	17	2 50	9–1
Maidment	W. Gilbert	£4,850	23	2 45½	3–1
F. Webb	R. Peck	£4,825	12	2 50	45–1
H. Custance	T. Leader	£5,350	20	2 46	9–1
Morris	J. Dawson	£4,950	18	2 48	2–1
Maidment	J. Hayhoe	£5,575	15	2 44	4–1
F. Archer	M. Dawson	£6,050	17	2 50	100–9
H. Constable	A. Taylor	£5,825	22	2 56	100–12
G. Fordham	J. Hayhoe	£7,025	23	3. 2	20–1
F. Archer	R. Peck	£6,375	19	2 46	2–1
F. Archer	J. Pincus	£5,925	15	2 50	11–2
T. Cannon	J. Porter	£4,775	14	2 45⅗	11–2
C. Wood	J. Porter	£5,150	12	2 48⅖	11–2
C. Wood	R. Sherwood	£4,900	15	2 46⅕	100–8
S. Loates	J. Jewitt				100–7
F. Archer	M. Dawson	£4,525	12	2 44⅕	75–40
F. Archer	J. Porter	£4,700	9	2 45⅗	4–9
J. Watts	M. Gurry	£4,525	11	2 43	100–9
F. Barrett	G. Dawson	£3,675	9	2 43	5–6
T. Loates	G. Dawson	£4,050	13	2 44⅖	8–11

Year	Winner	Second	Third
1890	Sir J. Miller's Sainfoin	Le Nord	Orwell
1891	Sir F. Johnstone's Common	Gouverneur	Martenhurst
1892	Lord Bradford's Sir Hugo	La Flèche	Bucentaure
1893	Mr H. McCalmont's Isinglass	Ravensbury	Raeburn
1894	Lord Rosebery's Ladas	Matchbox	Reminder
1895	Lord Rosebery's Sir Visto	Curzon	Kirkconnel
1896	H.R.H. the Prince of Wales's Persimmon	St Frusquin	Earwig
1897	Mr J. Gubbins's Galtee More	Velasquez	History
1898	Mr J. W. Larnach's Jeddah	Batt	Dunlop
1899	Duke of Westminster's Flying Fox	Damocles	Innocence
1900	H.R.H. the Prince of Wales's Diamond Jubilee	Simon Dale	Disguise II
1901	Mr W. C. Whitney's Volodyovski	William the Third	Veronese
1902	Mr J. Gubbins's Ard Patrick	Rising Glass	Friar Tuck
1903	Sir J. Miller's Rock Sand	Vinicius	Flotsam
1904	Mr L. de Rothschild's St Amant	John o' Gaunt	St Denis
1905	Lord Rosebery's Cicero	Jardy	Signorino
1906	Major E. Loder's Spearmint	Picton	Troutbeck
1907	Mr R. Croker's Orby	Wool Winder	Slieve Gallion
1908	Chev. E. Ginistrelli's Signorinetta	Primer	Llangwm
1909	H.M. King Edward VII's Minoru	Louviers	William the Fourth
1910	'Mr Fairie's' Lemberg	Greenback	Charles O'Malley
1911	Mr J. B. Joel's Sunstar	Stedfast	Royal Tender
1912	Mr W. Raphael's Tagalie	Jaeger	Tracery
1913	Mr A. P. Cunliffe's Aboyeur	Louvois	Great Sport
1914	Mr H. B. Duryea's Durbar II	Hapsburg	Peter the Hermit
1915*	Mr S. B. Joel's Pommern	Let Fly	Rossendale
1916*	Mr E. Hulton's Fifinella	Kwang-Su	Nassovian
1917*	'Mr Fairie's' Gay Crusader	Dansellon	Dark Legend
1918*	Lady James Douglas's Gainsborough	Blink	Treclare
1919	Lord Glanely's Grand Parade	Buchan	Paper Money
1920	Major G. Loder's Spion Kop	Archaic	Orpheus
1921	Mr J. B. Joel's Humorist	Craig an Eran	Lemonora

* Run at Newmarket on account of the war.

Jockey	Trainer	Value to Winner	Runners	Time m. s.	Starting Price
J. Watts	J. Porter	£5,940	8	2 49⅘	100–15
G. Barrett	J. Porter	£5,510	11	2 56⅘	10–11
F. Allsopp	T. Wadlow	£6,960	13	2 44	40–1
T. Loates	J. Jewitt	£5,515	11	2 43	4–9
J. Watts	M. Dawson	£5,450	7	2 45⅘	2–9
S. Loates	M. Dawson	£5,450	15	2 43⅖	9–1
J. Watts	R. Marsh	£5,450	11	2 42	5–1
C. Wood	S. Darling	£5,450	11	2 44	1–4
O. Madden	R. Marsh	£5,450	18	2 47	100–1
M. Cannon	J. Porter	£5,450	12	2 42⅘	2–5
H. Jones	R. Marsh	£5,450	14	2 42	6–4
L. Reiff	J. Huggins	£5,670	25	2 40⅘	5–2
J. H. Martin	S. Darling	£5,450	18	2 42⅕	100–14
D. Maher	S. Blackwell	£6,450	7	2 42⅘	4–6
K. Cannon	A. Hayhoe	£6,450	8	2 45⅖	5–1
D. Maher	P. Peck	£6,450	9	2 39⅗	4–11
D. Maher	P. P. Gilpin	£6,450	22	2 36⅘	6–1
J. Reiff	Colonel McCabe	£6,450	9	2 44	100–9
W. Bullock	Chev. E. Ginistrelli	£6,450	18	2 39⅘	100–1
H. Jones	R. Marsh	£6,450	15	2 42⅖	7–2
B. Dillon	A. Taylor	£6,450	15	2 35⅕	7–4
G. Stern	C. Morton	£6,450	26	2 36⅘	13–8
J. Reiff	D. Waugh	£6,450	20	2 38⅘	100–8
E. Piper	T. Lewis	£6,450	15	2 37⅗	100–1
M. MacGee	T. Murphy	£6,450	30	2 38⅖	20–1
S. Donoghue	C. Peck	£2,440	17	2 32⅗	11–10
J. Childs	R. C. Dawson	£2,900	10	2 36⅗	11–2
S. Donoghue	A. Taylor	£2,050	12	2 40⅗	7–4
J. Childs	A. Taylor	£4,000	13	2 33⅕	8–13
F. Templeman	F. Barling	£6,450	13	2 35⅘	33–1
F. O'Neill	P. P. Gilpin	£6,450	19	2 34⅘	100–6
S. Donoghue	C. Morton	£6,450	23	2 36⅕	6–1

Year	Winner	Second	Third
1922	Lord Woolavington's Captain Cuttle	Tamar	Craigangower
1923	Mr B. Irish's Papyrus	Pharos	Parth
1924	Lord Derby's Sansovino	St Germans	Hurstwood
1925	Mr H. E. Morriss's Manna	Zionist	The Sirdar
1926	Lord Woolavington's Coronach	Lancegaye	Colorado
1927	Mr F. Curzon's Call Boy	Hot Night	Shian Mor
1928	Sir H. Cunliffe-Owen's Felstead	Flamingo	Black Watch
1929	Mr W. Barnett's Trigo	Walter Gay	Brienz
1930	H.H. Aga Khan's Blenheim	Iliad	Diolite
1931	Mr J. A. Dewar's Cameronian	Orpen	Sandwich
1932	Mr T. Walls's April the Fifth	Dastur	Miracle
1933	Lord Derby's Hyperion	King Salmon	Statesman
1934	H.H. Maharaja of Rajpipla's Windsor Lad	Easton	Colombo
1935	H.H. Aga Khan's Bahram	Robin Goodfellow	Field Trial
1936	H.H. Aga Khan's Mahmoud	Taj Akbar	Thankerton
1937	Mrs G. B. Miller's Mid-day Sun	Sandsprite	Le Grand Duc
1938	Mr P. Beatty's Bois Roussel	Scottish Union	Pasch
1939	Lord Rosebery's Blue Peter	Fox Cub	Heliopolis
1940*	Mr F. Darling's Pont l'Evêque	Turkhan	Lighthouse II
1941*	Mrs Macdonald-Buchanan's Owen Tudor	Morogoro	Firoze Din
1942*	Lord Derby's Watling Street	Hyperides	Ujiji
1943*	Miss D. Paget's Straight Deal	Umiddad	Nasrullah
1944*	Lord Rosebery's Ocean Swell	Tehran	Happy Landing
1945*	Sir E. Ohlson's Dante	Midas	Court Martial
1946	Mr J. E. Ferguson's Airborne	Gulf Stream	Radiotherapy
1947	Baron G. de Waldner's Pearl Diver	Migoli	Sayajirao
1948	H.H. Aga Khan's My Love	Royal Drake	Noor
1949	Mrs M. Glenister's Nimbus	Amour Drake	Swallow Tail
1950	M. M. Boussac's Galcador	Prince Simon	Double Eclipse
1951	Mr J. McGrath's Arctic Prince	Sybil's Nephew	Signal Box
1952	H.H. Aga Khan's Tulyar	Gay Time	Faubourg II
1953	Sir V. Sassoon's Pinza	Aureole	Pink Horse

* Run over a mile and a half on the July Course, Newmarket, on account of the war.

APPENDIX I

Jockey	*Trainer*	*Value to Winner*	*Runners*	*Time m. s.*	*Starting Price*
S. Donoghue	F. Darling	£10,625	30	2 $34\frac{3}{5}$	10–1
S. Donoghue	B. Jarvis	£11,325	19	2 38	100–15
T. Weston	G. Lambton	£11,755	27	2 $46\frac{3}{5}$	9–2
S. Donoghue	F. Darling	£11,095	27	2 $40\frac{3}{5}$	9–1
J. Childs	F. Darling	£10,950	19	2 $47\frac{4}{5}$	11–2
E. C. Elliott	J. Watts	£12,615	23	2 $34\frac{2}{5}$	4–1
H. Wragg	O. Bell	£11,605	19	2 $34\frac{4}{5}$	33–1
J. Marshall	R. Dawson	£11,965	26	2 $36\frac{2}{5}$	33–1
H. Wragg	R. Dawson	£10,636 5s.	17	2 $38\frac{1}{5}$	18–1
F. Fox	F. Darling	£12,161 5s.	25	2 $36\frac{3}{5}$	7–2
F. Lane	T. Walls	£9,730 5s.	21	2 $43\frac{1}{5}$	100–6
T. Weston	G. Lambton	£9,836 10s.	24	2 34	6–1
C. Smirke	M. Marsh	£8,852	19	2 34	15–2
F. Fox	F. Butters	£9,216	16	2 36	5–4
C. Smirke	F. Butters	£9,934 5s.	22	2 $33\frac{4}{5}$*	100–8
M. Beary	F. S. Butters	£8,441 5s.	21	2 $37\frac{3}{5}$	100–7
E. C. Elliott	F. Darling	£8,728 15s.	22	2 $39\frac{1}{5}$	20–1
E. Smith	J. Jarvis	£10,625 10s.	27	2 $36\frac{4}{5}$	7–2
S. Wragg	F. Darling	£5,892 10s.	16	2 $30\frac{4}{5}$	10–1
W. Nevett	F. Darling	£4,473	20	2 32	25–1
H. Wragg	W. Earl	£3,844	13	2 $29\frac{3}{5}$	6–1
T. H. Carey	W. Nightingall	£4,388	23	2 $30\frac{2}{5}$	100–6
W. Nevett	J. Jarvis	£5,901	20	2 31	28–1
W. Nevett	M. Peacock	£8,339	27	2 $26\frac{3}{5}$	100–30
T. Lowrey	R. Perryman	£7,915 10s.	17	2 $44\frac{3}{5}$	50–1
G. Bridgland	C. Halsey	£9,101 5s.	15	2 $38\frac{2}{5}$	40–1
W. Johnstone	R. Carver	£13,059 5s.	32	2 40	100–9
E. C. Elliott	G. Colling	£14,245	32	2 42	7–1
W. Johnstone	C. H. Semblat	£17,010 10s.	25	2 $36\frac{4}{5}$	100–9
C. Spares	W. Stephenson	£19,386 5s.	33	2 $39\frac{2}{5}$	28–1
C. Smirke	M. Marsh	£20,487	33	2 $36\frac{2}{5}$	11–2
G. Richards	N. Bertie	£19,118 10s.	27	2 $35\frac{3}{5}$	5–1

* A record for the race.

APPENDIX I

Year	Winner	Second	Third
1954	Mr R. S. Clark's Never Say Die	Arabian Night	Darius
1955	Mme L. Volterra's Phil Drake	Panaslipper	Acropolis
1956	M. P. Wertheimer's Lavandin	Montaval	Roistar
1957	Sir V. Sassoon's Crepello	Ballymoss	Pipe of Peace
1958	Sir V. Sassoon's Hard Ridden	Paddy's Point	Nagami
1959	Sir H. de Trafford's Parthia	Fidalgo	Shantung
1960	Sir V. Sassoon's St Paddy	Alcaeus	Kythnos
1961	Mrs A. Plesch's Psidium	Dicta Drake	Pardao
1962	Mr R. Guest's Larkspur	Arcor	Le Cantilien
1963	M. F. Dupré's Relko	Merchant Venturer	Ragusa
1964	Mr J. Ismay's Santa Claus	Indiana	Dilettante II
1965	M. J. Ternynck's Sea Bird II	Meadow Court	I Say
1966	Lady Zia Wernher's Charlottown	Pretendre	Black Prince II
1967	Mr H. J. Joel's Royal Palace	Ribocco	Dart Board
1968	Mr R. Guest's Sir Ivor	Connaught	Mount Athos
1969	Mr A. M. Budgett's Blakeney	Shoemaker	Prince Regent
1970	Mr C. W. Engelhard's Nijinsky	Gyr	Stintino
1971	Mr P. Mellon's Mill Reef	Linden Tree	Irish Ball
1972	Mr J. W. Galbreath's Roberto	Rheingold	Pentland Firth
1973	Mr A. M. Budgett's Morston	Cavo Doro	Freefoot

Jockey	*Trainer*	*Value to Winner*	*Runners*	*Time m. s.*	*Starting Price*
L. Piggott	J. Lawson	£16,959 10s.	22	2 $35\frac{4}{5}$	33–1
F. Palmer	F. Mathet	£18,702	23	2 $39\frac{4}{5}$	100–8
W. Johnstone	A. Head	£17,282 10s.	27	2 $36\frac{2}{5}$	7–1
L. Piggott	N. Murless	£18,659 10s.	22	2 $35\frac{2}{5}$	6–4
C. Smirke	J. Rogers	£20,036 10s.	20	2 $41\frac{1}{5}$	18–1
W. H. Carr	C. Boyd-Rochfort	£36,078	20	2 36	10–1
L. Piggott	N. Murless	£33,052	17	2 $35\frac{3}{5}$	7–1
R. Poincelet	H. Wragg	£34,548	28	2 $36\frac{1}{2}$	66–1
N. Sellwood	M. V. O'Brien	£34,786	26	2 37·3	22–1
Y. Saint-Martin	F. Mathet	£35,338 10s.	26	2 39·4	5–1
A. Breasley	J. M. Rogers	£72,067	17	2 41·98	15–8
T. P. Glennon	E. Pollet	£65,301	22	2 38·41	7–4
A. Breasley	G. Smyth	£74,489 10s.	25	2 37·63	5–1
G. Moore	N. Murless	£61,918	22	2 38·30	7–4
L. Piggott	M. V. O'Brien	£58,525 10s.	13	2 38·7	4–5
E. Johnson	A. M. Budgett	£63,108 6s.	26	2 40·3	15–2
L. Piggott	M. V. O'Brien	£62,311	11	2 34·6	11–8
G. Lewis	I. Balding	£61,625.25	21	2 37·14	100–30
L. Piggott	M. V. O'Brien	£63,735·75	22	2 36·09	3–1
E. Hide	A. M. Budgett	£66,348.75	25	2 35·92	25–1

APPENDIX II

Miscellanea

MOST SUCCESSFUL OWNERS

Lord Egremont:	Assassin, 1782	H.H. Aga Khan:	Blenheim, 1930
	Hannibal, 1804		Bahram, 1935
	Cardinal Beaufort, 1805		Mahmoud, 1936
	Election, 1807		My Love, 1948
	Lapdog, 1826		Tulyar, 1952
Mr J. Bowes:	Mündig, 1835	Sir J. Hawley:	Teddington, 1851
	Cotherstone, 1843		Beadsman, 1858
	Daniel O'Rourke, 1852		Musjid, 1859
	West Australian, 1853		Blue Gown, 1868
First Duke of Westminster:	Bend Or, 1880	Sir V. Sassoon:	Pinza, 1953
	Shotover, 1882		Crepello, 1957
	Ormonde, 1886		Hard Ridden, 1958
	Flying Fox, 1899		St Paddy, 1960
Sir C. Bunbury:	Diomed, 1780	Fifth Duke of Bedford:	Skyscraper, 1789
	Eleanor, 1801		Eager, 1791
	Smolensko, 1813		Fidget colt, 1797
First Lord Grosvenor:	Rhadamanthus, 1790	Sir F. Standish:	Spread Eagle, 1795
	John Bull, 1792		Didelot, 1796
	Daedalus, 1794		Archduke, 1799
Third Duke of Grafton:	Tyrant, 1802	Fifth Earl of Jersey:	Middleton, 1825
	Pope, 1809		Mameluke, 1827
	Whalebone, 1810		Bay Middleton, 1836
Fifth Earl of Rosebery:	Ladas, 1894	King Edward VII:	Persimmon, 1896
	Sir Visto, 1895		Diamond Jubilee, 1900
	Cicero, 1905		Minoru, 1909
Seventeenth Earl of Derby:	Sansovino, 1924		
	Hyperion, 1933		
	Watling Street, 1942*		

* War substitute race at Newmarket.

The first woman to own a Derby winner was Lady James Douglas, who won a war substitute race with Gainsborough in 1918.

The first woman to own an Epsom Derby winner was Mrs G. B. Miller, whose Mid-day Sun, whom she owned in partnership with her mother, Mrs Talbot, won in 1937.

MOST SUCCESSFUL JOCKEYS

J. Robinson: Azor, 1817
Cedric, 1824
Middleton, 1825
Mameluke, 1827
Cadland, 1828
Bay Middleton, 1836

S. Donoghue: Pommern, 1915*
Gay Crusader, 1917*
Humorist, 1921
Captain Cuttle, 1922
Papyrus, 1923
Manna, 1925

L. Piggott: Never Say Die, 1954
Crepello, 1957
St Paddy, 1960
Sir Ivor, 1968
Nijinsky, 1970
Roberto, 1972

F. Buckle: John Bull, 1792
Daedalus, 1794
Tyrant, 1802
Phantom, 1811
Emilius, 1823

J. Arnull: Sergeant, 1784
Rhadamanthus, 1790
Didelot, 1796
Archduke, 1799
Election, 1807

F. Archer: Silvio, 1877
Bend Or, 1880
Iroquois, 1881
Melton, 1885
Ormonde, 1886

W. Clift: Waxy, 1793
Champion, 1800
Ditto, 1803
Whalebone, 1810
Tiresias, 1819

T. Goodisson: Pope, 1809
Smolensko, 1813
Whisker, 1815
Moses, 1822

S. Arnull: Diomed, 1780
Assassin, 1782
Sir Peter Teazle, 1787
Sir Harry, 1798

J. Watts: Merry Hampton, 1887
Sainfoin, 1890
Ladas, 1894
Persimmon, 1896

W. Scott: St Giles, 1832
Mündig, 1835
Attila, 1842
Cotherstone, 1843

C. Smirke: Windsor Lad, 1934
Mahmoud, 1936
Tulyar, 1952
Hard Ridden, 1958

* War substitute race at Newmarket.

W. Arnull:	Hannibal, 1804 Octavius, 1812 Blücher, 1814	W. Nevett:	Owen Tudor, 1941* Ocean Swell, 1944* Dante, 1945*
C. Hindley:	Young Eclipse, 1781 Saltram, 1783 Aimwell, 1785	J. Wells:	Beadsman, 1858 Musjid, 1859 Blue Gown, 1868
S. Day:	Gustavus, 1821 Priam, 1830 Pyrrhus the First, 1846	C. Wood:	St Blaise, 1883 St Gatien, 1884 Galtee More, 1897
S. Templeman:	Bloomsbury, 1839 Cossack, 1847 Surplice, 1848	J. Childs:	Fifinella, 1916* Gainsborough, 1918* Coronach, 1926
H. Custance:	Thormanby, 1860 Lord Lyon, 1866 George Frederick, 1874	H. Wragg:	Felstead, 1928 Blenheim, 1930 Watling Street, 1942*
D. Maher:	Rock Sand, 1903 Cicero, 1905 Spearmint, 1906	W. Johnstone:	My Love, 1948 Galcador, 1950 Lavandin, 1956
E. C. Elliott:	Call Boy, 1927 Bois Roussel, 1938 Nimbus, 1949		

The oldest winning rider is J. Forth, who was over sixty when he won on Frederick in 1829. The youngest, at any rate in this century, is L. Piggott, who was eighteen when he won on Never Say Die in 1954; the exact age of Parsons, who was only a boy when he won on Caractacus in 1862, is unknown.

* War substitute race at Newmarket.

MOST SUCCESSFUL TRAINERS

R. Robson: Waxy, 1793
Tyrant, 1802
Pope, 1809
Whalebone, 1810
Whisker, 1815
Azor, 1817
Emilius, 1823

John Porter: Blue Gown, 1868
Shotover, 1882
St Blaise, 1883
Ormonde, 1886
Sainfoin, 1890
Common, 1891
Flying Fox, 1899

F. Darling: Captain Cuttle, 1922
Manna, 1925
Coronach, 1926
Cameronian, 1931
Bois Roussel, 1938
Pont l'Evêque, 1940*
Owen Tudor, 1941*

M. Dawson: Thormanby, 1860
Kingcraft, 1870
Silvio, 1877
Melton, 1885
Ladas, 1894
Sir Visto, 1895

J. Scott: Mündig, 1835
Attila, 1842
Cotherstone, 1843
Daniel O'Rourke, 1852
West Australian, 1853

R. Marsh: Persimmon, 1896
Jeddah, 1898
Diamond Jubilee, 1900
Minoru, 1909

M. V. O'Brien: Larkspur, 1962
Sir Ivor, 1968
Nijinsky, 1970
Roberto, 1972

John Day: Pyrrhus the First, 1846
Cossack, 1847
Andover, 1854

W. Chifney: Sam, 1818
Sailor, 1820
Priam, 1830

A. Taylor: Lemberg, 1910
Gay Crusader, 1917*
Gainsborough, 1918*

J. Hayhoe: Favonius, 1871
Kisber, 1876
Sir Bevys, 1879

N. Murless: Crepello, 1957
St Paddy, 1960
Royal Palace, 1967

R. Dawson: Fifinella, 1916*
Trigo, 1929
Blenheim, 1930

* War substitute races at Newmarket.

MOST SUCCESSFUL SIRES

Sir Peter Teazle:	Sir Harry, 1798	Waxy:	Pope, 1809
	Archduke, 1799		Whalebone, 1810
	Ditto, 1803		Blücher, 1814
	Paris, 1806		Whisker, 1815
Cyllene:	Cicero, 1905	Blandford:	Trigo, 1929
	Minoru, 1909		Blenheim, 1930
	Lemberg, 1910		Windsor Lad, 1934
	Tagalie, 1912		Bahram, 1935

Eclipse, Highflyer, Pot-8-os, Touchstone, Stockwell, Polymelus, Hampton, and Hurry On all sired three Derby winners.

Sir Peter Teazle sired the first three to finish in the Derby of 1803; Stockwell accomplished the same feat in 1866.

*   *   *   *   *   *   *

The following owners have won the Derby and the Oaks in the same year:

Lord Clermont, 1785   Mr J. Gully, 1846
Duke of Bedford, 1791   Mr J. Merry, 1873
Sir F. Standish, 1796   M. M. Boussac, 1950

The following have owned the first two horses in the Derby in the same year:

Duke of Bedford, 1789   Colonel Peel, 1844
Earl Grosvenor, 1790   H.H. Aga Khan, 1936
Lord Jersey, 1827

The following fillies have won the Derby and the Oaks:

Eleanor, 1801   Signorinetta, 1908
Blink Bonny, 1857   Fifinella, 1916*

Other fillies to win the Derby are Shotover (1882) and Tagalie (1912).

Winner of the Two Thousand Guineas, Derby, St Leger, Grand Prix, and Gold Cup:

Gladiateur, 1865–6

* War substitute race at Newmarket.

Winners of the 'Triple Crown' (not counting the war years when substitute races were run):

West Australian, 1853	Galtee More, 1897
Gladiateur, 1865	Flying Fox, 1899
Lord Lyon, 1866	Diamond Jubilee, 1900
Ormonde, 1886	Rock Sand, 1903
Common, 1891	Bahram, 1935
Isinglass, 1893	Nijinsky, 1970

Pommern (1915), Gay Crusader (1917), and Gainsborough (1918) won war substitute races and are usually awarded 'Triple Crown' status.

Winners of the Two Thousand Guineas and the Derby (excluding winners of the 'Triple Crown'):

Smolensko, 1813	Minoru, 1909
Cadland, 1828	Sunstar, 1911
Bay Middleton, 1836	Manna, 1925
Cotherstone, 1843	Cameronian, 1931
Macaroni, 1863	Blue Peter, 1939
Pretender, 1869	Nimbus, 1949
Shotover, 1882	Crepello, 1957
Ayrshire, 1888	Royal Palace, 1967
Ladas, 1894	Sir Ivor, 1968
St Amant, 1904	

Winner of the One Thousand Guineas and the Derby:

Tagalie, 1912

Winners of the Derby and the St Leger ('Triple Crown' winners excluded):

Champion, 1800	Persimmon, 1896
Surplice, 1848	Coronach, 1926
The Flying Dutchman, 1849	Trigo, 1929
Voltigeur, 1850	Hyperion, 1933
Blair Athol, 1864	Windsor Lad, 1934
Silvio, 1877	Airborne, 1946
Iroquois, 1881	Tulyar, 1952
Melton, 1885	Never Say Die, 1954
Donovan, 1889	St Paddy, 1960
Sir Visto, 1895	

Winners of the Derby and the Grand Prix:

Gladiateur, 1865	Spearmint, 1906
Cremorne, 1872	My Love, 1948
Kisber, 1876	Phil Drake, 1955

Winners of the Derby and the Gold Cup:

The Flying Dutchman, 1849–50	Cremorne, 1872–3
Teddington, 1851–2	Doncaster, 1873–4
West Australian, 1853–4	St Gatien, 1884–5
Thormanby, 1860–1	Persimmon, 1896–7
Gladiateur, 1865–6	Owen Tudor, 1941–2*
Blue Gown, 1868–9	Ocean Swell, 1944–5†

Winners of the Derby and the King George VI and Queen Elizabeth Stakes:

Tulyar, 1952	Nijinsky, 1970
Pinza, 1953	Mill Reef, 1971
Royal Palace, 1968	

There have been four grey Derby winners:

Gustavus, 1821	Mahmoud, 1936
Tagalie, 1912	Airborne, 1946

Half-brothers that have won the Derby:

Spread Eagle, 1795, and Didelot, 1796	Mündig, 1835, and Cotherstone, 1843
Ditto, 1803, and Pan, 1808	Galtee More, 1897, and Ard Patrick, 1902

Full brothers that have won the Derby:

Rhadamanthus, 1790, and Daedalus, 1794
Archduke, 1799, and Paris, 1806
Whalebone, 1810, and Whisker, 1815
Persimmon, 1896, and Diamond Jubilee, 1900

Derby winners out of Oaks winners:

Bay Middleton, 1836 (Cobweb)	Humorist, 1921 (Jest)
Beadsman, 1858 (Mendicant)	Charlottown, 1966 (Meld)
Blair Athol, 1864 (Blink Bonny)	
(Blink Bonny also won the Derby)	

* Both war substitute races.
† War substitute Derby.

APPENDIX II

Derby winners sired by Derby winners:

Sir Harry, 1798 (Sir Peter Teazle)
Archduke, 1799 (Sir Peter Teazle)
Ditto, 1803 (Sir Peter Teazle)
Paris, 1806 (Sir Peter Teazle)
Pope, 1809 (Waxy)
Whalebone, 1810 (Waxy)
Blücher, 1814 (Waxy)
Whisker, 1815 (Waxy)
Gustavus, 1821 (Election)
Cedric, 1824 (Phantom)
Middleton, 1825 (Phantom)
Lapdog, 1826 (Whalebone)
Priam, 1830 (Emilius)
Plenipotentiary, 1834 (Emilius)
The Flying Dutchman, 1849 (Bay Middleton)
Teddington, 1851 (Orlando)
Andover, 1854 (Bay Middleton)

Ellington, 1856 (The Flying Dutchman)
Blue Gown, 1868 (Beadsman)
Silvio, 1877 (Blair Athol)
Sir Bevys, 1879 (Favonius)
Bend Or, 1880 (Doncaster)
Shotover, 1882 (Hermit)
St Blaise, 1883 (Hermit)
Ormonde, 1886 (Bend Or)
Donovan, 1889 (Galopin)
Rock Sand, 1903 (Sainfoin)
Grand Parade, 1919 (Orby)
Spion Kop, 1920 (Spearmint)
Felstead, 1928 (Spion Kop)
Hyperion, 1933 (Gainsborough)
Mahmoud, 1936 (Blenheim)
Owen Tudor, 1941 (Hyperion)
Ocean Swell, 1944 (Blue Peter)
Larkspur, 1962 (Never Say Die)

Exported Derby winners:

Diomed (U.S.A.)
Saltram (U.S.A.)
Spread Eagle (U.S.A.)
Gustavus (Prussia)
Middleton (Russia)
Mameluke (U.S.A.)
Cadland (France)
Priam (U.S.A.)
St Giles (U.S.A.)
Dangerous (France)
Phosphorus (Germany)
Bloomsbury (Germany)
Attila (Germany, died *en route*)
Cossack (France)
The Flying Dutchman (France)
Teddington (Hungary)

Daniel O'Rourke (Hungary)
West Australian (France)
Andover (Russia)
Blue Gown (U.S.A., died *en route*)
Kingcraft (U.S.A., died *en route*)
Doncaster (Austria)
George Frederick (U.S.A.)
Silvio (France)
St Blaise (U.S.A.)
St Gatien (Germany; later to U.S.A.)
Harvester (Austria)
Melton (Italy; returned to England)
Ormonde (Argentina; later to U.S.A.)
Galtee More (Russia; later to Germany)
Flying Fox (France)

Diamond Jubilee (Argentina)

Ard Patrick (Germany)

Rock Sand (U.S.A.; later to France)

Minoru (Russia)

Aboyeur (Russia)

Durbar II (exported from France to U.S.A.)

Captain Cuttle (Italy)

Coronach (New Zealand)

Blenheim (U.S.A.)

Cameronian (Argentina)

Bahram (U.S.A.)

Mahmoud (U.S.A.)

Mid-day Sun (New Zealand)

Pont l'Evêque (Argentina)

Watling Street (U.S.A.)

Pearl Diver (Japan)

My Love (Argentina)

Nimbus (Japan)

Galcador (Japan)

Arctic Prince (U.S.A.)

Tulyar (U.S.A.)

Lavandin (Japan)

Hard Ridden (Japan)

Parthia (Japan)

Psidium (Argentina)

Larkspur (Japan)

Sea Bird II (U.S.A.)

Sir Ivor (U.S.A.)*

Nijinsky (U.S.A.)†

Longest-priced winners: Jeddah (100–1) and Signorinetta (100–1).

Fastest time: Mahmoud, 2 minutes 33⅘ seconds, 1936.

Dead-heats: Cadland and The Colonel, 1828; Cadland won the run-off.
St Gatien and Harvester, 1884; the stakes were divided.

The Prince of Wales (later King Edward VII) won the Derby and the Grand National in 1900.

G. Blackwell, R. C. Dawson, J. Jewitt, W. Stephenson, and M. V. O'Brien have trained winners of the Derby and the Grand National.

In 1893 H. Barker rode the runner-up in both the Grand National and the Derby. The oldest mare to breed a Derby winner was Horatia, who was twenty-five when she produced Paris.

American-bred Derby winners are Iroquois (1881), Never Say Die (1954), Sir Ivor (1968), Mill Reef (1971), and Roberto (1972). Nijinsky (1970) was bred in Canada.

French-bred Derby winners are Gladiateur (1865), Durbar II (1914), Bois Roussel (1938), Pearl Diver (1947), My Love (1948), Galcador (1950), Phil Drake (1955), Lavandin (1956), Relko (1963), and Sea Bird II (1965).

Derby winners trained in Ireland are Orby (1907), Hard Ridden (1958), Larkspur (1962), Santa Claus (1964), Sir Ivor (1968), Nijinsky (1970), and Roberto (1972).

The smallest Derby field was four runners in 1794; the largest, thirty-four in 1862.

* Sir Ivor was bred in America. † Nijinsky was bred in Canada.

Indexes

D'Egville, 120–1
Deicoon, 159
Deimos, 496, 542
Deloraine, 148
Delville, 65
Democrat, 345–6, 348
Dervise, 85
Dervish, 171–2
Desmond, 340–2, 400–1,
  427, 473
Desmond's Song, 409
Desperation, 143
Despot, 107
D'Estournel, 220–1
Devil among the Tailors,
  132
Devonian, 532–4
Dewi Sant, 348
Dhoti, 525–6
Diadem, 299, 375, 423, 454
Diamond, 29
Diamond Jubilee, 299, 326–
  7, 330, 345–8, 524
Diamond Stud, 385
Dick Swiveller, 481
Dick Thornton, 139
Dicta Drake, 598, 625–8
Dictator (1818), 70
Dictator (1861), 195–7
Didelot, 30
Die Hard, 594, 620–3
Dieudonné (1898), 336, 338
Dieudonne (1969), 674
Digby Grand, 235–6
Dignity, 458–9
Dilettante II, 644–6
Diligence, 444–5, 642
Dingwall, 372
Diolite, 362, 430, 479–81, 486
Diomed, 5–6, 272
Diophantus, 196–7
Diophon, 450–2, 455, 477
Dirk Hatteraick, 176
Discussor, 41
Disguise II, 347–8
Disraeli (1830), 99
Disraeli (1898), 250, 336,
  338
Distin, 220–1
Ditto, 186
Djeddah, 561–4, 572
Doctor Busby, 68
Doctor Dolittle, 483, 485–7

Dr Quill, 444
Doleful, 141–3
Dominie, The, 72
Dominion, 427–9, 431
Dominion Day, 661, 663–4
Domino, 124
Don Carlos (1824), 81
Don Carlos (1877), 257
Don Fulano, 272
Don John, colt by, 146
Doncaster, 54, 164, 241–3;
  foals by, 265, 268, 290,
  450
Donello, 688
Donnybrook, 204
Donovan, 233, 250, 299,
  303–5, 369; foals by, 332,
  464
Donzelon, 453, 455
Dorcas, 310
Doric, 449
Doricles, 351–3, 364
Dormouse (1838), 120
Dormouse (1864), 208
Double Eclipse, 573–5
Double First, 444
Doudance, 641
Doutelle, 305, 540, 607–8,
  613, 637
Dragoman, 81
Dragon, 220–1
Dragsman, The, 124
Drake, The, 196–7
Dramatist, 178
Draw The Line, 691
Draycott, 269
Dreadnought, 41
Dream Man, 659
Drevno, 659
Dromoland, 647
Drone, 28
Drone, The, 193
Druid, 27
Druid, The, 240
Drum Major, 121
Drummer, The, 229–30
Drummond, 240
Dry Toast, 444–5
Dual, 626, 628
Duke, The (1820), 74
Duke, The (1867), 216
Duke of Beaufort, 229–30
Duke of Lancaster, 394

Duke of Ragusa, 691
Duke of Westminster, 257–8
Duke of York, 215
Dumfries, 186
Dumpling, 135
Dundee, 194–7
Dungannon, 11
Dungannon, colt by (Mr
  Lade's), 30
Dungannon, colt by (Mr
  Best's), 44–5
Dunlop, 336–8
Duplication, 637, 641
Duplicity, 637
Durbar II, 362, 407–10,
  518, 573
Durham Castle, 589
Dusty Miller, 183
Dutch Bells, 674
Dutch Oven, 274–6
Duxbury, 40
Dynamo, 435

Eager (1791), 19, 23, 30
Eager (1897), 334
Eagle, 33
Eagle, colt by, 63
Eaglehawk, 439
Eagles Plume, 151
Earl of Dartrey, 250
Earlston (1875), 250
Earlston (1907), 375, 377
Early Bird, The (1838), 121
Early Bird, The (1854), 171
Early Purl, 204
Earwig, 329, 331
East Langton, 186
Easton, 499, 501–2, 547
Eaton Lad, 381
Ebberston, 115
Ebony, 193
Ebury, 92
Eccleston, 55–6
Eclipse (1858), 184–6
Eclipse, colt by (Duke of
  Cumberland's, 1780), 6
Eclipse, colt by (Duke of
  Cumberland's, 1781), 8
Eclipse, colt by (Colonel
  O'Kelly's), 13
Eclipse, colt by (Mr
  Graham's), 23
Ecossais, 246–7

Iron Peg, 637–8, 641
Iroquois, 270–2
Ishmael, 12
Isinglass, 303–5, 316–19, 321, 583; pedigree, 217, 309, 316; foals by, 314, 318–19, 543
Italian, The, 159
Ivanhoe, 99
Izaak Walton, 268

Jack, 132
Jackdaw the Second, 492
Jacks Son, 466–7
Jacobite, 564
Jacopo, 483–7
Jacquot, 444
Jaeger, 397–9
Jaffa II, 587, 589
Jagellon, 257
Jai Hind, 570
Jameson, 405
Janitor, 215
Japetus, 507
Jardy, 301, 366–8
Jarnicoton, 204
Javelin, 398–9
Jeddah, 330, 335–8
Jeweller, 63
Jinglepot, 143
Jingling Geordie, 398–9
Jiweh, 492
Jo I So I, 342
Joachim, 129–30
Job Thornberry, 48
Jobson, 74
Jock the Laird's brother, 76
Joe Miller, 166–7
Joe's Dream, 683
John Bull (1792), 24–5
John Bull (1907), 377
John Davis, 143, 379
John de Bart, 90
John Frederick, 261
John o' Gaunt, 314, 319, 363–5, 388, 408
John of Paris, 66
Joinville, 145
Joker, 212
Jolter, 58
Jordan, 186
Josephus, 615, 617–18
Juggernaut, 683

Julian, 564–5
Julius, 219–21, 222
Julius Caesar, 252–3
Juniper, colt by, 78
Junius, 45
Jupiter, colt by, 18
Just Great, 625, 627–8
Justice, The, 85
Justice, colt by, 17

Kaiser, 241–3
Kangaroo, 212
Kara Tepe, 584
Kate, 104–5
Kate Hampton, 212
Kearsage, 357–8
Kedger, 141–2
Kel d'Or, 395
Kelpie, 186
Kennymore, 319, 364, 408–409
Kerasos, 435
Kettledrum, 194–7
Khaled, 458, 496, 553–5
Khalekan, 659
Khorassan (1843), 134–5
Khorassan (1950), 571–2, 574–5
Khor-Mousa, 584
Ki Ming, 517, 576–9, 657
Kildonan, 196–7
King Alfred, 225, 227
King Canute II, 632
King Charming, 212
King Cob, 143
King Cophetua, 228, 230
King David II, 601, 603
King Fergus, colt by, 30
King John, 425–6
King Legend, 526
King Log, 652
King of Kelton, 124
King of Sardinia, 186
King o' Scots, 232, 234
King of the Forest, 235–6
King of the Gipsies, 139
King of the Vale, 202, 204
King of Trumps, 167
King of Trumps II, 530
King of Tyne, 246–7
King of Utopia, 204
King Pepin, 166
King Priam, 414–15

King Salmon, 470–1, 494–7, 500; pedigree, 388, 453, 478; foals by, 496, 613
King Tom, 108, 164, 171–2, 174; foals by, 231, 235, 363
King William (1781), 8
King William (1911), 392, 395
Kingcraft, 231–4
Kingsloe, 595
Kingston, 161, 166–7, 198
Kingston Black, 423
Kingstown, 171, 174–6
Kingsway, 539, 541–2
Kingwood, 289
Kirkconnel, 324–5
Kirkham, 308
Kisber, 176, 251–3
Kiss of Life, 661, 664
Kite, 33
Klarikoff, 195–7
Knapsack, 215
Knave, The, 200
Knight of Gwynne, The, 159
Knight of St George, 172
Knight of Snowdon, 207
Knight of the Crescent, 215
Knight of the Cross, 261
Knight of the Grail, 466–7
Knight of the Thistle, 331
Knighthood, 261
Knightsbridge, 129–30
Knock Out, 691
Knockando, 447, 449, 514
Knoloma, 486
Knout, The, 155–6
Kookaburra, 599
Kopi, 433, 475–6
Kosciusko, 398–9
Ksar, 689–91
Kutusoff, 63
Kwang-Su, 386, 417, 420
Kythnos, 616, 620–3

La Flèche, 312–15, 318
La Varende, 583–4
Laburnum, 239–40
Ladas (1869), 229–30, 320
Ladas (1894), 229, 233, 297, 300, 318, 320–3, 428, 543; pedigree, 203, 265, 366; foals by, 314, 322

INDEX

Macanudo, 463

Macaroni, 201–4, 231, 290, 324

Macaroni, colt by (Repentance colt), 249–50

M'Adam, 81

Macbeth, 15

Maccabaeus—*see* Running Rein

Macgregor, 231–2, 234

McNeill, 426

Madagascar, 497

Magic, 57–8

Magna Charta, 135

Magnet, 511–12

Magnum, 188–9

Magnus Troil, 78

Magyar, 409

Maharajah, 200

Mahmoud (1830), 75, 96–7, 99

Mahmoud (1936), 145, 344, 477–8, 501, 508–12, 556, 665, 676; pedigree, 426, 473, 480, 508

Mahometan, 117–18

Mahu, 612

Maidstone, 167

Main Road, 574

Mainstone, 193

Major, The, 208

Major Brackey, 526

Malabar, 521

Malcolm, 146

Malek, 200

Malka's Boy, 576–9

Mallowry, 564

Malpas, 389–90

Malua, 370, 372–3

Mameluke, 83, 86–8

Man at Arms, 193

Man of Ross, 220

Manfred, 67–8

Mango, 65, 117–18

Manitoba, 494–7

Manitoulin, 685, 688

Manna, 413, 443, 456–8, 469, 494; foals by, 490, 585

Manorite, 521

Manuchehr, 550–1

Manuella, 59–60

Marc Anthony, 172

Marcellus, 78

Marco Polo II, 569–70

Marden, 273, 276

Marengo, 620, 622–3

Margery, 40

Margrave, 104–5

Mariner, 266, 268–9

Marionette, 187–9

Mark Ho!, 15

Marksman, 217–21

Marlborough Buck, 160–2

Marquis, The, 199–200

Marshal Bazaine, 240

Marshal Macdonald, 272

Marshal Neil, 435

Marshal Scott, 264

Marshal Soult, 128, 130

Marske, colt by, 8

Marsyad, 582, 584

Marsyas, 172, 244

Martagon, 308

Marten, 409

Martenhurst, 310–11

Martley, 298

Martyrdom, 230

Marwari, 599

Mask, 266, 268–9

Massif, 555

Master Butterfly, 220–1

Master Eagle, 40

Master of the Rolls, 115

Master Richard, 207

Matchbox, 320–3

Matchem, colt by, 6

Mathew, 38

Matoppo, 342

Mattygainmal, 574

Mauna Kea, 526

Mavors, 159

Mayor of Hull, The, 169

Mazarin, 534

M.D., 180–3

Mead, 360, 362

Meaden, 683

Meadow Court, 650–2

Meadow Mint, 685, 687–9

Meadowville, 676, 678

Mealy, 27

Medieval Knight, 499, 502

Medway, 578–9

Mehari, 658–9

Melbourne, 37, 50, 124; foals by, 144, 168, 180, 244

Melfort, 497

Melody colt, 125–7

Melton, 192, 286–9, 293, 514, 660

Mendicant Friar, 511

Mentor (1787), 17

Mentor (1845), 143

Merchant, 90

Merchant Navy, 540, 552

Merchant Venturer, 636–8, 640–1

Mercia Boy, 685, 688

Mercury, colt by (Lord Strathmore's), 27

Mercury, colt by (Lord Egremont's), 30

Mercutio, 381

Merry Hampton, 203, 296–298

Merry Minstrel, 584

Merry Monarch, The, 91, 141–2

Merry Quip, 560

Merrygoround, 57–8

Merrymaker, 68

Messenger, 104

Messmate, 607–8

Metaphysician, colt by, 8

Meteor, 15

Meter, 243

Mezzanine, 688

Michael Scott, 204

Michel Grove, 200

Mickle Fell, 118

Midas (1851), 162

Midas (1945), 548–51

Mid-day Sun, 458, 513–17, 543

Middlesex, 172

Middleton, 54, 57, 83–4

Midlander, 612

Midstream, 511–12

Migoli, 478, 559–60; pedigree, 505, 508, 520; foals by, 580, 601

Miguel, 304–5

Mildew, 157, 159

Mill Reef, 679–83

Millenium, 680, 683

Miller, 29

Millwall, 564

Milton, 431

Miner's Lamp, 611–12

736

GENERAL INDEX

Past and Present Derb

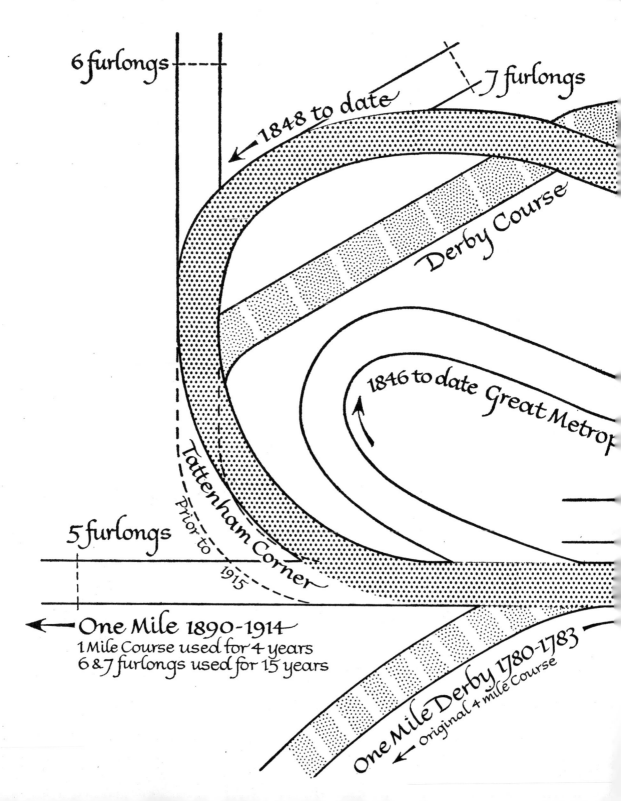

6 furlongs

7 furlongs

1848 to date

Derby Course

1846 to date Great Metrop

Tattenham Corner

Prior to 1915

5 furlongs

← One Mile 1890-1914 →
1 Mile Course used for 4 years
6 & 7 furlongs used for 15 years

One Mile Derby 1780-1783

original 4 mile Course